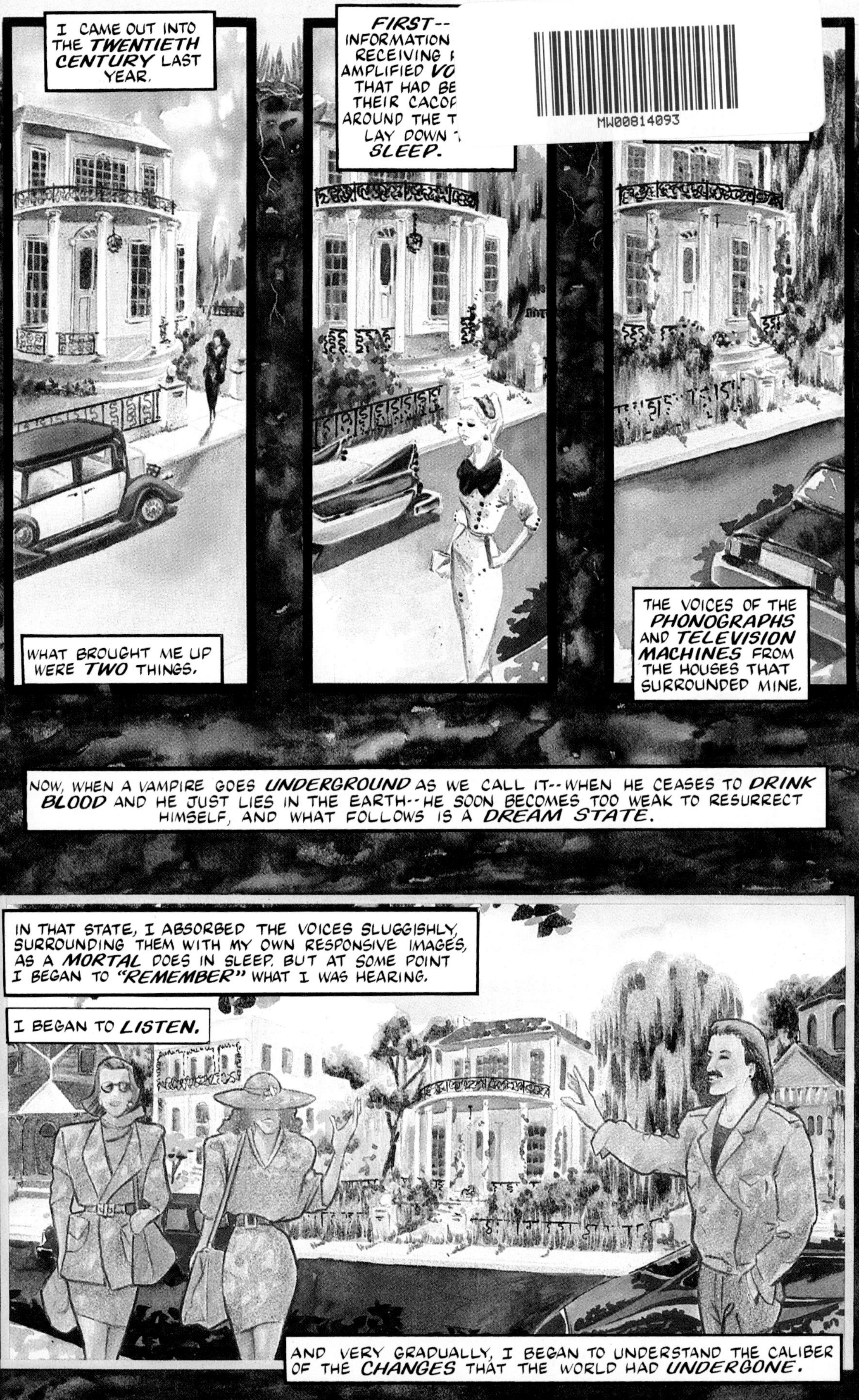

I CAME OUT INTO THE TWENTIETH CENTURY LAST YEAR.
WHAT BROUGHT ME UP WERE TWO THINGS.
FIRST-- INFORMATION RECEIVING AMPLIFIED THAT HAD THEIR AROUND THE LAY DOWN SLEEP.
THE VOICES OF THE PHONOGRAPHS AND TELEVISION MACHINES FROM THE HOUSES THAT SURROUNDED MINE.
NOW, WHEN A VAMPIRE GOES UNDERGROUND AS WE CALL IT--WHEN HE CEASES TO DRINK BLOOD AND HE JUST LIES IN THE EARTH--HE SOON BECOMES TOO WEAK TO RESURRECT HIMSELF, AND WHAT FOLLOWS IS A DREAM STATE.
IN THAT STATE, I ABSORBED THE VOICES SLUGGISHLY, SURROUNDING THEM WITH MY OWN RESPONSIVE IMAGES, AS A MORTAL DOES IN SLEEP. BUT AT SOME POINT I BEGAN TO "REMEMBER" WHAT I WAS HEARING.
I BEGAN TO LISTEN.
AND VERY GRADUALLY, I BEGAN TO UNDERSTAND THE CALIBER OF THE CHANGES THAT THE WORLD HAD UNDERGONE.

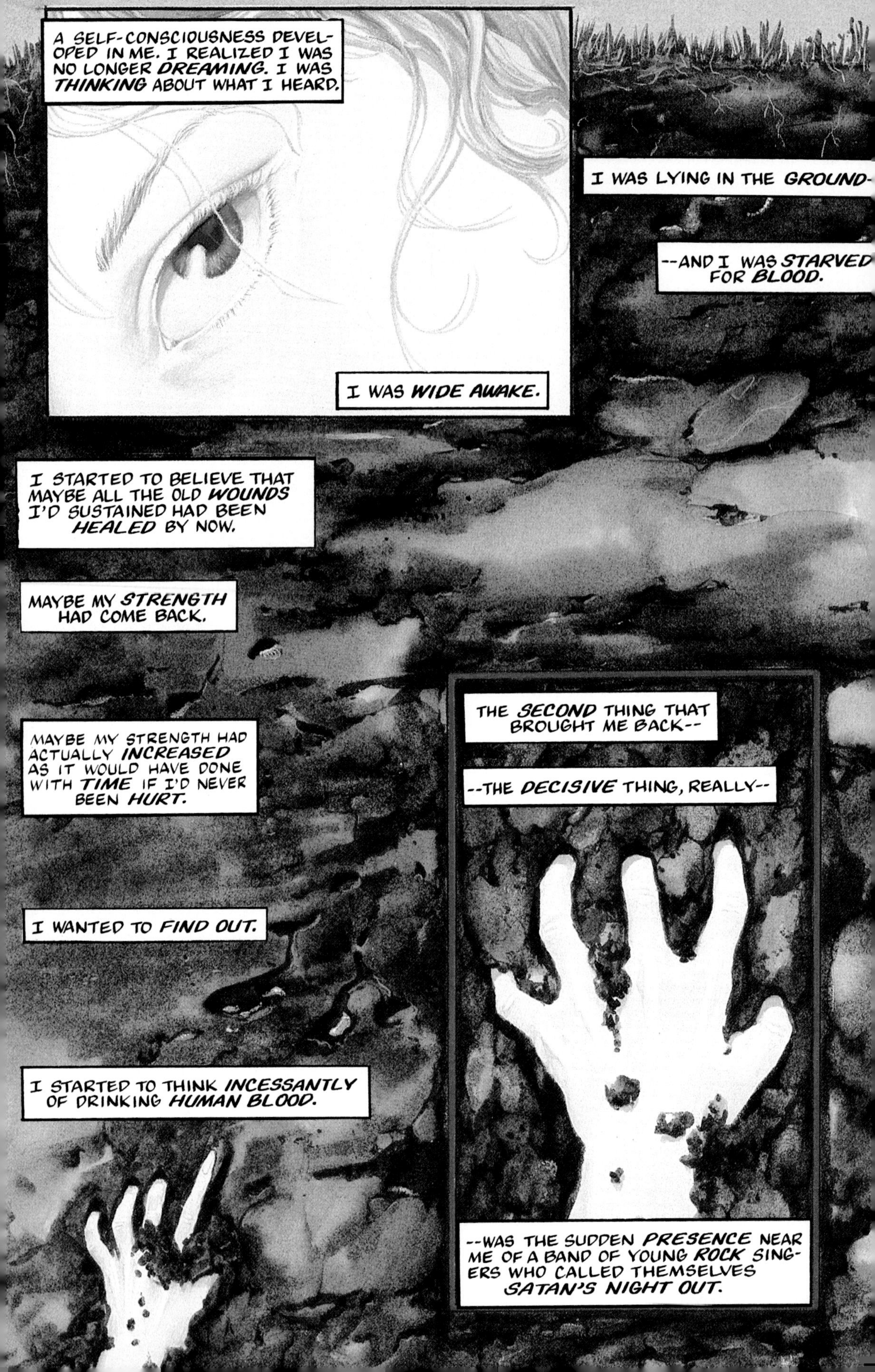
A SELF-CONSCIOUSNESS DEVELOPED IN ME. I REALIZED I WAS NO LONGER DREAMING. I WAS THINKING ABOUT WHAT I HEARD.
I WAS WIDE AWAKE.
I WAS LYING IN THE GROUND-
--AND I WAS STARVED FOR BLOOD.
I STARTED TO BELIEVE THAT MAYBE ALL THE OLD WOUNDS I'D SUSTAINED HAD BEEN HEALED BY NOW.
MAYBE MY STRENGTH HAD COME BACK.
MAYBE MY STRENGTH HAD ACTUALLY INCREASED AS IT WOULD HAVE DONE WITH TIME IF I'D NEVER BEEN HURT.
I WANTED TO FIND OUT.
I STARTED TO THINK INCESSANTLY OF DRINKING HUMAN BLOOD.
THE SECOND THING THAT BROUGHT ME BACK--
--THE DECISIVE THING, REALLY--
--WAS THE SUDDEN PRESENCE NEAR ME OF A BAND OF YOUNG ROCK SINGERS WHO CALLED THEMSELVES SATAN'S NIGHT OUT.

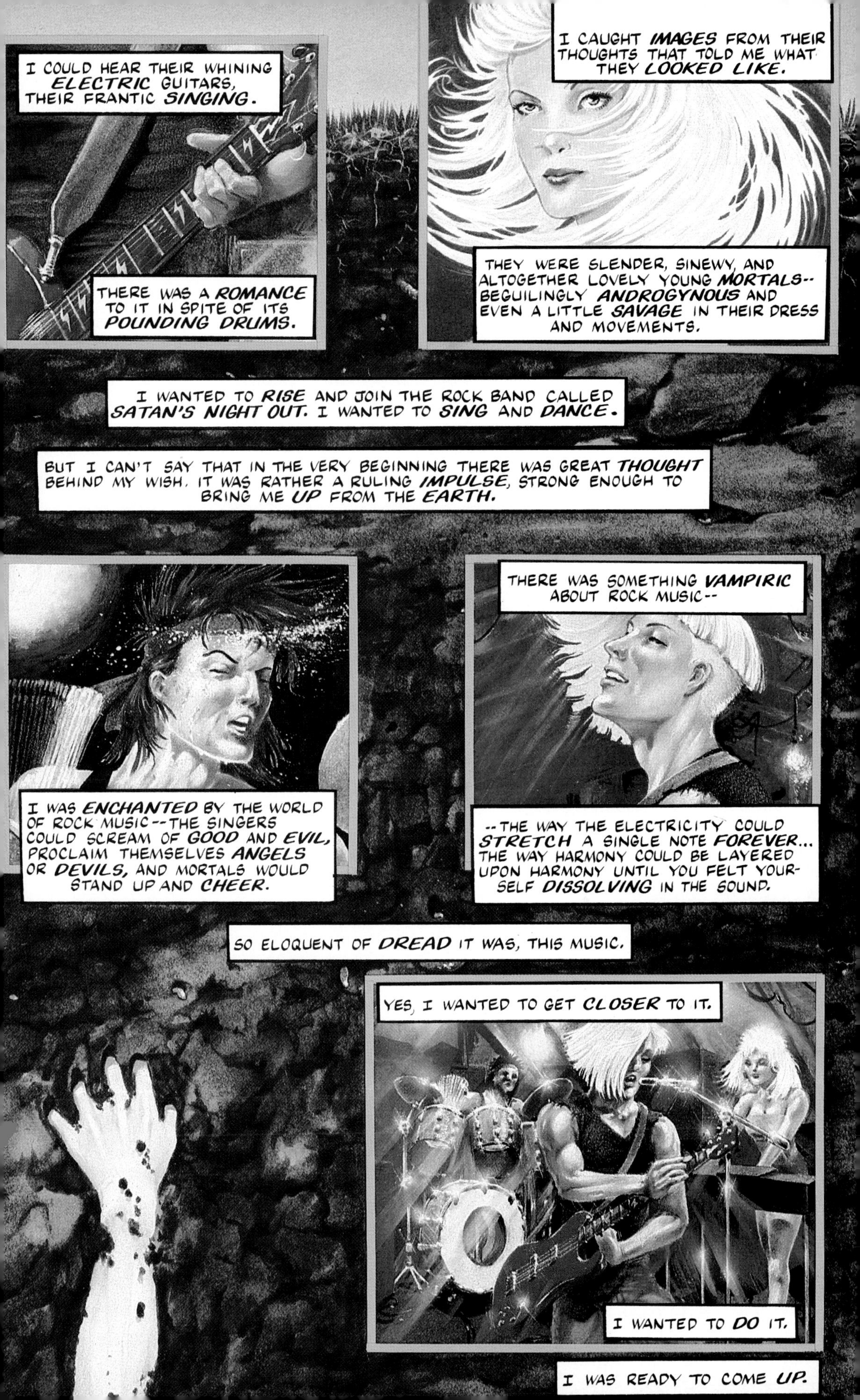

I COULD HEAR THEIR WHINING ELECTRIC GUITARS, THEIR FRANTIC SINGING.
THERE WAS A ROMANCE TO IT IN SPITE OF ITS POUNDING DRUMS.
I CAUGHT IMAGES FROM THEIR THOUGHTS THAT TOLD ME WHAT THEY LOOKED LIKE.
THEY WERE SLENDER, SINEWY, AND ALTOGETHER LOVELY YOUNG MORTALS-- BEGUILINGLY ANDROGYNOUS AND EVEN A LITTLE SAVAGE IN THEIR DRESS AND MOVEMENTS.
I WANTED TO RISE AND JOIN THE ROCK BAND CALLED SATAN'S NIGHT OUT. I WANTED TO SING AND DANCE.
BUT I CAN'T SAY THAT IN THE VERY BEGINNING THERE WAS GREAT THOUGHT BEHIND MY WISH. IT WAS RATHER A RULING IMPULSE, STRONG ENOUGH TO BRING ME UP FROM THE EARTH.
I WAS ENCHANTED BY THE WORLD OF ROCK MUSIC--THE SINGERS COULD SCREAM OF GOOD AND EVIL, PROCLAIM THEMSELVES ANGELS OR DEVILS, AND MORTALS WOULD STAND UP AND CHEER.
THERE WAS SOMETHING VAMPIRIC ABOUT ROCK MUSIC--
--THE WAY THE ELECTRICITY COULD STRETCH A SINGLE NOTE FOREVER... THE WAY HARMONY COULD BE LAYERED UPON HARMONY UNTIL YOU FELT YOURSELF DISSOLVING IN THE SOUND.
SO ELOQUENT OF DREAD IT WAS, THIS MUSIC.
YES, I WANTED TO GET CLOSER TO IT.
I WANTED TO DO IT.
I WAS READY TO COME UP.

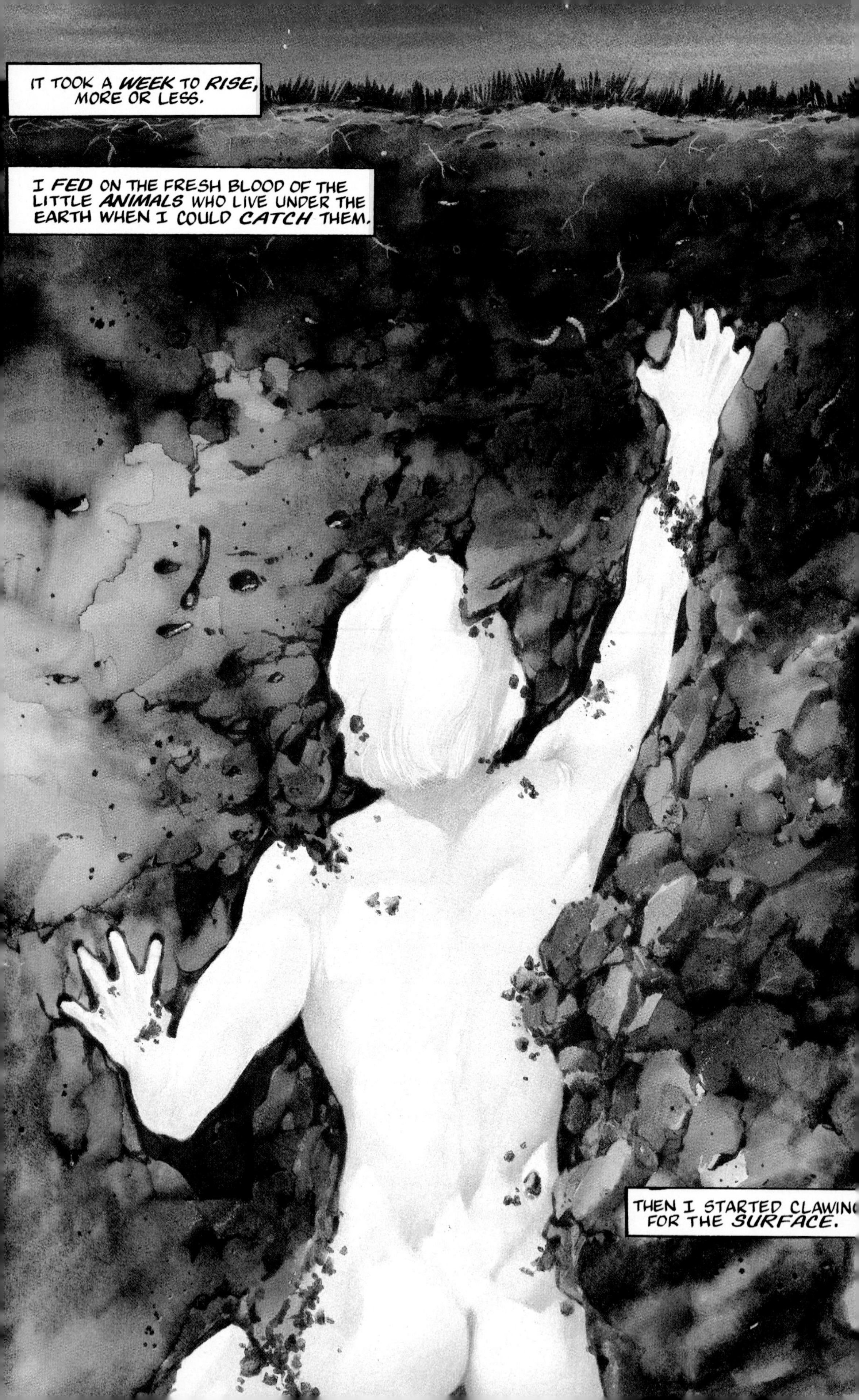
IT TOOK A WEEK TO RISE, MORE OR LESS.
I FED ON THE FRESH BLOOD OF THE LITTLE ANIMALS WHO LIVE UNDER THE EARTH WHEN I COULD CATCH THEM.
THEN I STARTED CLAWING FOR THE SURFACE.

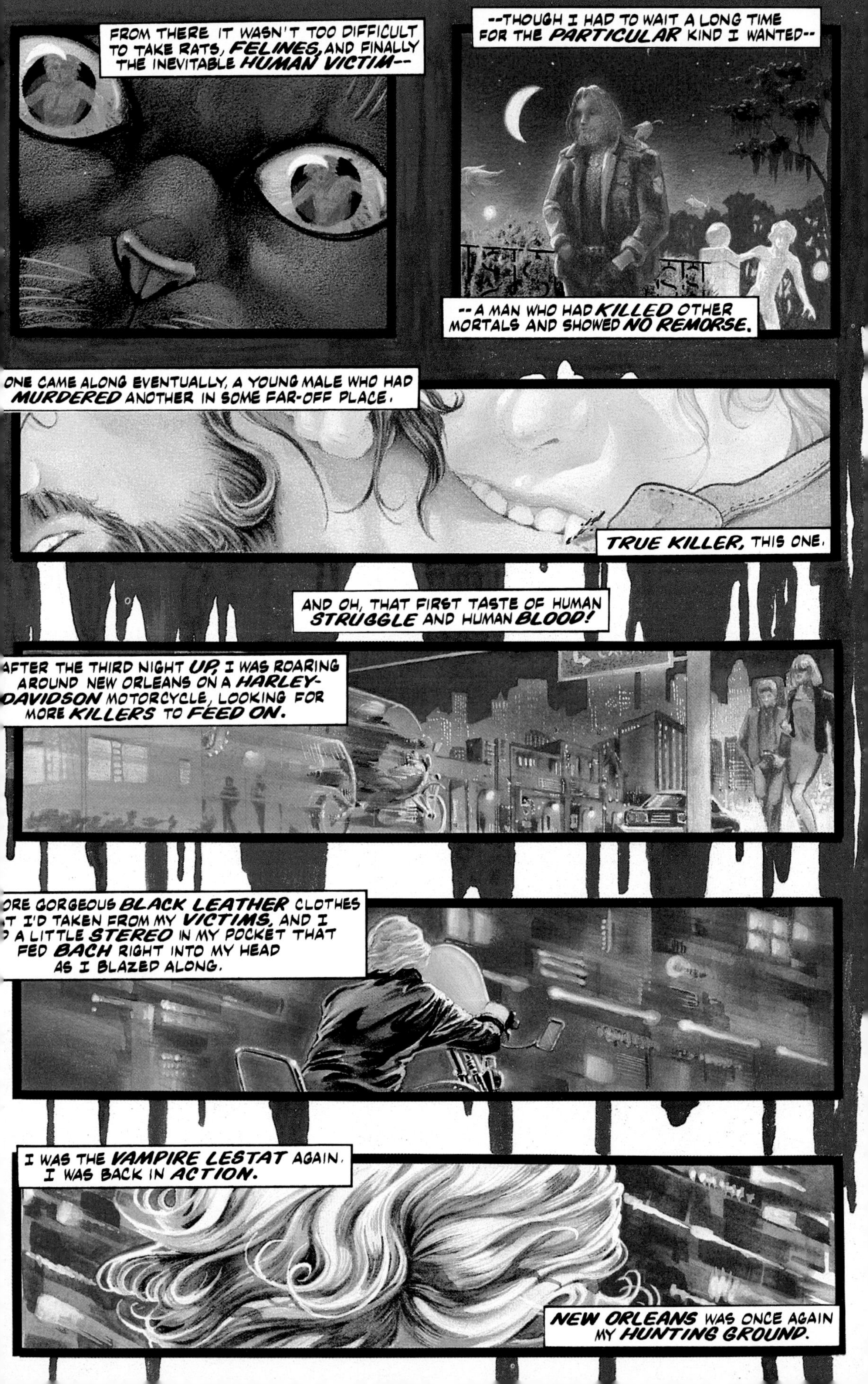

FROM THERE IT WASN'T TOO DIFFICULT TO TAKE RATS, FELINES, AND FINALLY THE INEVITABLE HUMAN VICTIM--
--THOUGH I HAD TO WAIT A LONG TIME FOR THE PARTICULAR KIND I WANTED--
--A MAN WHO HAD KILLED OTHER MORTALS AND SHOWED NO REMORSE.
ONE CAME ALONG EVENTUALLY, A YOUNG MALE WHO HAD MURDERED ANOTHER IN SOME FAR-OFF PLACE.
TRUE KILLER, THIS ONE.
AND OH, THAT FIRST TASTE OF HUMAN STRUGGLE AND HUMAN BLOOD!
AFTER THE THIRD NIGHT UP, I WAS ROARING AROUND NEW ORLEANS ON A HARLEY-DAVIDSON MOTORCYCLE, LOOKING FOR MORE KILLERS TO FEED ON.
ORE GORGEOUS BLACK LEATHER CLOTHES T I'D TAKEN FROM MY VICTIMS, AND I D A LITTLE STEREO IN MY POCKET THAT FED BACH RIGHT INTO MY HEAD AS I BLAZED ALONG.
I WAS THE VAMPIRE LESTAT AGAIN. I WAS BACK IN ACTION.
NEW ORLEANS WAS ONCE AGAIN MY HUNTING GROUND.

Anne Rice's
THE VAMPIRE LESTAT ™
A GRAPHIC NOVEL

Based on the novel by Anne Rice
Adapted and designed by Faye Perozich
Painted by Daerick Gross

BALLANTINE BOOKS • NEW YORK

INNOVATION BOOKS • WHEELING, WEST VIRGINIA

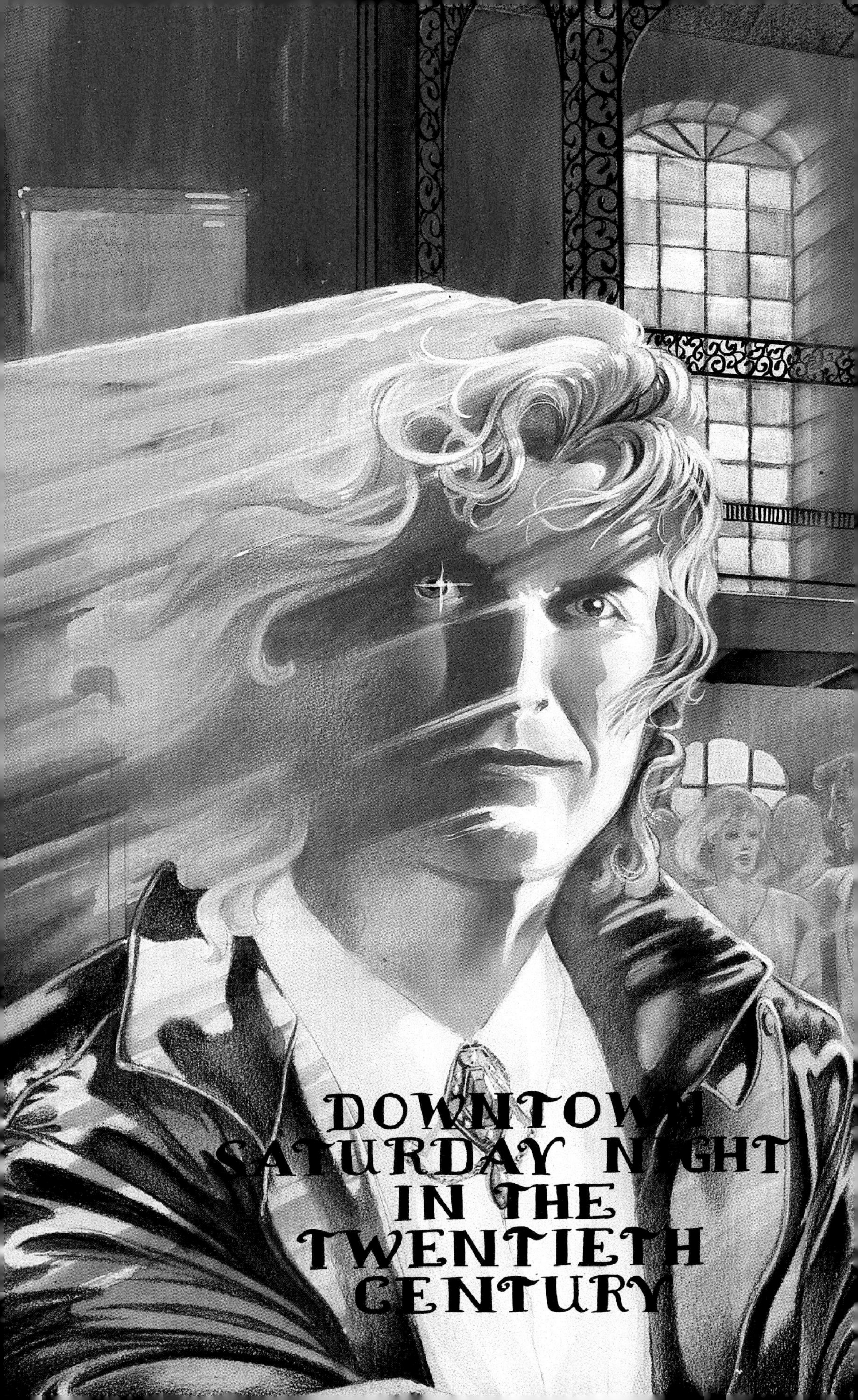
DOWNTOWN
SATURDAY NIGHT
IN THE
TWENTIETH
CENTURY

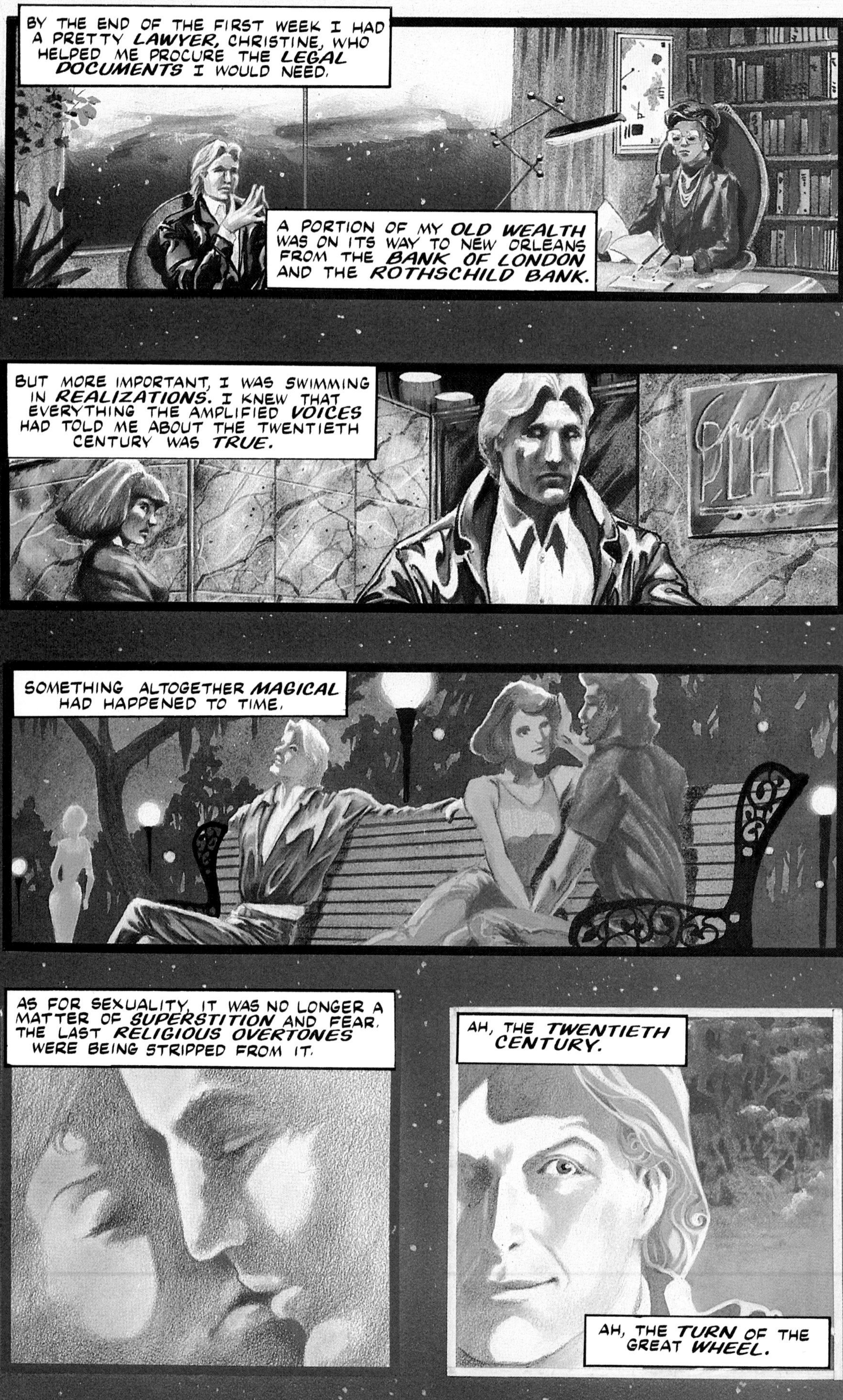
BY THE END OF THE FIRST WEEK I HAD A PRETTY LAWYER, CHRISTINE, WHO HELPED ME PROCURE THE LEGAL DOCUMENTS I WOULD NEED.
A PORTION OF MY OLD WEALTH WAS ON ITS WAY TO NEW ORLEANS FROM THE BANK OF LONDON AND THE ROTHSCHILD BANK.
BUT MORE IMPORTANT, I WAS SWIMMING IN REALIZATIONS. I KNEW THAT EVERYTHING THE AMPLIFIED VOICES HAD TOLD ME ABOUT THE TWENTIETH CENTURY WAS TRUE.
SOMETHING ALTOGETHER MAGICAL HAD HAPPENED TO TIME.
AS FOR SEXUALITY, IT WAS NO LONGER A MATTER OF SUPERSTITION AND FEAR. THE LAST RELIGIOUS OVERTONES WERE BEING STRIPPED FROM IT.
AH, THE TWENTIETH CENTURY.
AH, THE TURN OF THE GREAT WHEEL.

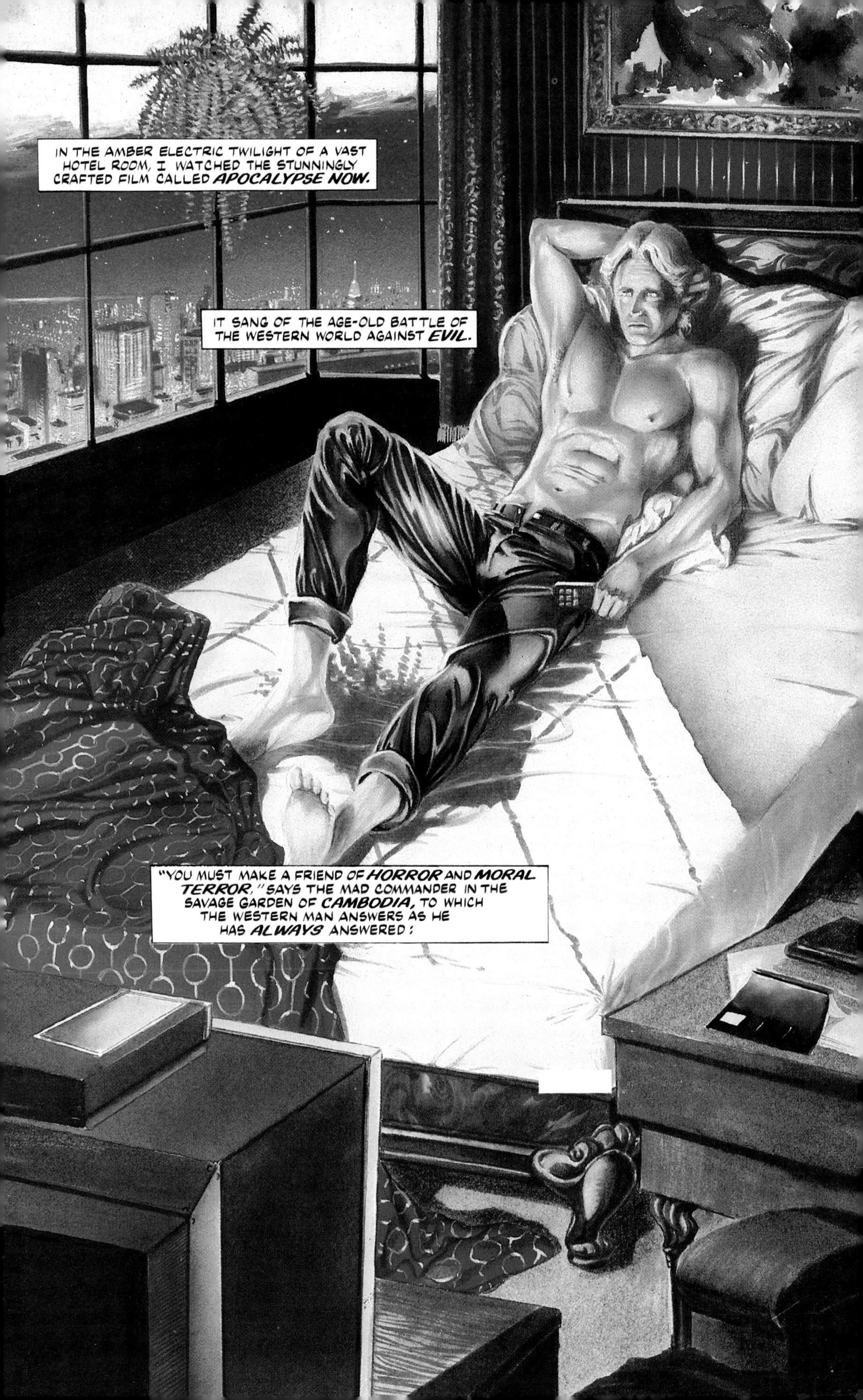
IN THE AMBER ELECTRIC TWILIGHT OF A VAST HOTEL ROOM, I WATCHED THE STUNNINGLY CRAFTED FILM CALLED APOCALYPSE NOW.
IT SANG OF THE AGE-OLD BATTLE OF THE WESTERN WORLD AGAINST EVIL.
"YOU MUST MAKE A FRIEND OF HORROR AND MORAL TERROR," SAYS THE MAD COMMANDER IN THE SAVAGE GARDEN OF CAMBODIA, TO WHICH THE WESTERN MAN ANSWERS AS HE HAS ALWAYS ANSWERED:

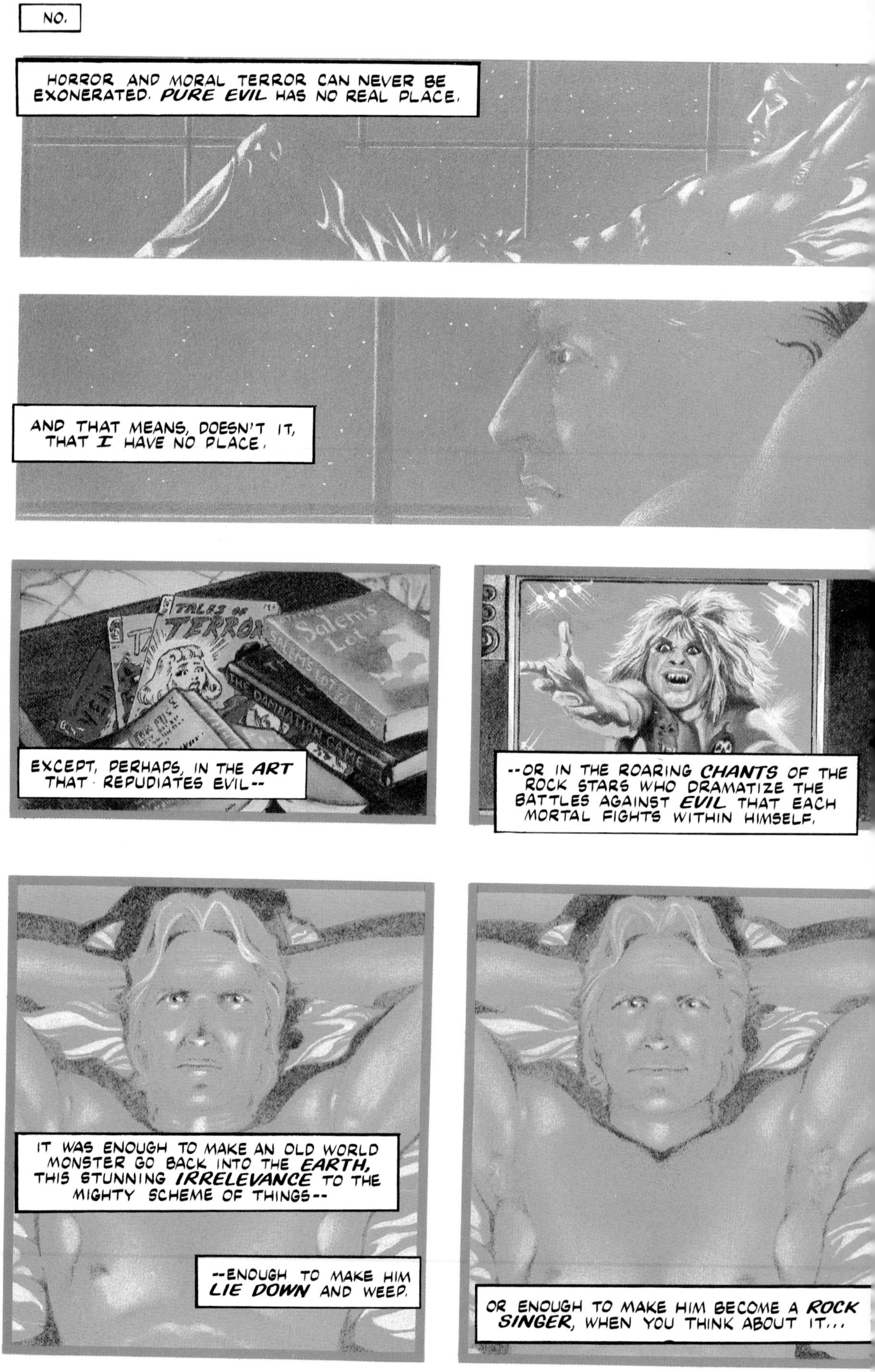
NO.
HORROR AND MORAL TERROR CAN NEVER BE EXONERATED. PURE EVIL HAS NO REAL PLACE.
AND THAT MEANS, DOESN'T IT, THAT I HAVE NO PLACE.
TALES OF TERROR
Salem's Lot
THE DAMNATION GAME
EXCEPT, PERHAPS, IN THE ART THAT REPUDIATES EVIL--
--OR IN THE ROARING CHANTS OF THE ROCK STARS WHO DRAMATIZE THE BATTLES AGAINST EVIL THAT EACH MORTAL FIGHTS WITHIN HIMSELF.
IT WAS ENOUGH TO MAKE AN OLD WORLD MONSTER GO BACK INTO THE EARTH, THIS STUNNING IRRELEVANCE TO THE MIGHTY SCHEME OF THINGS--
--ENOUGH TO MAKE HIM LIE DOWN AND WEEP.
OR ENOUGH TO MAKE HIM BECOME A ROCK SINGER, WHEN YOU THINK ABOUT IT...

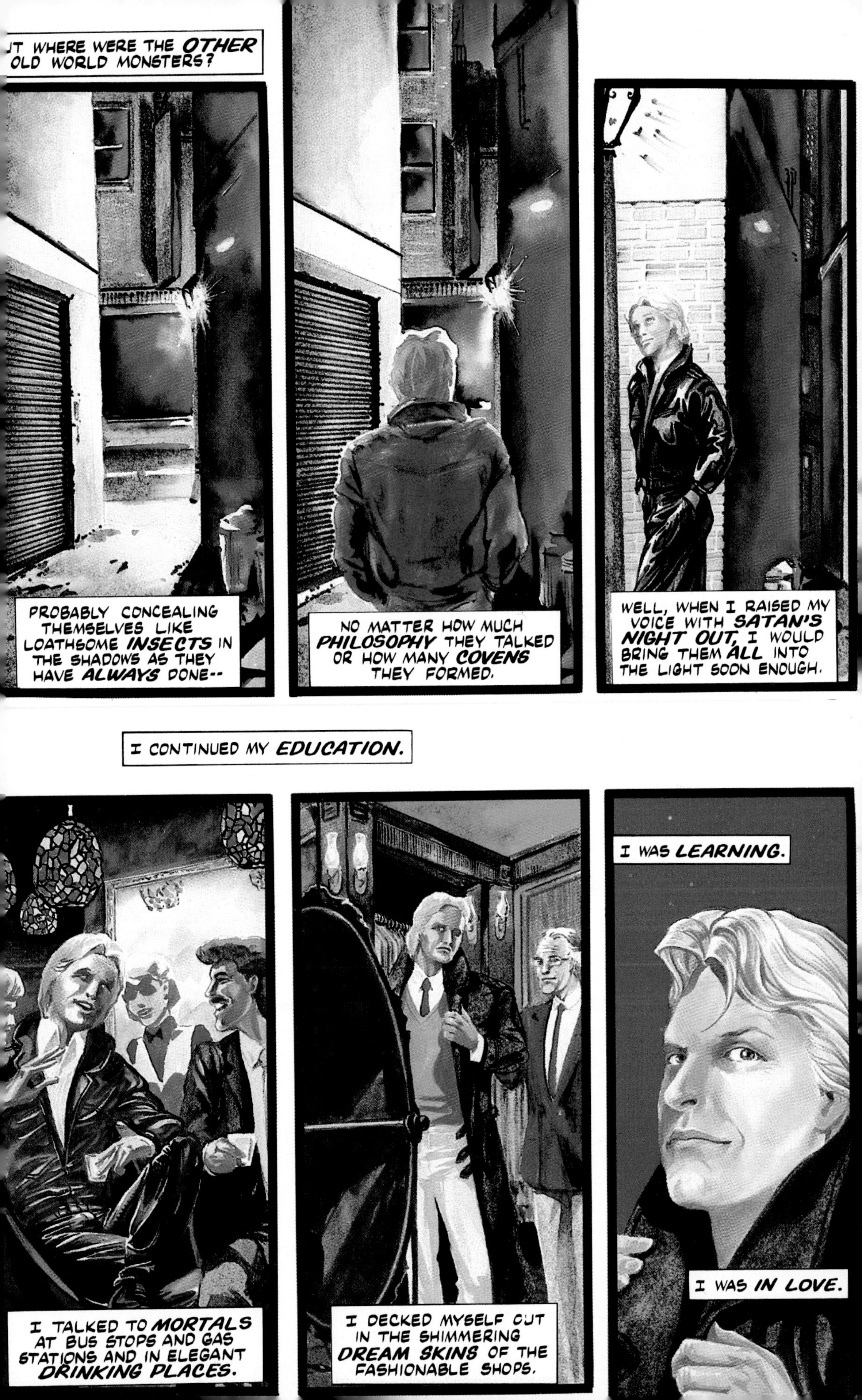

UT WHERE WERE THE OTHER OLD WORLD MONSTERS?
PROBABLY CONCEALING THEMSELVES LIKE LOATHSOME INSECTS IN THE SHADOWS AS THEY HAVE ALWAYS DONE--
NO MATTER HOW MUCH PHILOSOPHY THEY TALKED OR HOW MANY COVENS THEY FORMED.
WELL, WHEN I RAISED MY VOICE WITH SATAN'S NIGHT OUT, I WOULD BRING THEM ALL INTO THE LIGHT SOON ENOUGH.
I CONTINUED MY EDUCATION.
I TALKED TO MORTALS AT BUS STOPS AND GAS STATIONS AND IN ELEGANT DRINKING PLACES.
I DECKED MYSELF OUT IN THE SHIMMERING DREAM SKINS OF THE FASHIONABLE SHOPS.
I WAS LEARNING.
I WAS IN LOVE.

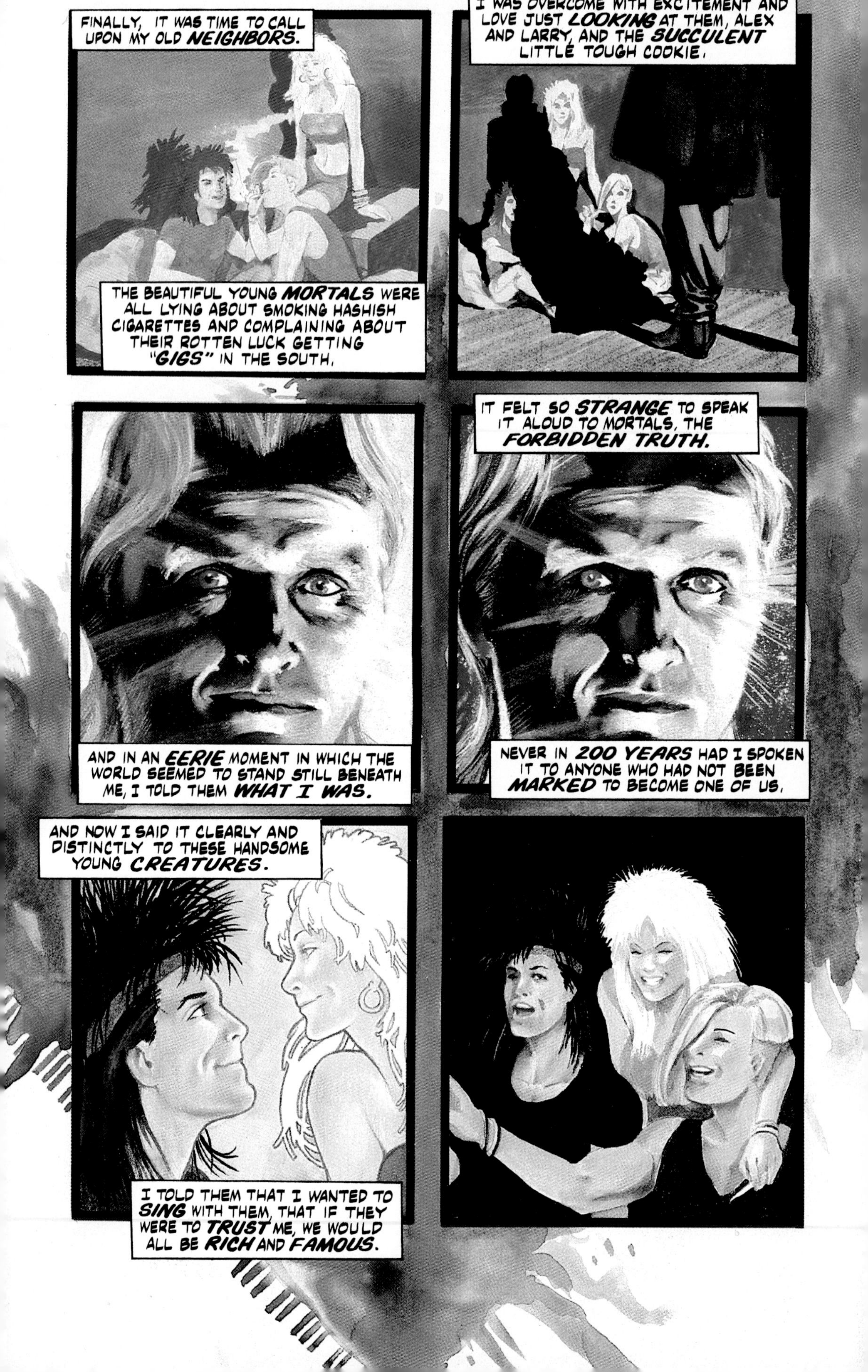
FINALLY, IT WAS TIME TO CALL UPON MY OLD NEIGHBORS.
THE BEAUTIFUL YOUNG MORTALS WERE ALL LYING ABOUT SMOKING HASHISH CIGARETTES AND COMPLAINING ABOUT THEIR ROTTEN LUCK GETTING "GIGS" IN THE SOUTH.
I WAS OVERCOME WITH EXCITEMENT AND LOVE JUST LOOKING AT THEM, ALEX AND LARRY, AND THE SUCCULENT LITTLE TOUGH COOKIE.
AND IN AN EERIE MOMENT IN WHICH THE WORLD SEEMED TO STAND STILL BENEATH ME, I TOLD THEM WHAT I WAS.
IT FELT SO STRANGE TO SPEAK IT ALOUD TO MORTALS, THE FORBIDDEN TRUTH.
NEVER IN 200 YEARS HAD I SPOKEN IT TO ANYONE WHO HAD NOT BEEN MARKED TO BECOME ONE OF US.
AND NOW I SAID IT CLEARLY AND DISTINCTLY TO THESE HANDSOME YOUNG CREATURES.
I TOLD THEM THAT I WANTED TO SING WITH THEM, THAT IF THEY WERE TO TRUST ME, WE WOULD ALL BE RICH AND FAMOUS.

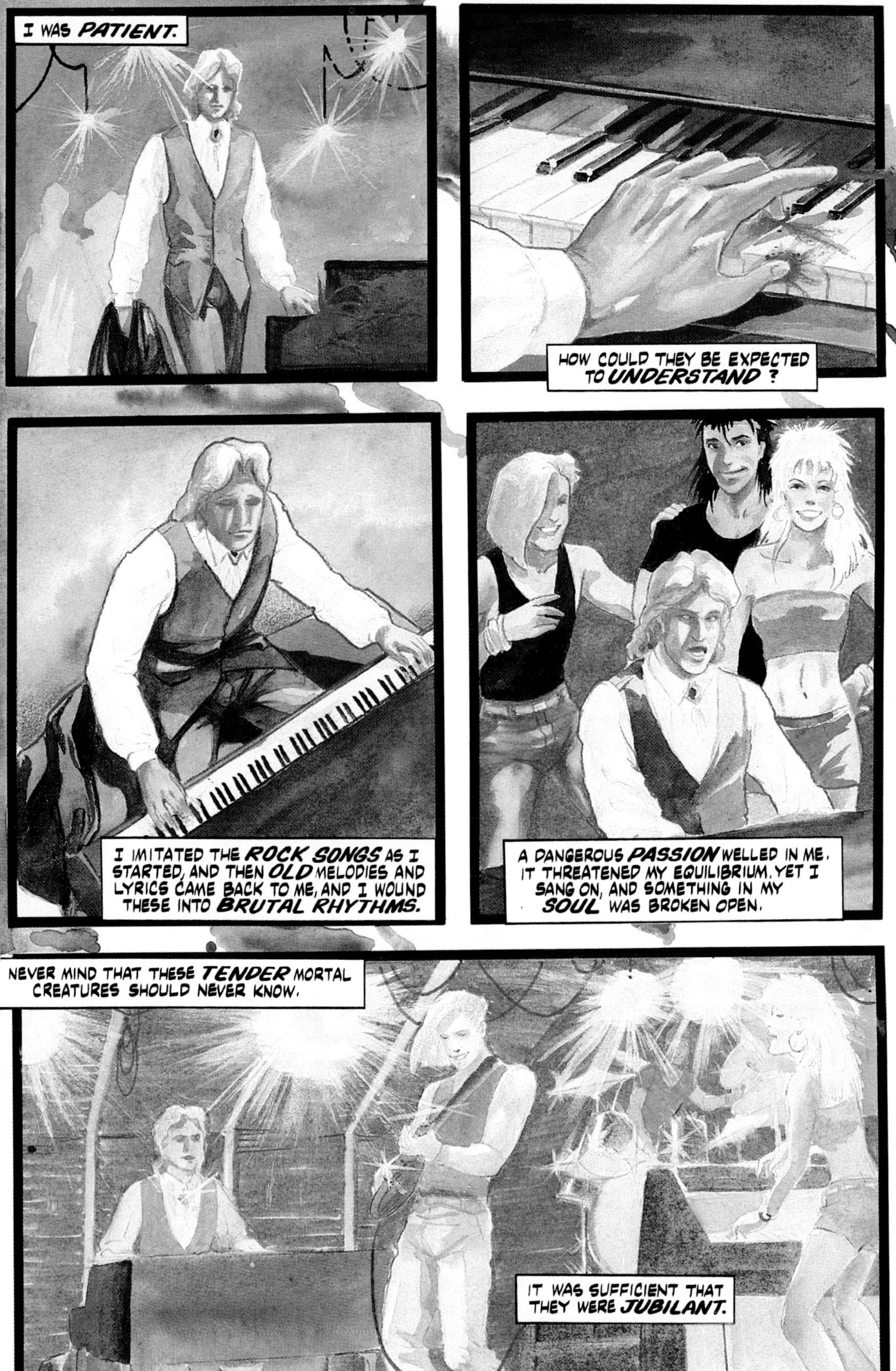
I WAS PATIENT.
HOW COULD THEY BE EXPECTED TO UNDERSTAND ?
I IMITATED THE ROCK SONGS AS I STARTED, AND THEN OLD MELODIES AND LYRICS CAME BACK TO ME, AND I WOUND THESE INTO BRUTAL RHYTHMS.
A DANGEROUS PASSION WELLED IN ME. IT THREATENED MY EQUILIBRIUM. YET I SANG ON, AND SOMETHING IN MY SOUL WAS BROKEN OPEN.
NEVER MIND THAT THESE TENDER MORTAL CREATURES SHOULD NEVER KNOW.
IT WAS SUFFICIENT THAT THEY WERE JUBILANT.

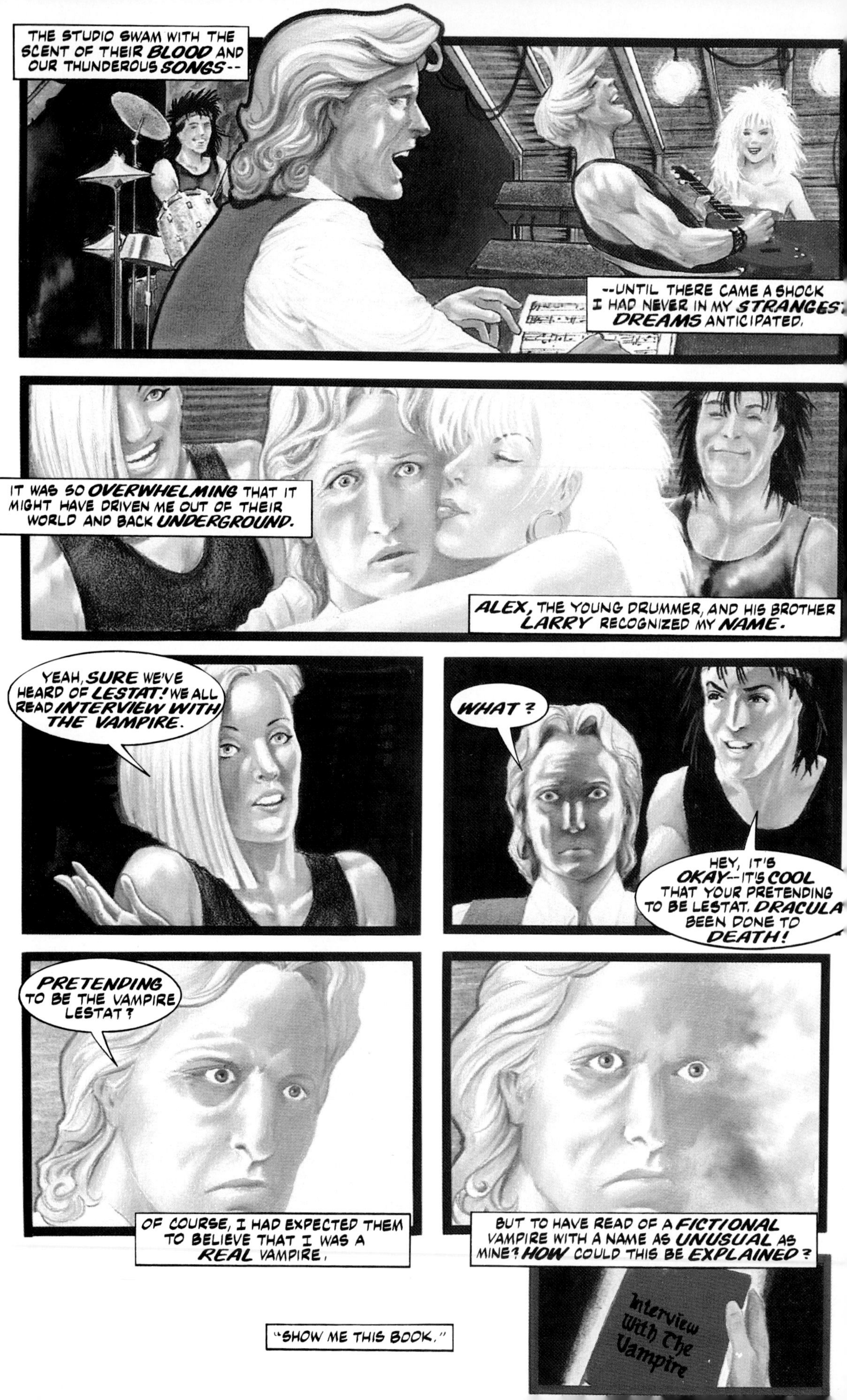
THE STUDIO SWAM WITH THE SCENT OF THEIR BLOOD AND OUR THUNDEROUS SONGS--
--UNTIL THERE CAME A SHOCK I HAD NEVER IN MY STRANGEST DREAMS ANTICIPATED.
IT WAS SO OVERWHELMING THAT IT MIGHT HAVE DRIVEN ME OUT OF THEIR WORLD AND BACK UNDERGROUND.
ALEX, THE YOUNG DRUMMER, AND HIS BROTHER LARRY RECOGNIZED MY NAME.
YEAH, SURE WE'VE HEARD OF LESTAT! WE ALL READ INTERVIEW WITH THE VAMPIRE.
WHAT?
HEY, IT'S OKAY--IT'S COOL THAT YOUR PRETENDING TO BE LESTAT. DRACULA BEEN DONE TO DEATH!
PRETENDING TO BE THE VAMPIRE LESTAT?
OF COURSE, I HAD EXPECTED THEM TO BELIEVE THAT I WAS A REAL VAMPIRE.
BUT TO HAVE READ OF A FICTIONAL VAMPIRE WITH A NAME AS UNUSUAL AS MINE? HOW COULD THIS BE EXPLAINED?
"SHOW ME THIS BOOK."
Interview With The Vampire

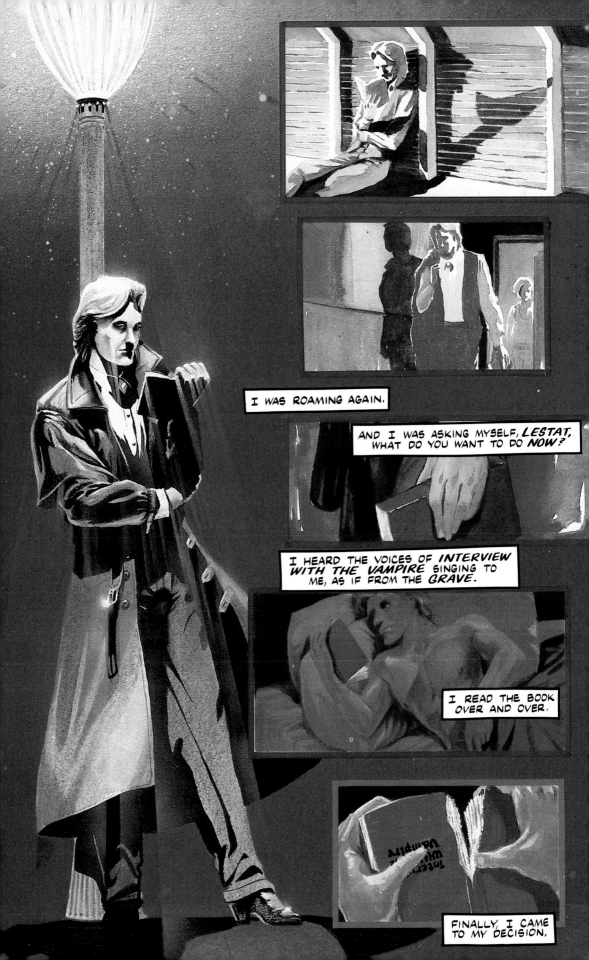

I WAS ROAMING AGAIN.

AND I WAS ASKING MYSELF, *LESTAT*, WHAT DO YOU WANT TO DO *NOW*?

I HEARD THE VOICES OF *INTERVIEW WITH THE VAMPIRE* SINGING TO ME, AS IF FROM THE *GRAVE*.

I READ THE BOOK OVER AND OVER.

FINALLY, I CAME TO MY DECISION.

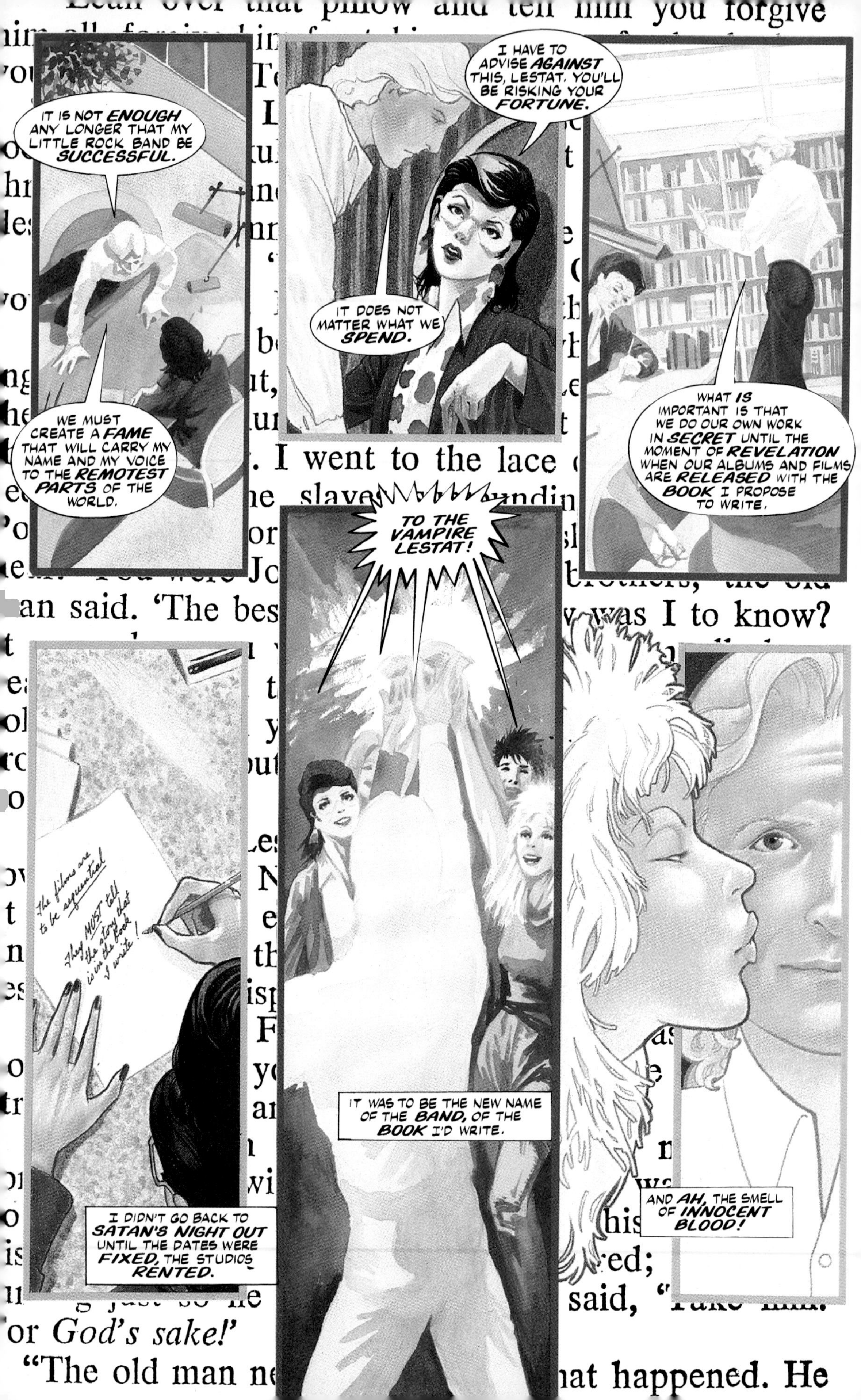
IT IS NOT ENOUGH ANY LONGER THAT MY LITTLE ROCK BAND BE SUCCESSFUL.
WE MUST CREATE A FAME THAT WILL CARRY MY NAME AND MY VOICE TO THE REMOTEST PARTS OF THE WORLD.
I HAVE TO ADVISE AGAINST THIS, LESTAT. YOU'LL BE RISKING YOUR FORTUNE.
IT DOES NOT MATTER WHAT WE SPEND.
WHAT IS IMPORTANT IS THAT WE DO OUR OWN WORK IN SECRET UNTIL THE MOMENT OF REVELATION WHEN OUR ALBUMS AND FILMS ARE RELEASED WITH THE BOOK I PROPOSE TO WRITE.
The films are to be sequential
They MUST tell the story that is in the book I write!
I DIDN'T GO BACK TO SATAN'S NIGHT OUT UNTIL THE DATES WERE FIXED, THE STUDIOS RENTED.
TO THE VAMPIRE LESTAT!
IT WAS TO BE THE NEW NAME OF THE BAND, OF THE BOOK I'D WRITE.
AND AH, THE SMELL OF INNOCENT BLOOD!

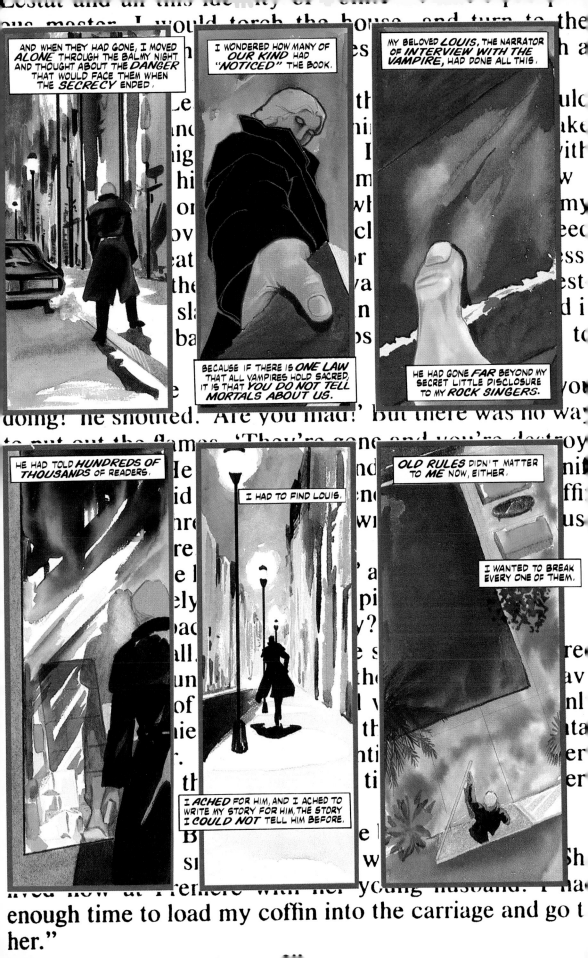

Lestat and all this identity of things whoever happens master. I would torch the house, and turn to the ...

AND WHEN THEY HAD GONE, I MOVED *ALONE* THROUGH THE BALMY NIGHT AND THOUGHT ABOUT THE *DANGER* THAT WOULD FACE THEM WHEN THE *SECRECY* ENDED.

I WONDERED HOW MANY OF *OUR KIND* HAD "*NOTICED*" THE BOOK.

BECAUSE IF THERE IS *ONE LAW* THAT ALL VAMPIRES HOLD SACRED, IT IS THAT *YOU DO NOT TELL MORTALS ABOUT US*.

MY BELOVED *LOUIS*, THE NARRATOR OF *INTERVIEW WITH THE VAMPIRE*, HAD DONE ALL THIS.

HE HAD GONE *FAR* BEYOND MY SECRET LITTLE DISCLOSURE TO MY *ROCK SINGERS*.

doing!' he shouted. 'Are you mad!' But there was no way to put out the flames. 'They're gone and you're destroy...

HE HAD TOLD *HUNDREDS OF THOUSANDS* OF READERS.

I HAD TO FIND LOUIS.

I *ACHED* FOR HIM, AND I ACHED TO WRITE MY STORY FOR HIM, THE STORY I *COULD NOT* TELL HIM BEFORE.

OLD RULES DIDN'T MATTER TO *ME* NOW, EITHER.

I WANTED TO BREAK EVERY ONE OF THEM.

enough time to load my coffin into the carriage and go t her."

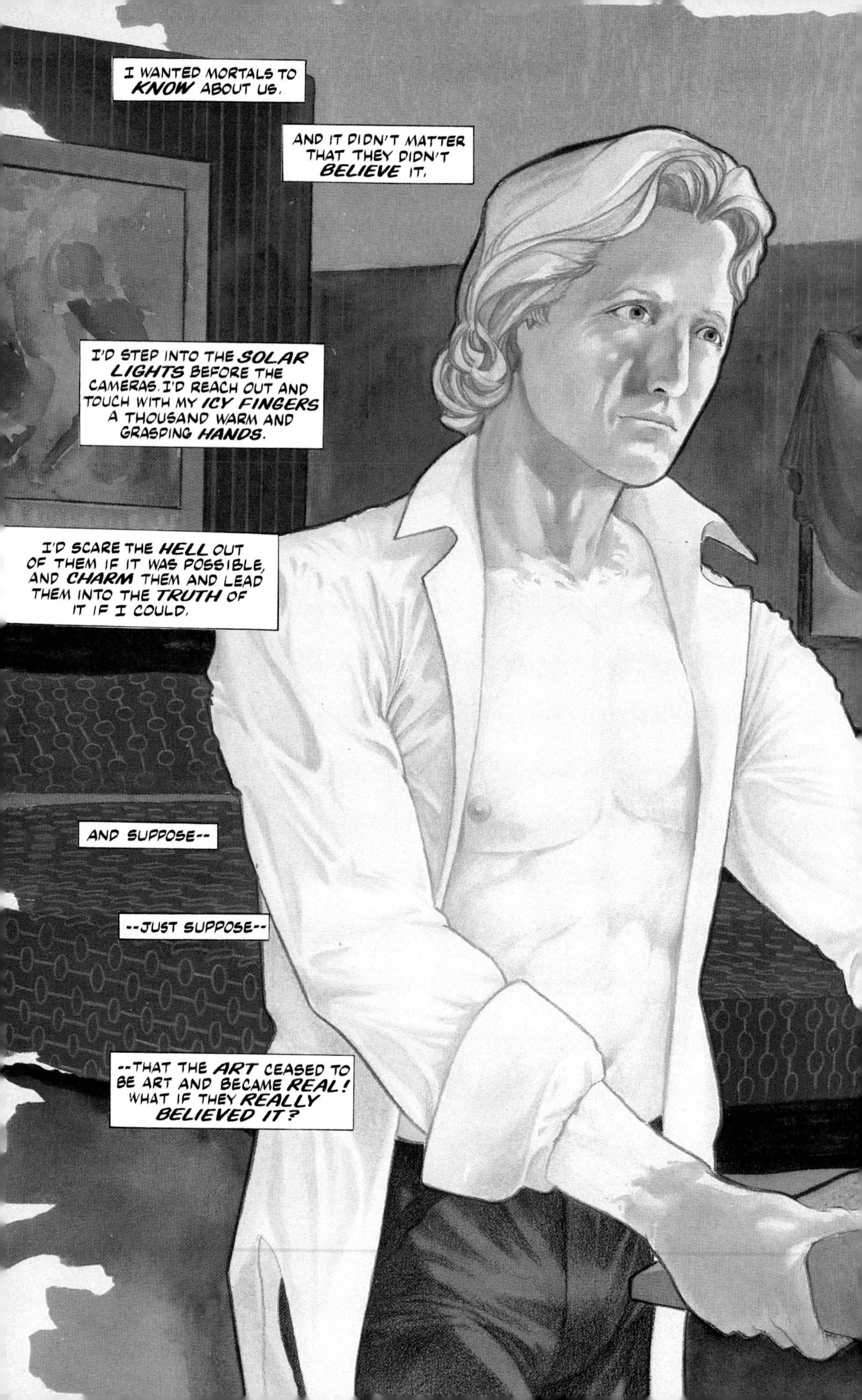
I WANTED MORTALS TO KNOW ABOUT US.
AND IT DIDN'T MATTER THAT THEY DIDN'T BELIEVE IT.
I'D STEP INTO THE SOLAR LIGHTS BEFORE THE CAMERAS. I'D REACH OUT AND TOUCH WITH MY ICY FINGERS A THOUSAND WARM AND GRASPING HANDS.
I'D SCARE THE HELL OUT OF THEM IF IT WAS POSSIBLE, AND CHARM THEM AND LEAD THEM INTO THE TRUTH OF IT IF I COULD.
AND SUPPOSE--
--JUST SUPPOSE--
--THAT THE ART CEASED TO BE ART AND BECAME REAL! WHAT IF THEY REALLY BELIEVED IT?

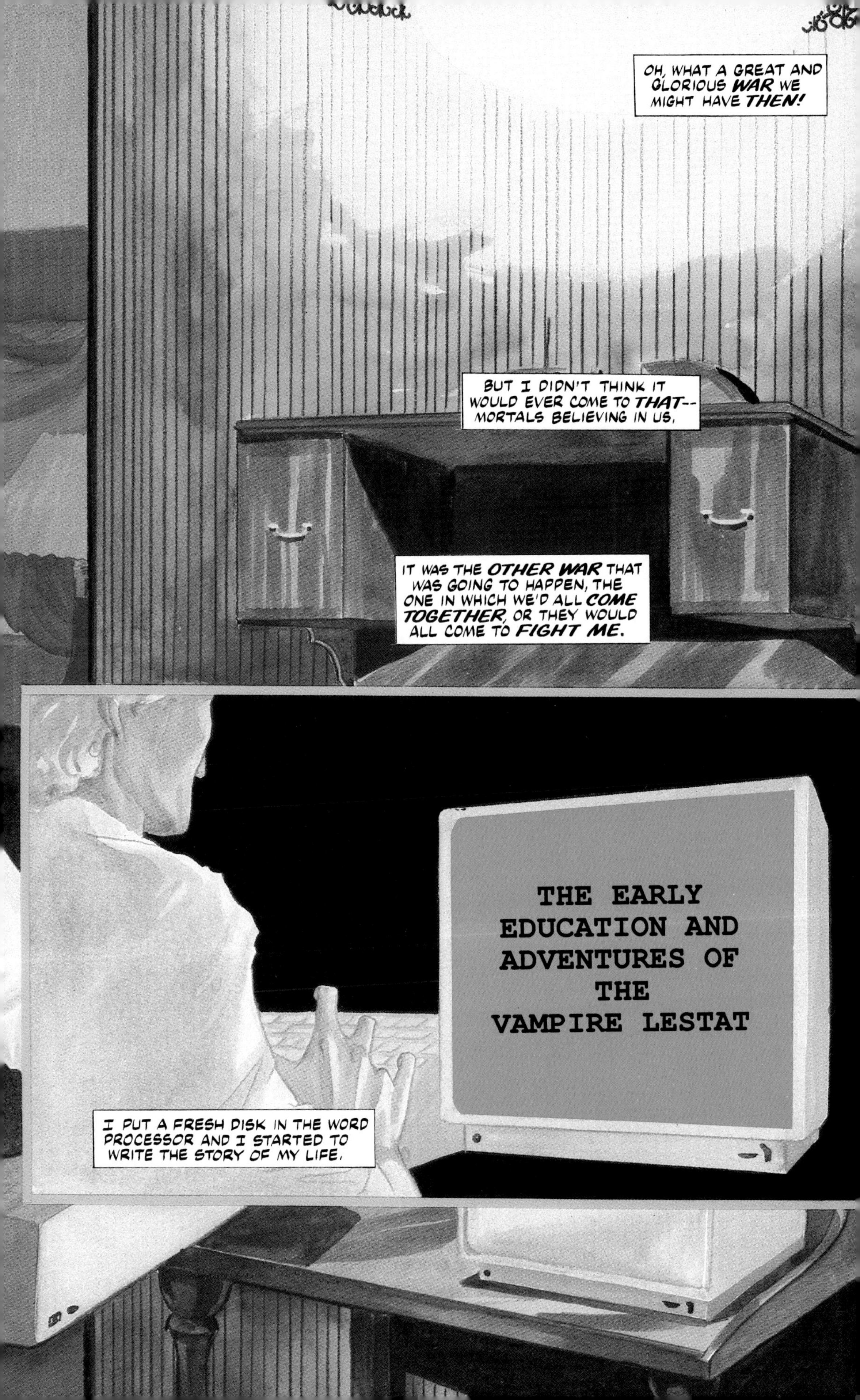
OH, WHAT A GREAT AND GLORIOUS WAR WE MIGHT HAVE THEN!
BUT I DIDN'T THINK IT WOULD EVER COME TO THAT-- MORTALS BELIEVING IN US.
IT WAS THE OTHER WAR THAT WAS GOING TO HAPPEN, THE ONE IN WHICH WE'D ALL COME TOGETHER, OR THEY WOULD ALL COME TO FIGHT ME.
THE EARLY EDUCATION AND ADVENTURES OF THE VAMPIRE LESTAT
I PUT A FRESH DISK IN THE WORD PROCESSOR AND I STARTED TO WRITE THE STORY OF MY LIFE.

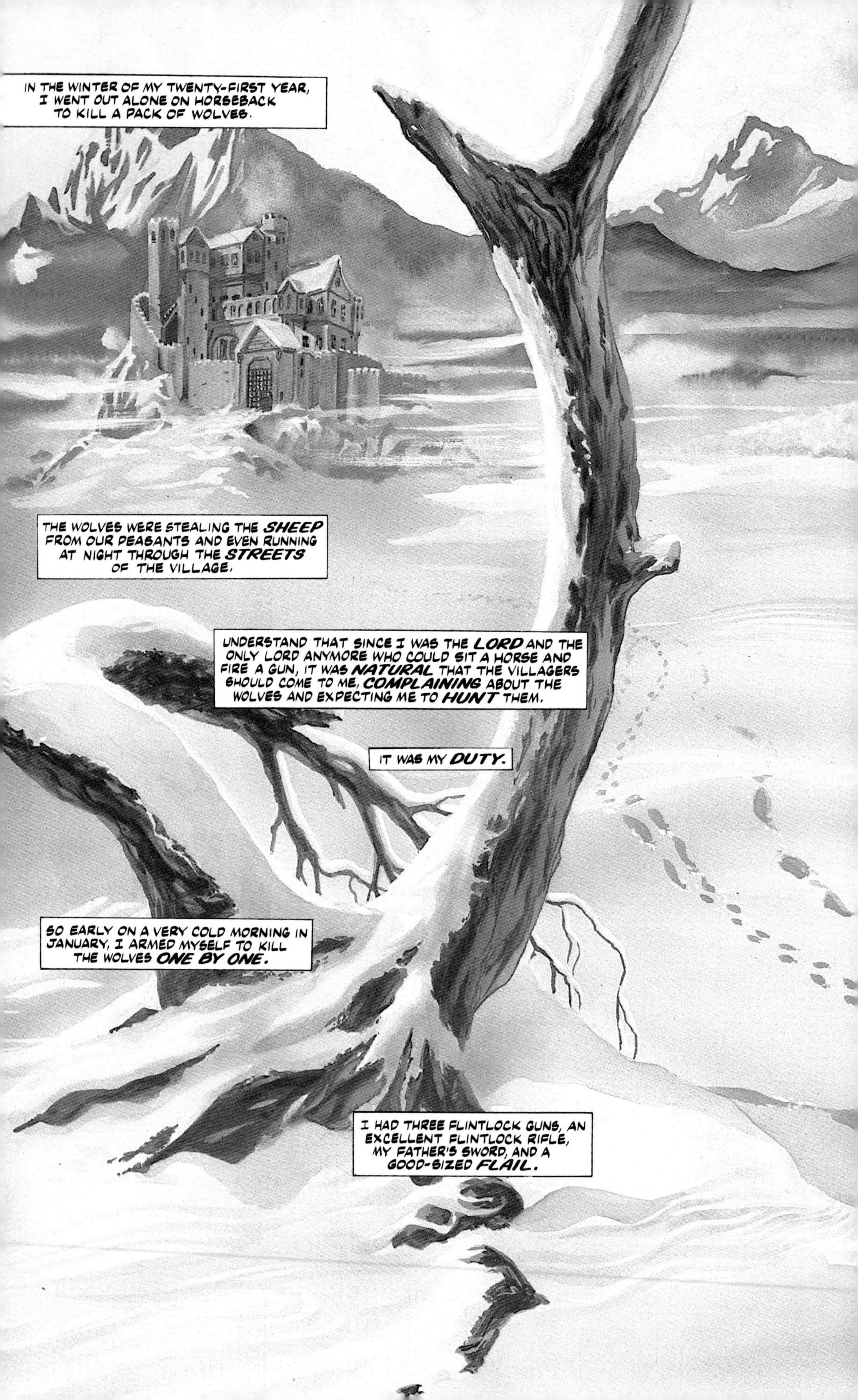
IN THE WINTER OF MY TWENTY-FIRST YEAR, I WENT OUT ALONE ON HORSEBACK TO KILL A PACK OF WOLVES.
THE WOLVES WERE STEALING THE SHEEP FROM OUR PEASANTS AND EVEN RUNNING AT NIGHT THROUGH THE STREETS OF THE VILLAGE.
UNDERSTAND THAT SINCE I WAS THE LORD AND THE ONLY LORD ANYMORE WHO COULD SIT A HORSE AND FIRE A GUN, IT WAS NATURAL THAT THE VILLAGERS SHOULD COME TO ME, COMPLAINING ABOUT THE WOLVES AND EXPECTING ME TO HUNT THEM.
IT WAS MY DUTY.
SO EARLY ON A VERY COLD MORNING IN JANUARY, I ARMED MYSELF TO KILL THE WOLVES ONE BY ONE.
I HAD THREE FLINTLOCK GUNS, AN EXCELLENT FLINTLOCK RIFLE, MY FATHER'S SWORD, AND A GOOD-SIZED FLAIL.

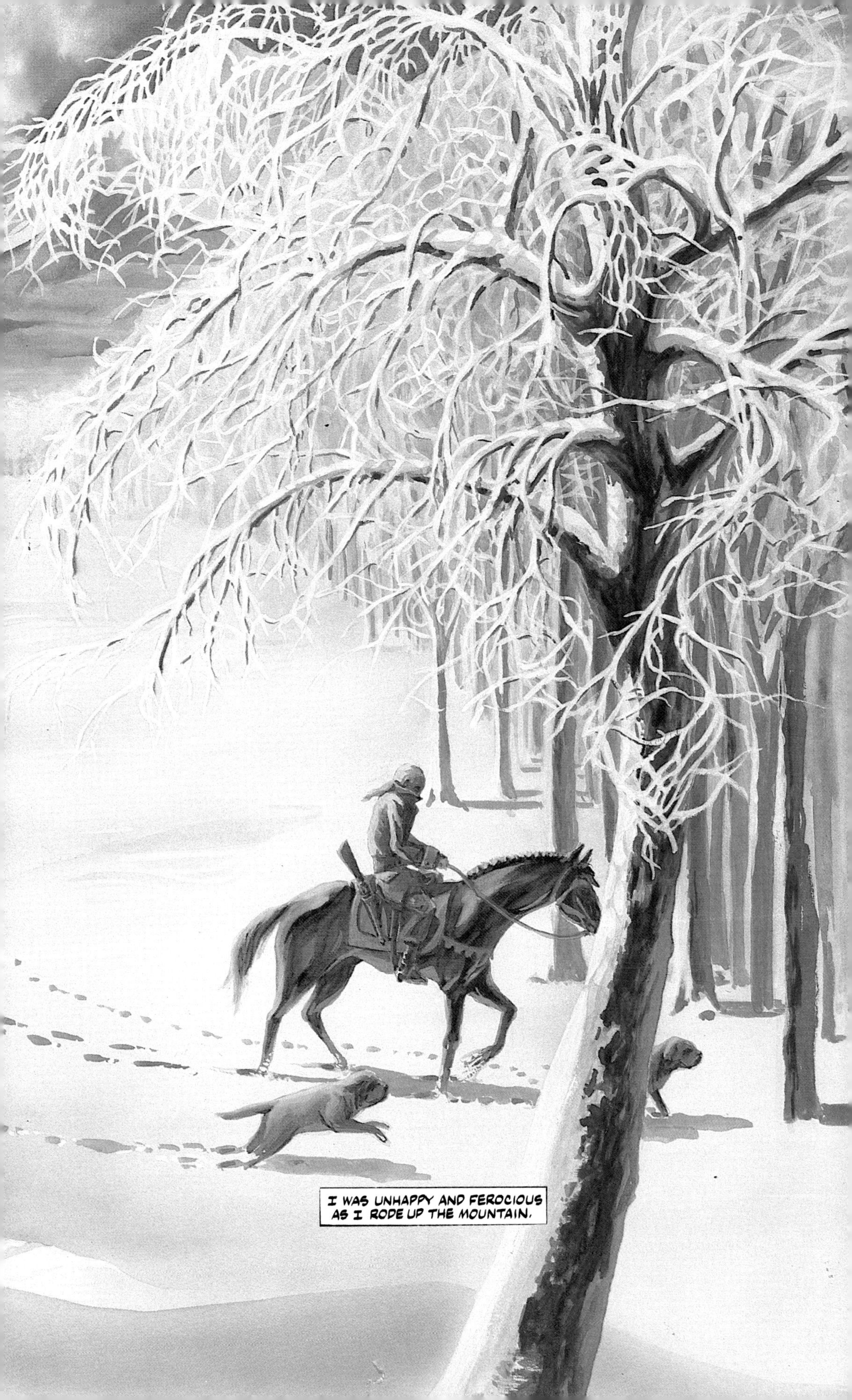
I WAS UNHAPPY AND FEROCIOUS AS I RODE UP THE MOUNTAIN.

AS I STARTED ACROSS A BROAD EMPTY FIELD TOWARD THE BARREN WOOD, I HEARD THE FIRST *HOWLING*.

I BROKE INTO A RUN FOR THE FOREST.

IT SEEMED I WOULD MAKE IT *EASILY* BEFORE THE THREE REACHED ME--

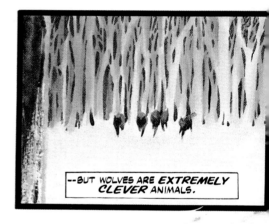

--BUT WOLVES ARE *EXTREMELY CLEVER* ANIMALS.

IT WAS AN *AMBUSH,* AND I COULD NEVER MAKE IT TO THE FOREST *IN TIME.*

I GOT READY FOR BATTLE.

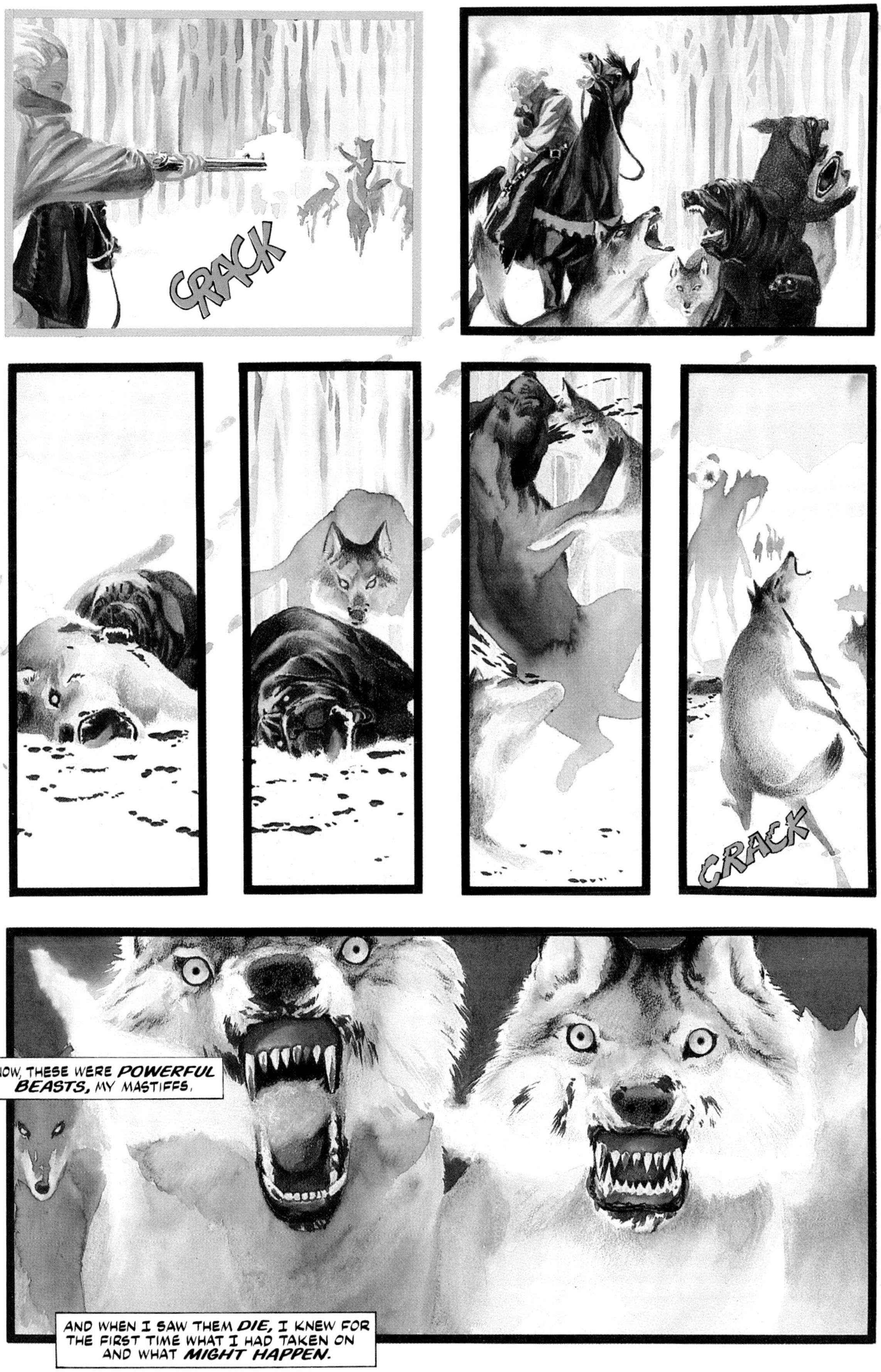
CRACK
CRACK
NOW, THESE WERE POWERFUL BEASTS, MY MASTIFFS.
AND WHEN I SAW THEM DIE, I KNEW FOR THE FIRST TIME WHAT I HAD TAKEN ON AND WHAT MIGHT HAPPEN.

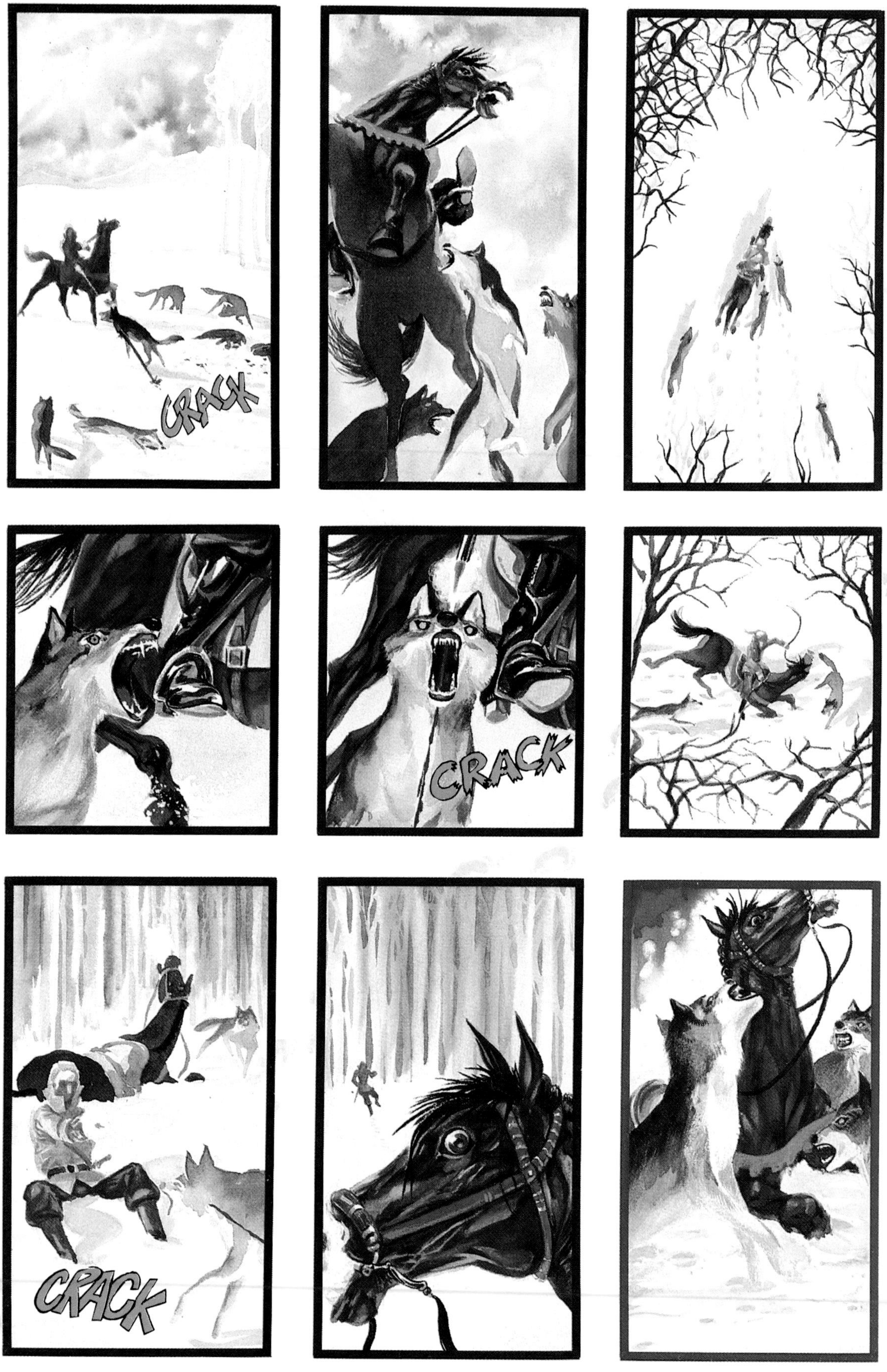
CRACK
CRACK
CRACK

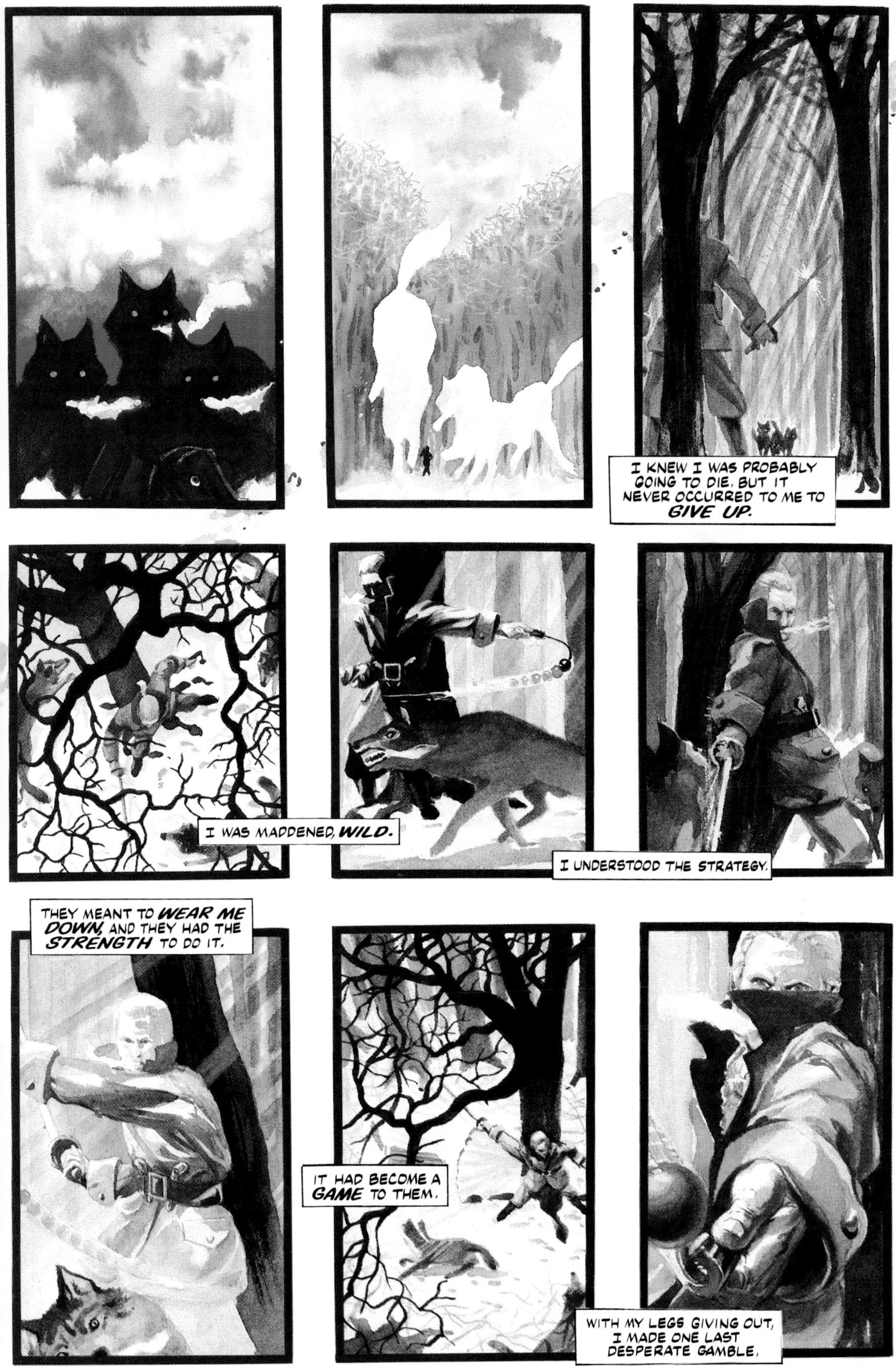
I KNEW I WAS PROBABLY GOING TO DIE, BUT IT NEVER OCCURRED TO ME TO GIVE UP.
I WAS MADDENED, WILD.
I UNDERSTOOD THE STRATEGY.
THEY MEANT TO WEAR ME DOWN, AND THEY HAD THE STRENGTH TO DO IT.
IT HAD BECOME A GAME TO THEM.
WITH MY LEGS GIVING OUT, I MADE ONE LAST DESPERATE GAMBLE.

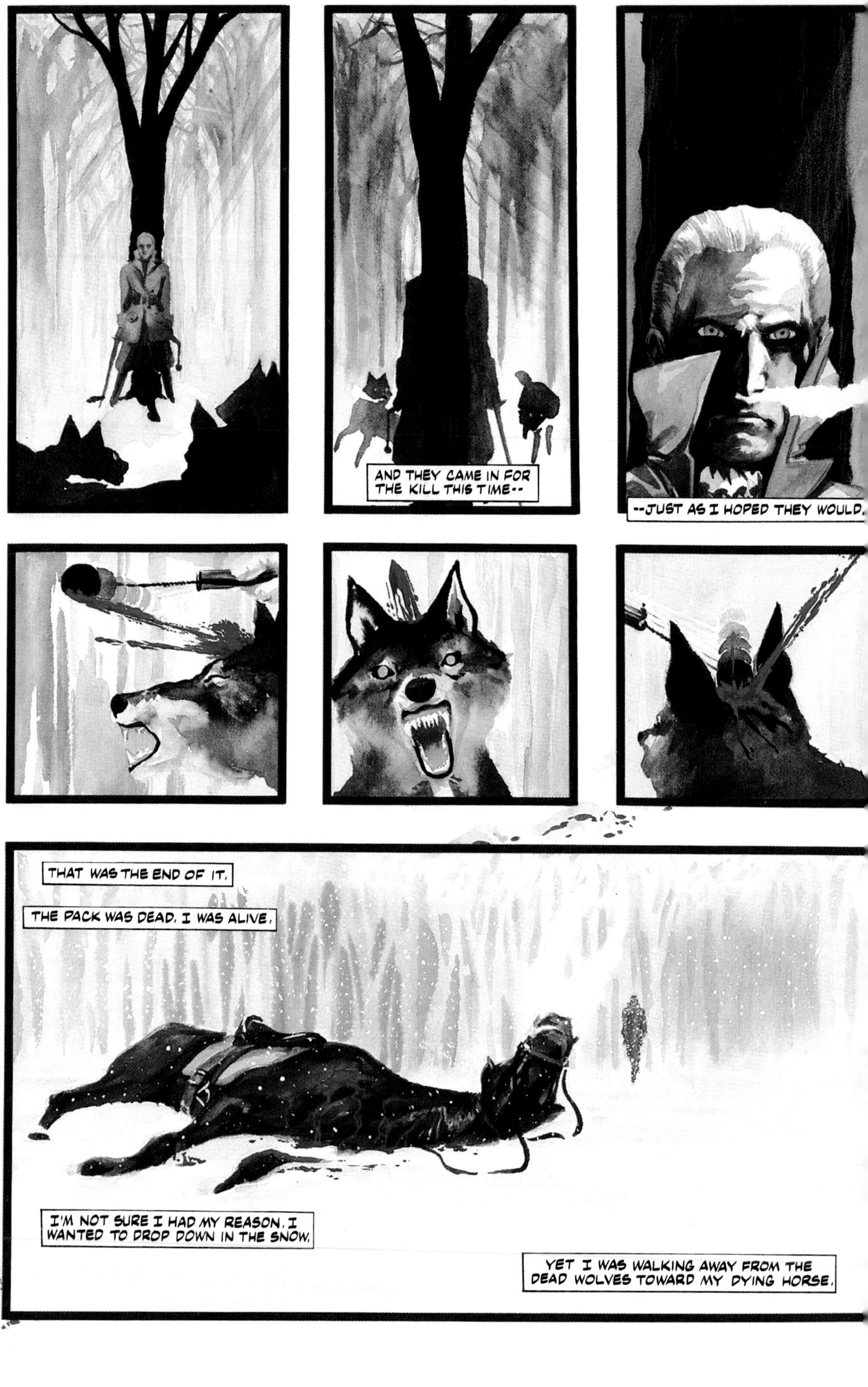
AND THEY CAME IN FOR THE KILL THIS TIME--
--JUST AS I HOPED THEY WOULD.
THAT WAS THE END OF IT.
THE PACK WAS DEAD. I WAS ALIVE.
I'M NOT SURE I HAD MY REASON. I WANTED TO DROP DOWN IN THE SNOW.
YET I WAS WALKING AWAY FROM THE DEAD WOLVES TOWARD MY DYING HORSE.

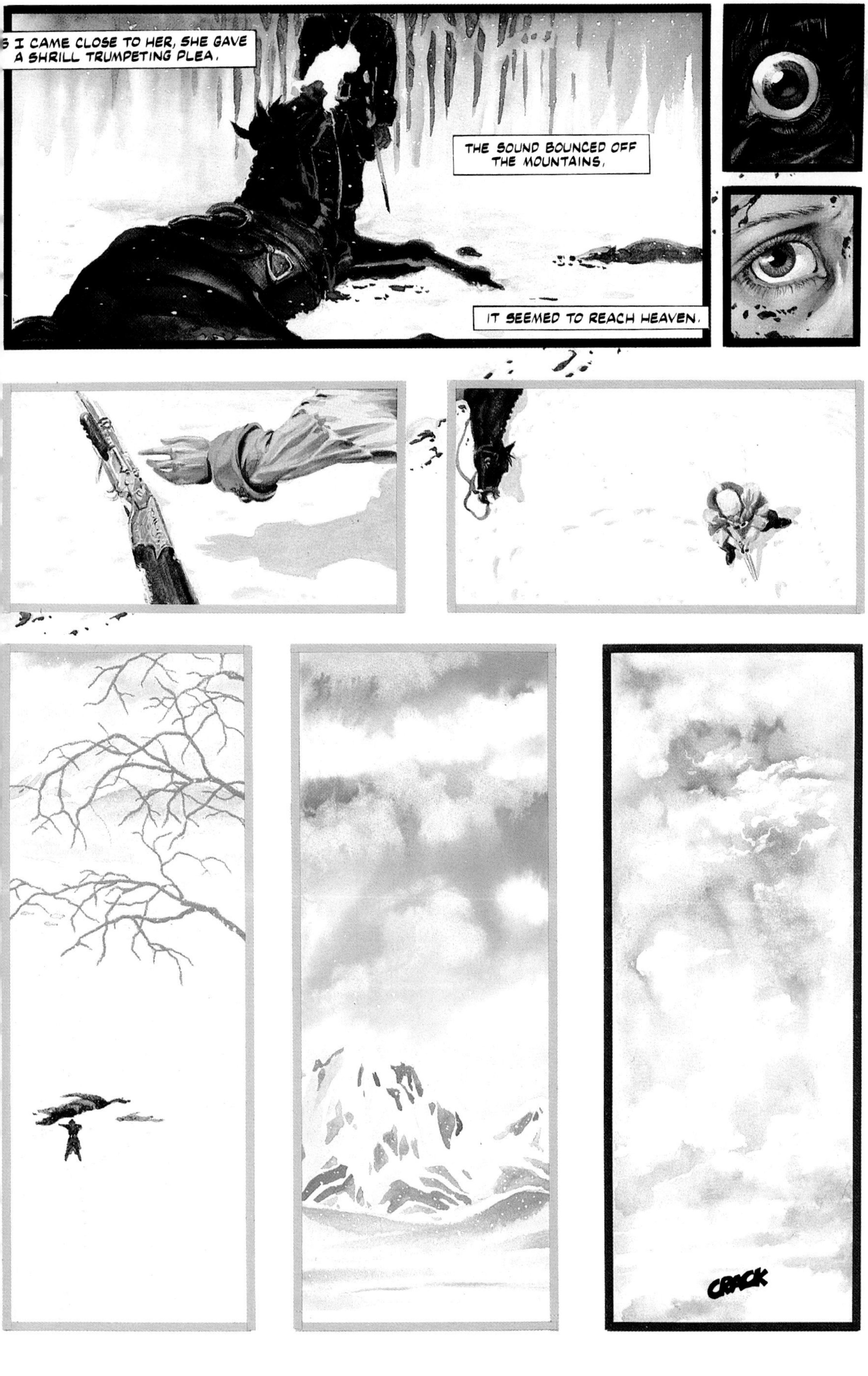
S I CAME CLOSE TO HER, SHE GAVE A SHRILL TRUMPETING PLEA.
THE SOUND BOUNCED OFF THE MOUNTAINS,
IT SEEMED TO REACH HEAVEN.
CRACK

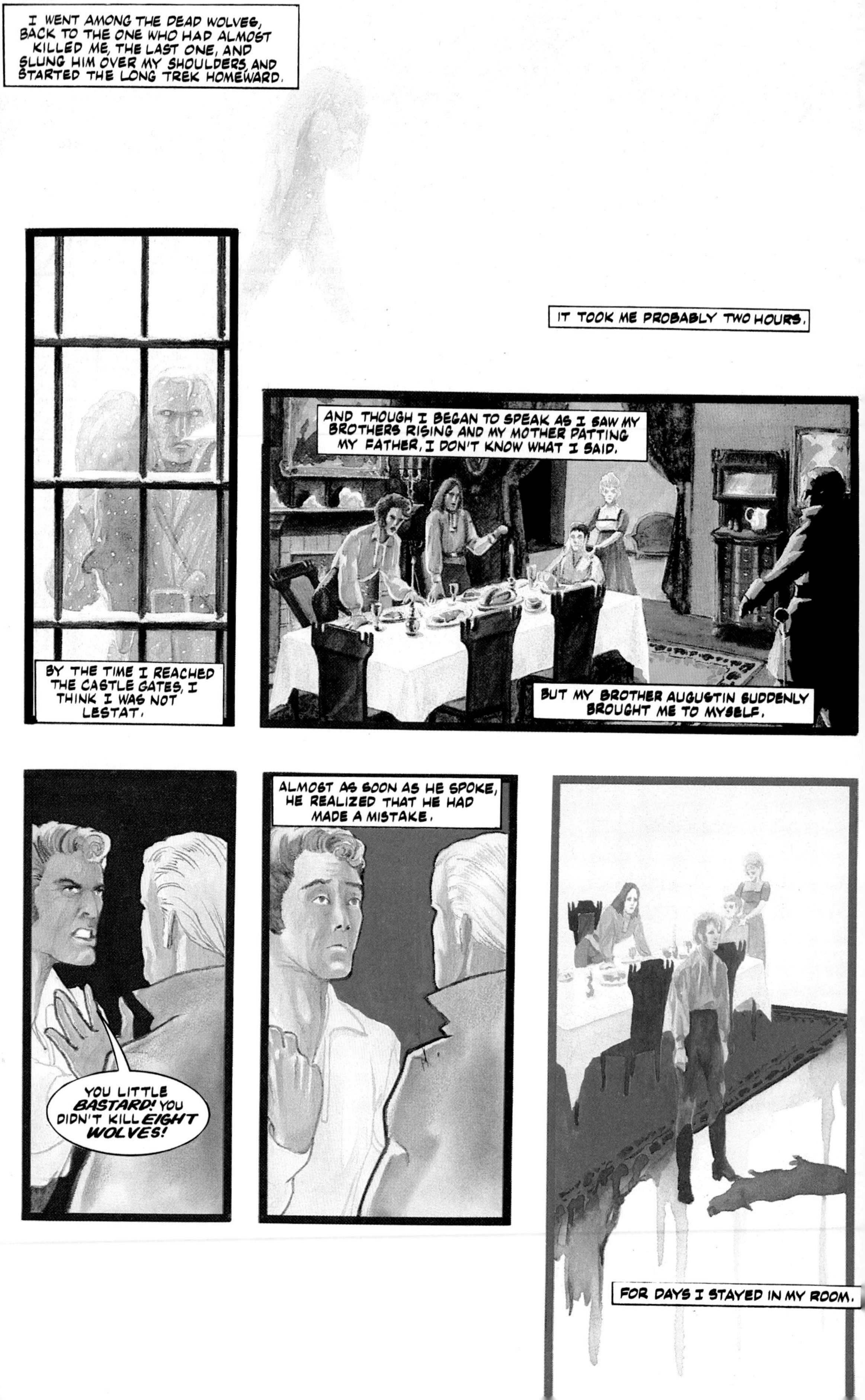
I WENT AMONG THE DEAD WOLVES, BACK TO THE ONE WHO HAD ALMOST KILLED ME, THE LAST ONE, AND SLUNG HIM OVER MY SHOULDERS, AND STARTED THE LONG TREK HOMEWARD.
IT TOOK ME PROBABLY TWO HOURS.
BY THE TIME I REACHED THE CASTLE GATES, I THINK I WAS NOT LESTAT.
AND THOUGH I BEGAN TO SPEAK AS I SAW MY BROTHERS RISING AND MY MOTHER PATTING MY FATHER, I DON'T KNOW WHAT I SAID.
BUT MY BROTHER AUGUSTIN SUDDENLY BROUGHT ME TO MYSELF.
YOU LITTLE BASTARD! YOU DIDN'T KILL EIGHT WOLVES!
ALMOST AS SOON AS HE SPOKE, HE REALIZED THAT HE HAD MADE A MISTAKE.
FOR DAYS I STAYED IN MY ROOM.

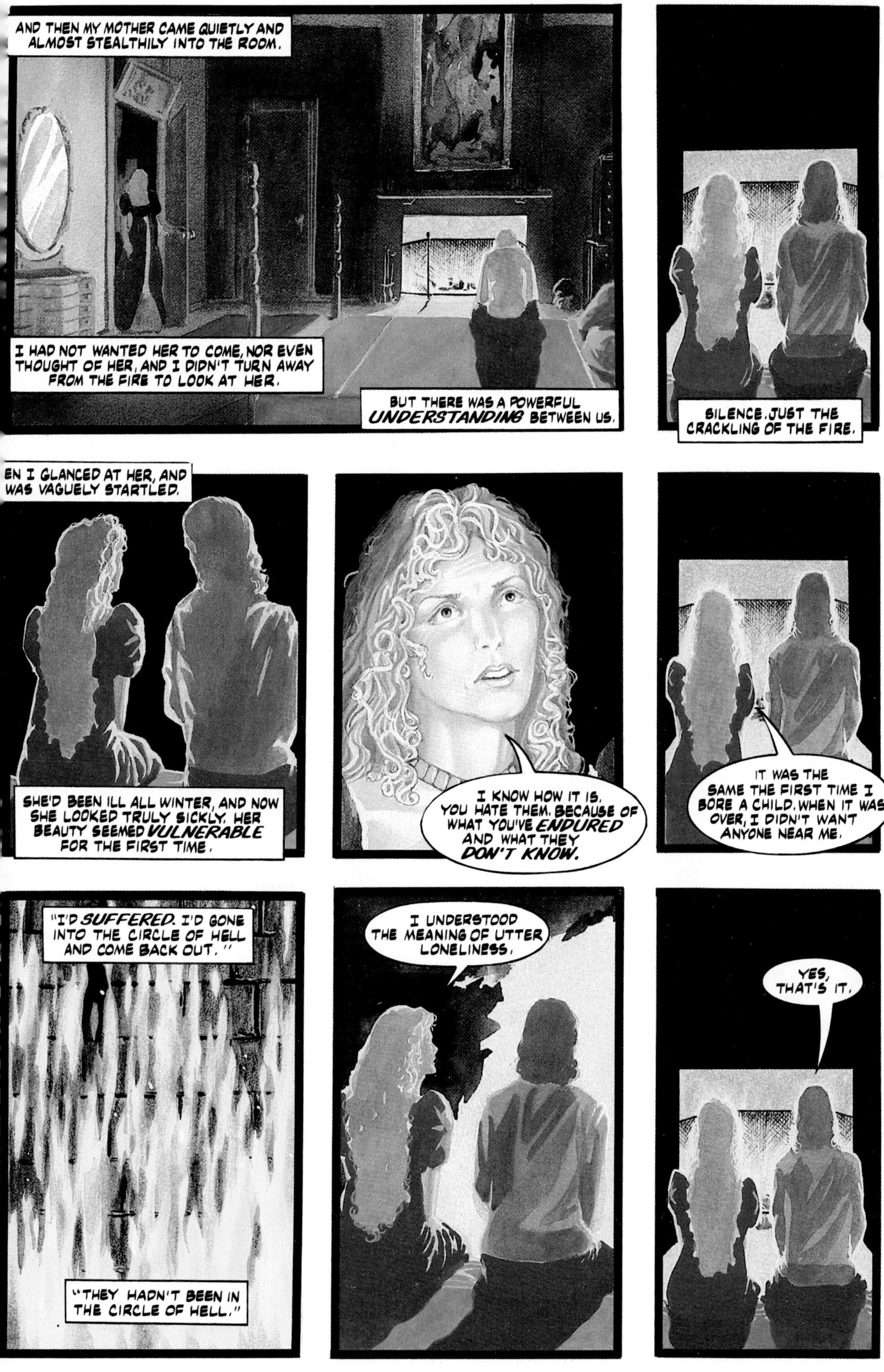
AND THEN MY MOTHER CAME QUIETLY AND ALMOST STEALTHILY INTO THE ROOM.
I HAD NOT WANTED HER TO COME, NOR EVEN THOUGHT OF HER, AND I DIDN'T TURN AWAY FROM THE FIRE TO LOOK AT HER.
BUT THERE WAS A POWERFUL UNDERSTANDING BETWEEN US.
SILENCE. JUST THE CRACKLING OF THE FIRE.
EN I GLANCED AT HER, AND WAS VAGUELY STARTLED.
SHE'D BEEN ILL ALL WINTER, AND NOW SHE LOOKED TRULY SICKLY. HER BEAUTY SEEMED VULNERABLE FOR THE FIRST TIME.
I KNOW HOW IT IS. YOU HATE THEM. BECAUSE OF WHAT YOU'VE ENDURED AND WHAT THEY DON'T KNOW.
IT WAS THE SAME THE FIRST TIME I BORE A CHILD. WHEN IT WAS OVER, I DIDN'T WANT ANYONE NEAR ME.
"I'D SUFFERED. I'D GONE INTO THE CIRCLE OF HELL AND COME BACK OUT."
"THEY HADN'T BEEN IN THE CIRCLE OF HELL."
I UNDERSTOOD THE MEANING OF UTTER LONELINESS.
YES, THAT'S IT.

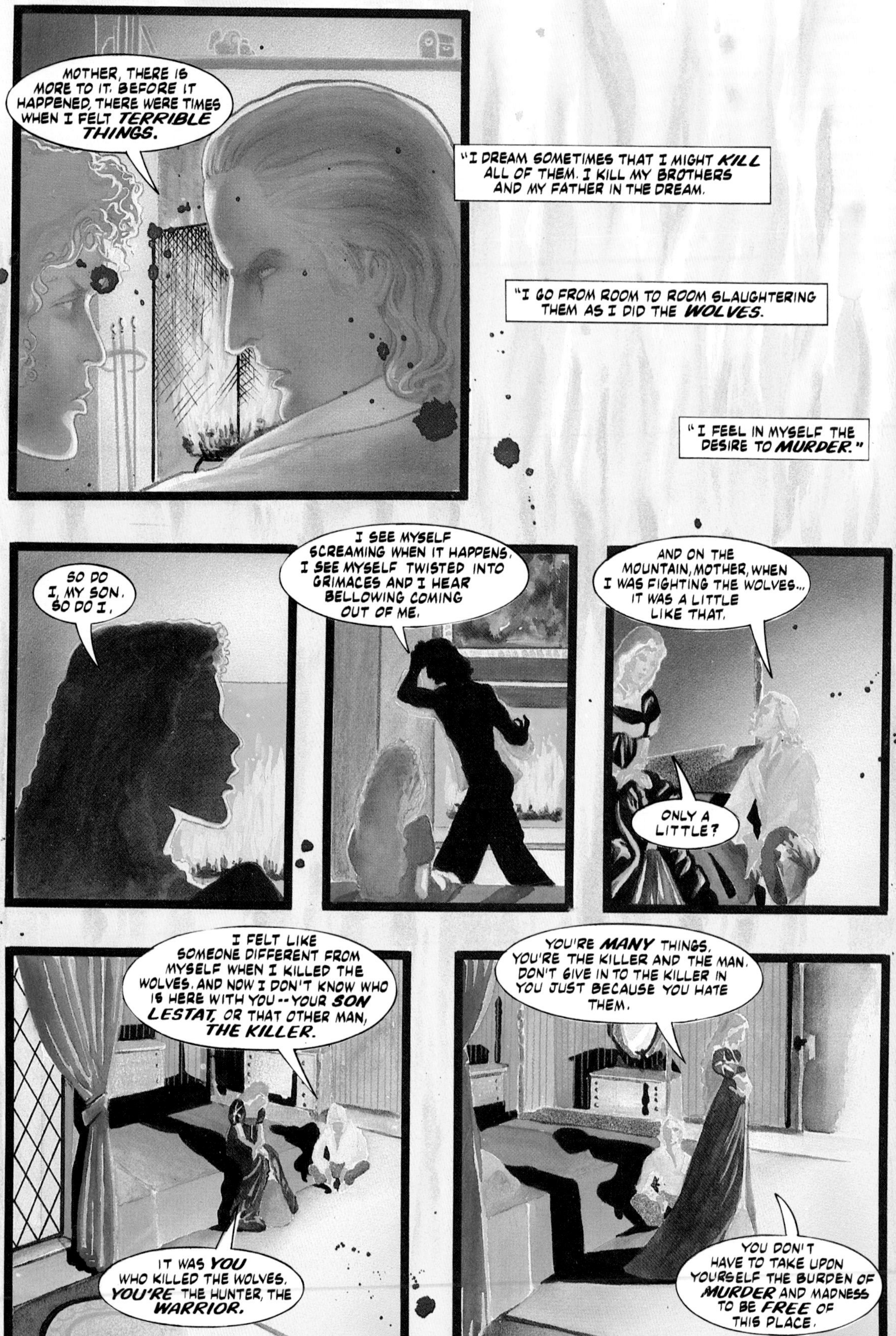

MOTHER, THERE IS MORE TO IT. BEFORE IT HAPPENED, THERE WERE TIMES WHEN I FELT TERRIBLE THINGS.
"I DREAM SOMETIMES THAT I MIGHT KILL ALL OF THEM. I KILL MY BROTHERS AND MY FATHER IN THE DREAM.
"I GO FROM ROOM TO ROOM SLAUGHTERING THEM AS I DID THE WOLVES.
"I FEEL IN MYSELF THE DESIRE TO MURDER."
SO DO I, MY SON. SO DO I.
I SEE MYSELF SCREAMING WHEN IT HAPPENS. I SEE MYSELF TWISTED INTO GRIMACES AND I HEAR BELLOWING COMING OUT OF ME.
AND ON THE MOUNTAIN, MOTHER, WHEN I WAS FIGHTING THE WOLVES... IT WAS A LITTLE LIKE THAT.
ONLY A LITTLE?
I FELT LIKE SOMEONE DIFFERENT FROM MYSELF WHEN I KILLED THE WOLVES. AND NOW I DON'T KNOW WHO IS HERE WITH YOU -- YOUR SON LESTAT, OR THAT OTHER MAN, THE KILLER.
IT WAS YOU WHO KILLED THE WOLVES. YOU'RE THE HUNTER, THE WARRIOR.
YOU'RE MANY THINGS. YOU'RE THE KILLER AND THE MAN. DON'T GIVE IN TO THE KILLER IN YOU JUST BECAUSE YOU HATE THEM.
YOU DON'T HAVE TO TAKE UPON YOURSELF THE BURDEN OF MURDER AND MADNESS TO BE FREE OF THIS PLACE.
"SURELY, THERE MUST BE OTHER WAYS."

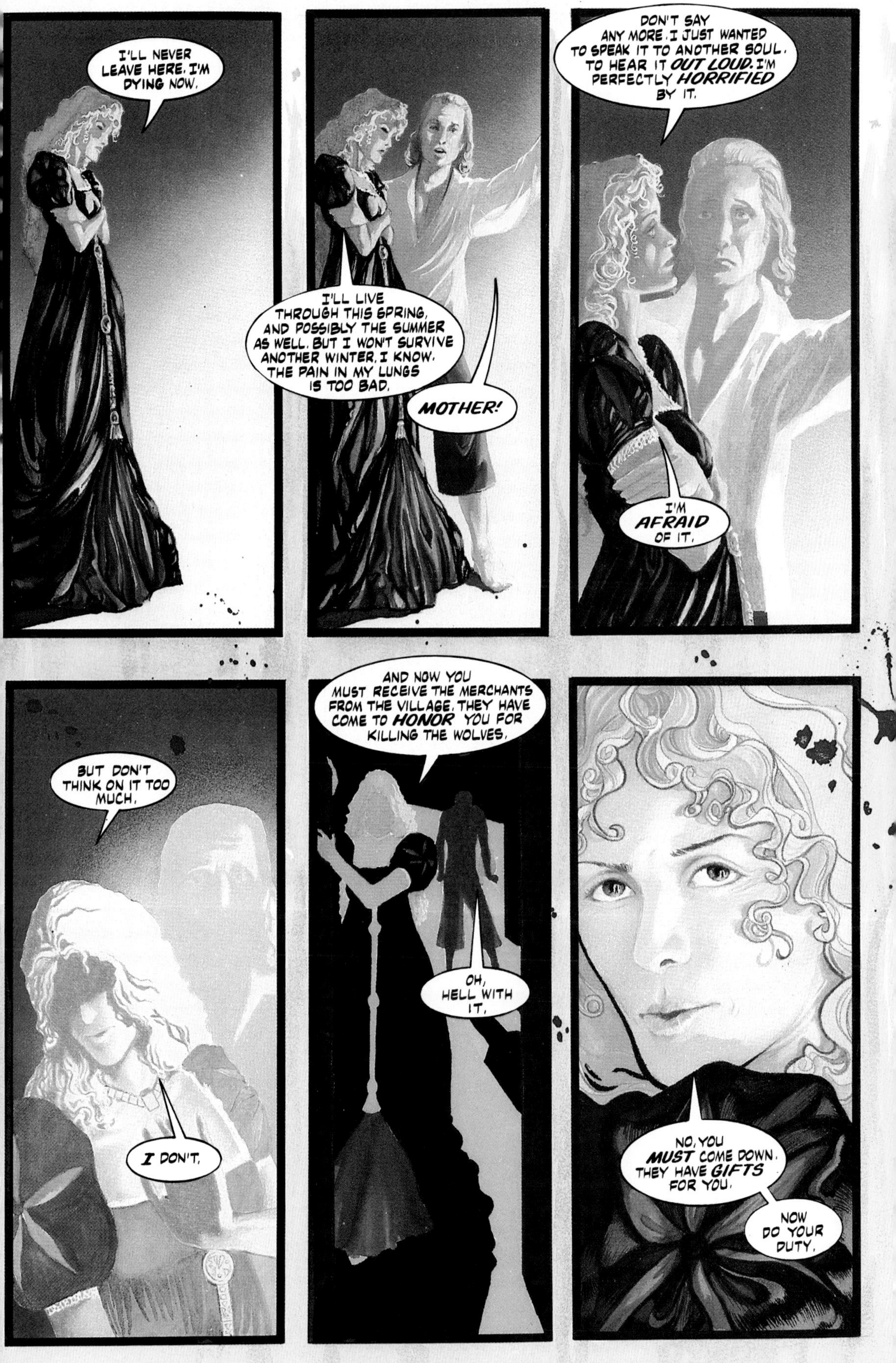
I'LL NEVER LEAVE HERE. I'M DYING NOW.
I'LL LIVE THROUGH THIS SPRING, AND POSSIBLY THE SUMMER AS WELL. BUT I WON'T SURVIVE ANOTHER WINTER, I KNOW. THE PAIN IN MY LUNGS IS TOO BAD.
MOTHER!
DON'T SAY ANY MORE. I JUST WANTED TO SPEAK IT TO ANOTHER SOUL. TO HEAR IT OUT LOUD. I'M PERFECTLY HORRIFIED BY IT.
I'M AFRAID OF IT.
BUT DON'T THINK ON IT TOO MUCH.
I DON'T.
AND NOW YOU MUST RECEIVE THE MERCHANTS FROM THE VILLAGE. THEY HAVE COME TO HONOR YOU FOR KILLING THE WOLVES.
OH, HELL WITH IT.
NO, YOU MUST COME DOWN. THEY HAVE GIFTS FOR YOU.
NOW DO YOUR DUTY.

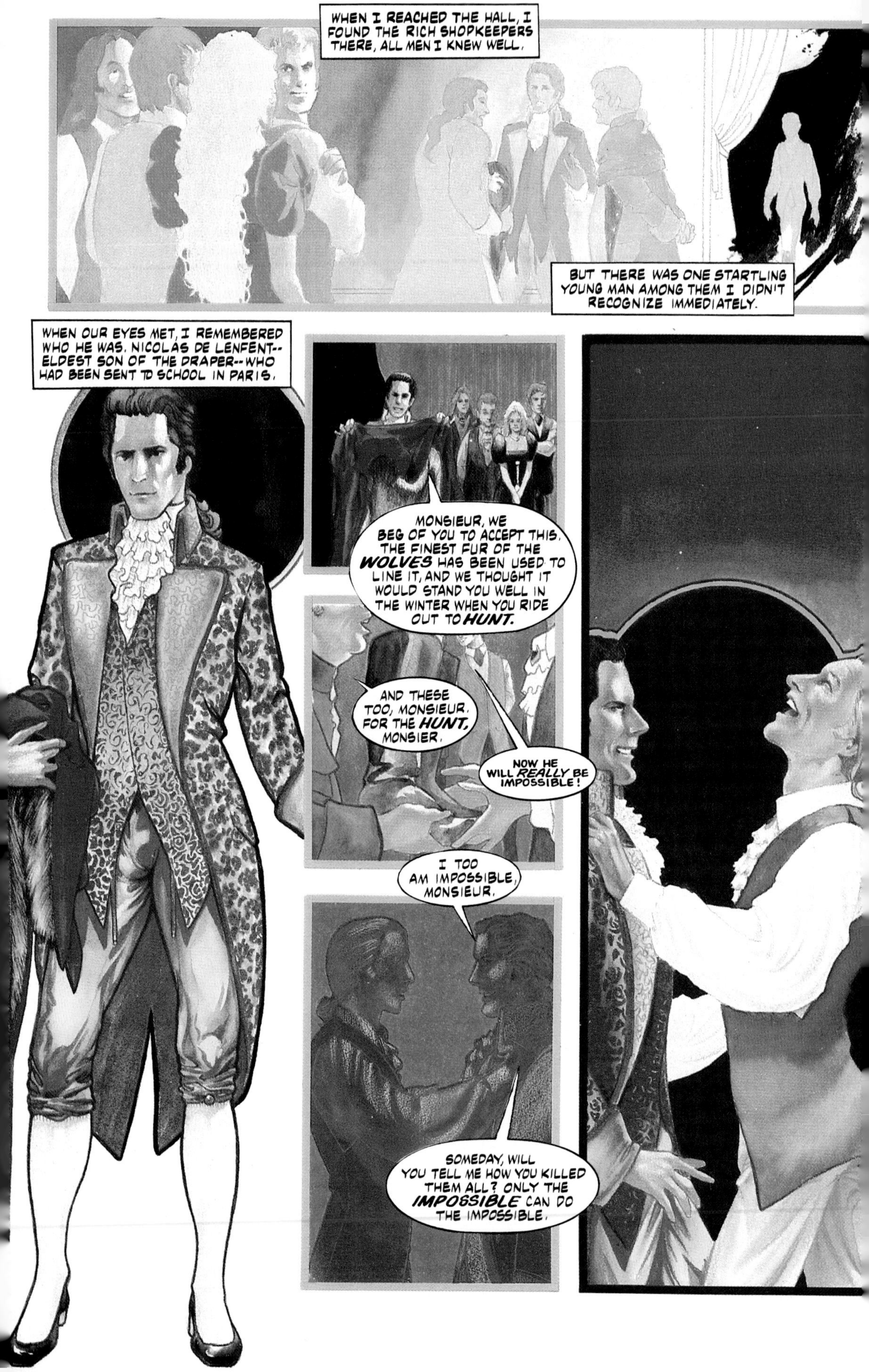
WHEN I REACHED THE HALL, I FOUND THE RICH SHOPKEEPERS THERE, ALL MEN I KNEW WELL.
BUT THERE WAS ONE STARTLING YOUNG MAN AMONG THEM I DIDN'T RECOGNIZE IMMEDIATELY.
WHEN OUR EYES MET, I REMEMBERED WHO HE WAS. NICOLAS DE LENFENT-- ELDEST SON OF THE DRAPER--WHO HAD BEEN SENT TO SCHOOL IN PARIS.
MONSIEUR, WE BEG OF YOU TO ACCEPT THIS. THE FINEST FUR OF THE WOLVES HAS BEEN USED TO LINE IT, AND WE THOUGHT IT WOULD STAND YOU WELL IN THE WINTER WHEN YOU RIDE OUT TO HUNT.
AND THESE TOO, MONSIEUR. FOR THE HUNT, MONSIER.
NOW HE WILL REALLY BE IMPOSSIBLE!
I TOO AM IMPOSSIBLE, MONSIEUR.
SOMEDAY, WILL YOU TELL ME HOW YOU KILLED THEM ALL? ONLY THE IMPOSSIBLE CAN DO THE IMPOSSIBLE.

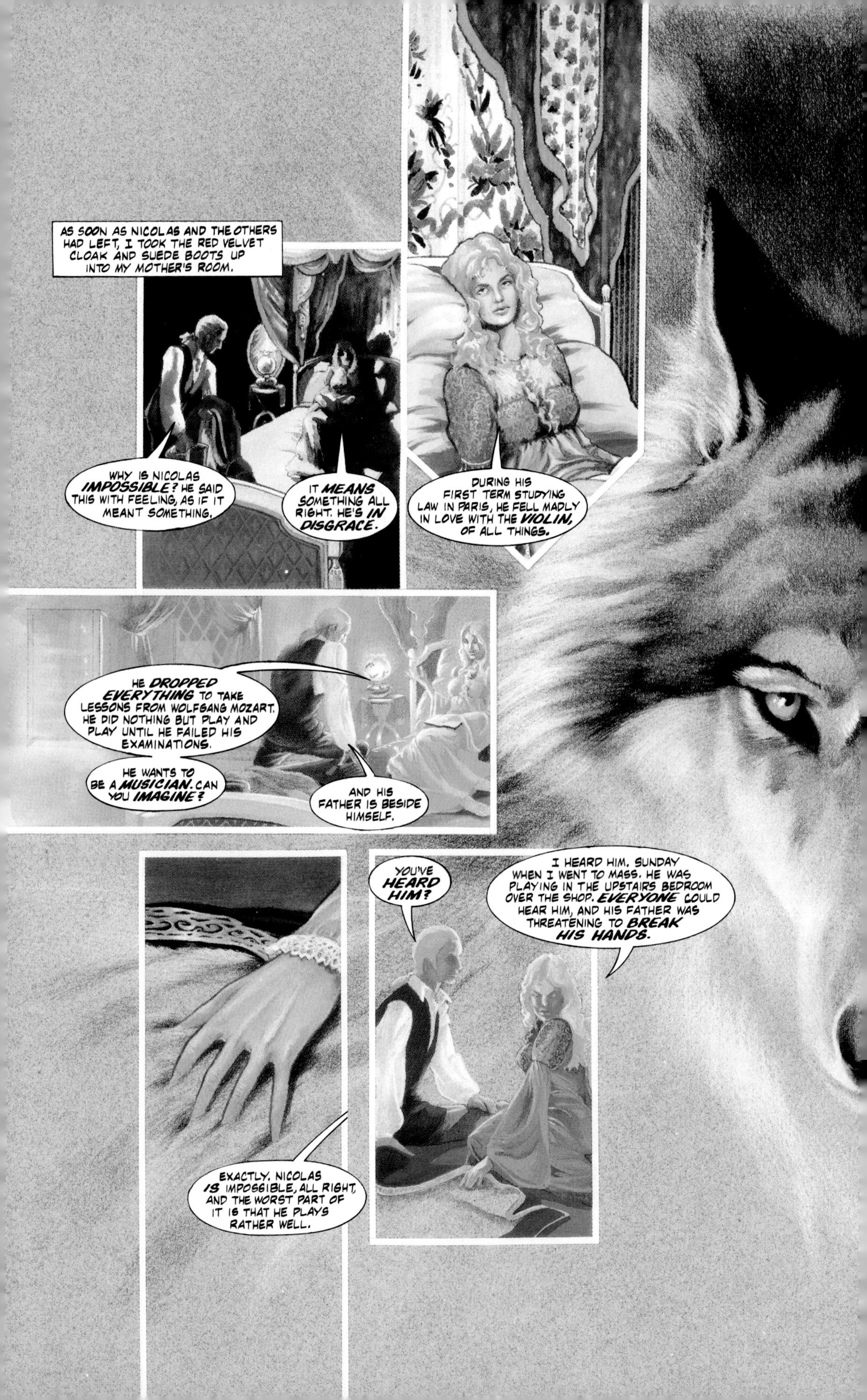
AS SOON AS NICOLAS AND THE OTHERS HAD LEFT, I TOOK THE RED VELVET CLOAK AND SUEDE BOOTS UP INTO MY MOTHER'S ROOM.
WHY IS NICOLAS IMPOSSIBLE? HE SAID THIS WITH FEELING, AS IF IT MEANT SOMETHING.
IT MEANS SOMETHING ALL RIGHT. HE'S IN DISGRACE.
DURING HIS FIRST TERM STUDYING LAW IN PARIS, HE FELL MADLY IN LOVE WITH THE VIOLIN, OF ALL THINGS.
HE DROPPED EVERYTHING TO TAKE LESSONS FROM WOLFGANG MOZART. HE DID NOTHING BUT PLAY AND PLAY UNTIL HE FAILED HIS EXAMINATIONS.
HE WANTS TO BE A MUSICIAN. CAN YOU IMAGINE?
AND HIS FATHER IS BESIDE HIMSELF.
YOU'VE HEARD HIM?
I HEARD HIM. SUNDAY WHEN I WENT TO MASS. HE WAS PLAYING IN THE UPSTAIRS BEDROOM OVER THE SHOP. EVERYONE COULD HEAR HIM, AND HIS FATHER WAS THREATENING TO BREAK HIS HANDS.
EXACTLY. NICOLAS IS IMPOSSIBLE, ALL RIGHT, AND THE WORST PART OF IT IS THAT HE PLAYS RATHER WELL.

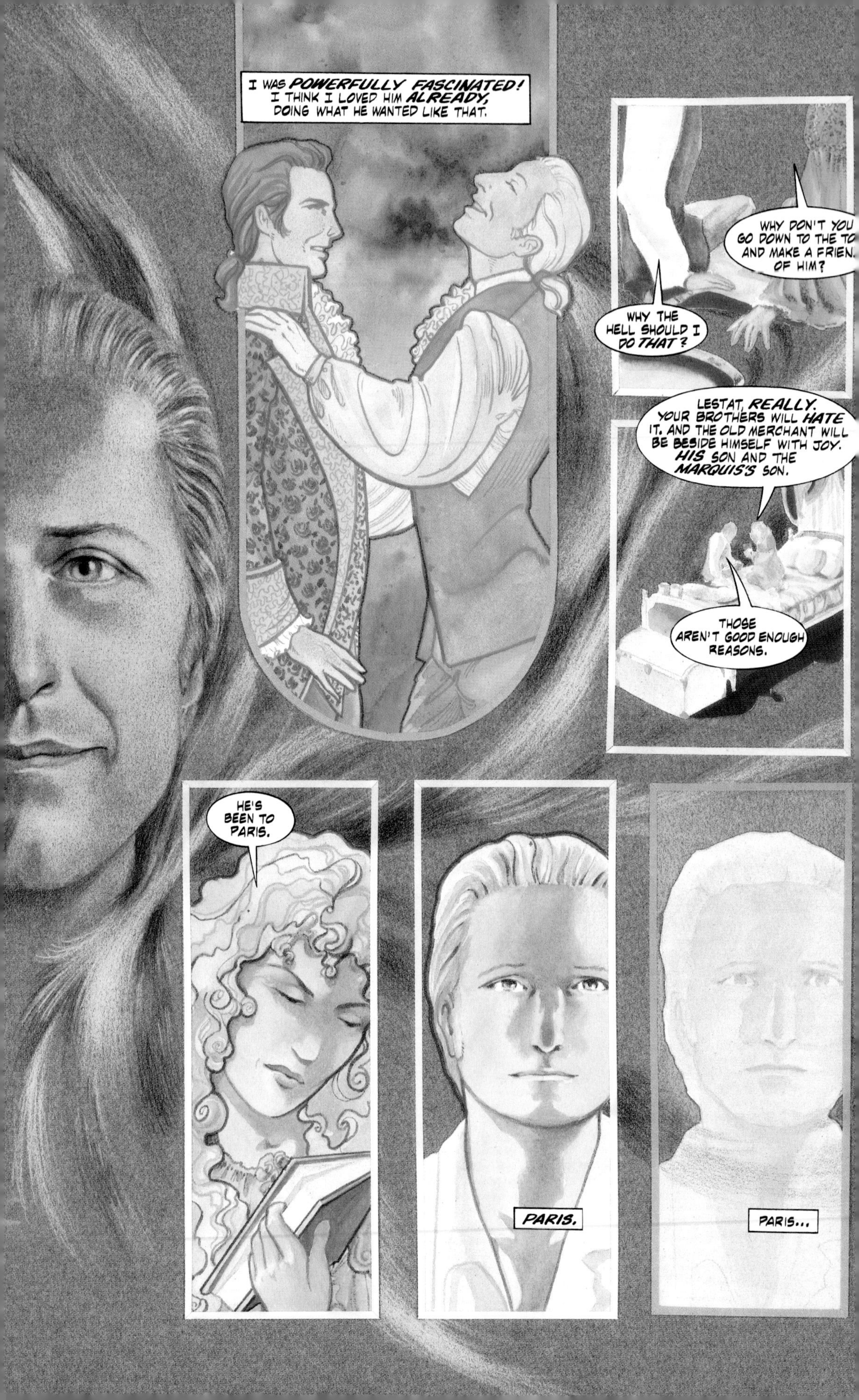

I WAS POWERFULLY FASCINATED! I THINK I LOVED HIM ALREADY, DOING WHAT HE WANTED LIKE THAT.
WHY DON'T YOU GO DOWN TO THE TO AND MAKE A FRIEN OF HIM?
WHY THE HELL SHOULD I DO THAT?
LESTAT, REALLY. YOUR BROTHERS WILL HATE IT. AND THE OLD MERCHANT WILL BE BESIDE HIMSELF WITH JOY. HIS SON AND THE MARQUIS'S SON.
THOSE AREN'T GOOD ENOUGH REASONS.
HE'S BEEN TO PARIS.
PARIS.
PARIS...

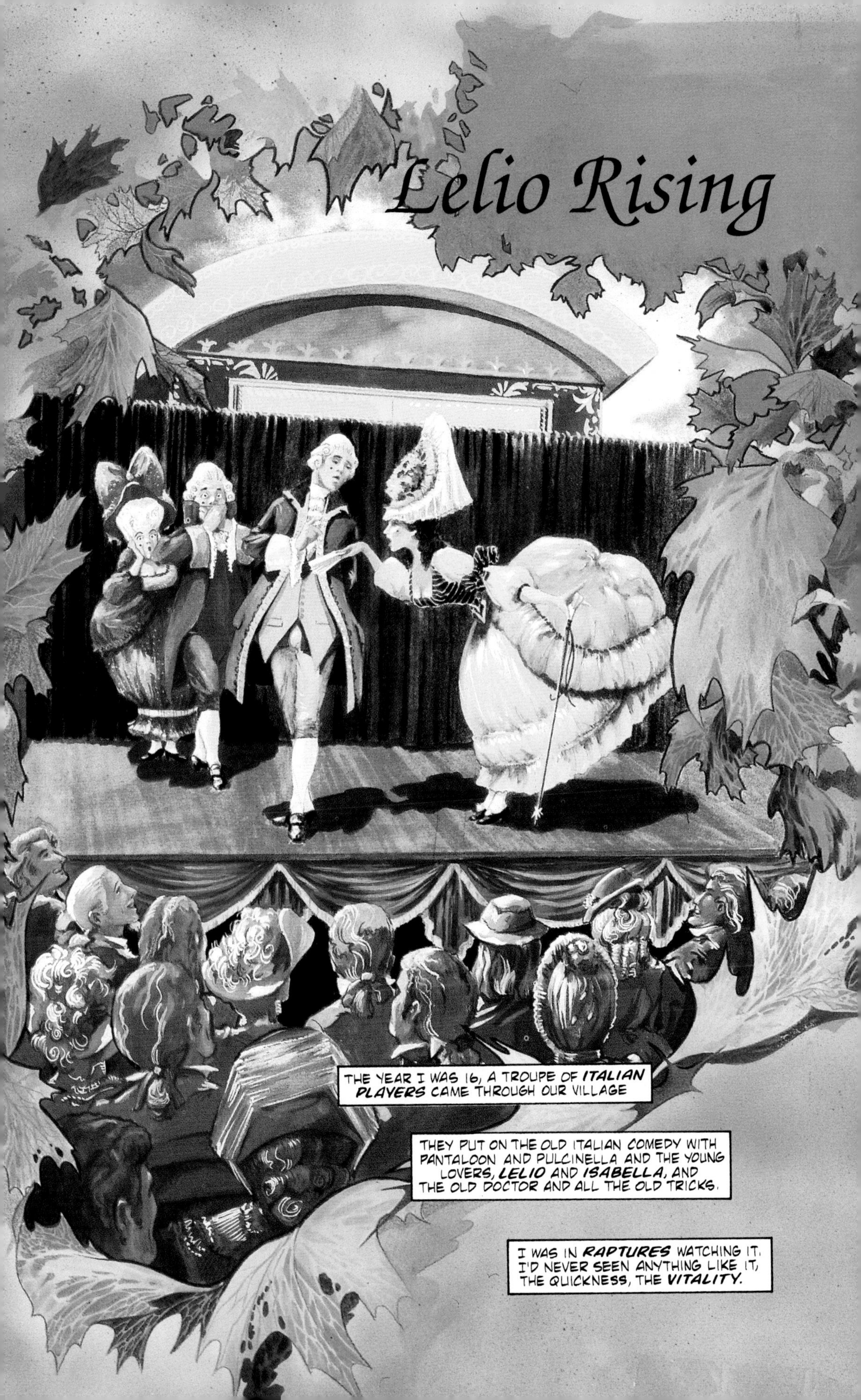
Lelio Rising
THE YEAR I WAS 16, A TROUPE OF ITALIAN PLAYERS CAME THROUGH OUR VILLAGE
THEY PUT ON THE OLD ITALIAN COMEDY WITH PANTALOON AND PULCINELLA AND THE YOUNG LOVERS, LELIO AND ISABELLA, AND THE OLD DOCTOR AND ALL THE OLD TRICKS.
I WAS IN RAPTURES WATCHING IT. I'D NEVER SEEN ANYTHING LIKE IT, THE QUICKNESS, THE VITALITY.

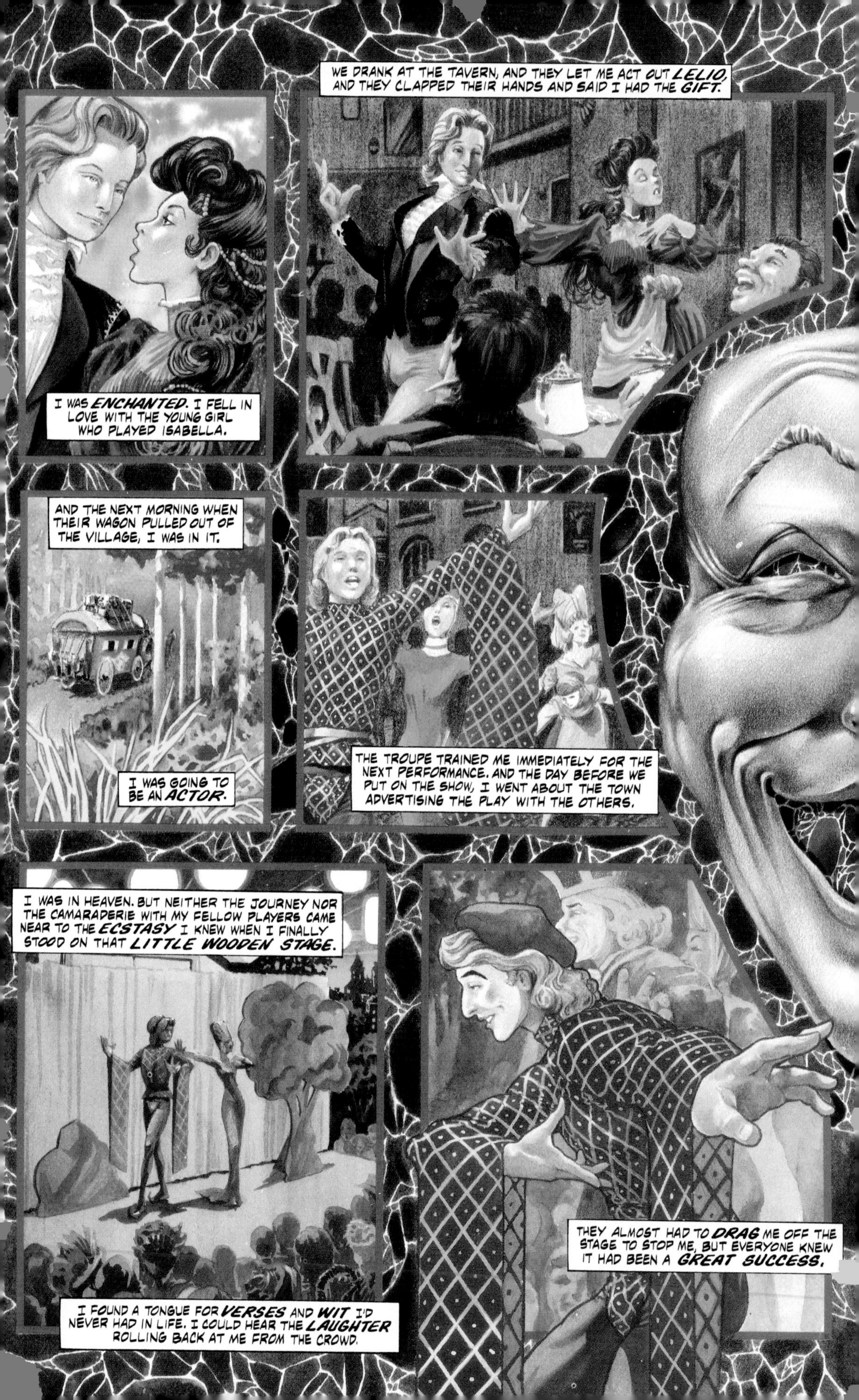
WE DRANK AT THE TAVERN, AND THEY LET ME ACT OUT LELIO, AND THEY CLAPPED THEIR HANDS AND SAID I HAD THE GIFT.
I WAS ENCHANTED. I FELL IN LOVE WITH THE YOUNG GIRL WHO PLAYED ISABELLA.
AND THE NEXT MORNING WHEN THEIR WAGON PULLED OUT OF THE VILLAGE, I WAS IN IT.
I WAS GOING TO BE AN ACTOR.
THE TROUPE TRAINED ME IMMEDIATELY FOR THE NEXT PERFORMANCE. AND THE DAY BEFORE WE PUT ON THE SHOW, I WENT ABOUT THE TOWN ADVERTISING THE PLAY WITH THE OTHERS.
I WAS IN HEAVEN. BUT NEITHER THE JOURNEY NOR THE CAMARADERIE WITH MY FELLOW PLAYERS CAME NEAR TO THE ECSTASY I KNEW WHEN I FINALLY STOOD ON THAT LITTLE WOODEN STAGE.
I FOUND A TONGUE FOR VERSES AND WIT I'D NEVER HAD IN LIFE. I COULD HEAR THE LAUGHTER ROLLING BACK AT ME FROM THE CROWD.
THEY ALMOST HAD TO DRAG ME OFF THE STAGE TO STOP ME, BUT EVERYONE KNEW IT HAD BEEN A GREAT SUCCESS.

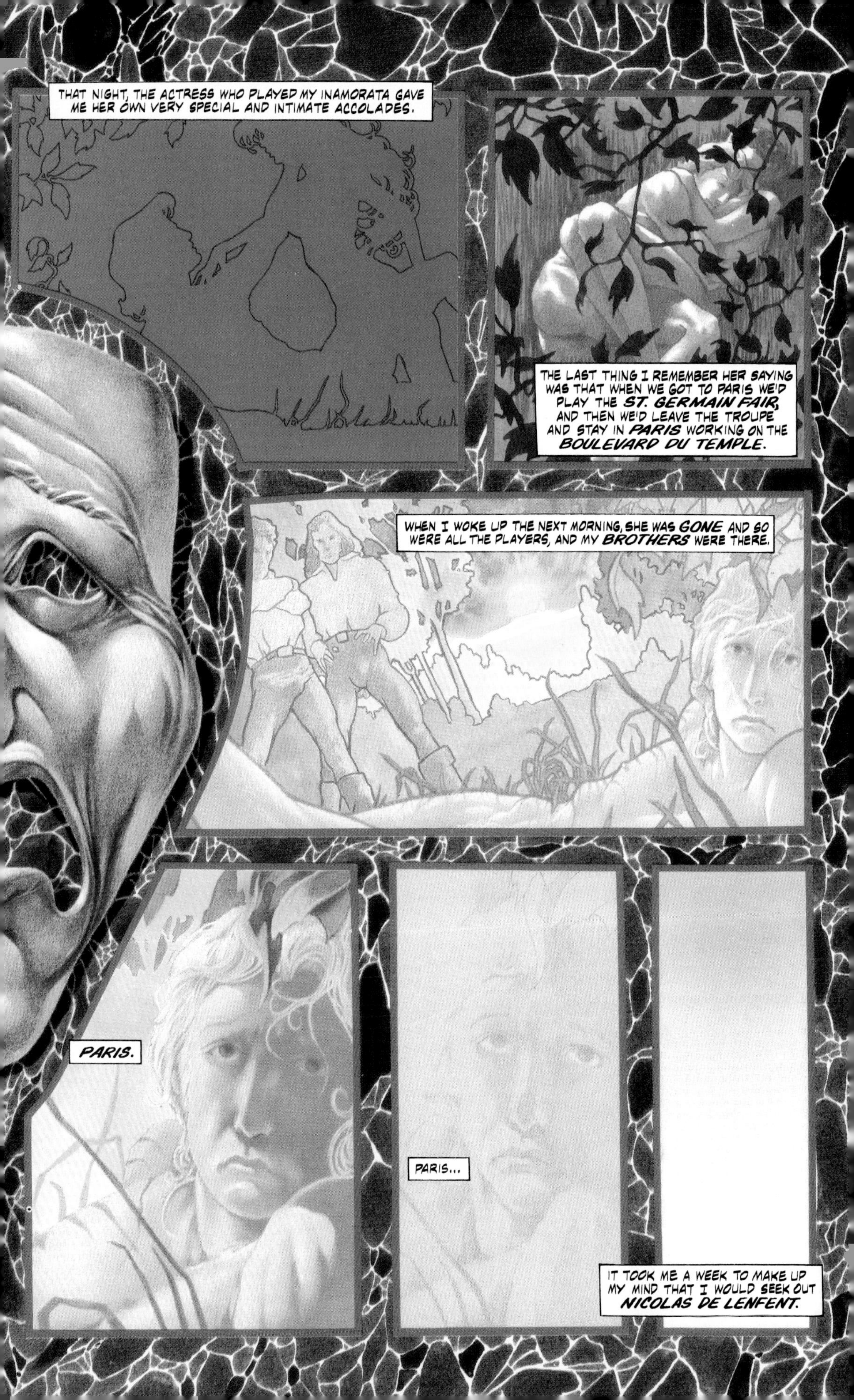
THAT NIGHT, THE ACTRESS WHO PLAYED MY INAMORATA GAVE ME HER OWN VERY SPECIAL AND INTIMATE ACCOLADES.
THE LAST THING I REMEMBER HER SAYING WAS THAT WHEN WE GOT TO PARIS WE'D PLAY THE ST. GERMAIN FAIR, AND THEN WE'D LEAVE THE TROUPE AND STAY IN PARIS WORKING ON THE BOULEVARD DU TEMPLE.
WHEN I WOKE UP THE NEXT MORNING, SHE WAS GONE AND SO WERE ALL THE PLAYERS, AND MY BROTHERS WERE THERE.
PARIS.
PARIS...
IT TOOK ME A WEEK TO MAKE UP MY MIND THAT I WOULD SEEK OUT NICOLAS DE LENFENT.

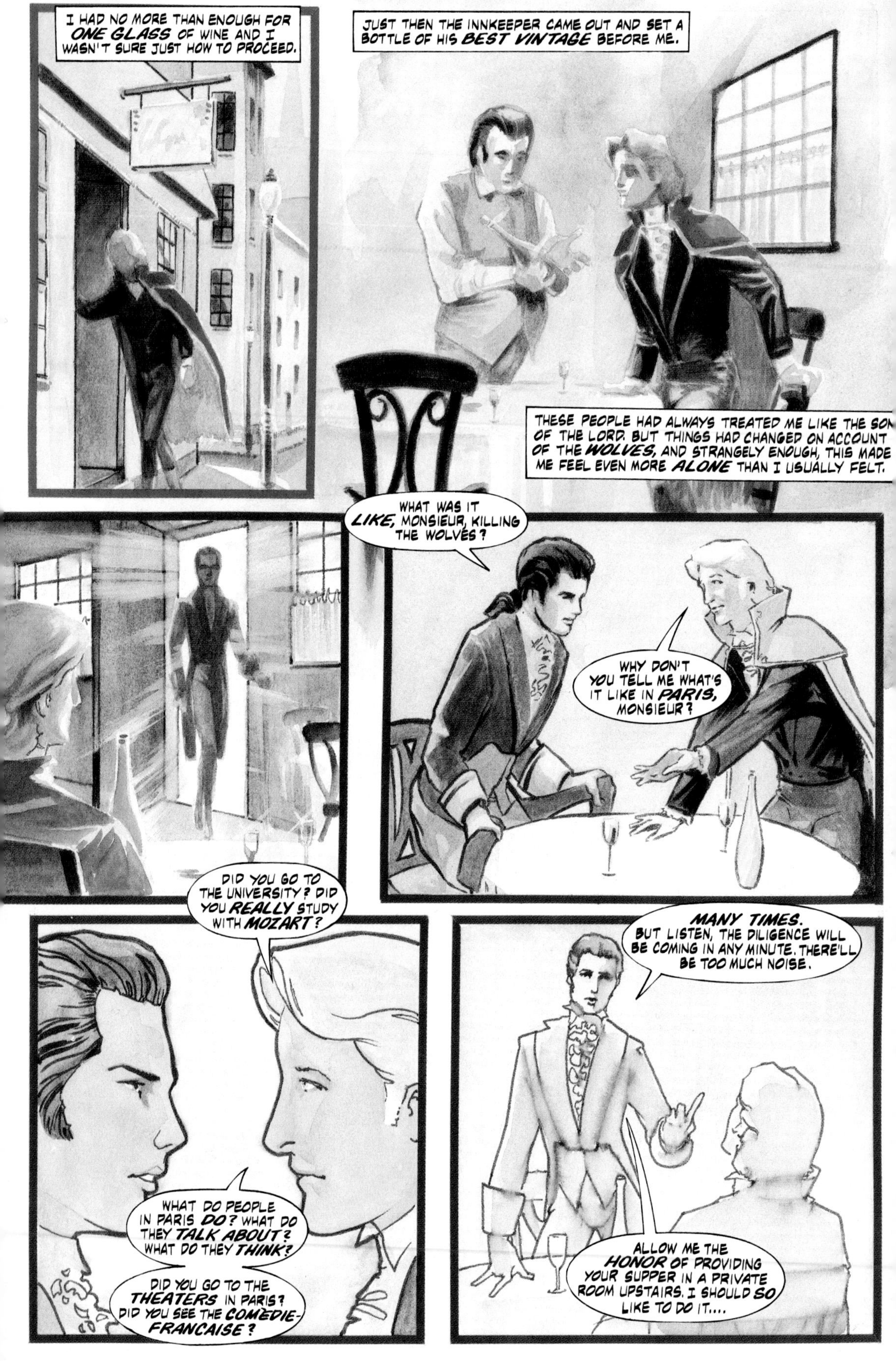
I HAD NO MORE THAN ENOUGH FOR ONE GLASS OF WINE AND I WASN'T SURE JUST HOW TO PROCEED.
JUST THEN THE INNKEEPER CAME OUT AND SET A BOTTLE OF HIS BEST VINTAGE BEFORE ME.
THESE PEOPLE HAD ALWAYS TREATED ME LIKE THE SON OF THE LORD. BUT THINGS HAD CHANGED ON ACCOUNT OF THE WOLVES, AND STRANGELY ENOUGH, THIS MADE ME FEEL EVEN MORE ALONE THAN I USUALLY FELT.
WHAT WAS IT LIKE, MONSIEUR, KILLING THE WOLVES?
WHY DON'T YOU TELL ME WHAT'S IT LIKE IN PARIS, MONSIEUR?
DID YOU GO TO THE UNIVERSITY? DID YOU REALLY STUDY WITH MOZART?
WHAT DO PEOPLE IN PARIS DO? WHAT DO THEY TALK ABOUT? WHAT DO THEY THINK?
DID YOU GO TO THE THEATERS IN PARIS? DID YOU SEE THE COMEDIE-FRANCAISE?
MANY TIMES. BUT LISTEN, THE DILIGENCE WILL BE COMING IN ANY MINUTE. THERE'LL BE TOO MUCH NOISE.
ALLOW ME THE HONOR OF PROVIDING YOUR SUPPER IN A PRIVATE ROOM UPSTAIRS. I SHOULD SO LIKE TO DO IT....

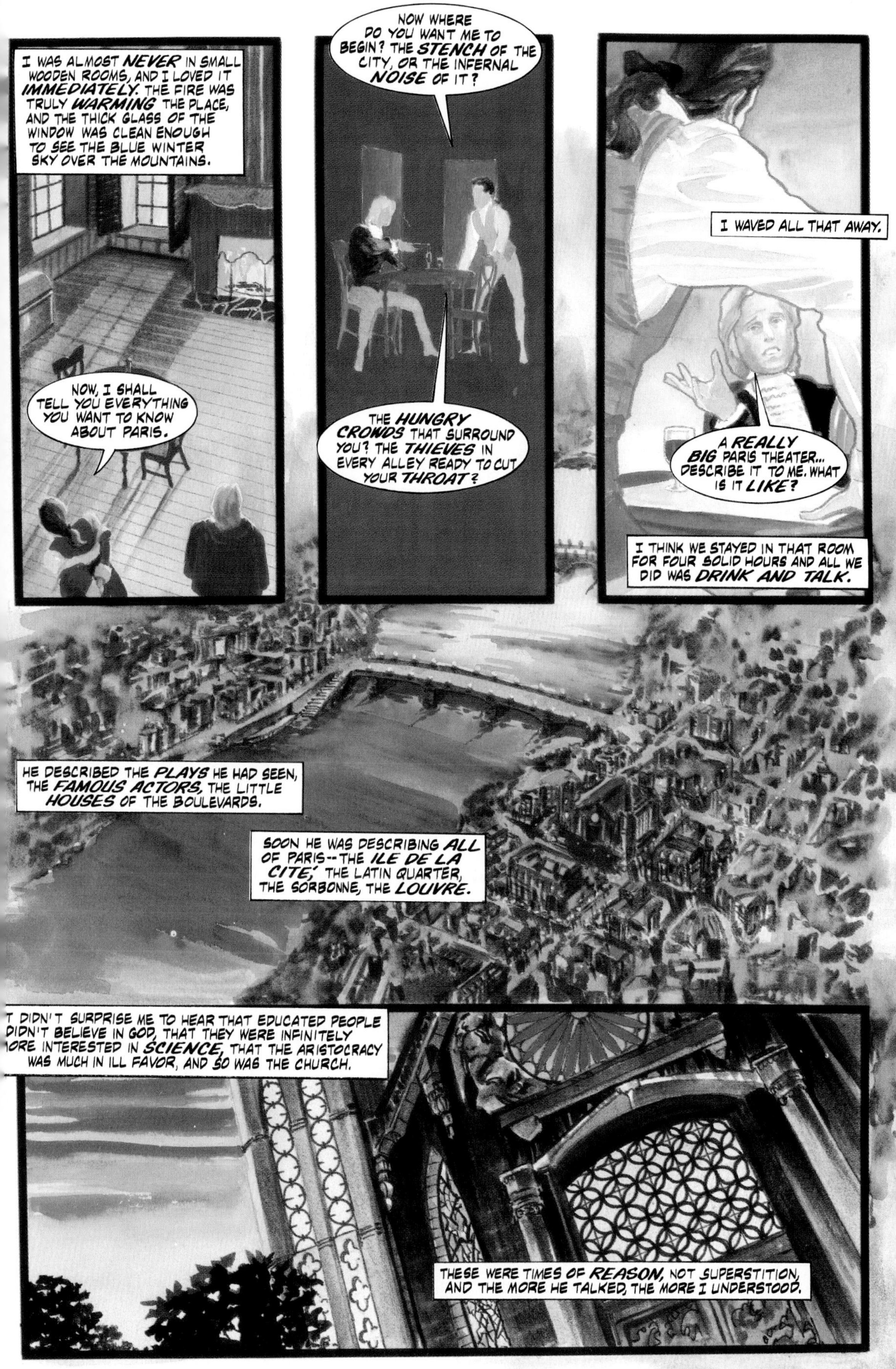

I WAS ALMOST NEVER IN SMALL WOODEN ROOMS, AND I LOVED IT IMMEDIATELY. THE FIRE WAS TRULY WARMING THE PLACE, AND THE THICK GLASS OF THE WINDOW WAS CLEAN ENOUGH TO SEE THE BLUE WINTER SKY OVER THE MOUNTAINS.
NOW, I SHALL TELL YOU EVERYTHING YOU WANT TO KNOW ABOUT PARIS.
NOW WHERE DO YOU WANT ME TO BEGIN? THE STENCH OF THE CITY, OR THE INFERNAL NOISE OF IT?
THE HUNGRY CROWDS THAT SURROUND YOU? THE THIEVES IN EVERY ALLEY READY TO CUT YOUR THROAT?
I WAVED ALL THAT AWAY.
A REALLY BIG PARIS THEATER... DESCRIBE IT TO ME. WHAT IS IT LIKE?
I THINK WE STAYED IN THAT ROOM FOR FOUR SOLID HOURS AND ALL WE DID WAS DRINK AND TALK.
HE DESCRIBED THE PLAYS HE HAD SEEN, THE FAMOUS ACTORS, THE LITTLE HOUSES OF THE BOULEVARDS.
SOON HE WAS DESCRIBING ALL OF PARIS--THE ILE DE LA CITE, THE LATIN QUARTER, THE SORBONNE, THE LOUVRE.
T DIDN'T SURPRISE ME TO HEAR THAT EDUCATED PEOPLE DIDN'T BELIEVE IN GOD, THAT THEY WERE INFINITELY IORE INTERESTED IN SCIENCE, THAT THE ARISTOCRACY WAS MUCH IN ILL FAVOR, AND SO WAS THE CHURCH.
THESE WERE TIMES OF REASON, NOT SUPERSTITION, AND THE MORE HE TALKED, THE MORE I UNDERSTOOD.

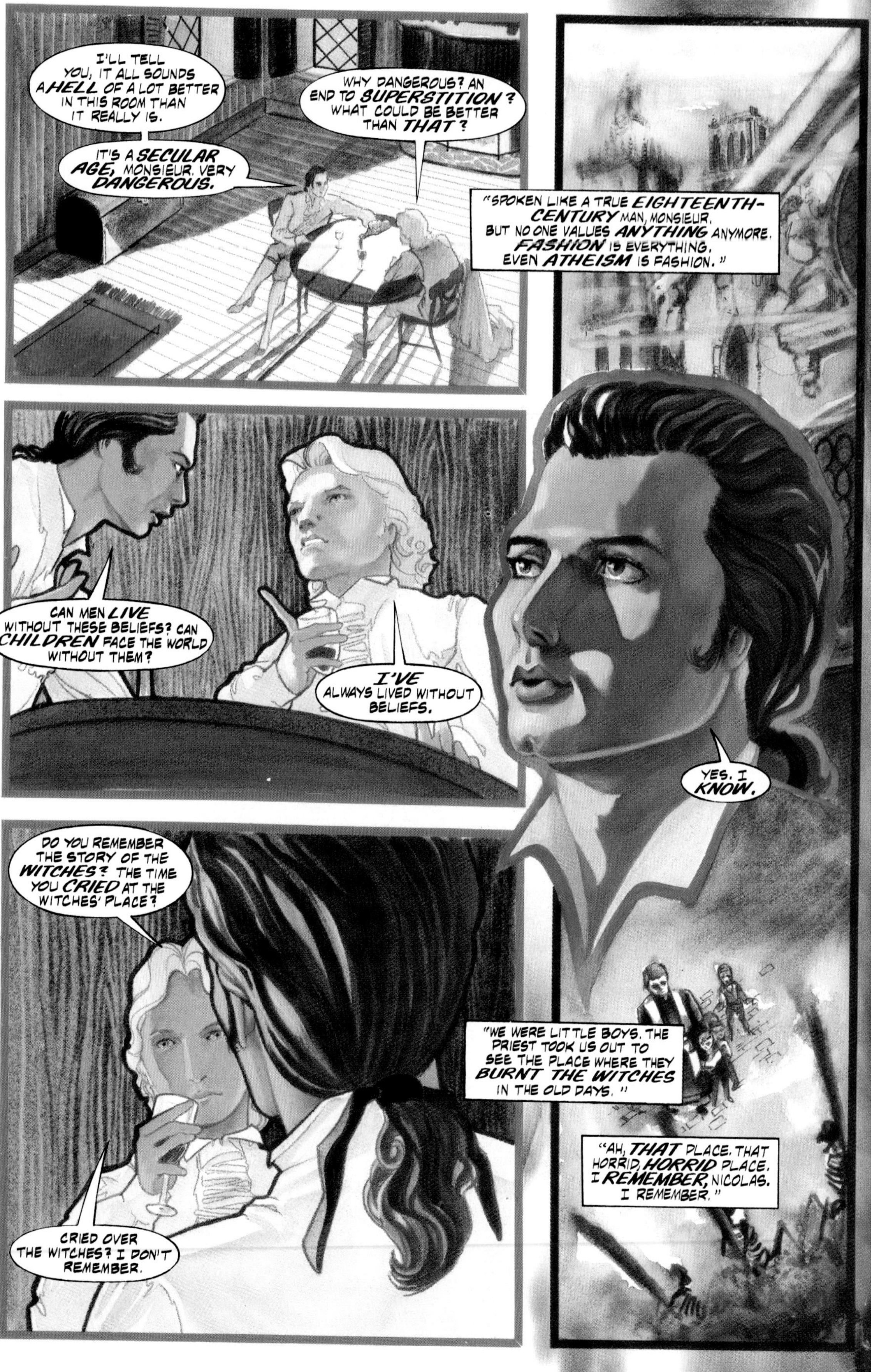
I'LL TELL YOU, IT ALL SOUNDS A HELL OF A LOT BETTER IN THIS ROOM THAN IT REALLY IS.
IT'S A SECULAR AGE, MONSIEUR. VERY DANGEROUS.
WHY DANGEROUS? AN END TO SUPERSTITION? WHAT COULD BE BETTER THAN THAT?
"SPOKEN LIKE A TRUE EIGHTEENTH-CENTURY MAN, MONSIEUR. BUT NO ONE VALUES ANYTHING ANYMORE. FASHION IS EVERYTHING. EVEN ATHEISM IS FASHION."
CAN MEN LIVE WITHOUT THESE BELIEFS? CAN CHILDREN FACE THE WORLD WITHOUT THEM?
I'VE ALWAYS LIVED WITHOUT BELIEFS.
YES. I KNOW.
DO YOU REMEMBER THE STORY OF THE WITCHES? THE TIME YOU CRIED AT THE WITCHES' PLACE?
CRIED OVER THE WITCHES? I DON'T REMEMBER.
"WE WERE LITTLE BOYS. THE PRIEST TOOK US OUT TO SEE THE PLACE WHERE THEY BURNT THE WITCHES IN THE OLD DAYS."
"AH, THAT PLACE. THAT HORRID, HORRID PLACE. I REMEMBER, NICOLAS. I REMEMBER."

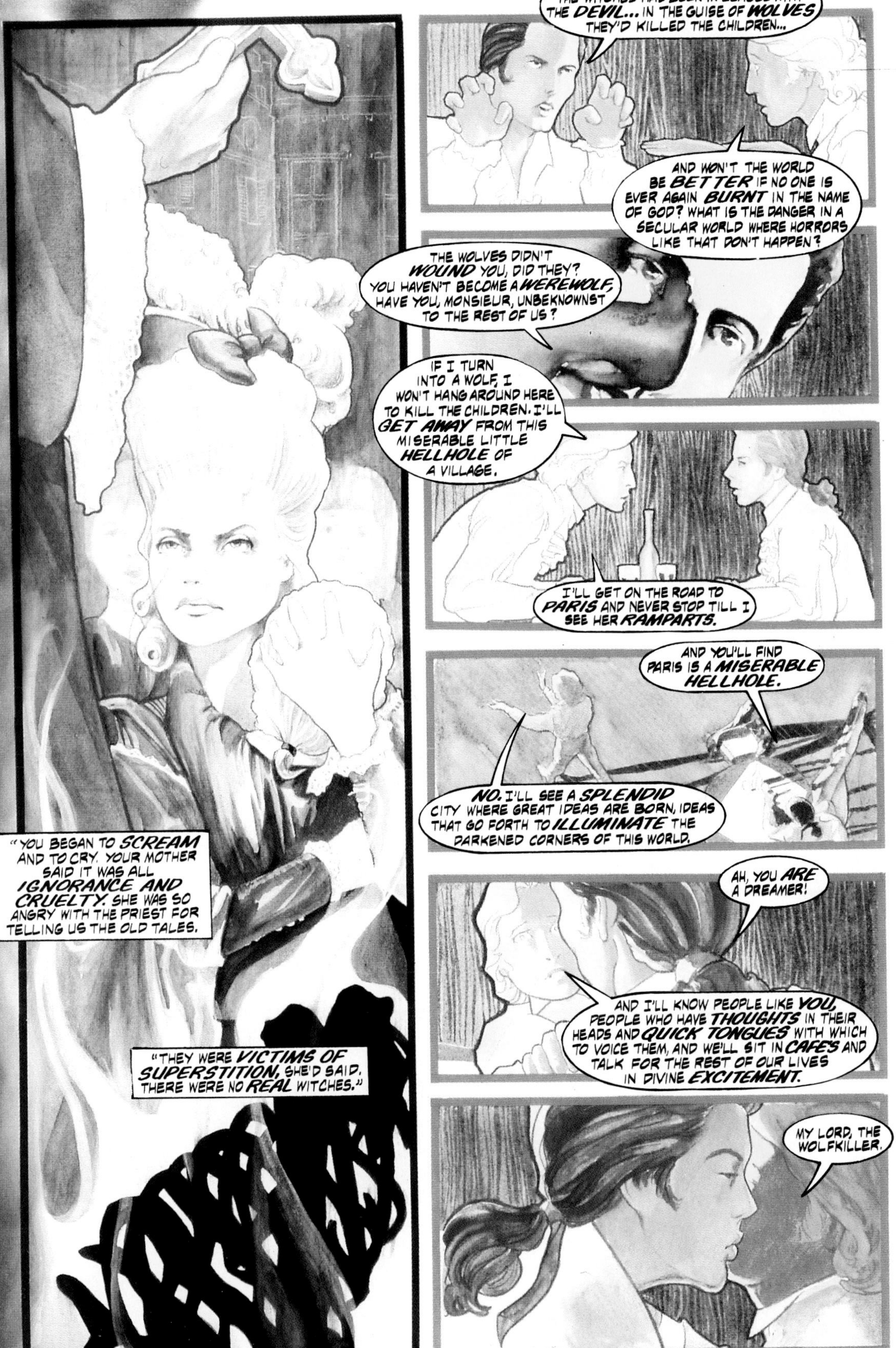
"YOU BEGAN TO SCREAM AND TO CRY. YOUR MOTHER SAID IT WAS ALL IGNORANCE AND CRUELTY. SHE WAS SO ANGRY WITH THE PRIEST FOR TELLING US THE OLD TALES.
"THEY WERE VICTIMS OF SUPERSTITION, SHE'D SAID. THERE WERE NO REAL WITCHES."
BUT MY MOTHER SAID THAT THE WITCHES HAD BEEN IN LEAGUE WITH THE DEVIL... IN THE GUISE OF WOLVES THEY'D KILLED THE CHILDREN...
AND WON'T THE WORLD BE BETTER IF NO ONE IS EVER AGAIN BURNT IN THE NAME OF GOD? WHAT IS THE DANGER IN A SECULAR WORLD WHERE HORRORS LIKE THAT DON'T HAPPEN?
THE WOLVES DIDN'T WOUND YOU, DID THEY? YOU HAVEN'T BECOME A WEREWOLF, HAVE YOU, MONSIEUR, UNBEKNOWNST TO THE REST OF US?
IF I TURN INTO A WOLF, I WON'T HANG AROUND HERE TO KILL THE CHILDREN. I'LL GET AWAY FROM THIS MISERABLE LITTLE HELLHOLE OF A VILLAGE.
I'LL GET ON THE ROAD TO PARIS AND NEVER STOP TILL I SEE HER RAMPARTS.
AND YOU'LL FIND PARIS IS A MISERABLE HELLHOLE.
NO. I'LL SEE A SPLENDID CITY WHERE GREAT IDEAS ARE BORN, IDEAS THAT GO FORTH TO ILLUMINATE THE DARKENED CORNERS OF THIS WORLD.
AH, YOU ARE A DREAMER!
AND I'LL KNOW PEOPLE LIKE YOU, PEOPLE WHO HAVE THOUGHTS IN THEIR HEADS AND QUICK TONGUES WITH WHICH TO VOICE THEM, AND WE'LL SIT IN CAFÉS AND TALK FOR THE REST OF OUR LIVES IN DIVINE EXCITEMENT.
MY LORD, THE WOLFKILLER.

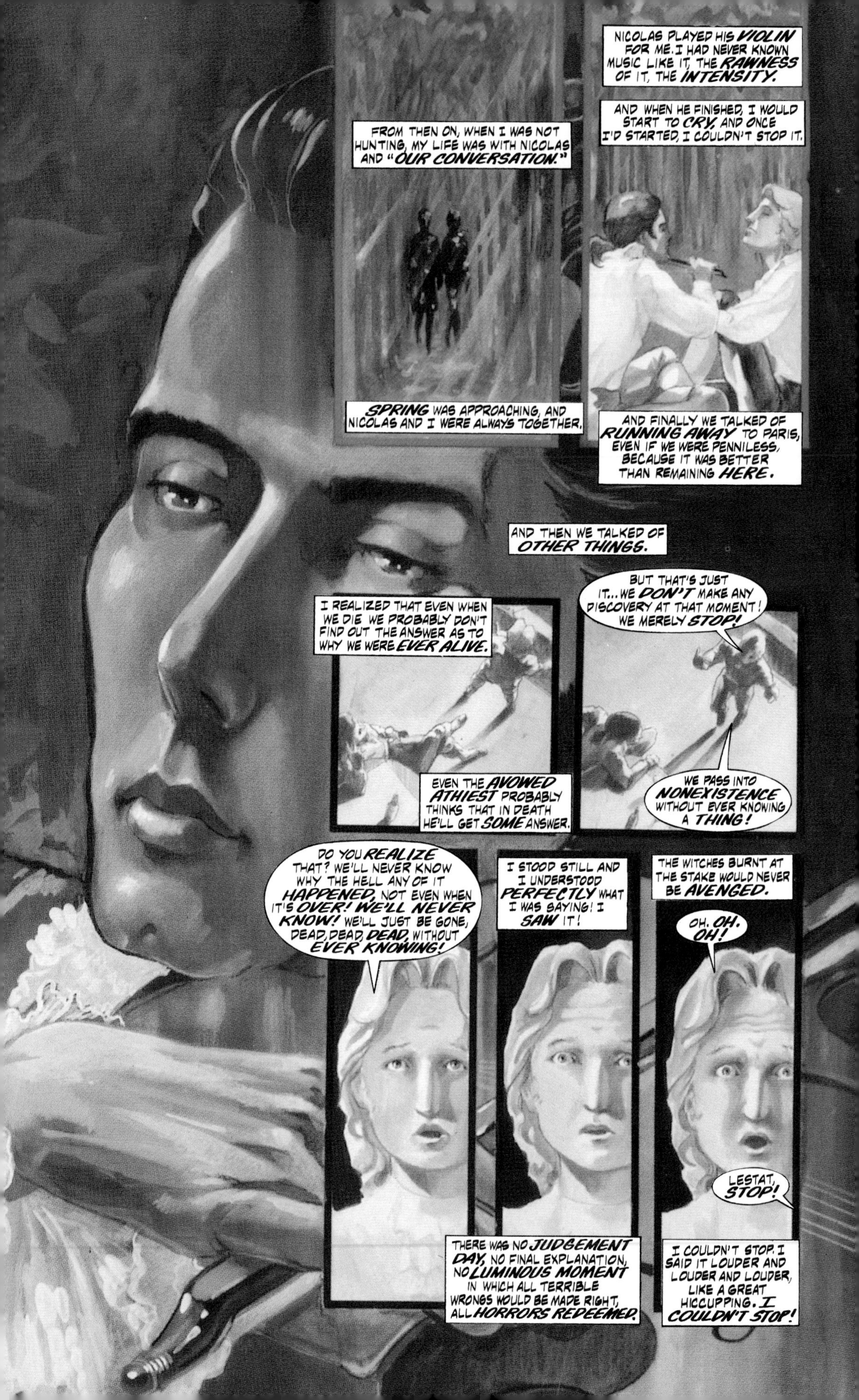
FROM THEN ON, WHEN I WAS NOT HUNTING, MY LIFE WAS WITH NICOLAS AND "OUR CONVERSATION."
SPRING WAS APPROACHING, AND NICOLAS AND I WERE ALWAYS TOGETHER.
NICOLAS PLAYED HIS VIOLIN FOR ME. I HAD NEVER KNOWN MUSIC LIKE IT, THE RAWNESS OF IT, THE INTENSITY.
AND WHEN HE FINISHED, I WOULD START TO CRY, AND ONCE I'D STARTED, I COULDN'T STOP IT.
AND FINALLY WE TALKED OF RUNNING AWAY TO PARIS, EVEN IF WE WERE PENNILESS, BECAUSE IT WAS BETTER THAN REMAINING HERE.
AND THEN WE TALKED OF OTHER THINGS.
I REALIZED THAT EVEN WHEN WE DIE WE PROBABLY DON'T FIND OUT THE ANSWER AS TO WHY WE WERE EVER ALIVE.
EVEN THE AVOWED ATHIEST PROBABLY THINKS THAT IN DEATH HE'LL GET SOME ANSWER.
BUT THAT'S JUST IT... WE DON'T MAKE ANY DISCOVERY AT THAT MOMENT! WE MERELY STOP!
WE PASS INTO NONEXISTENCE WITHOUT EVER KNOWING A THING!
DO YOU REALIZE THAT? WE'LL NEVER KNOW WHY THE HELL ANY OF IT HAPPENED, NOT EVEN WHEN IT'S OVER! WE'LL NEVER KNOW! WE'LL JUST BE GONE, DEAD, DEAD, DEAD, WITHOUT EVER KNOWING!
I STOOD STILL AND I UNDERSTOOD PERFECTLY WHAT I WAS SAYING! I SAW IT!
THERE WAS NO JUDGEMENT DAY, NO FINAL EXPLANATION, NO LUMINOUS MOMENT IN WHICH ALL TERRIBLE WRONGS WOULD BE MADE RIGHT, ALL HORRORS REDEEMED.
THE WITCHES BURNT AT THE STAKE WOULD NEVER BE AVENGED.
OH. OH. OH!
LESTAT, STOP!
I COULDN'T STOP. I SAID IT LOUDER AND LOUDER AND LOUDER, LIKE A GREAT HICCUPPING. I COULDN'T STOP!

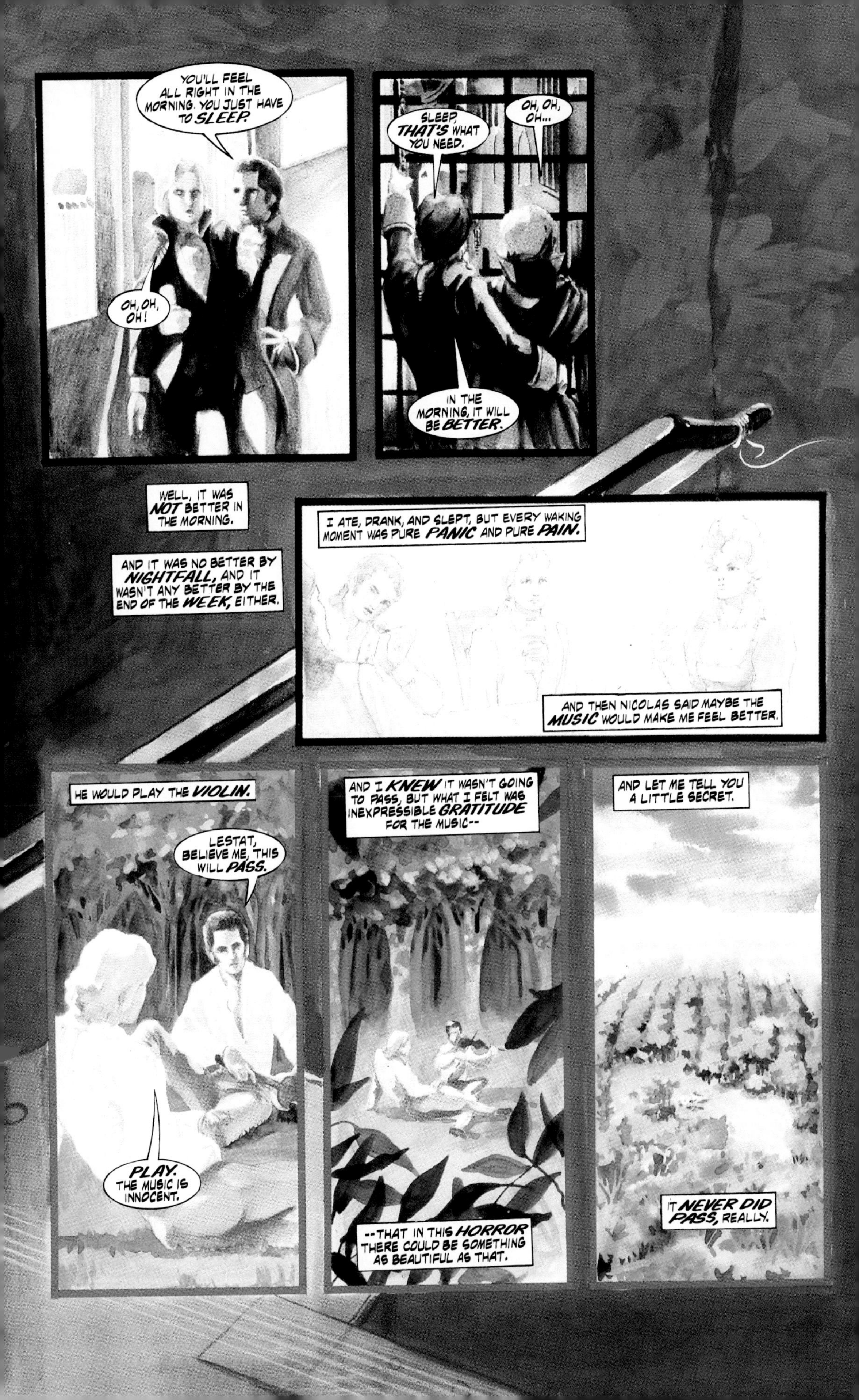
YOU'LL FEEL ALL RIGHT IN THE MORNING. YOU JUST HAVE TO SLEEP.
OH, OH, OH!
SLEEP, THAT'S WHAT YOU NEED.
OH, OH, OH...
IN THE MORNING, IT WILL BE BETTER.
WELL, IT WAS NOT BETTER IN THE MORNING.
AND IT WAS NO BETTER BY NIGHTFALL, AND IT WASN'T ANY BETTER BY THE END OF THE WEEK, EITHER.
I ATE, DRANK, AND SLEPT, BUT EVERY WAKING MOMENT WAS PURE PANIC AND PURE PAIN.
AND THEN NICOLAS SAID MAYBE THE MUSIC WOULD MAKE ME FEEL BETTER.
HE WOULD PLAY THE VIOLIN.
LESTAT, BELIEVE ME, THIS WILL PASS.
PLAY. THE MUSIC IS INNOCENT.
AND I KNEW IT WASN'T GOING TO PASS, BUT WHAT I FELT WAS INEXPRESSIBLE GRATITUDE FOR THE MUSIC--
--THAT IN THIS HORROR THERE COULD BE SOMETHING AS BEAUTIFUL AS THAT.
AND LET ME TELL YOU A LITTLE SECRET.
IT NEVER DID PASS, REALLY.

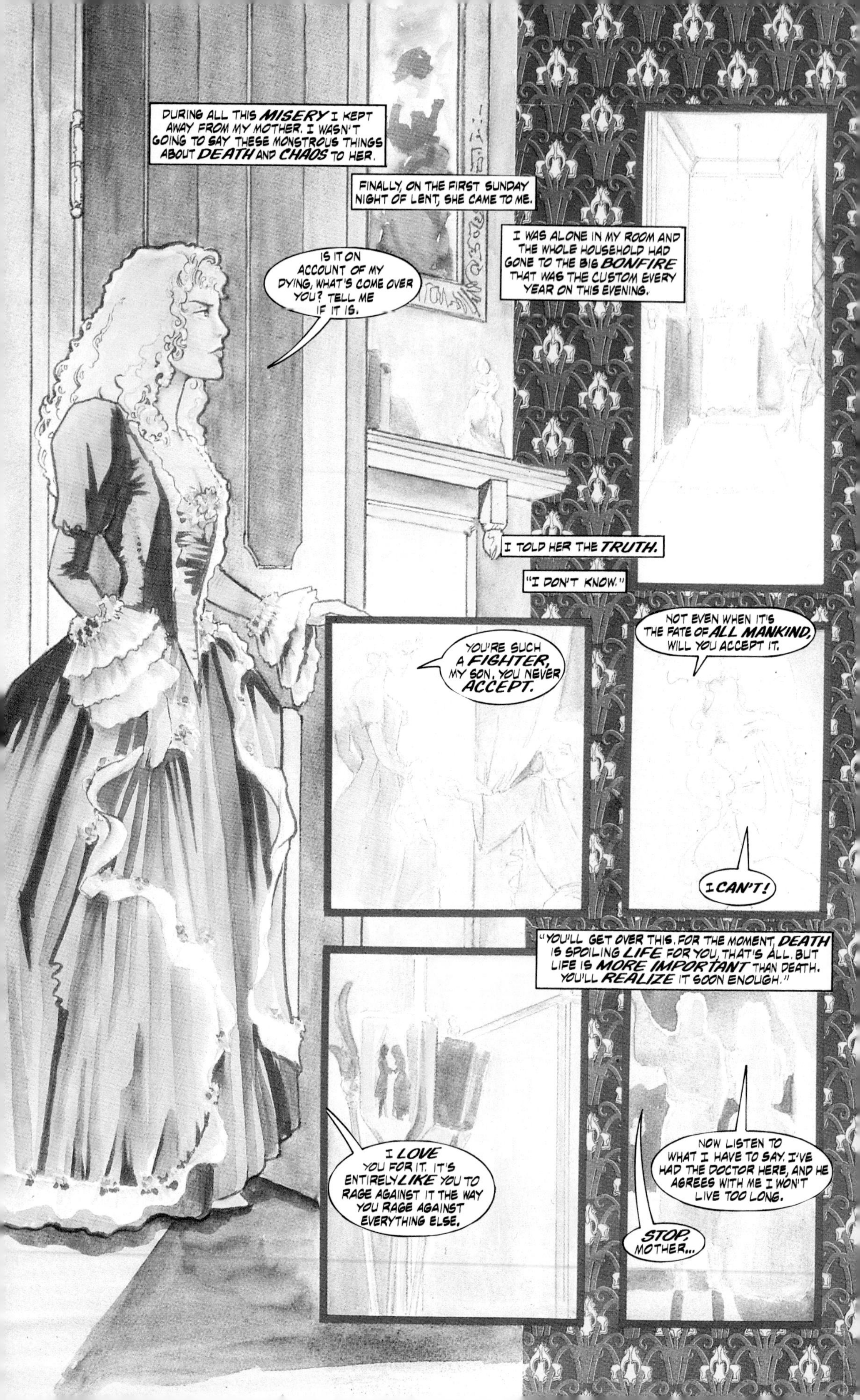
DURING ALL THIS MISERY I KEPT AWAY FROM MY MOTHER. I WASN'T GOING TO SAY THESE MONSTROUS THINGS ABOUT DEATH AND CHAOS TO HER.
FINALLY, ON THE FIRST SUNDAY NIGHT OF LENT, SHE CAME TO ME.
I WAS ALONE IN MY ROOM AND THE WHOLE HOUSEHOLD HAD GONE TO THE BIG BONFIRE THAT WAS THE CUSTOM EVERY YEAR ON THIS EVENING.
IS IT ON ACCOUNT OF MY DYING, WHAT'S COME OVER YOU? TELL ME IF IT IS.
I TOLD HER THE TRUTH.
"I DON'T KNOW."
YOU'RE SUCH A FIGHTER, MY SON, YOU NEVER ACCEPT.
NOT EVEN WHEN IT'S THE FATE OF ALL MANKIND, WILL YOU ACCEPT IT.
I CAN'T!
"YOU'LL GET OVER THIS. FOR THE MOMENT, DEATH IS SPOILING LIFE FOR YOU, THAT'S ALL. BUT LIFE IS MORE IMPORTANT THAN DEATH. YOU'LL REALIZE IT SOON ENOUGH."
I LOVE YOU FOR IT. IT'S ENTIRELY LIKE YOU TO RAGE AGAINST IT THE WAY YOU RAGE AGAINST EVERYTHING ELSE.
NOW LISTEN TO WHAT I HAVE TO SAY. I'VE HAD THE DOCTOR HERE, AND HE AGREES WITH ME I WON'T LIVE TOO LONG.
STOP, MOTHER...

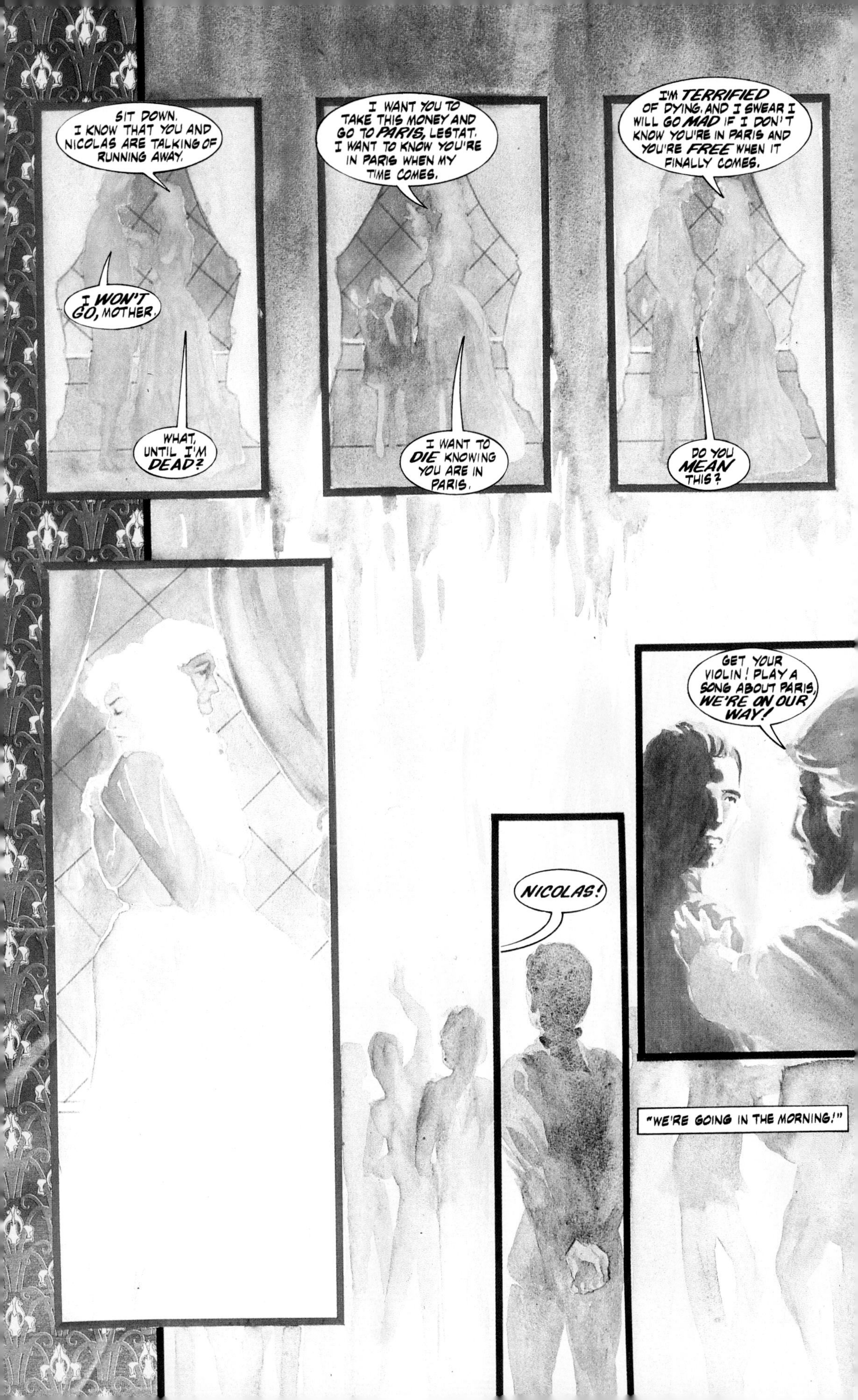
SIT DOWN. I KNOW THAT YOU AND NICOLAS ARE TALKING OF RUNNING AWAY.
I WON'T GO, MOTHER.
WHAT, UNTIL I'M DEAD?
I WANT YOU TO TAKE THIS MONEY AND GO TO PARIS, LESTAT. I WANT TO KNOW YOU'RE IN PARIS WHEN MY TIME COMES.
I WANT TO DIE KNOWING YOU ARE IN PARIS.
I'M TERRIFIED OF DYING, AND I SWEAR I WILL GO MAD IF I DON'T KNOW YOU'RE IN PARIS AND YOU'RE FREE WHEN IT FINALLY COMES.
DO YOU MEAN THIS?
NICOLAS!
GET YOUR VIOLIN! PLAY A SONG ABOUT PARIS, WE'RE ON OUR WAY!
"WE'RE GOING IN THE MORNING!"

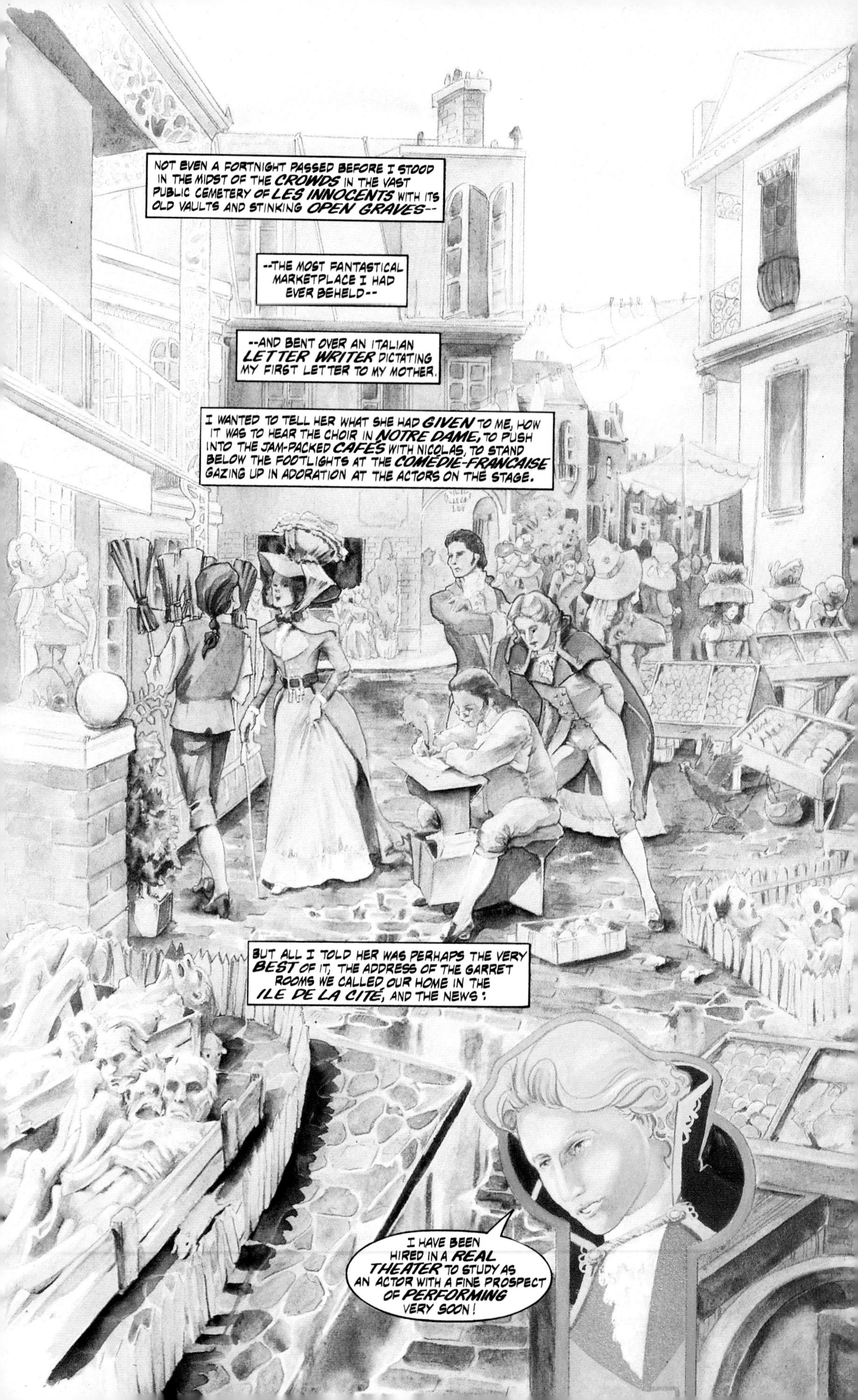
NOT EVEN A FORTNIGHT PASSED BEFORE I STOOD IN THE MIDST OF THE CROWDS IN THE VAST PUBLIC CEMETERY OF LES INNOCENTS WITH ITS OLD VAULTS AND STINKING OPEN GRAVES--
--THE MOST FANTASTICAL MARKETPLACE I HAD EVER BEHELD--
--AND BENT OVER AN ITALIAN LETTER WRITER DICTATING MY FIRST LETTER TO MY MOTHER.
I WANTED TO TELL HER WHAT SHE HAD GIVEN TO ME, HOW IT WAS TO HEAR THE CHOIR IN NOTRE DAME, TO PUSH INTO THE JAM-PACKED CAFÉS WITH NICOLAS, TO STAND BELOW THE FOOTLIGHTS AT THE COMÉDIE-FRANCAISE GAZING UP IN ADORATION AT THE ACTORS ON THE STAGE.
BUT ALL I TOLD HER WAS PERHAPS THE VERY BEST OF IT, THE ADDRESS OF THE GARRET ROOMS WE CALLED OUR HOME IN THE ILE DE LA CITÉ, AND THE NEWS:
I HAVE BEEN HIRED IN A REAL THEATER TO STUDY AS AN ACTOR WITH A FINE PROSPECT OF PERFORMING VERY SOON!

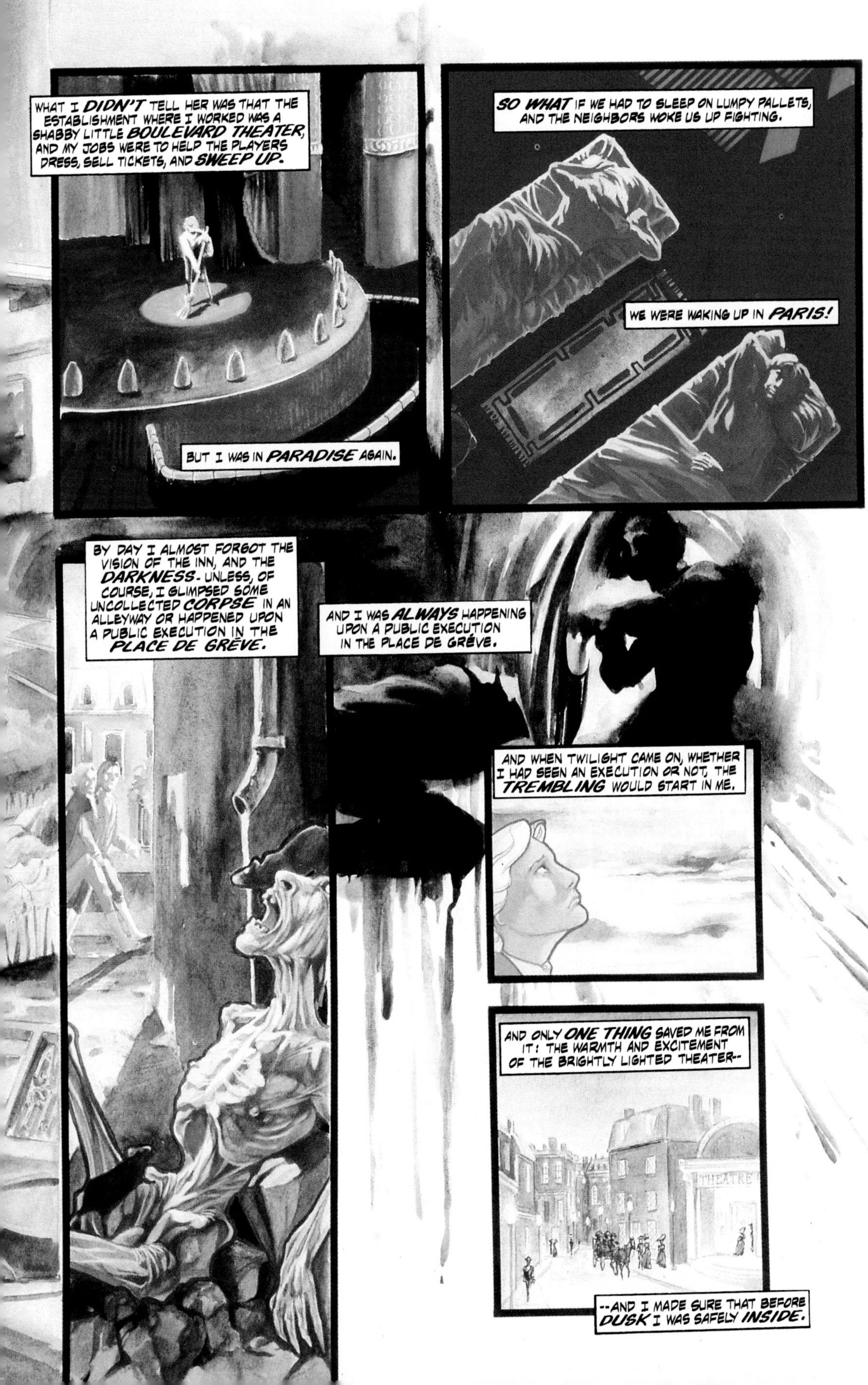
WHAT I DIDN'T TELL HER WAS THAT THE ESTABLISHMENT WHERE I WORKED WAS A SHABBY LITTLE BOULEVARD THEATER, AND MY JOBS WERE TO HELP THE PLAYERS DRESS, SELL TICKETS, AND SWEEP UP.
BUT I WAS IN PARADISE AGAIN.
SO WHAT IF WE HAD TO SLEEP ON LUMPY PALLETS, AND THE NEIGHBORS WOKE US UP FIGHTING.
WE WERE WAKING UP IN PARIS!
BY DAY I ALMOST FORGOT THE VISION OF THE INN, AND THE DARKNESS- UNLESS, OF COURSE, I GLIMPSED SOME UNCOLLECTED CORPSE IN AN ALLEYWAY OR HAPPENED UPON A PUBLIC EXECUTION IN THE PLACE DE GRÈVE.
AND I WAS ALWAYS HAPPENING UPON A PUBLIC EXECUTION IN THE PLACE DE GRÈVE.
AND WHEN TWILIGHT CAME ON, WHETHER I HAD SEEN AN EXECUTION OR NOT, THE TREMBLING WOULD START IN ME.
AND ONLY ONE THING SAVED ME FROM IT: THE WARMTH AND EXCITEMENT OF THE BRIGHTLY LIGHTED THEATER--
THEATRE
--AND I MADE SURE THAT BEFORE DUSK I WAS SAFELY INSIDE.

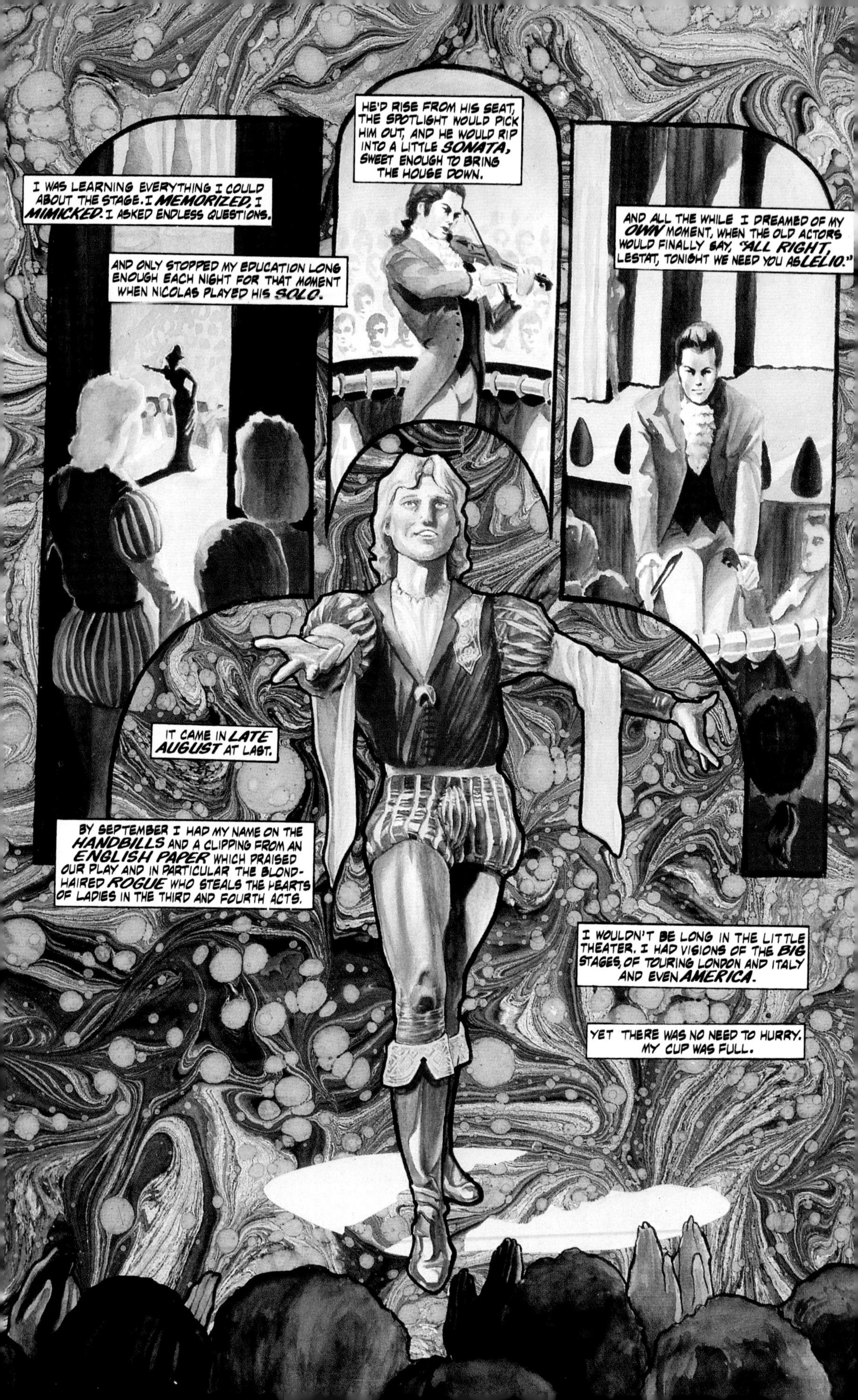
I WAS LEARNING EVERYTHING I COULD ABOUT THE STAGE. I MEMORIZED, I MIMICKED. I ASKED ENDLESS QUESTIONS.
AND ONLY STOPPED MY EDUCATION LONG ENOUGH EACH NIGHT FOR THAT MOMENT WHEN NICOLAS PLAYED HIS SOLO.
HE'D RISE FROM HIS SEAT, THE SPOTLIGHT WOULD PICK HIM OUT, AND HE WOULD RIP INTO A LITTLE SONATA, SWEET ENOUGH TO BRING THE HOUSE DOWN.
AND ALL THE WHILE I DREAMED OF MY OWN MOMENT, WHEN THE OLD ACTORS WOULD FINALLY SAY, "ALL RIGHT, LESTAT, TONIGHT WE NEED YOU AS LELIO."
IT CAME IN LATE AUGUST AT LAST.
BY SEPTEMBER I HAD MY NAME ON THE HANDBILLS AND A CLIPPING FROM AN ENGLISH PAPER WHICH PRAISED OUR PLAY AND IN PARTICULAR THE BLOND-HAIRED ROGUE WHO STEALS THE HEARTS OF LADIES IN THE THIRD AND FOURTH ACTS.
I WOULDN'T BE LONG IN THE LITTLE THEATER. I HAD VISIONS OF THE BIG STAGES, OF TOURING LONDON AND ITALY AND EVEN AMERICA.
YET THERE WAS NO NEED TO HURRY. MY CUP WAS FULL.

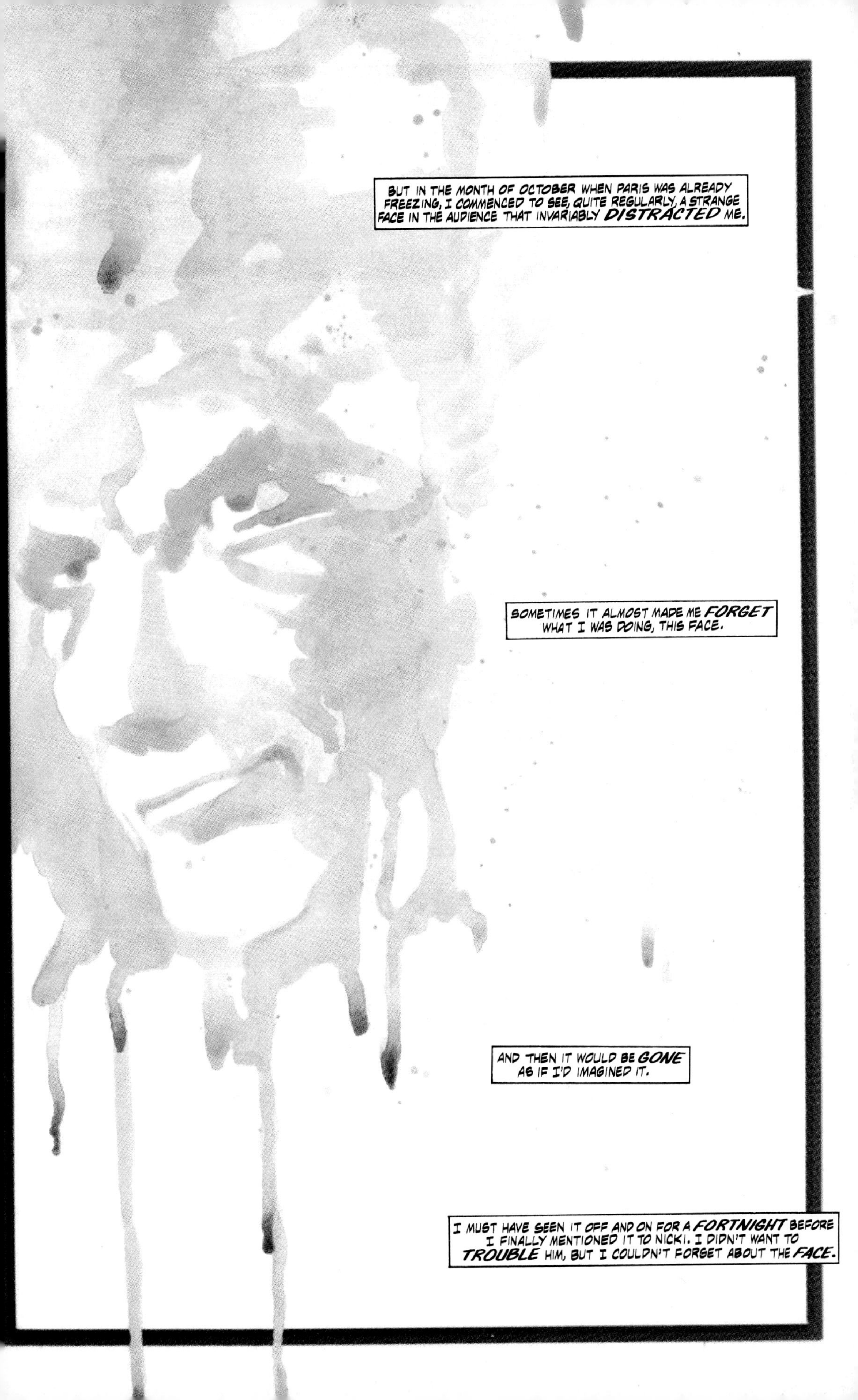

BUT IN THE MONTH OF OCTOBER WHEN PARIS WAS ALREADY FREEZING, I COMMENCED TO SEE, QUITE REGULARLY, A STRANGE FACE IN THE AUDIENCE THAT INVARIABLY DISTRACTED ME.
SOMETIMES IT ALMOST MADE ME FORGET WHAT I WAS DOING, THIS FACE.
AND THEN IT WOULD BE GONE AS IF I'D IMAGINED IT.
I MUST HAVE SEEN IT OFF AND ON FOR A FORTNIGHT BEFORE I FINALLY MENTIONED IT TO NICKI. I DIDN'T WANT TO TROUBLE HIM, BUT I COULDN'T FORGET ABOUT THE FACE.

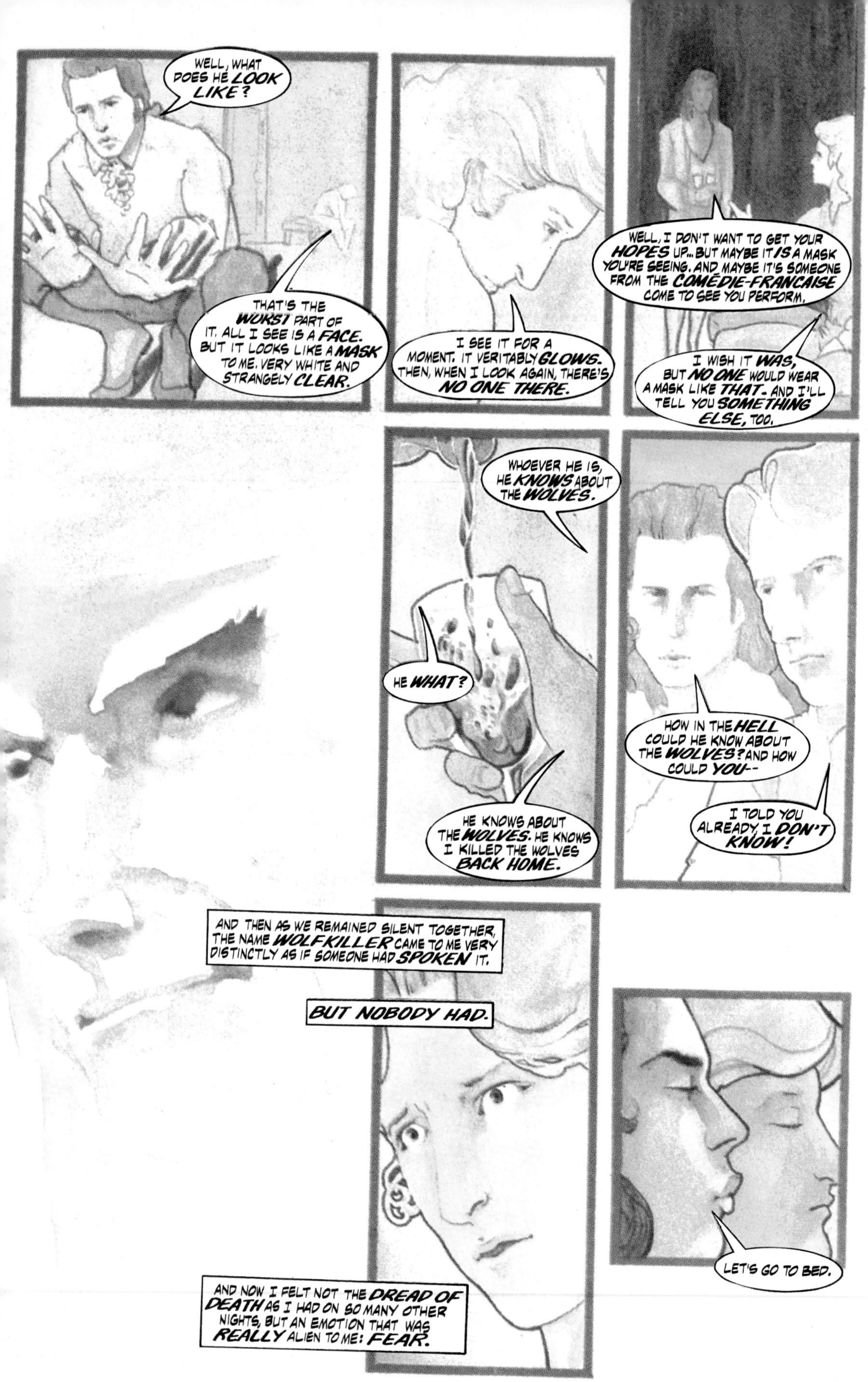
WELL, WHAT DOES HE LOOK LIKE?
THAT'S THE WORST PART OF IT. ALL I SEE IS A FACE. BUT IT LOOKS LIKE A MASK TO ME. VERY WHITE AND STRANGELY CLEAR.
I SEE IT FOR A MOMENT. IT VERITABLY GLOWS. THEN, WHEN I LOOK AGAIN, THERE'S NO ONE THERE.
WELL, I DON'T WANT TO GET YOUR HOPES UP.. BUT MAYBE IT IS A MASK YOU'RE SEEING. AND MAYBE IT'S SOMEONE FROM THE COMÉDIE-FRANCAISE COME TO SEE YOU PERFORM.
I WISH IT WAS, BUT NO ONE WOULD WEAR A MASK LIKE THAT.. AND I'LL TELL YOU SOMETHING ELSE, TOO.
WHOEVER HE IS, HE KNOWS ABOUT THE WOLVES.
HE WHAT?
HE KNOWS ABOUT THE WOLVES. HE KNOWS I KILLED THE WOLVES BACK HOME.
HOW IN THE HELL COULD HE KNOW ABOUT THE WOLVES? AND HOW COULD YOU--
I TOLD YOU ALREADY, I DON'T KNOW!
AND THEN AS WE REMAINED SILENT TOGETHER, THE NAME WOLFKILLER CAME TO ME VERY DISTINCTLY AS IF SOMEONE HAD SPOKEN IT.
BUT NOBODY HAD.
AND NOW I FELT NOT THE DREAD OF DEATH AS I HAD ON SO MANY OTHER NIGHTS, BUT AN EMOTION THAT WAS REALLY ALIEN TO ME: FEAR.
LET'S GO TO BED.

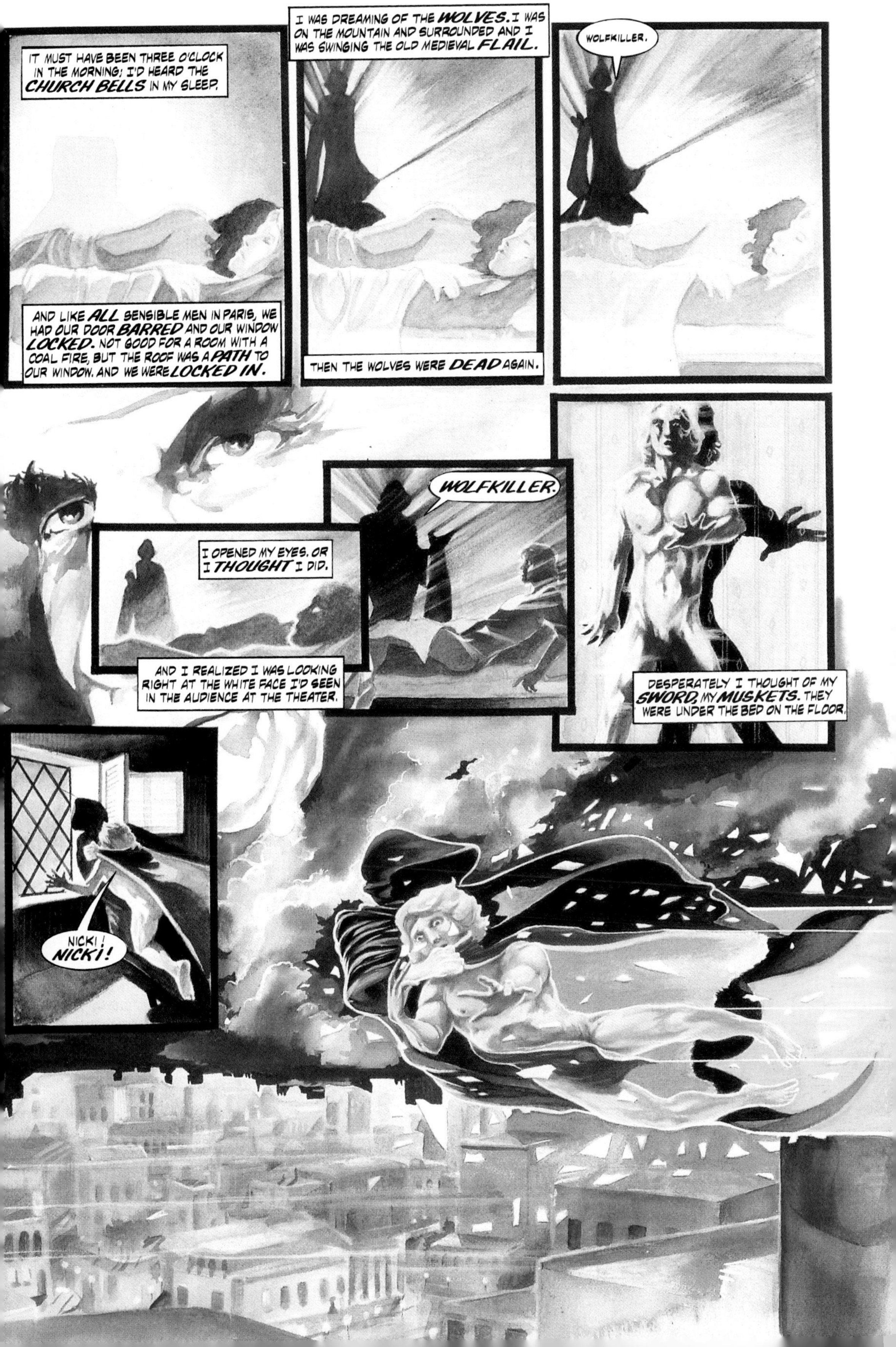

IT MUST HAVE BEEN THREE O'CLOCK IN THE MORNING; I'D HEARD THE CHURCH BELLS IN MY SLEEP.
AND LIKE ALL SENSIBLE MEN IN PARIS, WE HAD OUR DOOR BARRED AND OUR WINDOW LOCKED. NOT GOOD FOR A ROOM WITH A COAL FIRE, BUT THE ROOF WAS A PATH TO OUR WINDOW. AND WE WERE LOCKED IN.
I WAS DREAMING OF THE WOLVES. I WAS ON THE MOUNTAIN AND SURROUNDED AND I WAS SWINGING THE OLD MEDIEVAL FLAIL.
THEN THE WOLVES WERE DEAD AGAIN.
WOLFKILLER.
I OPENED MY EYES. OR I THOUGHT I DID.
AND I REALIZED I WAS LOOKING RIGHT AT THE WHITE FACE I'D SEEN IN THE AUDIENCE AT THE THEATER.
WOLFKILLER.
DESPERATELY I THOUGHT OF MY SWORD, MY MUSKETS. THEY WERE UNDER THE BED ON THE FLOOR.
NICKI! NICKI!

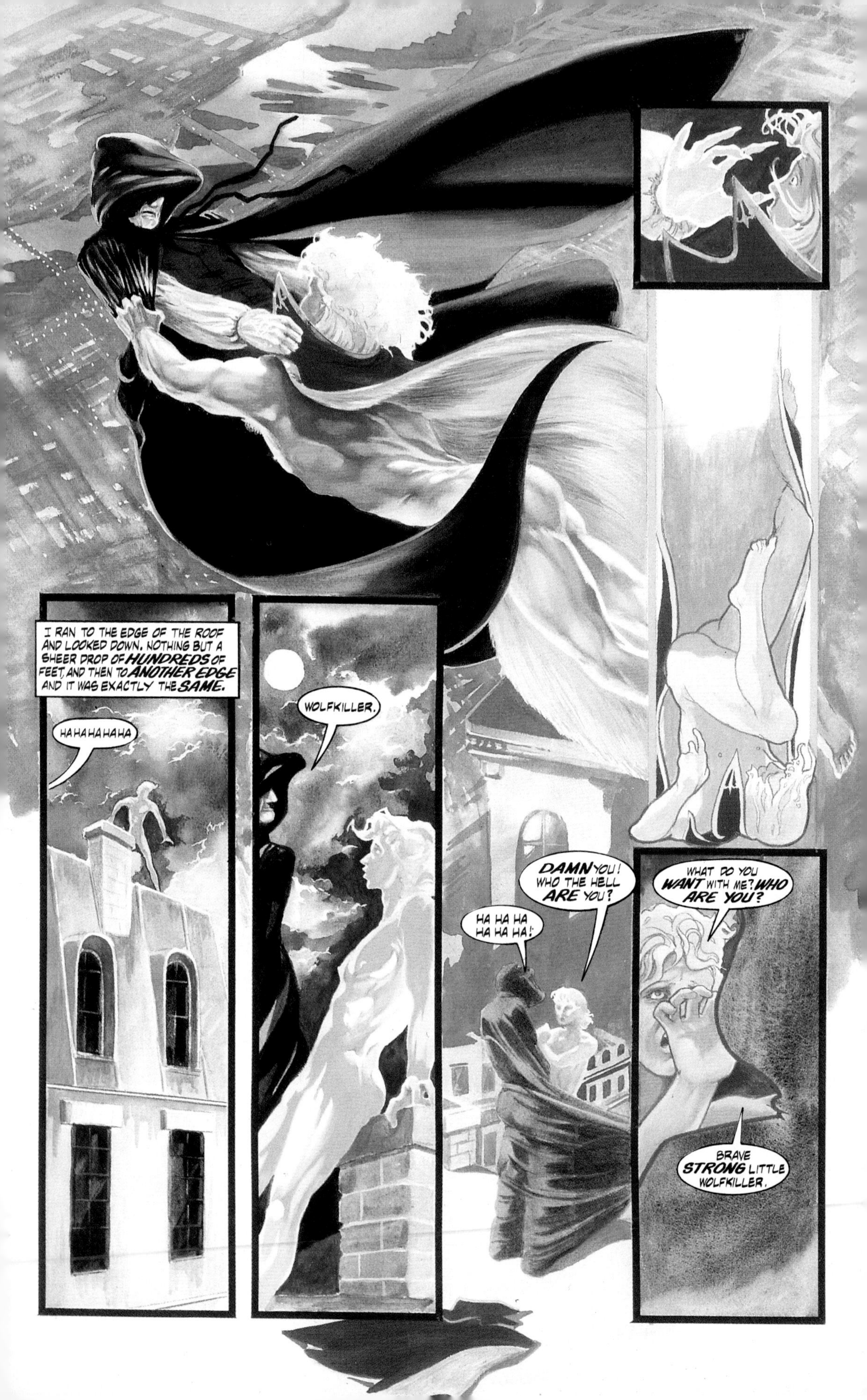
I RAN TO THE EDGE OF THE ROOF AND LOOKED DOWN. NOTHING BUT A SHEER DROP OF HUNDREDS OF FEET, AND THEN TO ANOTHER EDGE AND IT WAS EXACTLY THE SAME.
HA HA HA HA HA
WOLFKILLER.
HA HA HA HA HA HA!
DAMN YOU! WHO THE HELL ARE YOU?
WHAT DO YOU WANT WITH ME? WHO ARE YOU?
BRAVE STRONG LITTLE WOLFKILLER.

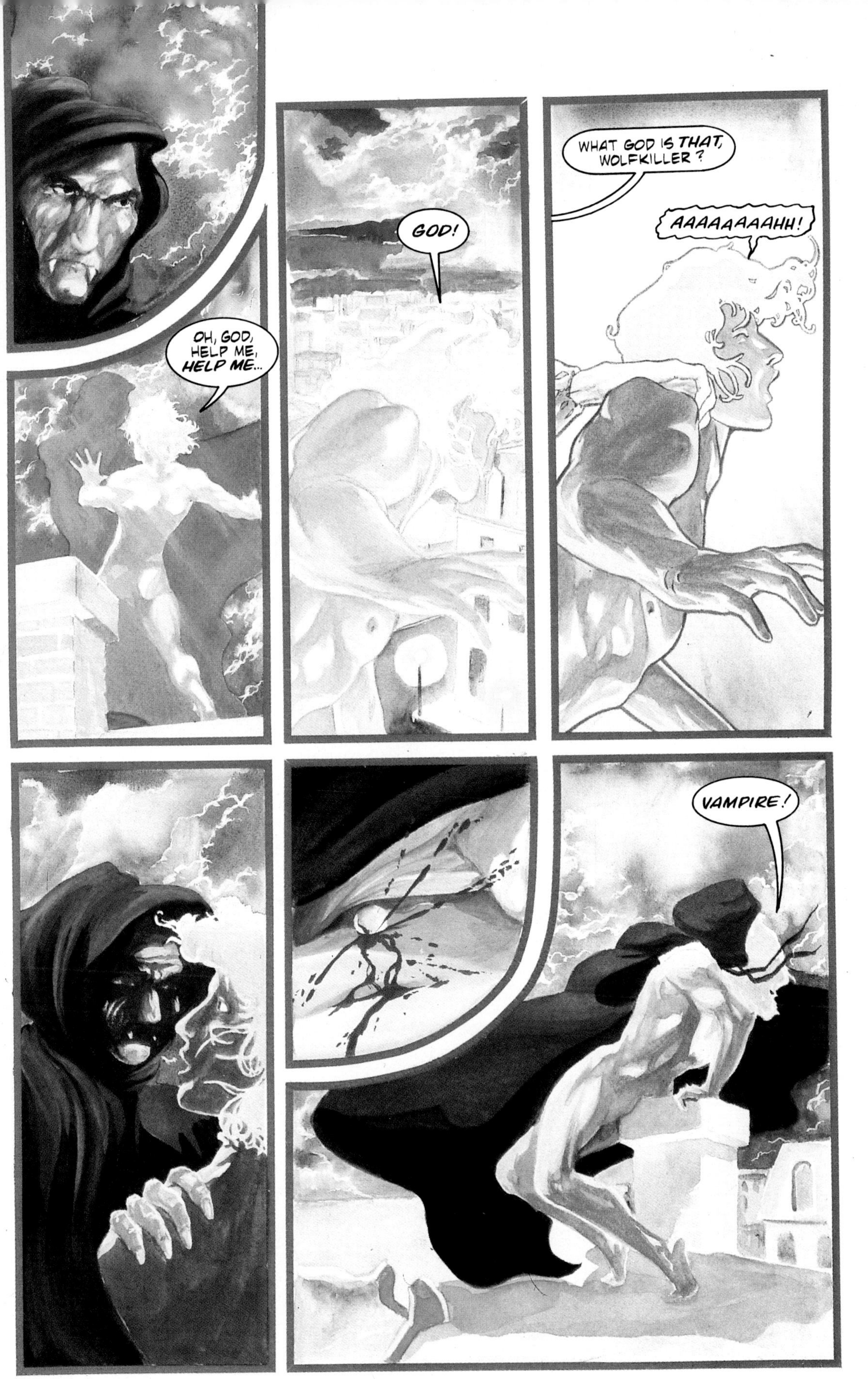
OH, GOD, HELP ME, HELP ME...
GOD!
WHAT GOD IS THAT, WOLFKILLER?
AAAAAAAAHH!
VAMPIRE!

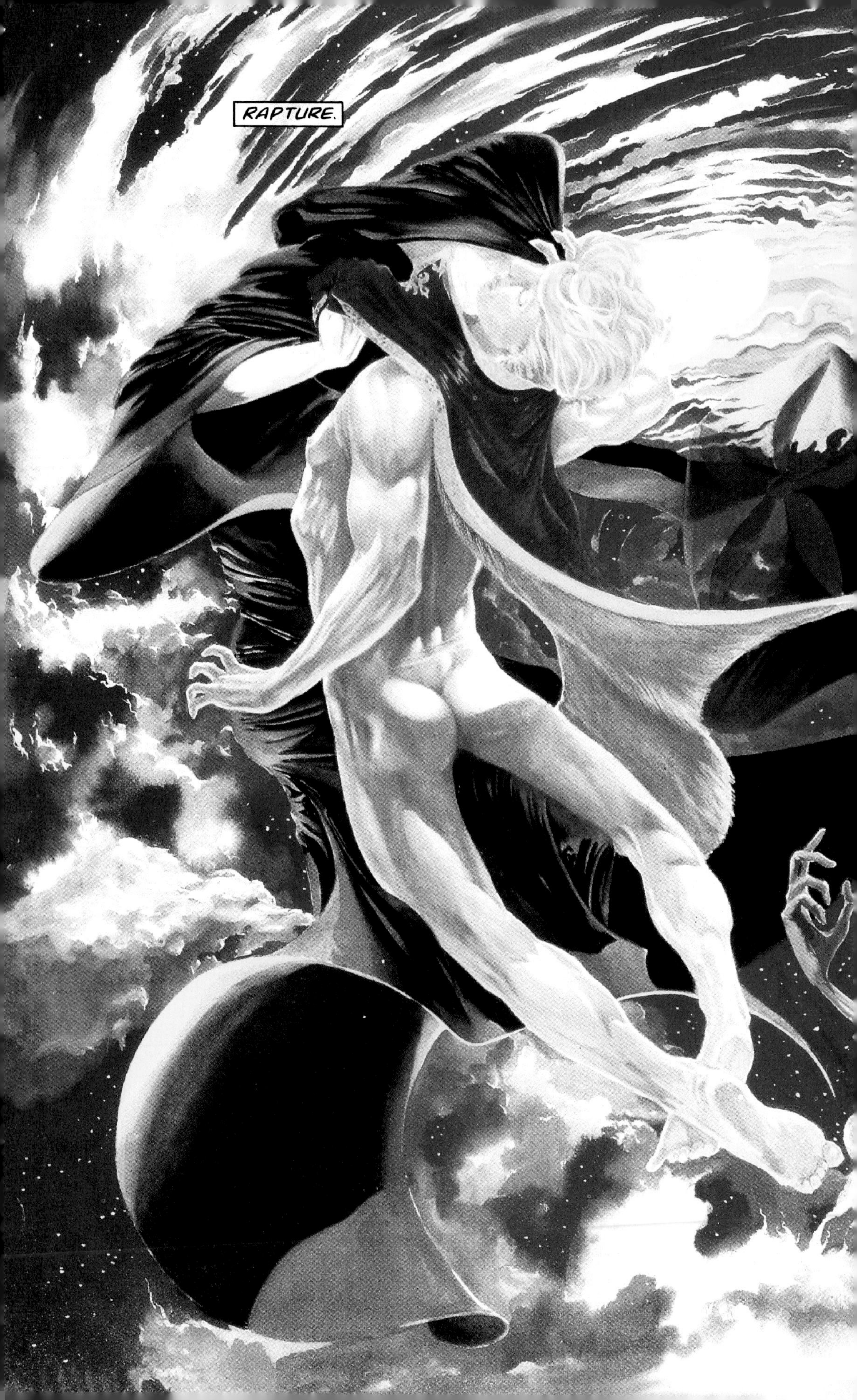
RAPTURE.

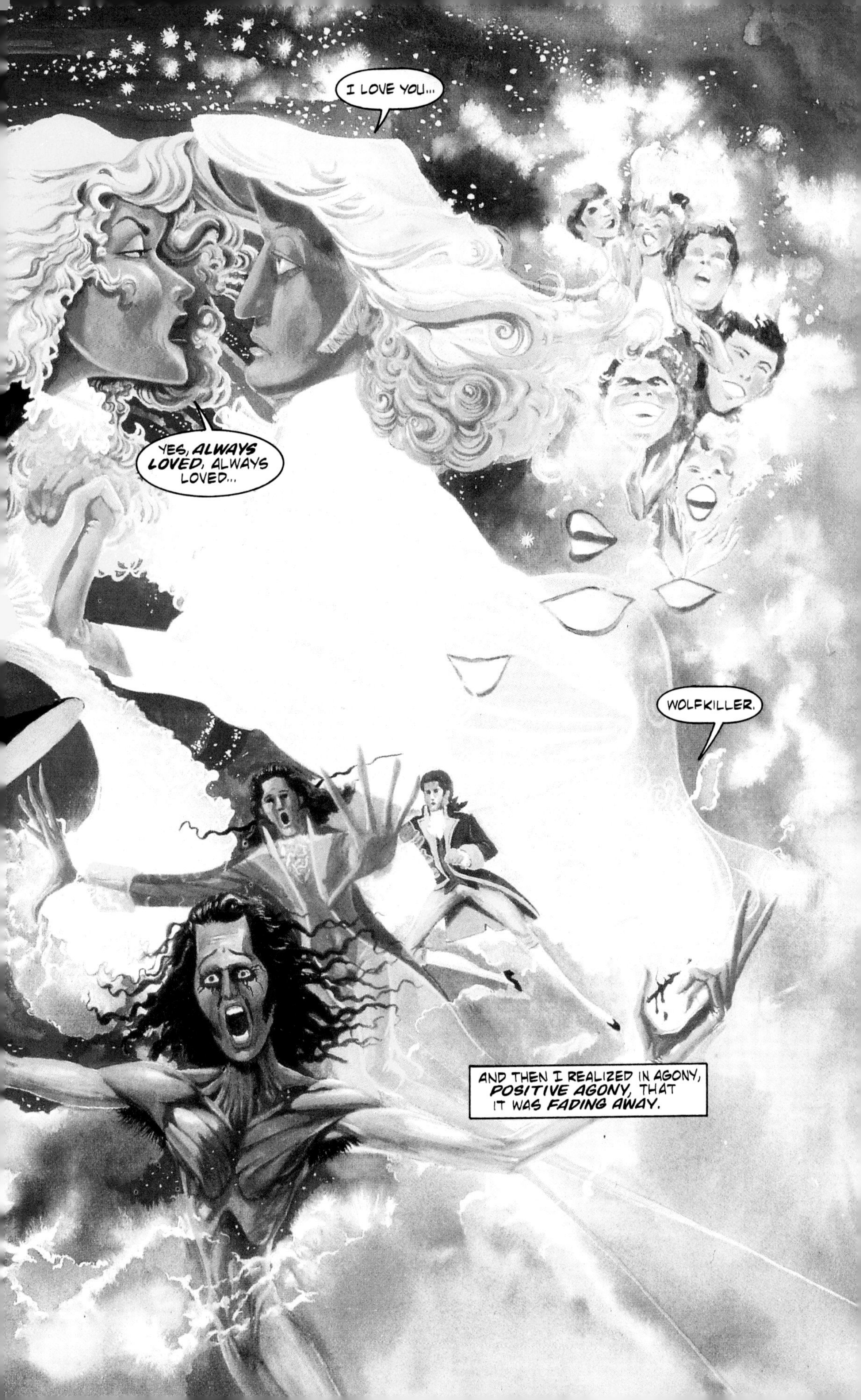
I LOVE YOU...
YES, ALWAYS LOVED, ALWAYS LOVED...
WOLFKILLER.
AND THEN I REALIZED IN AGONY, POSITIVE AGONY, THAT IT WAS FADING AWAY.

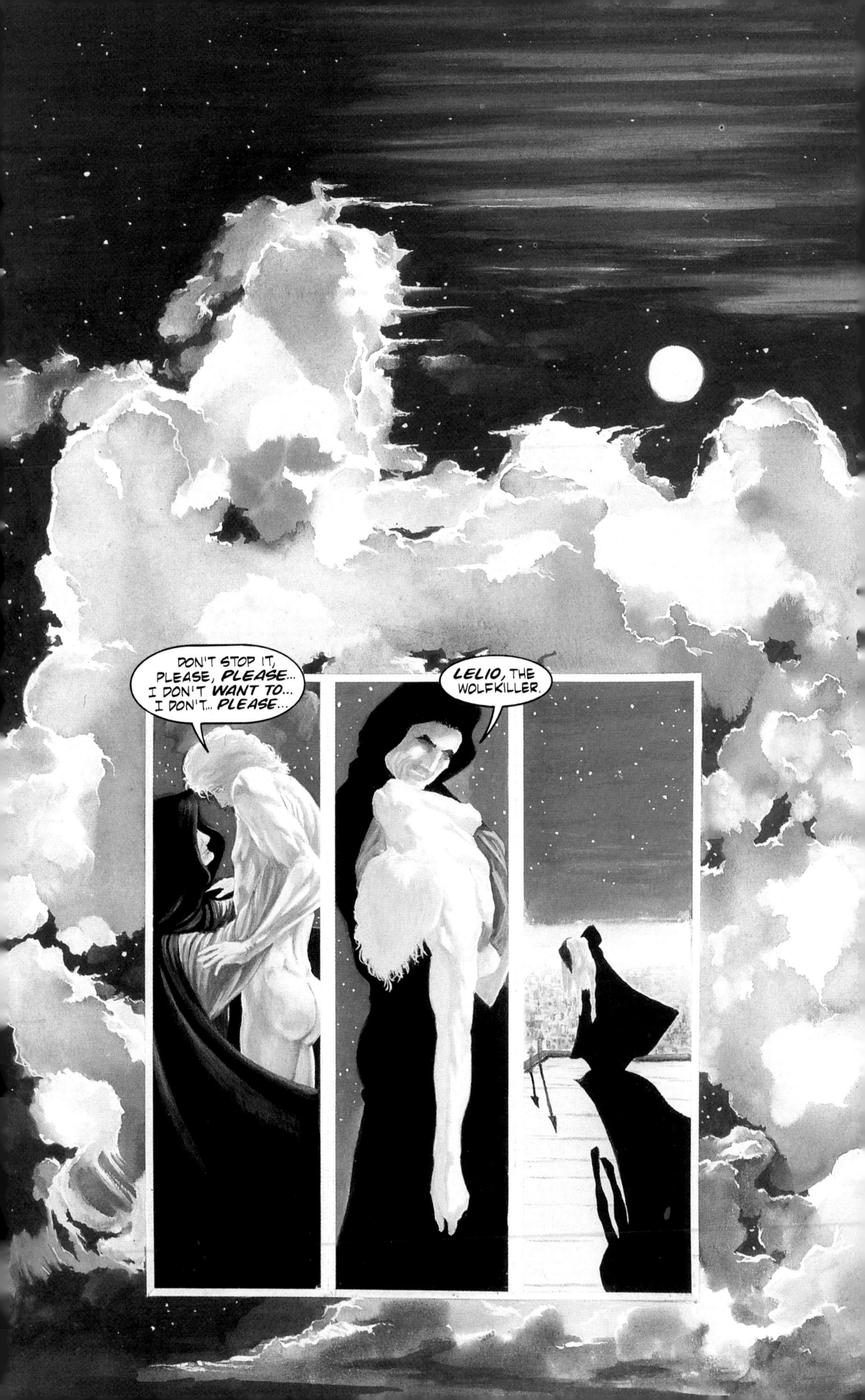

DON'T STOP IT, PLEASE, PLEASE... I DON'T WANT TO... I DON'T... PLEASE...
LELIO, THE WOLFKILLER.

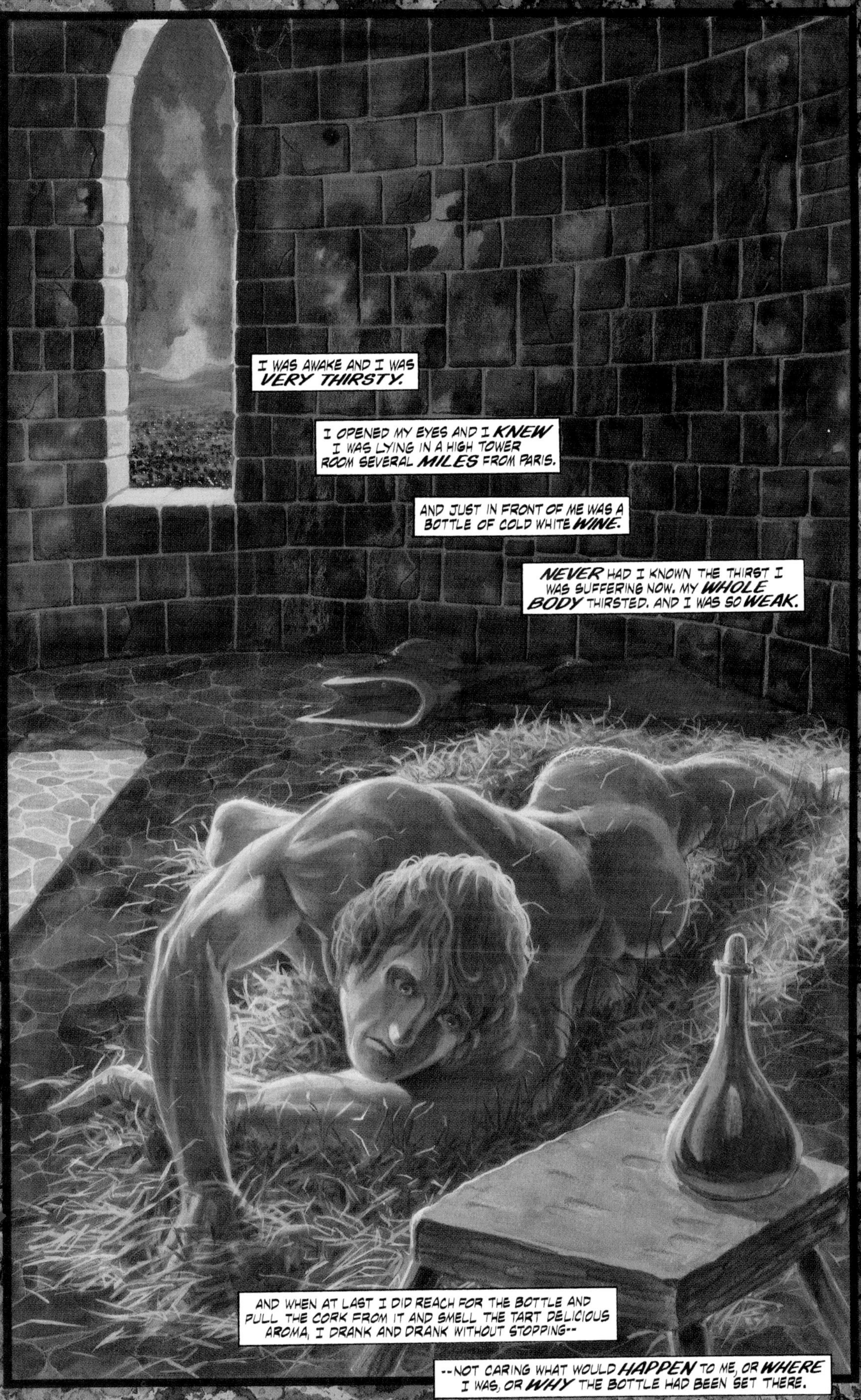
I WAS AWAKE AND I WAS VERY THIRSTY.
I OPENED MY EYES AND I KNEW I WAS LYING IN A HIGH TOWER ROOM SEVERAL MILES FROM PARIS.
AND JUST IN FRONT OF ME WAS A BOTTLE OF COLD WHITE WINE.
NEVER HAD I KNOWN THE THIRST I WAS SUFFERING NOW. MY WHOLE BODY THIRSTED. AND I WAS SO WEAK.
AND WHEN AT LAST I DID REACH FOR THE BOTTLE AND PULL THE CORK FROM IT AND SMELL THE TART DELICIOUS AROMA, I DRANK AND DRANK WITHOUT STOPPING--
--NOT CARING WHAT WOULD HAPPEN TO ME, OR WHERE I WAS, OR WHY THE BOTTLE HAD BEEN SET THERE.

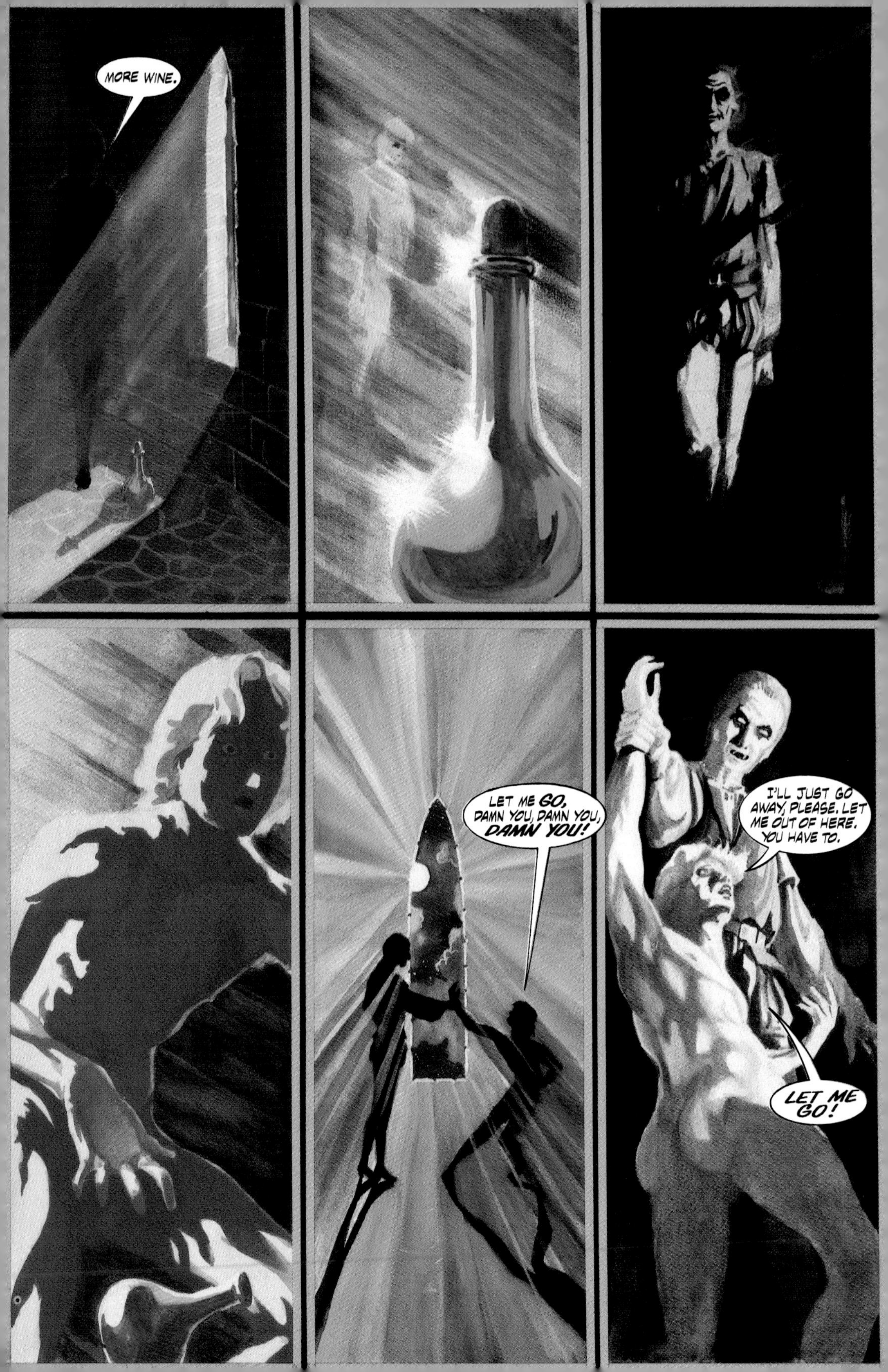
MORE WINE.
LET ME GO, DAMN YOU, DAMN YOU, DAMN YOU!
I'LL JUST GO AWAY, PLEASE. LET ME OUT OF HERE. YOU HAVE TO.
LET ME GO!

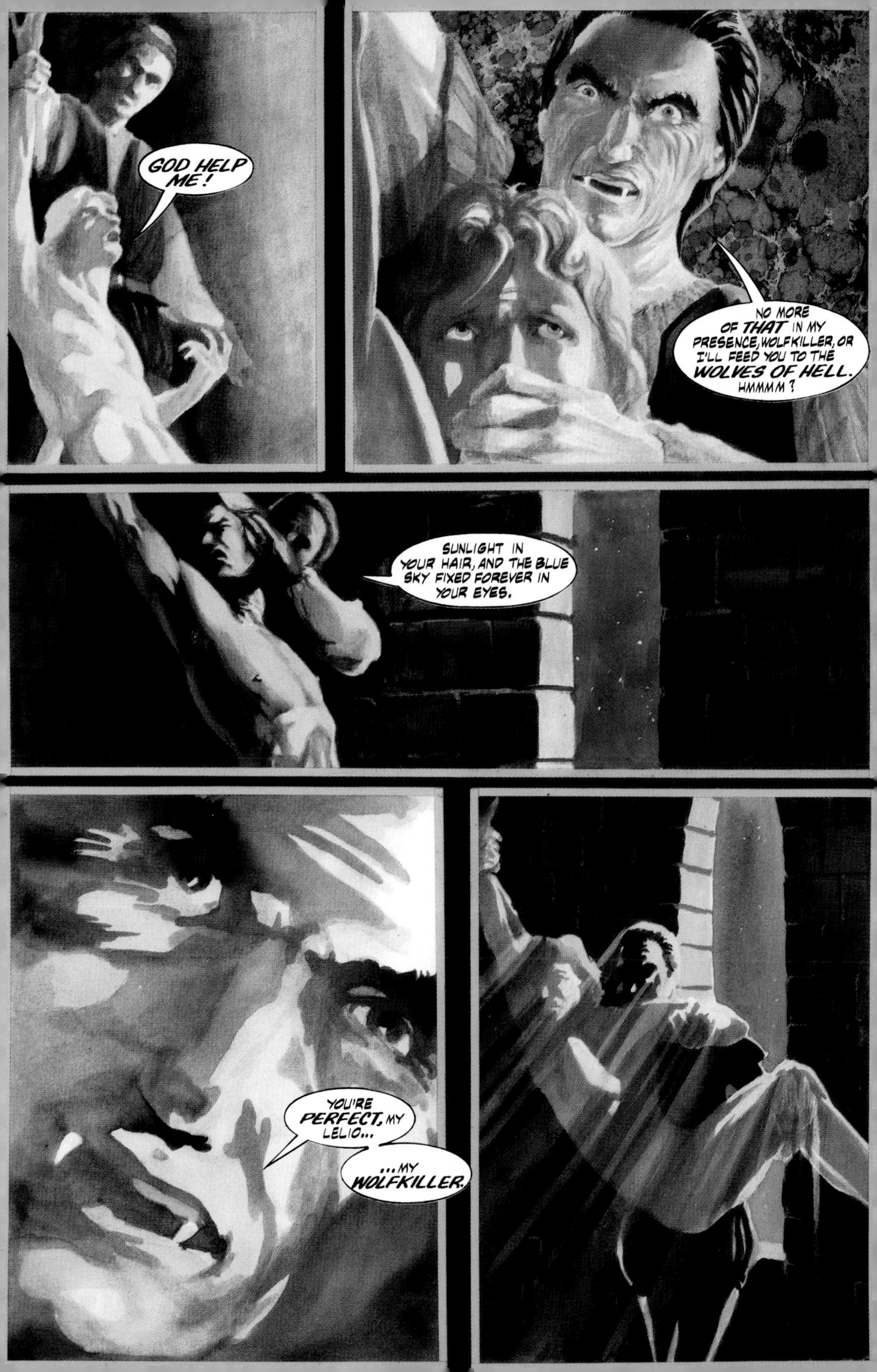
GOD HELP ME!
NO MORE OF THAT IN MY PRESENCE, WOLFKILLER, OR I'LL FEED YOU TO THE WOLVES OF HELL. HMMMM?
SUNLIGHT IN YOUR HAIR, AND THE BLUE SKY FIXED FOREVER IN YOUR EYES.
YOU'RE PERFECT, MY LELIO...
...MY WOLFKILLER.

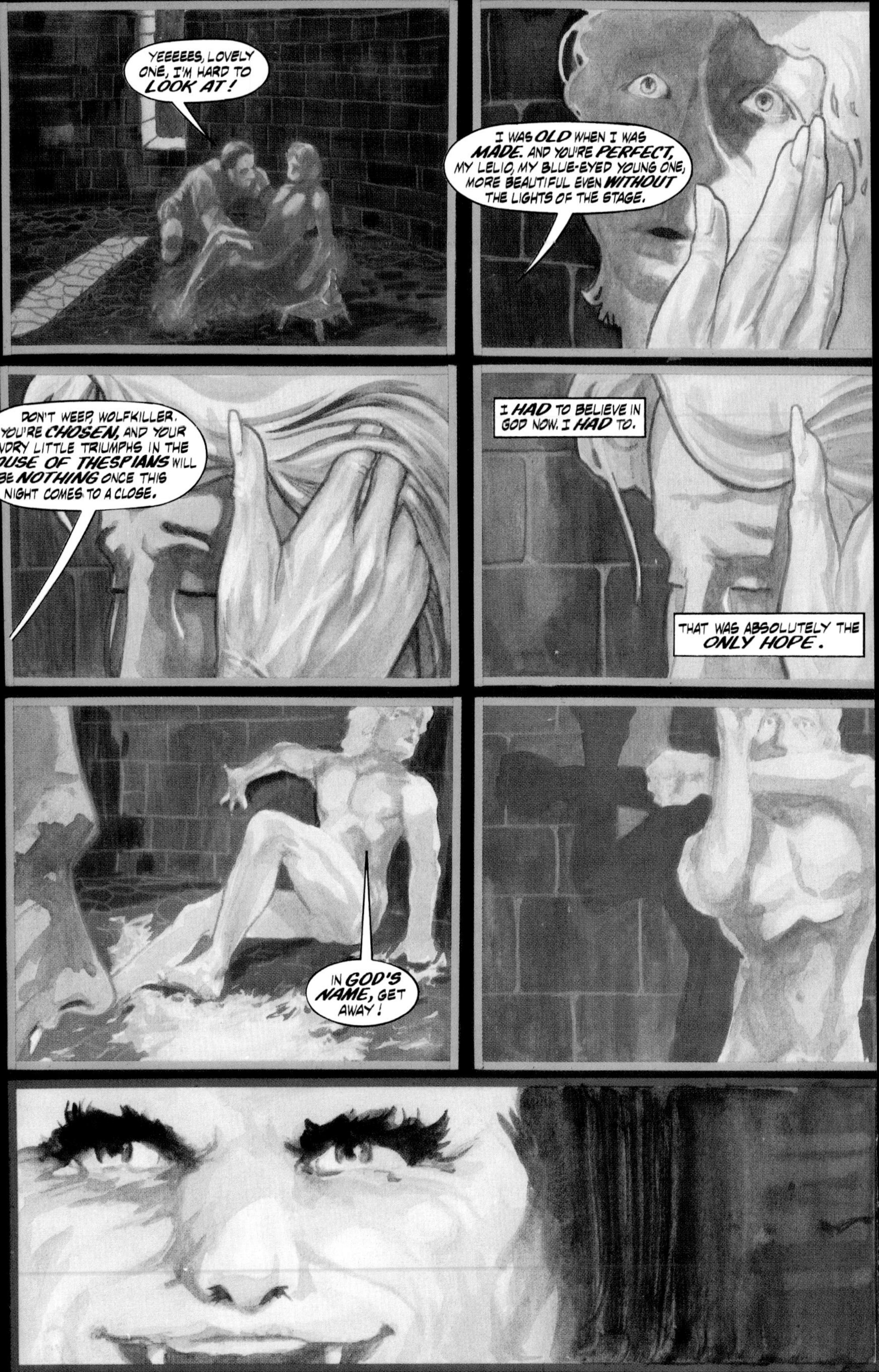
YEEEEES, LOVELY ONE, I'M HARD TO LOOK AT!
I WAS OLD WHEN I WAS MADE. AND YOU'RE PERFECT, MY LELIO, MY BLUE-EYED YOUNG ONE, MORE BEAUTIFUL EVEN WITHOUT THE LIGHTS OF THE STAGE.
DON'T WEEP, WOLFKILLER. YOU'RE CHOSEN, AND YOUR TAWDRY LITTLE TRIUMPHS IN THE HOUSE OF THESPIANS WILL BE NOTHING ONCE THIS NIGHT COMES TO A CLOSE.
I HAD TO BELIEVE IN GOD NOW. I HAD TO.
THAT WAS ABSOLUTELY THE ONLY HOPE.
IN GOD'S NAME, GET AWAY!

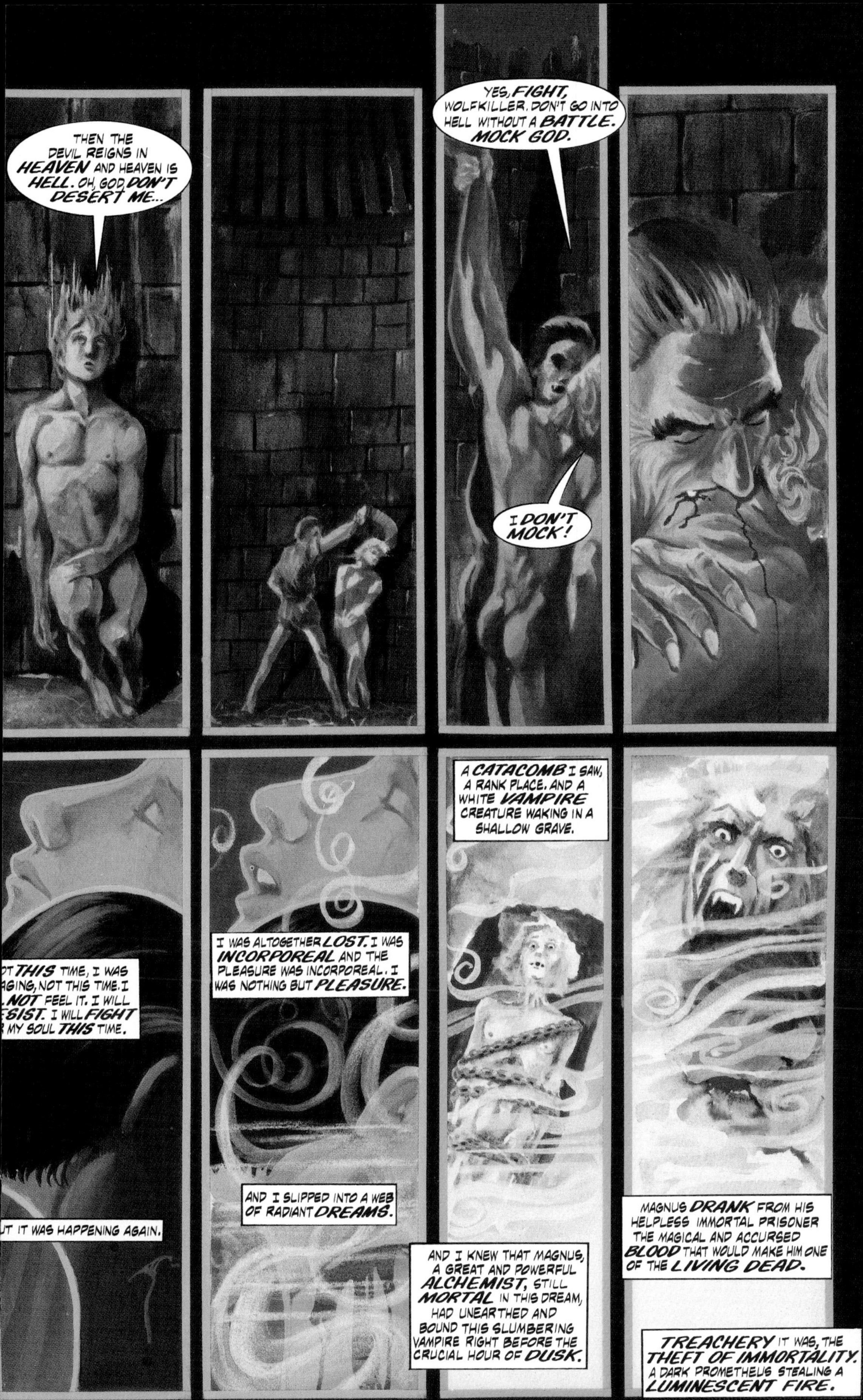
THEN THE DEVIL REIGNS IN HEAVEN AND HEAVEN IS HELL. OH, GOD, DON'T DESERT ME...
YES, FIGHT, WOLFKILLER. DON'T GO INTO HELL WITHOUT A BATTLE. MOCK GOD.
I DON'T MOCK!
OT THIS TIME, I WAS AGING, NOT THIS TIME. I NOT FEEL IT. I WILL ESIST. I WILL FIGHT R MY SOUL THIS TIME.
UT IT WAS HAPPENING AGAIN.
I WAS ALTOGETHER LOST. I WAS INCORPOREAL AND THE PLEASURE WAS INCORPOREAL. I WAS NOTHING BUT PLEASURE.
AND I SLIPPED INTO A WEB OF RADIANT DREAMS.
A CATACOMB I SAW, A RANK PLACE. AND A WHITE VAMPIRE CREATURE WAKING IN A SHALLOW GRAVE.
AND I KNEW THAT MAGNUS, A GREAT AND POWERFUL ALCHEMIST, STILL MORTAL IN THIS DREAM, HAD UNEARTHED AND BOUND THIS SLUMBERING VAMPIRE RIGHT BEFORE THE CRUCIAL HOUR OF DUSK.
MAGNUS DRANK FROM HIS HELPLESS IMMORTAL PRISONER THE MAGICAL AND ACCURSED BLOOD THAT WOULD MAKE HIM ONE OF THE LIVING DEAD.
TREACHERY IT WAS, THE THEFT OF IMMORTALITY. A DARK PROMETHEUS STEALING A LUMINESCENT FIRE.

LAUGHTER IN THE DARKNESS. AND THE STENCH OF THE GRAVE.

AND THE *ECSTASY*, ABSOLUTELY FATHOMLESS, AND IRRESISTIBLE, AND THEN DRAWING TO A FINISH.

PLEASE, DON'T STOP IT...

I TRIED TO MOVE. I WAS *CRAVING*. MY WHOLE BODY WAS THIRSTY.

YOU'RE DYING, *WOLFKILLER*. THE LIGHT'S GOING OUT OF YOUR BLUE EYES AS IF ALL THE SUMMER DAYS ARE GONE...

NO, *PLEASE*...

ASK FOR IT, CHILD. ASK AND YOU SHALL *RECEIVE*.

HELP ME. PLEASE.

I SHALL GIVE YOU THE *WATER* OF ALL WATERS, THE *WINE* OF ALL WINES.

THIS IS MY *BODY*, THIS IS MY *BLOOD*.

ASK FOR WOLFKILLE YOU WILL L FOREVE

THE *GREAT DESPAIR* I FEARED SO MUCH LAY BEFORE ME, THE EMPTINESS THAT WAS *DEATH*, AND STILL I SAID *NO*. IN PURE HORROR I SAID *NO*.

I WILL *NOT* BOW DOWN TO IT, THE CHAOS AND THE HORROR. I SAID *NO*.

STUBBORN WOLFKILLER.

NOT STUBBORN. *BRAVE*. NOT STUBBORN.

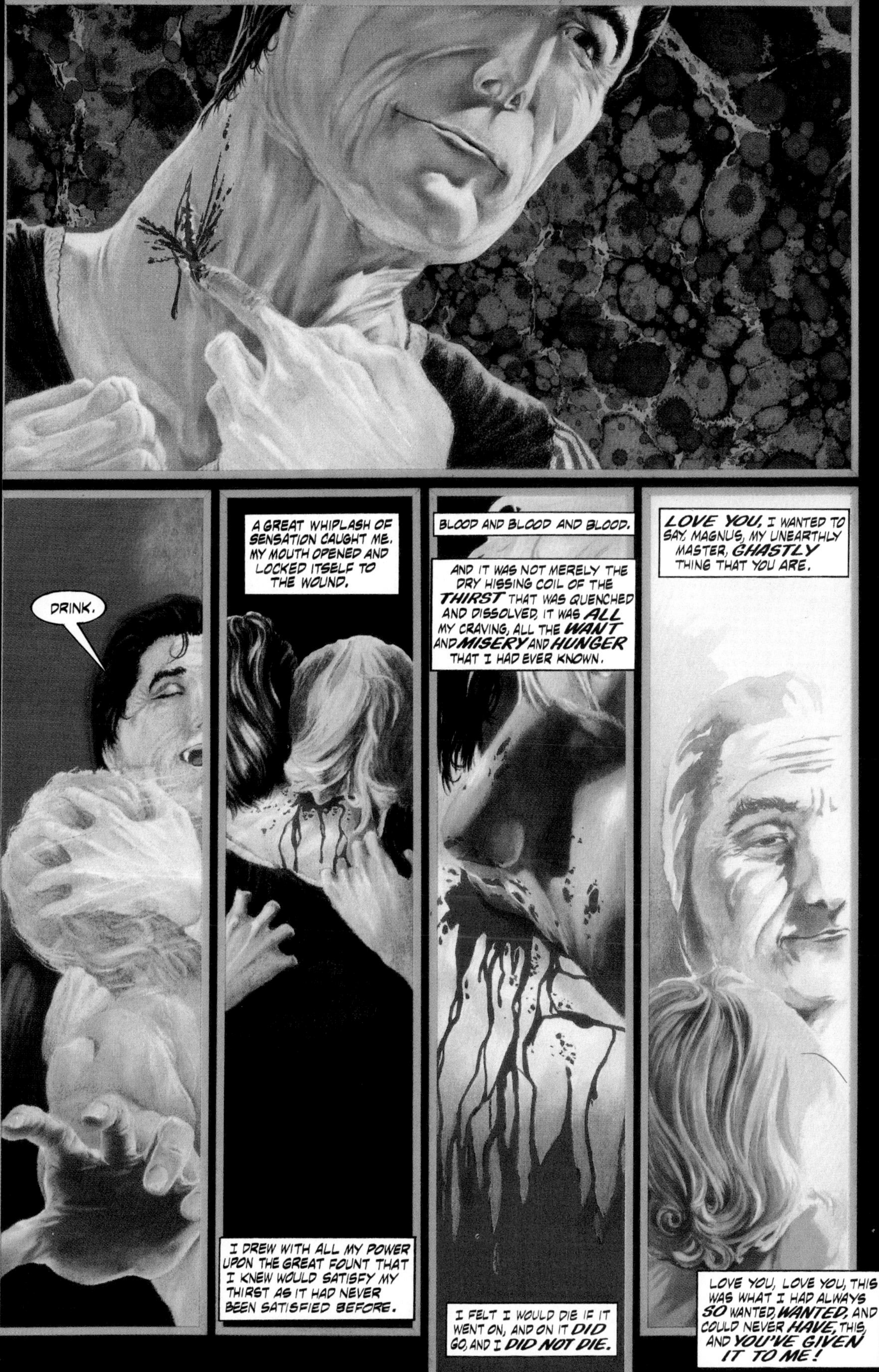

DRINK.
A GREAT WHIPLASH OF SENSATION CAUGHT ME. MY MOUTH OPENED AND LOCKED ITSELF TO THE WOUND.
I DREW WITH ALL MY POWER UPON THE GREAT FOUNT THAT I KNEW WOULD SATISFY MY THIRST AS IT HAD NEVER BEEN SATISFIED BEFORE.
BLOOD AND BLOOD AND BLOOD.
AND IT WAS NOT MERELY THE DRY HISSING COIL OF THE THIRST THAT WAS QUENCHED AND DISSOLVED, IT WAS ALL MY CRAVING, ALL THE WANT AND MISERY AND HUNGER THAT I HAD EVER KNOWN.
I FELT I WOULD DIE IF IT WENT ON, AND ON IT DID GO, AND I DID NOT DIE.
LOVE YOU, I WANTED TO SAY, MAGNUS, MY UNEARTHLY MASTER, GHASTLY THING THAT YOU ARE.
LOVE YOU, LOVE YOU, THIS WAS WHAT I HAD ALWAYS SO WANTED, WANTED, AND COULD NEVER HAVE, THIS, AND YOU'VE GIVEN IT TO ME!

OH, WHAT HAVE YOU *DONE*, WHAT IS THIS THAT YOU'VE *GIVEN* TO ME?!

AH, DON'T YOU *SEE*? MY *HEIR* CHOSEN TO TAKE THE *DARK GIFT* FROM ME WITH MORE FIBER AND COURAGE THAN TEN *MORTAL MEN*--

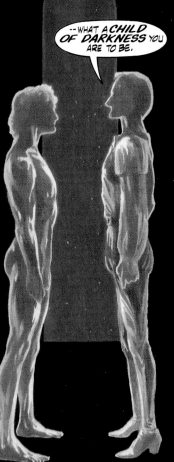

--WHAT A *CHILD OF DARKNESS* YOU ARE TO BE.

HE WAS NO *GHASTLY THING* TO ME NOW BUT MERELY THAT WHICH WAS *STRANGE* AND *WHITE*, AND FULL OF SOME DEEPER LESSON PERHAPS THAN THE *SIGHING TREES* BELOW OR THE *SHIMMERING CITY* CALLING ME OVER THE MILES.

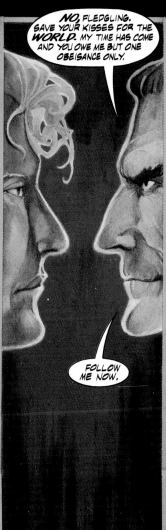

NO, FLEDGLING. SAVE YOUR KISSES FOR THE *WORLD*. MY TIME HAS COME AND YOU OWE ME BUT ONE *OBEISANCE* ONLY.

FOLLOW ME NOW.

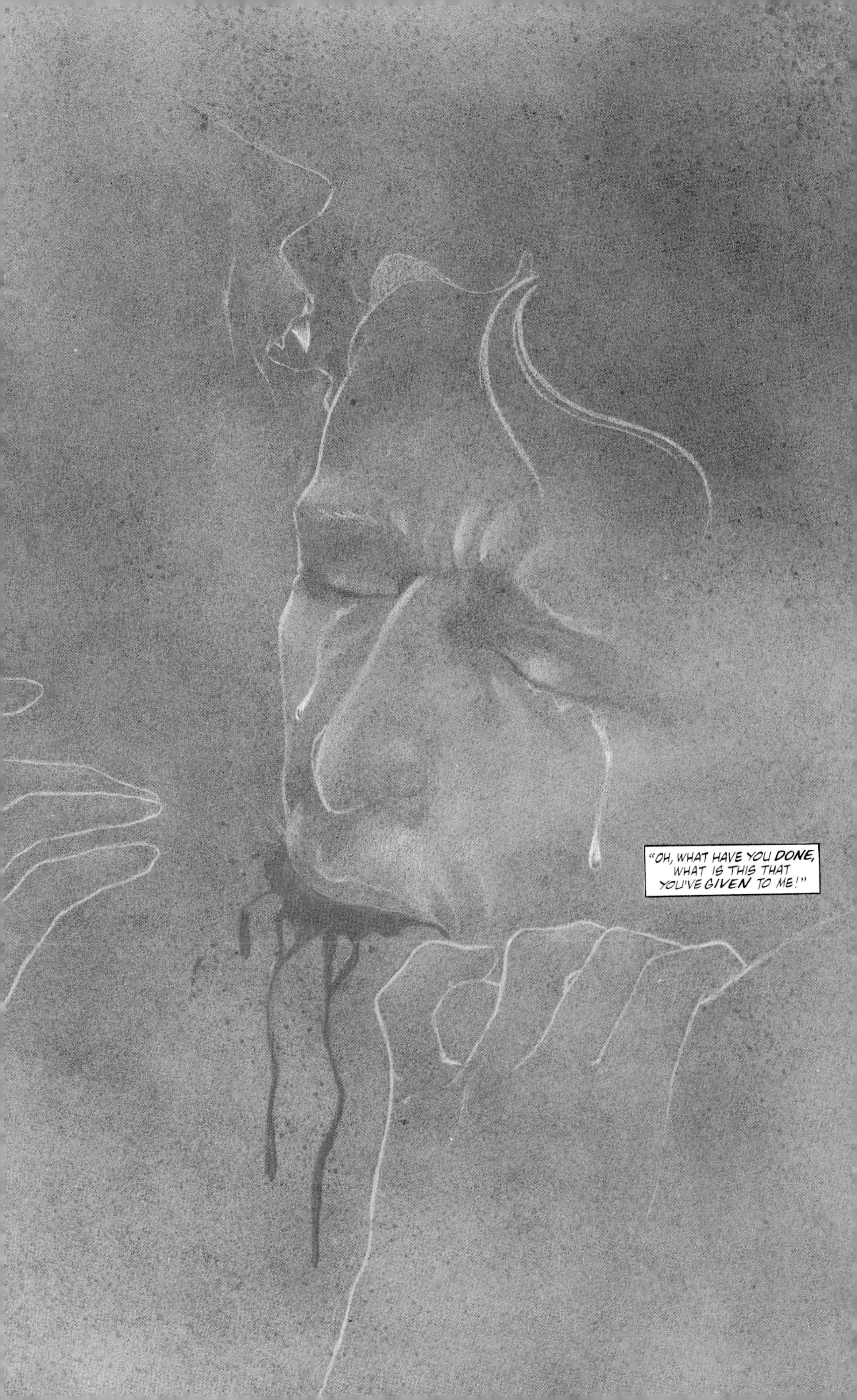
"OH, WHAT HAVE YOU DONE, WHAT IS THIS THAT YOU'VE GIVEN TO ME!"

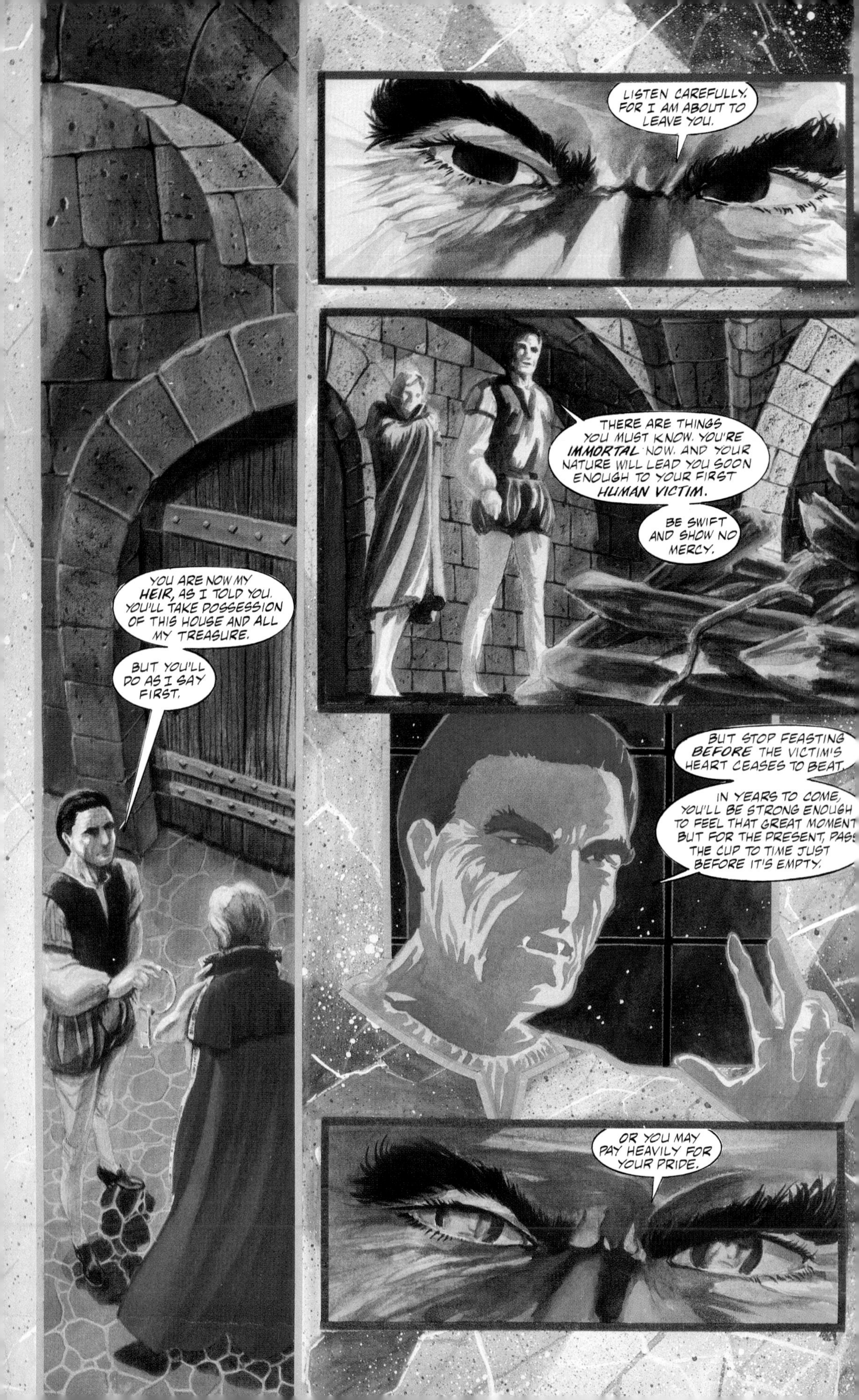
YOU ARE NOW MY HEIR, AS I TOLD YOU. YOU'LL TAKE POSSESSION OF THIS HOUSE AND ALL MY TREASURE.
BUT YOU'LL DO AS I SAY FIRST.
LISTEN CAREFULLY, FOR I AM ABOUT TO LEAVE YOU.
THERE ARE THINGS YOU MUST KNOW. YOU'RE IMMORTAL NOW. AND YOUR NATURE WILL LEAD YOU SOON ENOUGH TO YOUR FIRST HUMAN VICTIM.
BE SWIFT AND SHOW NO MERCY.
BUT STOP FEASTING BEFORE THE VICTIM'S HEART CEASES TO BEAT.
IN YEARS TO COME, YOU'LL BE STRONG ENOUGH TO FEEL THAT GREAT MOMENT BUT FOR THE PRESENT, PASS THE CUP TO TIME JUST BEFORE IT'S EMPTY.
OR YOU MAY PAY HEAVILY FOR YOUR PRIDE.

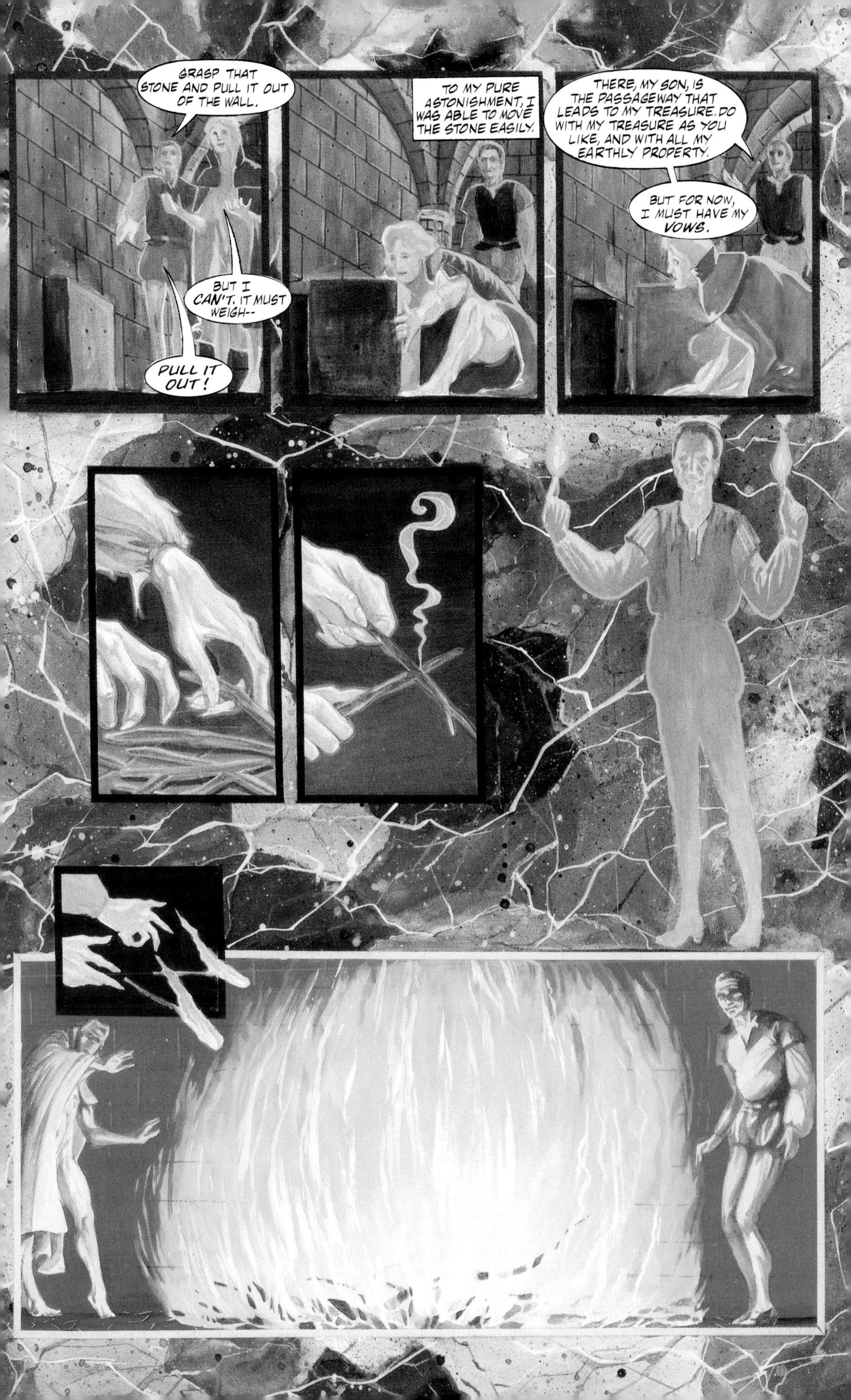
GRASP THAT STONE AND PULL IT OUT OF THE WALL.
BUT I CAN'T. IT MUST WEIGH--
PULL IT OUT!
TO MY PURE ASTONISHMENT, I WAS ABLE TO MOVE THE STONE EASILY.
THERE, MY SON, IS THE PASSAGEWAY THAT LEADS TO MY TREASURE. DO WITH MY TREASURE AS YOU LIKE, AND WITH ALL MY EARTHLY PROPERTY.
BUT FOR NOW, I MUST HAVE MY VOWS.

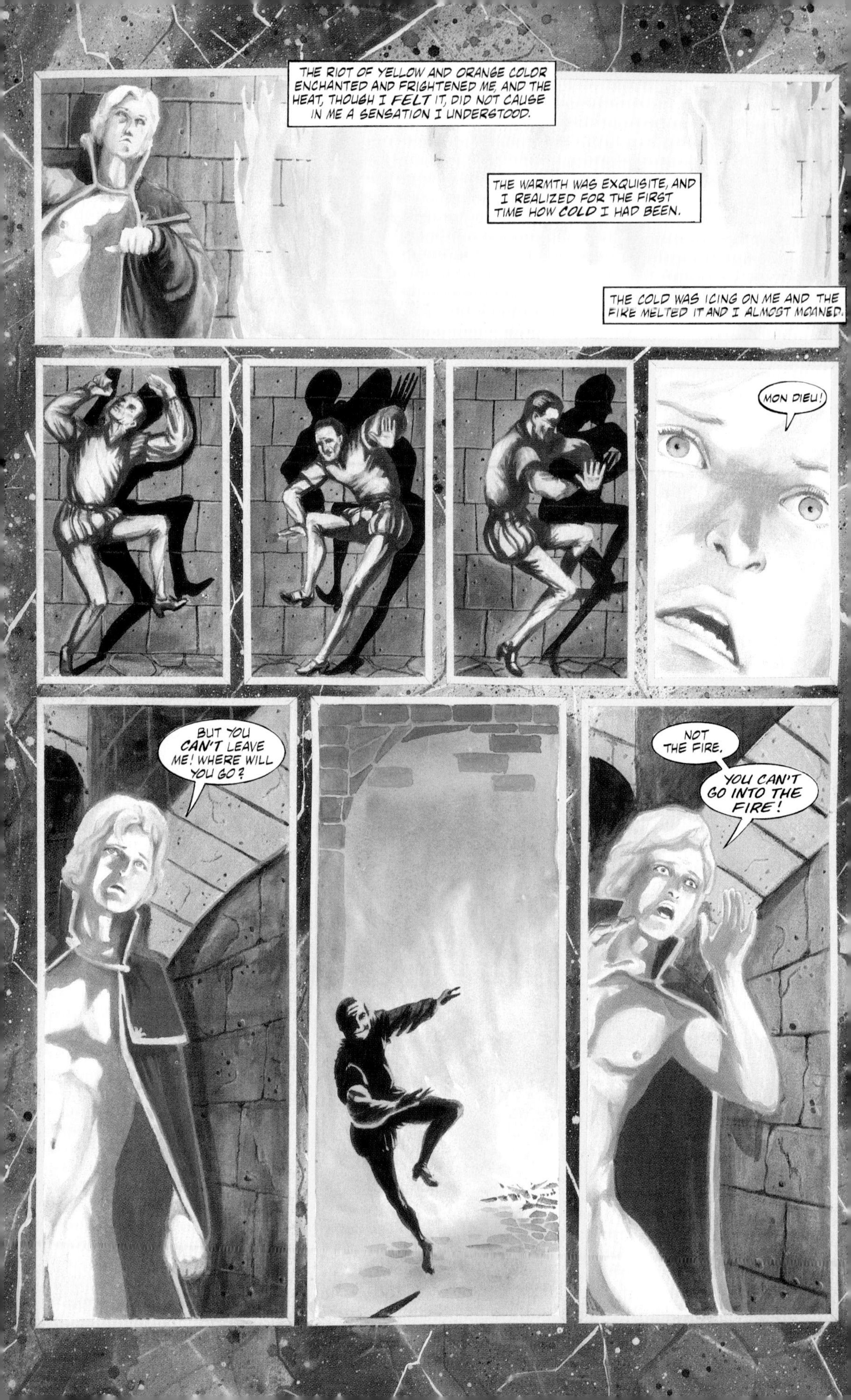
THE RIOT OF YELLOW AND ORANGE COLOR ENCHANTED AND FRIGHTENED ME, AND THE HEAT, THOUGH I FELT IT, DID NOT CAUSE IN ME A SENSATION I UNDERSTOOD.
THE WARMTH WAS EXQUISITE, AND I REALIZED FOR THE FIRST TIME HOW COLD I HAD BEEN.
THE COLD WAS ICING ON ME AND THE FIRE MELTED IT AND I ALMOST MOANED.
MON DIEU!
BUT YOU CAN'T LEAVE ME! WHERE WILL YOU GO?
NOT THE FIRE.
YOU CAN'T GO INTO THE FIRE!

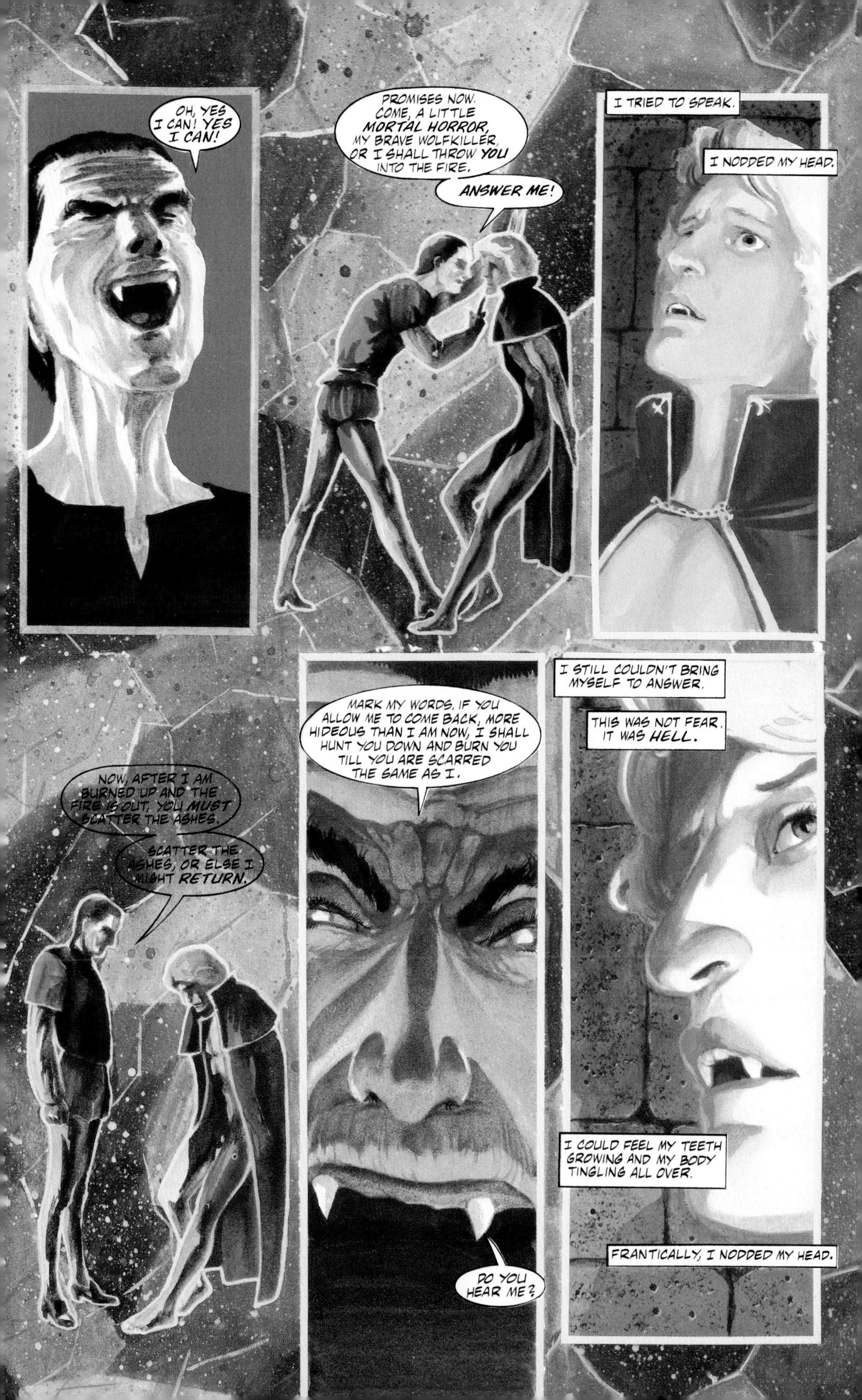
OH, YES I CAN! YES I CAN!
PROMISES NOW. COME, A LITTLE MORTAL HORROR, MY BRAVE WOLFKILLER, OR I SHALL THROW YOU INTO THE FIRE.
ANSWER ME!
I TRIED TO SPEAK.
I NODDED MY HEAD.
NOW, AFTER I AM BURNED UP AND THE FIRE IS OUT, YOU MUST SCATTER THE ASHES.
SCATTER THE ASHES, OR ELSE I MIGHT RETURN.
MARK MY WORDS, IF YOU ALLOW ME TO COME BACK, MORE HIDEOUS THAN I AM NOW, I SHALL HUNT YOU DOWN AND BURN YOU TILL YOU ARE SCARRED THE SAME AS I.
DO YOU HEAR ME?
I STILL COULDN'T BRING MYSELF TO ANSWER.
THIS WAS NOT FEAR. IT WAS HELL.
I COULD FEEL MY TEETH GROWING AND MY BODY TINGLING ALL OVER.
FRANTICALLY, I NODDED MY HEAD.

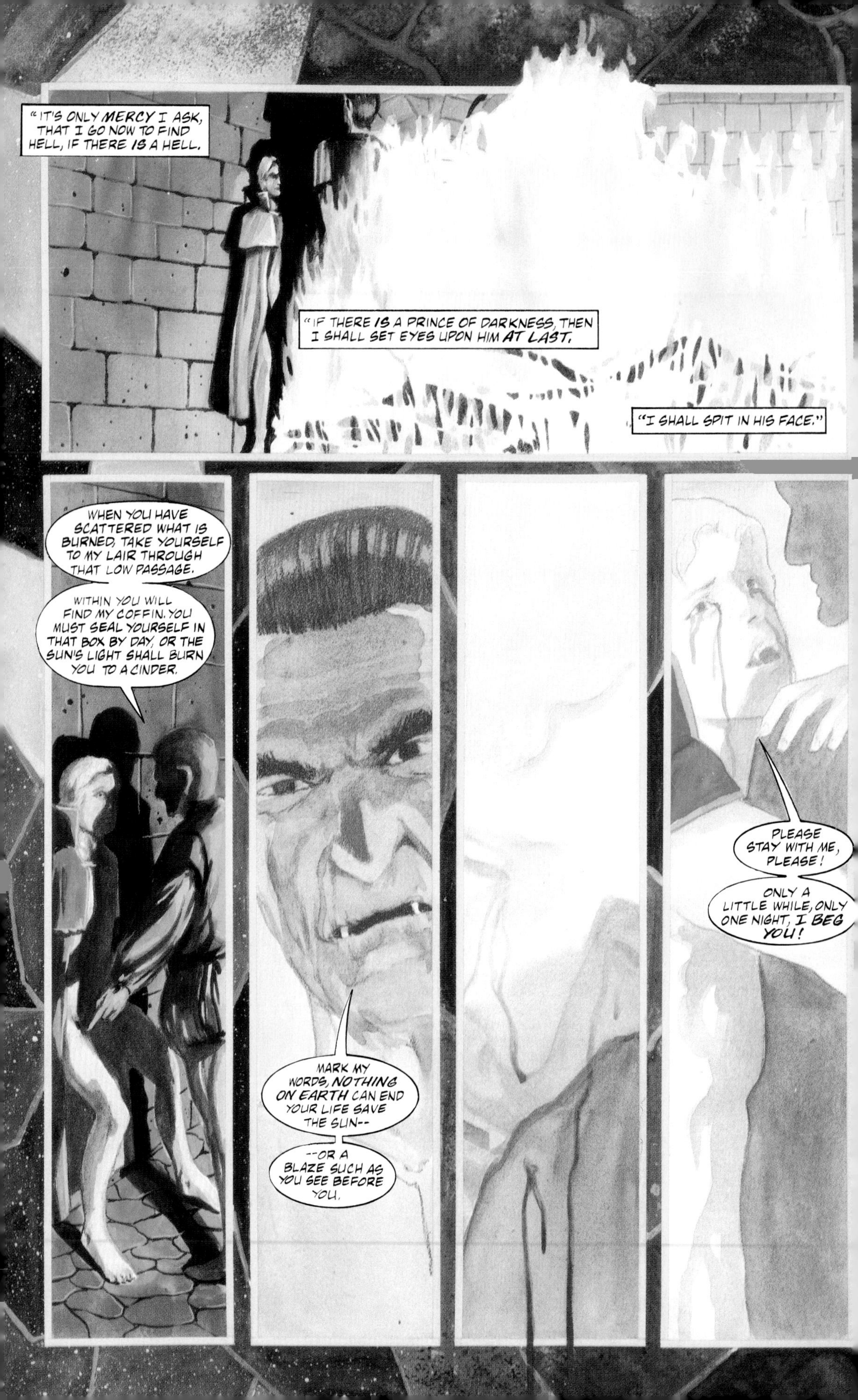
"IT'S ONLY MERCY I ASK, THAT I GO NOW TO FIND HELL, IF THERE IS A HELL.
"IF THERE IS A PRINCE OF DARKNESS, THEN I SHALL SET EYES UPON HIM AT LAST.
"I SHALL SPIT IN HIS FACE."
WHEN YOU HAVE SCATTERED WHAT IS BURNED, TAKE YOURSELF TO MY LAIR THROUGH THAT LOW PASSAGE.
WITHIN YOU WILL FIND MY COFFIN. YOU MUST SEAL YOURSELF IN THAT BOX BY DAY, OR THE SUN'S LIGHT SHALL BURN YOU TO A CINDER.
MARK MY WORDS, NOTHING ON EARTH CAN END YOUR LIFE SAVE THE SUN--
--OR A BLAZE SUCH AS YOU SEE BEFORE YOU.
PLEASE STAY WITH ME, PLEASE!
ONLY A LITTLE WHILE, ONLY ONE NIGHT, I BEG YOU!

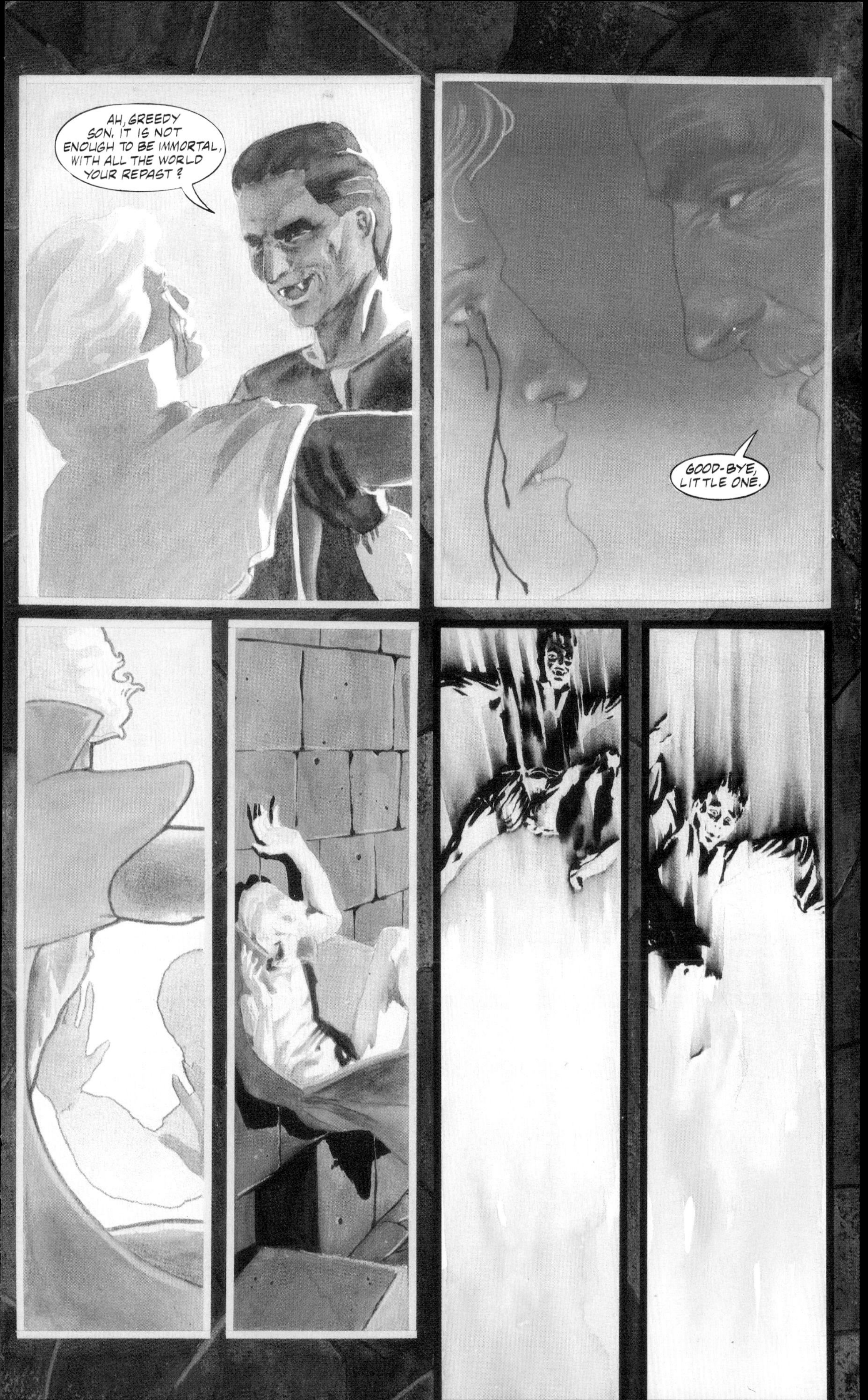
AH, GREEDY SON, IT IS NOT ENOUGH TO BE IMMORTAL, WITH ALL THE WORLD YOUR REPAST?
GOOD-BYE, LITTLE ONE.

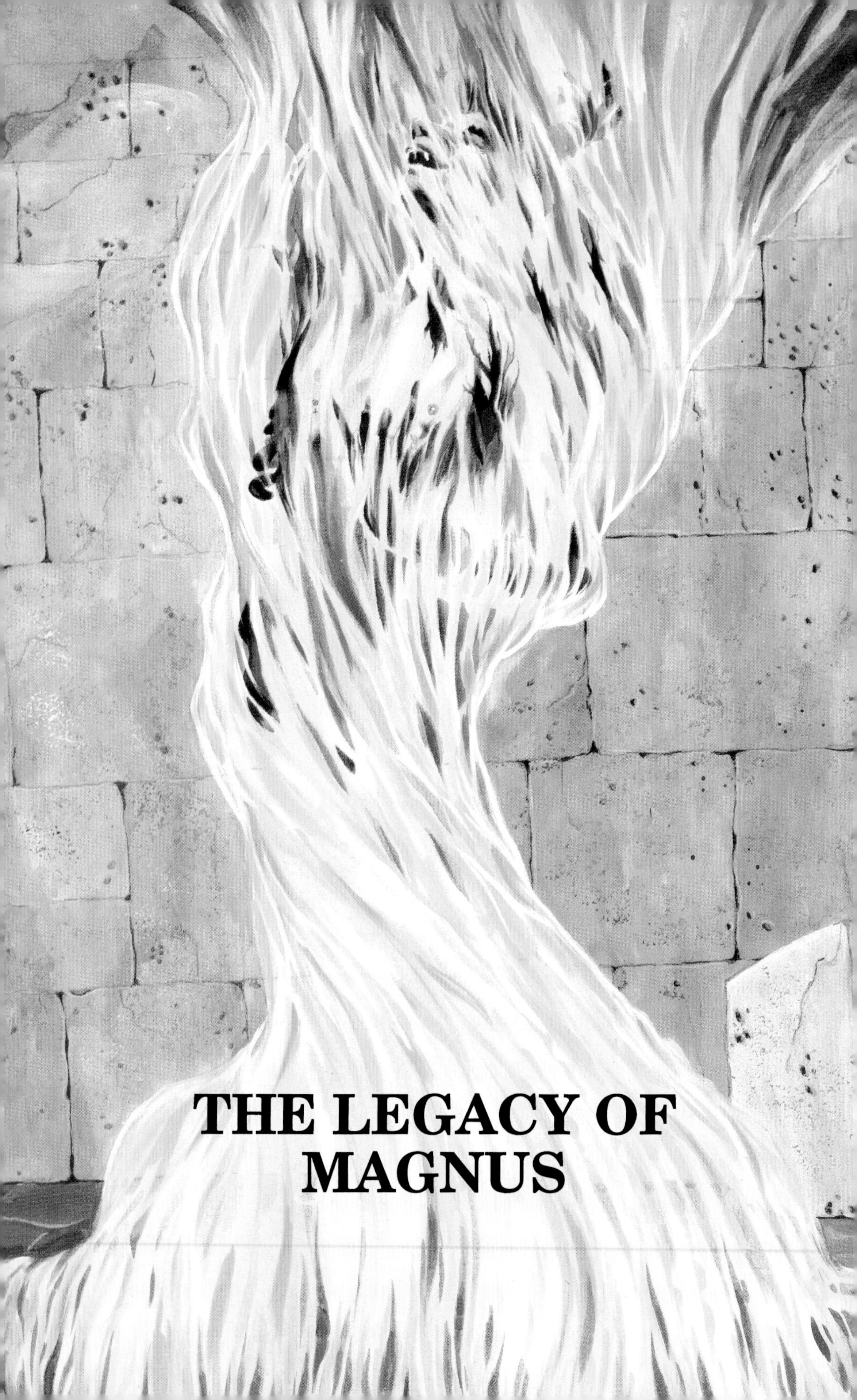

THE LEGACY OF MAGNUS

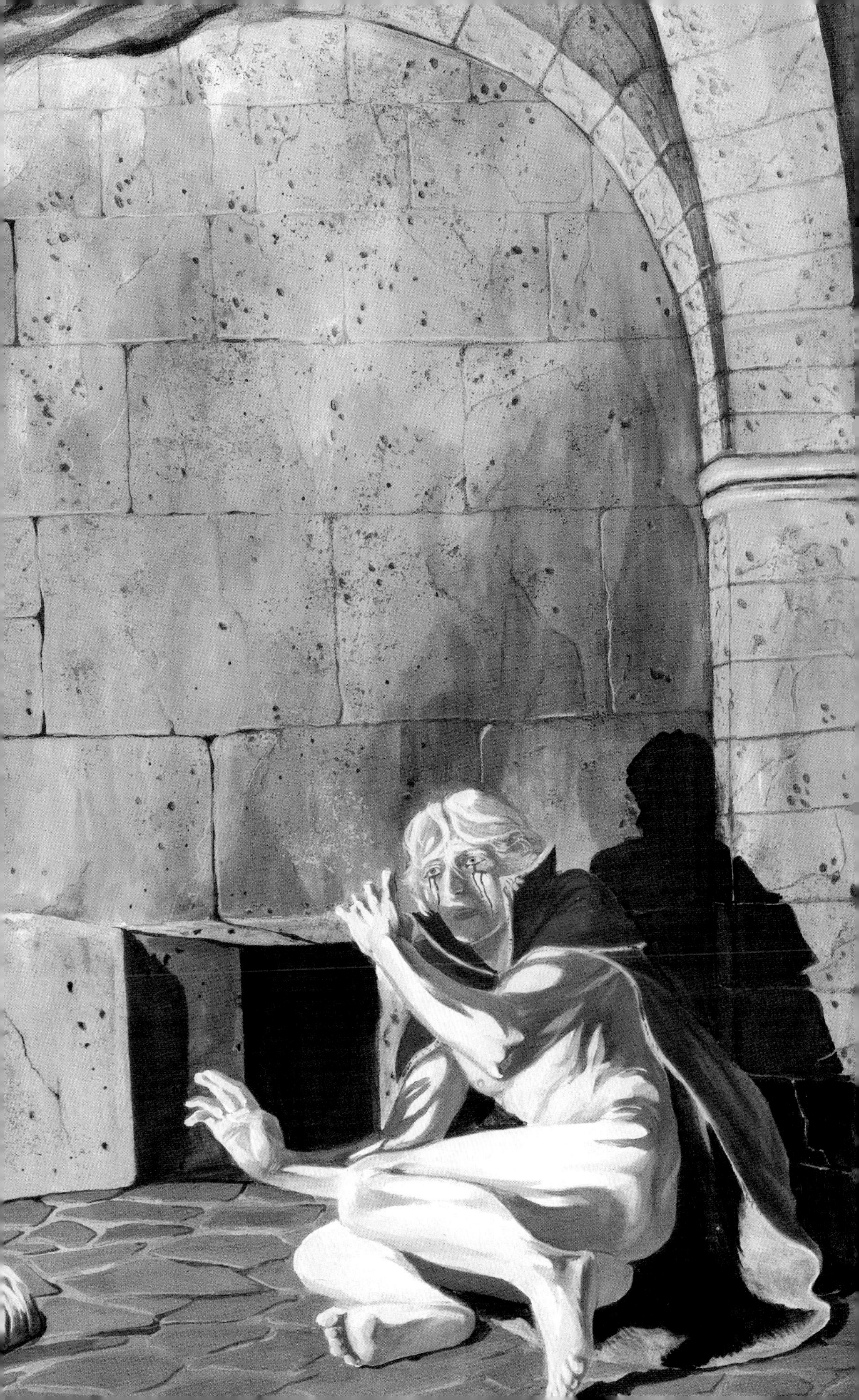

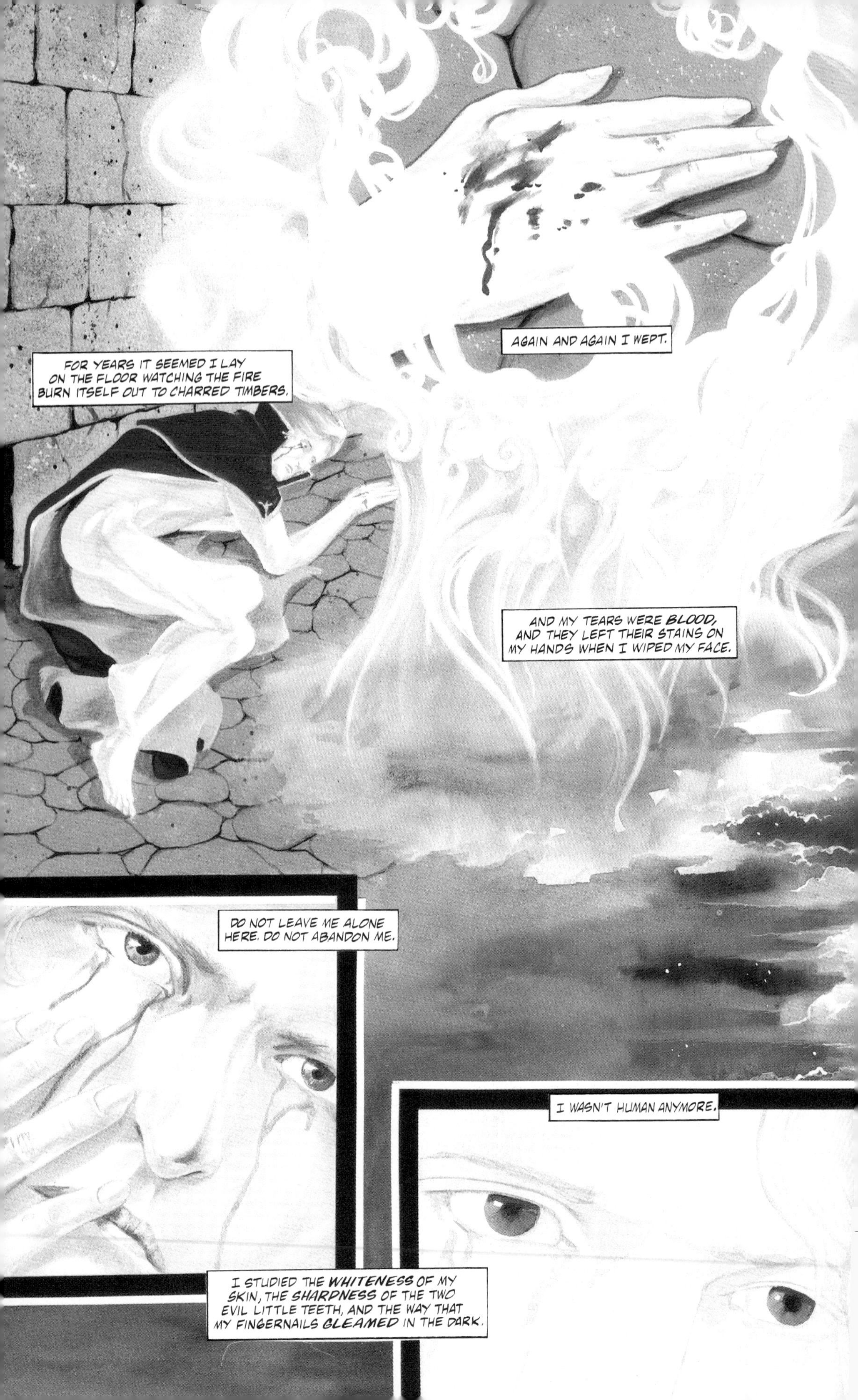
FOR YEARS IT SEEMED I LAY ON THE FLOOR WATCHING THE FIRE BURN ITSELF OUT TO CHARRED TIMBERS.
AGAIN AND AGAIN I WEPT.
AND MY TEARS WERE BLOOD, AND THEY LEFT THEIR STAINS ON MY HANDS WHEN I WIPED MY FACE.
DO NOT LEAVE ME ALONE HERE. DO NOT ABANDON ME.
I WASN'T HUMAN ANYMORE.
I STUDIED THE WHITENESS OF MY SKIN, THE SHARPNESS OF THE TWO EVIL LITTLE TEETH, AND THE WAY THAT MY FINGERNAILS GLEAMED IN THE DARK.

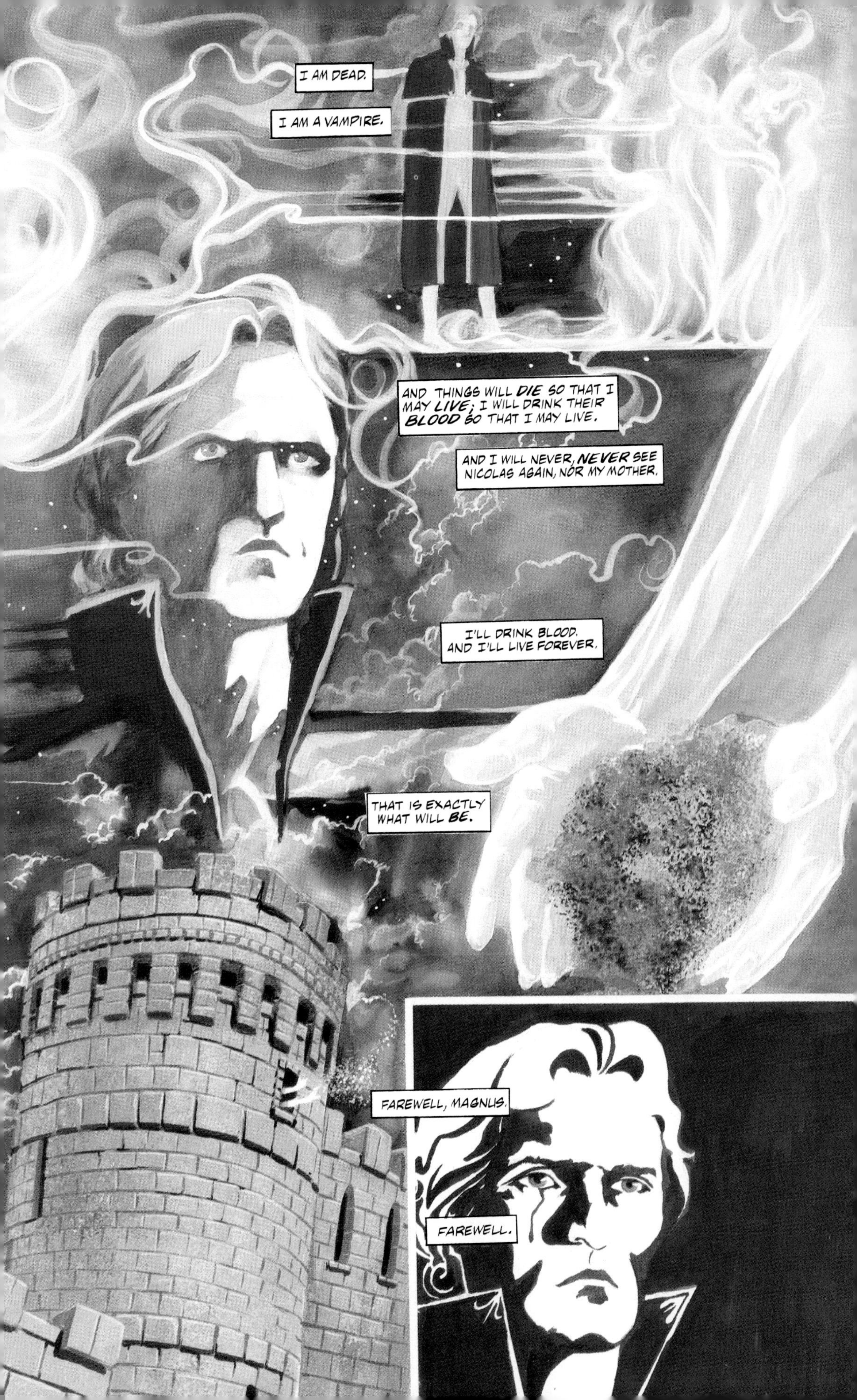

I AM DEAD.
I AM A VAMPIRE.
AND THINGS WILL DIE SO THAT I MAY LIVE; I WILL DRINK THEIR BLOOD SO THAT I MAY LIVE.
AND I WILL NEVER, NEVER SEE NICOLAS AGAIN, NOR MY MOTHER.
I'LL DRINK BLOOD. AND I'LL LIVE FOREVER.
THAT IS EXACTLY WHAT WILL BE.
FAREWELL, MAGNUS.
FAREWELL.

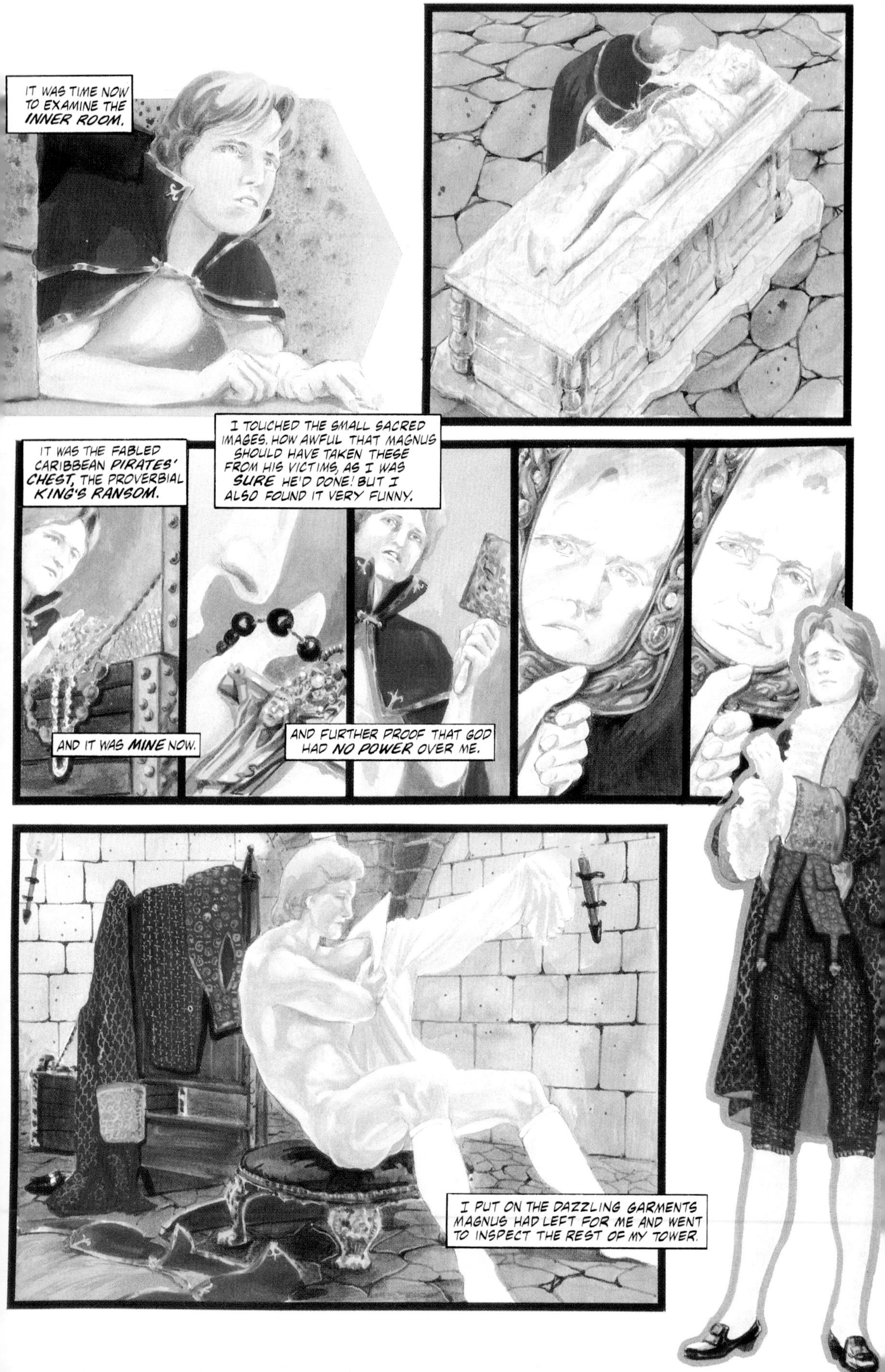
IT WAS TIME NOW TO EXAMINE THE INNER ROOM.
IT WAS THE FABLED CARIBBEAN PIRATES' CHEST, THE PROVERBIAL KING'S RANSOM.
AND IT WAS MINE NOW.
I TOUCHED THE SMALL SACRED IMAGES. HOW AWFUL THAT MAGNUS SHOULD HAVE TAKEN THESE FROM HIS VICTIMS, AS I WAS SURE HE'D DONE! BUT I ALSO FOUND IT VERY FUNNY.
AND FURTHER PROOF THAT GOD HAD NO POWER OVER ME.
I PUT ON THE DAZZLING GARMENTS MAGNUS HAD LEFT FOR ME AND WENT TO INSPECT THE REST OF MY TOWER.

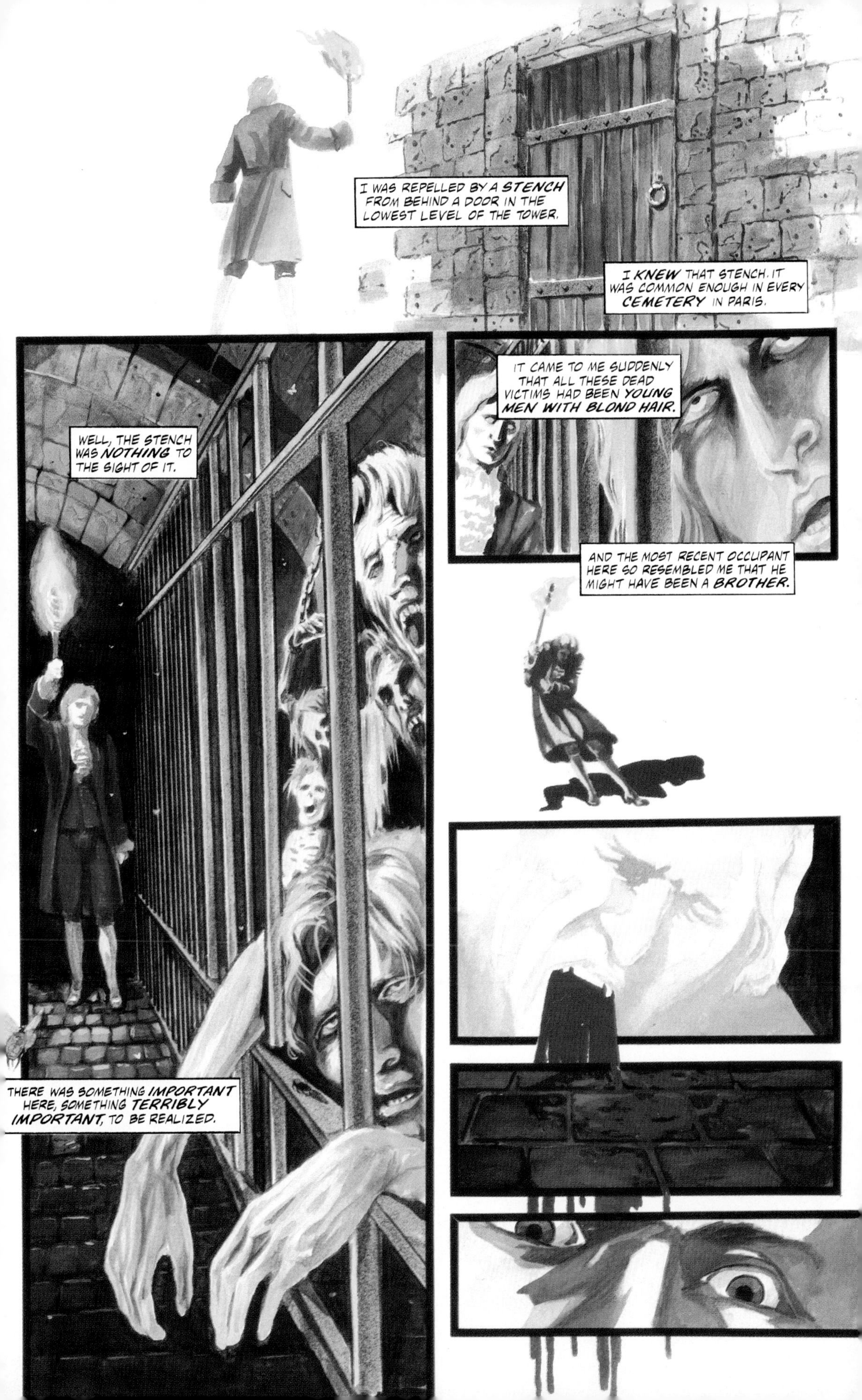
I WAS REPELLED BY A STENCH FROM BEHIND A DOOR IN THE LOWEST LEVEL OF THE TOWER.
I KNEW THAT STENCH. IT WAS COMMON ENOUGH IN EVERY CEMETERY IN PARIS.
WELL, THE STENCH WAS NOTHING TO THE SIGHT OF IT.
THERE WAS SOMETHING IMPORTANT HERE, SOMETHING TERRIBLY IMPORTANT, TO BE REALIZED.
IT CAME TO ME SUDDENLY THAT ALL THESE DEAD VICTIMS HAD BEEN YOUNG MEN WITH BLOND HAIR.
AND THE MOST RECENT OCCUPANT HERE SO RESEMBLED ME THAT HE MIGHT HAVE BEEN A BROTHER.

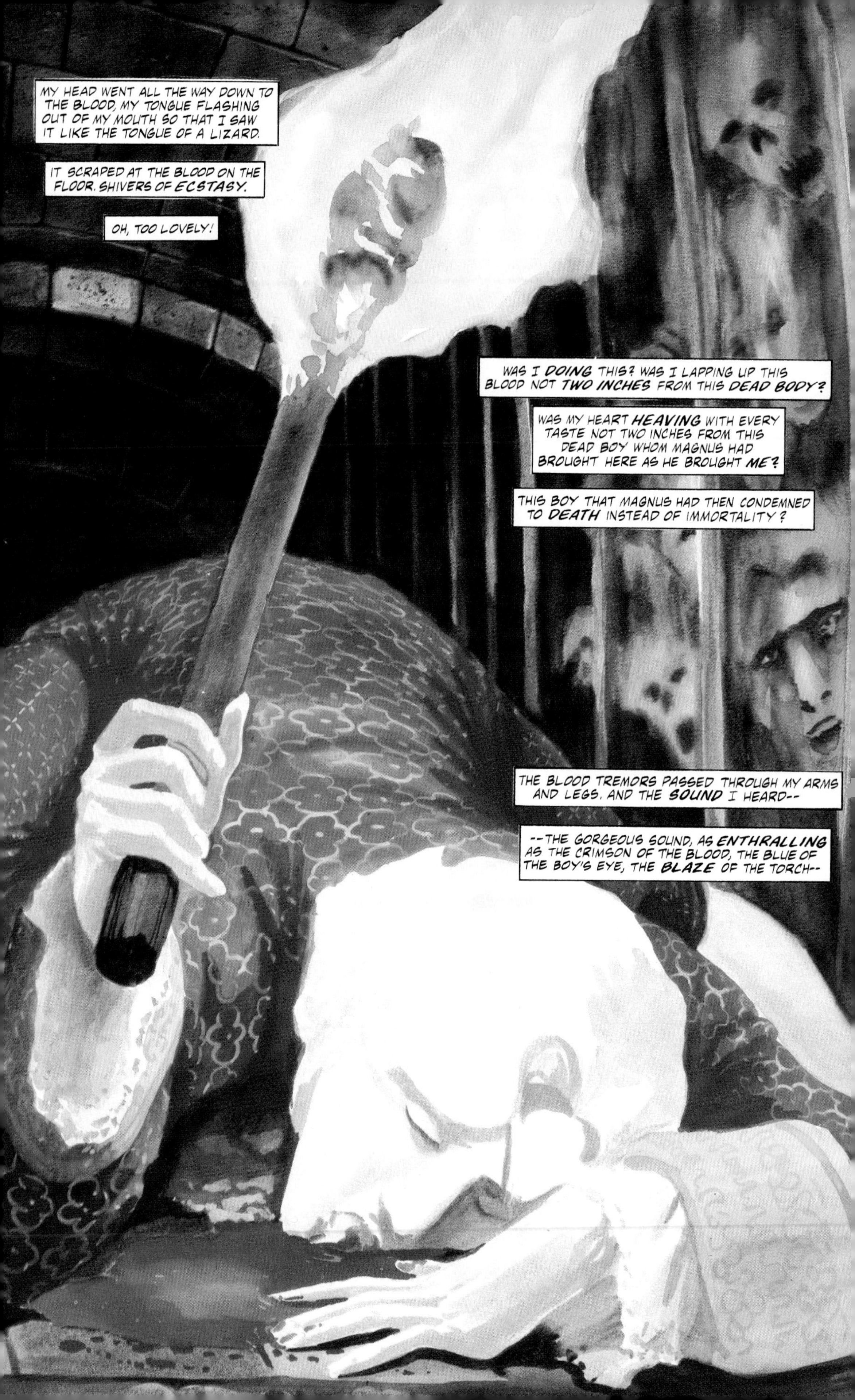

MY HEAD WENT ALL THE WAY DOWN TO THE BLOOD, MY TONGUE FLASHING OUT OF MY MOUTH SO THAT I SAW IT LIKE THE TONGUE OF A LIZARD.
IT SCRAPED AT THE BLOOD ON THE FLOOR. SHIVERS OF ECSTASY.
OH, TOO LOVELY!
WAS I DOING THIS? WAS I LAPPING UP THIS BLOOD NOT TWO INCHES FROM THIS DEAD BODY?
WAS MY HEART HEAVING WITH EVERY TASTE NOT TWO INCHES FROM THIS DEAD BOY WHOM MAGNUS HAD BROUGHT HERE AS HE BROUGHT ME?
THIS BOY THAT MAGNUS HAD THEN CONDEMNED TO DEATH INSTEAD OF IMMORTALITY?
THE BLOOD TREMORS PASSED THROUGH MY ARMS AND LEGS. AND THE SOUND I HEARD--
--THE GORGEOUS SOUND, AS ENTHRALLING AS THE CRIMSON OF THE BLOOD, THE BLUE OF THE BOY'S EYE, THE BLAZE OF THE TORCH--

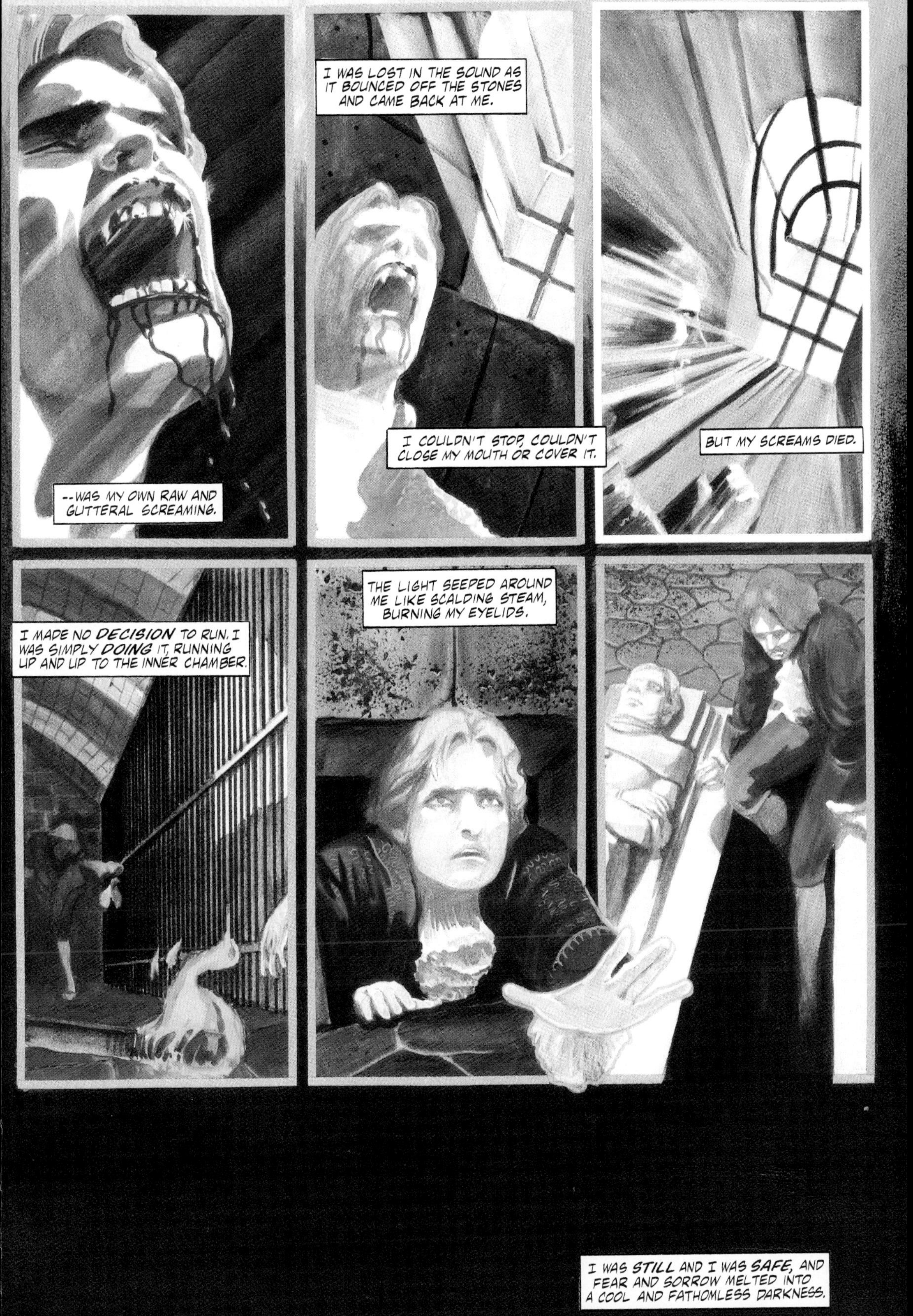
--WAS MY OWN RAW AND GUTTERAL SCREAMING.
I WAS LOST IN THE SOUND AS IT BOUNCED OFF THE STONES AND CAME BACK AT ME.
I COULDN'T STOP, COULDN'T CLOSE MY MOUTH OR COVER IT.
BUT MY SCREAMS DIED.
I MADE NO DECISION TO RUN. I WAS SIMPLY DOING IT, RUNNING UP AND UP TO THE INNER CHAMBER.
THE LIGHT SEEPED AROUND ME LIKE SCALDING STEAM, BURNING MY EYELIDS.
I WAS STILL AND I WAS SAFE, AND FEAR AND SORROW MELTED INTO A COOL AND FATHOMLESS DARKNESS.

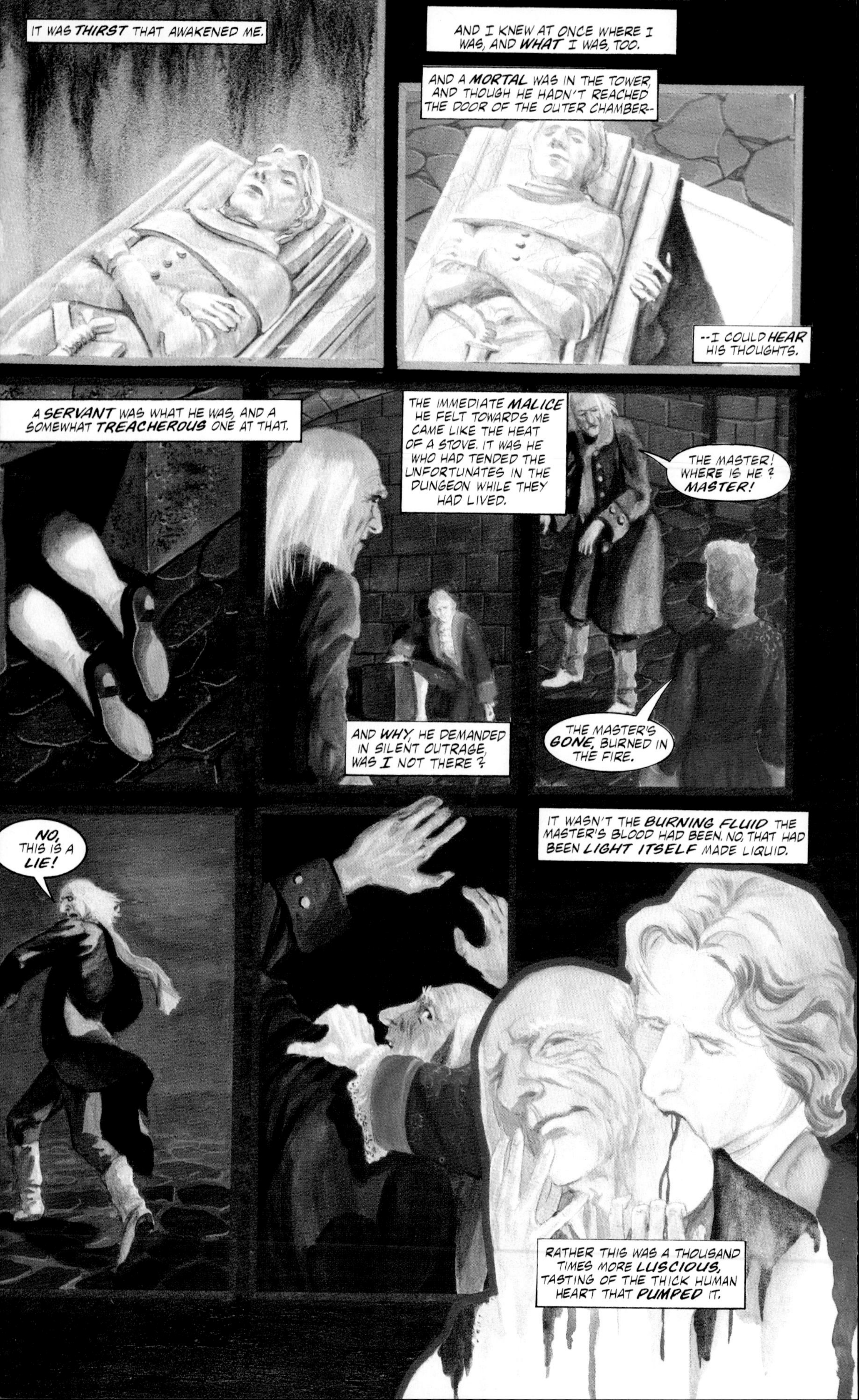
IT WAS THIRST THAT AWAKENED ME.
AND I KNEW AT ONCE WHERE I WAS, AND WHAT I WAS, TOO.
AND A MORTAL WAS IN THE TOWER, AND THOUGH HE HADN'T REACHED THE DOOR OF THE OUTER CHAMBER--
--I COULD HEAR HIS THOUGHTS.
A SERVANT WAS WHAT HE WAS, AND A SOMEWHAT TREACHEROUS ONE AT THAT.
THE IMMEDIATE MALICE HE FELT TOWARDS ME CAME LIKE THE HEAT OF A STOVE. IT WAS HE WHO HAD TENDED THE UNFORTUNATES IN THE DUNGEON WHILE THEY HAD LIVED.
AND WHY, HE DEMANDED IN SILENT OUTRAGE, WAS I NOT THERE?
THE MASTER! WHERE IS HE? MASTER!
THE MASTER'S GONE, BURNED IN THE FIRE.
NO, THIS IS A LIE!
IT WASN'T THE BURNING FLUID THE MASTER'S BLOOD HAD BEEN. NO, THAT HAD BEEN LIGHT ITSELF MADE LIQUID.
RATHER THIS WAS A THOUSAND TIMES MORE LUSCIOUS, TASTING OF THE THICK HUMAN HEART THAT PUMPED IT.

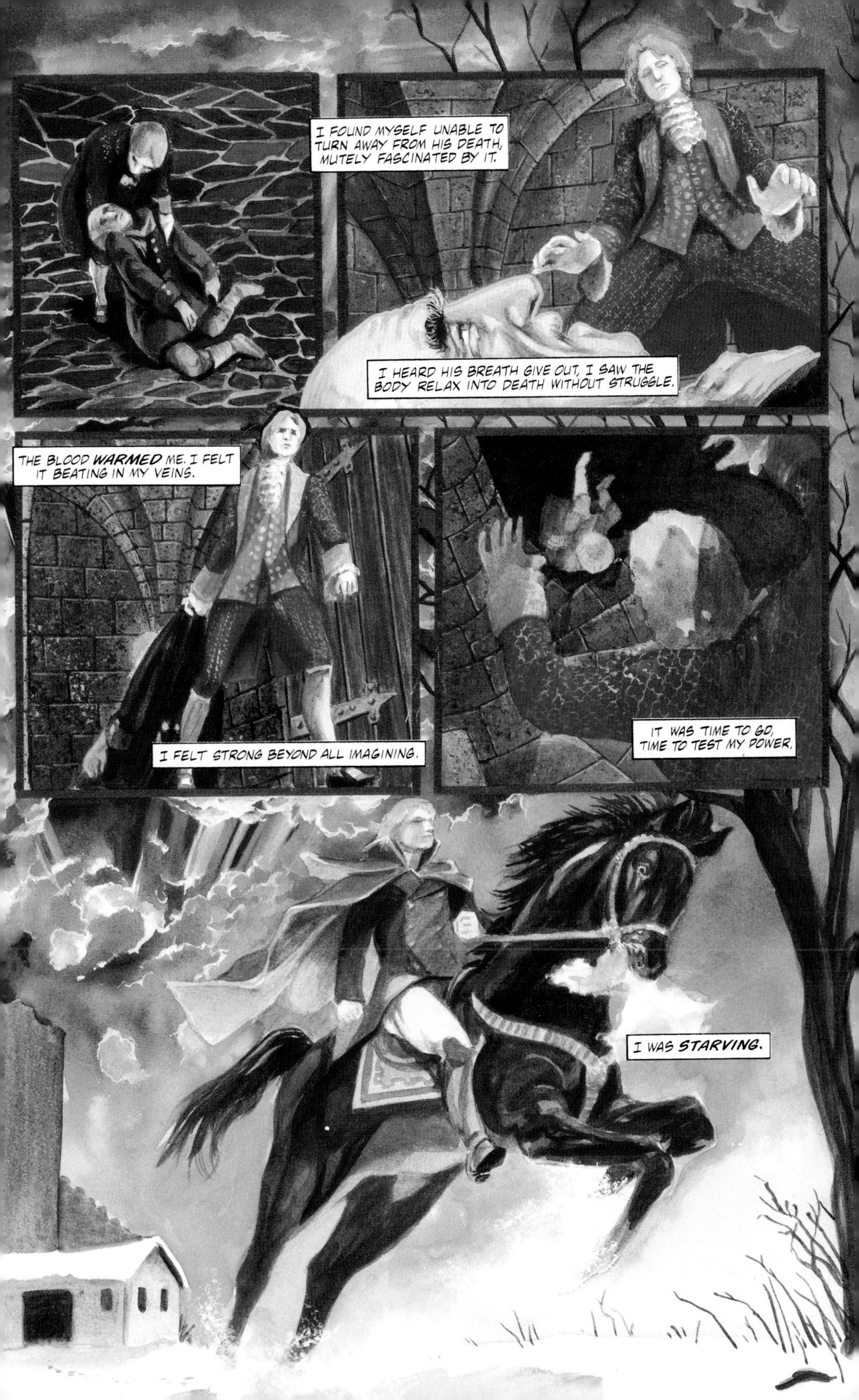
I FOUND MYSELF UNABLE TO TURN AWAY FROM HIS DEATH, MUTELY FASCINATED BY IT.
I HEARD HIS BREATH GIVE OUT, I SAW THE BODY RELAX INTO DEATH WITHOUT STRUGGLE.
THE BLOOD WARMED ME. I FELT IT BEATING IN MY VEINS.
I FELT STRONG BEYOND ALL IMAGINING.
IT WAS TIME TO GO, TIME TO TEST MY POWER.
I WAS STARVING.

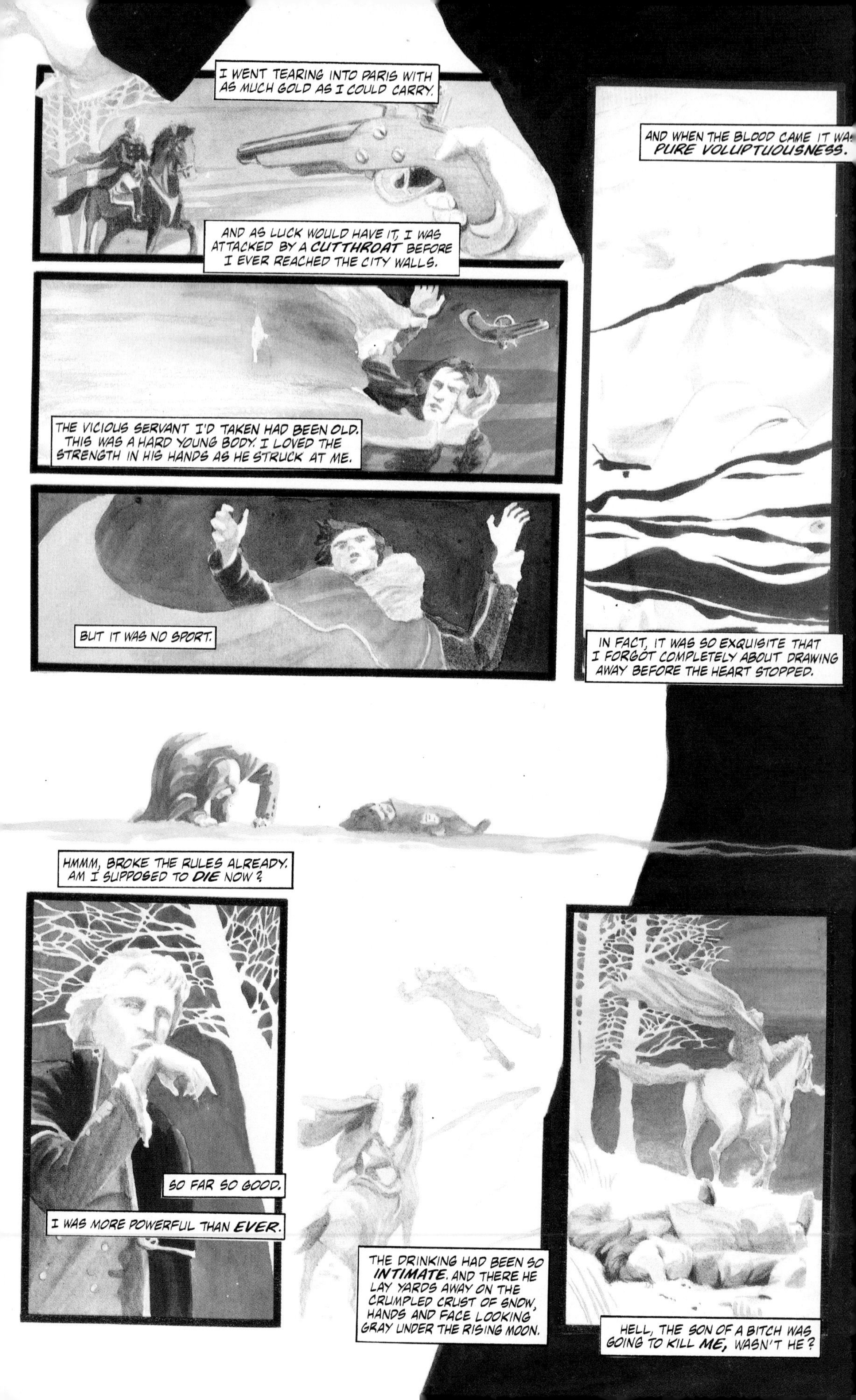
I WENT TEARING INTO PARIS WITH AS MUCH GOLD AS I COULD CARRY.
AND AS LUCK WOULD HAVE IT, I WAS ATTACKED BY A CUTTHROAT BEFORE I EVER REACHED THE CITY WALLS.
THE VICIOUS SERVANT I'D TAKEN HAD BEEN OLD. THIS WAS A HARD YOUNG BODY. I LOVED THE STRENGTH IN HIS HANDS AS HE STRUCK AT ME.
BUT IT WAS NO SPORT.
AND WHEN THE BLOOD CAME IT WAS PURE VOLUPTUOUSNESS.
IN FACT, IT WAS SO EXQUISITE THAT I FORGOT COMPLETELY ABOUT DRAWING AWAY BEFORE THE HEART STOPPED.
HMMM, BROKE THE RULES ALREADY. AM I SUPPOSED TO DIE NOW?
SO FAR SO GOOD.
I WAS MORE POWERFUL THAN EVER.
THE DRINKING HAD BEEN SO INTIMATE. AND THERE HE LAY YARDS AWAY ON THE CRUMPLED CRUST OF SNOW, HANDS AND FACE LOOKING GRAY UNDER THE RISING MOON.
HELL, THE SON OF A BITCH WAS GOING TO KILL ME, WASN'T HE?

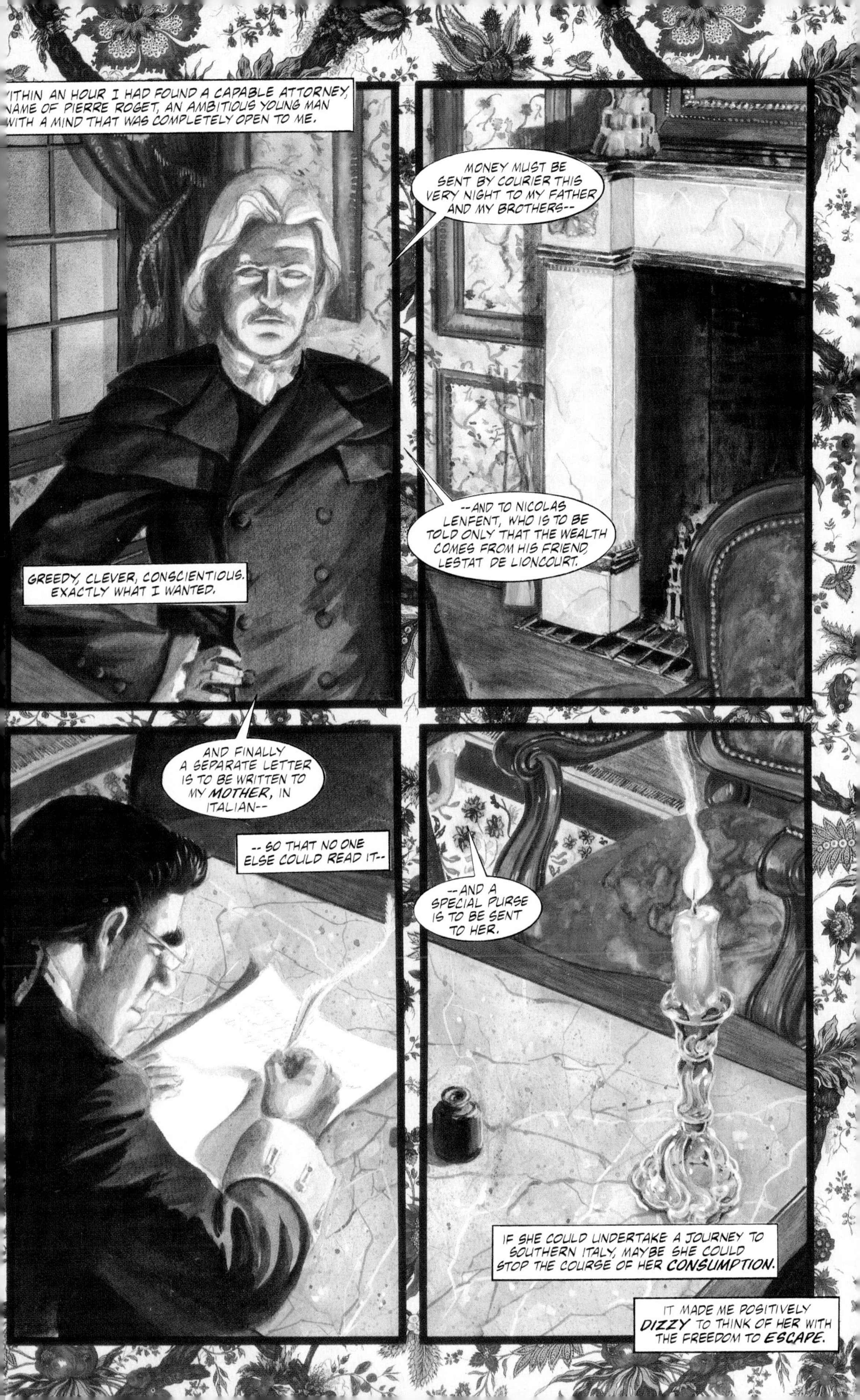
WITHIN AN HOUR I HAD FOUND A CAPABLE ATTORNEY, NAME OF PIERRE ROGET, AN AMBITIOUS YOUNG MAN WITH A MIND THAT WAS COMPLETELY OPEN TO ME.
GREEDY, CLEVER, CONSCIENTIOUS. EXACTLY WHAT I WANTED.
MONEY MUST BE SENT BY COURIER THIS VERY NIGHT TO MY FATHER AND MY BROTHERS--
--AND TO NICOLAS LENFENT, WHO IS TO BE TOLD ONLY THAT THE WEALTH COMES FROM HIS FRIEND, LESTAT DE LIONCOURT.
AND FINALLY A SEPARATE LETTER IS TO BE WRITTEN TO MY MOTHER, IN ITALIAN--
-- SO THAT NO ONE ELSE COULD READ IT--
--AND A SPECIAL PURSE IS TO BE SENT TO HER.
IF SHE COULD UNDERTAKE A JOURNEY TO SOUTHERN ITALY, MAYBE SHE COULD STOP THE COURSE OF HER CONSUMPTION.
IT MADE ME POSITIVELY DIZZY TO THINK OF HER WITH THE FREEDOM TO ESCAPE.

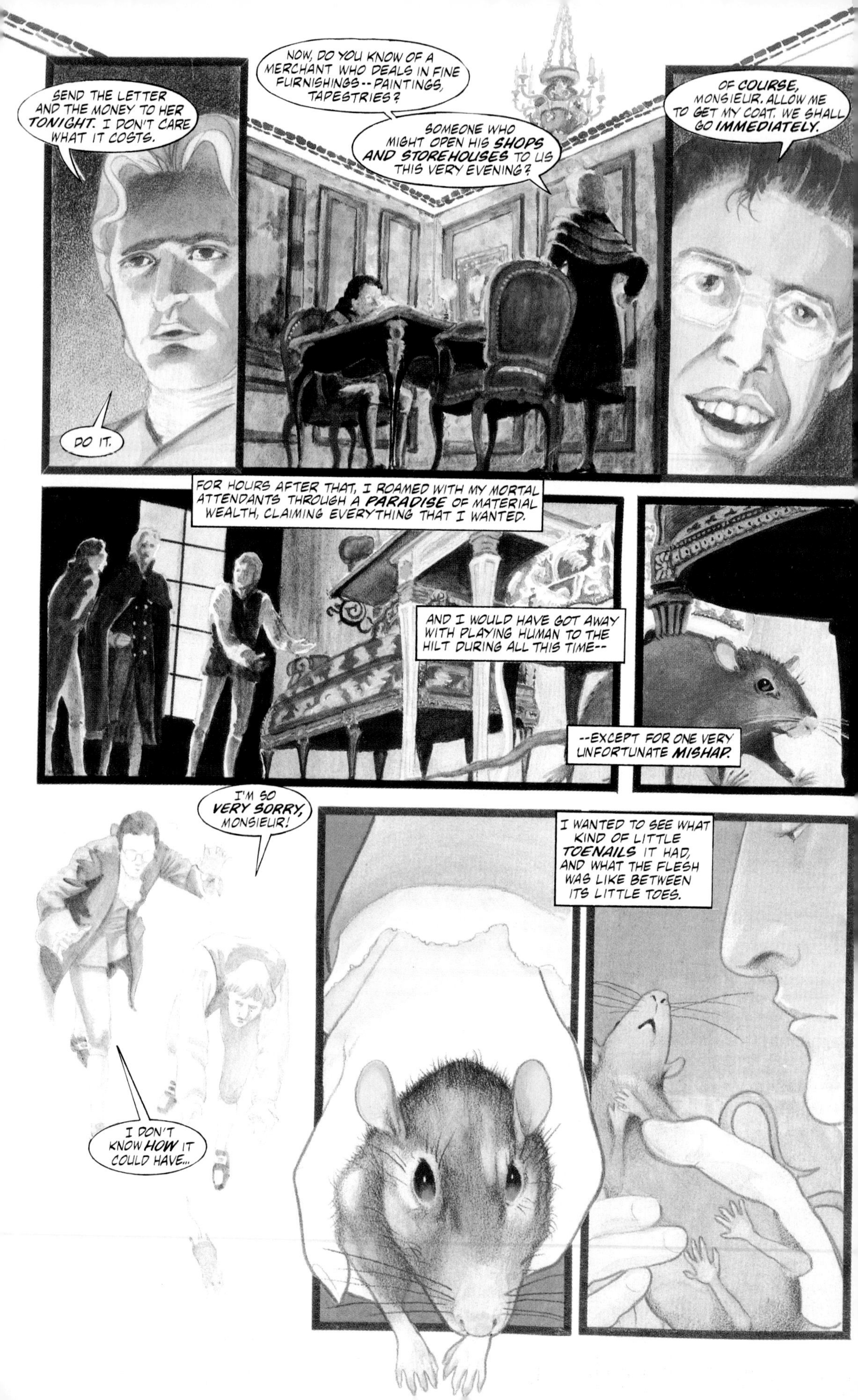
SEND THE LETTER AND THE MONEY TO HER TONIGHT. I DON'T CARE WHAT IT COSTS.
DO IT.
NOW, DO YOU KNOW OF A MERCHANT WHO DEALS IN FINE FURNISHINGS--PAINTINGS, TAPESTRIES?
SOMEONE WHO MIGHT OPEN HIS SHOPS AND STOREHOUSES TO US THIS VERY EVENING?
OF COURSE, MONSIEUR. ALLOW ME TO GET MY COAT. WE SHALL GO IMMEDIATELY.
FOR HOURS AFTER THAT, I ROAMED WITH MY MORTAL ATTENDANTS THROUGH A PARADISE OF MATERIAL WEALTH, CLAIMING EVERYTHING THAT I WANTED.
AND I WOULD HAVE GOT AWAY WITH PLAYING HUMAN TO THE HILT DURING ALL THIS TIME--
--EXCEPT FOR ONE VERY UNFORTUNATE MISHAP.
I'M SO VERY SORRY, MONSIEUR!
I DON'T KNOW HOW IT COULD HAVE...
I WANTED TO SEE WHAT KIND OF LITTLE TOENAILS IT HAD, AND WHAT THE FLESH WAS LIKE BETWEEN ITS LITTLE TOES.

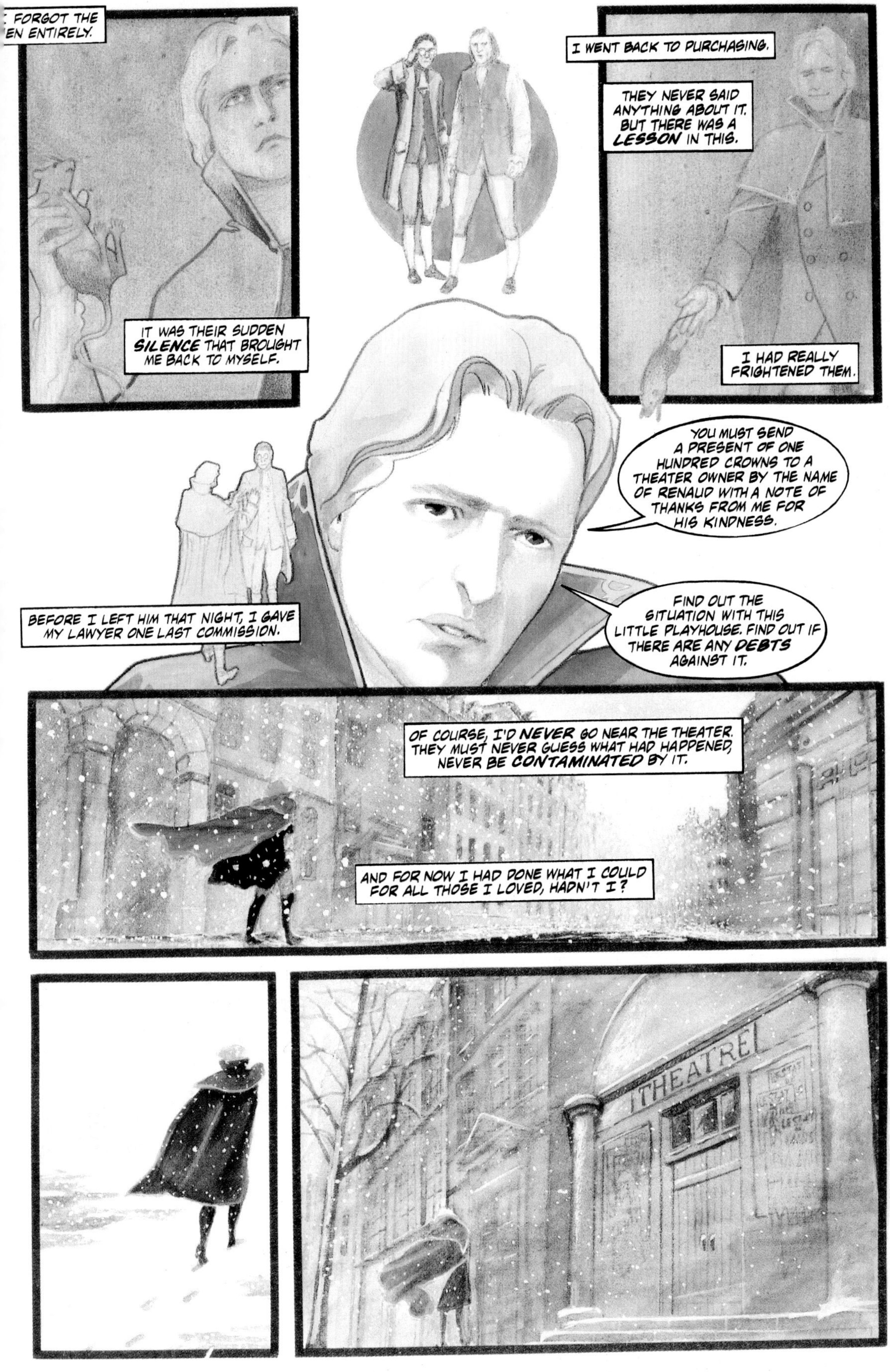

FORGOT THE
EN ENTIRELY.
IT WAS THEIR SUDDEN SILENCE THAT BROUGHT ME BACK TO MYSELF.
I WENT BACK TO PURCHASING.
THEY NEVER SAID ANYTHING ABOUT IT. BUT THERE WAS A LESSON IN THIS.
I HAD REALLY FRIGHTENED THEM.
BEFORE I LEFT HIM THAT NIGHT, I GAVE MY LAWYER ONE LAST COMMISSION.
YOU MUST SEND A PRESENT OF ONE HUNDRED CROWNS TO A THEATER OWNER BY THE NAME OF RENAUD WITH A NOTE OF THANKS FROM ME FOR HIS KINDNESS.
FIND OUT THE SITUATION WITH THIS LITTLE PLAYHOUSE. FIND OUT IF THERE ARE ANY DEBTS AGAINST IT.
OF COURSE, I'D NEVER GO NEAR THE THEATER. THEY MUST NEVER GUESS WHAT HAD HAPPENED, NEVER BE CONTAMINATED BY IT.
AND FOR NOW I HAD DONE WHAT I COULD FOR ALL THOSE I LOVED, HADN'T I?
THEATRE

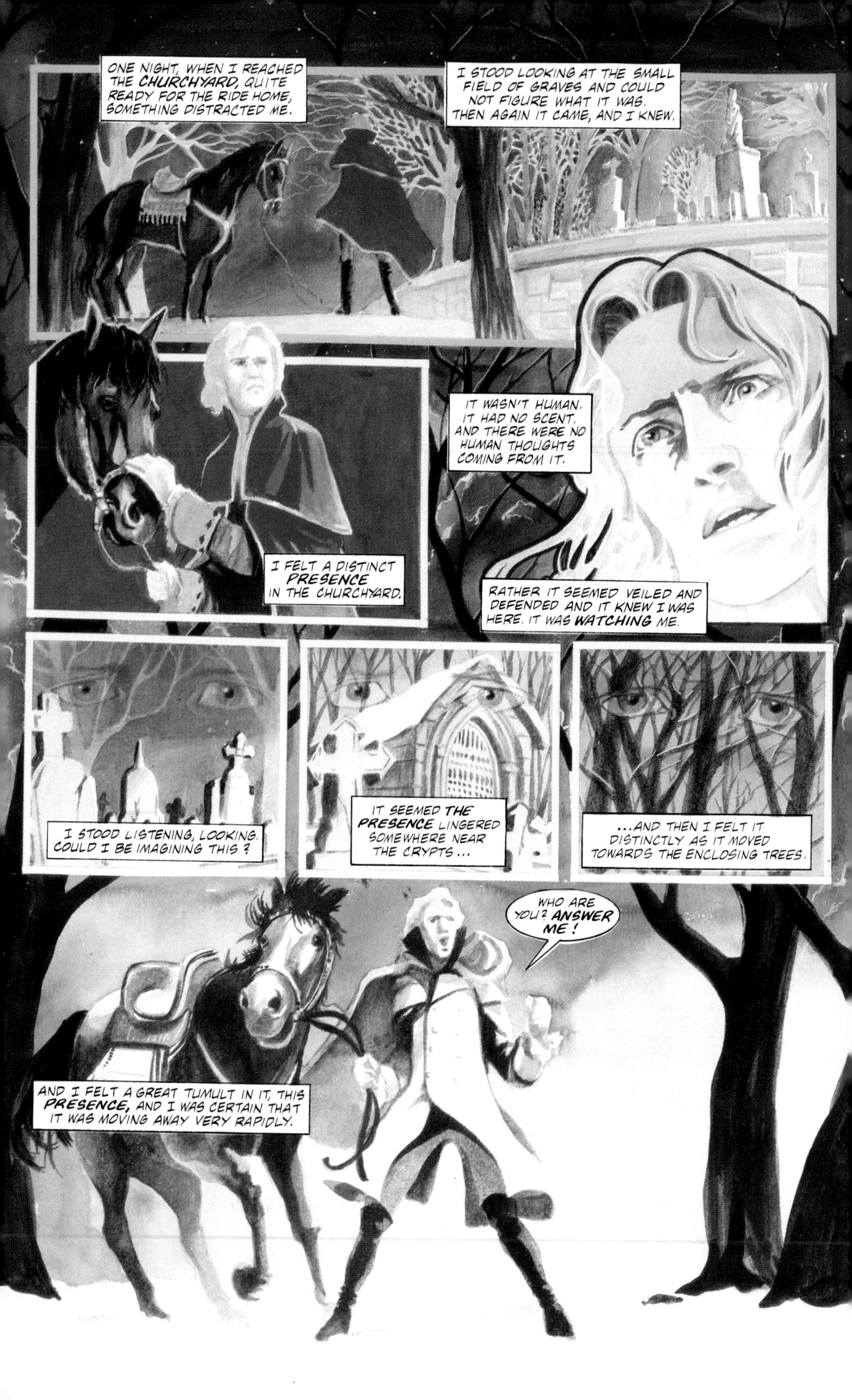
ONE NIGHT, WHEN I REACHED THE CHURCHYARD, QUITE READY FOR THE RIDE HOME, SOMETHING DISTRACTED ME.
I STOOD LOOKING AT THE SMALL FIELD OF GRAVES AND COULD NOT FIGURE WHAT IT WAS. THEN AGAIN IT CAME, AND I KNEW.
I FELT A DISTINCT PRESENCE IN THE CHURCHYARD.
IT WASN'T HUMAN. IT HAD NO SCENT. AND THERE WERE NO HUMAN THOUGHTS COMING FROM IT.
RATHER IT SEEMED VEILED AND DEFENDED AND IT KNEW I WAS HERE. IT WAS WATCHING ME.
I STOOD LISTENING, LOOKING. COULD I BE IMAGINING THIS ?
IT SEEMED THE PRESENCE LINGERED SOMEWHERE NEAR THE CRYPTS ...
...AND THEN I FELT IT DISTINCTLY AS IT MOVED TOWARDS THE ENCLOSING TREES.
WHO ARE YOU? ANSWER ME !
AND I FELT A GREAT TUMULT IN IT, THIS PRESENCE, AND I WAS CERTAIN THAT IT WAS MOVING AWAY VERY RAPIDLY.

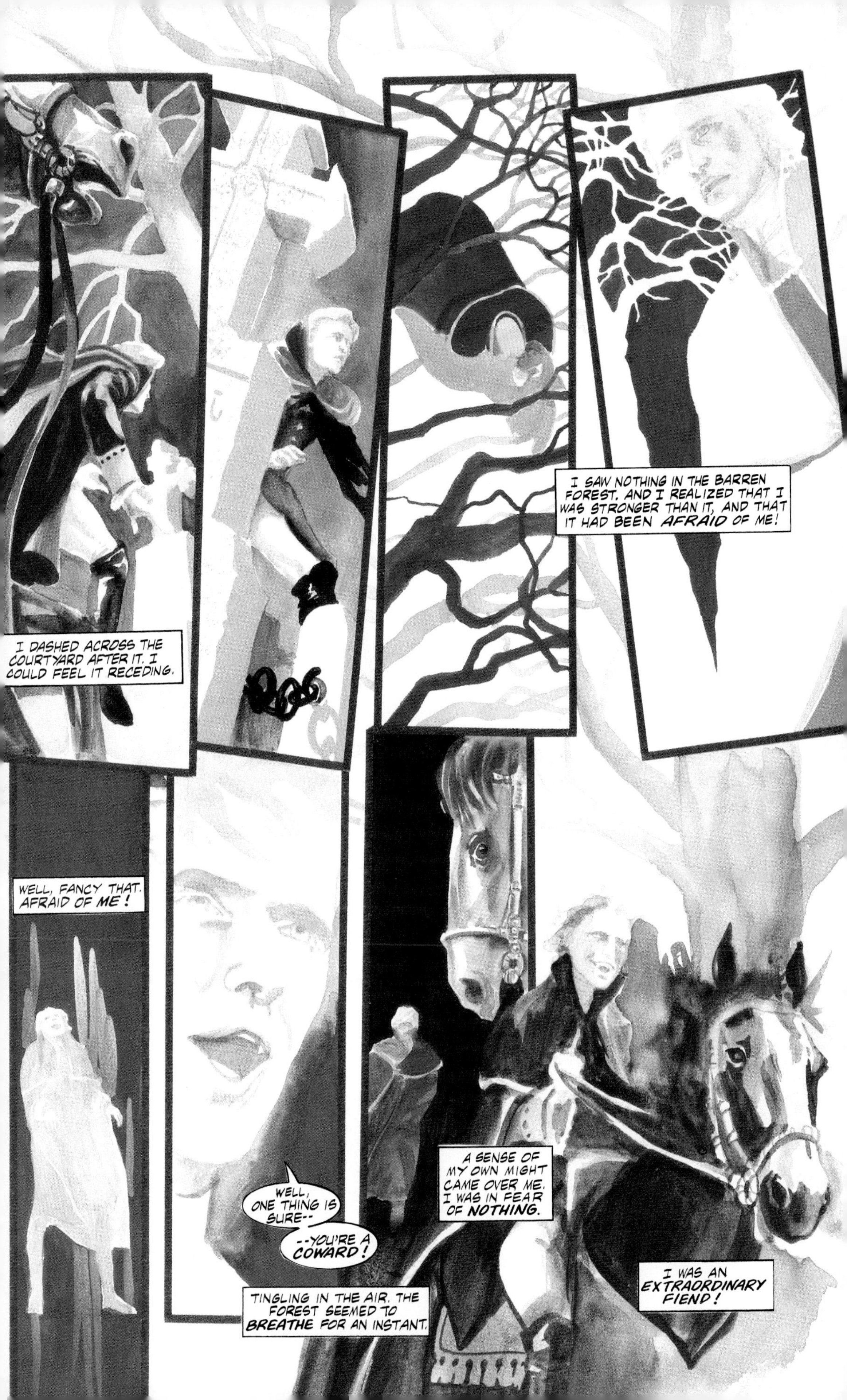
I DASHED ACROSS THE COURTYARD AFTER IT. I COULD FEEL IT RECEDING.
I SAW NOTHING IN THE BARREN FOREST. AND I REALIZED THAT I WAS STRONGER THAN IT, AND THAT IT HAD BEEN AFRAID OF ME!
WELL, FANCY THAT. AFRAID OF ME!
WELL, ONE THING IS SURE--
--YOU'RE A COWARD!
TINGLING IN THE AIR. THE FOREST SEEMED TO BREATHE FOR AN INSTANT.
A SENSE OF MY OWN MIGHT CAME OVER ME. I WAS IN FEAR OF NOTHING.
I WAS AN EXTRAORDINARY FIEND!

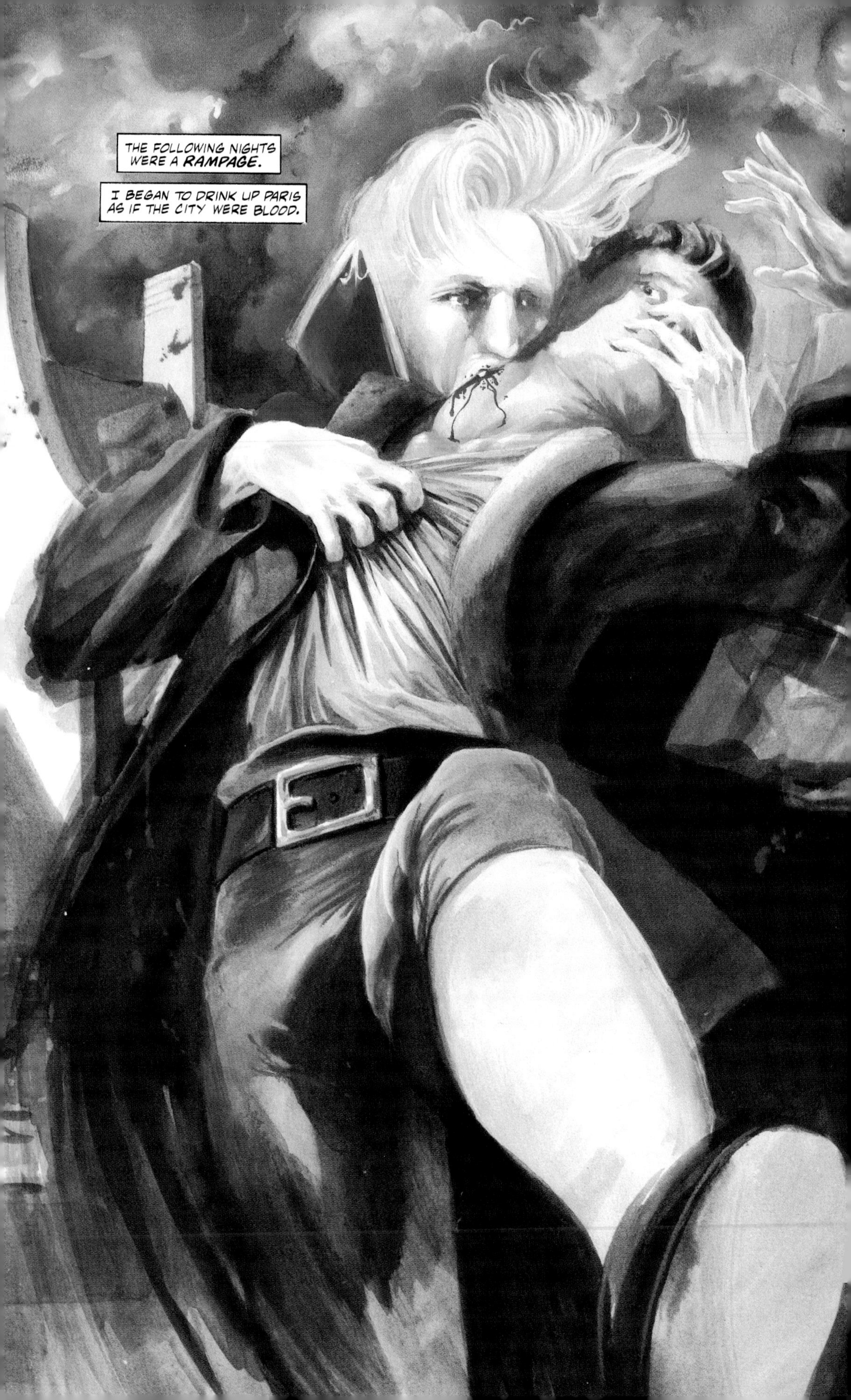
THE FOLLOWING NIGHTS WERE A RAMPAGE.
I BEGAN TO DRINK UP PARIS AS IF THE CITY WERE BLOOD.

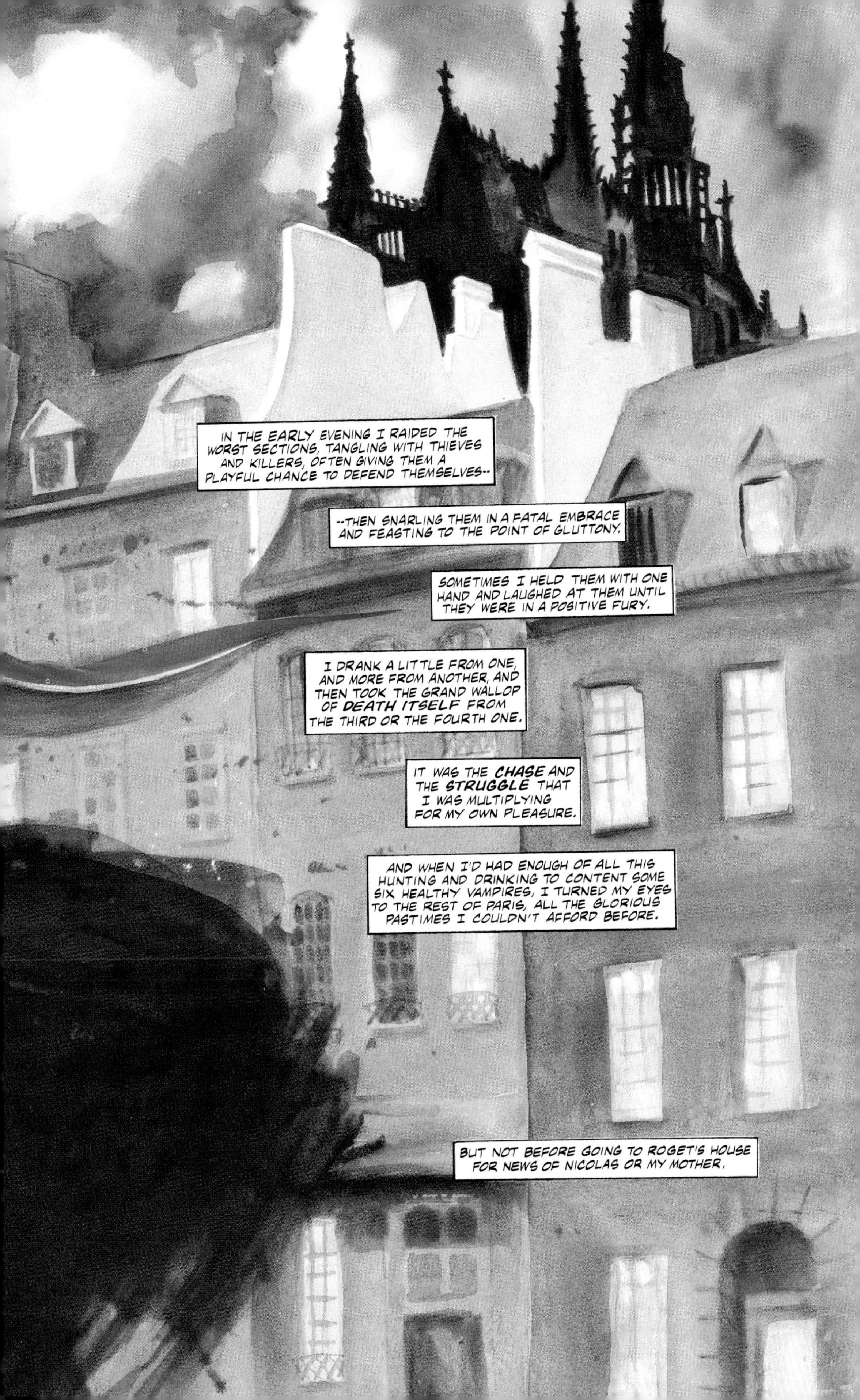
IN THE EARLY EVENING I RAIDED THE WORST SECTIONS, TANGLING WITH THIEVES AND KILLERS, OFTEN GIVING THEM A PLAYFUL CHANCE TO DEFEND THEMSELVES--
--THEN SNARLING THEM IN A FATAL EMBRACE AND FEASTING TO THE POINT OF GLUTTONY.
SOMETIMES I HELD THEM WITH ONE HAND AND LAUGHED AT THEM UNTIL THEY WERE IN A POSITIVE FURY.
I DRANK A LITTLE FROM ONE, AND MORE FROM ANOTHER, AND THEN TOOK THE GRAND WALLOP OF DEATH ITSELF FROM THE THIRD OR THE FOURTH ONE.
IT WAS THE CHASE AND THE STRUGGLE THAT I WAS MULTIPLYING FOR MY OWN PLEASURE.
AND WHEN I'D HAD ENOUGH OF ALL THIS HUNTING AND DRINKING TO CONTENT SOME SIX HEALTHY VAMPIRES, I TURNED MY EYES TO THE REST OF PARIS, ALL THE GLORIOUS PASTIMES I COULDN'T AFFORD BEFORE.
BUT NOT BEFORE GOING TO ROGET'S HOUSE FOR NEWS OF NICOLAS OR MY MOTHER.

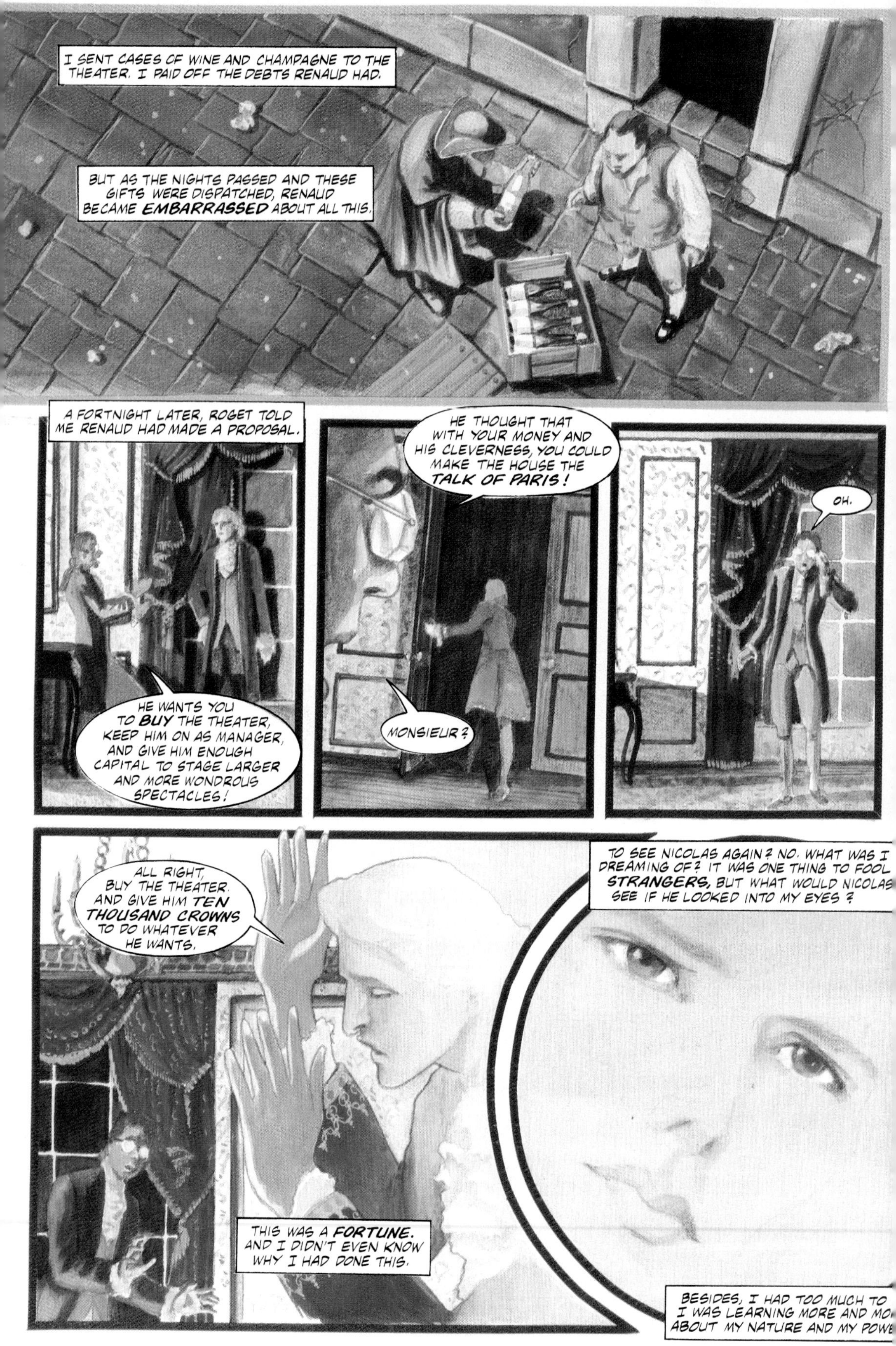

I SENT CASES OF WINE AND CHAMPAGNE TO THE THEATER. I PAID OFF THE DEBTS RENAUD HAD.
BUT AS THE NIGHTS PASSED AND THESE GIFTS WERE DISPATCHED, RENAUD BECAME EMBARRASSED ABOUT ALL THIS.
A FORTNIGHT LATER, ROGET TOLD ME RENAUD HAD MADE A PROPOSAL.
HE WANTS YOU TO BUY THE THEATER, KEEP HIM ON AS MANAGER, AND GIVE HIM ENOUGH CAPITAL TO STAGE LARGER AND MORE WONDROUS SPECTACLES!
HE THOUGHT THAT WITH YOUR MONEY AND HIS CLEVERNESS, YOU COULD MAKE THE HOUSE THE TALK OF PARIS!
MONSIEUR?
OH.
ALL RIGHT, BUY THE THEATER. AND GIVE HIM TEN THOUSAND CROWNS TO DO WHATEVER HE WANTS.
THIS WAS A FORTUNE. AND I DIDN'T EVEN KNOW WHY I HAD DONE THIS.
TO SEE NICOLAS AGAIN? NO. WHAT WAS I DREAMING OF? IT WAS ONE THING TO FOOL STRANGERS, BUT WHAT WOULD NICOLAS SEE IF HE LOOKED INTO MY EYES?
BESIDES, I HAD TOO MUCH TO I WAS LEARNING MORE AND MO ABOUT MY NATURE AND MY POWE

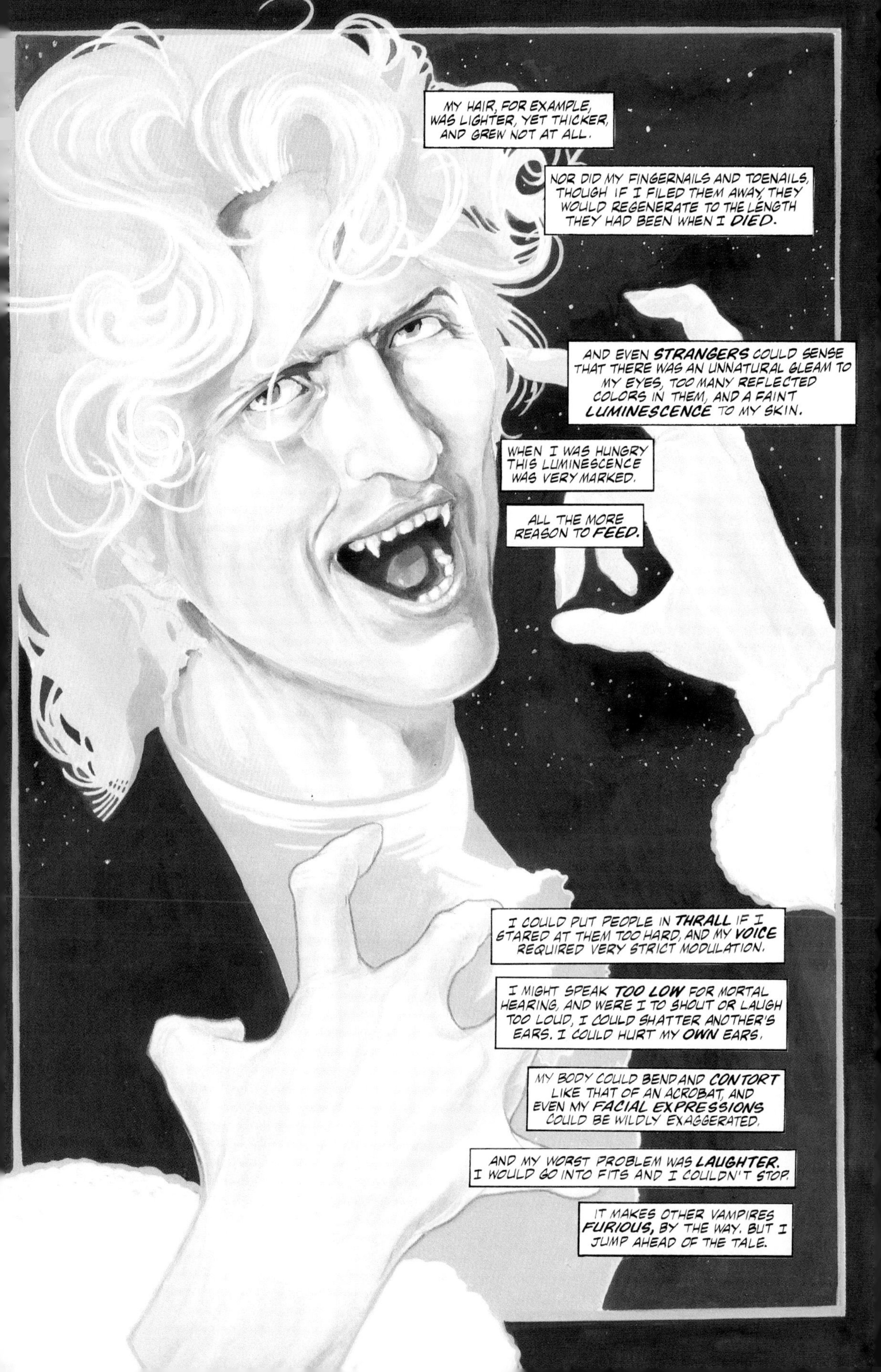

MY HAIR, FOR EXAMPLE, WAS LIGHTER, YET THICKER, AND GREW NOT AT ALL.
NOR DID MY FINGERNAILS AND TOENAILS, THOUGH IF I FILED THEM AWAY, THEY WOULD REGENERATE TO THE LENGTH THEY HAD BEEN WHEN I DIED.
AND EVEN STRANGERS COULD SENSE THAT THERE WAS AN UNNATURAL GLEAM TO MY EYES, TOO MANY REFLECTED COLORS IN THEM, AND A FAINT LUMINESCENCE TO MY SKIN.
WHEN I WAS HUNGRY THIS LUMINESCENCE WAS VERY MARKED.
ALL THE MORE REASON TO FEED.
I COULD PUT PEOPLE IN THRALL IF I STARED AT THEM TOO HARD, AND MY VOICE REQUIRED VERY STRICT MODULATION.
I MIGHT SPEAK TOO LOW FOR MORTAL HEARING, AND WERE I TO SHOUT OR LAUGH TOO LOUD, I COULD SHATTER ANOTHER'S EARS. I COULD HURT MY OWN EARS.
MY BODY COULD BEND AND CONTORT LIKE THAT OF AN ACROBAT, AND EVEN MY FACIAL EXPRESSIONS COULD BE WILDLY EXAGGERATED.
AND MY WORST PROBLEM WAS LAUGHTER. I WOULD GO INTO FITS AND I COULDN'T STOP.
IT MAKES OTHER VAMPIRES FURIOUS, BY THE WAY. BUT I JUMP AHEAD OF THE TALE.

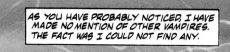

AS YOU HAVE PROBABLY NOTICED, I HAVE MADE NO MENTION OF OTHER VAMPIRES. THE FACT WAS I COULD NOT FIND ANY.

BUT NOW AND THEN, I'D FEEL THAT VAGUE AND MADDENINGLY ELUSIVE *PRESENCE*.

INVARIABLY IT WAS IN THE VICINITY OF A *PARIS CEMETERY*.

I HAD THE DISTINCT IMPRESSION THAT *THE PRESENCE* WAS WATCHING ME, MAYBE EVEN *DELIBERATELY REVEALING* ITSELF TO ME.

WHATEVER THE CASE, I SAW NO OTHER VAMPIRES IN PARIS.

MORTALS TO THE LEFT OF ME, MORTALS TO THE RIGHT OF ME.

AND ONE NIGHT IN MARCH, I DASHED TO ROGET'S HOUSE WITHOUT EVEN THINKING OF WHAT I WAS DOING AND DEMANDED HE TELL ME WHERE NICOLAS LIVED.

IT WAS ON THE ILE ST.-LOUIS, AND VERY IMPRESSIVE, JUST AS I'D WANTED.

I WOULD JUST HAVE A LOOK AT HIM, MAKE CERTAIN HE WAS IN GOOD HEALTH, BE CERTAIN THE HOUSE WAS FINE ENOUGH.

I STOOD WATCHING IT FOR A LONG TIME.

AND I KNEW THAT I *HAD* TO SEE NICKI.

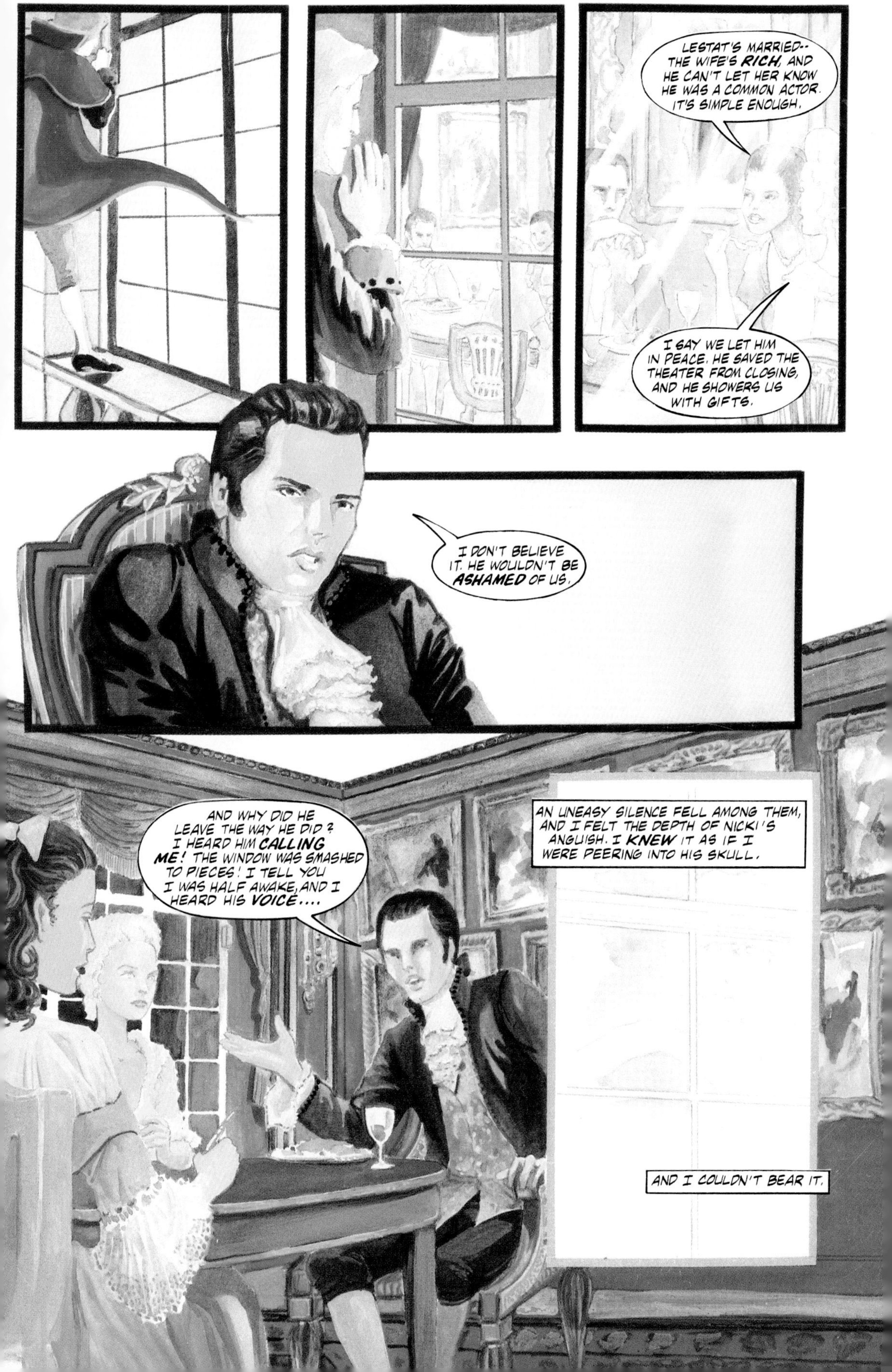
LESTAT'S MARRIED-- THE WIFE'S RICH, AND HE CAN'T LET HER KNOW HE WAS A COMMON ACTOR. IT'S SIMPLE ENOUGH.
I SAY WE LET HIM IN PEACE. HE SAVED THE THEATER FROM CLOSING, AND HE SHOWERS US WITH GIFTS.
I DON'T BELIEVE IT. HE WOULDN'T BE ASHAMED OF US.
AND WHY DID HE LEAVE THE WAY HE DID? I HEARD HIM CALLING ME! THE WINDOW WAS SMASHED TO PIECES! I TELL YOU I WAS HALF AWAKE, AND I HEARD HIS VOICE....
AN UNEASY SILENCE FELL AMONG THEM, AND I FELT THE DEPTH OF NICKI'S ANGUISH. I KNEW IT AS IF I WERE PEERING INTO HIS SKULL.
AND I COULDN'T BEAR IT.

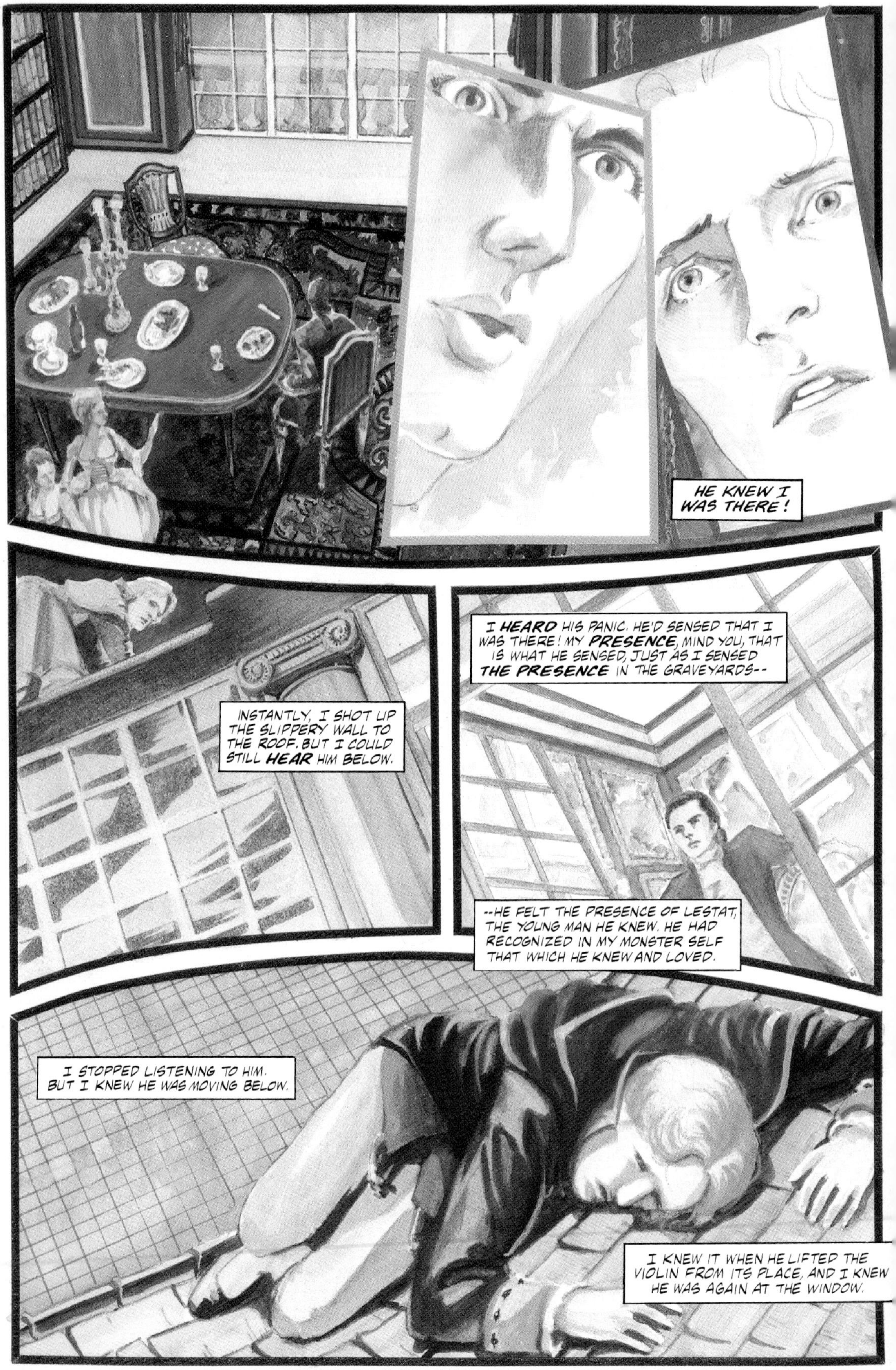
HE KNEW I WAS THERE!
INSTANTLY, I SHOT UP THE SLIPPERY WALL TO THE ROOF. BUT I COULD STILL HEAR HIM BELOW.
I HEARD HIS PANIC. HE'D SENSED THAT I WAS THERE! MY PRESENCE, MIND YOU, THAT IS WHAT HE SENSED, JUST AS I SENSED THE PRESENCE IN THE GRAVEYARDS--
--HE FELT THE PRESENCE OF LESTAT, THE YOUNG MAN HE KNEW. HE HAD RECOGNIZED IN MY MONSTER SELF THAT WHICH HE KNEW AND LOVED.
I STOPPED LISTENING TO HIM. BUT I KNEW HE WAS MOVING BELOW.
I KNEW IT WHEN HE LIFTED THE VIOLIN FROM ITS PLACE, AND I KNEW HE WAS AGAIN AT THE WINDOW.

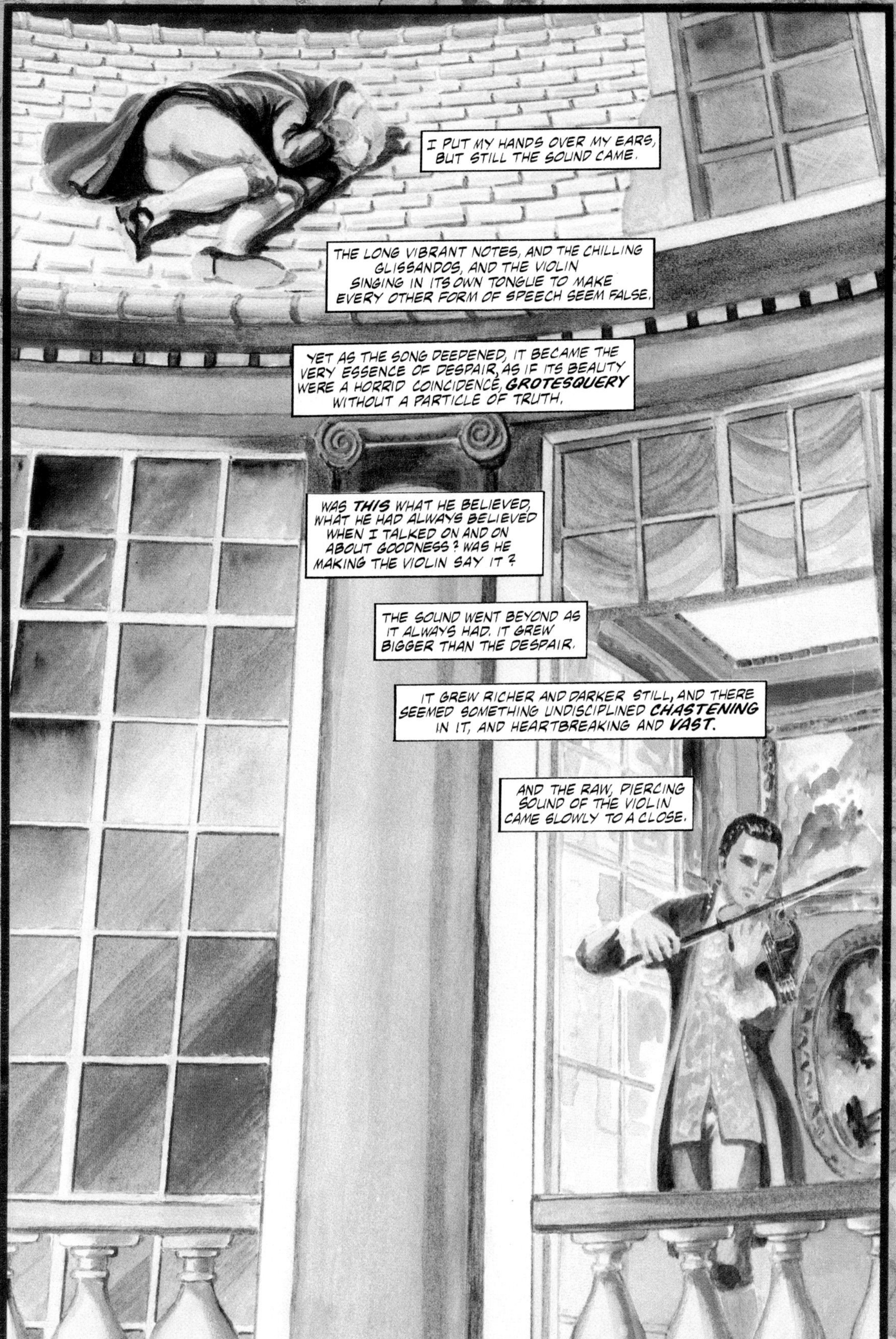
I PUT MY HANDS OVER MY EARS, BUT STILL THE SOUND CAME.
THE LONG VIBRANT NOTES, AND THE CHILLING GLISSANDOS, AND THE VIOLIN SINGING IN ITS OWN TONGUE TO MAKE EVERY OTHER FORM OF SPEECH SEEM FALSE.
YET AS THE SONG DEEPENED, IT BECAME THE VERY ESSENCE OF DESPAIR, AS IF ITS BEAUTY WERE A HORRID COINCIDENCE, GROTESQUERY WITHOUT A PARTICLE OF TRUTH.
WAS THIS WHAT HE BELIEVED, WHAT HE HAD ALWAYS BELIEVED WHEN I TALKED ON AND ON ABOUT GOODNESS? WAS HE MAKING THE VIOLIN SAY IT?
THE SOUND WENT BEYOND AS IT ALWAYS HAD. IT GREW BIGGER THAN THE DESPAIR.
IT GREW RICHER AND DARKER STILL, AND THERE SEEMED SOMETHING UNDISCIPLINED CHASTENING IN IT, AND HEARTBREAKING AND VAST.
AND THE RAW, PIERCING SOUND OF THE VIOLIN CAME SLOWLY TO A CLOSE.

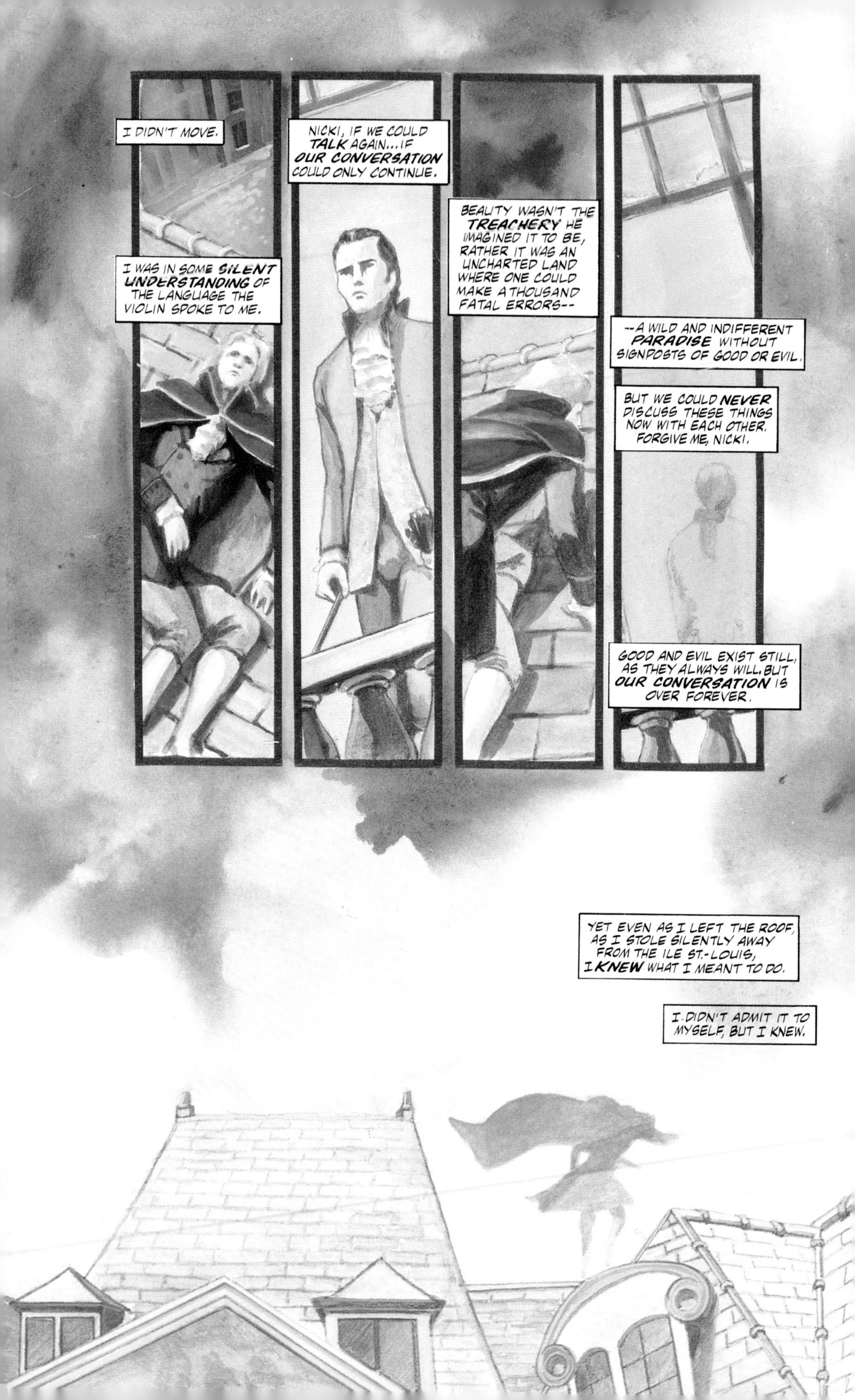
I DIDN'T MOVE.
I WAS IN SOME SILENT UNDERSTANDING OF THE LANGUAGE THE VIOLIN SPOKE TO ME.
NICKI, IF WE COULD TALK AGAIN...IF OUR CONVERSATION COULD ONLY CONTINUE.
BEAUTY WASN'T THE TREACHERY HE IMAGINED IT TO BE, RATHER IT WAS AN UNCHARTED LAND WHERE ONE COULD MAKE A THOUSAND FATAL ERRORS--
--A WILD AND INDIFFERENT PARADISE WITHOUT SIGNPOSTS OF GOOD OR EVIL.
BUT WE COULD NEVER DISCUSS THESE THINGS NOW WITH EACH OTHER. FORGIVE ME, NICKI.
GOOD AND EVIL EXIST STILL, AS THEY ALWAYS WILL. BUT OUR CONVERSATION IS OVER FOREVER.
YET EVEN AS I LEFT THE ROOF, AS I STOLE SILENTLY AWAY FROM THE ILE ST.-LOUIS, I KNEW WHAT I MEANT TO DO.
I DIDN'T ADMIT IT TO MYSELF, BUT I KNEW.

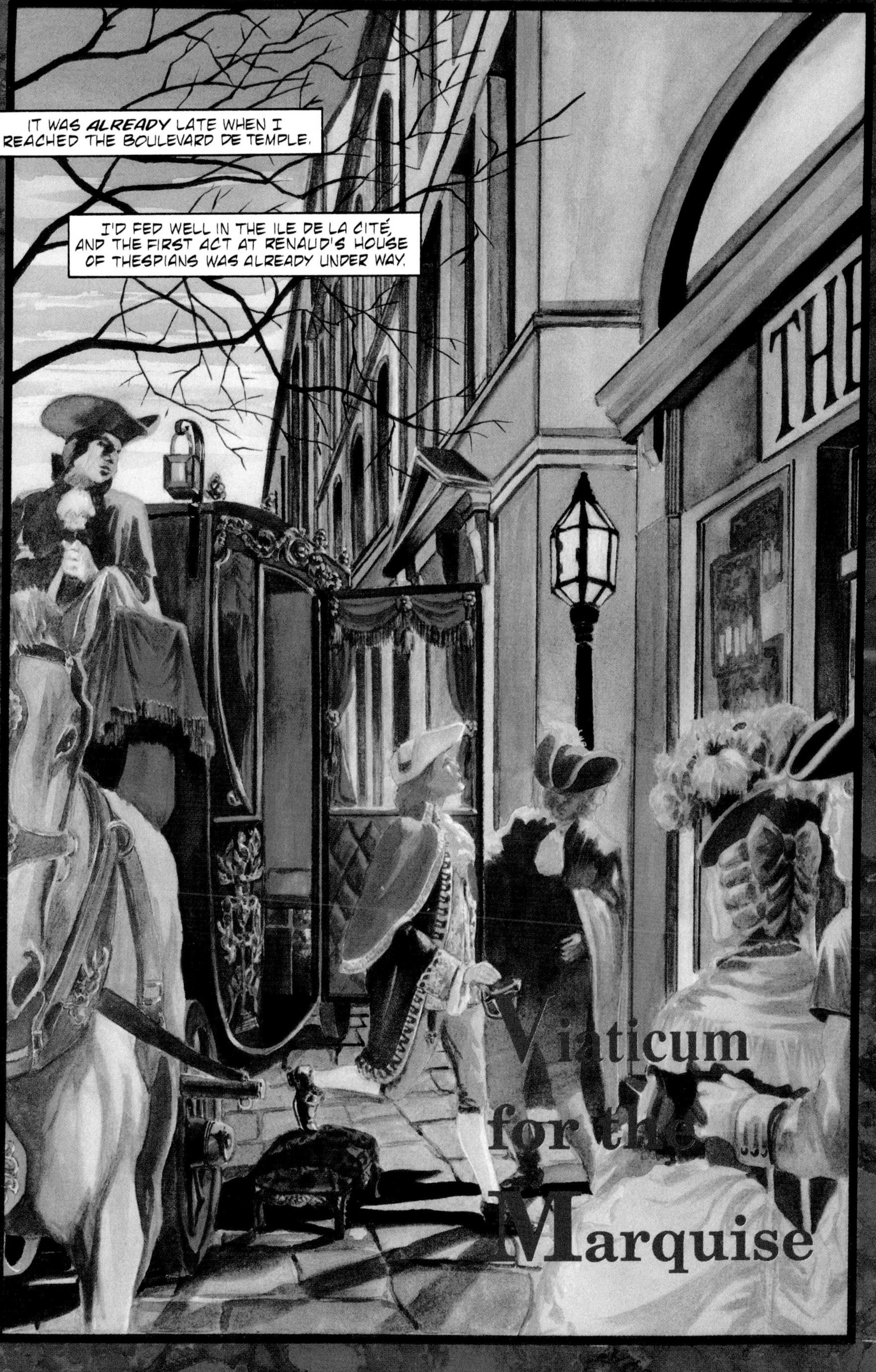

IT WAS ALREADY LATE WHEN I REACHED THE BOULEVARD DE TEMPLE.
I'D FED WELL IN THE ILE DE LA CITÉ, AND THE FIRST ACT AT RENAUD'S HOUSE OF THESPIANS WAS ALREADY UNDER WAY.
THE
Viaticum for the Marquise

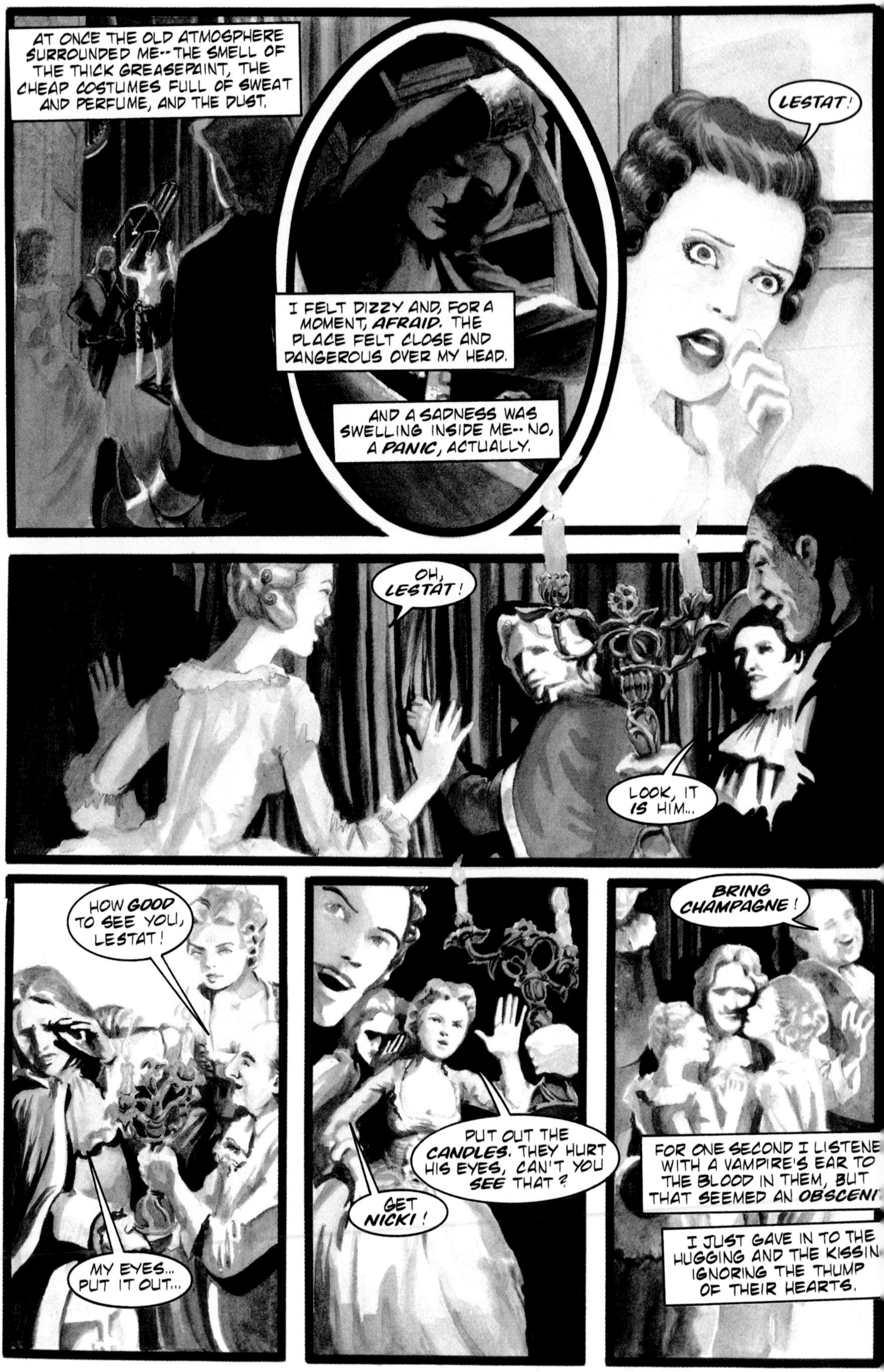
AT ONCE THE OLD ATMOSPHERE SURROUNDED ME--THE SMELL OF THE THICK GREASEPAINT, THE CHEAP COSTUMES FULL OF SWEAT AND PERFUME, AND THE DUST.
I FELT DIZZY AND, FOR A MOMENT, AFRAID. THE PLACE FELT CLOSE AND DANGEROUS OVER MY HEAD.
AND A SADNESS WAS SWELLING INSIDE ME-- NO, A PANIC, ACTUALLY.
LESTAT!
OH, LESTAT!
LOOK, IT IS HIM...
HOW GOOD TO SEE YOU, LESTAT!
MY EYES... PUT IT OUT...
PUT OUT THE CANDLES. THEY HURT HIS EYES, CAN'T YOU SEE THAT?
GET NICKI!
BRING CHAMPAGNE!
FOR ONE SECOND I LISTENE WITH A VAMPIRE'S EAR TO THE BLOOD IN THEM, BUT THAT SEEMED AN OBSCENI
I JUST GAVE IN TO THE HUGGING AND THE KISSIN IGNORING THE THUMP OF THEIR HEARTS.

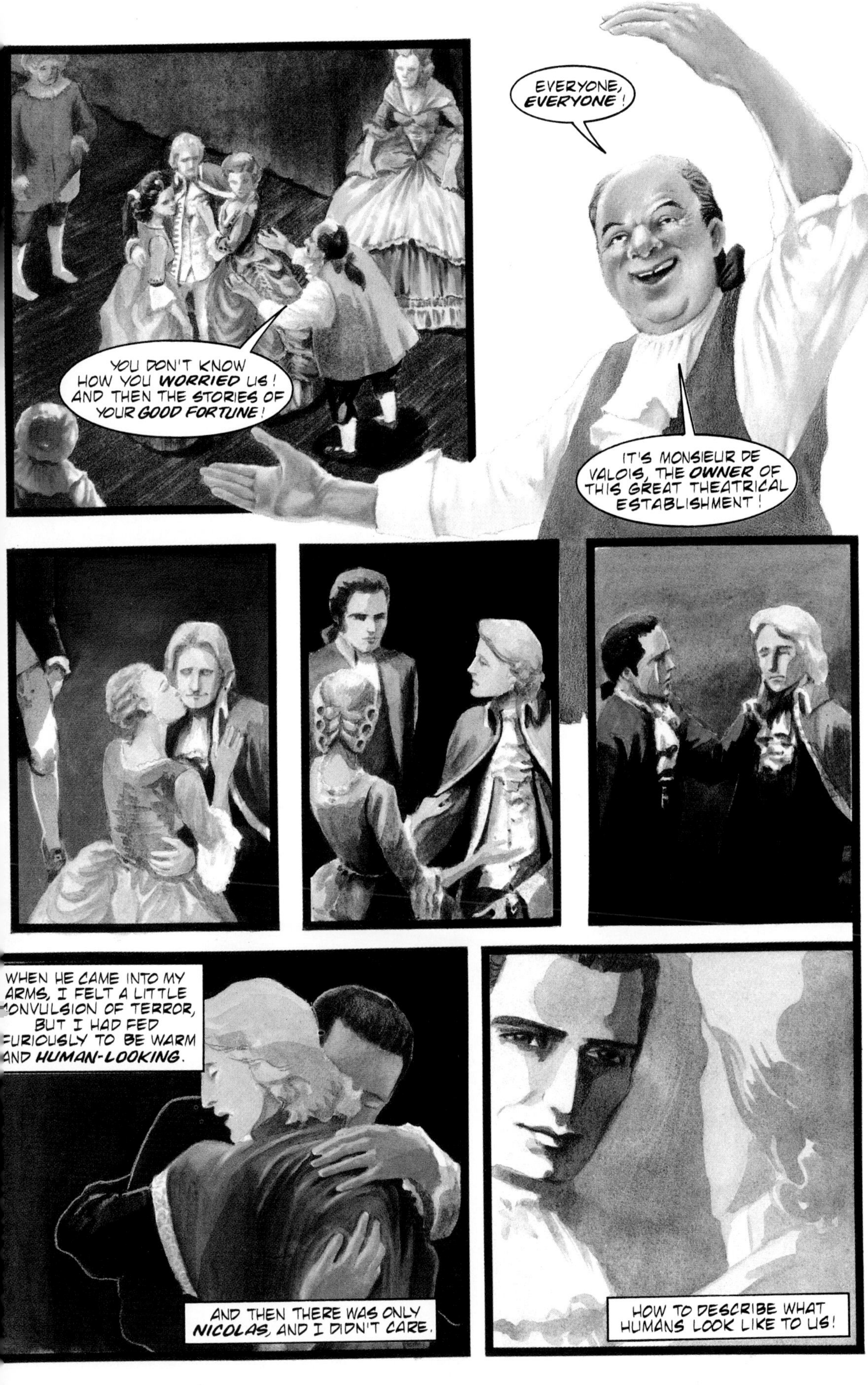
EVERYONE, EVERYONE!
YOU DON'T KNOW HOW YOU WORRIED US! AND THEN THE STORIES OF YOUR GOOD FORTUNE!
IT'S MONSIEUR DE VALOIS, THE OWNER OF THIS GREAT THEATRICAL ESTABLISHMENT!
WHEN HE CAME INTO MY ARMS, I FELT A LITTLE CONVULSION OF TERROR, BUT I HAD FED FURIOUSLY TO BE WARM AND HUMAN-LOOKING.
AND THEN THERE WAS ONLY NICOLAS, AND I DIDN'T CARE.
HOW TO DESCRIBE WHAT HUMANS LOOK LIKE TO US!

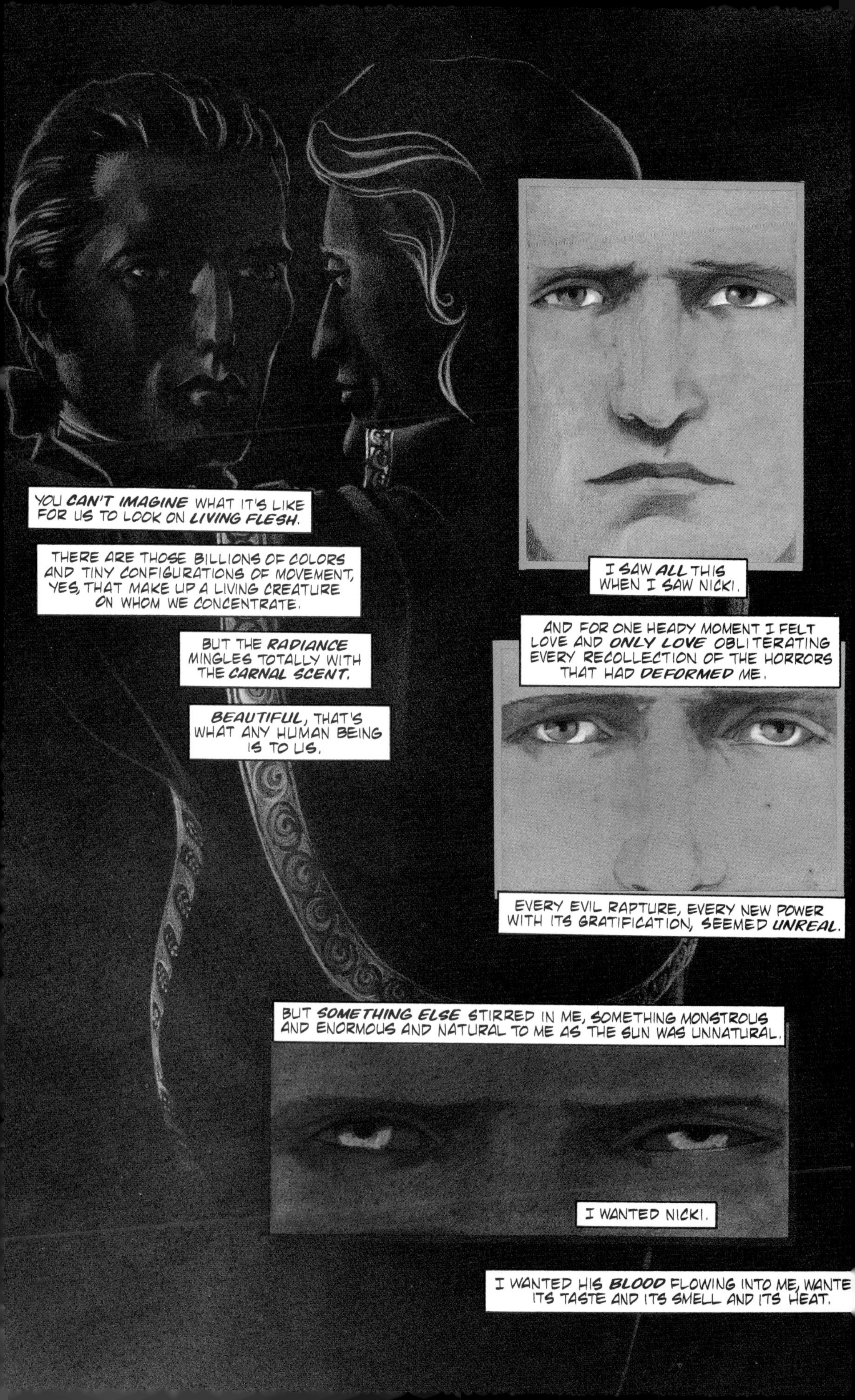
YOU CAN'T IMAGINE WHAT IT'S LIKE FOR US TO LOOK ON LIVING FLESH.
THERE ARE THOSE BILLIONS OF COLORS AND TINY CONFIGURATIONS OF MOVEMENT, YES, THAT MAKE UP A LIVING CREATURE ON WHOM WE CONCENTRATE.
BUT THE RADIANCE MINGLES TOTALLY WITH THE CARNAL SCENT.
BEAUTIFUL, THAT'S WHAT ANY HUMAN BEING IS TO US.
I SAW ALL THIS WHEN I SAW NICKI.
AND FOR ONE HEADY MOMENT I FELT LOVE AND ONLY LOVE OBLITERATING EVERY RECOLLECTION OF THE HORRORS THAT HAD DEFORMED ME.
EVERY EVIL RAPTURE, EVERY NEW POWER WITH ITS GRATIFICATION, SEEMED UNREAL.
BUT SOMETHING ELSE STIRRED IN ME, SOMETHING MONSTROUS AND ENORMOUS AND NATURAL TO ME AS THE SUN WAS UNNATURAL.
I WANTED NICKI.
I WANTED HIS BLOOD FLOWING INTO ME, WANTE
ITS TASTE AND ITS SMELL AND ITS HEAT.

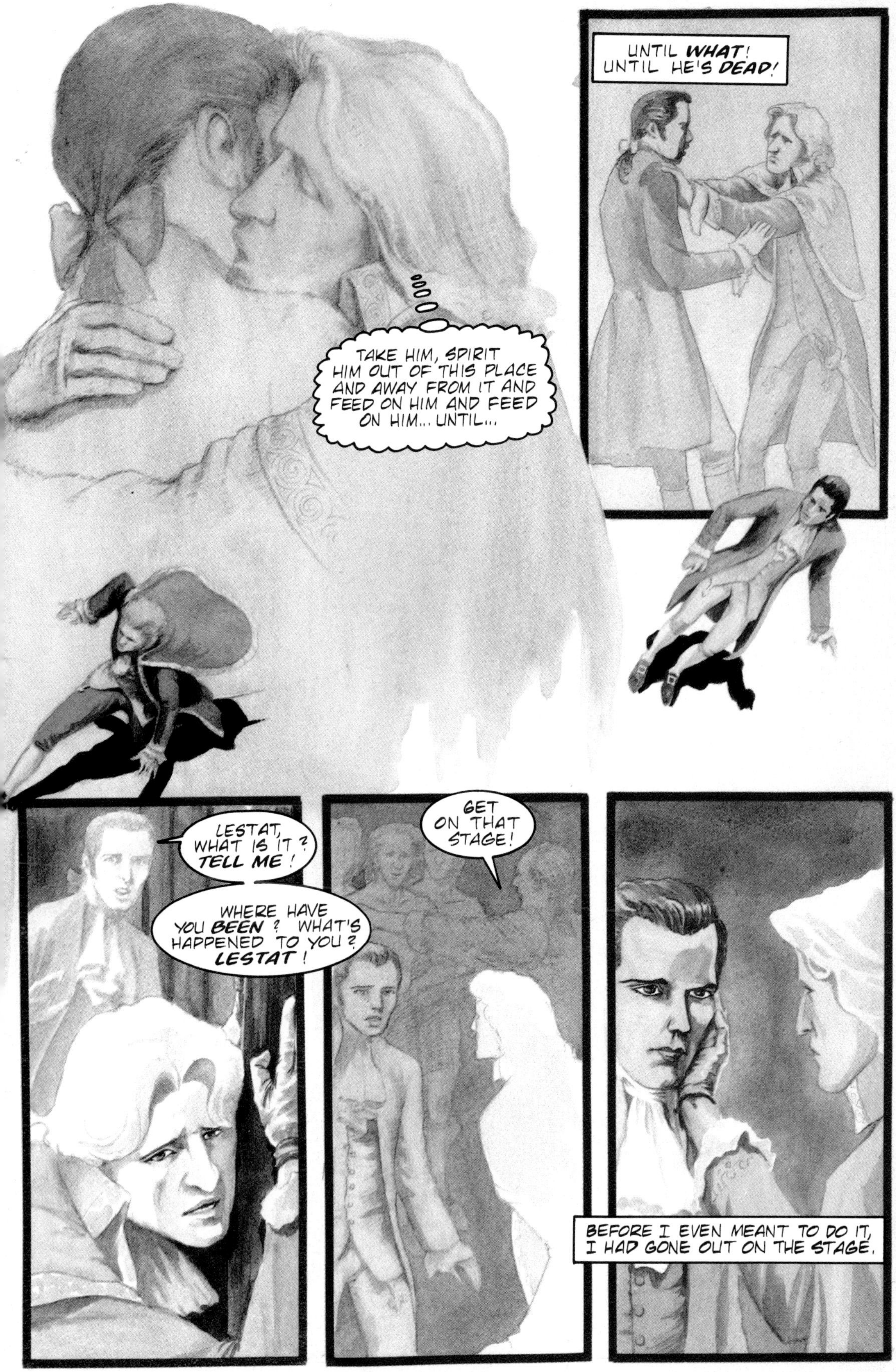

UNTIL **WHAT**! UNTIL HE'S **DEAD**!
TAKE HIM, SPIRIT HIM OUT OF THIS PLACE AND AWAY FROM IT AND FEED ON HIM AND FEED ON HIM... UNTIL...
LESTAT, WHAT IS IT ? **TELL ME** !
WHERE HAVE YOU **BEEN** ? WHAT'S HAPPENED TO YOU ? **LESTAT** !
GET ON THAT STAGE!
BEFORE I EVEN MEANT TO DO IT, I HAD GONE OUT ON THE **STAGE**.

I STARED AT THE CROWDED GALLERY, THE SCREENED BOXES, THE ROWS AND ROWS OF *SPECTATORS* TO THE BACK WALL.

I WAS STANDING IN THE VERY CENTER, FEELING THE *HEAT* OF THE FOOTLIGHTS, THE *SMOKE* STINGING MY EYES.

ON WITH THE PERFORMANCE!

YOU'RE *HANDSOME ENOUGH*, NOW LET'S SEE SOME *ACTION*!

"HANDSOME ENOUGH" IS THIS GRIM REAPER, WHO CAN SNUFF ALL THESE "BRIEF CANDLES," EVERY FLUTTERING SOUL SUCKING AIR FROM THIS HALL.

I BEGAN TURNING ROUND AND ROUND, EFFORTLESSLY, GOING FASTER AND FASTER, UNTIL I BROKE--

--FLIPPING BACKWARDS INTO A CIRCLE OF CARTWHEELS, AND THEN SOMERSAULTS, IMITATING EVERYTHING I HAD EVER SEEN THE PLAYERS PERFORM.

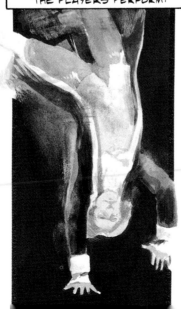

THEN, GAZING AT THE CEILING, I WILLED MY BODY UPWARDS AS I BENT MY KNEES TO SPRING.

IN AN INSTANT, I TOUCHED THE *RAFTERS*.

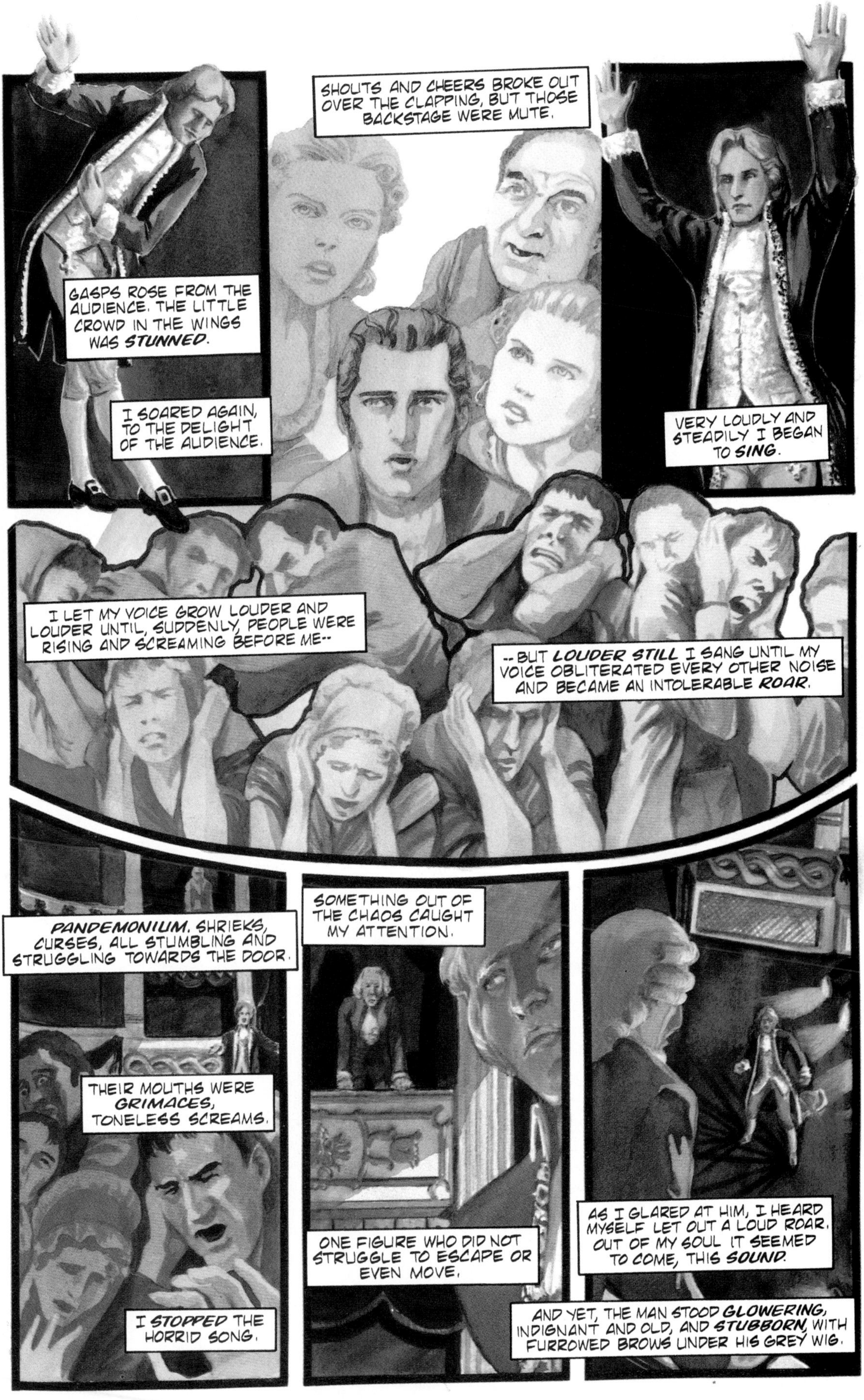
GASPS ROSE FROM THE AUDIENCE. THE LITTLE CROWD IN THE WINGS WAS **STUNNED**.
I SOARED AGAIN, TO THE DELIGHT OF THE AUDIENCE.
SHOUTS AND CHEERS BROKE OUT OVER THE CLAPPING, BUT THOSE BACKSTAGE WERE MUTE.
VERY LOUDLY AND STEADILY I BEGAN TO **SING**.
I LET MY VOICE GROW LOUDER AND LOUDER UNTIL, SUDDENLY, PEOPLE WERE RISING AND SCREAMING BEFORE ME--
--BUT **LOUDER STILL** I SANG UNTIL MY VOICE OBLITERATED EVERY OTHER NOISE AND BECAME AN INTOLERABLE **ROAR**.
PANDEMONIUM. SHRIEKS, CURSES, ALL STUMBLING AND STRUGGLING TOWARDS THE DOOR.
THEIR MOUTHS WERE **GRIMACES**, TONELESS SCREAMS.
I **STOPPED** THE HORRID SONG.
SOMETHING OUT OF THE CHAOS CAUGHT MY ATTENTION.
ONE FIGURE WHO DID NOT STRUGGLE TO ESCAPE OR EVEN MOVE.
AS I GLARED AT HIM, I HEARD MYSELF LET OUT A LOUD ROAR. OUT OF MY SOUL IT SEEMED TO COME, THIS **SOUND**.
AND YET, THE MAN STOOD **GLOWERING**, INDIGNANT AND OLD, AND **STUBBORN**, WITH FURROWED BROWS UNDER HIS GREY WIG.

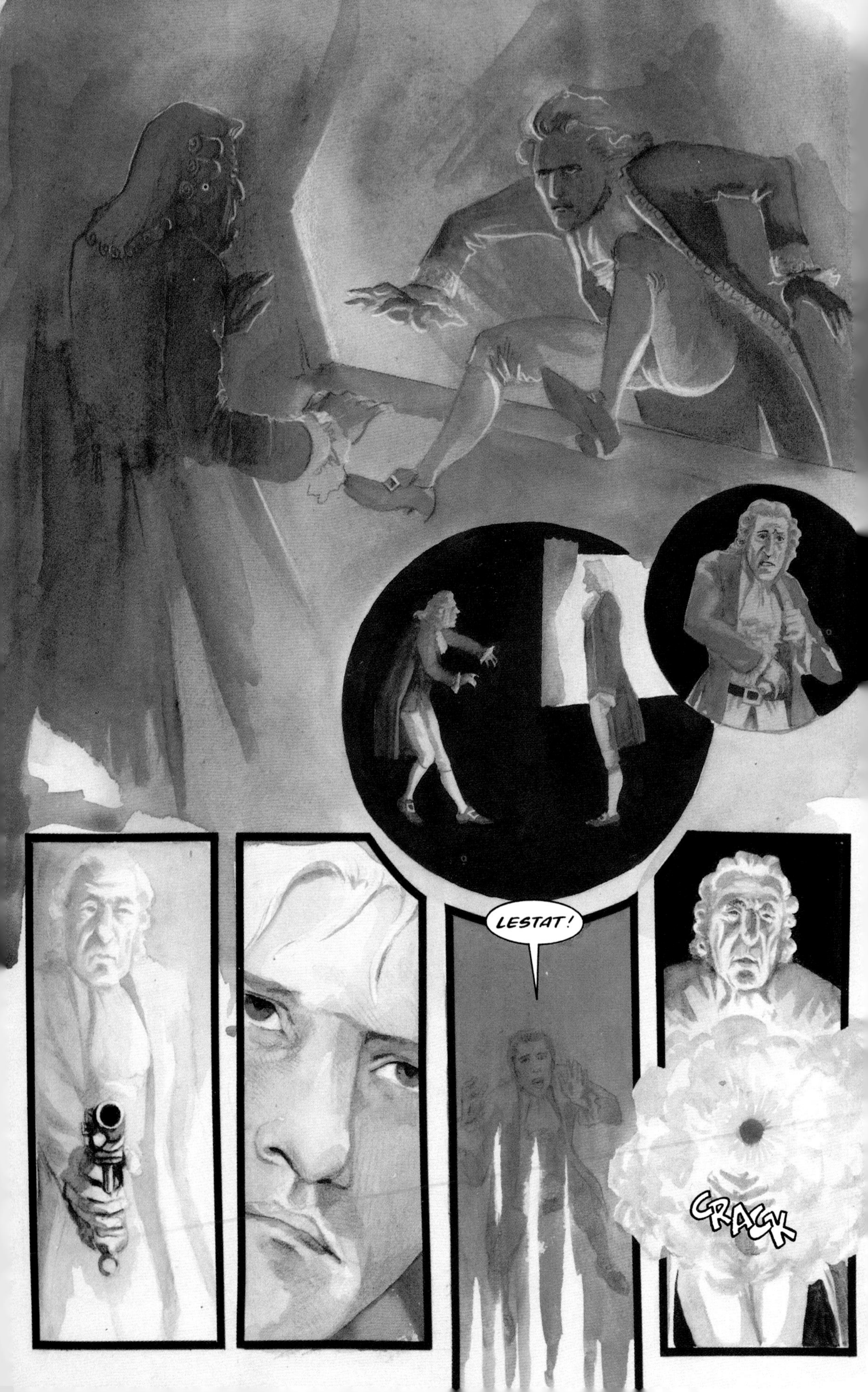
LESTAT!
CRACK

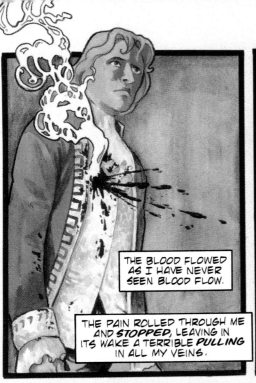

THE BLOOD FLOWED AS I HAVE NEVER SEEN BLOOD FLOW.

THE PAIN ROLLED THROUGH ME AND *STOPPED*, LEAVING IN ITS WAKE A TERRIBLE *PULLING* IN ALL MY VEINS.

I STOOD STILL HEARKENING TO MY BODY IN THAT *TERRIBLE SOLITUDE* THAT HAD BEEN MINE SINCE MAGNUS MADE ME THE VAMPIRE,

AND I KNEW THE WOUNDS WERE NO LONGER THERE.

LESTAT...?

MY BODY *THROBBED* AND MY VEINS WERE *ALIVE* WITH THE PULLING, BUT THE INJURY WAS *NO MORE*.

LESTAT!

LET GO OF ME!

GET *AWAY* FROM ME, NICKI!

MONSIEUR!

IT IS *NOTHING*, MY DEAR RENAUD.

BUT THERE *WAS* SOMETHING. SOMETHING DISTRACTED ME AS I SPOKE.

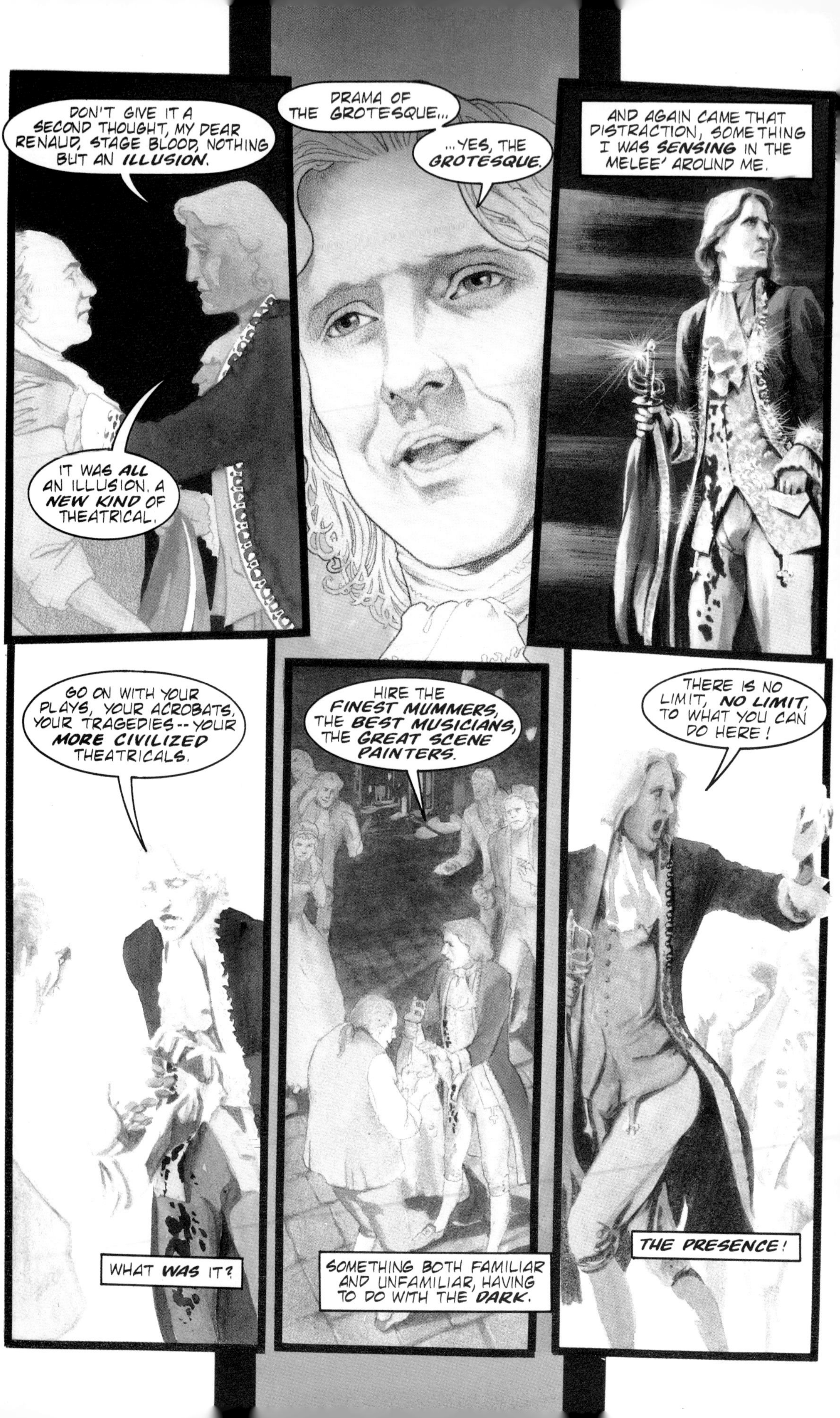
DON'T GIVE IT A SECOND THOUGHT, MY DEAR RENAUD, STAGE BLOOD, NOTHING BUT AN ILLUSION.
IT WAS ALL AN ILLUSION. A NEW KIND OF THEATRICAL.
DRAMA OF THE GROTESQUE...
...YES, THE GROTESQUE.
AND AGAIN CAME THAT DISTRACTION, SOMETHING I WAS SENSING IN THE MELEE' AROUND ME.
GO ON WITH YOUR PLAYS, YOUR ACROBATS, YOUR TRAGEDIES--YOUR MORE CIVILIZED THEATRICALS.
WHAT WAS IT?
HIRE THE FINEST MUMMERS, THE BEST MUSICIANS, THE GREAT SCENE PAINTERS.
SOMETHING BOTH FAMILIAR AND UNFAMILIAR, HAVING TO DO WITH THE DARK.
THERE IS NO LIMIT, NO LIMIT, TO WHAT YOU CAN DO HERE!
THE PRESENCE!

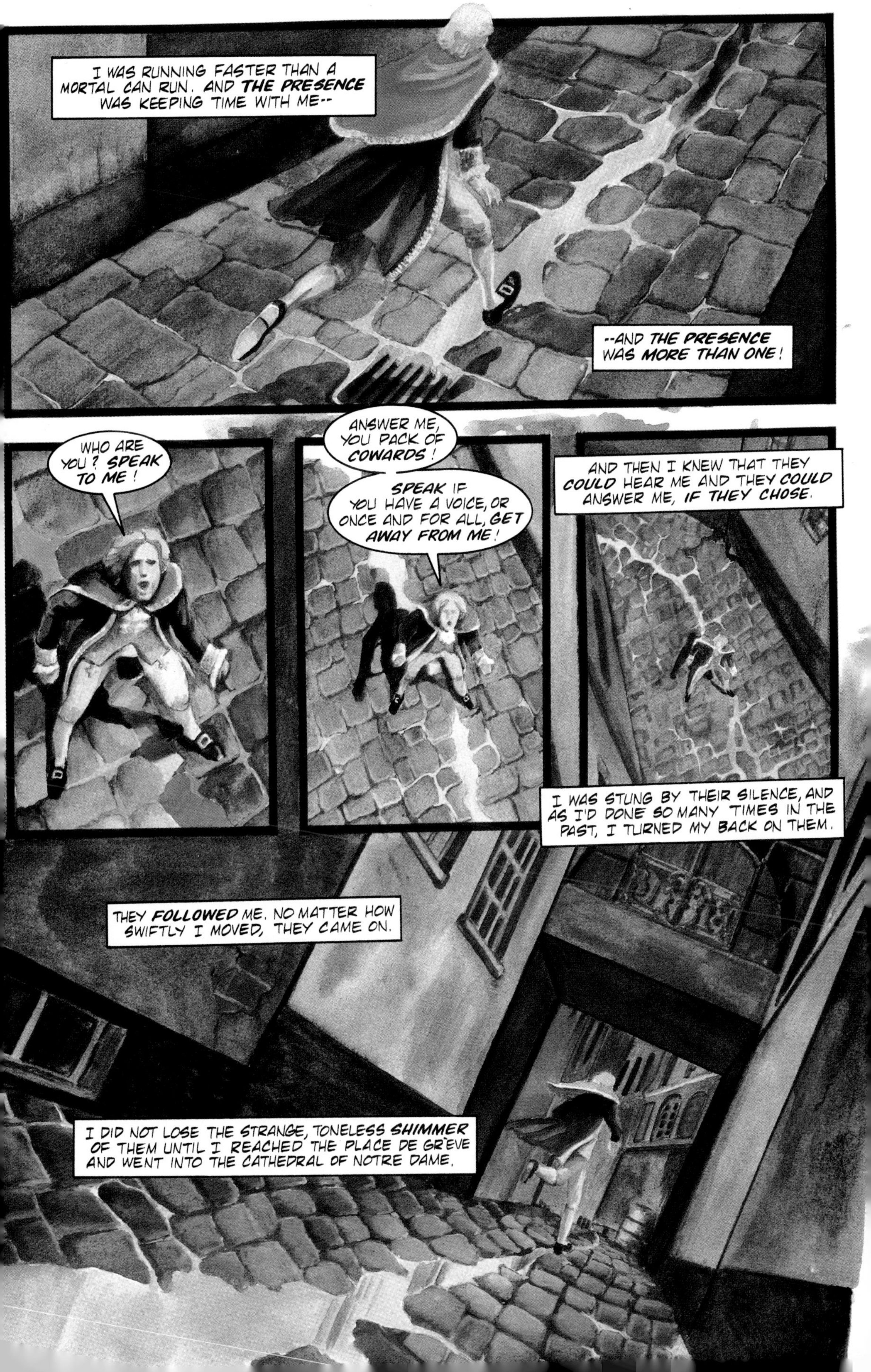
I WAS RUNNING FASTER THAN A MORTAL CAN RUN. AND THE PRESENCE WAS KEEPING TIME WITH ME--
--AND THE PRESENCE WAS MORE THAN ONE!
WHO ARE YOU? SPEAK TO ME!
ANSWER ME, YOU PACK OF COWARDS!
SPEAK IF YOU HAVE A VOICE, OR ONCE AND FOR ALL, GET AWAY FROM ME!
AND THEN I KNEW THAT THEY COULD HEAR ME AND THEY COULD ANSWER ME, IF THEY CHOSE.
I WAS STUNG BY THEIR SILENCE, AND AS I'D DONE SO MANY TIMES IN THE PAST, I TURNED MY BACK ON THEM.
THEY FOLLOWED ME. NO MATTER HOW SWIFTLY I MOVED, THEY CAME ON.
I DID NOT LOSE THE STRANGE, TONELESS SHIMMER OF THEM UNTIL I REACHED THE PLACE DE GRÈVE AND WENT INTO THE CATHEDRAL OF NOTRE DAME.

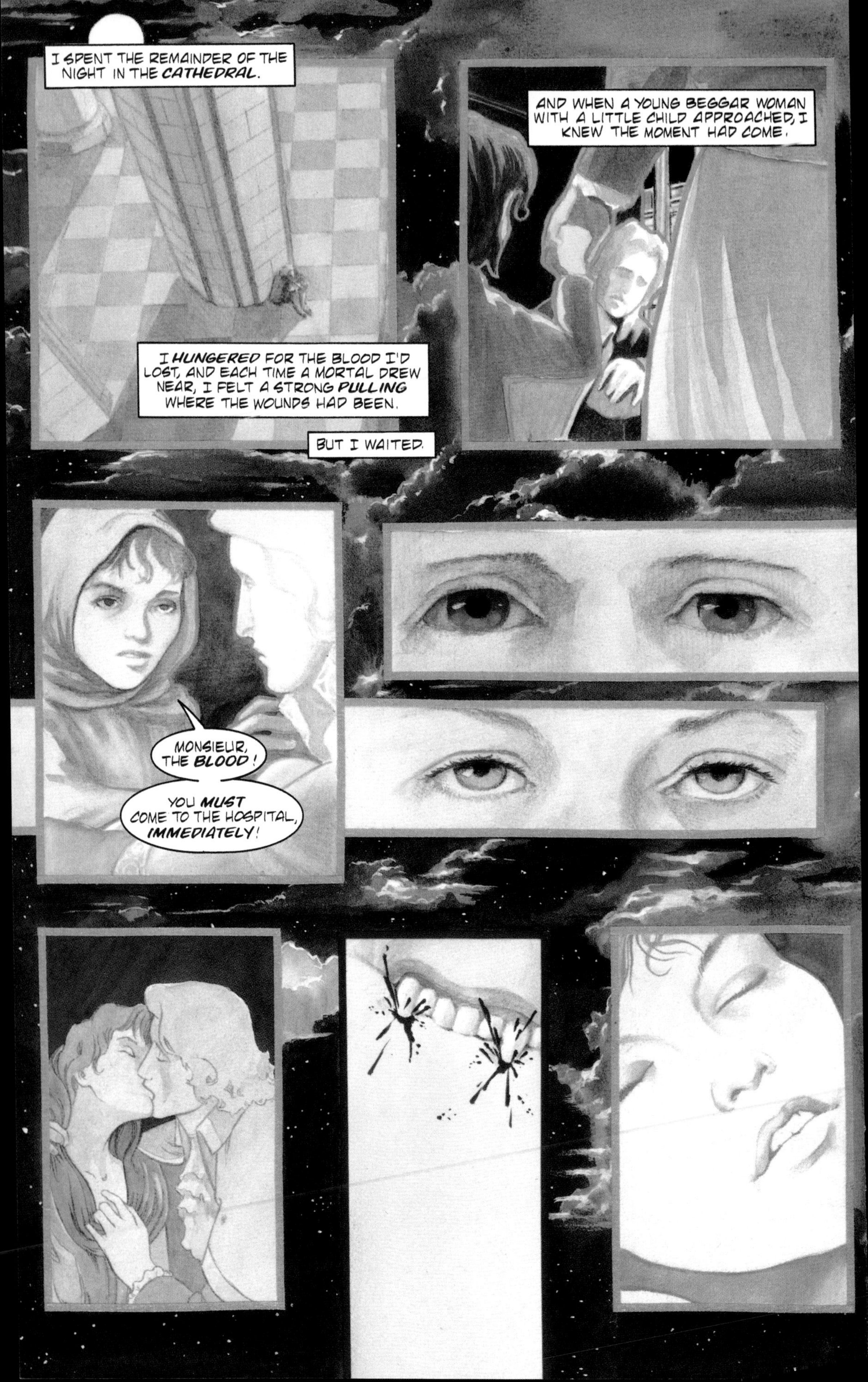
I SPENT THE REMAINDER OF THE NIGHT IN THE CATHEDRAL.
I HUNGERED FOR THE BLOOD I'D LOST, AND EACH TIME A MORTAL DREW NEAR, I FELT A STRONG PULLING WHERE THE WOUNDS HAD BEEN.
BUT I WAITED.
AND WHEN A YOUNG BEGGAR WOMAN WITH A LITTLE CHILD APPROACHED, I KNEW THE MOMENT HAD COME.
MONSIEUR, THE BLOOD!
YOU MUST COME TO THE HOSPITAL, IMMEDIATELY!

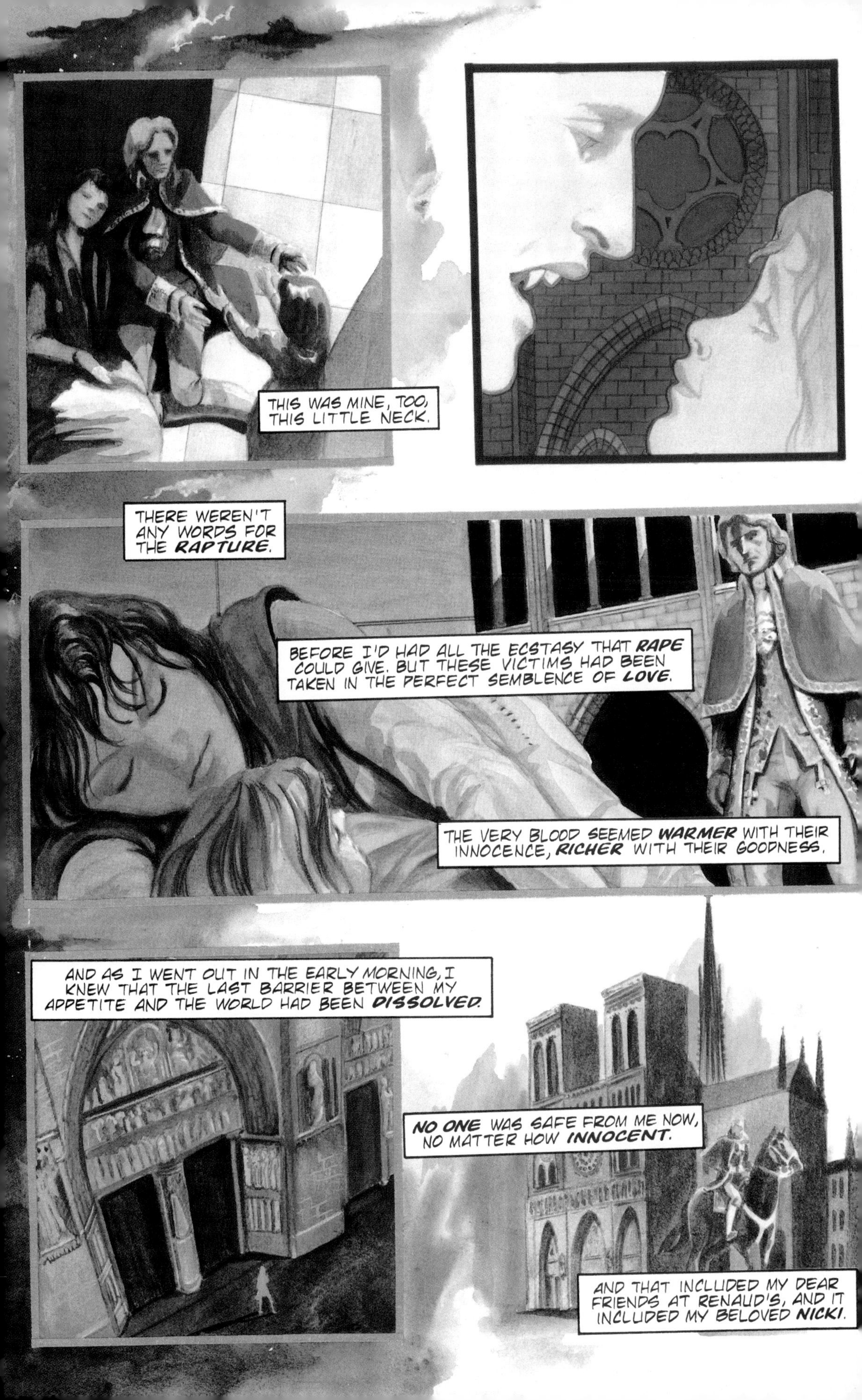
THIS WAS MINE, TOO, THIS LITTLE NECK.
THERE WEREN'T ANY WORDS FOR THE RAPTURE.
BEFORE I'D HAD ALL THE ECSTASY THAT RAPE COULD GIVE. BUT THESE VICTIMS HAD BEEN TAKEN IN THE PERFECT SEMBLENCE OF LOVE.
THE VERY BLOOD SEEMED WARMER WITH THEIR INNOCENCE, RICHER WITH THEIR GOODNESS.
AND AS I WENT OUT IN THE EARLY MORNING, I KNEW THAT THE LAST BARRIER BETWEEN MY APPETITE AND THE WORLD HAD BEEN DISSOLVED.
NO ONE WAS SAFE FROM ME NOW, NO MATTER HOW INNOCENT.
AND THAT INCLUDED MY DEAR FRIENDS AT RENAUD'S, AND IT INCLUDED MY BELOVED NICKI.

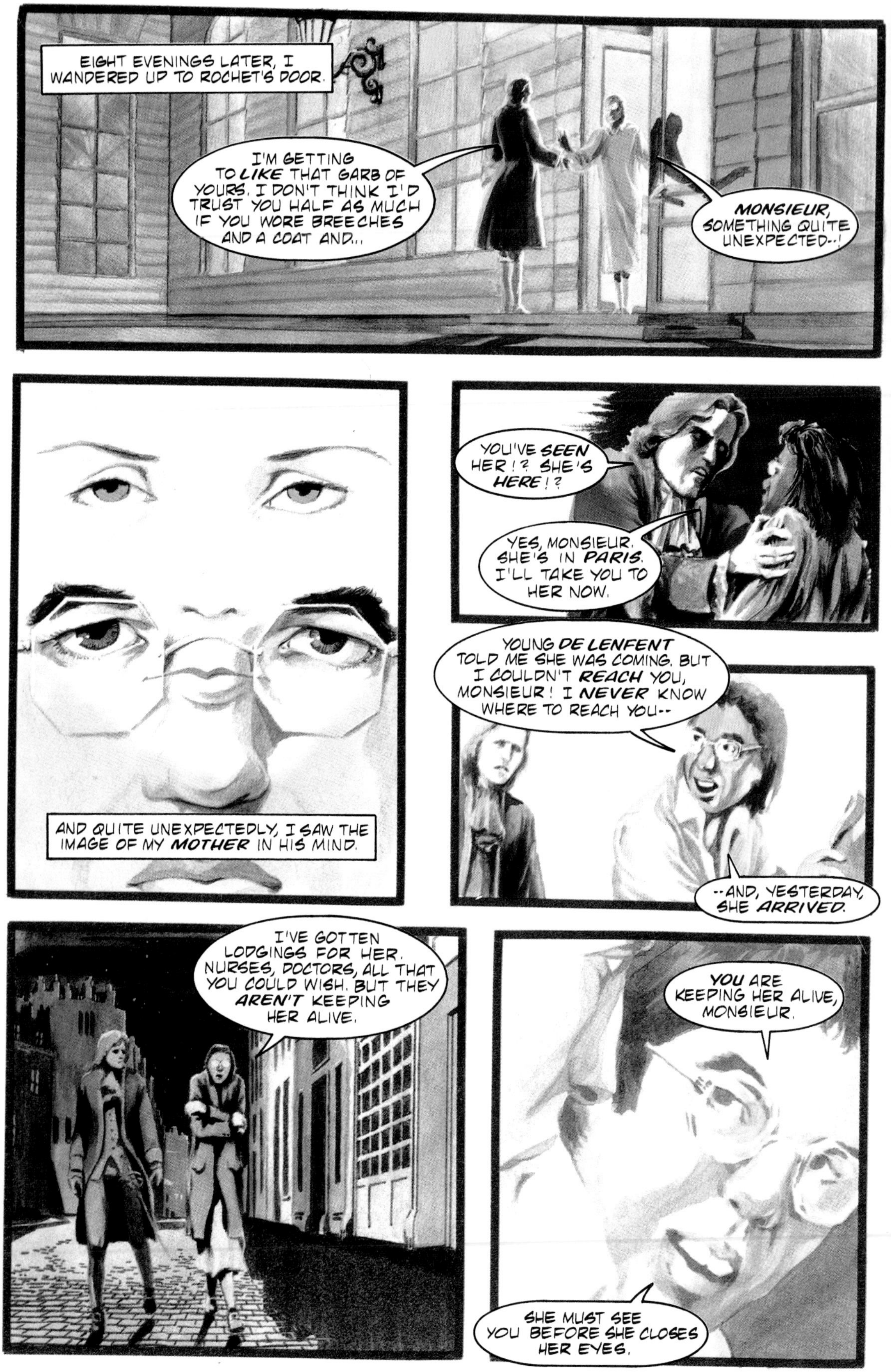
EIGHT EVENINGS LATER, I WANDERED UP TO ROCHET'S DOOR.
I'M GETTING TO **LIKE** THAT GARB OF YOURS. I DON'T THINK I'D TRUST YOU HALF AS MUCH IF YOU WORE BREECHES AND A COAT AND...
MONSIEUR, SOMETHING QUITE UNEXPECTED--!
AND QUITE UNEXPECTEDLY, I SAW THE IMAGE OF MY **MOTHER** IN HIS MIND.
YOU'VE **SEEN** HER!? SHE'S **HERE**!?
YES, MONSIEUR. SHE'S IN **PARIS**. I'LL TAKE YOU TO HER NOW.
YOUNG **DE LENFENT** TOLD ME SHE WAS COMING. BUT I COULDN'T **REACH** YOU, MONSIEUR! I **NEVER** KNOW WHERE TO REACH YOU--
--AND, YESTERDAY, SHE **ARRIVED**.
I'VE GOTTEN LODGINGS FOR HER. NURSES, DOCTORS, ALL THAT YOU COULD WISH. BUT THEY **AREN'T** KEEPING HER ALIVE.
YOU ARE KEEPING HER ALIVE, MONSIEUR.
SHE MUST SEE YOU BEFORE SHE CLOSES HER EYES.

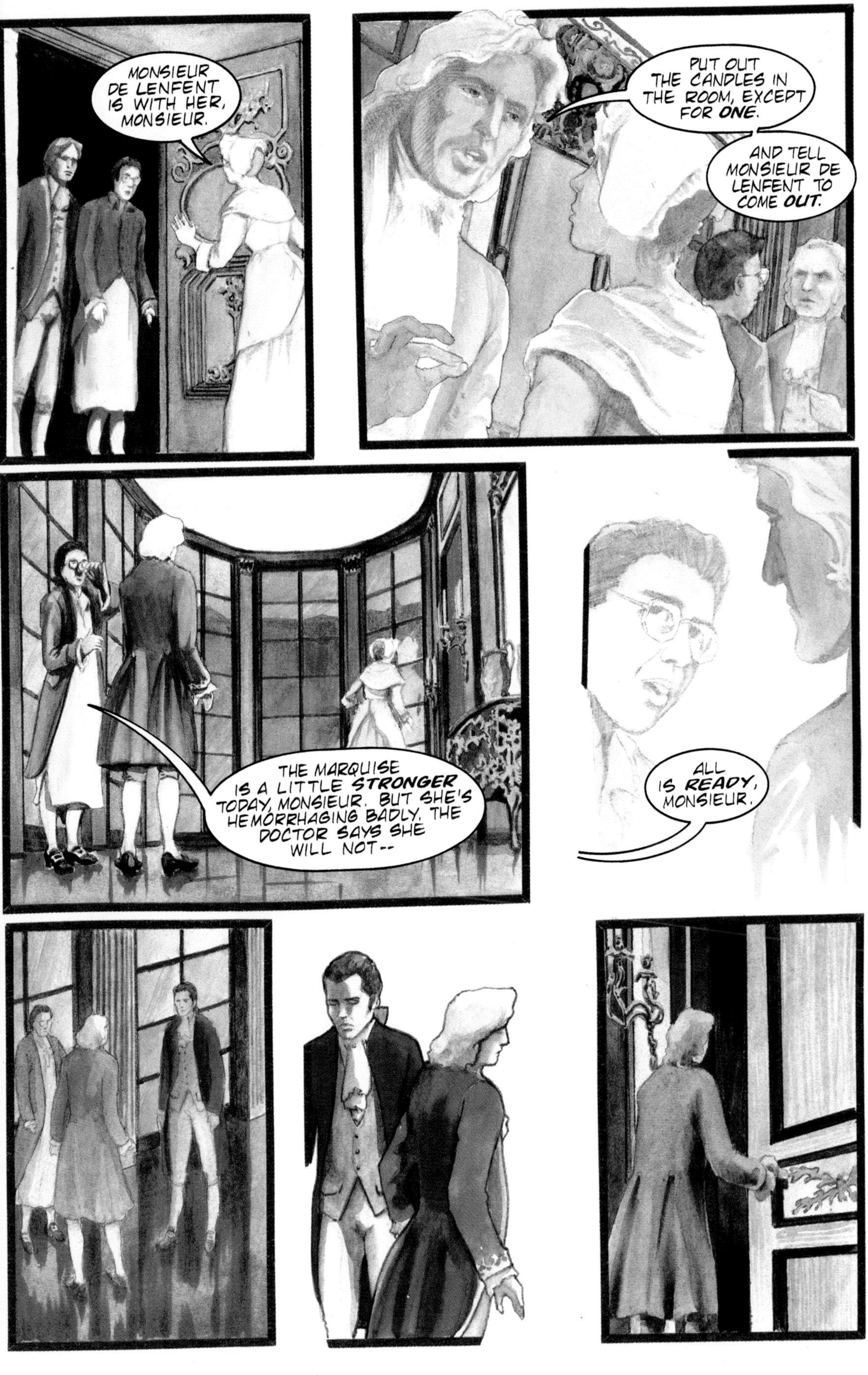

MONSIEUR DE LENFENT IS WITH HER, MONSIEUR.
PUT OUT THE CANDLES IN THE ROOM, EXCEPT FOR **ONE**.
AND TELL MONSIEUR DE LENFENT TO COME **OUT**.
THE MARQUISE IS A LITTLE **STRONGER** TODAY, MONSIEUR. BUT SHE'S HEMORRHAGING BADLY. THE DOCTOR **SAYS** SHE WILL NOT--
ALL IS **READY**, MONSIEUR.

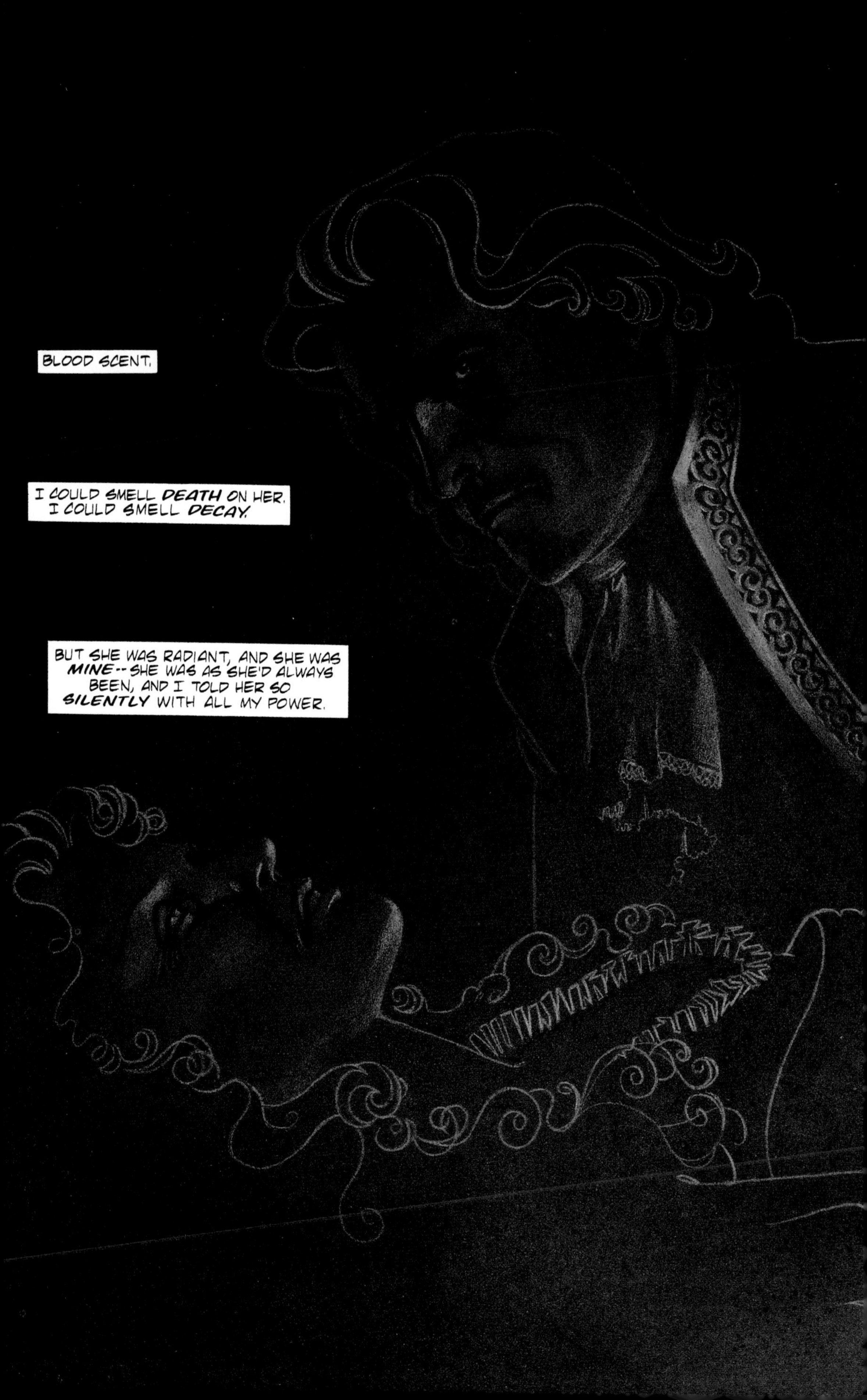
BLOOD SCENT.
I COULD SMELL DEATH ON HER. I COULD SMELL DECAY.
BUT SHE WAS RADIANT, AND SHE WAS MINE-- SHE WAS AS SHE'D ALWAYS BEEN, AND I TOLD HER SO SILENTLY WITH ALL MY POWER.

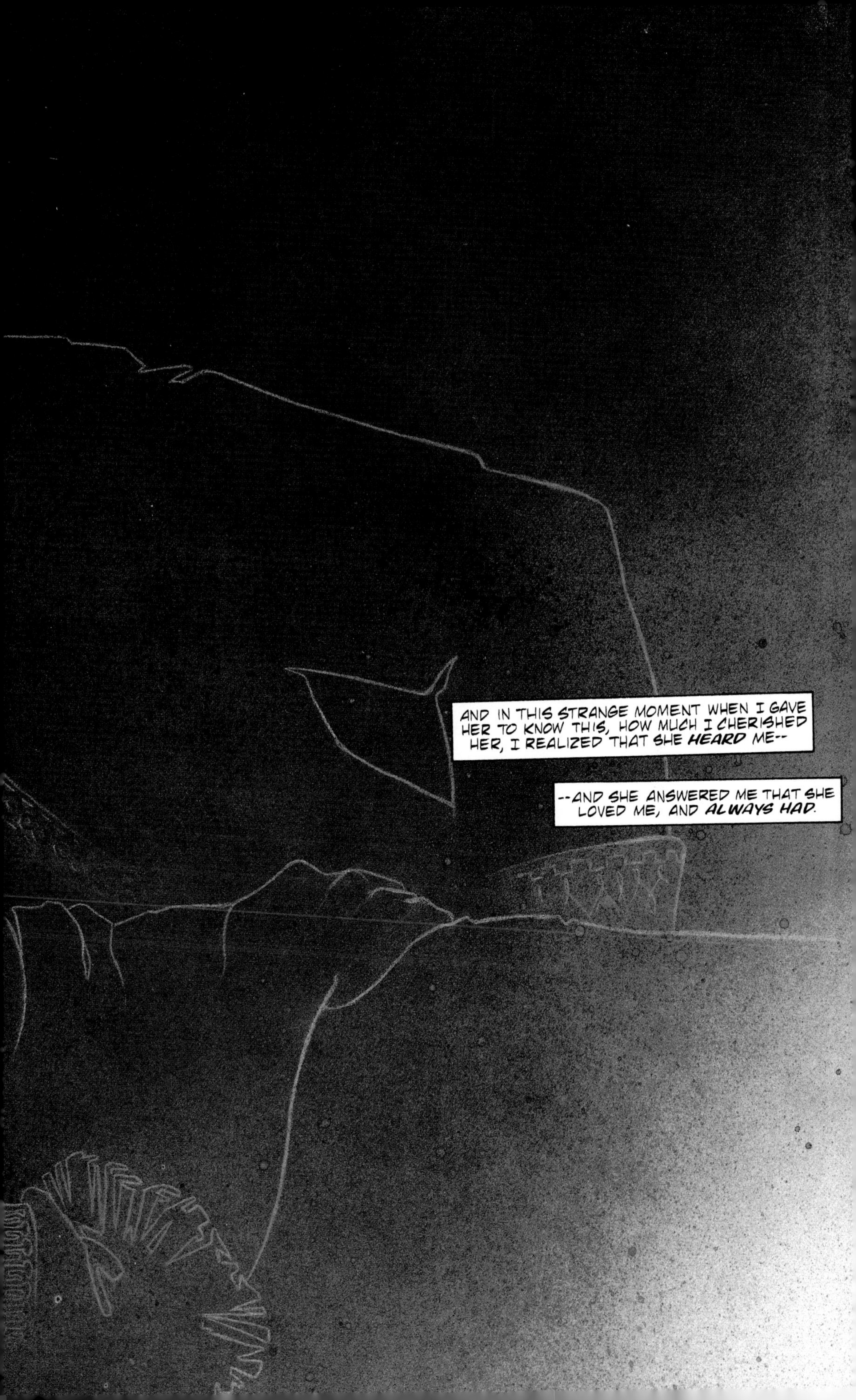
AND IN THIS STRANGE MOMENT WHEN I GAVE HER TO KNOW THIS, HOW MUCH I CHERISHED HER, I REALIZED THAT SHE HEARD ME--
--AND SHE ANSWERED ME THAT SHE LOVED ME, AND ALWAYS HAD.

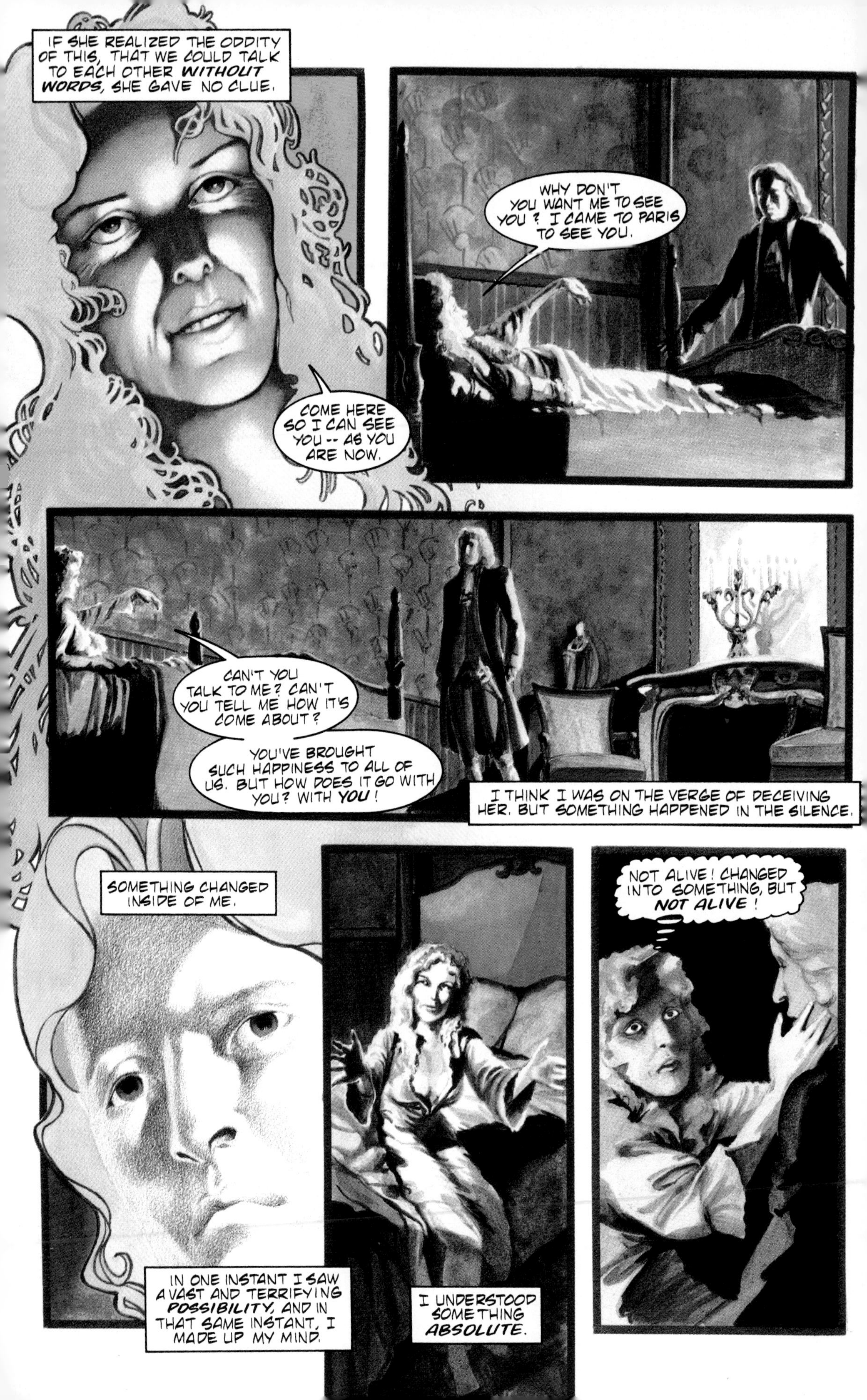
IF SHE REALIZED THE ODDITY OF THIS, THAT WE COULD TALK TO EACH OTHER WITHOUT WORDS, SHE GAVE NO CLUE.
COME HERE SO I CAN SEE YOU -- AS YOU ARE NOW.
WHY DON'T YOU WANT ME TO SEE YOU ? I CAME TO PARIS TO SEE YOU.
CAN'T YOU TALK TO ME? CAN'T YOU TELL ME HOW IT'S COME ABOUT?
YOU'VE BROUGHT SUCH HAPPINESS TO ALL OF US. BUT HOW DOES IT GO WITH YOU? WITH YOU!
I THINK I WAS ON THE VERGE OF DECEIVING HER. BUT SOMETHING HAPPENED IN THE SILENCE.
SOMETHING CHANGED INSIDE OF ME.
IN ONE INSTANT I SAW A VAST AND TERRIFYING POSSIBILITY, AND IN THAT SAME INSTANT, I MADE UP MY MIND.
I UNDERSTOOD SOMETHING ABSOLUTE.
NOT ALIVE! CHANGED INTO SOMETHING, BUT NOT ALIVE!

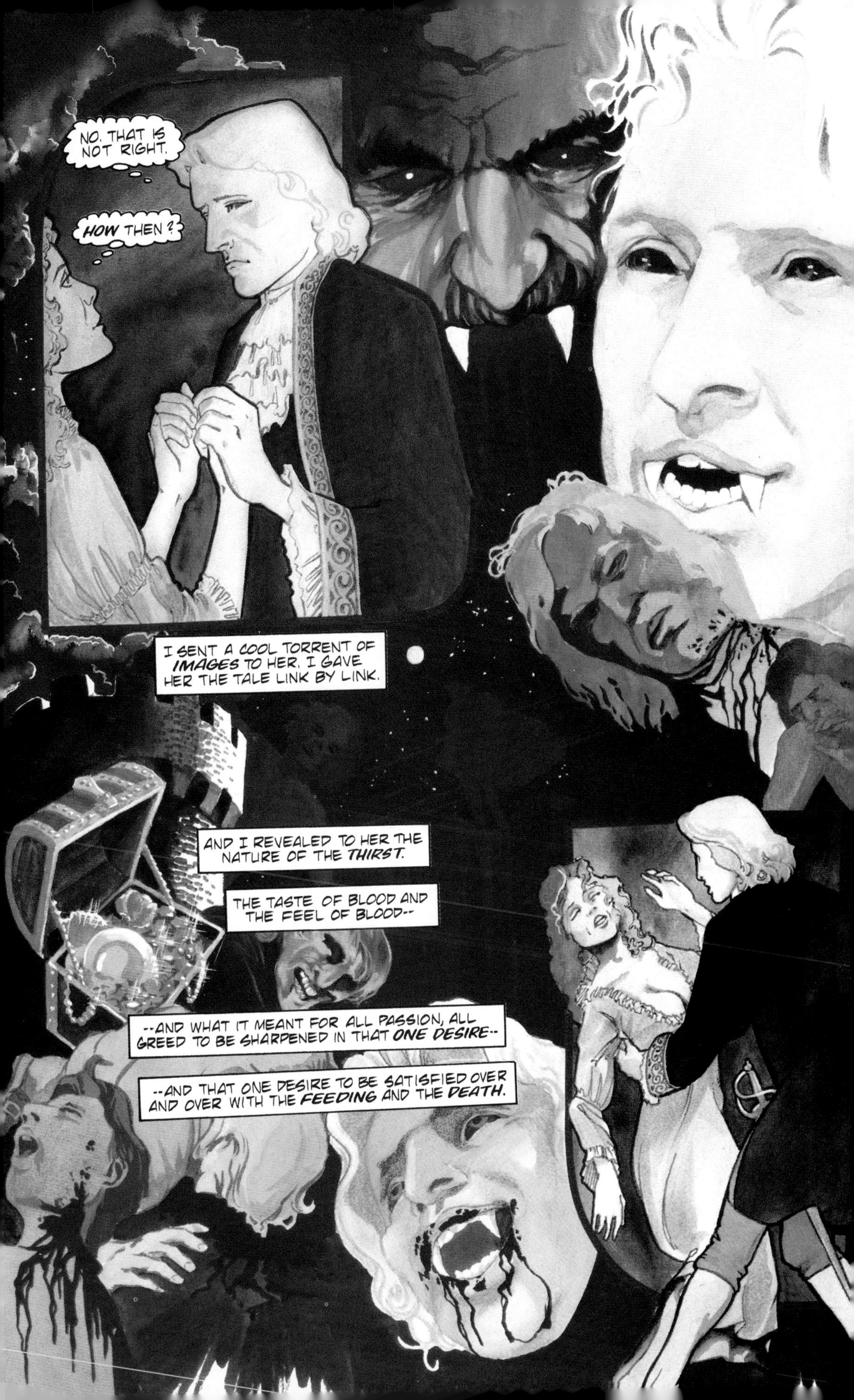
NO. THAT IS NOT RIGHT.
HOW THEN?
I SENT A COOL TORRENT OF IMAGES TO HER. I GAVE HER THE TALE LINK BY LINK.
AND I REVEALED TO HER THE NATURE OF THE THIRST.
THE TASTE OF BLOOD AND THE FEEL OF BLOOD--
--AND WHAT IT MEANT FOR ALL PASSION, ALL GREED TO BE SHARPENED IN THAT ONE DESIRE--
--AND THAT ONE DESIRE TO BE SATISFIED OVER AND OVER WITH THE FEEDING AND THE DEATH.

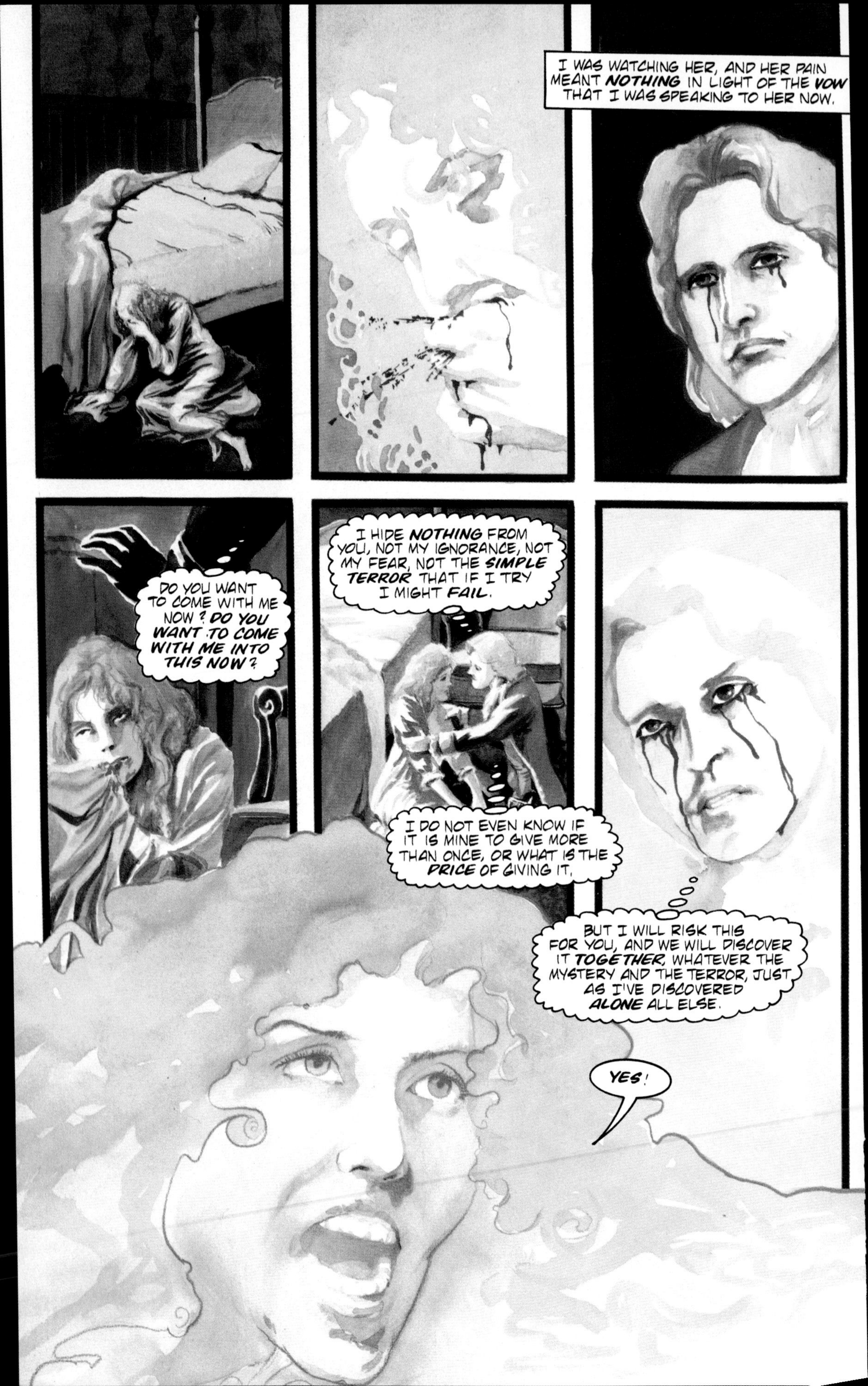
I WAS WATCHING HER, AND HER PAIN MEANT NOTHING IN LIGHT OF THE VOW THAT I WAS SPEAKING TO HER NOW.
DO YOU WANT TO COME WITH ME NOW? DO YOU WANT TO COME WITH ME INTO THIS NOW?
I HIDE NOTHING FROM YOU, NOT MY IGNORANCE, NOT MY FEAR, NOT THE SIMPLE TERROR THAT IF I TRY I MIGHT FAIL.
I DO NOT EVEN KNOW IF IT IS MINE TO GIVE MORE THAN ONCE, OR WHAT IS THE PRICE OF GIVING IT.
BUT I WILL RISK THIS FOR YOU, AND WE WILL DISCOVER IT TOGETHER, WHATEVER THE MYSTERY AND THE TERROR, JUST AS I'VE DISCOVERED ALONE ALL ELSE.
YES!

ALL THE MEMORIES OF MY LIFE WITH HER SURROUNDED US--

--THE NEED OF HER AND THE TERROR OF HER AND HER COMPLEXITY AND HER INDIFFERENCE AND HER STRENGTH.

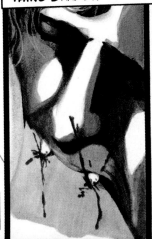

SHE WAS FLESH AND BLOOD AND MOTHER AND LOVER AND ALL THINGS BENEATH THE CRUEL PRESSURE OF MY LIPS, *EVERY-THING* I HAD EVER DESIRED.

HER HEART AND SOUL SPLIT OPEN. THERE WAS NO AGE TO HER, NO *SINGLE MOMENT.*

AND THEN THERE WAS NO *MOTHER* ANYMORE, NO PETTY NEED AND PETTY TERROR-- SHE SIMPLY *WAS* WHO SHE WAS.

SHE WAS *GABRIELLE.*

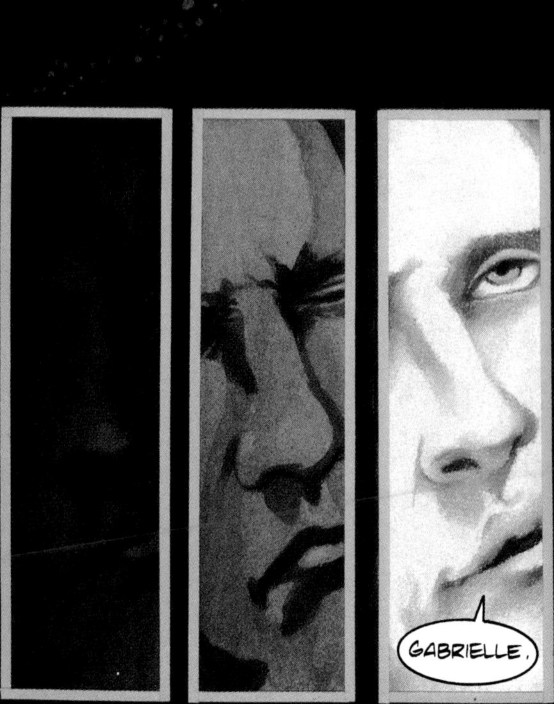
GABRIELLE.

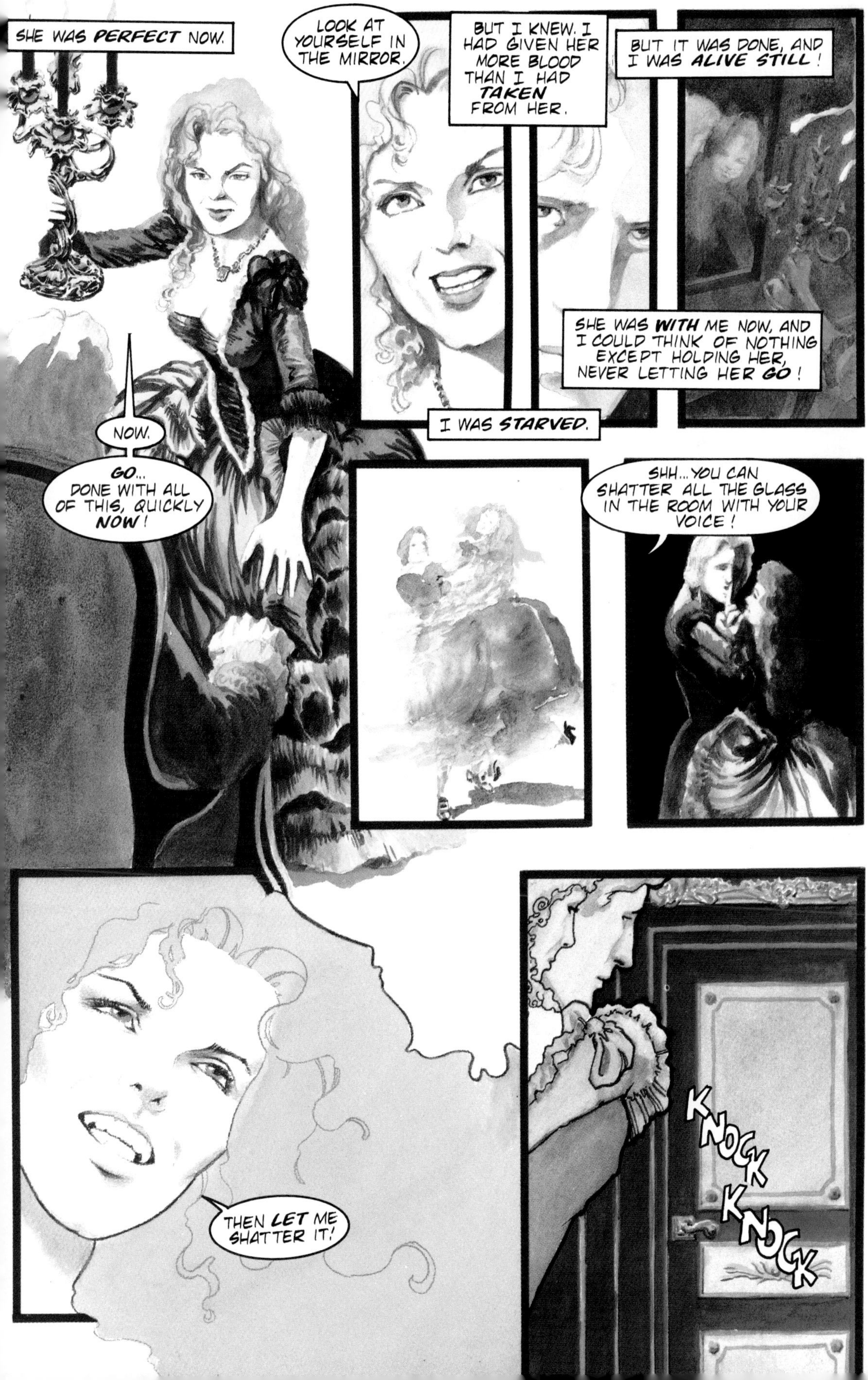
SHE WAS PERFECT NOW.
NOW.
GO... DONE WITH ALL OF THIS, QUICKLY NOW!
LOOK AT YOURSELF IN THE MIRROR.
BUT I KNEW. I HAD GIVEN HER MORE BLOOD THAN I HAD TAKEN FROM HER.
I WAS STARVED.
BUT IT WAS DONE, AND I WAS ALIVE STILL!
SHE WAS WITH ME NOW, AND I COULD THINK OF NOTHING EXCEPT HOLDING HER, NEVER LETTING HER GO!
SHH... YOU CAN SHATTER ALL THE GLASS IN THE ROOM WITH YOUR VOICE!
THEN LET ME SHATTER IT!
KNOCK KNOCK

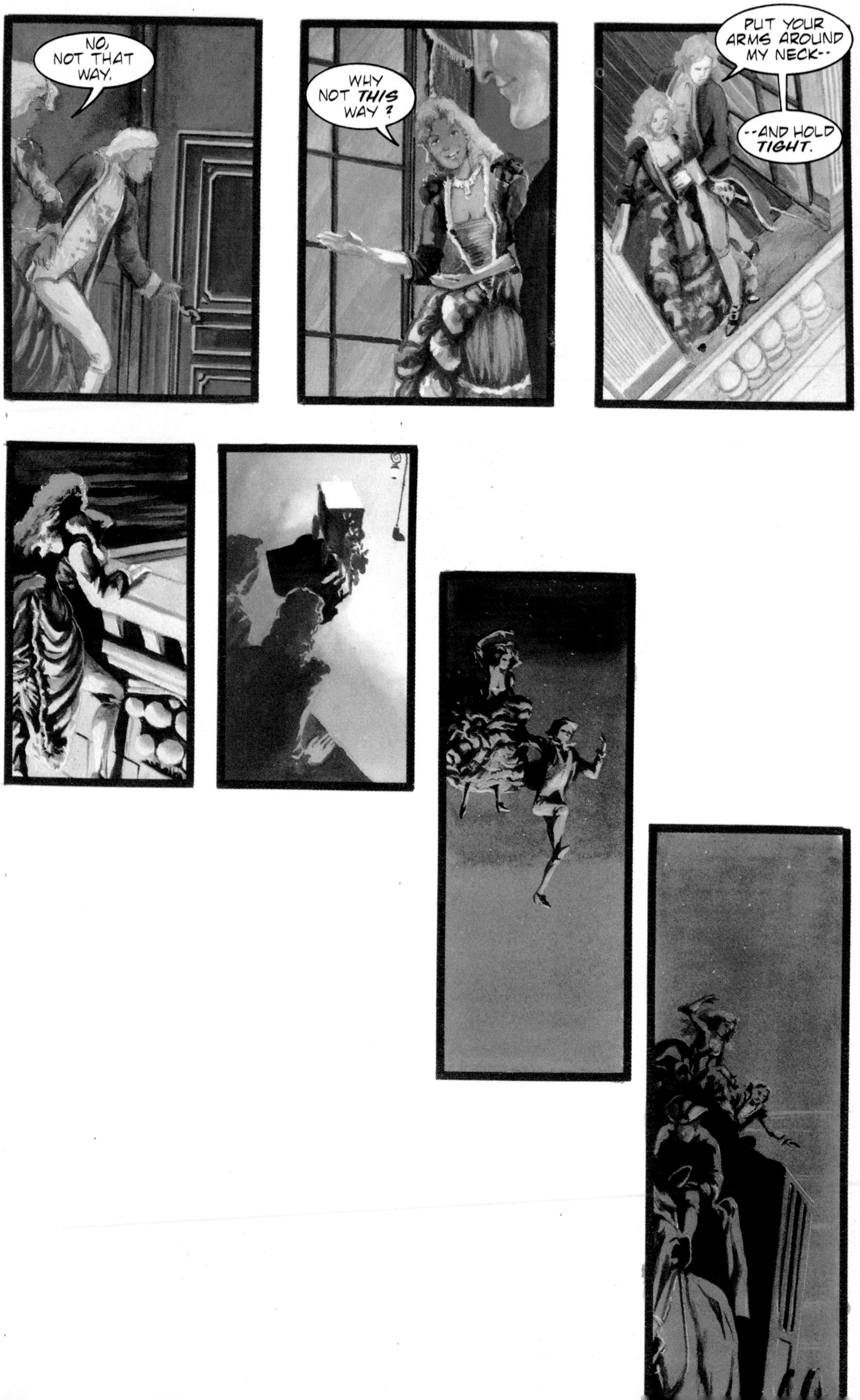
NO, NOT THAT WAY.
WHY NOT THIS WAY?
PUT YOUR ARMS AROUND MY NECK--
--AND HOLD TIGHT.

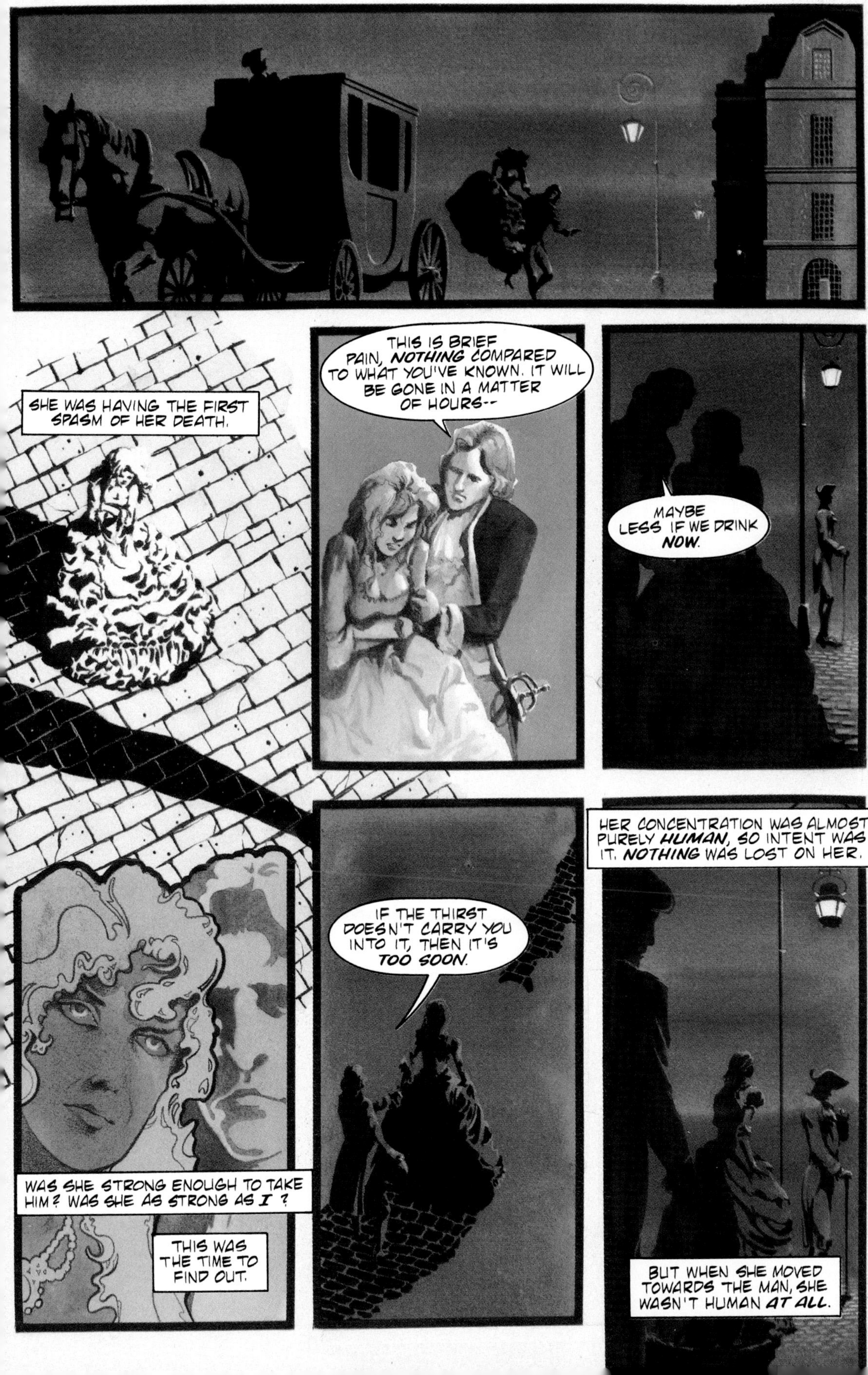
SHE WAS HAVING THE FIRST SPASM OF HER DEATH.
THIS IS BRIEF PAIN, NOTHING COMPARED TO WHAT YOU'VE KNOWN. IT WILL BE GONE IN A MATTER OF HOURS--
MAYBE LESS IF WE DRINK NOW.
WAS SHE STRONG ENOUGH TO TAKE HIM? WAS SHE AS STRONG AS I ?
THIS WAS THE TIME TO FIND OUT.
IF THE THIRST DOESN'T CARRY YOU INTO IT, THEN IT'S TOO SOON.
HER CONCENTRATION WAS ALMOST PURELY HUMAN, SO INTENT WAS IT. NOTHING WAS LOST ON HER.
BUT WHEN SHE MOVED TOWARDS THE MAN, SHE WASN'T HUMAN AT ALL.

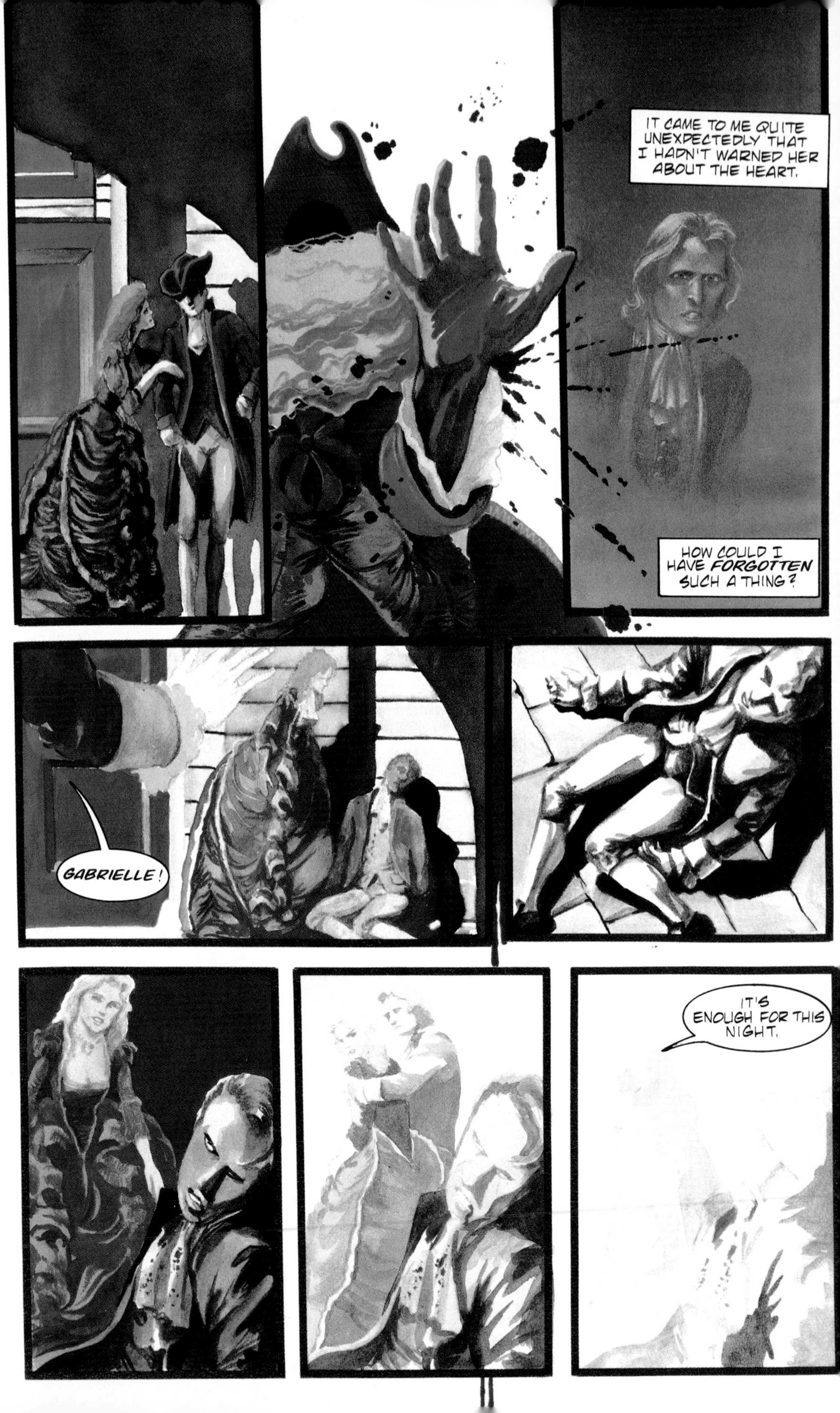
IT CAME TO ME QUITE UNEXPECTEDLY THAT I HADN'T WARNED HER ABOUT THE HEART.
HOW COULD I HAVE FORGOTTEN SUCH A THING?
GABRIELLE!
IT'S ENOUGH FOR THIS NIGHT.

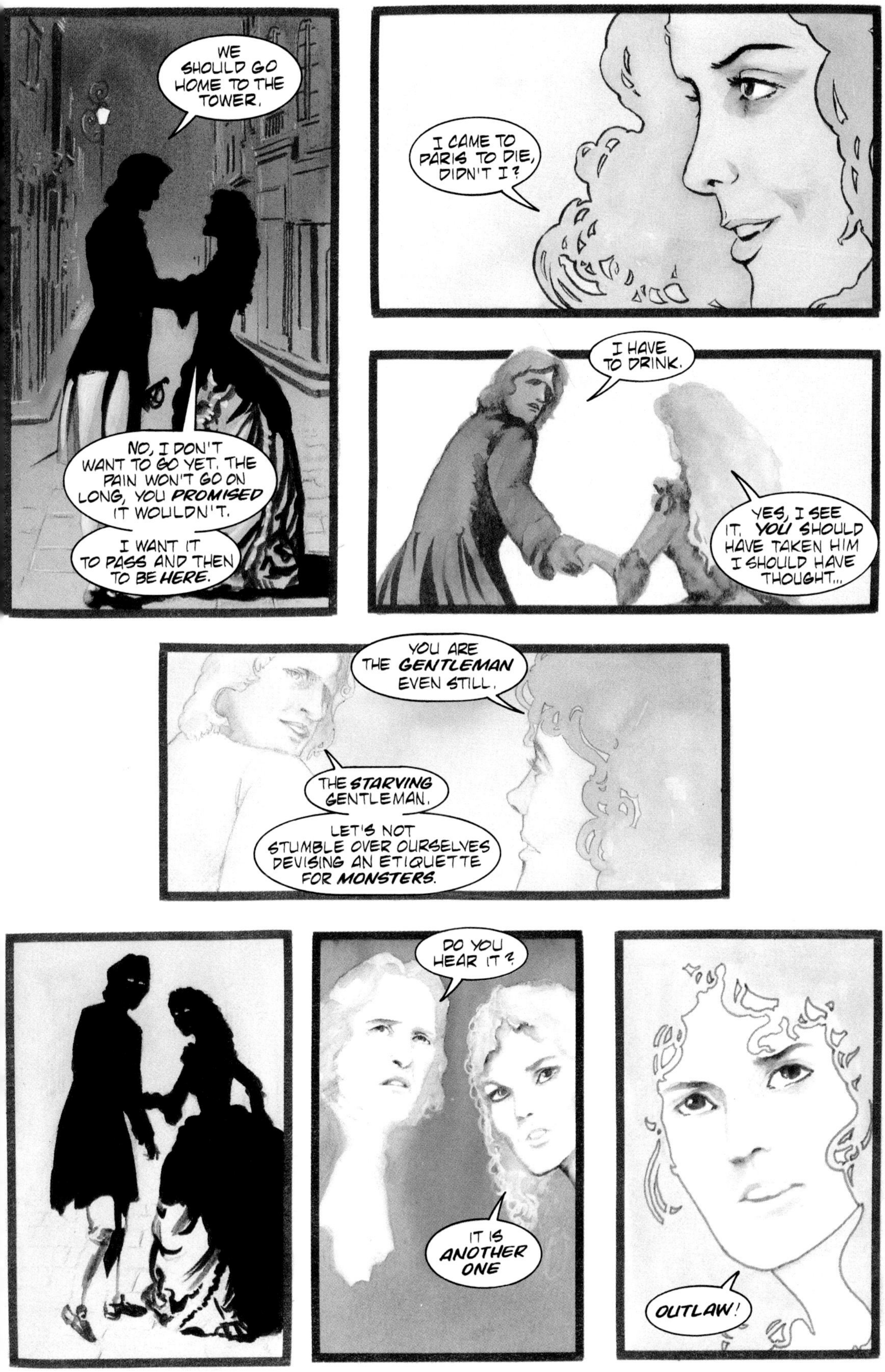
WE SHOULD GO HOME TO THE TOWER.
NO, I DON'T WANT TO GO YET. THE PAIN WON'T GO ON LONG, YOU PROMISED IT WOULDN'T.
I WANT IT TO PASS AND THEN TO BE HERE.
I CAME TO PARIS TO DIE, DIDN'T I?
I HAVE TO DRINK.
YES, I SEE IT. YOU SHOULD HAVE TAKEN HIM I SHOULD HAVE THOUGHT...
YOU ARE THE GENTLEMAN EVEN STILL.
THE STARVING GENTLEMAN.
LET'S NOT STUMBLE OVER OURSELVES DEVISING AN ETIQUETTE FOR MONSTERS.
DO YOU HEAR IT?
IT IS ANOTHER ONE
OUTLAW!

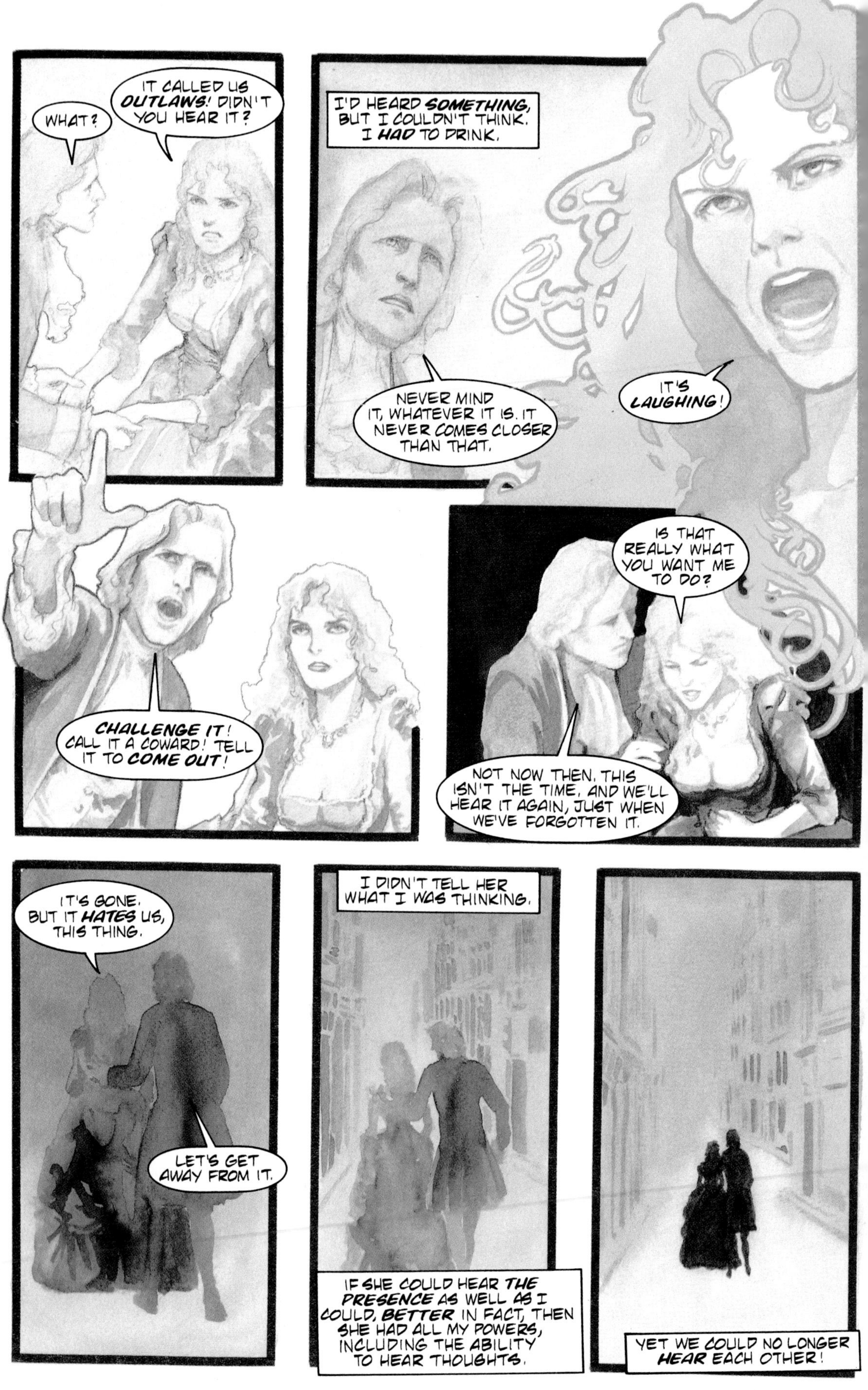
WHAT?
IT CALLED US OUTLAWS! DIDN'T YOU HEAR IT?
I'D HEARD SOMETHING, BUT I COULDN'T THINK. I HAD TO DRINK.
NEVER MIND IT, WHATEVER IT IS. IT NEVER COMES CLOSER THAN THAT.
IT'S LAUGHING!
CHALLENGE IT! CALL IT A COWARD! TELL IT TO COME OUT!
IS THAT REALLY WHAT YOU WANT ME TO DO?
NOT NOW THEN. THIS ISN'T THE TIME, AND WE'LL HEAR IT AGAIN, JUST WHEN WE'VE FORGOTTEN IT.
IT'S GONE. BUT IT HATES US, THIS THING.
LET'S GET AWAY FROM IT.
I DIDN'T TELL HER WHAT I WAS THINKING.
IF SHE COULD HEAR THE PRESENCE AS WELL AS I COULD, BETTER IN FACT, THEN SHE HAD ALL MY POWERS, INCLUDING THE ABILITY TO HEAR THOUGHTS.
YET WE COULD NO LONGER HEAR EACH OTHER!

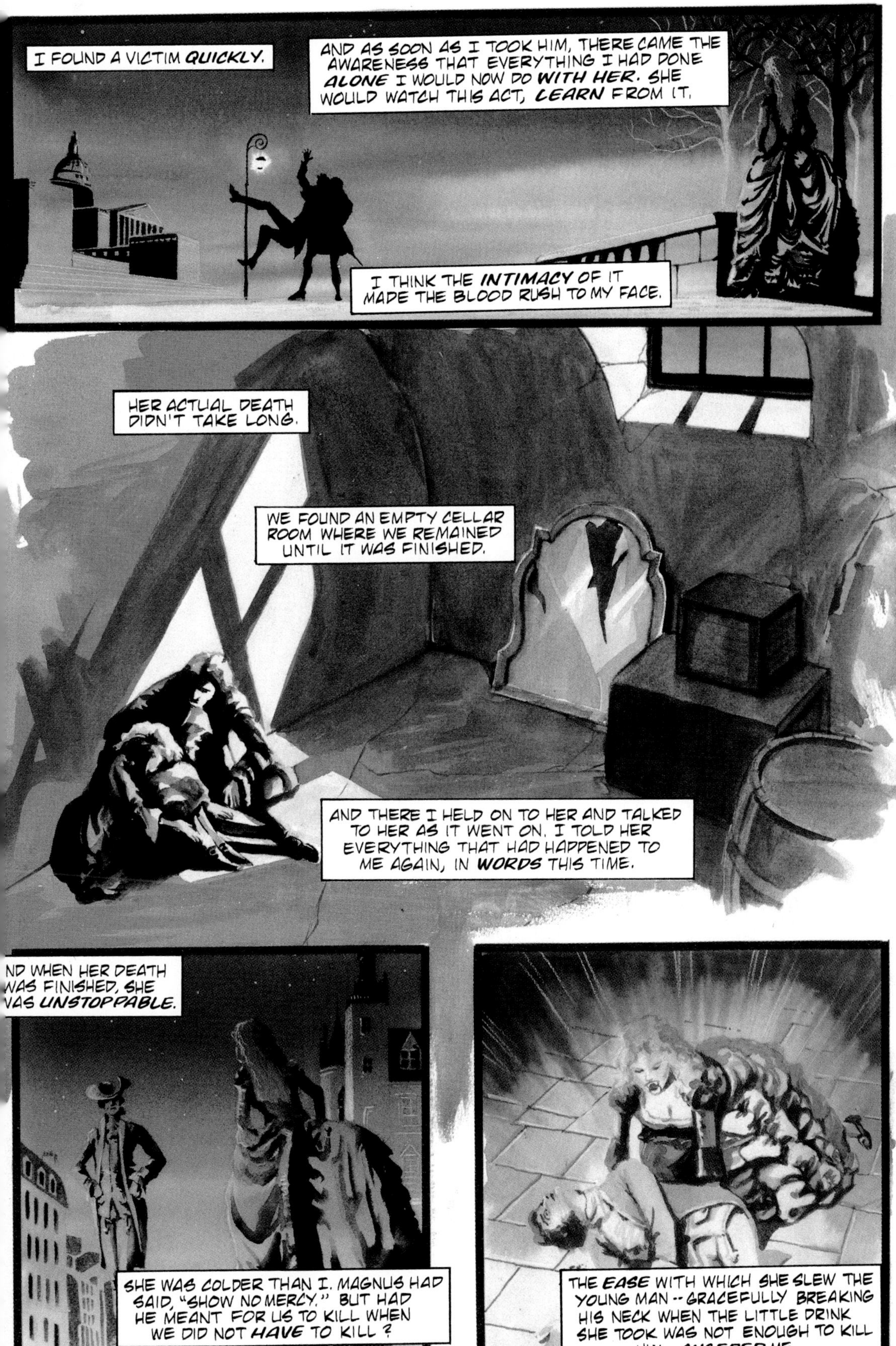
I FOUND A VICTIM QUICKLY.
AND AS SOON AS I TOOK HIM, THERE CAME THE AWARENESS THAT EVERYTHING I HAD DONE ALONE I WOULD NOW DO WITH HER. SHE WOULD WATCH THIS ACT, LEARN FROM IT.
I THINK THE INTIMACY OF IT MADE THE BLOOD RUSH TO MY FACE.
HER ACTUAL DEATH DIDN'T TAKE LONG.
WE FOUND AN EMPTY CELLAR ROOM WHERE WE REMAINED UNTIL IT WAS FINISHED.
AND THERE I HELD ON TO HER AND TALKED TO HER AS IT WENT ON. I TOLD HER EVERYTHING THAT HAD HAPPENED TO ME AGAIN, IN WORDS THIS TIME.
ND WHEN HER DEATH WAS FINISHED, SHE VAS UNSTOPPABLE.
SHE WAS COLDER THAN I. MAGNUS HAD SAID, "SHOW NO MERCY." BUT HAD HE MEANT FOR US TO KILL WHEN WE DID NOT HAVE TO KILL?
THE EASE WITH WHICH SHE SLEW THE YOUNG MAN -- GRACEFULLY BREAKING HIS NECK WHEN THE LITTLE DRINK SHE TOOK WAS NOT ENOUGH TO KILL HIM -- ANGERED ME.

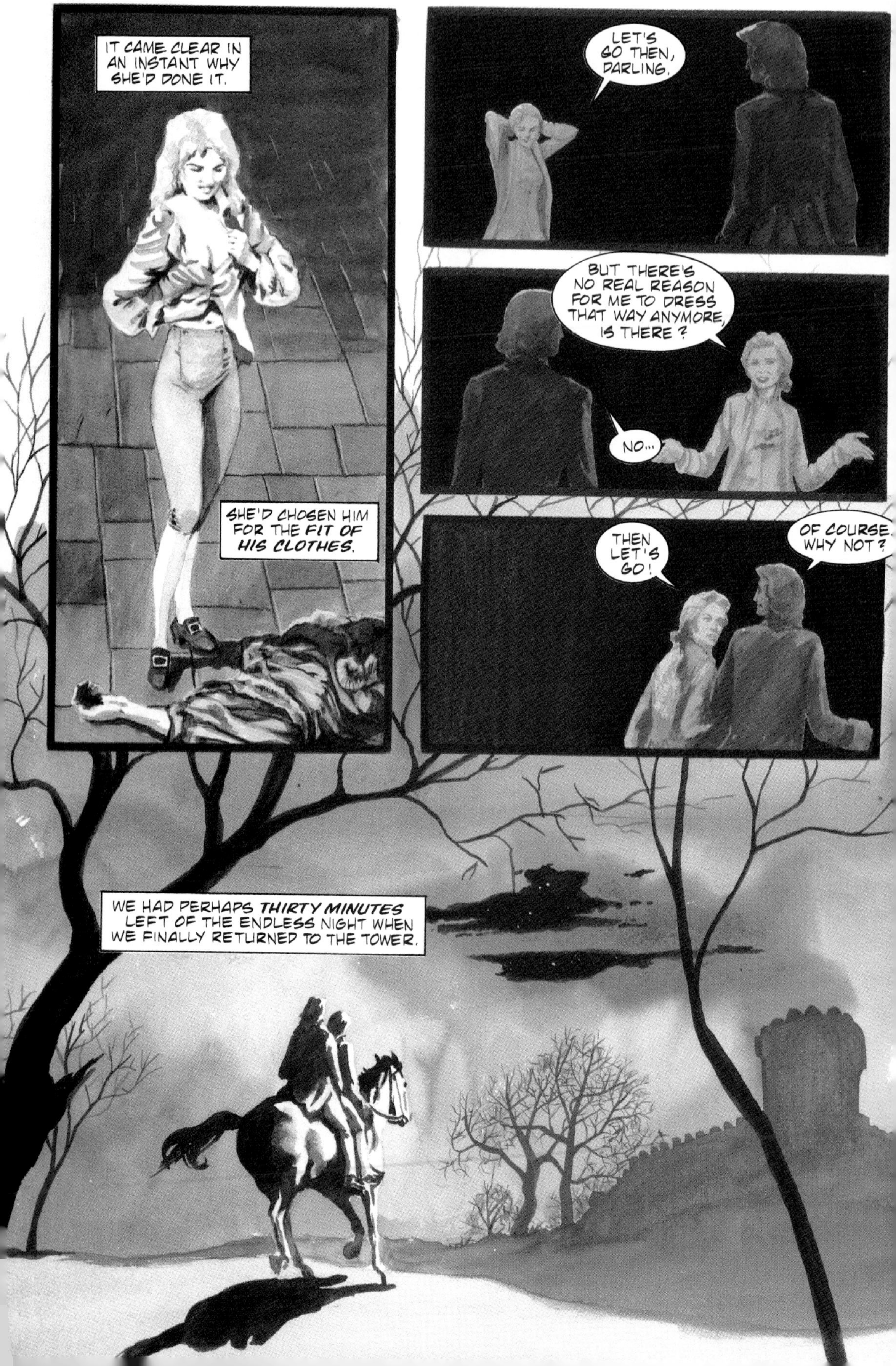

IT CAME CLEAR IN AN INSTANT WHY SHE'D DONE IT.
SHE'D CHOSEN HIM FOR THE FIT OF HIS CLOTHES.
LET'S GO THEN, DARLING.
BUT THERE'S NO REAL REASON FOR ME TO DRESS THAT WAY ANYMORE, IS THERE ?
NO...
THEN LET'S GO!
OF COURSE. WHY NOT ?
WE HAD PERHAPS THIRTY MINUTES LEFT OF THE ENDLESS NIGHT WHEN WE FINALLY RETURNED TO THE TOWER.

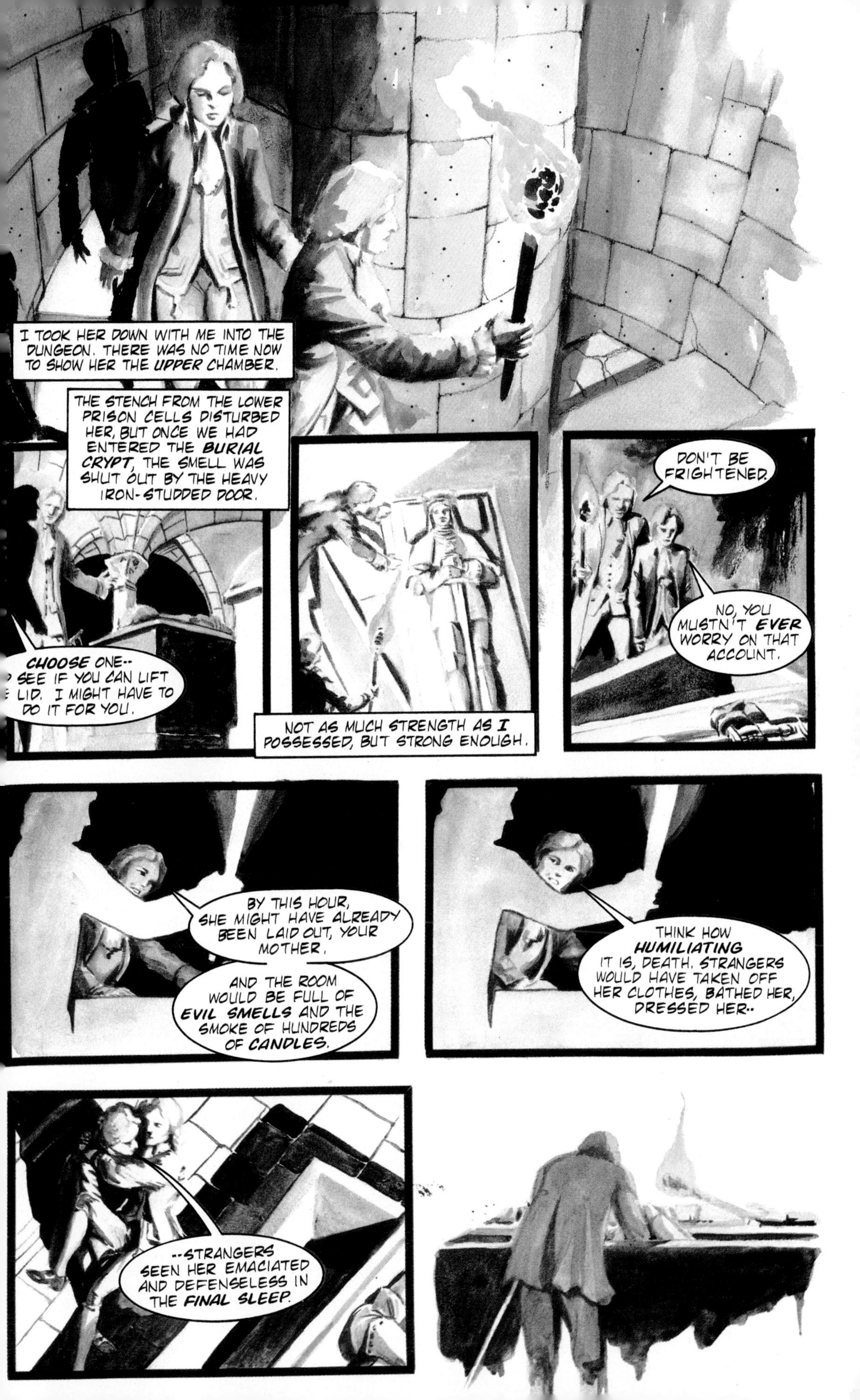
I TOOK HER DOWN WITH ME INTO THE DUNGEON. THERE WAS NO TIME NOW TO SHOW HER THE UPPER CHAMBER.
THE STENCH FROM THE LOWER PRISON CELLS DISTURBED HER, BUT ONCE WE HAD ENTERED THE BURIAL CRYPT, THE SMELL WAS SHUT OUT BY THE HEAVY IRON-STUDDED DOOR.
CHOOSE ONE-- SEE IF YOU CAN LIFT LID. I MIGHT HAVE TO DO IT FOR YOU.
NOT AS MUCH STRENGTH AS I POSSESSED, BUT STRONG ENOUGH.
DON'T BE FRIGHTENED.
NO, YOU MUSTN'T EVER WORRY ON THAT ACCOUNT.
BY THIS HOUR, SHE MIGHT HAVE ALREADY BEEN LAID OUT, YOUR MOTHER.
AND THE ROOM WOULD BE FULL OF EVIL SMELLS AND THE SMOKE OF HUNDREDS OF CANDLES.
THINK HOW HUMILIATING IT IS, DEATH. STRANGERS WOULD HAVE TAKEN OFF HER CLOTHES, BATHED HER, DRESSED HER--
--STRANGERS SEEN HER EMACIATED AND DEFENSELESS IN THE FINAL SLEEP.

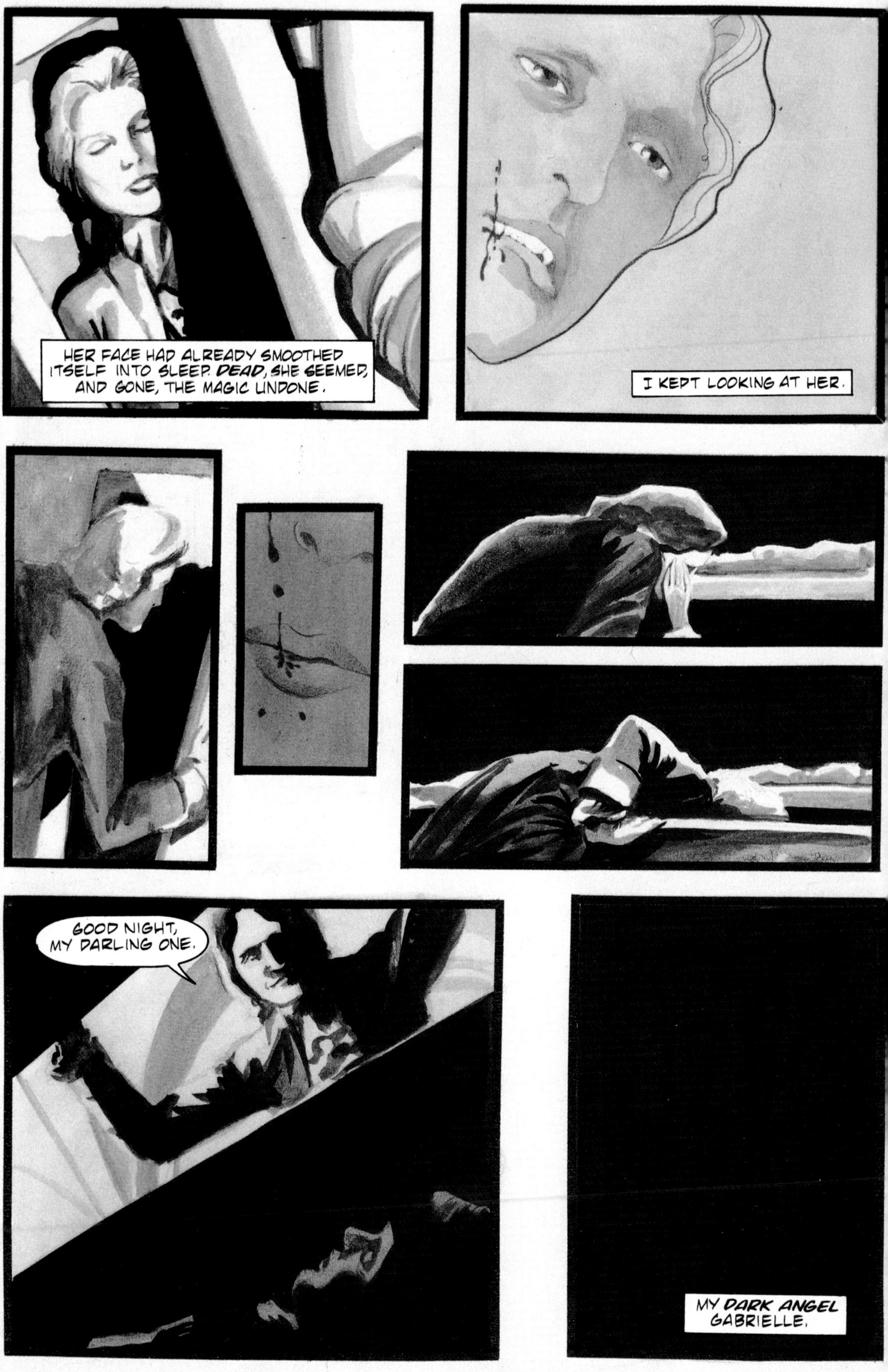
HER FACE HAD ALREADY SMOOTHED ITSELF INTO SLEEP. DEAD, SHE SEEMED, AND GONE, THE MAGIC UNDONE.
I KEPT LOOKING AT HER.
GOOD NIGHT, MY DARLING ONE.
MY DARK ANGEL GABRIELLE.

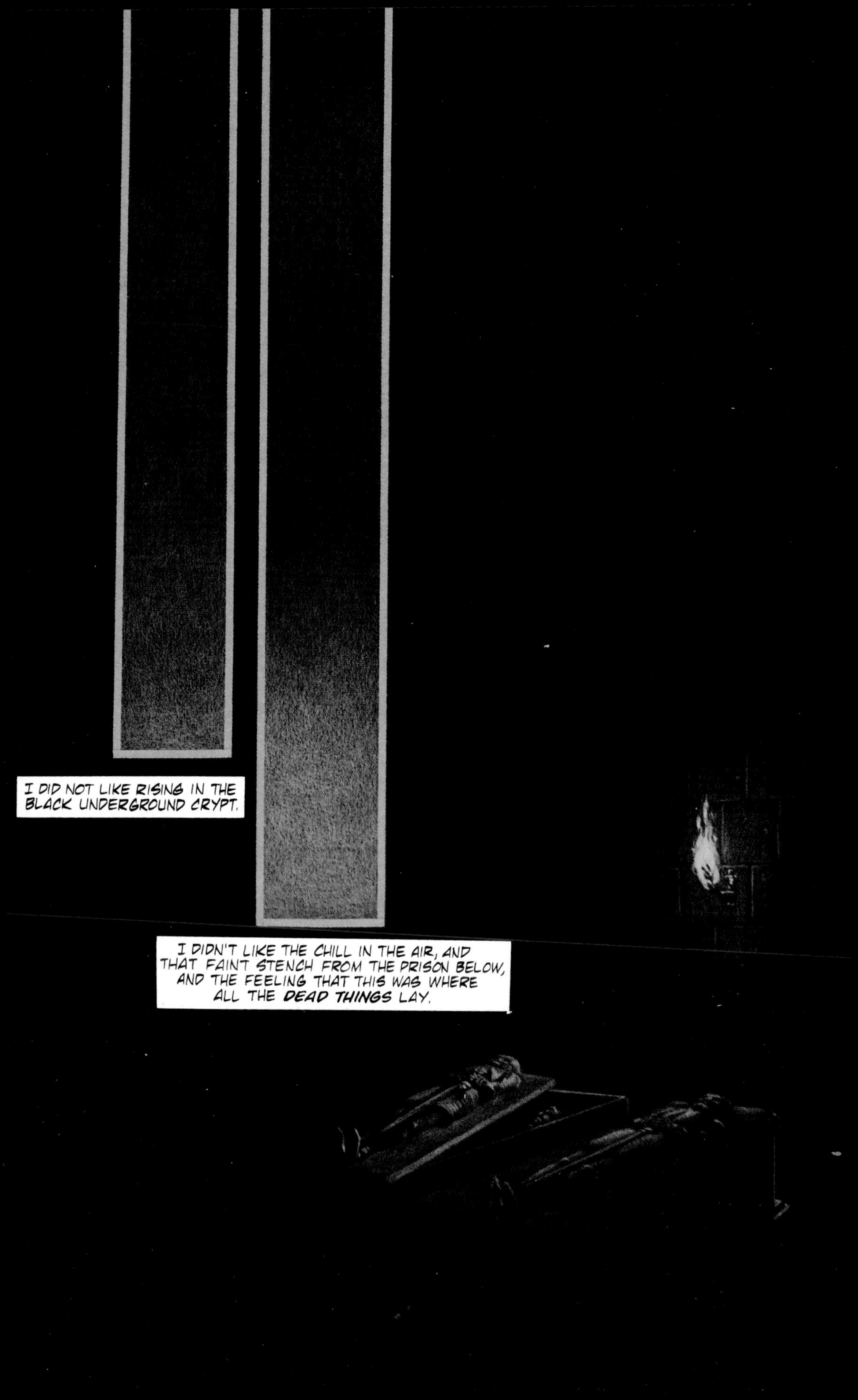
I DID NOT LIKE RISING IN THE BLACK UNDERGROUND CRYPT.
I DIDN'T LIKE THE CHILL IN THE AIR, AND THAT FAINT STENCH FROM THE PRISON BELOW, AND THE FEELING THAT THIS WAS WHERE ALL THE DEAD THINGS LAY.

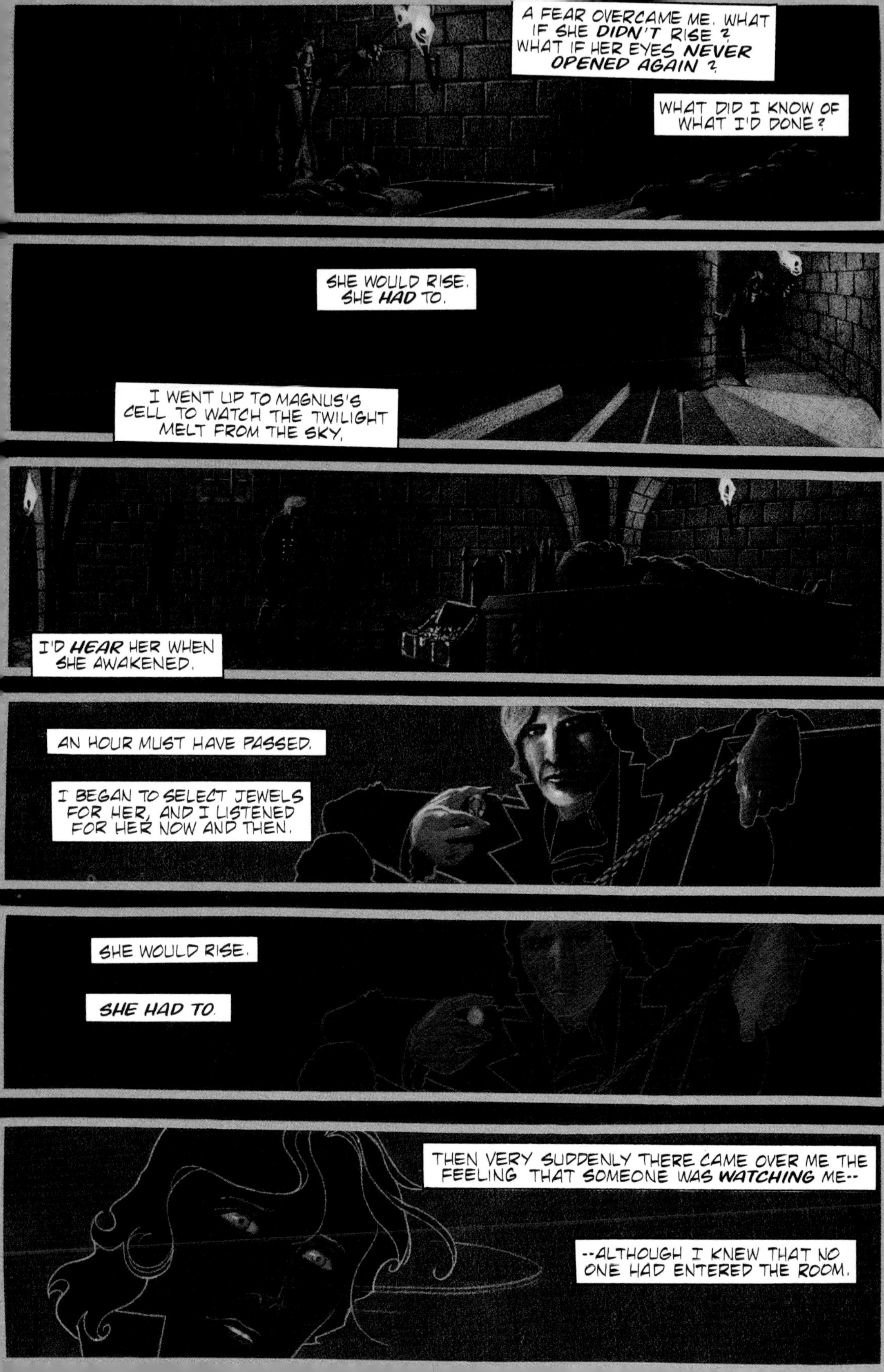
A FEAR OVERCAME ME. WHAT IF SHE DIDN'T RISE? WHAT IF HER EYES NEVER OPENED AGAIN?
WHAT DID I KNOW OF WHAT I'D DONE?
SHE WOULD RISE. SHE HAD TO.
I WENT UP TO MAGNUS'S CELL TO WATCH THE TWILIGHT MELT FROM THE SKY.
I'D HEAR HER WHEN SHE AWAKENED.
AN HOUR MUST HAVE PASSED.
I BEGAN TO SELECT JEWELS FOR HER, AND I LISTENED FOR HER NOW AND THEN.
SHE WOULD RISE.
SHE HAD TO.
THEN VERY SUDDENLY THERE CAME OVER ME THE FEELING THAT SOMEONE WAS WATCHING ME--
--ALTHOUGH I KNEW THAT NO ONE HAD ENTERED THE ROOM.

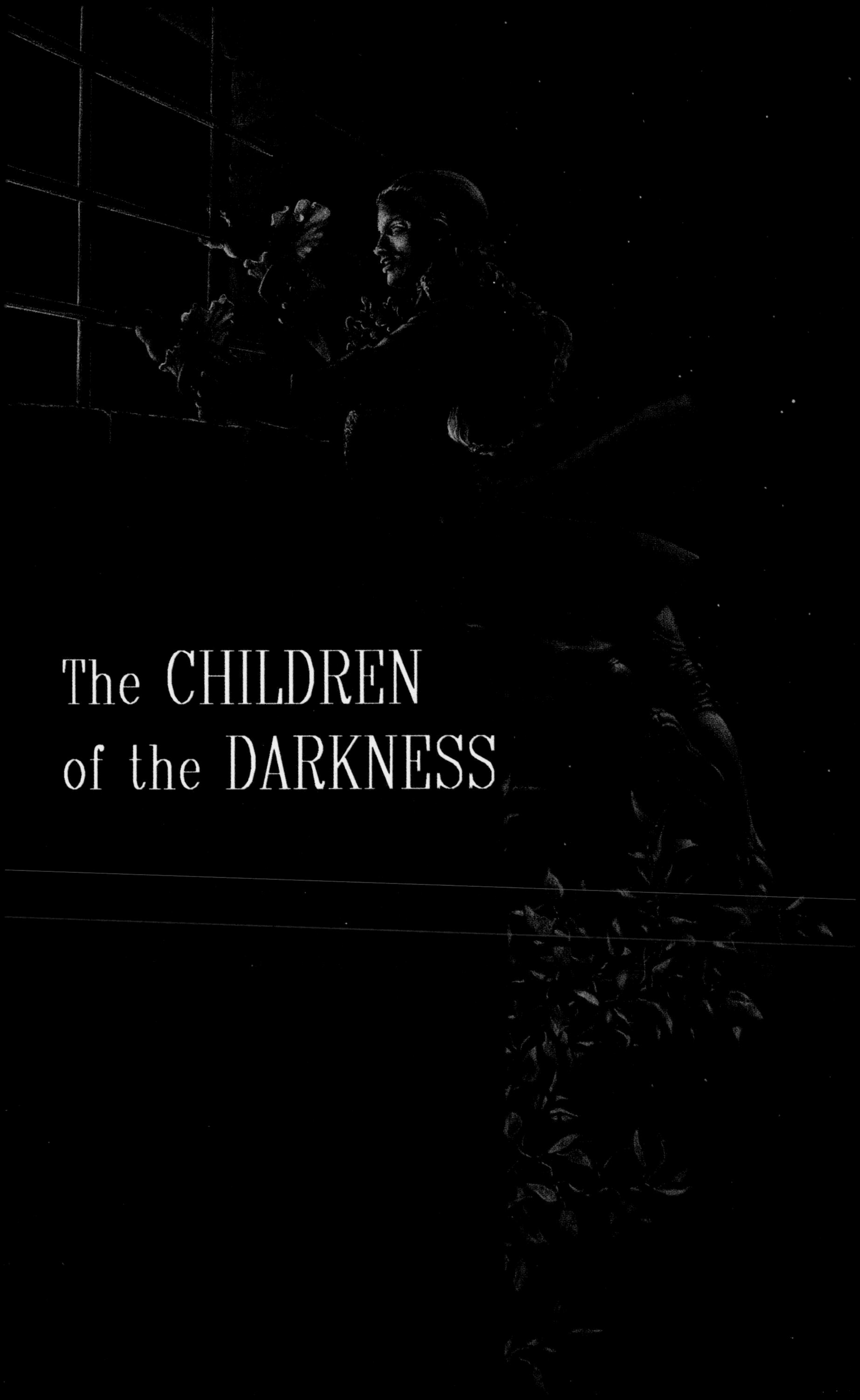

The CHILDREN of the DARKNESS

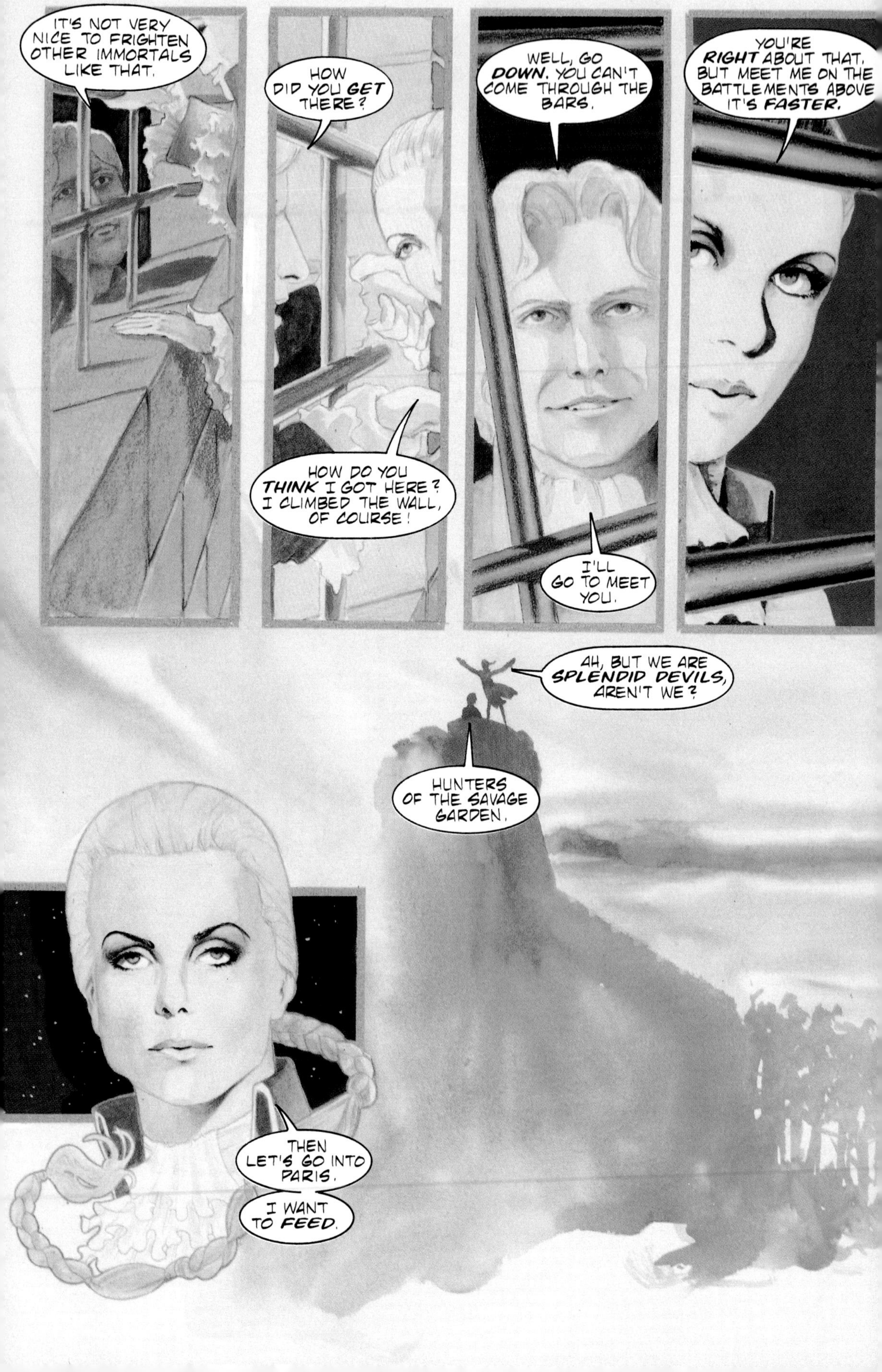
IT'S NOT VERY NICE TO FRIGHTEN OTHER IMMORTALS LIKE THAT.
HOW DID YOU GET THERE?
HOW DO YOU THINK I GOT HERE? I CLIMBED THE WALL, OF COURSE!
WELL, GO DOWN. YOU CAN'T COME THROUGH THE BARS.
I'LL GO TO MEET YOU.
YOU'RE RIGHT ABOUT THAT. BUT MEET ME ON THE BATTLEMENTS ABOVE IT'S FASTER.
AH, BUT WE ARE SPLENDID DEVILS, AREN'T WE?
HUNTERS OF THE SAVAGE GARDEN.
THEN LET'S GO INTO PARIS.
I WANT TO FEED.

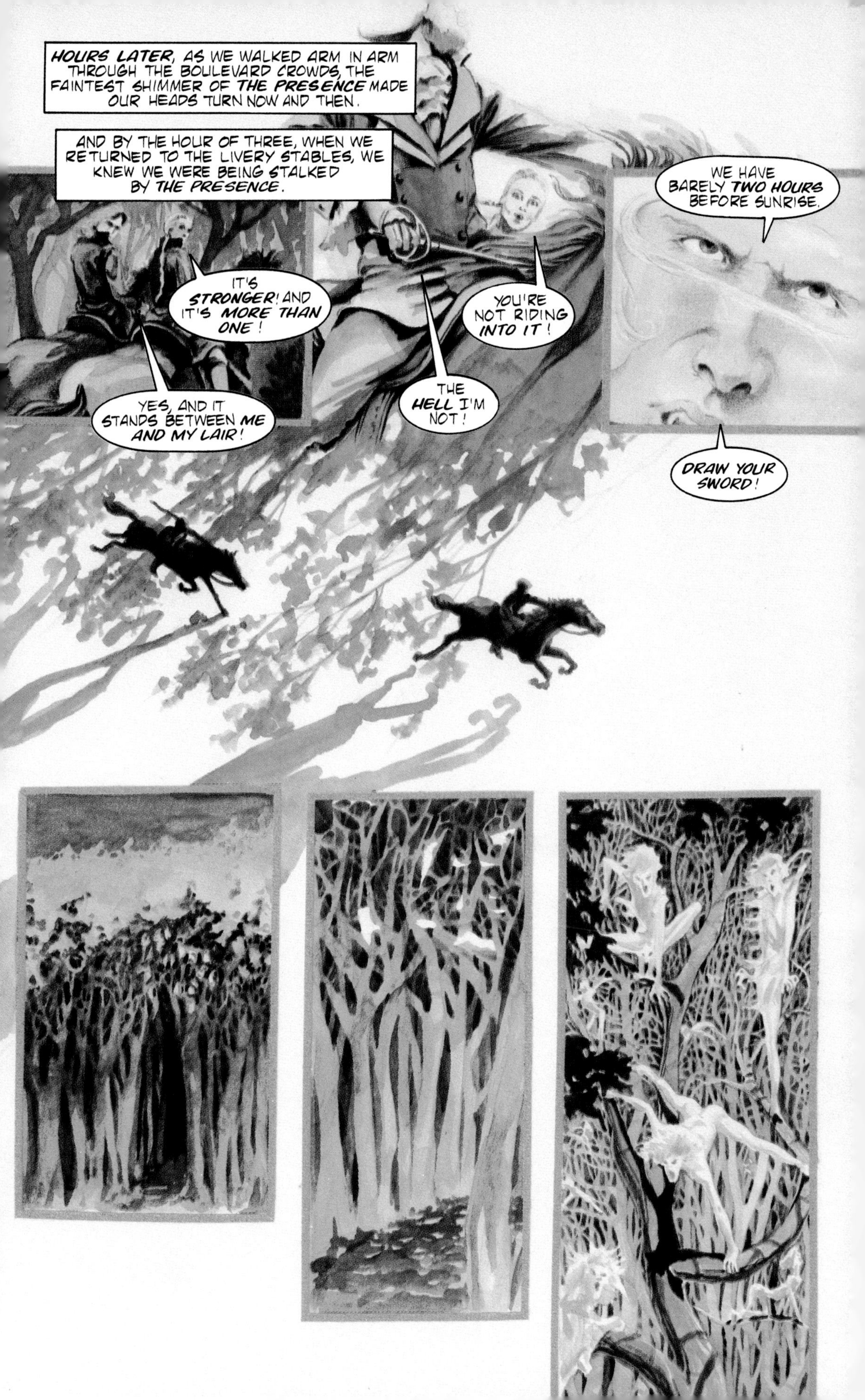
HOURS LATER, AS WE WALKED ARM IN ARM THROUGH THE BOULEVARD CROWDS, THE FAINTEST SHIMMER OF THE PRESENCE MADE OUR HEADS TURN NOW AND THEN.
AND BY THE HOUR OF THREE, WHEN WE RETURNED TO THE LIVERY STABLES, WE KNEW WE WERE BEING STALKED BY THE PRESENCE.
IT'S STRONGER! AND IT'S MORE THAN ONE!
YES, AND IT STANDS BETWEEN ME AND MY LAIR!
YOU'RE NOT RIDING INTO IT!
THE HELL I'M NOT!
WE HAVE BARELY TWO HOURS BEFORE SUNRISE.
DRAW YOUR SWORD!

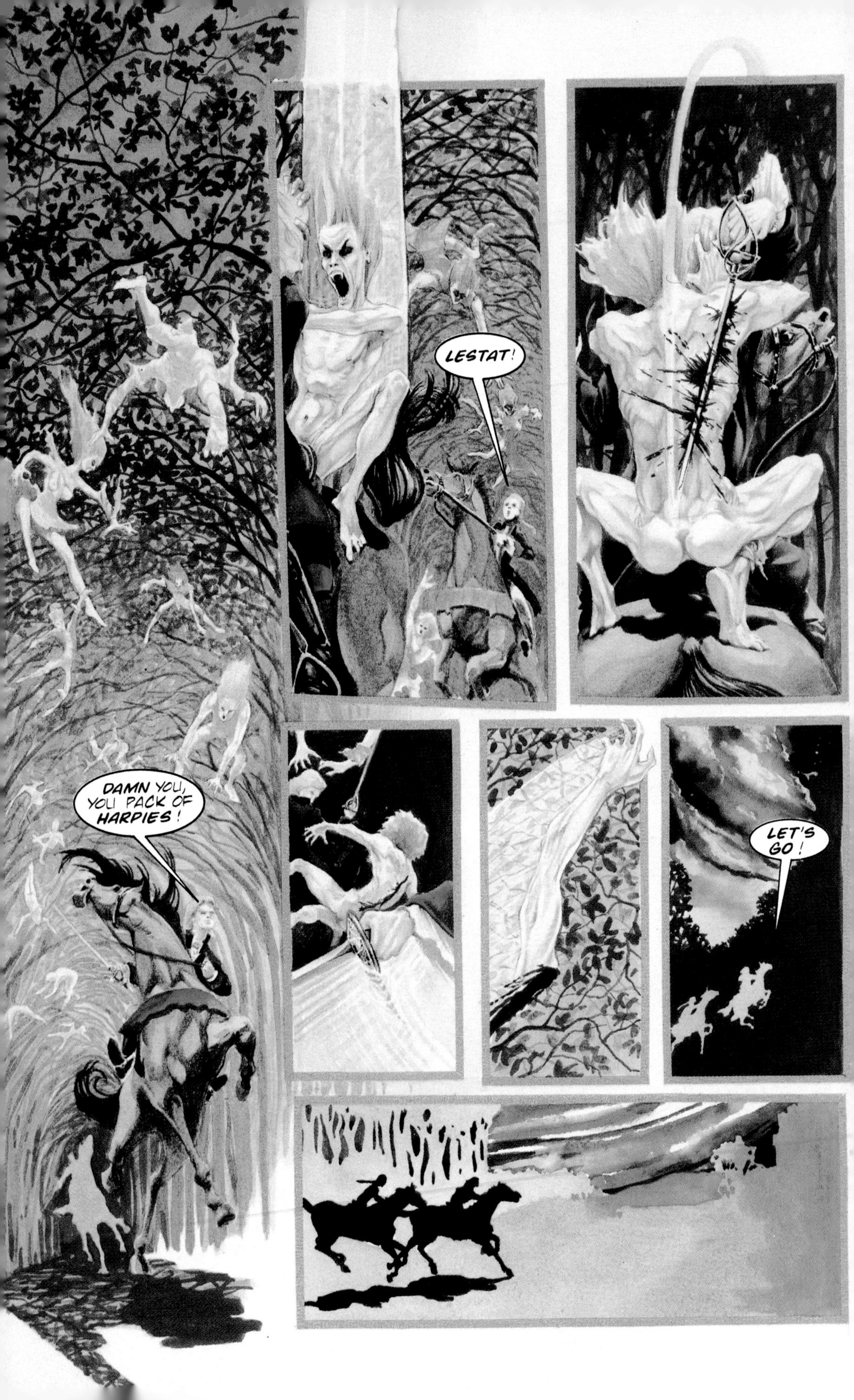
DAMN YOU, YOU PACK OF HARPIES!
LESTAT!
LET'S GO!

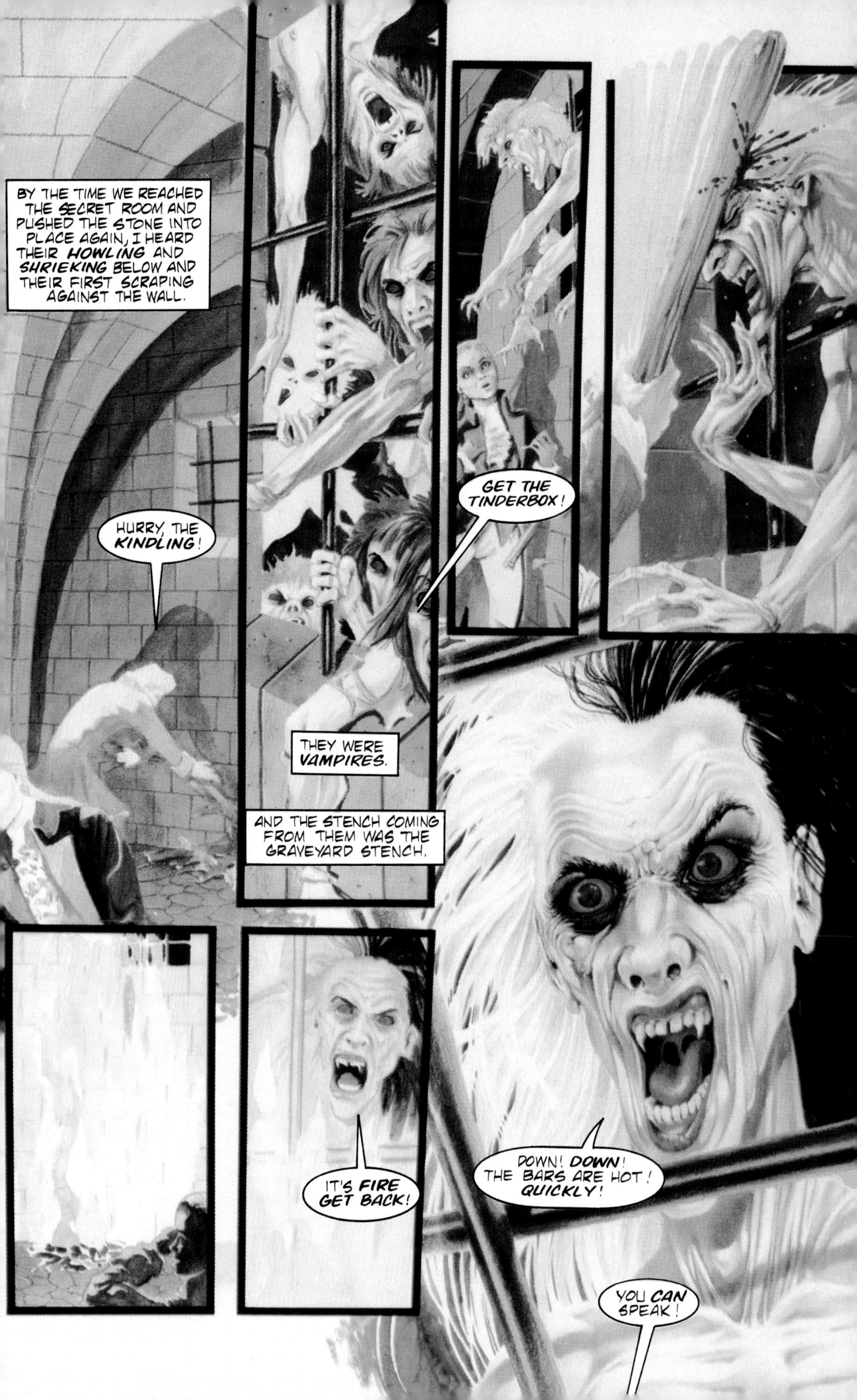
BY THE TIME WE REACHED THE SECRET ROOM AND PUSHED THE STONE INTO PLACE AGAIN, I HEARD THEIR HOWLING AND SHRIEKING BELOW AND THEIR FIRST SCRAPING AGAINST THE WALL.
HURRY, THE KINDLING!
GET THE TINDERBOX!
THEY WERE VAMPIRES.
AND THE STENCH COMING FROM THEM WAS THE GRAVEYARD STENCH.
IT'S FIRE GET BACK!
DOWN! DOWN! THE BARS ARE HOT! QUICKLY!
YOU CAN SPEAK!

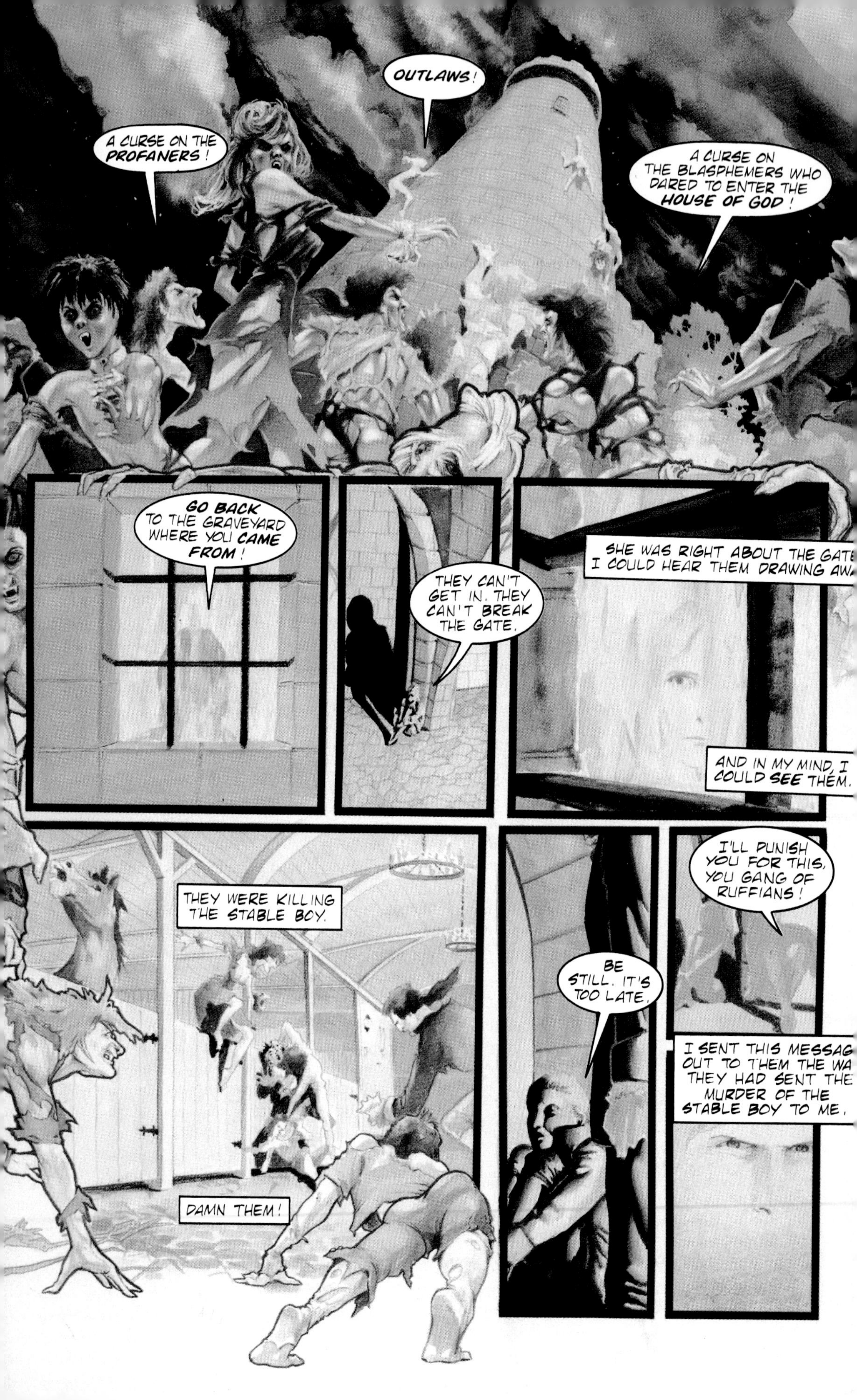
A CURSE ON THE PROFANERS!
OUTLAWS!
A CURSE ON THE BLASPHEMERS WHO DARED TO ENTER THE HOUSE OF GOD!
GO BACK TO THE GRAVEYARD WHERE YOU CAME FROM!
THEY CAN'T GET IN. THEY CAN'T BREAK THE GATE.
SHE WAS RIGHT ABOUT THE GATE
I COULD HEAR THEM DRAWING AWA
AND IN MY MIND, I COULD SEE THEM.
THEY WERE KILLING THE STABLE BOY.
DAMN THEM!
BE STILL. IT'S TOO LATE.
I'LL PUNISH YOU FOR THIS, YOU GANG OF RUFFIANS!
I SENT THIS MESSAG OUT TO THEM THE WA THEY HAD SENT THE MURDER OF THE STABLE BOY TO ME.

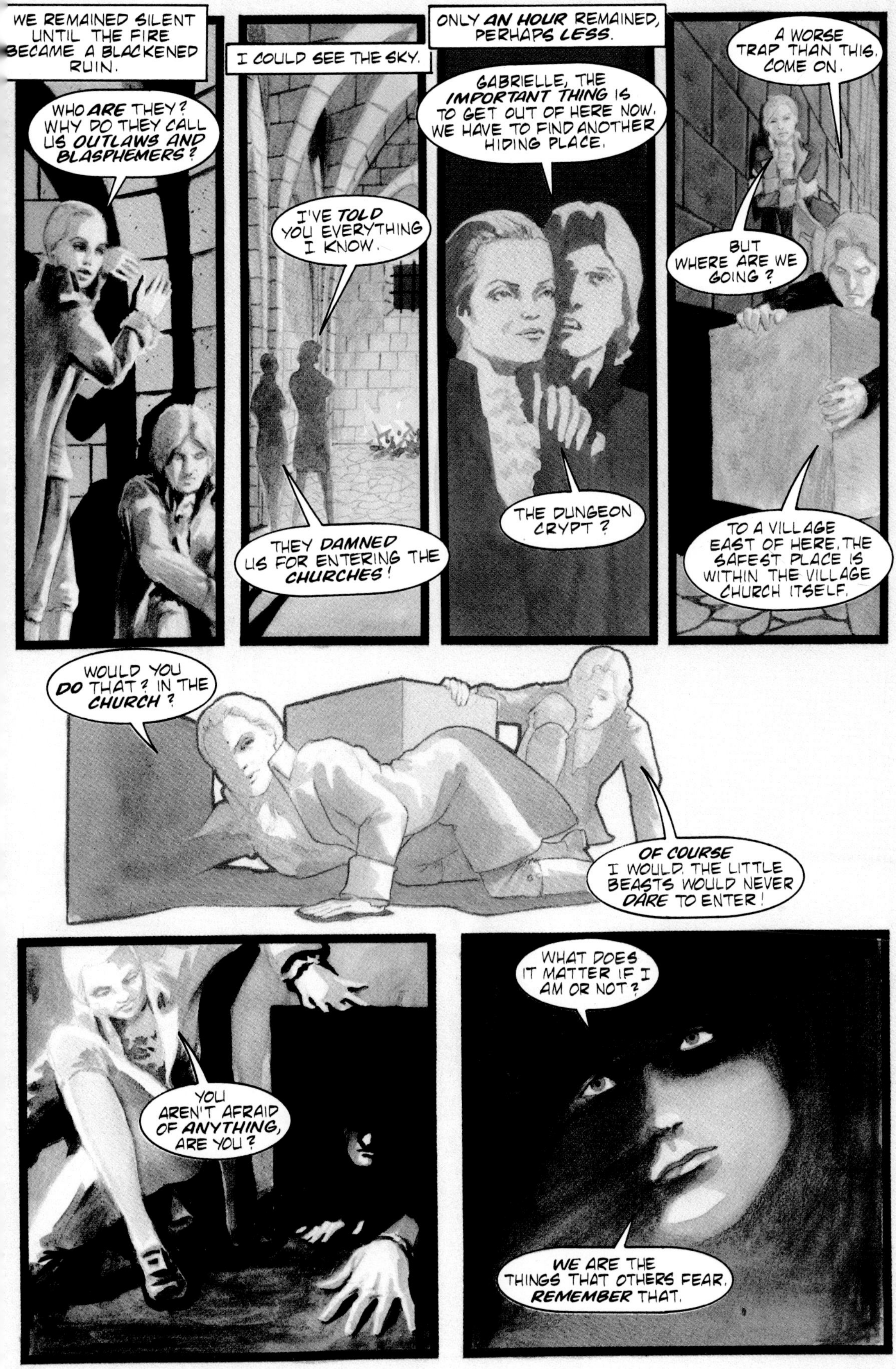
WE REMAINED SILENT UNTIL THE FIRE BECAME A BLACKENED RUIN.
WHO ARE THEY? WHY DO THEY CALL US OUTLAWS AND BLASPHEMERS?
I COULD SEE THE SKY.
I'VE TOLD YOU EVERYTHING I KNOW.
THEY DAMNED US FOR ENTERING THE CHURCHES!
ONLY AN HOUR REMAINED, PERHAPS LESS.
GABRIELLE, THE IMPORTANT THING IS TO GET OUT OF HERE NOW. WE HAVE TO FIND ANOTHER HIDING PLACE.
THE DUNGEON CRYPT?
A WORSE TRAP THAN THIS. COME ON.
BUT WHERE ARE WE GOING?
TO A VILLAGE EAST OF HERE. THE SAFEST PLACE IS WITHIN THE VILLAGE CHURCH ITSELF.
WOULD YOU DO THAT? IN THE CHURCH?
OF COURSE I WOULD. THE LITTLE BEASTS WOULD NEVER DARE TO ENTER!
YOU AREN'T AFRAID OF ANYTHING, ARE YOU?
WHAT DOES IT MATTER IF I AM OR NOT?
WE ARE THE THINGS THAT OTHERS FEAR. REMEMBER THAT.

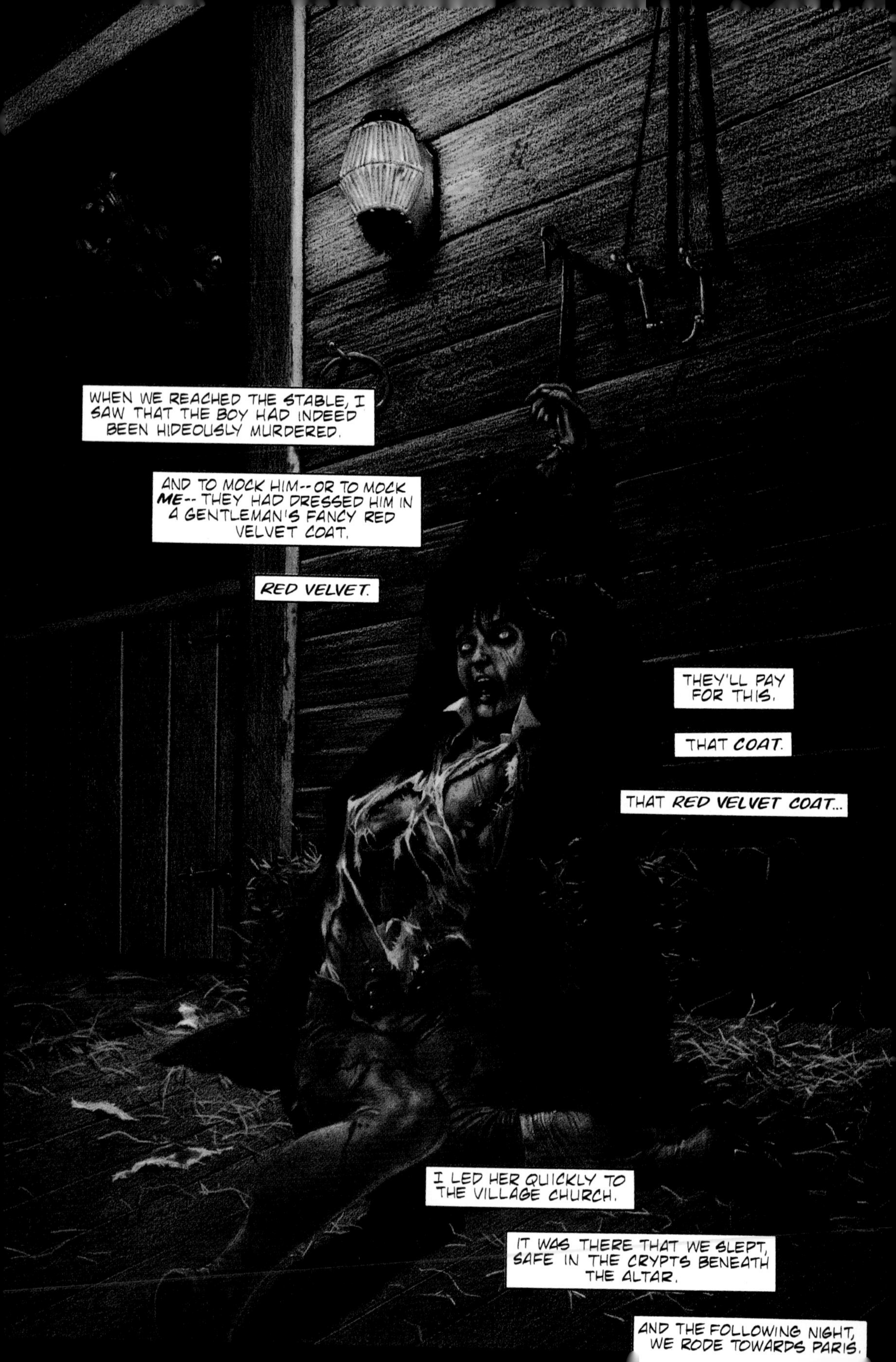

WHEN WE REACHED THE STABLE, I SAW THAT THE BOY HAD INDEED BEEN HIDEOUSLY MURDERED.
AND TO MOCK HIM--OR TO MOCK ME-- THEY HAD DRESSED HIM IN A GENTLEMAN'S FANCY RED VELVET COAT.
RED VELVET.
THEY'LL PAY FOR THIS.
THAT COAT.
THAT RED VELVET COAT...
I LED HER QUICKLY TO THE VILLAGE CHURCH.
IT WAS THERE THAT WE SLEPT, SAFE IN THE CRYPTS BENEATH THE ALTAR.
AND THE FOLLOWING NIGHT, WE RODE TOWARDS PARIS.

WE MUST GO INTO PARIS TO FACE THESE LITTLE BEASTS HEAD-ON. THERE ARE THINGS I MUST DO.
I HAVE TO THINK ABOUT NICKI AND TALK TO ROGET.
THIS ISN'T THE TIME FOR THAT MORTAL NONSENSE.
I WON'T HAVE THEM COME BETWEEN ME AND WHAT I MEAN TO DO.
DO YOU WANT TO LEAD THESE CREATURES TO YOUR BELOVED MONSIEUR ROGET?
ALL RIGHT! NOTHING CAN BE DONE UNTIL THIS IS FINISHED!
INJURY ONLY SPURS YOU ON, DOESN'T IT? IT WOULD ONLY STRENGTHEN YOU, WHATEVER THEY DO.
NOW THIS IS WHAT I CALL MORTAL NONSENSE!
LESTAT, THEY PUT YOUR STABLE BOY IN A FROCK COAT AFTER THEY KILLED HIM.
DID YOU SEE IT? HAVEN'T YOU SEEN IT BEFORE?
THAT DAMNED RED VELVET COAT...
I HAVE SEEN IT. I LOOKED AT IT FOR HOURS AT MY BEDSIDE IN PARIS.
IT WAS NICOLAS DE LENFENT'S COAT.
"I'M GOING AFTER THEM."

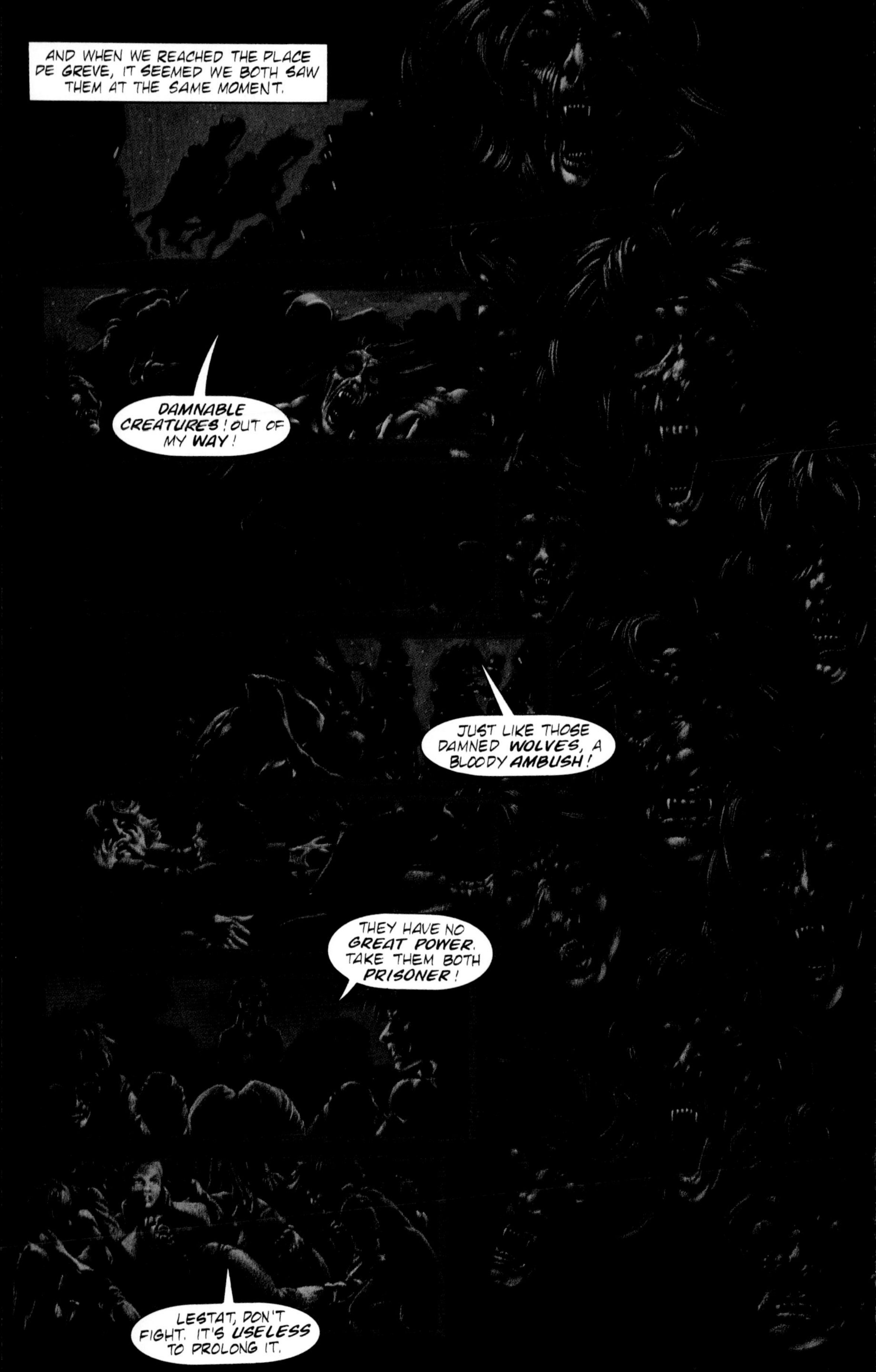
AND WHEN WE REACHED THE PLACE DE GREVE, IT SEEMED WE BOTH SAW THEM AT THE SAME MOMENT.
DAMNABLE CREATURES! OUT OF MY WAY!
JUST LIKE THOSE DAMNED WOLVES, A BLOODY AMBUSH!
THEY HAVE NO GREAT POWER. TAKE THEM BOTH PRISONER!
LESTAT, DON'T FIGHT. IT'S USELESS TO PROLONG IT.

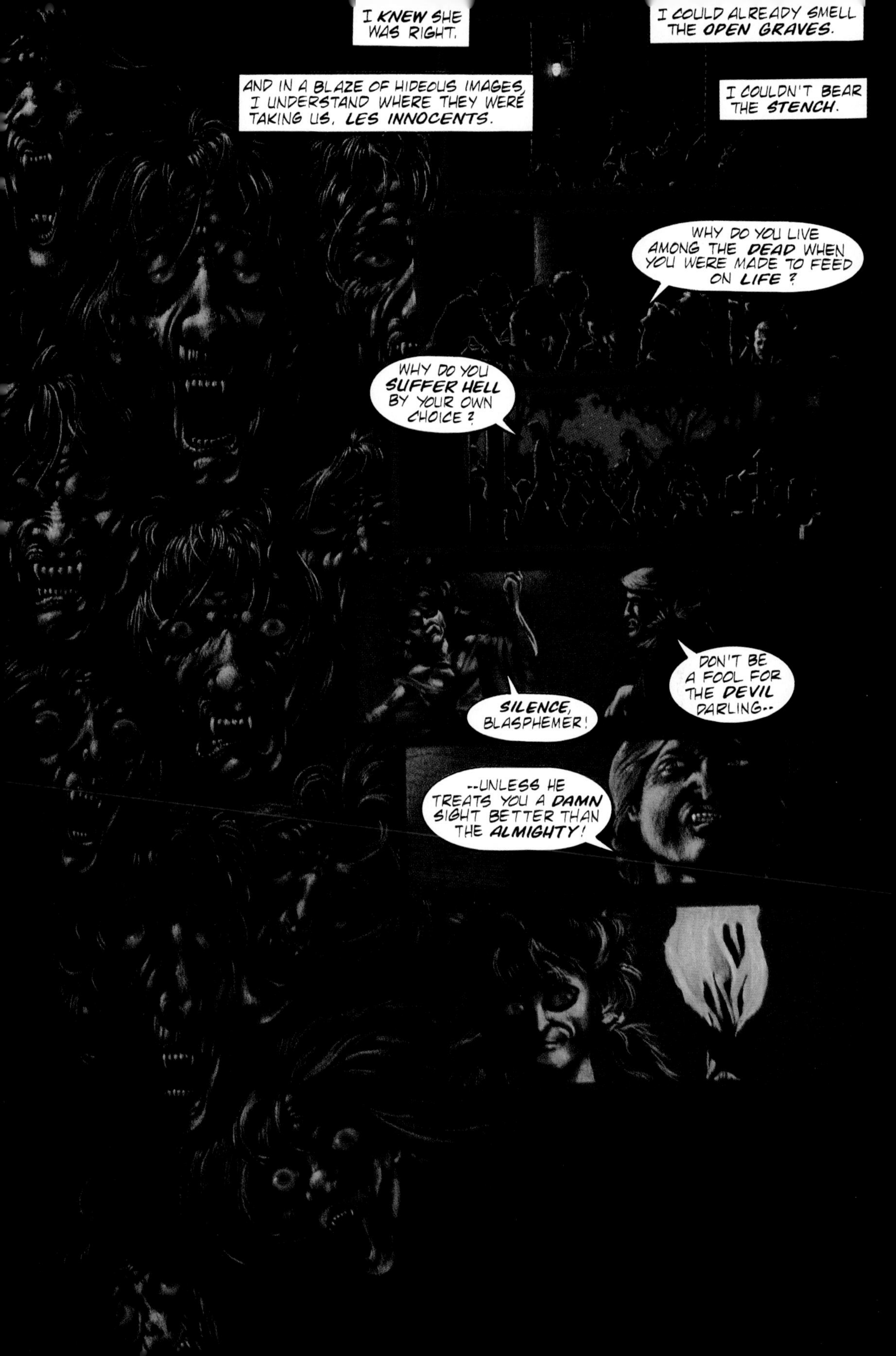
I KNEW SHE WAS RIGHT.
I COULD ALREADY SMELL THE OPEN GRAVES.
AND IN A BLAZE OF HIDEOUS IMAGES, I UNDERSTAND WHERE THEY WERE TAKING US. LES INNOCENTS.
I COULDN'T BEAR THE STENCH.
WHY DO YOU LIVE AMONG THE DEAD WHEN YOU WERE MADE TO FEED ON LIFE ?
WHY DO YOU SUFFER HELL BY YOUR OWN CHOICE ?
DON'T BE A FOOL FOR THE DEVIL DARLING--
SILENCE, BLASPHEMER!
--UNLESS HE TREATS YOU A DAMN SIGHT BETTER THAN THE ALMIGHTY!

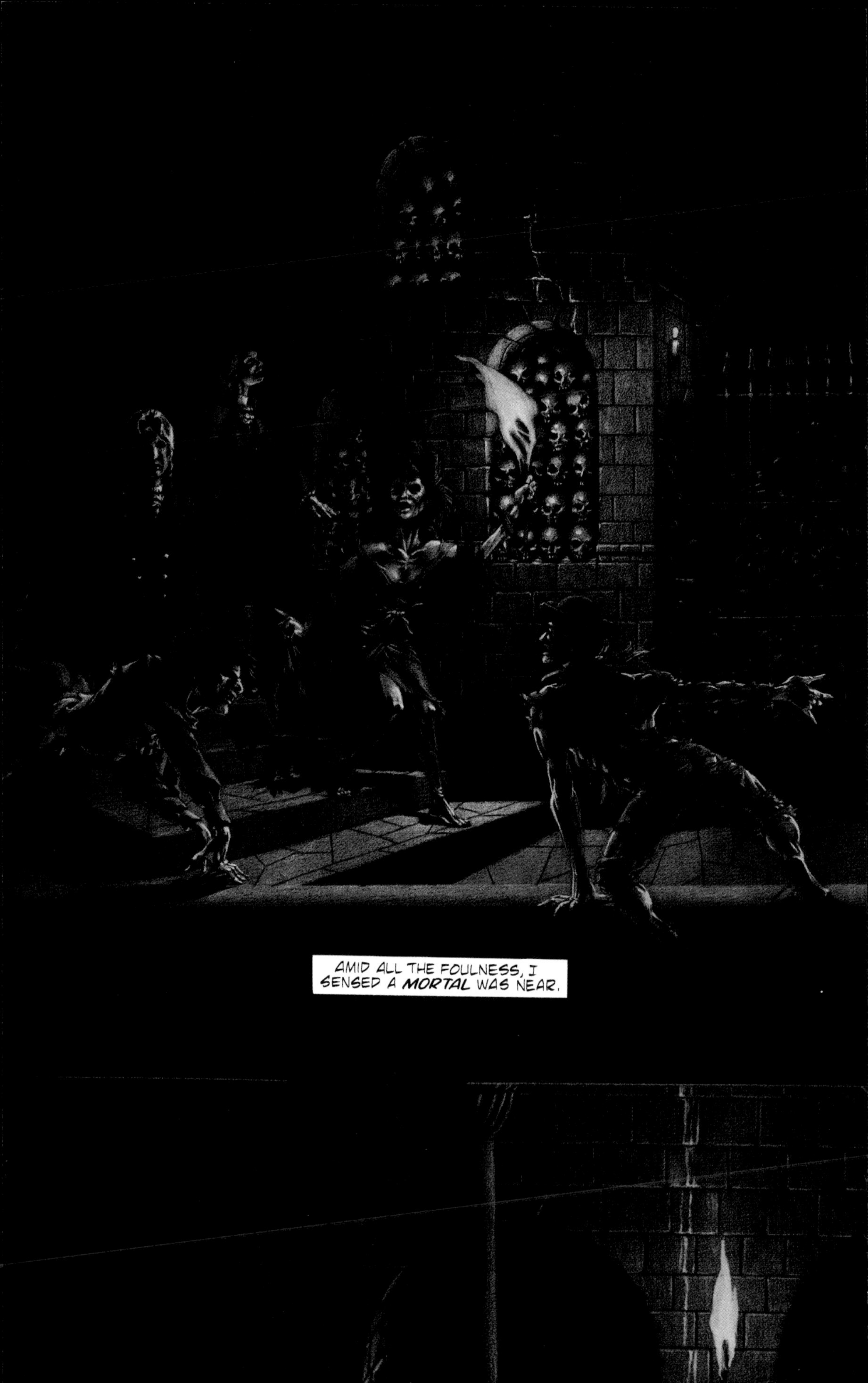
AMID ALL THE FOULNESS, I SENSED A MORTAL WAS NEAR.

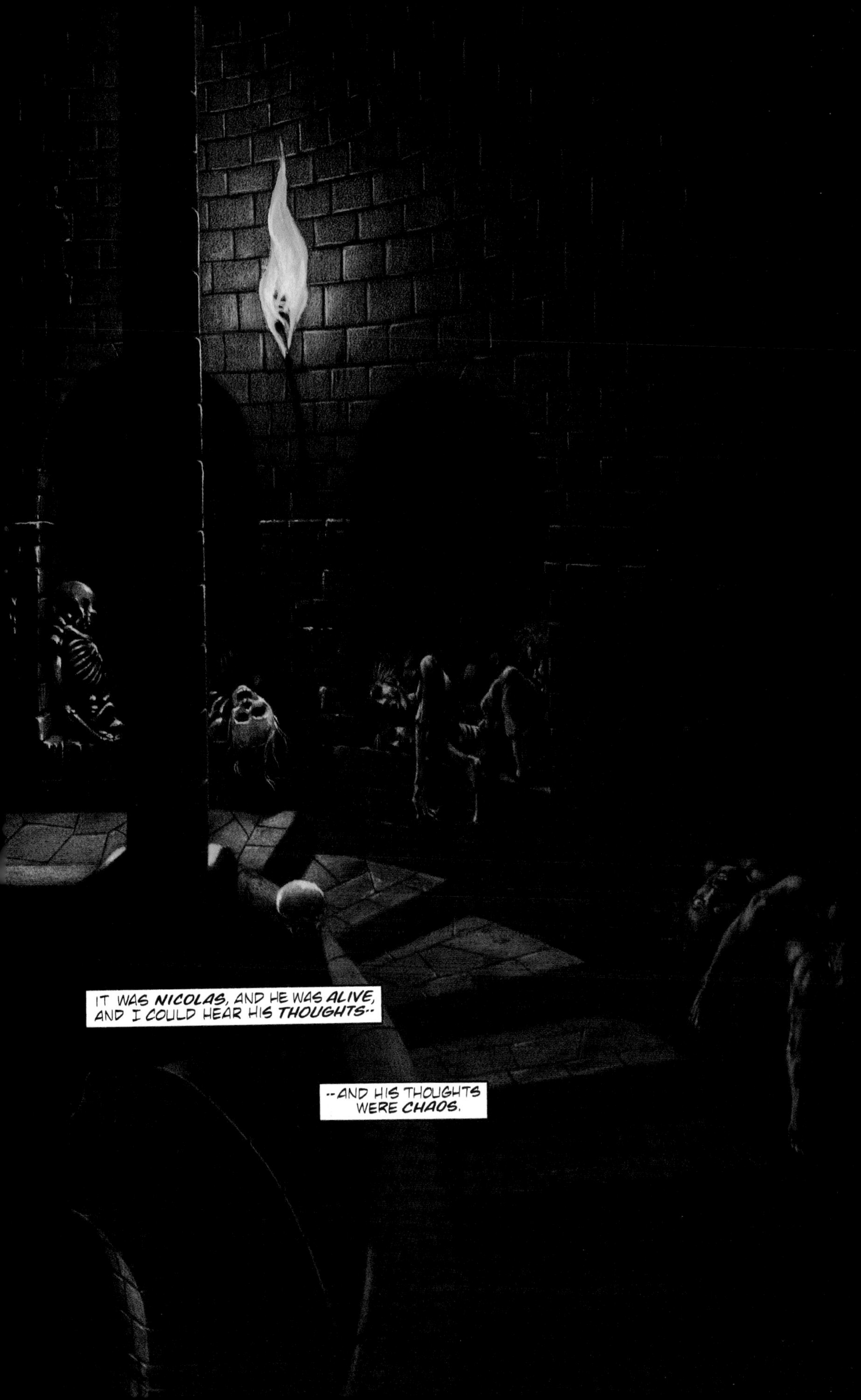
IT WAS NICOLAS, AND HE WAS ALIVE, AND I COULD HEAR HIS THOUGHTS--
--AND HIS THOUGHTS WERE CHAOS.

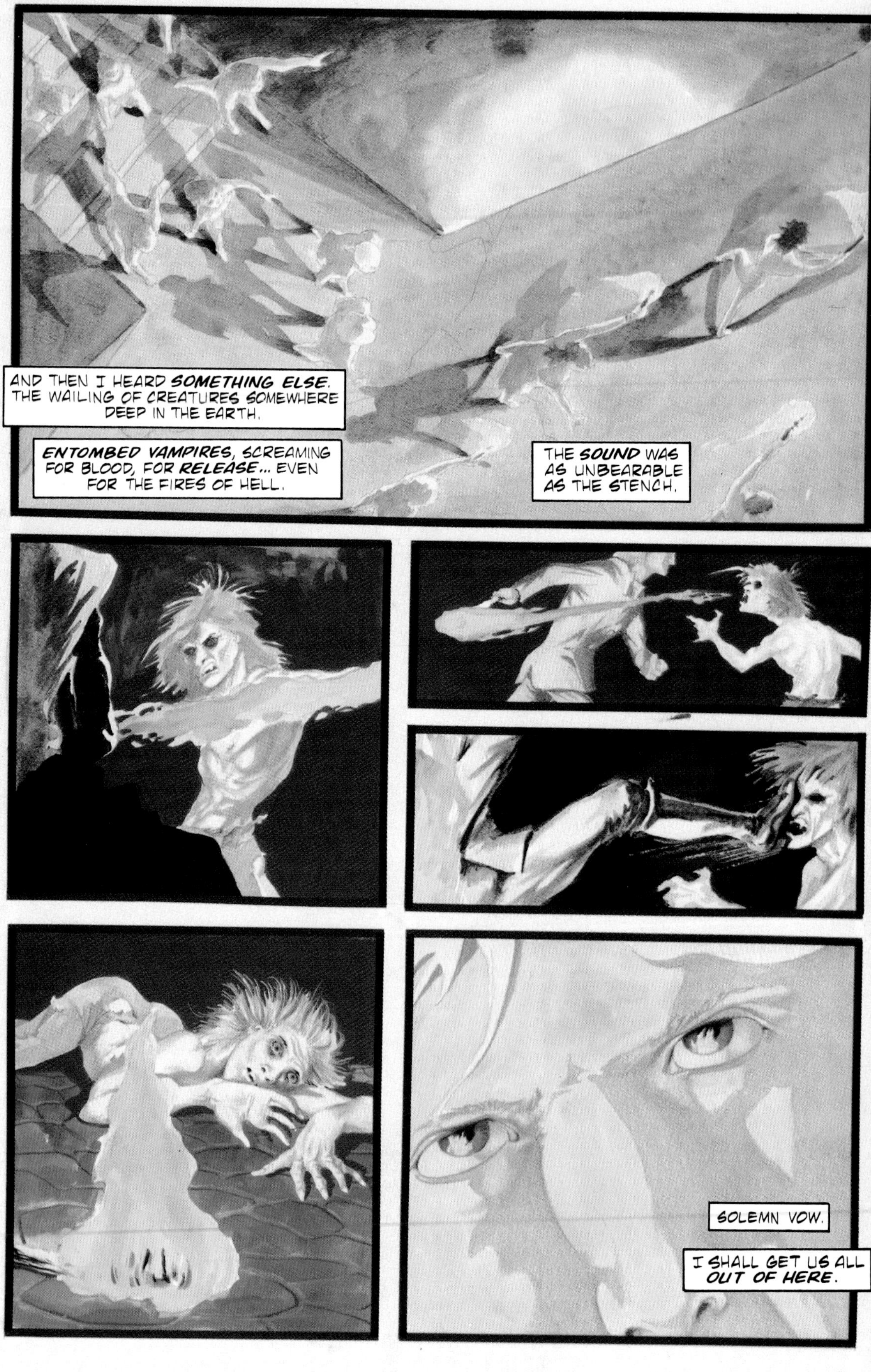
AND THEN I HEARD SOMETHING ELSE. THE WAILING OF CREATURES SOMEWHERE DEEP IN THE EARTH.
ENTOMBED VAMPIRES, SCREAMING FOR BLOOD, FOR RELEASE... EVEN FOR THE FIRES OF HELL.
THE SOUND WAS AS UNBEARABLE AS THE STENCH.
SOLEMN VOW.
I SHALL GET US ALL OUT OF HERE.

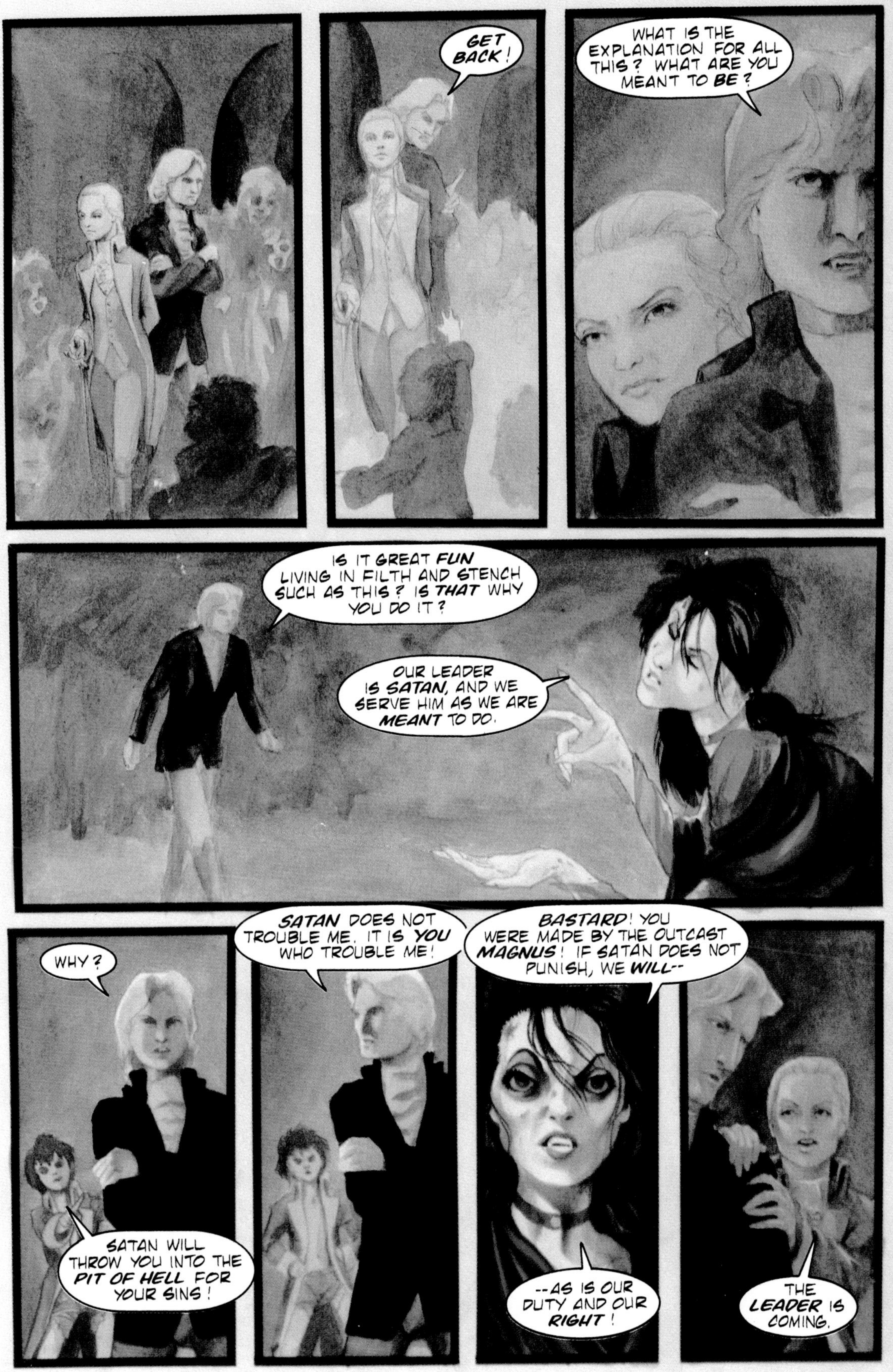
GET BACK!
WHAT IS THE EXPLANATION FOR ALL THIS? WHAT ARE YOU MEANT TO BE?
IS IT GREAT FUN LIVING IN FILTH AND STENCH SUCH AS THIS? IS THAT WHY YOU DO IT?
OUR LEADER IS SATAN, AND WE SERVE HIM AS WE ARE MEANT TO DO.
WHY?
SATAN WILL THROW YOU INTO THE PIT OF HELL FOR YOUR SINS!
SATAN DOES NOT TROUBLE ME. IT IS YOU WHO TROUBLE ME!
BASTARD! YOU WERE MADE BY THE OUTCAST MAGNUS! IF SATAN DOES NOT PUNISH, WE WILL--
--AS IS OUR DUTY AND OUR RIGHT!
THE LEADER IS COMING.

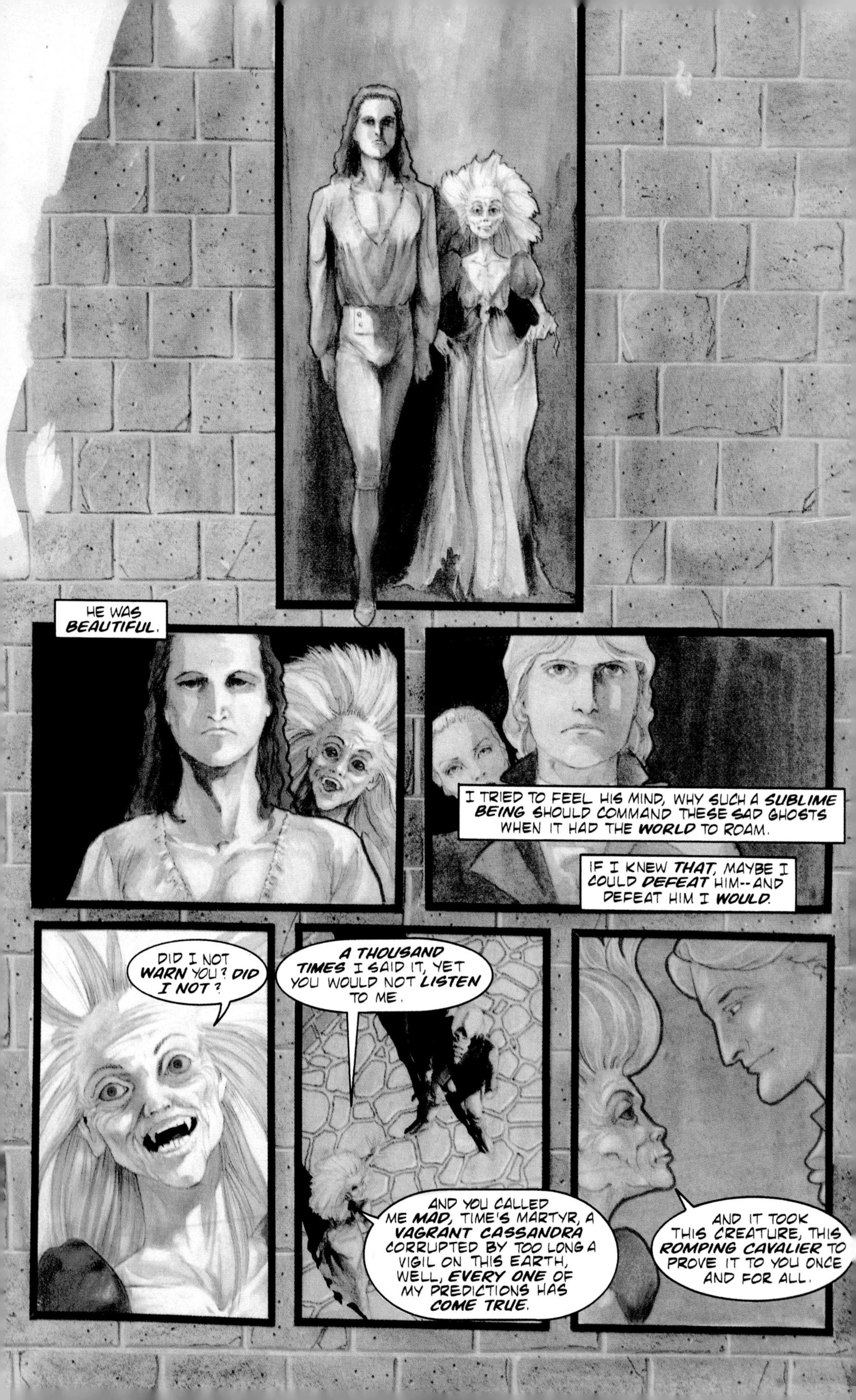

HE WAS BEAUTIFUL.
I TRIED TO FEEL HIS MIND, WHY SUCH A SUBLIME BEING SHOULD COMMAND THESE SAD GHOSTS WHEN IT HAD THE WORLD TO ROAM.
IF I KNEW THAT, MAYBE I COULD DEFEAT HIM--AND DEFEAT HIM I WOULD.
DID I NOT WARN YOU? DID I NOT?
A THOUSAND TIMES I SAID IT, YET YOU WOULD NOT LISTEN TO ME.
AND YOU CALLED ME MAD, TIME'S MARTYR, A VAGRANT CASSANDRA CORRUPTED BY TOO LONG A VIGIL ON THIS EARTH. WELL, EVERY ONE OF MY PREDICTIONS HAS COME TRUE.
AND IT TOOK THIS CREATURE, THIS ROMPING CAVALIER TO PROVE IT TO YOU ONCE AND FOR ALL.

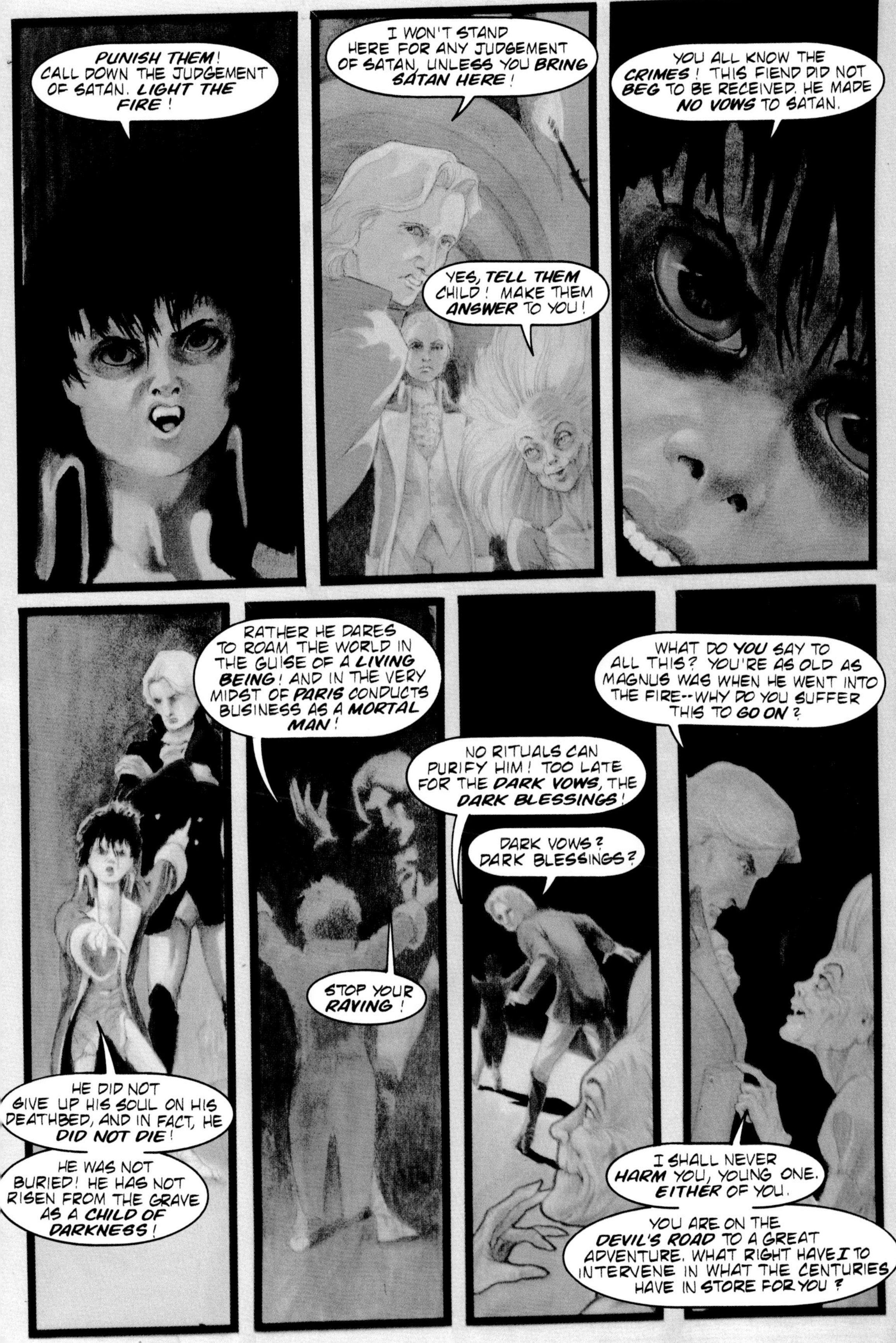
PUNISH THEM! CALL DOWN THE JUDGEMENT OF SATAN. LIGHT THE FIRE!
I WON'T STAND HERE FOR ANY JUDGEMENT OF SATAN, UNLESS YOU BRING SATAN HERE!
YES, TELL THEM CHILD! MAKE THEM ANSWER TO YOU!
YOU ALL KNOW THE CRIMES! THIS FIEND DID NOT BEG TO BE RECEIVED. HE MADE NO VOWS TO SATAN.
HE DID NOT GIVE UP HIS SOUL ON HIS DEATHBED, AND IN FACT, HE DID NOT DIE!
HE WAS NOT BURIED! HE HAS NOT RISEN FROM THE GRAVE AS A CHILD OF DARKNESS!
RATHER HE DARES TO ROAM THE WORLD IN THE GUISE OF A LIVING BEING! AND IN THE VERY MIDST OF PARIS CONDUCTS BUSINESS AS A MORTAL MAN!
STOP YOUR RAVING!
NO RITUALS CAN PURIFY HIM! TOO LATE FOR THE DARK VOWS, THE DARK BLESSINGS!
DARK VOWS? DARK BLESSINGS?
WHAT DO YOU SAY TO ALL THIS? YOU'RE AS OLD AS MAGNUS WAS WHEN HE WENT INTO THE FIRE--WHY DO YOU SUFFER THIS TO GO ON?
I SHALL NEVER HARM YOU, YOUNG ONE. EITHER OF YOU.
YOU ARE ON THE DEVIL'S ROAD TO A GREAT ADVENTURE. WHAT RIGHT HAVE I TO INTERVENE IN WHAT THE CENTURIES HAVE IN STORE FOR YOU?

THE DEVIL'S ROAD.

SHOW IT TO ME, CHILD, THE **STRENGTH** MAGNUS GAVE YOU. DO YOU KNOW WHAT IT MEANS TO BE MADE A VAMPIRE BY ONE THAT **POWERFUL**, WHO HAS NEVER GIVEN THE GIFT BEFORE?

IT'S FORBIDDEN HERE, CHILD, *NO ONE* OF SUCH AGE CONVEYS HIS POWER!

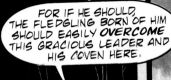

FOR IF HE SHOULD, THE FLEDGLING BORN OF HIM SHOULD EASILY **OVERCOME** THIS GRACIOUS LEADER AND HIS COVEN HERE.

STOP THIS NONSENSE!

WHAT HAPPENED IN THE **GREAT CATHEDRAL** WHEN YOU ENTERED IT? TELL ME NOW!

ABSOLUTELY **NOTHING**, MADAME!

AH, BUT IT IS **TOO** SUBLIME!

DISPENSE WITH THE TRIAL, LIGHT THE PYRE **NOW**!

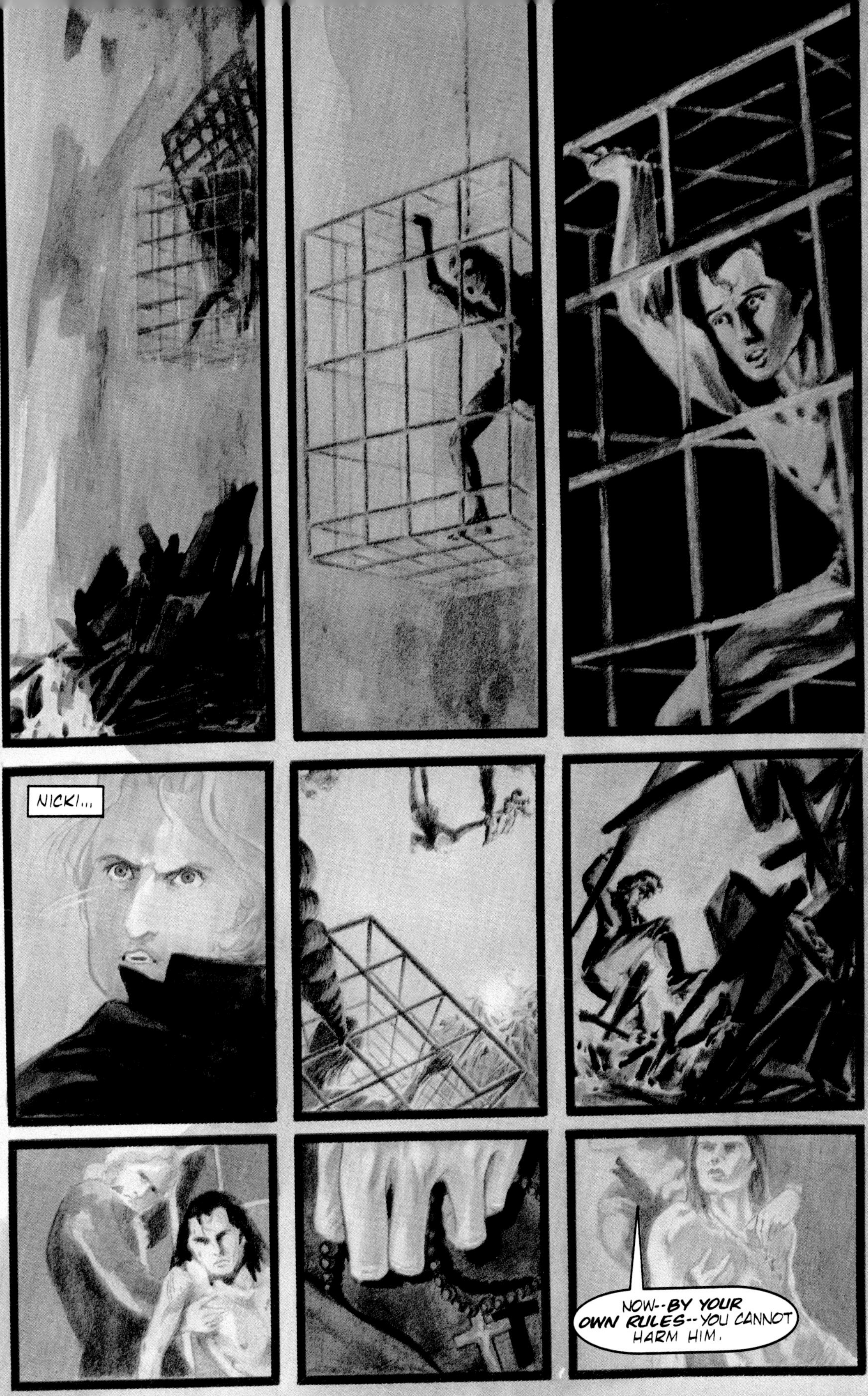
NICKI...
NOW--BY YOUR OWN RULES--YOU CANNOT HARM HIM.

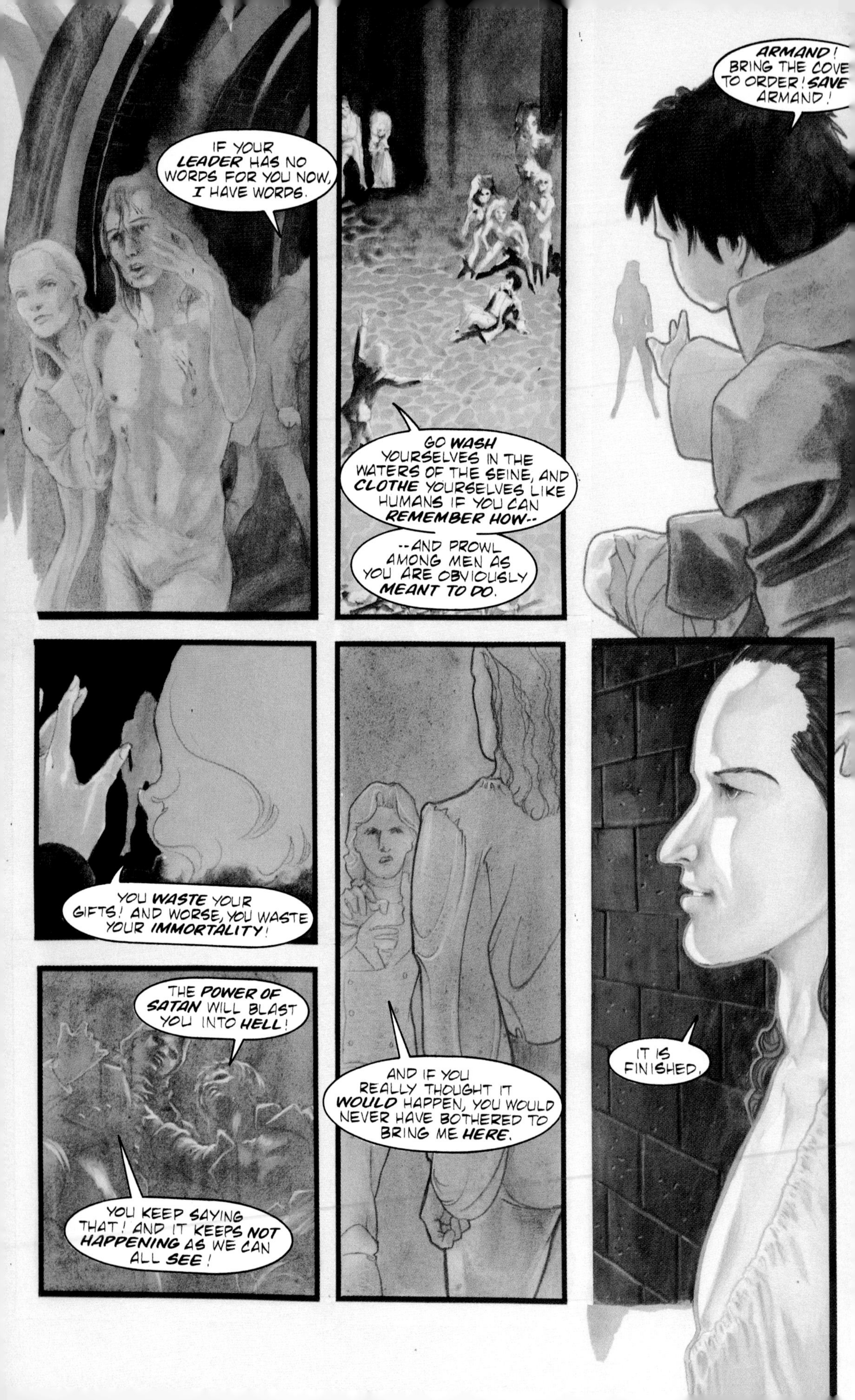
IF YOUR LEADER HAS NO WORDS FOR YOU NOW, I HAVE WORDS.
GO WASH YOURSELVES IN THE WATERS OF THE SEINE, AND CLOTHE YOURSELVES LIKE HUMANS IF YOU CAN REMEMBER HOW--
--AND PROWL AMONG MEN AS YOU ARE OBVIOUSLY MEANT TO DO.
ARMAND! BRING THE COVE TO ORDER! SAVE ARMAND!
YOU WASTE YOUR GIFTS! AND WORSE, YOU WASTE YOUR IMMORTALITY!
THE POWER OF SATAN WILL BLAST YOU INTO HELL!
YOU KEEP SAYING THAT! AND IT KEEPS NOT HAPPENING AS WE CAN ALL SEE!
AND IF YOU REALLY THOUGHT IT WOULD HAPPEN, YOU WOULD NEVER HAVE BOTHERED TO BRING ME HERE.
IT IS FINISHED.

GO NOW--ALL OF YOU. IT IS AT AN END.

ARMAND, NO!

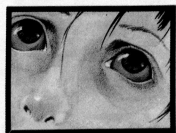

ARMAND? MAY I ADDRESS YOU IN THIS WAY?

YOU ARE OBVIOUSLY THE LEADER. AND YOU ARE THE ONE WHO CAN EXPLAIN ALL THIS TO US.

ARMAND, WHAT IS THE MEANING OF ALL THIS?

YOU TURN TO ME FOR EXPLANATIONS?

I COULD SPEAK UNTIL THE END OF THE WORLD, AND I COULD NEVER TELL YOU WHAT YOU HAVE DESTROYED HERE,

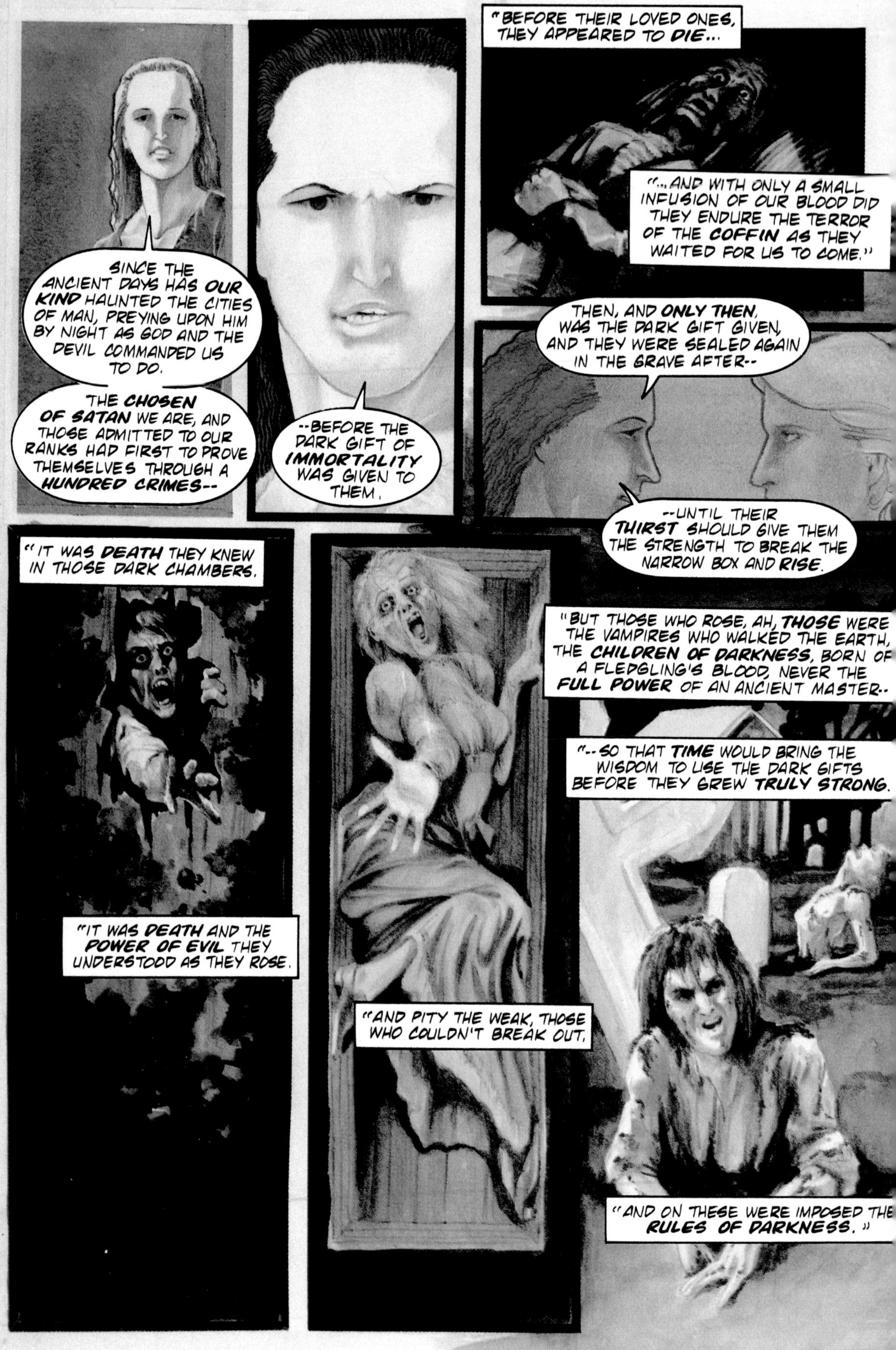
SINCE THE ANCIENT DAYS HAS OUR KIND HAUNTED THE CITIES OF MAN, PREYING UPON HIM BY NIGHT AS GOD AND THE DEVIL COMMANDED US TO DO.
THE CHOSEN OF SATAN WE ARE, AND THOSE ADMITTED TO OUR RANKS HAD FIRST TO PROVE THEMSELVES THROUGH A HUNDRED CRIMES--
--BEFORE THE DARK GIFT OF IMMORTALITY WAS GIVEN TO THEM.
"BEFORE THEIR LOVED ONES, THEY APPEARED TO DIE...
"...AND WITH ONLY A SMALL INFUSION OF OUR BLOOD DID THEY ENDURE THE TERROR OF THE COFFIN AS THEY WAITED FOR US TO COME."
THEN, AND ONLY THEN, WAS THE DARK GIFT GIVEN, AND THEY WERE SEALED AGAIN IN THE GRAVE AFTER--
--UNTIL THEIR THIRST SHOULD GIVE THEM THE STRENGTH TO BREAK THE NARROW BOX AND RISE.
"IT WAS DEATH THEY KNEW IN THOSE DARK CHAMBERS.
"IT WAS DEATH AND THE POWER OF EVIL THEY UNDERSTOOD AS THEY ROSE.
"AND PITY THE WEAK, THOSE WHO COULDN'T BREAK OUT.
"BUT THOSE WHO ROSE, AH, THOSE WERE THE VAMPIRES WHO WALKED THE EARTH, THE CHILDREN OF DARKNESS, BORN OF A FLEDGLING'S BLOOD, NEVER THE FULL POWER OF AN ANCIENT MASTER--
"--SO THAT TIME WOULD BRING THE WISDOM TO USE THE DARK GIFTS BEFORE THEY GREW TRULY STRONG.
"AND ON THESE WERE IMPOSED THE RULES OF DARKNESS."

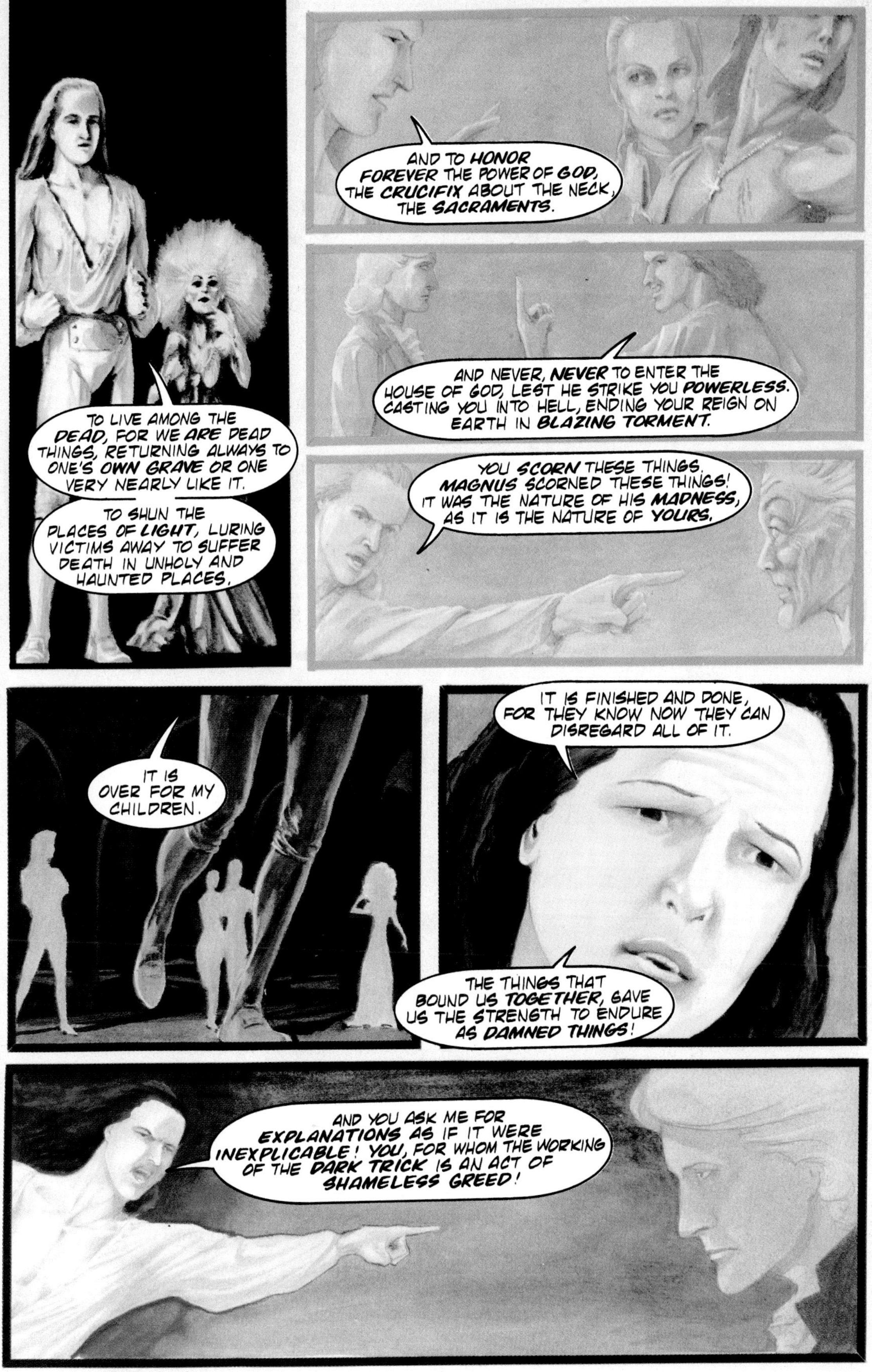
AND TO HONOR FOREVER THE POWER OF GOD, THE CRUCIFIX ABOUT THE NECK, THE SACRAMENTS.
TO LIVE AMONG THE DEAD, FOR WE ARE DEAD THINGS, RETURNING ALWAYS TO ONE'S OWN GRAVE OR ONE VERY NEARLY LIKE IT.
TO SHUN THE PLACES OF LIGHT, LURING VICTIMS AWAY TO SUFFER DEATH IN UNHOLY AND HAUNTED PLACES.
AND NEVER, NEVER TO ENTER THE HOUSE OF GOD, LEST HE STRIKE YOU POWERLESS. CASTING YOU INTO HELL, ENDING YOUR REIGN ON EARTH IN BLAZING TORMENT.
YOU SCORN THESE THINGS. MAGNUS SCORNED THESE THINGS! IT WAS THE NATURE OF HIS MADNESS, AS IT IS THE NATURE OF YOURS.
IT IS OVER FOR MY CHILDREN.
IT IS FINISHED AND DONE, FOR THEY KNOW NOW THEY CAN DISREGARD ALL OF IT.
THE THINGS THAT BOUND US TOGETHER, GAVE US THE STRENGTH TO ENDURE AS DAMNED THINGS!
AND YOU ASK ME FOR EXPLANATIONS AS IF IT WERE INEXPLICABLE! YOU, FOR WHOM THE WORKING OF THE DARK TRICK IS AN ACT OF SHAMELESS GREED!

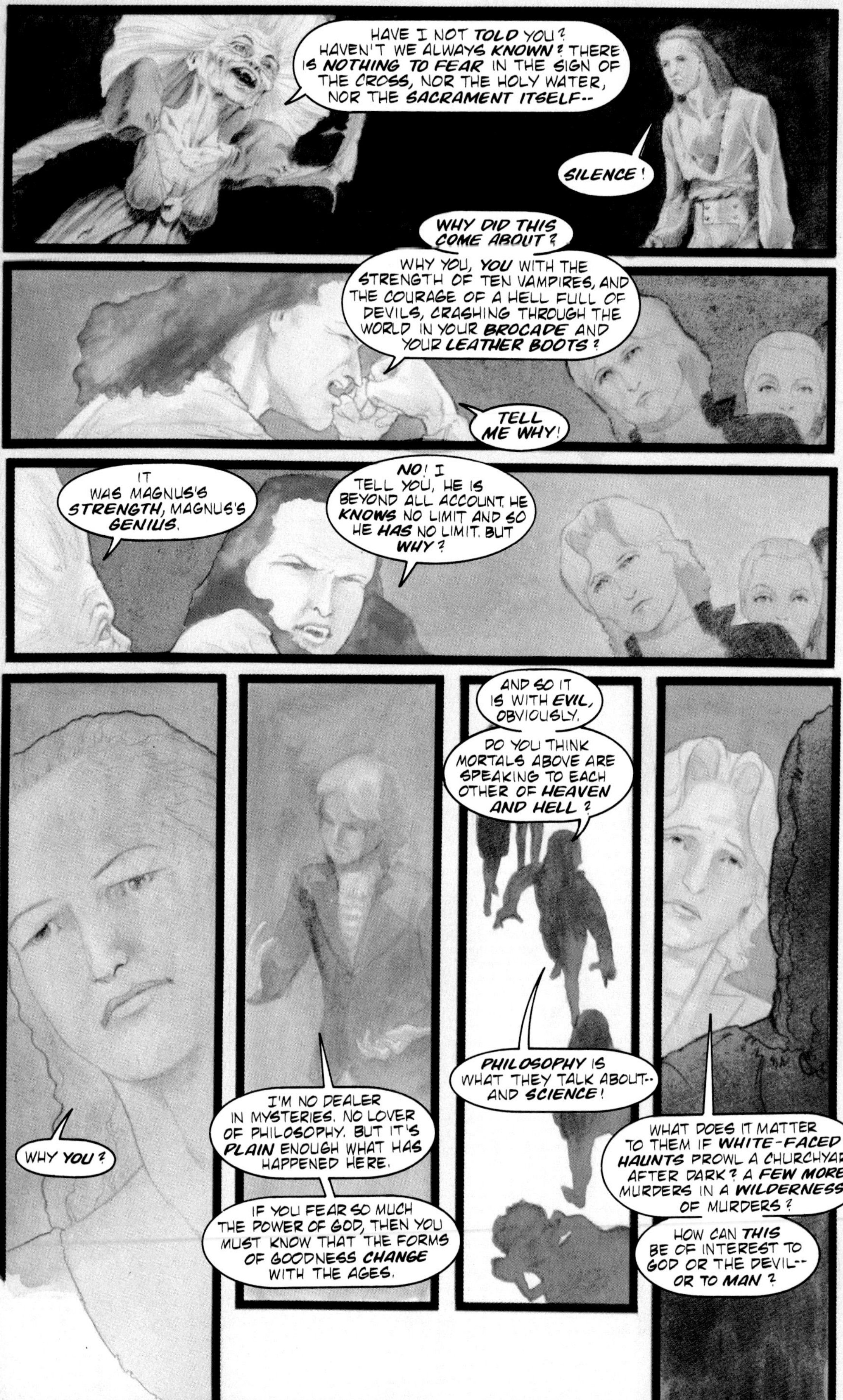
HAVE I NOT TOLD YOU? HAVEN'T WE ALWAYS KNOWN? THERE IS NOTHING TO FEAR IN THE SIGN OF THE CROSS, NOR THE HOLY WATER, NOR THE SACRAMENT ITSELF--
SILENCE!
WHY DID THIS COME ABOUT?
WHY YOU, YOU WITH THE STRENGTH OF TEN VAMPIRES, AND THE COURAGE OF A HELL FULL OF DEVILS, CRASHING THROUGH THE WORLD IN YOUR BROCADE AND YOUR LEATHER BOOTS?
TELL ME WHY!
IT WAS MAGNUS'S STRENGTH, MAGNUS'S GENIUS.
NO! I TELL YOU, HE IS BEYOND ALL ACCOUNT. HE KNOWS NO LIMIT AND SO HE HAS NO LIMIT. BUT WHY?
WHY YOU?
I'M NO DEALER IN MYSTERIES. NO LOVER OF PHILOSOPHY. BUT IT'S PLAIN ENOUGH WHAT HAS HAPPENED HERE.
IF YOU FEAR SO MUCH THE POWER OF GOD, THEN YOU MUST KNOW THAT THE FORMS OF GOODNESS CHANGE WITH THE AGES.
AND SO IT IS WITH EVIL, OBVIOUSLY.
DO YOU THINK MORTALS ABOVE ARE SPEAKING TO EACH OTHER OF HEAVEN AND HELL?
PHILOSOPHY IS WHAT THEY TALK ABOUT-- AND SCIENCE!
WHAT DOES IT MATTER TO THEM IF WHITE-FACED HAUNTS PROWL A CHURCHYARD AFTER DARK? A FEW MORE MURDERS IN A WILDERNESS OF MURDERS?
HOW CAN THIS BE OF INTEREST TO GOD OR THE DEVIL-- OR TO MAN?

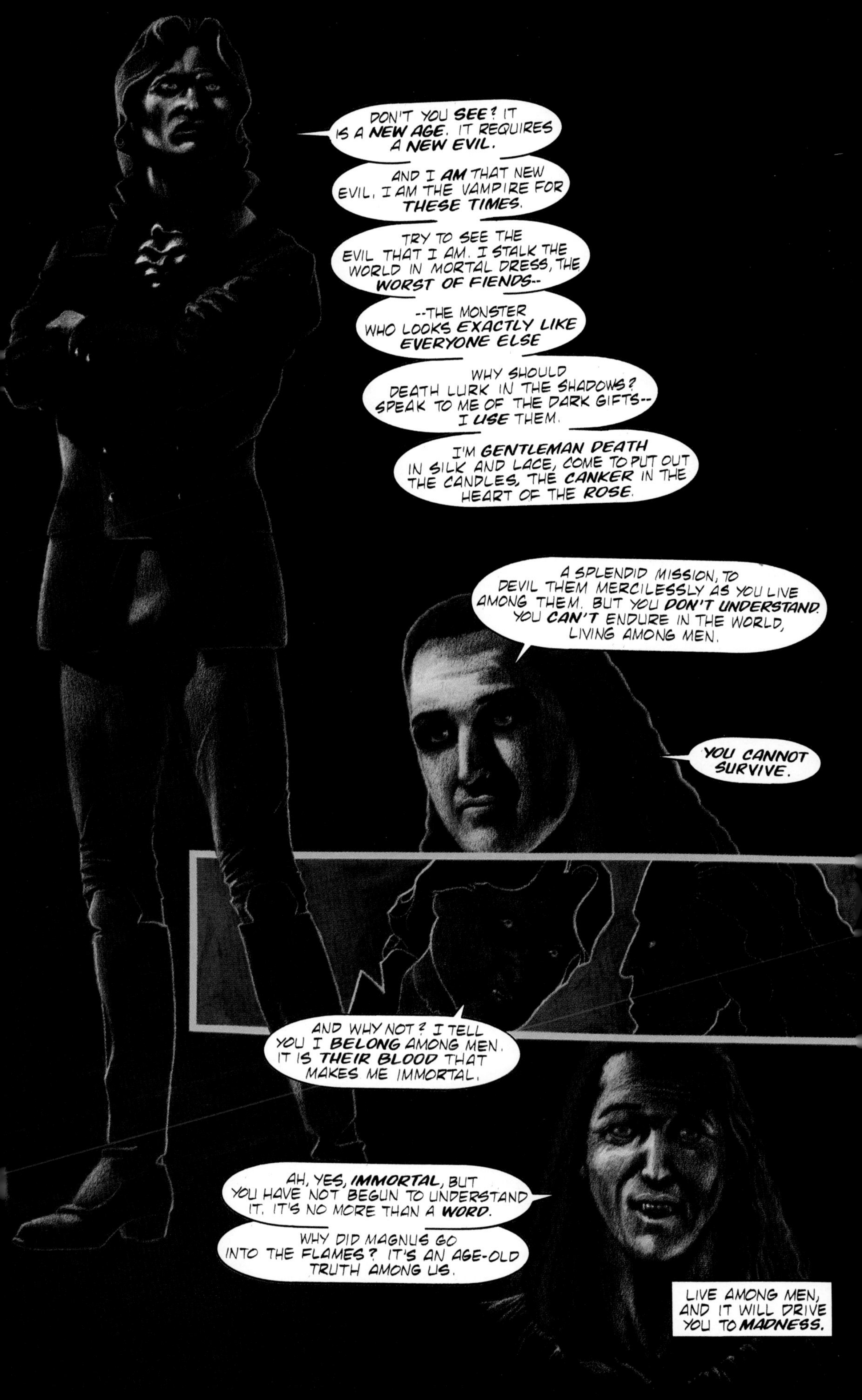
DON'T YOU SEE? IT IS A NEW AGE. IT REQUIRES A NEW EVIL.
AND I AM THAT NEW EVIL. I AM THE VAMPIRE FOR THESE TIMES.
TRY TO SEE THE EVIL THAT I AM. I STALK THE WORLD IN MORTAL DRESS, THE WORST OF FIENDS--
--THE MONSTER WHO LOOKS EXACTLY LIKE EVERYONE ELSE
WHY SHOULD DEATH LURK IN THE SHADOWS? SPEAK TO ME OF THE DARK GIFTS-- I USE THEM.
I'M GENTLEMAN DEATH IN SILK AND LACE, COME TO PUT OUT THE CANDLES, THE CANKER IN THE HEART OF THE ROSE.
A SPLENDID MISSION, TO DEVIL THEM MERCILESSLY AS YOU LIVE AMONG THEM. BUT YOU DON'T UNDERSTAND. YOU CAN'T ENDURE IN THE WORLD, LIVING AMONG MEN.
YOU CANNOT SURVIVE.
AND WHY NOT? I TELL YOU I BELONG AMONG MEN. IT IS THEIR BLOOD THAT MAKES ME IMMORTAL.
AH, YES, IMMORTAL, BUT YOU HAVE NOT BEGUN TO UNDERSTAND IT. IT'S NO MORE THAN A WORD.
WHY DID MAGNUS GO INTO THE FLAMES? IT'S AN AGE-OLD TRUTH AMONG US.
LIVE AMONG MEN, AND IT WILL DRIVE YOU TO MADNESS.

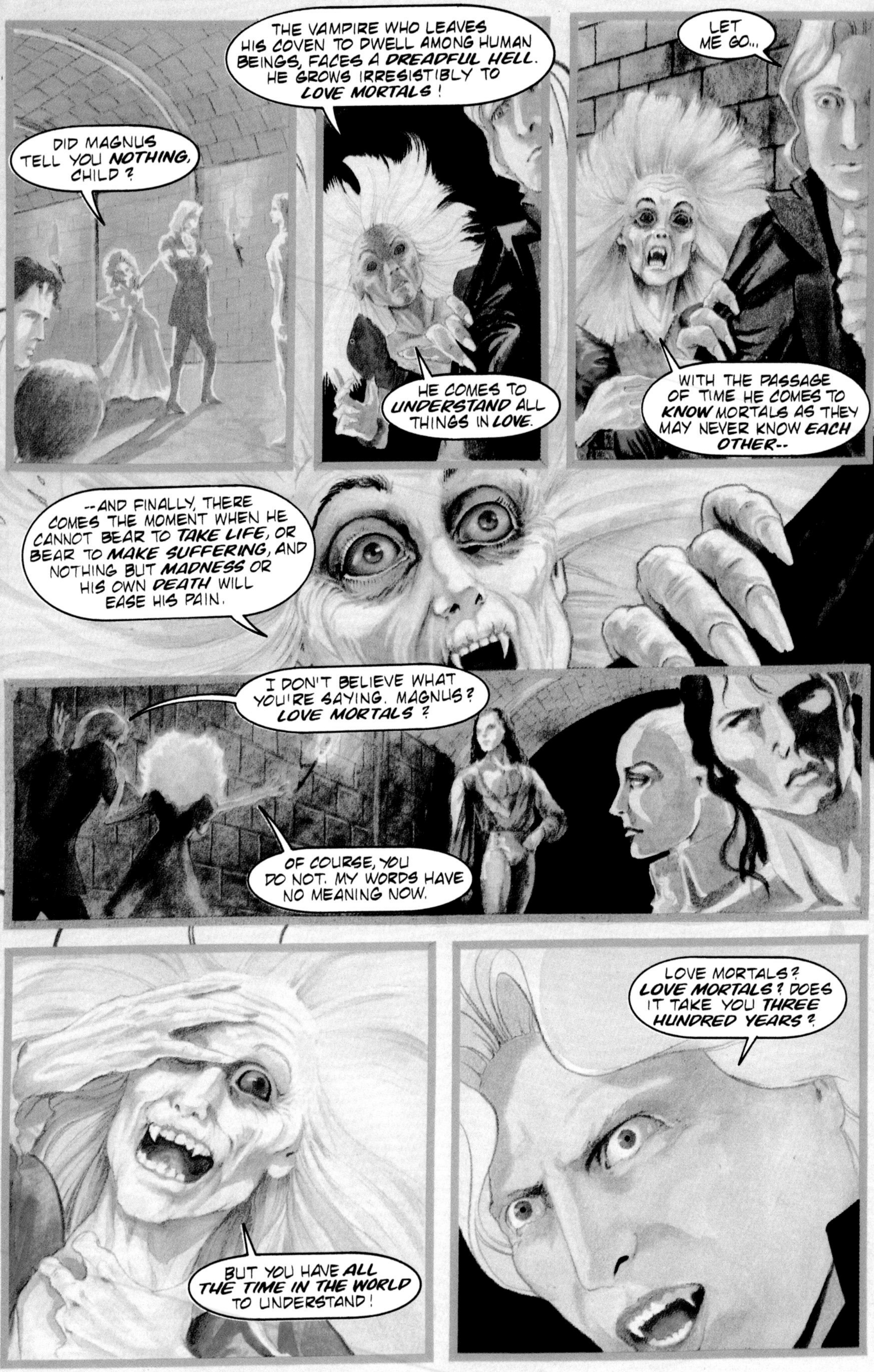
DID MAGNUS TELL YOU NOTHING, CHILD ?
THE VAMPIRE WHO LEAVES HIS COVEN TO DWELL AMONG HUMAN BEINGS, FACES A DREADFUL HELL. HE GROWS IRRESISTIBLY TO LOVE MORTALS !
HE COMES TO UNDERSTAND ALL THINGS IN LOVE.
LET ME GO...
WITH THE PASSAGE OF TIME HE COMES TO KNOW MORTALS AS THEY MAY NEVER KNOW EACH OTHER--
--AND FINALLY, THERE COMES THE MOMENT WHEN HE CANNOT BEAR TO TAKE LIFE, OR BEAR TO MAKE SUFFERING, AND NOTHING BUT MADNESS OR HIS OWN DEATH WILL EASE HIS PAIN.
I DON'T BELIEVE WHAT YOU'RE SAYING. MAGNUS? LOVE MORTALS ?
OF COURSE, YOU DO NOT. MY WORDS HAVE NO MEANING NOW.
BUT YOU HAVE ALL THE TIME IN THE WORLD TO UNDERSTAND !
LOVE MORTALS? LOVE MORTALS? DOES IT TAKE YOU THREE HUNDRED YEARS ?

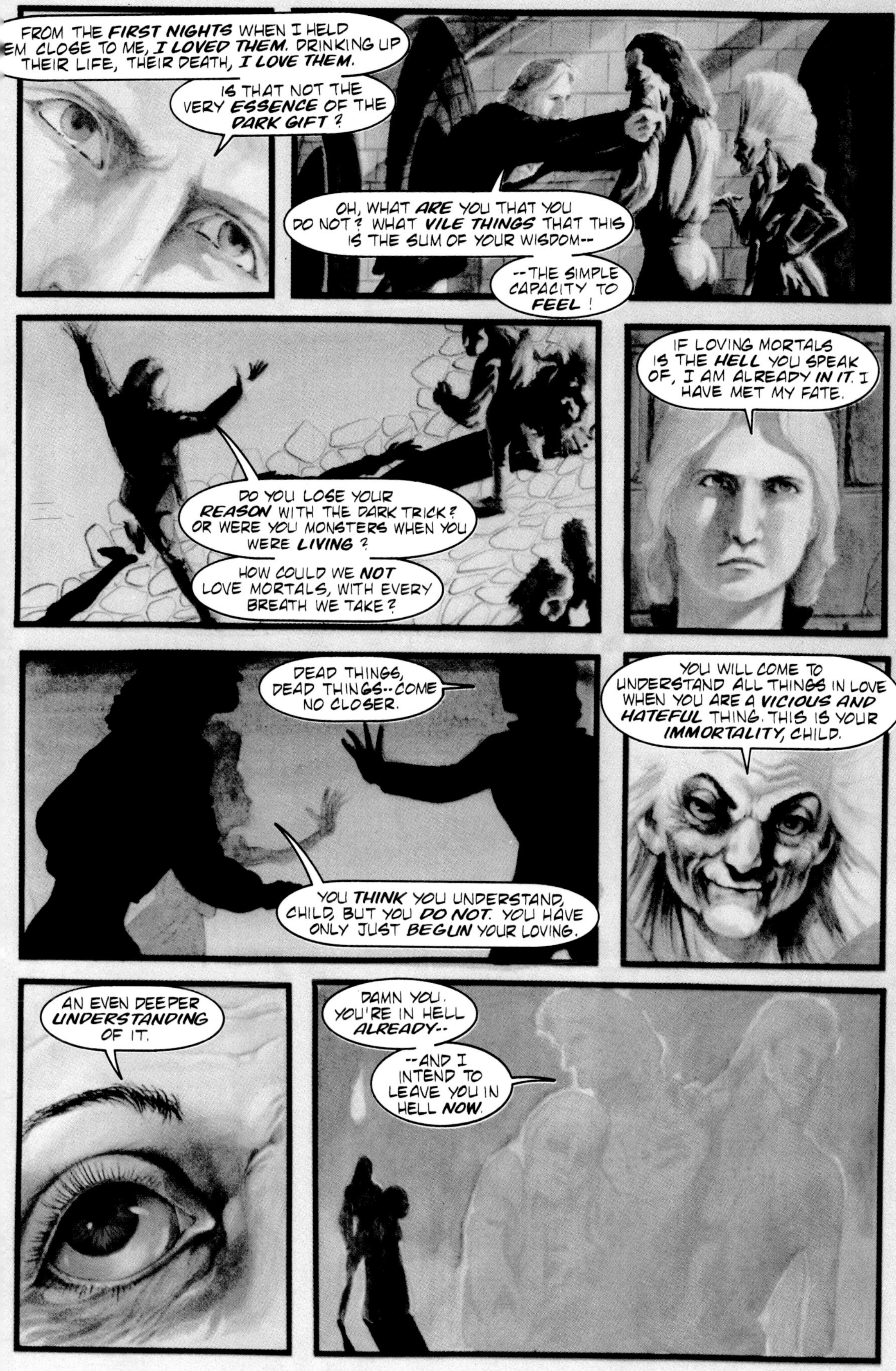
FROM THE FIRST NIGHTS WHEN I HELD EM CLOSE TO ME, I LOVED THEM. DRINKING UP THEIR LIFE, THEIR DEATH, I LOVE THEM.
IS THAT NOT THE VERY ESSENCE OF THE DARK GIFT?
OH, WHAT ARE YOU THAT YOU DO NOT? WHAT VILE THINGS THAT THIS IS THE SUM OF YOUR WISDOM--
--THE SIMPLE CAPACITY TO FEEL!
DO YOU LOSE YOUR REASON WITH THE DARK TRICK? OR WERE YOU MONSTERS WHEN YOU WERE LIVING?
HOW COULD WE NOT LOVE MORTALS, WITH EVERY BREATH WE TAKE?
IF LOVING MORTALS IS THE HELL YOU SPEAK OF, I AM ALREADY IN IT. I HAVE MET MY FATE.
DEAD THINGS, DEAD THINGS--COME NO CLOSER.
YOU THINK YOU UNDERSTAND, CHILD, BUT YOU DO NOT. YOU HAVE ONLY JUST BEGUN YOUR LOVING.
YOU WILL COME TO UNDERSTAND ALL THINGS IN LOVE WHEN YOU ARE A VICIOUS AND HATEFUL THING. THIS IS YOUR IMMORTALITY, CHILD.
AN EVEN DEEPER UNDERSTANDING OF IT.
DAMN YOU. YOU'RE IN HELL ALREADY--
--AND I INTEND TO LEAVE YOU IN HELL NOW.

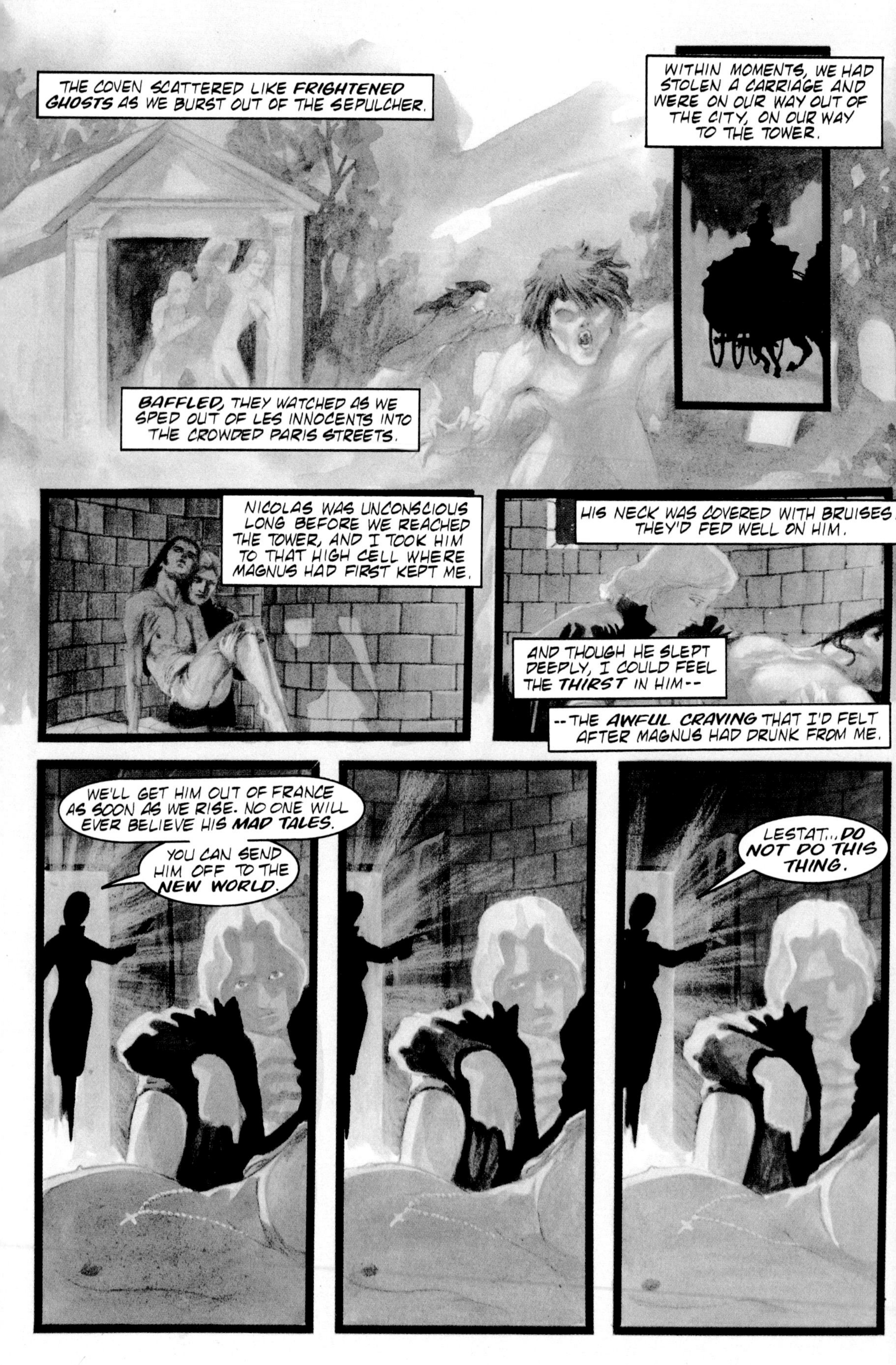
THE COVEN SCATTERED LIKE FRIGHTENED GHOSTS AS WE BURST OUT OF THE SEPULCHER.
BAFFLED, THEY WATCHED AS WE SPED OUT OF LES INNOCENTS INTO THE CROWDED PARIS STREETS.
WITHIN MOMENTS, WE HAD STOLEN A CARRIAGE AND WERE ON OUR WAY OUT OF THE CITY, ON OUR WAY TO THE TOWER.
NICOLAS WAS UNCONSCIOUS LONG BEFORE WE REACHED THE TOWER, AND I TOOK HIM TO THAT HIGH CELL WHERE MAGNUS HAD FIRST KEPT ME.
HIS NECK WAS COVERED WITH BRUISES. THEY'D FED WELL ON HIM.
AND THOUGH HE SLEPT DEEPLY, I COULD FEEL THE THIRST IN HIM--
--THE AWFUL CRAVING THAT I'D FELT AFTER MAGNUS HAD DRUNK FROM ME.
WE'LL GET HIM OUT OF FRANCE AS SOON AS WE RISE. NO ONE WILL EVER BELIEVE HIS MAD TALES.
YOU CAN SEND HIM OFF TO THE NEW WORLD.
LESTAT... DO NOT DO THIS THING.

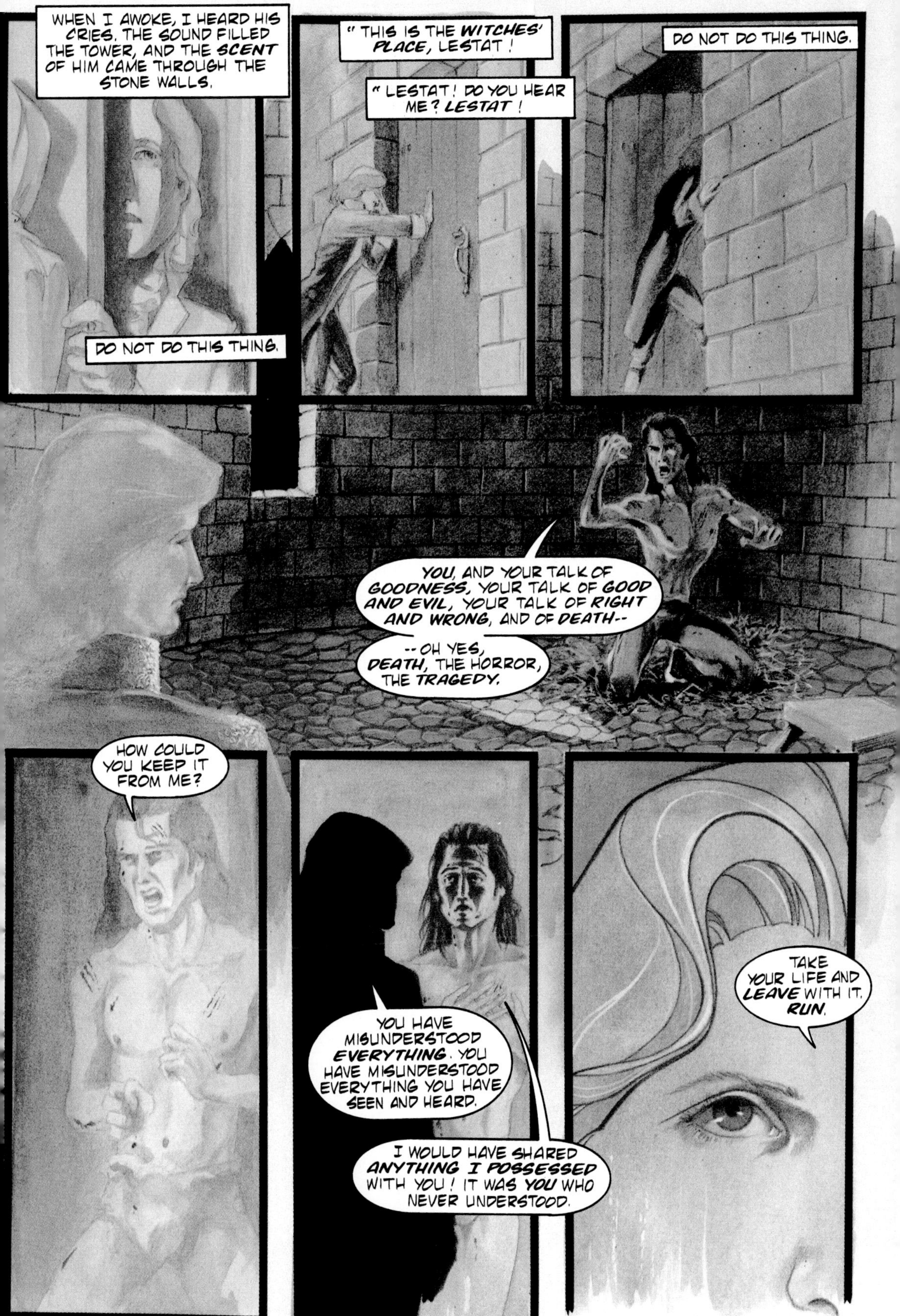
WHEN I AWOKE, I HEARD HIS CRIES. THE SOUND FILLED THE TOWER, AND THE SCENT OF HIM CAME THROUGH THE STONE WALLS.
DO NOT DO THIS THING.
"THIS IS THE WITCHES' PLACE, LESTAT!
"LESTAT! DO YOU HEAR ME? LESTAT!
DO NOT DO THIS THING.
YOU, AND YOUR TALK OF GOODNESS, YOUR TALK OF GOOD AND EVIL, YOUR TALK OF RIGHT AND WRONG, AND OF DEATH--
--OH YES, DEATH, THE HORROR, THE TRAGEDY.
HOW COULD YOU KEEP IT FROM ME?
YOU HAVE MISUNDERSTOOD EVERYTHING. YOU HAVE MISUNDERSTOOD EVERYTHING YOU HAVE SEEN AND HEARD.
I WOULD HAVE SHARED ANYTHING I POSSESSED WITH YOU! IT WAS YOU WHO NEVER UNDERSTOOD.
TAKE YOUR LIFE AND LEAVE WITH IT. RUN.

DON'T YOU SEE, IT'S THE CONFIRMATION OF EVERYTHING? THAT IT EXISTS IS THE CONFIRMATION-- PURE EVIL, SUBLIME EVIL!
DON'T TAUNT ME!
WHEN IT WAS OFFERED ME I SAID NO. WITH MY LAST BREATH, I SAID NO.
YOU ALWAYS WERE THE FOOL. I TOLD YOU THAT.
YOU BELIEVED THINGS THAT DIDN'T MATTER. THERE WAS SOMETHING YOU FAILED TO SEE.
IS IT IMPOSSIBLE YOU DON'T KNOW YOURSELF WHAT YOU POSSESS NOW?
COME TO ME, NICKI. IF YOU WANT IT, YOU MUST COME...
DO NOT DO THIS THING.

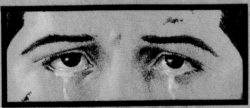

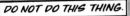

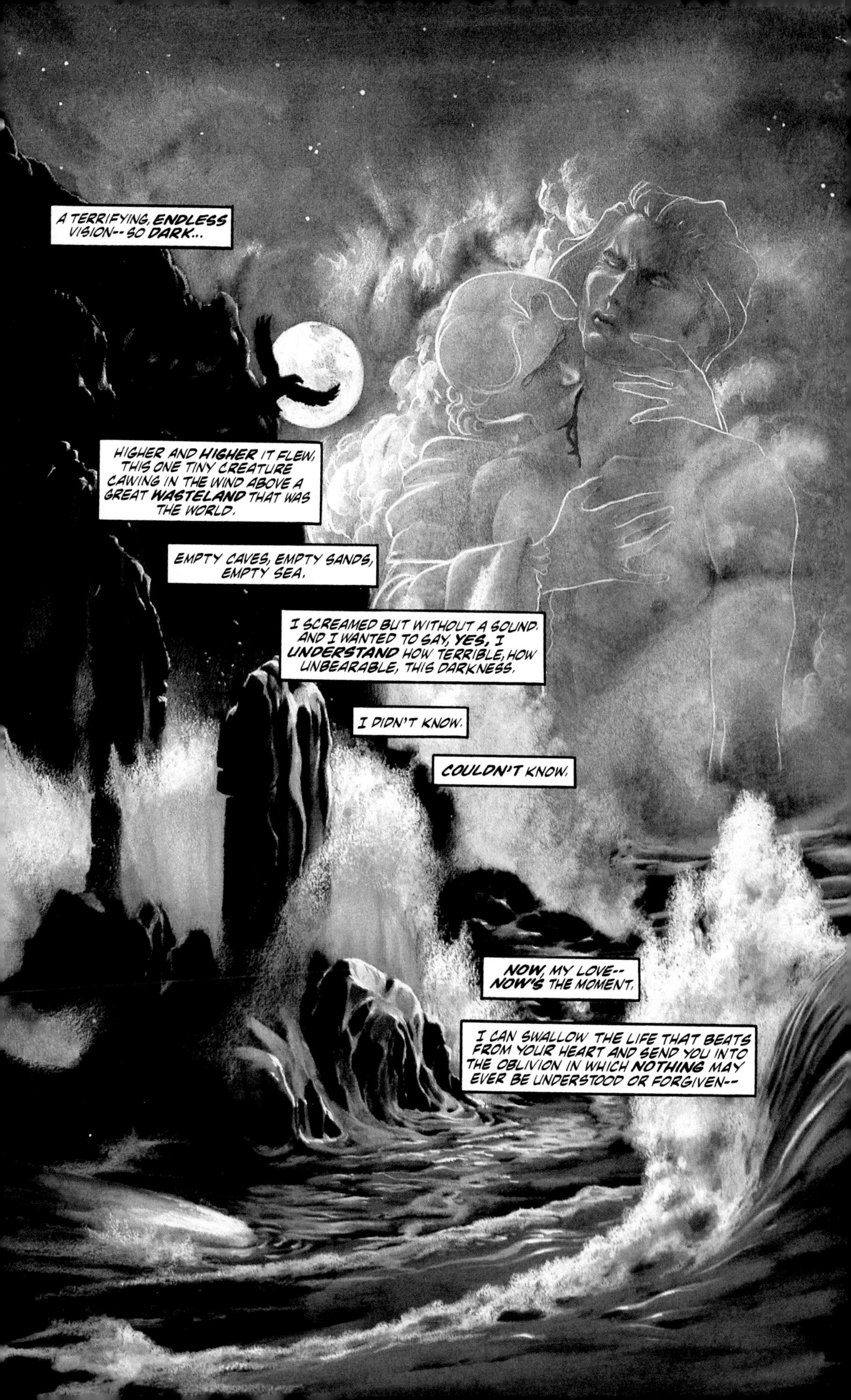
A TERRIFYING, ENDLESS VISION-- SO DARK...
HIGHER AND HIGHER IT FLEW, THIS ONE TINY CREATURE CAWING IN THE WIND ABOVE A GREAT WASTELAND THAT WAS THE WORLD.
EMPTY CAVES, EMPTY SANDS, EMPTY SEA.
I SCREAMED BUT WITHOUT A SOUND. AND I WANTED TO SAY, YES, I UNDERSTAND HOW TERRIBLE, HOW UNBEARABLE, THIS DARKNESS.
I DIDN'T KNOW.
COULDN'T KNOW.
NOW, MY LOVE-- NOW'S THE MOMENT.
I CAN SWALLOW THE LIFE THAT BEATS FROM YOUR HEART AND SEND YOU INTO THE OBLIVION IN WHICH NOTHING MAY EVER BE UNDERSTOOD OR FORGIVEN--

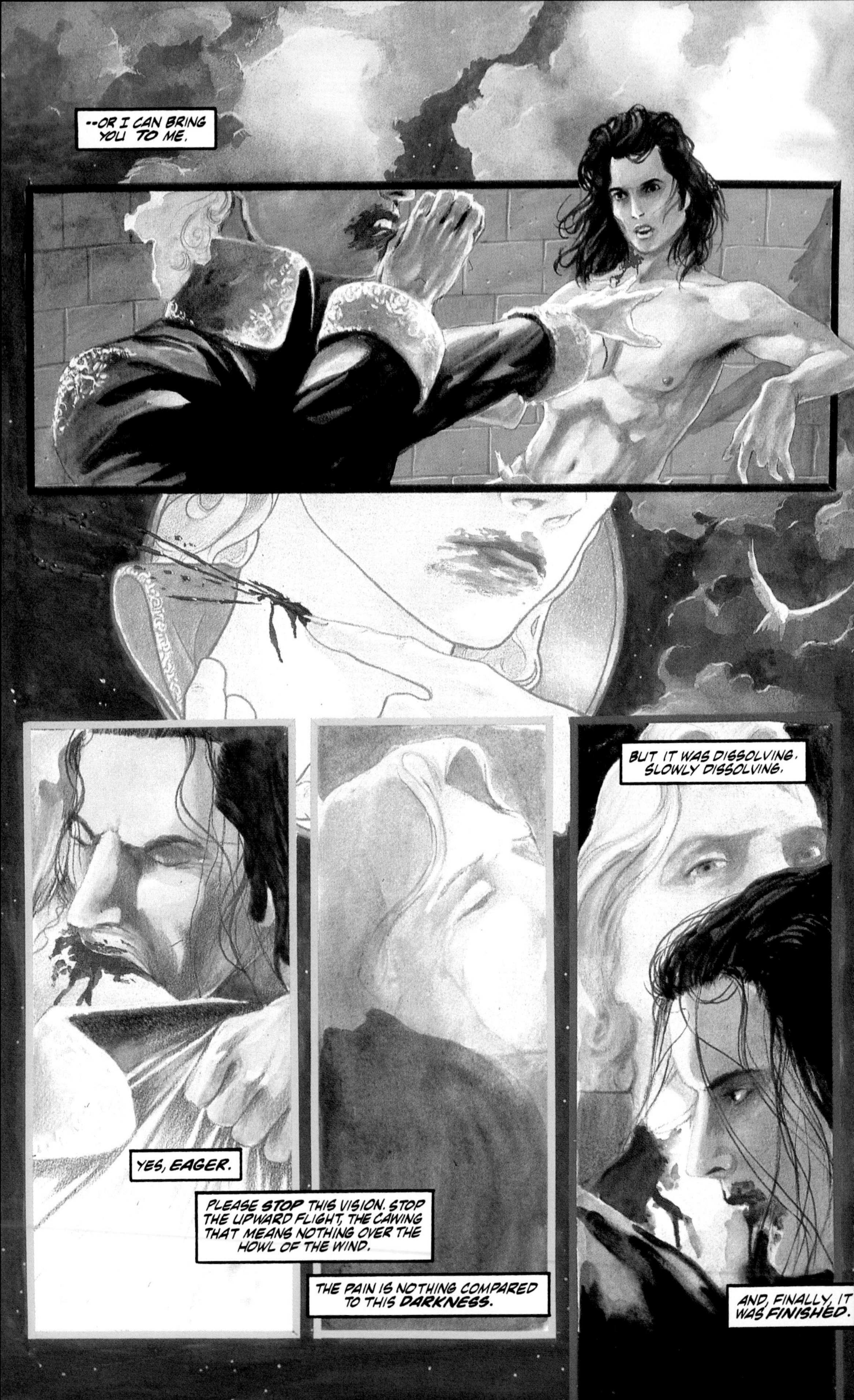
--OR I CAN BRING YOU TO ME.
BUT IT WAS DISSOLVING. SLOWLY DISSOLVING.
YES, EAGER.
PLEASE STOP THIS VISION. STOP THE UPWARD FLIGHT, THE CAWING THAT MEANS NOTHING OVER THE HOWL OF THE WIND.
THE PAIN IS NOTHING COMPARED TO THIS DARKNESS.
AND, FINALLY, IT WAS FINISHED.

DISASTER, MY SON.

A DRY SOUND CAME OUT OF HIS MOUTH-- IN SPITE OF THE BLOOD, A *DRY SCREAM.*

AND BEYOND HIM, *BEYOND THE REMEMBERED VISION OF THE DARK SEA AND THE LONE BIRD WHO WAS ITS ONLY WITNESS, I SAW* HER IN THE DOORWAY.

BY MIDNIGHT IT WAS CLEAR THAT HE WOULD NOT SPEAK OR ANSWER TO ANY VOICE, OR MOVE OF HIS OWN VOLITION.

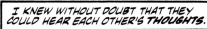

I KNEW WITHOUT DOUBT THAT THEY COULD HEAR EACH OTHER'S *THOUGHTS.*

I COULD NOT APPROACH HIM, AND SO *GABRIELLE* TOOK HIM IN HAND.

HE SHOULD HUNT NOW.

THE EMPTINESS OF THE NIGHT WAS AN INDISSOLUBLE *COLD* SETTLING OVER ME, CLOSING ME IN.

NOT EVEN THE *FIRE* WARMED ME.

EMPTINESS HERE. AND *QUIET.*

QUIET, AND THE REALIZATION GNAWING AT MY INSIDES LIKE A *STARVED ANIMAL*--

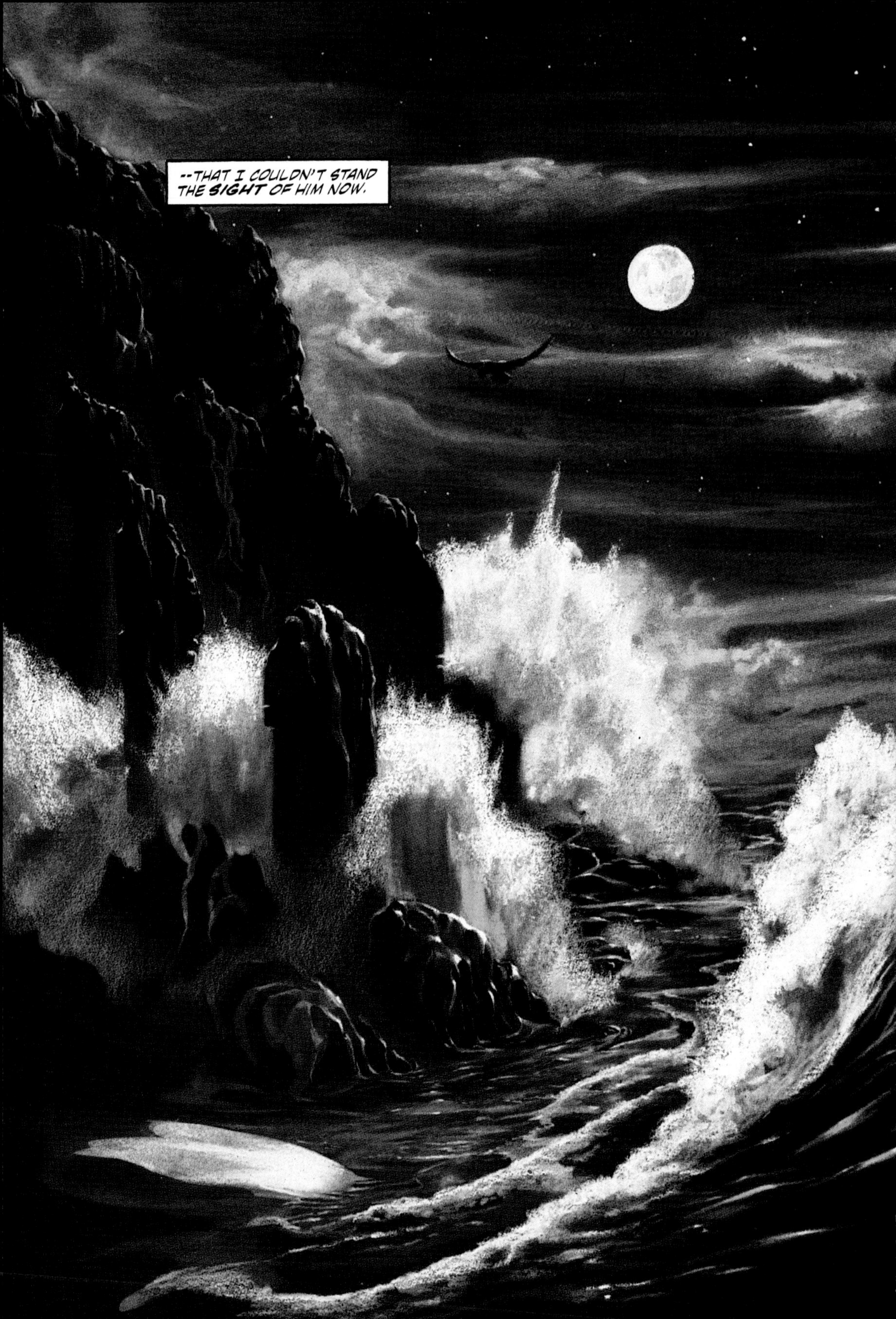
--THAT I COULDN'T STAND THE SIGHT OF HIM NOW.

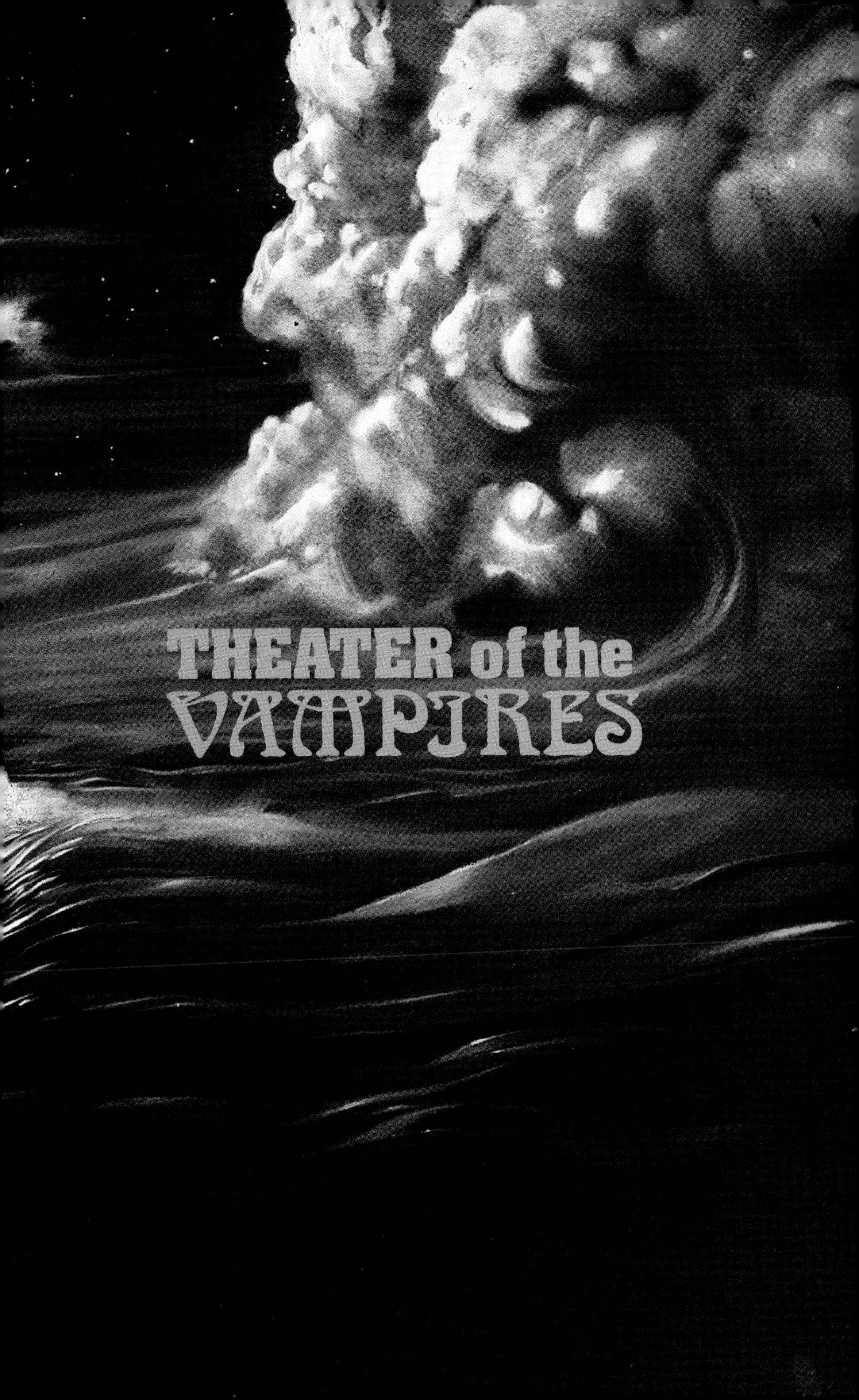
THEATER of the
VAMPIRES

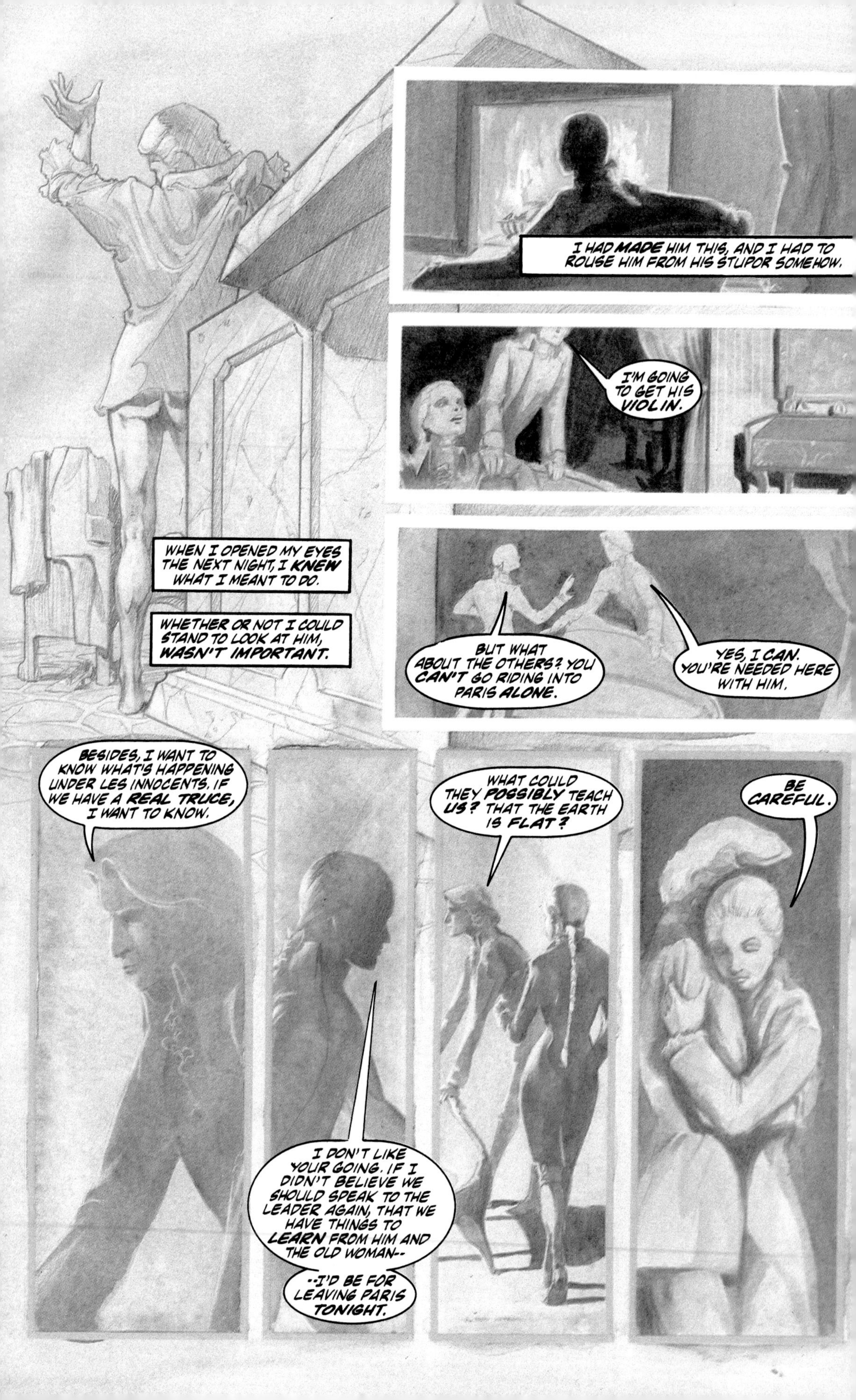
I HAD MADE HIM THIS, AND I HAD TO ROUSE HIM FROM HIS STUPOR SOMEHOW.
I'M GOING TO GET HIS VIOLIN.
WHEN I OPENED MY EYES THE NEXT NIGHT, I KNEW WHAT I MEANT TO DO.
WHETHER OR NOT I COULD STAND TO LOOK AT HIM, WASN'T IMPORTANT.
BUT WHAT ABOUT THE OTHERS? YOU CAN'T GO RIDING INTO PARIS ALONE.
YES, I CAN. YOU'RE NEEDED HERE WITH HIM.
BESIDES, I WANT TO KNOW WHAT'S HAPPENING UNDER LES INNOCENTS. IF WE HAVE A REAL TRUCE, I WANT TO KNOW.
I DON'T LIKE YOUR GOING. IF I DIDN'T BELIEVE WE SHOULD SPEAK TO THE LEADER AGAIN, THAT WE HAVE THINGS TO LEARN FROM HIM AND THE OLD WOMAN--
--I'D BE FOR LEAVING PARIS TONIGHT.
WHAT COULD THEY POSSIBLY TEACH US? THAT THE EARTH IS FLAT?
BE CAREFUL.

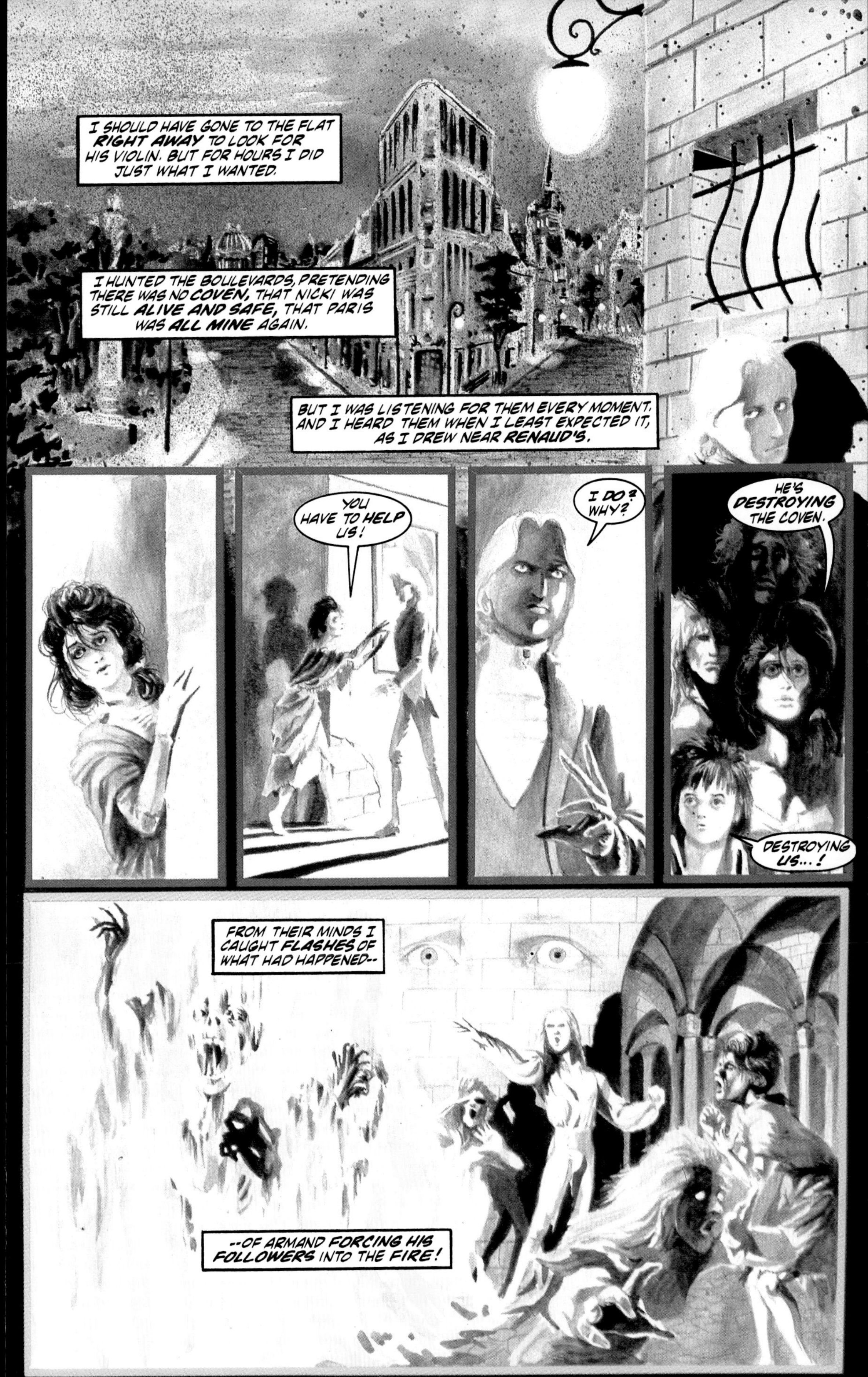
I SHOULD HAVE GONE TO THE FLAT RIGHT AWAY TO LOOK FOR HIS VIOLIN. BUT FOR HOURS I DID JUST WHAT I WANTED.
I HUNTED THE BOULEVARDS, PRETENDING THERE WAS NO COVEN, THAT NICKI WAS STILL ALIVE AND SAFE, THAT PARIS WAS ALL MINE AGAIN.
BUT I WAS LISTENING FOR THEM EVERY MOMENT. AND I HEARD THEM WHEN I LEAST EXPECTED IT, AS I DREW NEAR RENAUD'S.
YOU HAVE TO HELP US!
I DO? WHY?
HE'S DESTROYING THE COVEN.
DESTROYING US...!
FROM THEIR MINDS I CAUGHT FLASHES OF WHAT HAD HAPPENED--
--OF ARMAND FORCING HIS FOLLOWERS INTO THE FIRE!

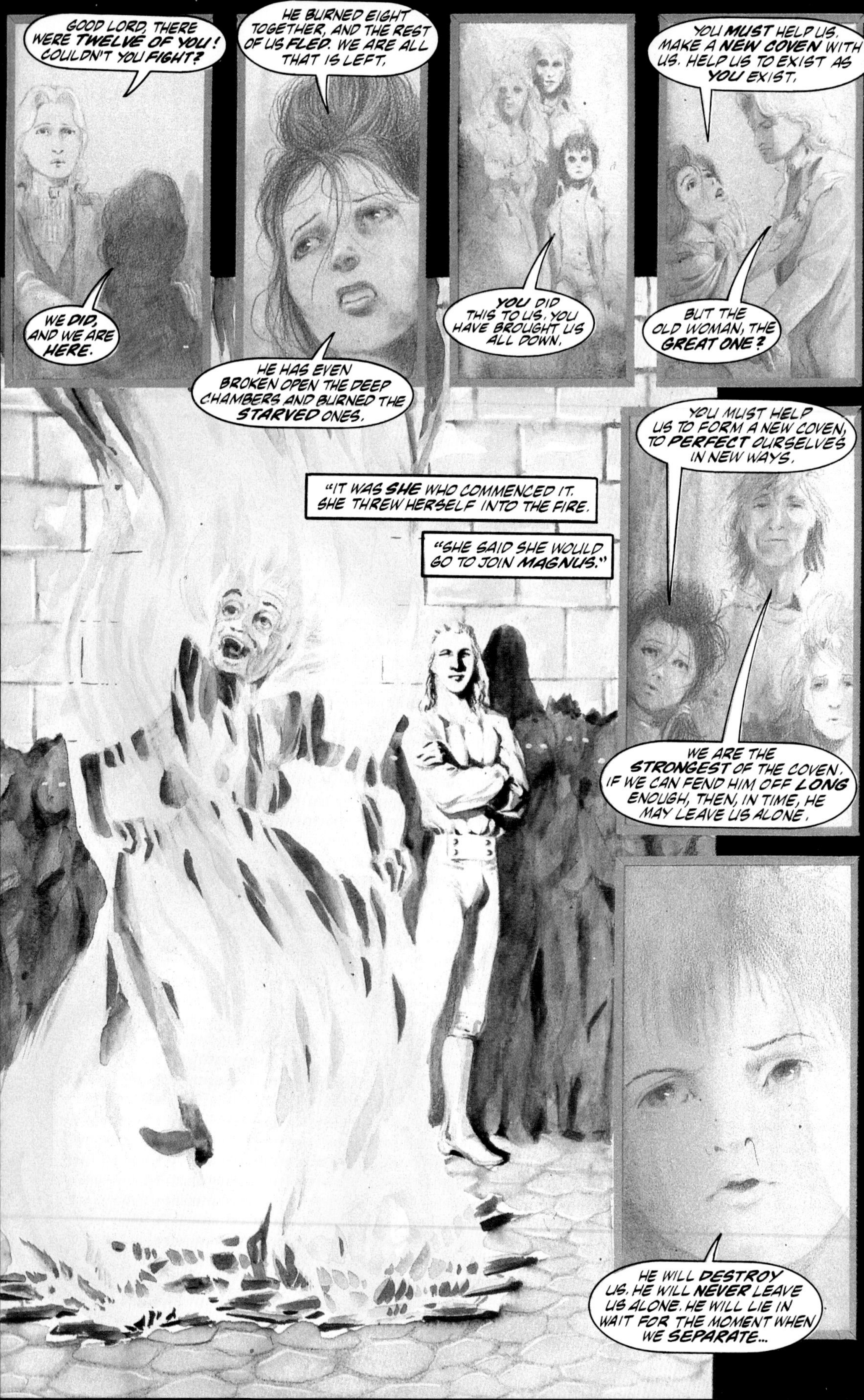

GOOD LORD, THERE WERE TWELVE OF YOU! COULDN'T YOU FIGHT?
WE DID, AND WE ARE HERE.
HE BURNED EIGHT TOGETHER, AND THE REST OF US FLED. WE ARE ALL THAT IS LEFT.
HE HAS EVEN BROKEN OPEN THE DEEP CHAMBERS AND BURNED THE STARVED ONES.
YOU DID THIS TO US. YOU HAVE BROUGHT US ALL DOWN.
YOU MUST HELP US. MAKE A NEW COVEN WITH US. HELP US TO EXIST AS YOU EXIST.
BUT THE OLD WOMAN, THE GREAT ONE?
"IT WAS SHE WHO COMMENCED IT. SHE THREW HERSELF INTO THE FIRE.
"SHE SAID SHE WOULD GO TO JOIN MAGNUS."
YOU MUST HELP US TO FORM A NEW COVEN, TO PERFECT OURSELVES IN NEW WAYS.
WE ARE THE STRONGEST OF THE COVEN. IF WE CAN FEND HIM OFF LONG ENOUGH, THEN, IN TIME, HE MAY LEAVE US ALONE.
HE WILL DESTROY US. HE WILL NEVER LEAVE US ALONE. HE WILL LIE IN WAIT FOR THE MOMENT WHEN WE SEPARATE...

HE ISN'T INVINCIBLE. AND HE'S LOST ALL CONVICTION. *REMEMBER* THAT.

YOU HAVE MAGNUS' *TOWER*, A SAFE PLACE...

NO, *THAT* I CAN'T SHARE WITH YOU. YOU HAVE TO WIN THIS BATTLE ON YOUR *OWN*.

BUT SURELY YOU CAN *GUIDE* US--!

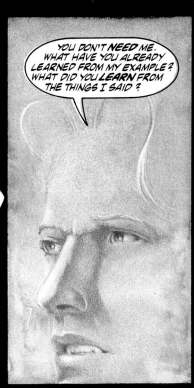

YOU DON'T *NEED* ME. WHAT HAVE YOU ALREADY LEARNED FROM MY EXAMPLE? WHAT DID YOU *LEARN* FROM THE THINGS I SAID?

WE LEARNED MORE FROM WHAT YOU SAID TO HIM *AFTERWARDS*.

WE HEARD YOU SPEAK TO HIM OF A *NEW EVIL*, AN EVIL FOR THESE TIMES DESTINED TO MOVE THROUGH THE WORLD IN HANDSOME *HUMAN GUISE*.

SO TAKE ON THE GUISE, TAKE THE *GARMENTS* OF YOUR VICTIMS, TAKE THE *MONEY* FROM THEIR POCKETS,

THEN *YOU* CAN MOVE AMONG MORTALS AS I DO.

BUT, OUR *SKIN*, THE TIMBRE OF OUR *VOICES*...

YOU CAN *FOOL* MORTALS. IT'S VERY EASY. IT JUST TAKES A LITTLE *SKILL*.

BUT HOW DO WE START? WHAT *SORT* OF MORTALS DO WE *PRETEND* TO BE?

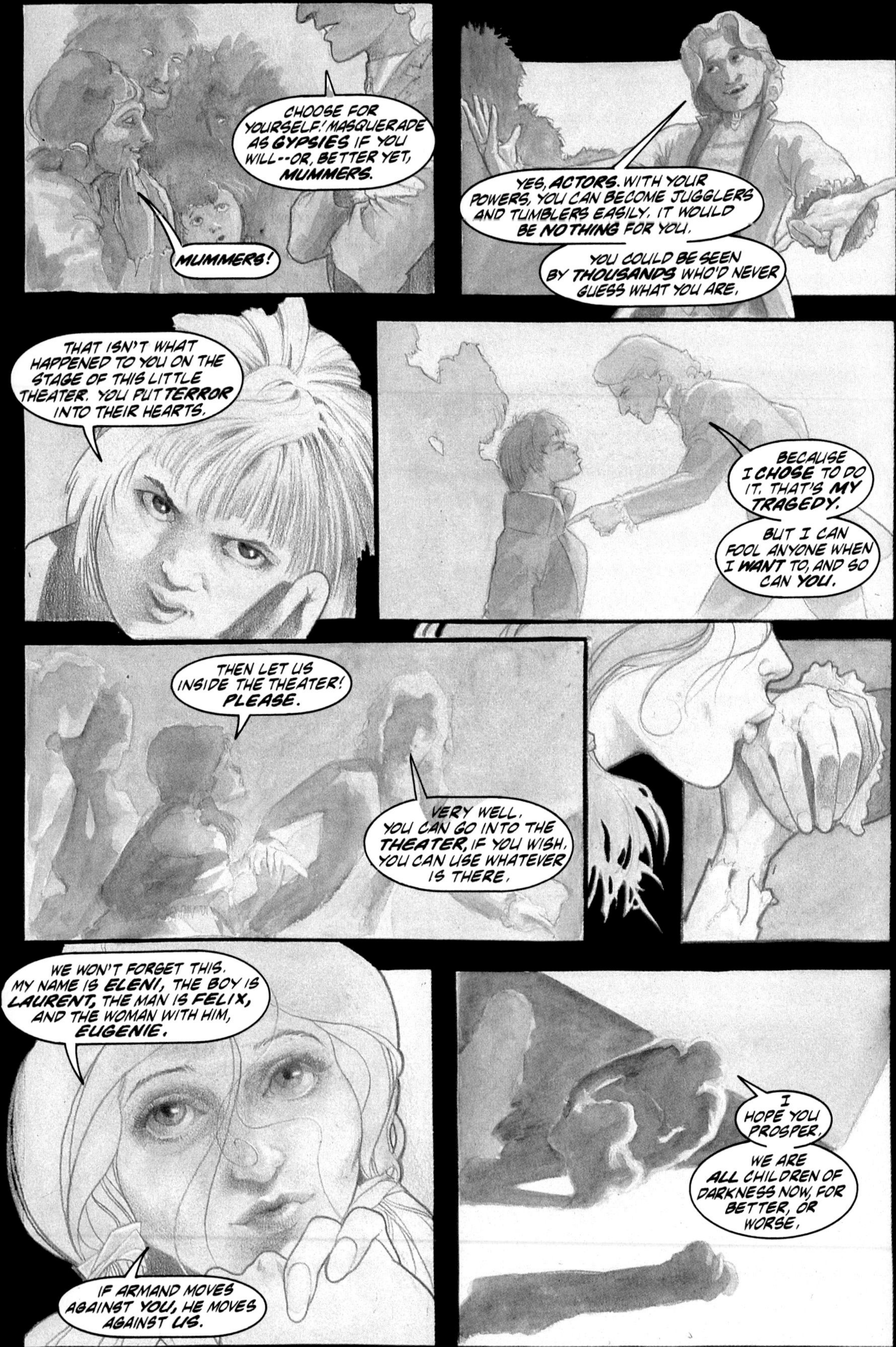
CHOOSE FOR YOURSELF! MASQUERADE AS GYPSIES IF YOU WILL--OR, BETTER YET, MUMMERS.
MUMMERS!
YES, ACTORS. WITH YOUR POWERS, YOU CAN BECOME JUGGLERS AND TUMBLERS EASILY. IT WOULD BE NOTHING FOR YOU.
YOU COULD BE SEEN BY THOUSANDS WHO'D NEVER GUESS WHAT YOU ARE.
THAT ISN'T WHAT HAPPENED TO YOU ON THE STAGE OF THIS LITTLE THEATER. YOU PUT TERROR INTO THEIR HEARTS.
BECAUSE I CHOSE TO DO IT. THAT'S MY TRAGEDY.
BUT I CAN FOOL ANYONE WHEN I WANT TO, AND SO CAN YOU.
THEN LET US INSIDE THE THEATER! PLEASE.
VERY WELL. YOU CAN GO INTO THE THEATER, IF YOU WISH. YOU CAN USE WHATEVER IS THERE.
WE WON'T FORGET THIS. MY NAME IS ELENI, THE BOY IS LAURENT, THE MAN IS FELIX, AND THE WOMAN WITH HIM, EUGENIE.
IF ARMAND MOVES AGAINST YOU, HE MOVES AGAINST US.
I HOPE YOU PROSPER.
WE ARE ALL CHILDREN OF DARKNESS NOW, FOR BETTER, OR WORSE.

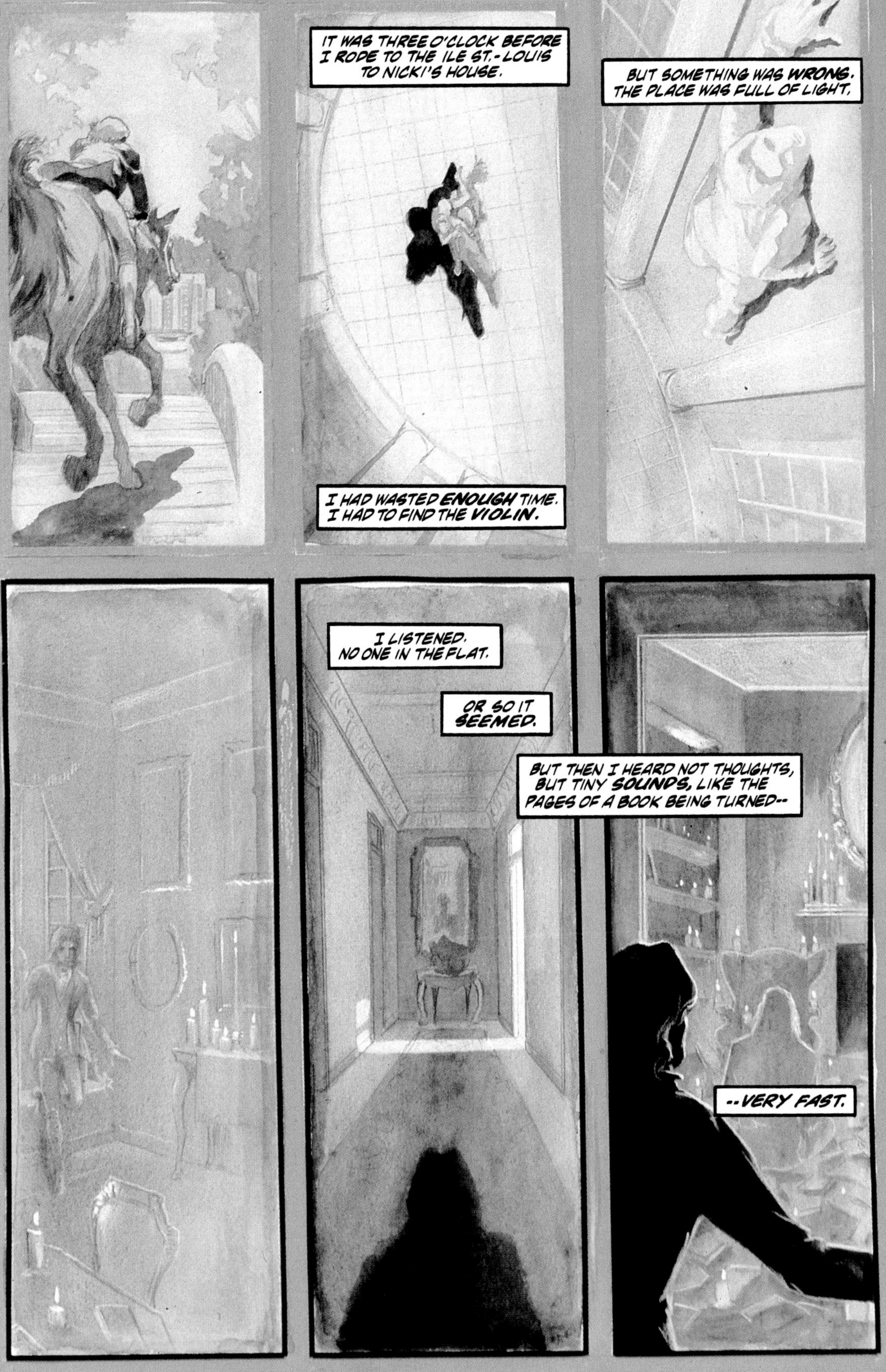
IT WAS THREE O'CLOCK BEFORE I RODE TO THE ILE ST.-LOUIS TO NICKI'S HOUSE.
I HAD WASTED ENOUGH TIME. I HAD TO FIND THE VIOLIN.
BUT SOMETHING WAS WRONG. THE PLACE WAS FULL OF LIGHT.
I LISTENED. NO ONE IN THE FLAT.
OR SO IT SEEMED.
BUT THEN I HEARD NOT THOUGHTS, BUT TINY SOUNDS, LIKE THE PAGES OF A BOOK BEING TURNED--
--VERY FAST.

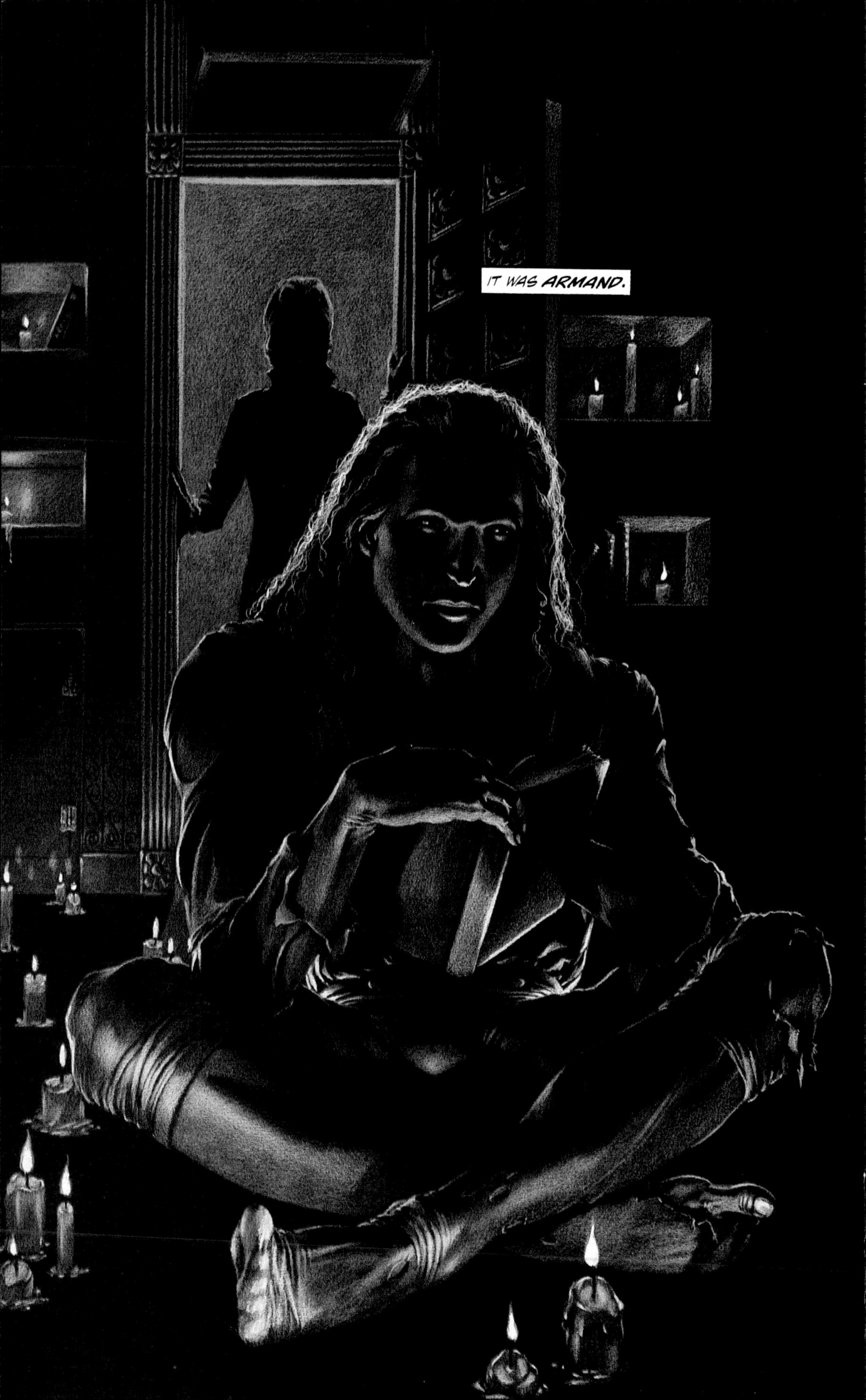
IT WAS ARMAND.

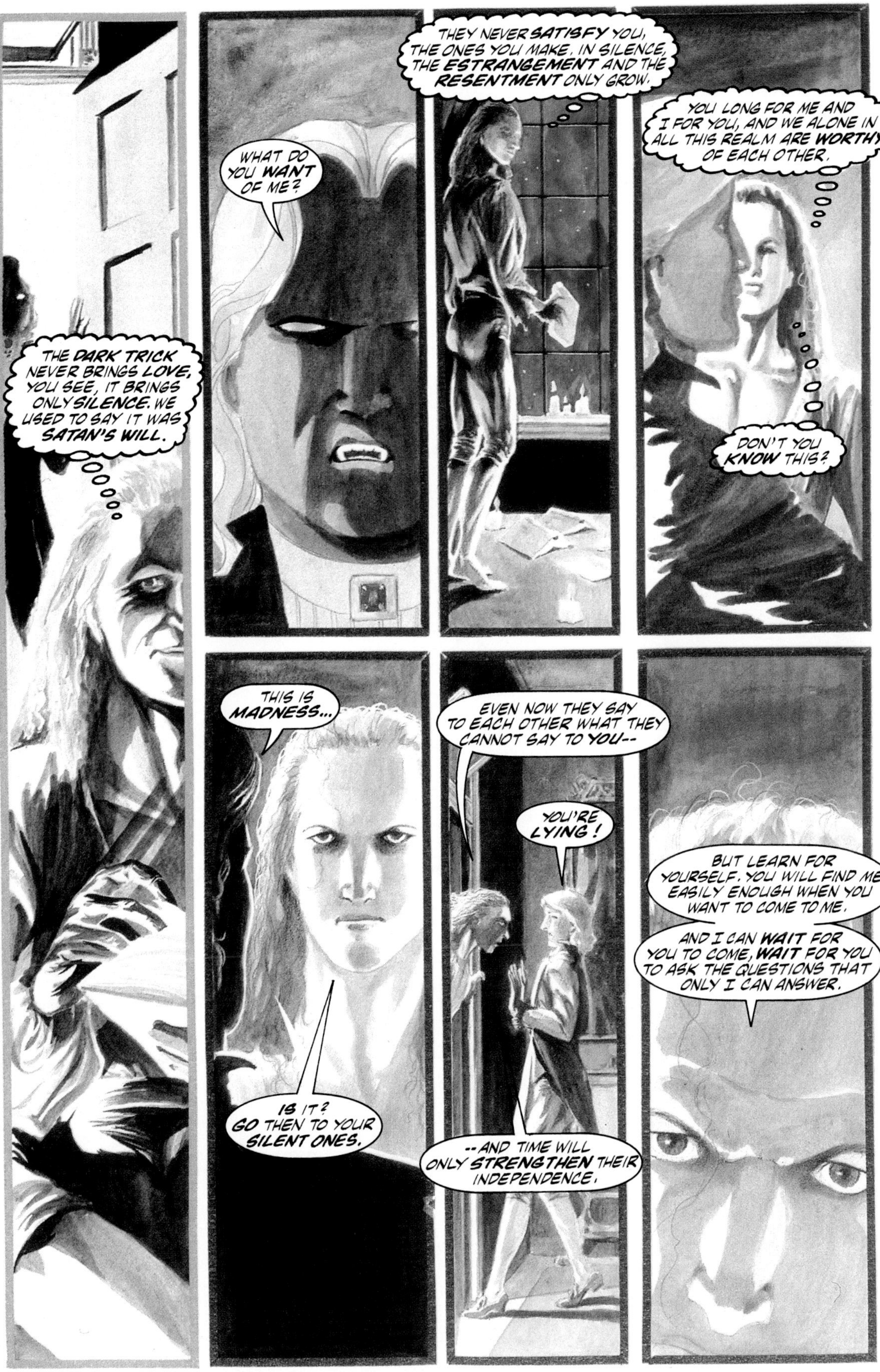
THE DARK TRICK NEVER BRINGS LOVE, YOU SEE, IT BRINGS ONLY SILENCE. WE USED TO SAY IT WAS SATAN'S WILL.
WHAT DO YOU WANT OF ME?
THEY NEVER SATISFY YOU, THE ONES YOU MAKE. IN SILENCE, THE ESTRANGEMENT AND THE RESENTMENT ONLY GROW.
YOU LONG FOR ME AND I FOR YOU, AND WE ALONE IN ALL THIS REALM ARE WORTHY OF EACH OTHER.
DON'T YOU KNOW THIS?
THIS IS MADNESS...
IS IT? GO THEN TO YOUR SILENT ONES.
EVEN NOW THEY SAY TO EACH OTHER WHAT THEY CANNOT SAY TO YOU--
YOU'RE LYING!
--AND TIME WILL ONLY STRENGTHEN THEIR INDEPENDENCE.
BUT LEARN FOR YOURSELF. YOU WILL FIND ME EASILY ENOUGH WHEN YOU WANT TO COME TO ME.
AND I CAN WAIT FOR YOU TO COME, WAIT FOR YOU TO ASK THE QUESTIONS THAT ONLY I CAN ANSWER.

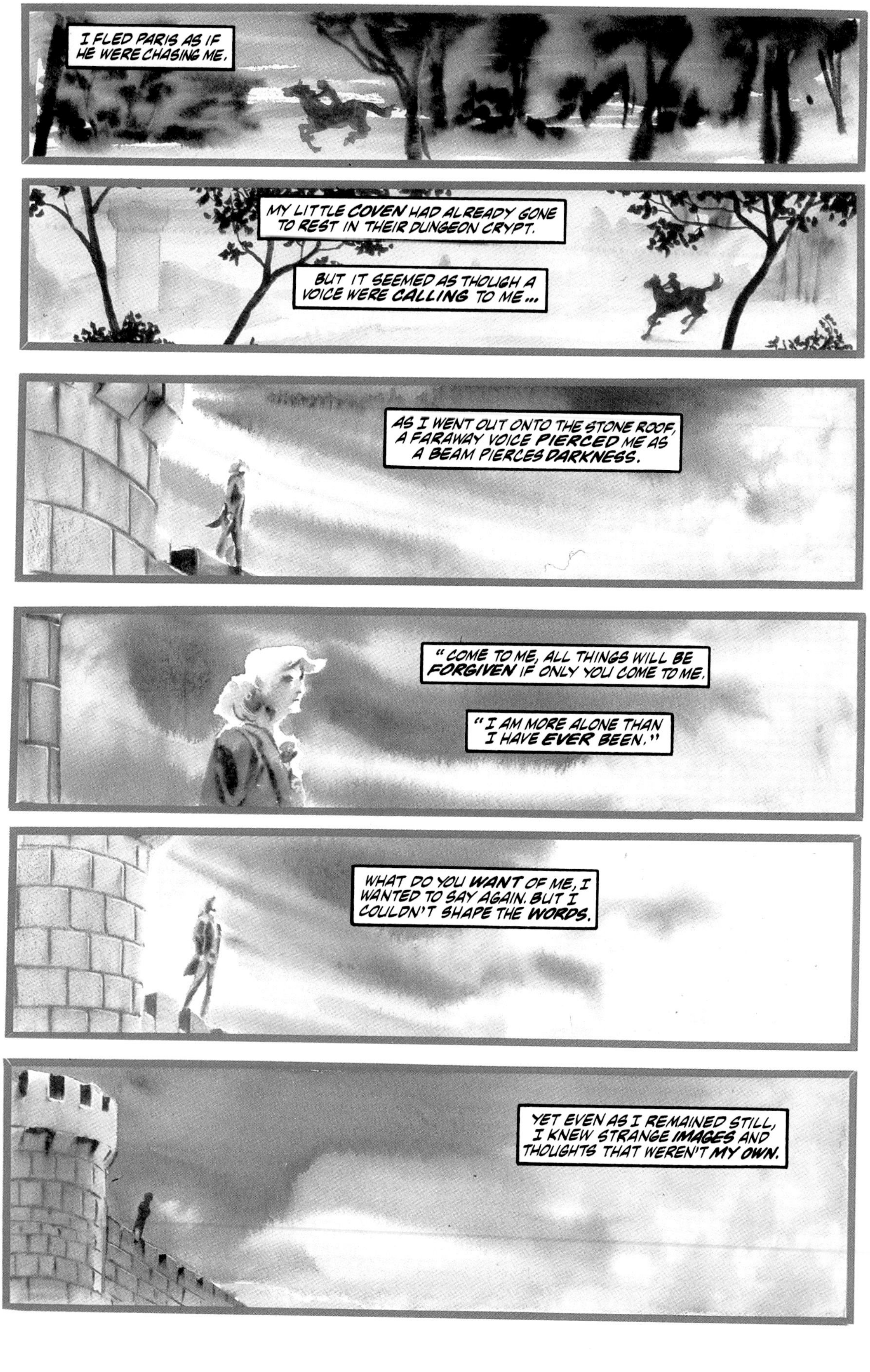
I FLED PARIS AS IF HE WERE CHASING ME.
MY LITTLE COVEN HAD ALREADY GONE TO REST IN THEIR DUNGEON CRYPT.
BUT IT SEEMED AS THOUGH A VOICE WERE CALLING TO ME...
AS I WENT OUT ONTO THE STONE ROOF, A FARAWAY VOICE PIERCED ME AS A BEAM PIERCES DARKNESS.
"COME TO ME, ALL THINGS WILL BE FORGIVEN IF ONLY YOU COME TO ME.
"I AM MORE ALONE THAN I HAVE EVER BEEN."
WHAT DO YOU WANT OF ME, I WANTED TO SAY AGAIN. BUT I COULDN'T SHAPE THE WORDS.
YET EVEN AS I REMAINED STILL, I KNEW STRANGE IMAGES AND THOUGHTS THAT WEREN'T MY OWN.

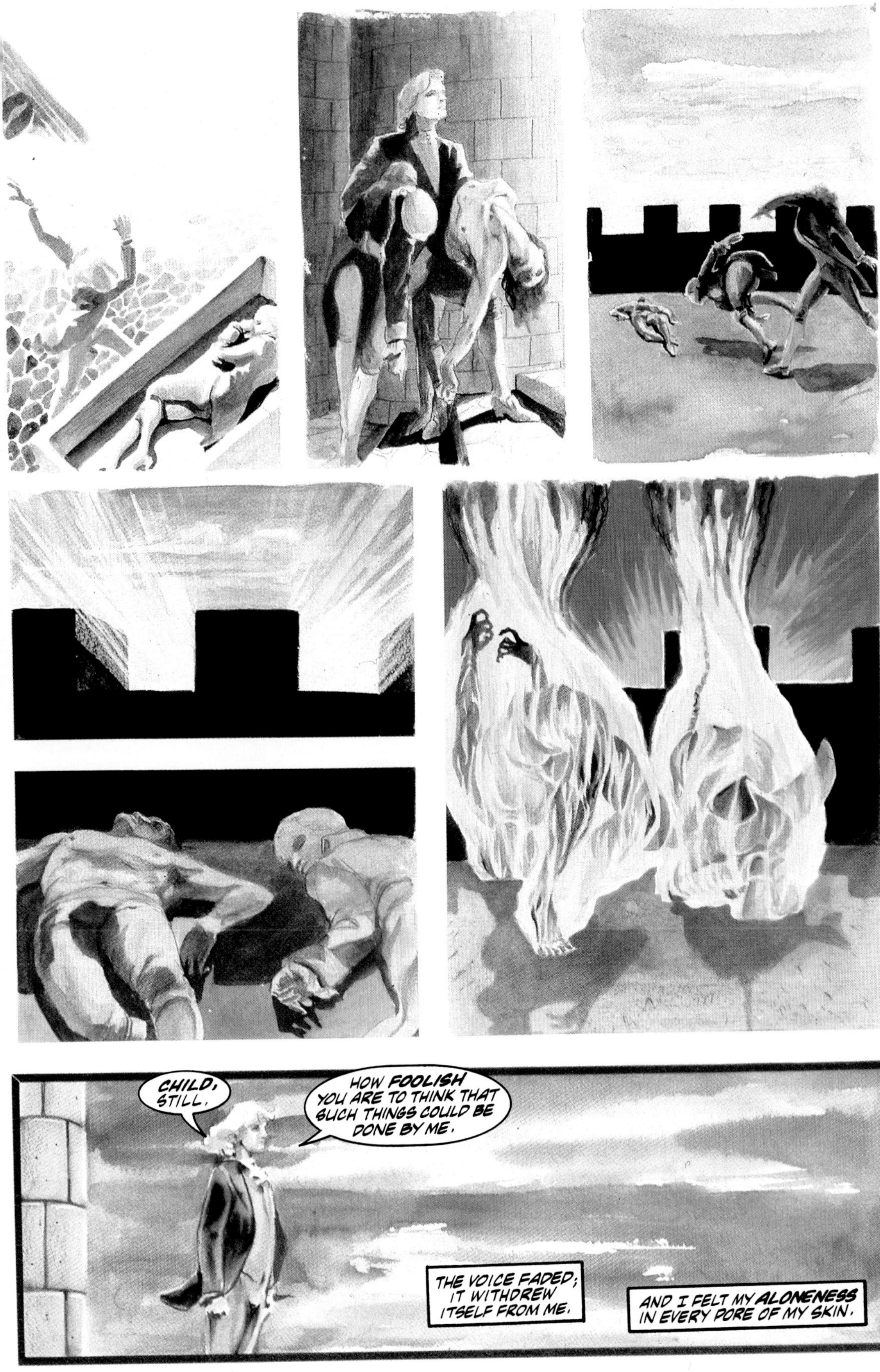
CHILD, STILL.
HOW FOOLISH YOU ARE TO THINK THAT SUCH THINGS COULD BE DONE BY ME.
THE VOICE FADED; IT WITHDREW ITSELF FROM ME.
AND I FELT MY ALONENESS IN EVERY PORE OF MY SKIN.

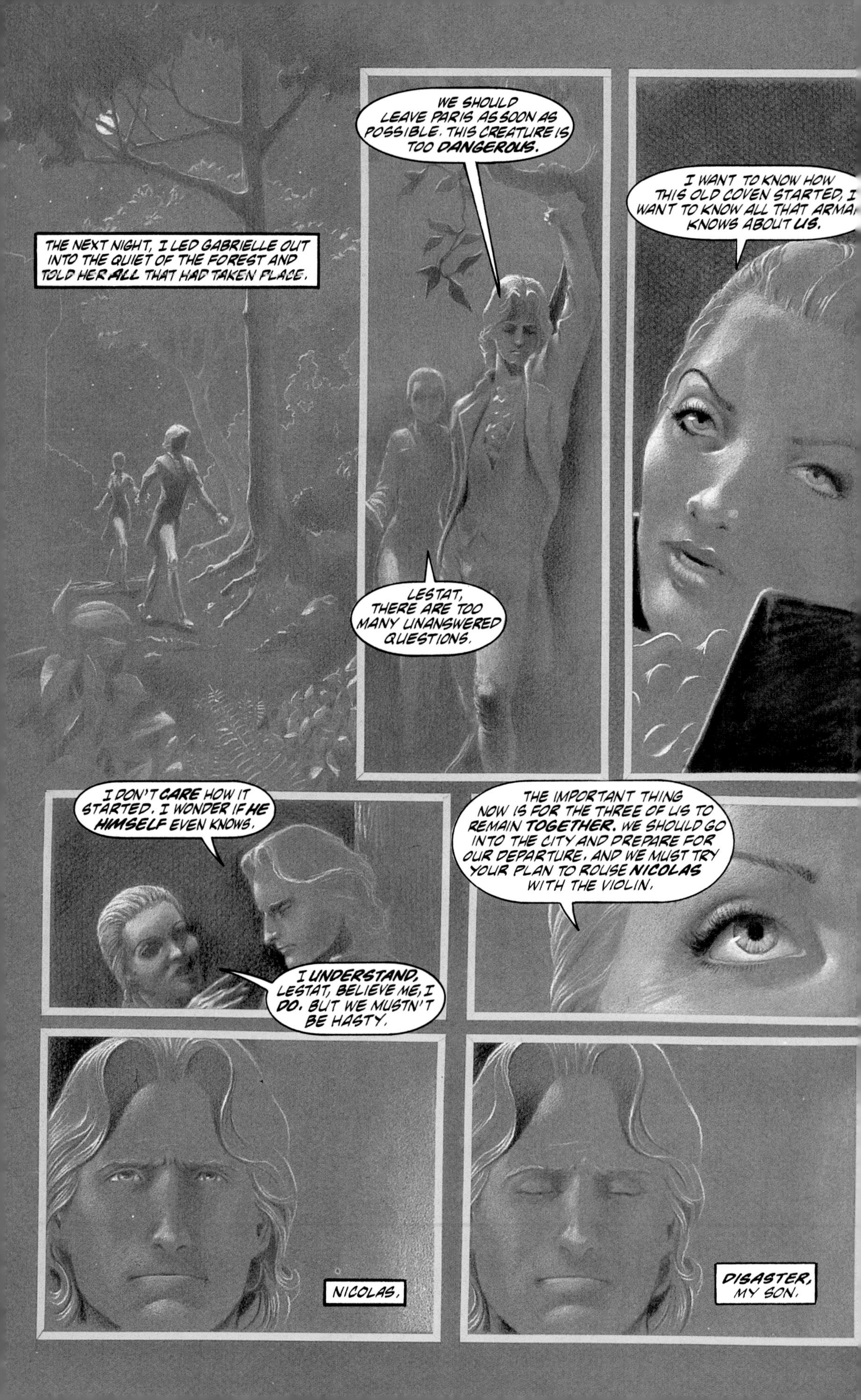

THE NEXT NIGHT, I LED GABRIELLE OUT INTO THE QUIET OF THE FOREST AND TOLD HER ALL THAT HAD TAKEN PLACE.
WE SHOULD LEAVE PARIS AS SOON AS POSSIBLE. THIS CREATURE IS TOO DANGEROUS.
LESTAT, THERE ARE TOO MANY UNANSWERED QUESTIONS.
I WANT TO KNOW HOW THIS OLD COVEN STARTED, I WANT TO KNOW ALL THAT ARMA KNOWS ABOUT US.
I DON'T CARE HOW IT STARTED. I WONDER IF HE HIMSELF EVEN KNOWS.
I UNDERSTAND, LESTAT, BELIEVE ME, I DO. BUT WE MUSTN'T BE HASTY.
THE IMPORTANT THING NOW IS FOR THE THREE OF US TO REMAIN TOGETHER. WE SHOULD GO INTO THE CITY AND PREPARE FOR OUR DEPARTURE. AND WE MUST TRY YOUR PLAN TO ROUSE NICOLAS WITH THE VIOLIN.
NICOLAS.
DISASTER, MY SON.

IT WAS AS EASY TO TAKE NICOLAS INTO PARIS AS TO LEAD HIM IN EVERYTHING ELSE.

LIKE A **GHOST** HE RODE ALONGSIDE OF US, ONLY HIS DARK HAIR AND CAPE SEEMINGLY ANIMATE, WHIPPED ABOUT BY THE WIND.

A VISIT TO ROGET HAD TO COME **FIRST**.

BUT WHEN I STEPPED OUT OF THE LAWYER'S HOUSE:

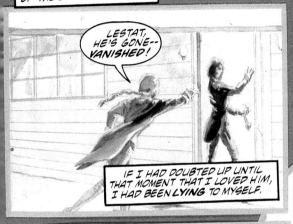

LESTAT, HE'S GONE-- **VANISHED**!

IF I HAD DOUBTED UP UNTIL THAT MOMENT THAT I LOVED HIM, I HAD BEEN **LYING** TO MYSELF.

I TURNED MY BACK, AND IT WAS **THAT** QUICK, I TELL YOU!

THERE ARE ONLY **TWO THINGS** THAT GO ROUND IN HIS MIND. ONE IS THE PYRE UNDER LES INNOCENTS...

...THE OTHER IS A **SMALL THEATER**-- FOOTLIGHTS, A STAGE.

RENAUD'S.

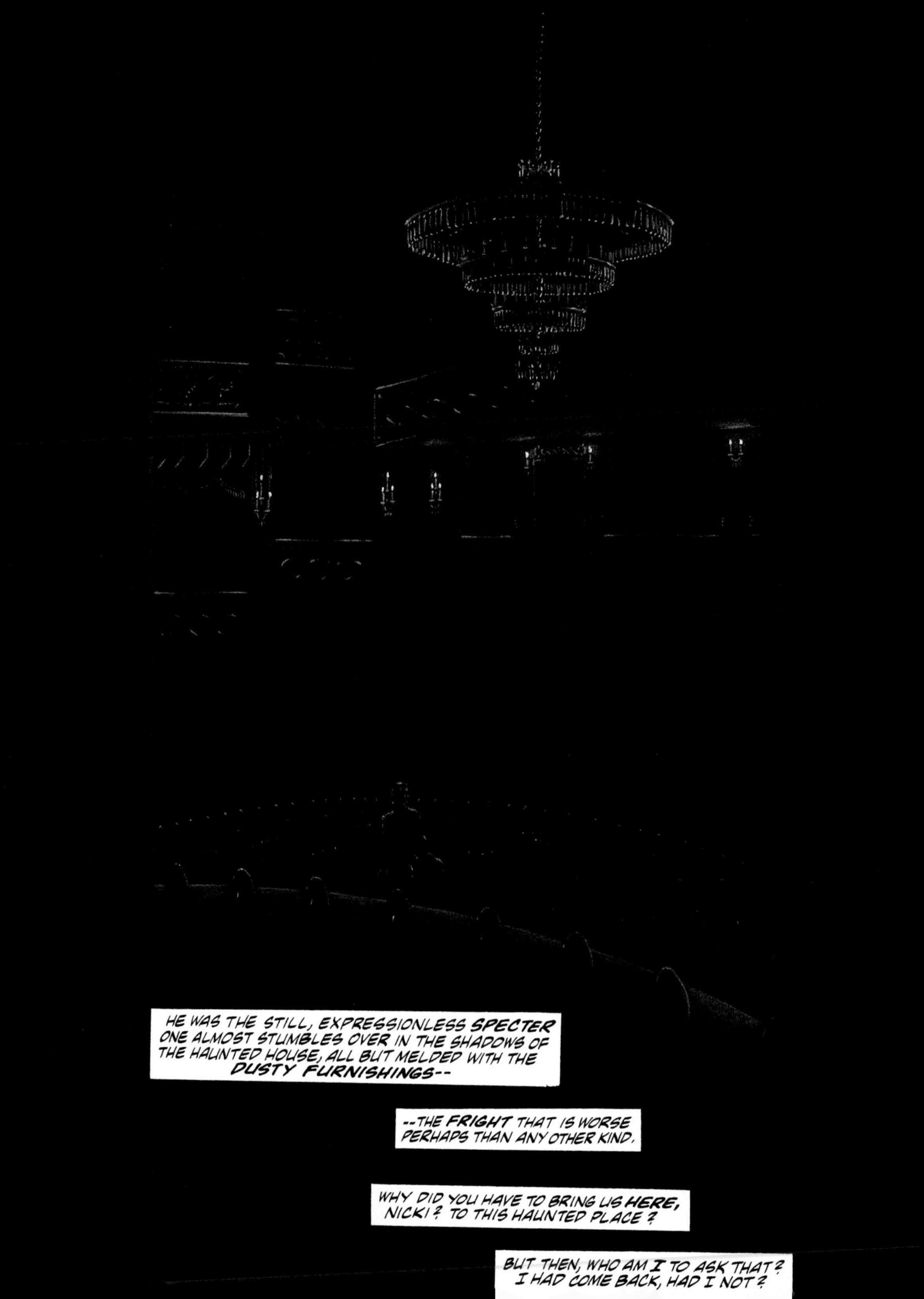
HE WAS THE STILL, EXPRESSIONLESS SPECTER ONE ALMOST STUMBLES OVER IN THE SHADOWS OF THE HAUNTED HOUSE, ALL BUT MELDED WITH THE DUSTY FURNISHINGS--
--THE FRIGHT THAT IS WORSE PERHAPS THAN ANY OTHER KIND.
WHY DID YOU HAVE TO BRING US HERE, NICKI? TO THIS HAUNTED PLACE?
BUT THEN, WHO AM I TO ASK THAT? I HAD COME BACK, HAD I NOT?

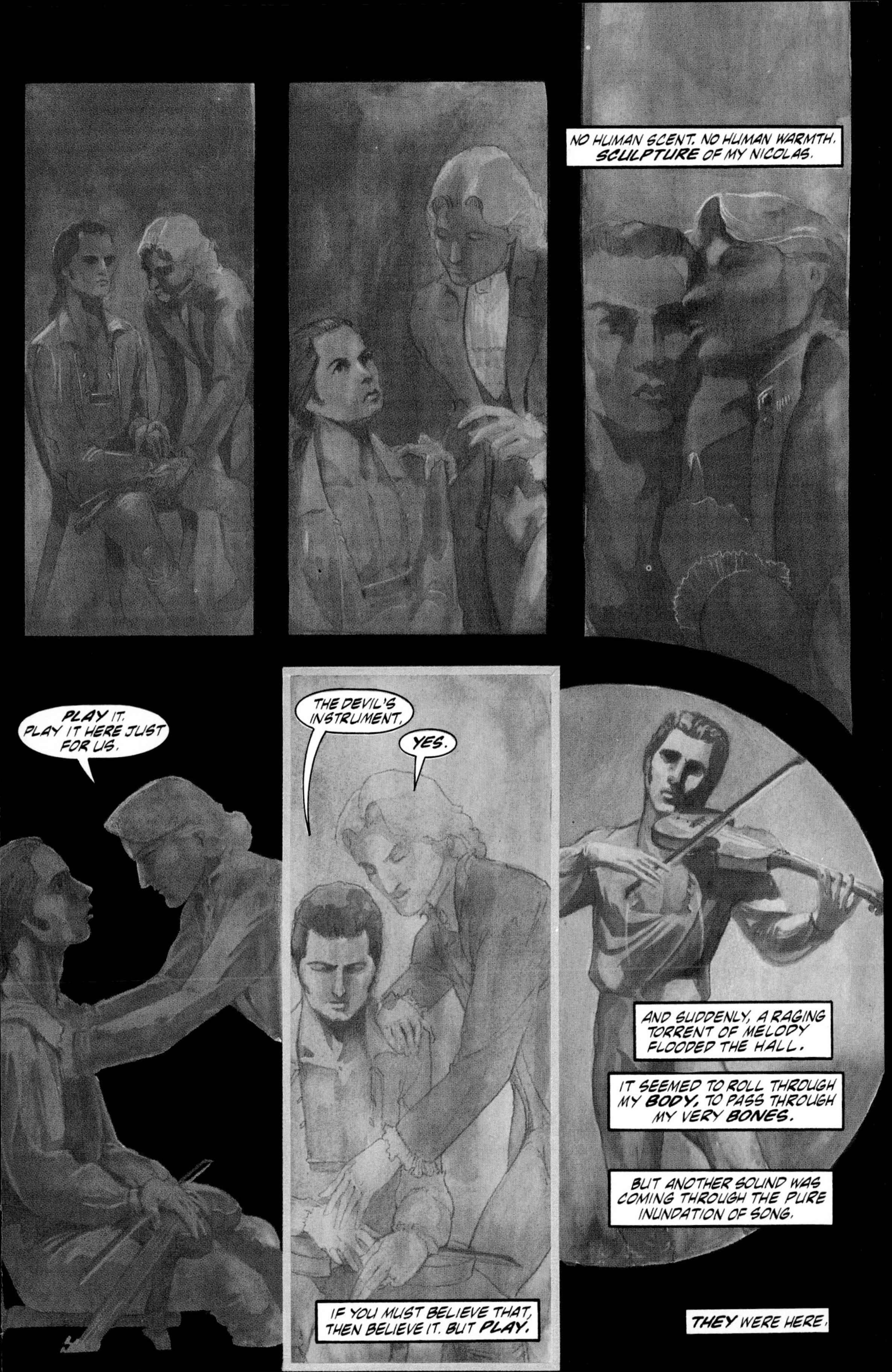
NO HUMAN SCENT. NO HUMAN WARMTH. SCULPTURE OF MY NICOLAS.
PLAY IT. PLAY IT HERE JUST FOR US.
THE DEVIL'S INSTRUMENT.
YES.
IF YOU MUST BELIEVE THAT, THEN BELIEVE IT. BUT PLAY.
AND SUDDENLY, A RAGING TORRENT OF MELODY FLOODED THE HALL.
IT SEEMED TO ROLL THROUGH MY BODY, TO PASS THROUGH MY VERY BONES.
BUT ANOTHER SOUND WAS COMING THROUGH THE PURE INUNDATION OF SONG.
THEY WERE HERE.

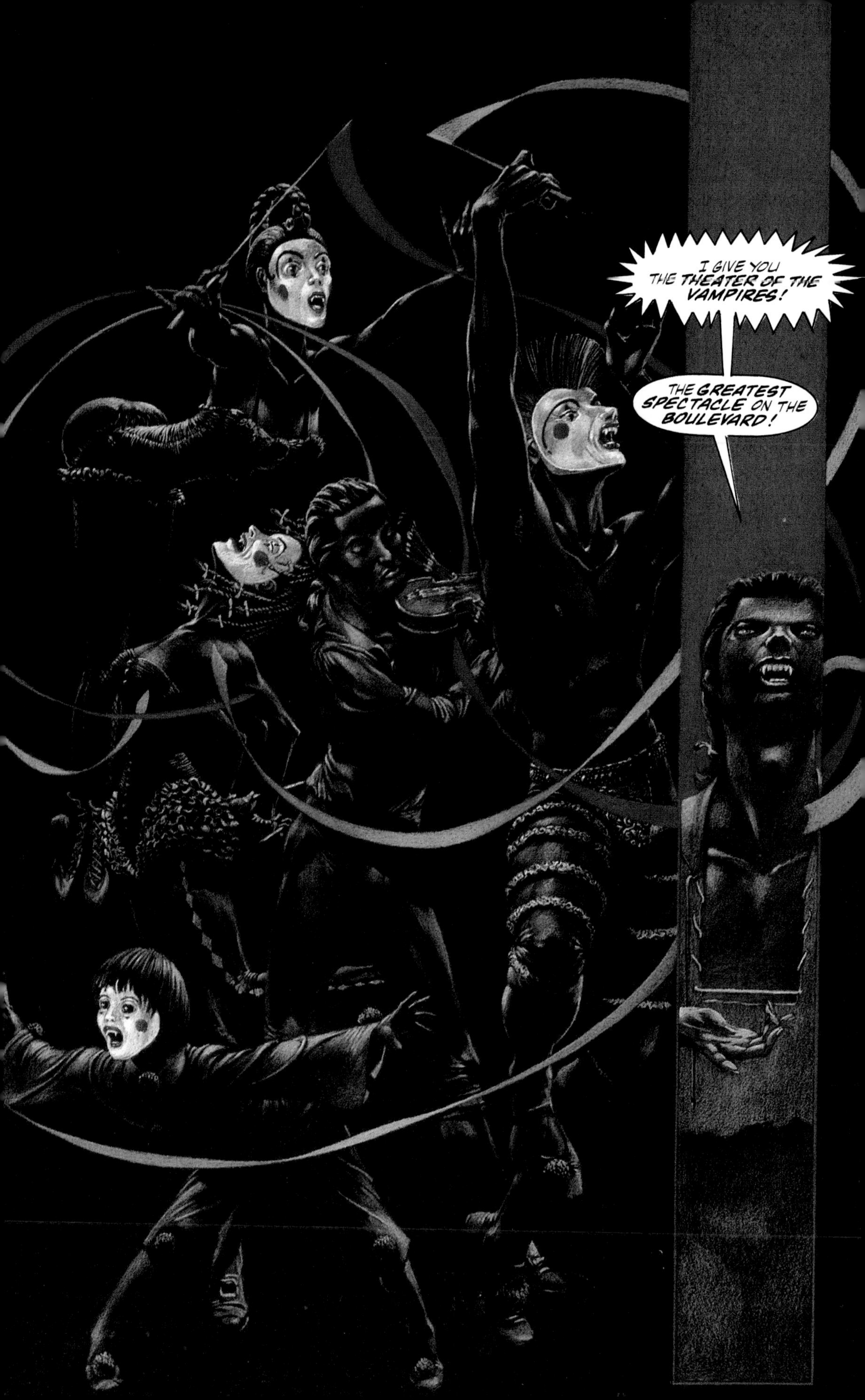
I GIVE YOU THE THEATER OF THE VAMPIRES!
THE GREATEST SPECTACLE ON THE BOULEVARD!

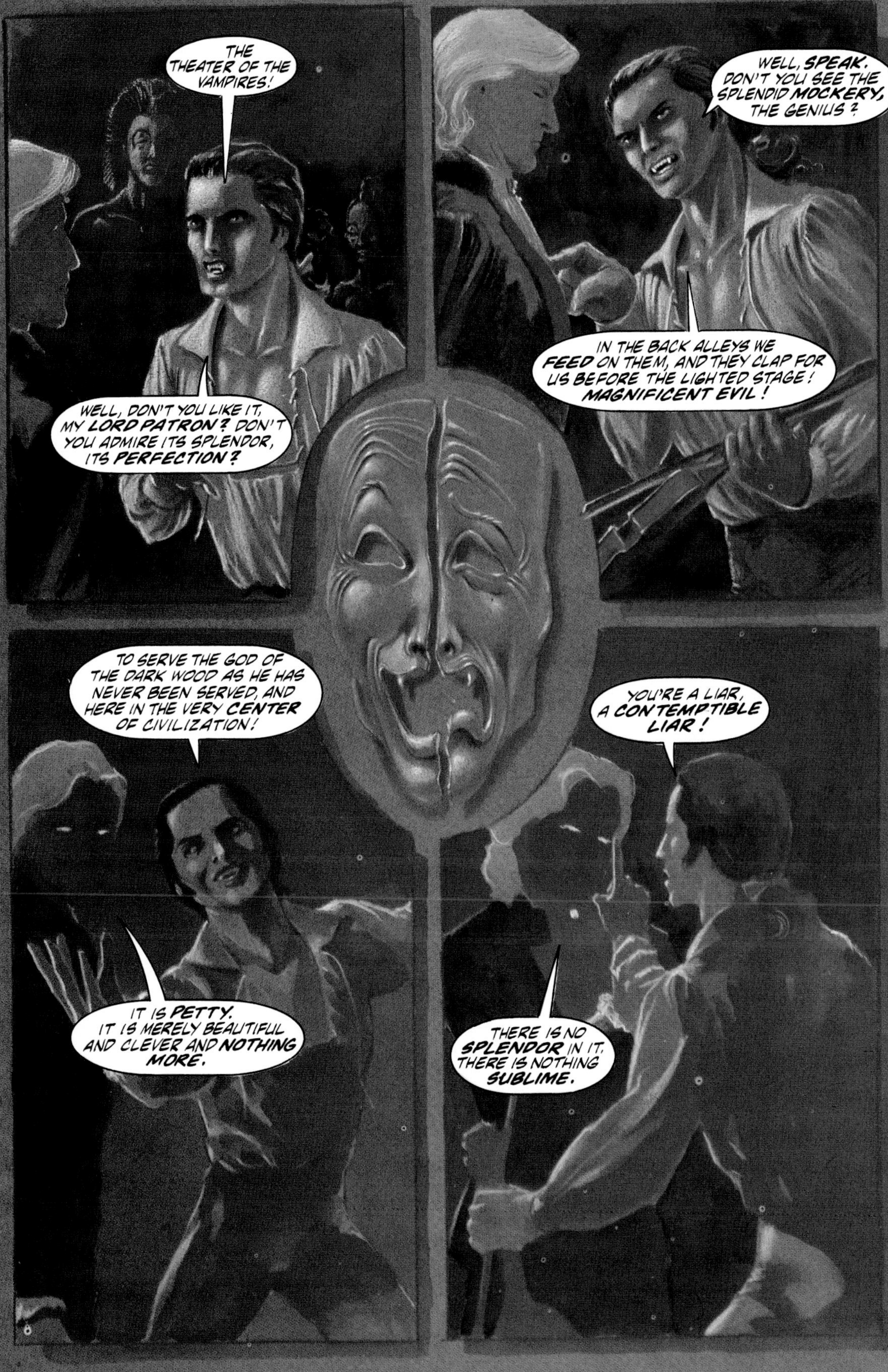
THE THEATER OF THE VAMPIRES!
WELL, DON'T YOU LIKE IT, MY LORD PATRON? DON'T YOU ADMIRE ITS SPLENDOR, ITS PERFECTION?
WELL, SPEAK. DON'T YOU SEE THE SPLENDID MOCKERY, THE GENIUS?
IN THE BACK ALLEYS WE FEED ON THEM, AND THEY CLAP FOR US BEFORE THE LIGHTED STAGE! MAGNIFICENT EVIL!
TO SERVE THE GOD OF THE DARK WOOD AS HE HAS NEVER BEEN SERVED, AND HERE IN THE VERY CENTER OF CIVILIZATION!
IT IS PETTY. IT IS MERELY BEAUTIFUL AND CLEVER AND NOTHING MORE.
YOU'RE A LIAR, A CONTEMPTIBLE LIAR!
THERE IS NO SPLENDOR IN IT. THERE IS NOTHING SUBLIME.

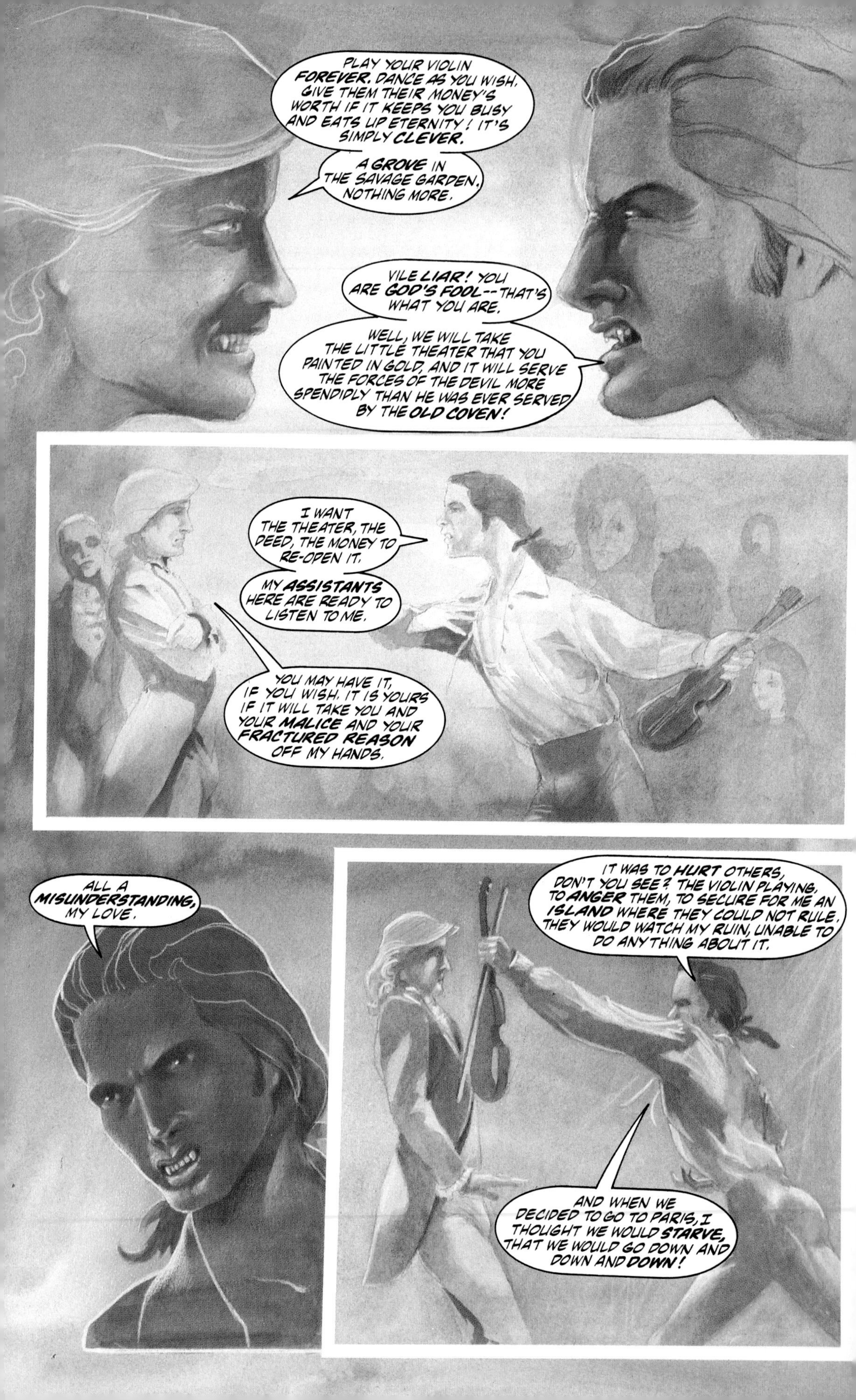
PLAY YOUR VIOLIN FOREVER. DANCE AS YOU WISH. GIVE THEM THEIR MONEY'S WORTH IF IT KEEPS YOU BUSY AND EATS UP ETERNITY! IT'S SIMPLY CLEVER.
A GROVE IN THE SAVAGE GARDEN. NOTHING MORE.
VILE LIAR! YOU ARE GOD'S FOOL--THAT'S WHAT YOU ARE.
WELL, WE WILL TAKE THE LITTLE THEATER THAT YOU PAINTED IN GOLD, AND IT WILL SERVE THE FORCES OF THE DEVIL MORE SPENDIDLY THAN HE WAS EVER SERVED BY THE OLD COVEN!
I WANT THE THEATER, THE DEED, THE MONEY TO RE-OPEN IT.
MY ASSISTANTS HERE ARE READY TO LISTEN TO ME.
YOU MAY HAVE IT, IF YOU WISH. IT IS YOURS IF IT WILL TAKE YOU AND YOUR MALICE AND YOUR FRACTURED REASON OFF MY HANDS.
ALL A MISUNDERSTANDING, MY LOVE.
IT WAS TO HURT OTHERS, DON'T YOU SEE? THE VIOLIN PLAYING, TO ANGER THEM, TO SECURE FOR ME AN ISLAND WHERE THEY COULD NOT RULE. THEY WOULD WATCH MY RUIN, UNABLE TO DO ANYTHING ABOUT IT.
AND WHEN WE DECIDED TO GO TO PARIS, I THOUGHT WE WOULD STARVE, THAT WE WOULD GO DOWN AND DOWN AND DOWN!

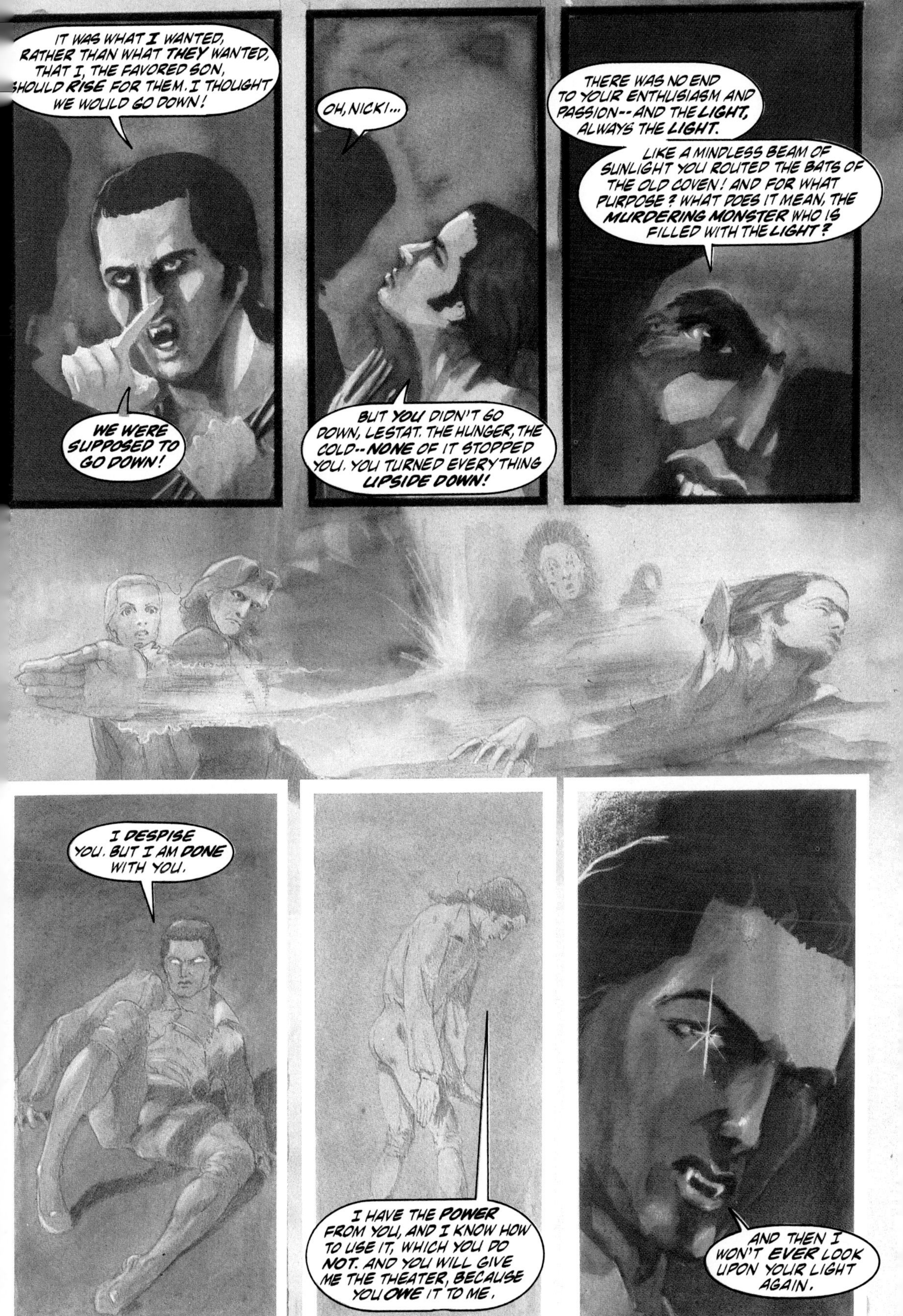
IT WAS WHAT I WANTED, RATHER THAN WHAT THEY WANTED, THAT I, THE FAVORED SON, SHOULD RISE FOR THEM. I THOUGHT WE WOULD GO DOWN!
WE WERE SUPPOSED TO GO DOWN!
OH, NICKI...
BUT YOU DIDN'T GO DOWN, LESTAT. THE HUNGER, THE COLD--NONE OF IT STOPPED YOU. YOU TURNED EVERYTHING UPSIDE DOWN!
THERE WAS NO END TO YOUR ENTHUSIASM AND PASSION--AND THE LIGHT, ALWAYS THE LIGHT.
LIKE A MINDLESS BEAM OF SUNLIGHT YOU ROUTED THE BATS OF THE OLD COVEN! AND FOR WHAT PURPOSE? WHAT DOES IT MEAN, THE MURDERING MONSTER WHO IS FILLED WITH THE LIGHT?
I DESPISE YOU. BUT I AM DONE WITH YOU.
I HAVE THE POWER FROM YOU, AND I KNOW HOW TO USE IT, WHICH YOU DO NOT. AND YOU WILL GIVE ME THE THEATER, BECAUSE YOU OWE IT TO ME.
AND THEN I WON'T EVER LOOK UPON YOUR LIGHT AGAIN.

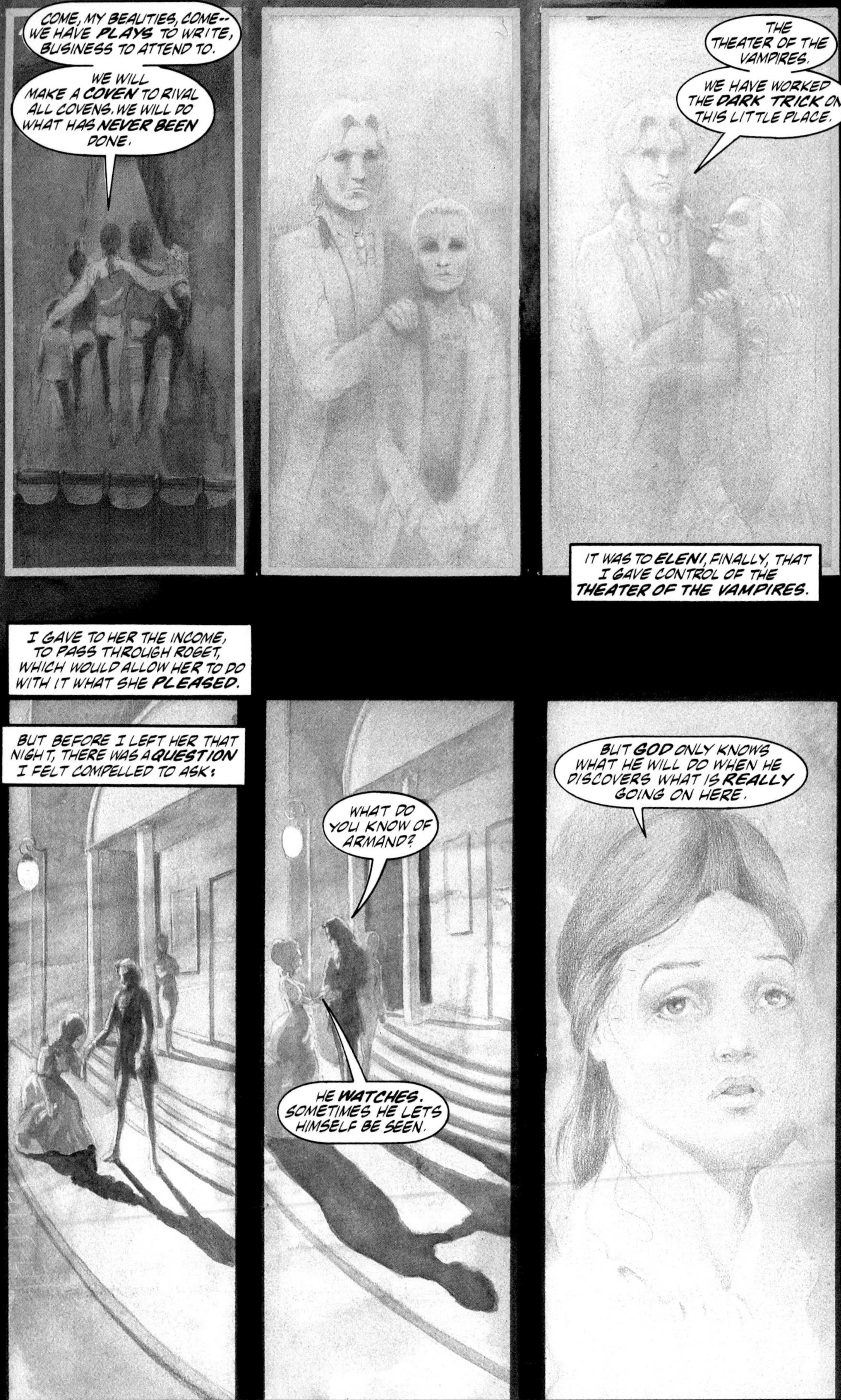
COME, MY BEAUTIES, COME-- WE HAVE PLAYS TO WRITE, BUSINESS TO ATTEND TO.
WE WILL MAKE A COVEN TO RIVAL ALL COVENS. WE WILL DO WHAT HAS NEVER BEEN DONE.
THE THEATER OF THE VAMPIRES.
WE HAVE WORKED THE DARK TRICK ON THIS LITTLE PLACE.
IT WAS TO ELENI, FINALLY, THAT I GAVE CONTROL OF THE THEATER OF THE VAMPIRES.
I GAVE TO HER THE INCOME, TO PASS THROUGH ROGET, WHICH WOULD ALLOW HER TO DO WITH IT WHAT SHE PLEASED.
BUT BEFORE I LEFT HER THAT NIGHT, THERE WAS A QUESTION I FELT COMPELLED TO ASK:
WHAT DO YOU KNOW OF ARMAND?
HE WATCHES. SOMETIMES HE LETS HIMSELF BE SEEN.
BUT GOD ONLY KNOWS WHAT HE WILL DO WHEN HE DISCOVERS WHAT IS REALLY GOING ON HERE.

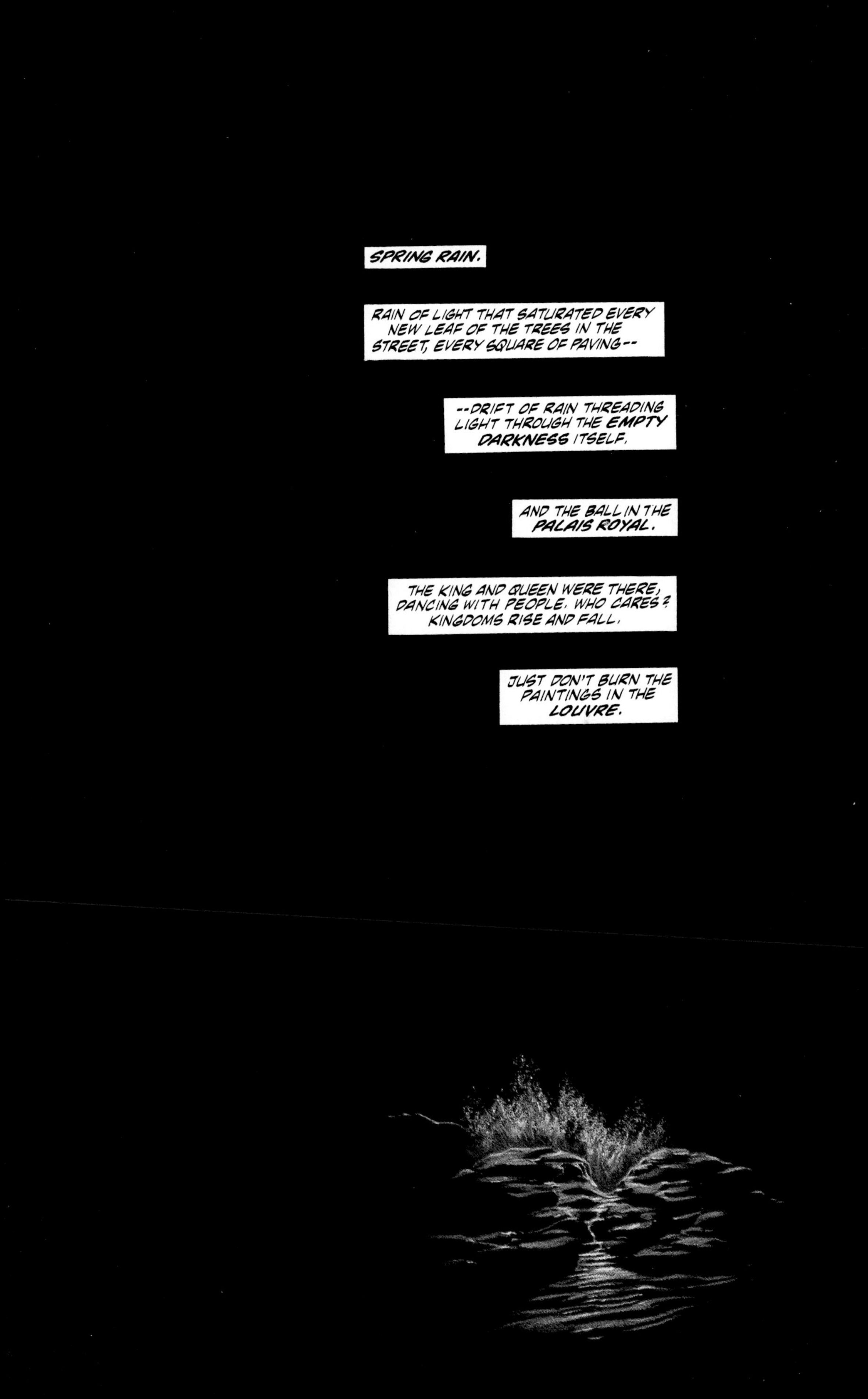
SPRING RAIN.
RAIN OF LIGHT THAT SATURATED EVERY NEW LEAF OF THE TREES IN THE STREET, EVERY SQUARE OF PAVING--
--DRIFT OF RAIN THREADING LIGHT THROUGH THE EMPTY DARKNESS ITSELF.
AND THE BALL IN THE PALAIS ROYAL.
THE KING AND QUEEN WERE THERE, DANCING WITH PEOPLE. WHO CARES? KINGDOMS RISE AND FALL.
JUST DON'T BURN THE PAINTINGS IN THE LOUVRE.

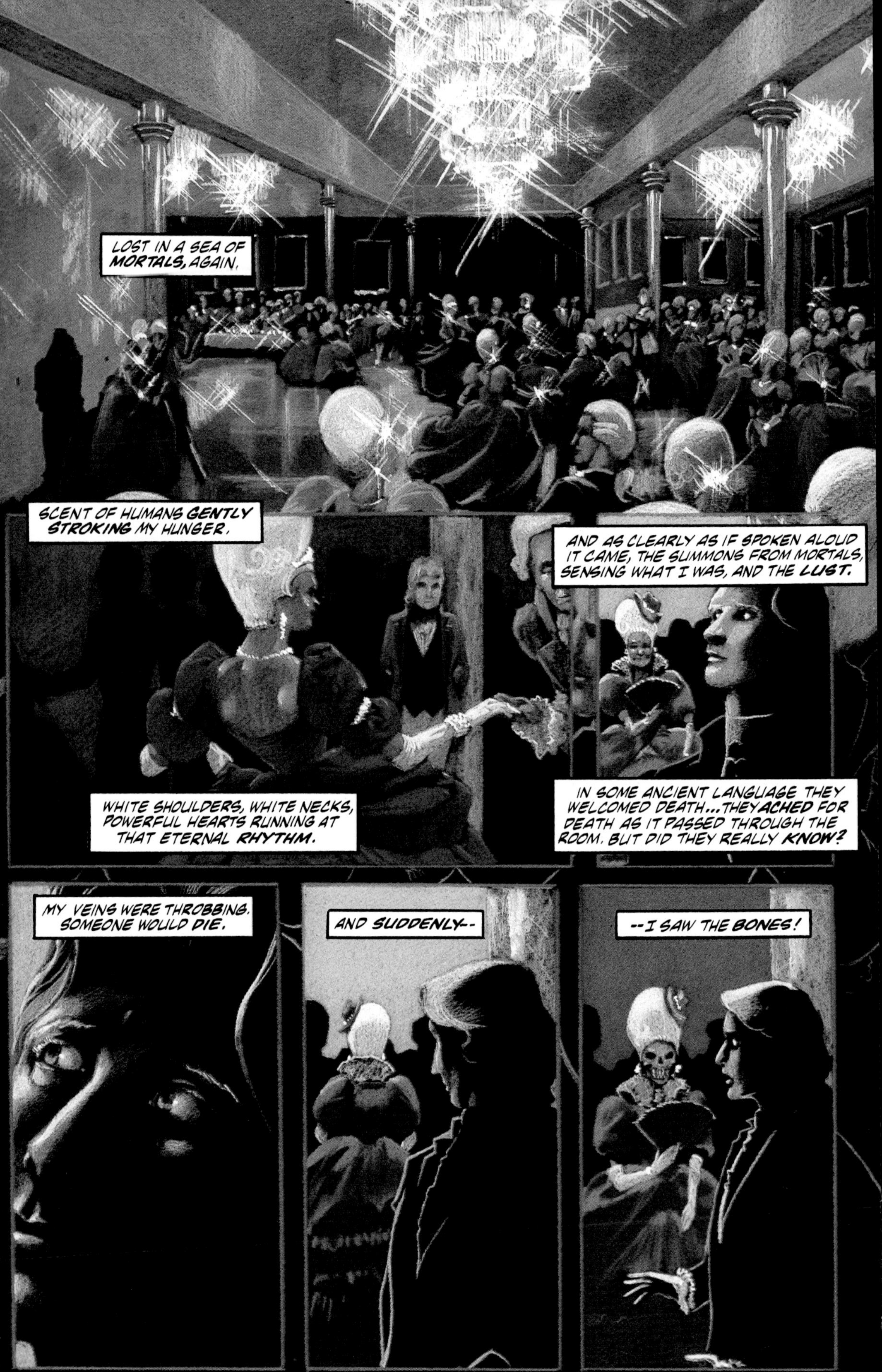
LOST IN A SEA OF MORTALS, AGAIN.
SCENT OF HUMANS GENTLY STROKING MY HUNGER.
WHITE SHOULDERS, WHITE NECKS, POWERFUL HEARTS RUNNING AT THAT ETERNAL RHYTHM.
AND AS CLEARLY AS IF SPOKEN ALOUD IT CAME, THE SUMMONS FROM MORTALS, SENSING WHAT I WAS, AND THE LUST.
IN SOME ANCIENT LANGUAGE THEY WELCOMED DEATH... THEY ACHED FOR DEATH AS IT PASSED THROUGH THE ROOM. BUT DID THEY REALLY KNOW?
MY VEINS WERE THROBBING. SOMEONE WOULD DIE.
AND SUDDENLY--
--I SAW THE BONES!

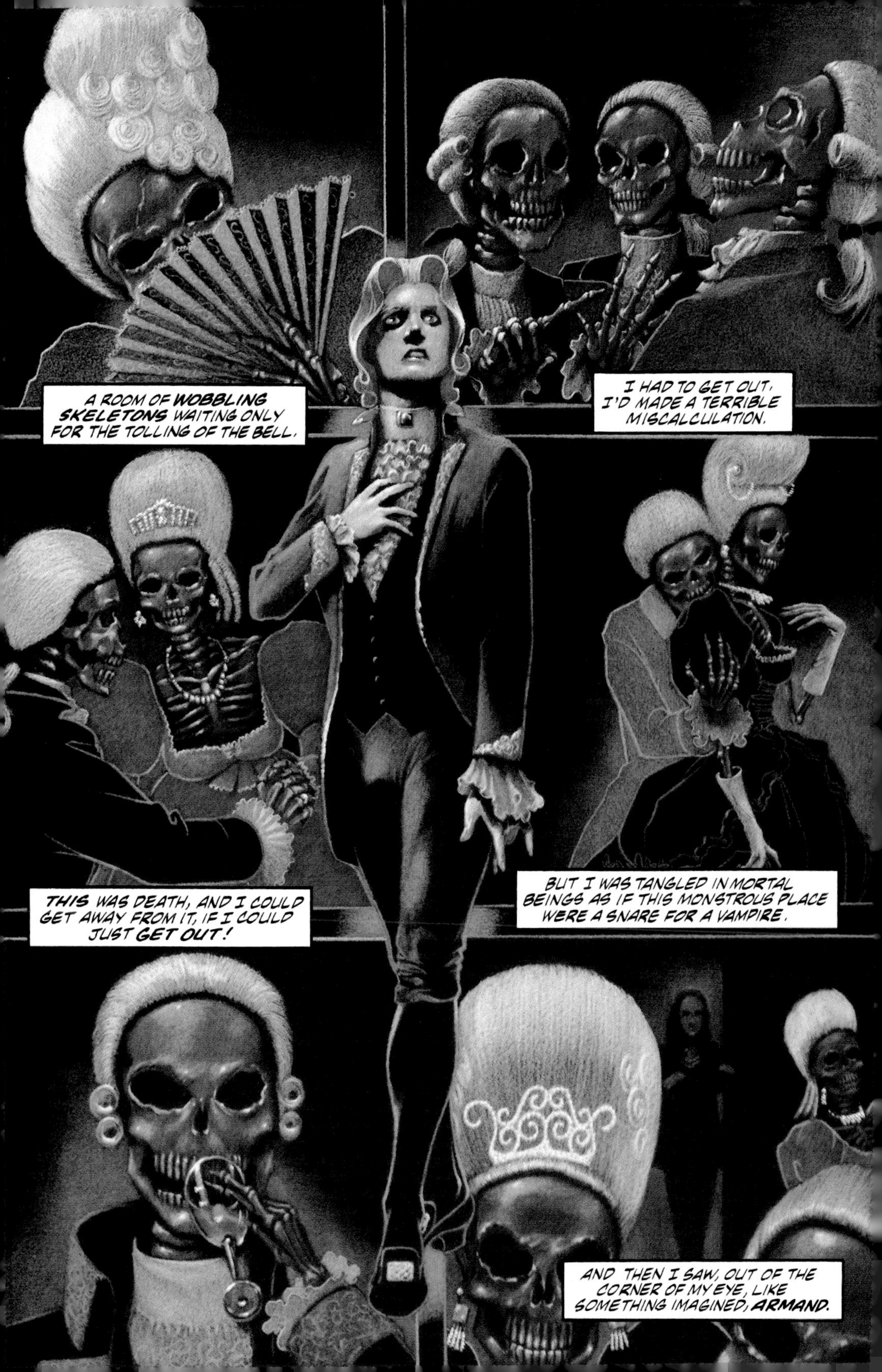

A ROOM OF WOBBLING SKELETONS WAITING ONLY FOR THE TOLLING OF THE BELL.
I HAD TO GET OUT. I'D MADE A TERRIBLE MISCALCULATION.
THIS WAS DEATH, AND I COULD GET AWAY FROM IT, IF I COULD JUST GET OUT!
BUT I WAS TANGLED IN MORTAL BEINGS AS IF THIS MONSTROUS PLACE WERE A SNARE FOR A VAMPIRE.
AND THEN I SAW, OUT OF THE CORNER OF MY EYE, LIKE SOMETHING IMAGINED, ARMAND.

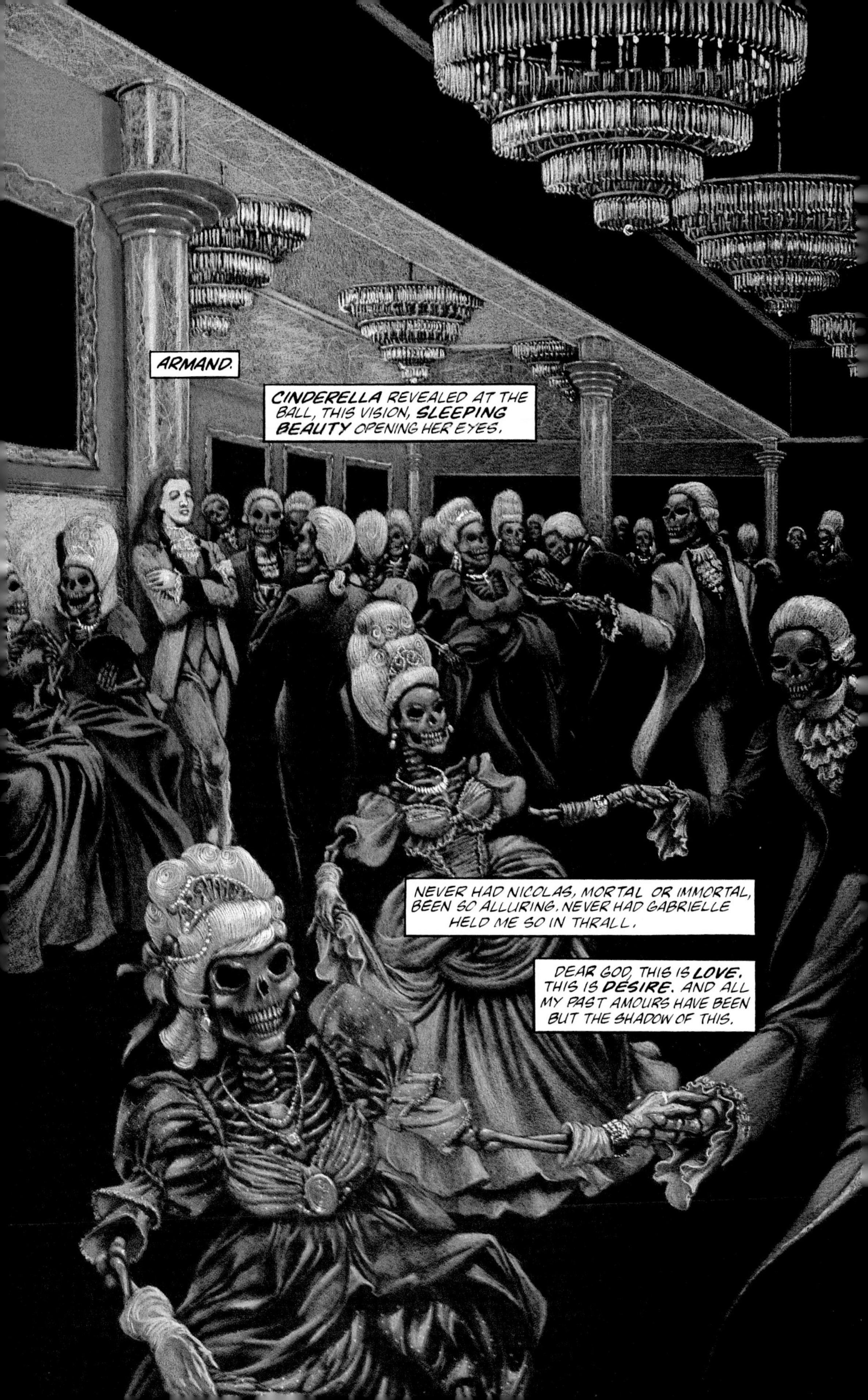
ARMAND.
CINDERELLA REVEALED AT THE BALL, THIS VISION, SLEEPING BEAUTY OPENING HER EYES.
NEVER HAD NICOLAS, MORTAL OR IMMORTAL, BEEN SO ALLURING. NEVER HAD GABRIELLE HELD ME SO IN THRALL.
DEAR GOD, THIS IS LOVE. THIS IS DESIRE. AND ALL MY PAST AMOURS HAVE BEEN BUT THE SHADOW OF THIS.

A MAD THOUGHT CAME TO ME AS I FOLLOWED HIM. NONE OF THE OTHER THINGS HAD HAPPENED.

WHO CAN LOVE US, YOU AND I, AS WE CAN LOVE EACH OTHER?

THERE WAS NO *CRYPT* UNDER LES INNOCENTS, AND HE HAD NOT BEEN THAT ANCIENT FEARFUL *FRIEND.*

WE WERE SOMEHOW *SAFE.*

YES, YES, HIS LIPS TASTED LIKE BLOOD, BUT IT WAS NOT HUMAN BLOOD. IT WAS THE *ELIXIR* THAT MAGNUS HAD GIVEN ME!

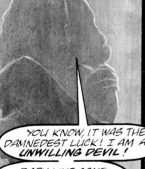

YOU KNOW, IT WAS THE DAMNEDEST LUCK! I AM AN *UNWILLING DEVIL!*

I CRY LIKE SOME VAGRANT CHILD. I WANT TO GO *HOME.*

I HAD *NEVER DIED.* I HAD *ANOTHER CHANCE.* I COULD GET AWAY THIS TIME. THE WHEEL HAD TURNED FULL ROUND.

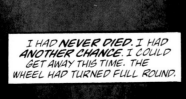

I WAS CRYING OUT THAT I WOULDN'T DRINK, I WOULDN'T, AND THEN I FELT THE TWO HOT SHAFTS DRIVEN HARD THROUGH MY NECK AND DOWN TO MY SOUL.

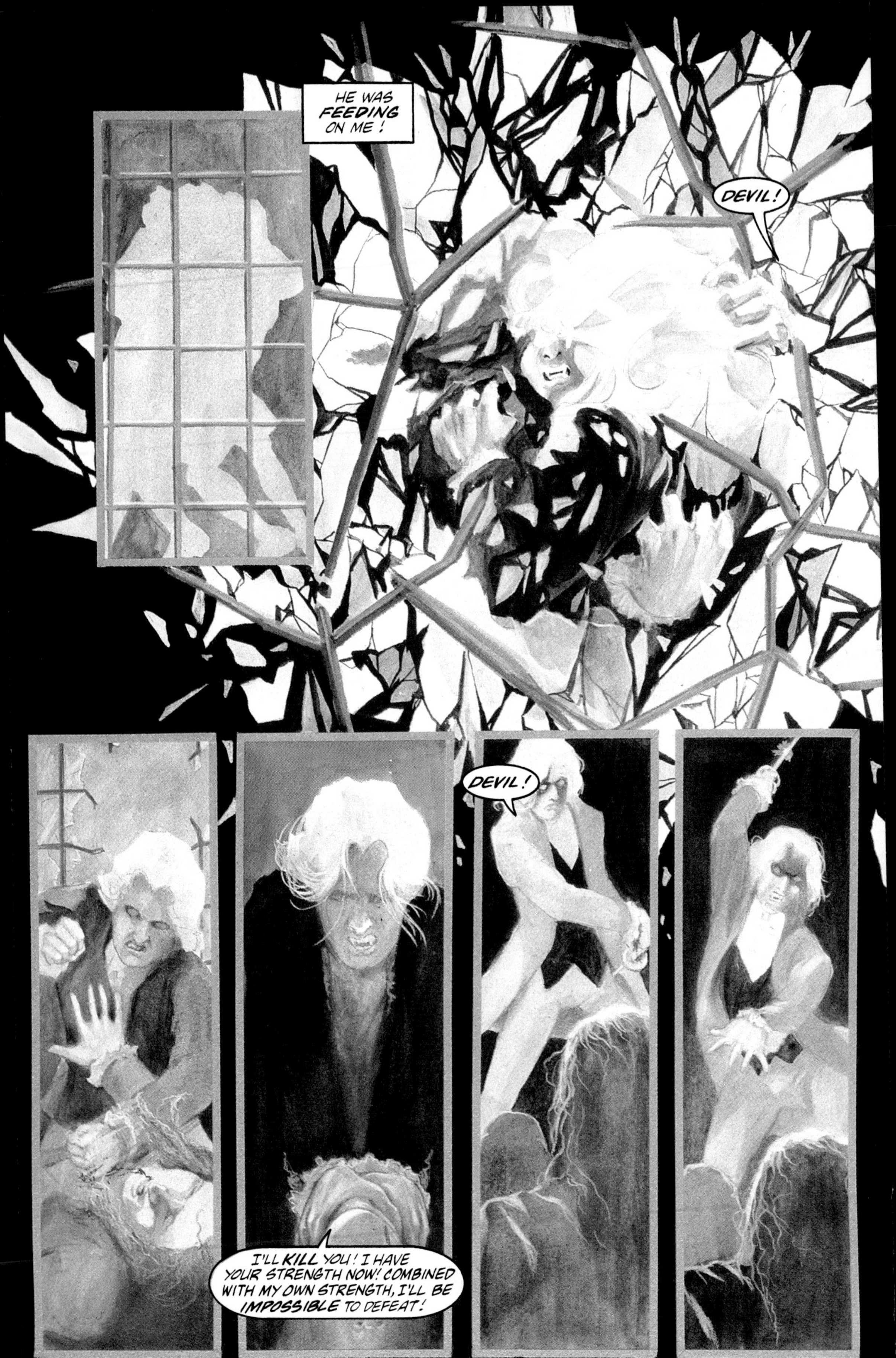
HE WAS FEEDING ON ME!
DEVIL!
I'LL KILL YOU! I HAVE YOUR STRENGTH NOW! COMBINED WITH MY OWN STRENGTH, I'LL BE IMPOSSIBLE TO DEFEAT!
DEVIL!

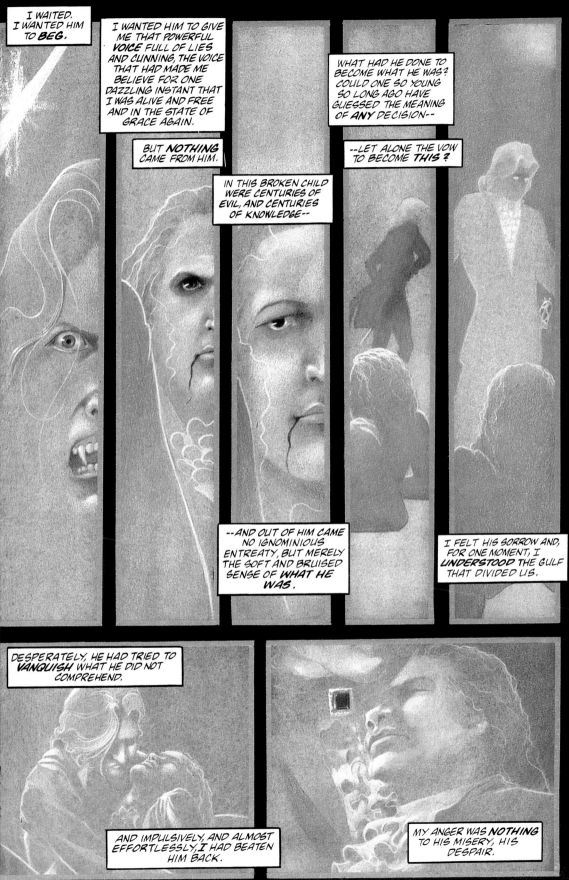

I WAITED.
I WANTED HIM
TO **BEG.**

I WANTED HIM TO GIVE
ME THAT POWERFUL
VOICE FULL OF LIES
AND CUNNING, THE VOICE
THAT HAD MADE ME
BELIEVE FOR ONE
DAZZLING INSTANT THAT
I WAS ALIVE AND FREE
AND IN THE STATE OF
GRACE AGAIN.

WHAT HAD HE DONE TO
BECOME WHAT HE WAS?
COULD ONE SO YOUNG
SO LONG AGO HAVE
GUESSED THE MEANING
OF **ANY** DECISION--

BUT **NOTHING**
CAME FROM HIM.

--LET ALONE THE VOW
TO BECOME **THIS?**

IN THIS BROKEN CHILD
WERE CENTURIES OF
EVIL, AND CENTURIES
OF KNOWLEDGE--

--AND OUT OF HIM CAME
NO IGNOMINIOUS
ENTREATY, BUT MERELY
THE SOFT AND BRUISED
SENSE OF **WHAT HE
WAS.**

I FELT HIS SORROW AND,
FOR ONE MOMENT, I
UNDERSTOOD THE GULF
THAT DIVIDED US.

DESPERATELY, HE HAD TRIED TO
VANQUISH WHAT HE DID NOT
COMPREHEND.

AND IMPULSIVELY, AND ALMOST
EFFORTLESSLY, **I** HAD BEATEN
HIM BACK.

MY ANGER WAS **NOTHING**
TO HIS MISERY, HIS
DESPAIR.

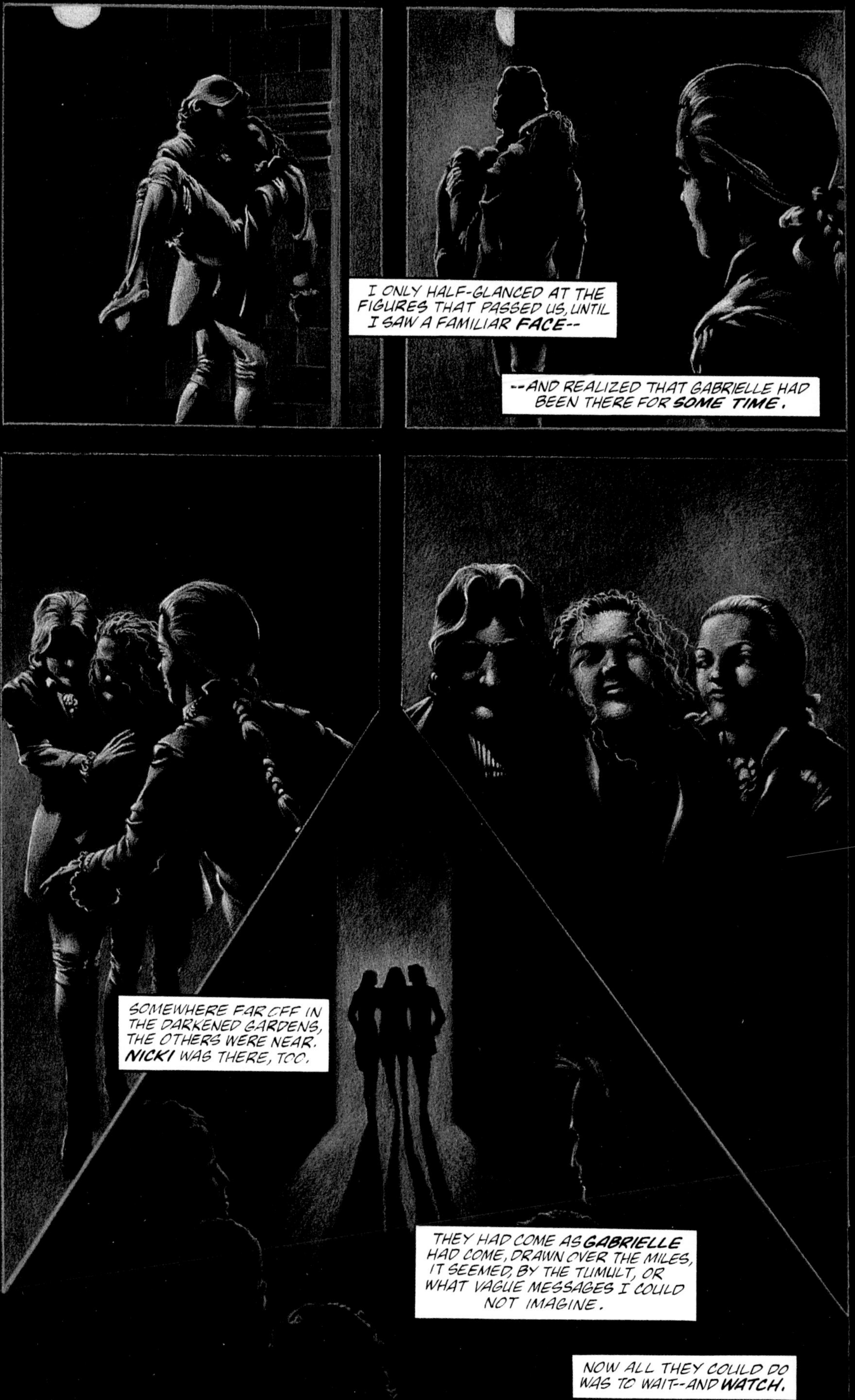
I ONLY HALF-GLANCED AT THE FIGURES THAT PASSED US, UNTIL I SAW A FAMILIAR FACE--
--AND REALIZED THAT GABRIELLE HAD BEEN THERE FOR SOME TIME.
SOMEWHERE FAR OFF IN THE DARKENED GARDENS, THE OTHERS WERE NEAR. NICKI WAS THERE, TOO.
THEY HAD COME AS GABRIELLE HAD COME, DRAWN OVER THE MILES, IT SEEMED, BY THE TUMULT, OR WHAT VAGUE MESSAGES I COULD NOT IMAGINE.
NOW ALL THEY COULD DO WAS TO WAIT--AND WATCH.

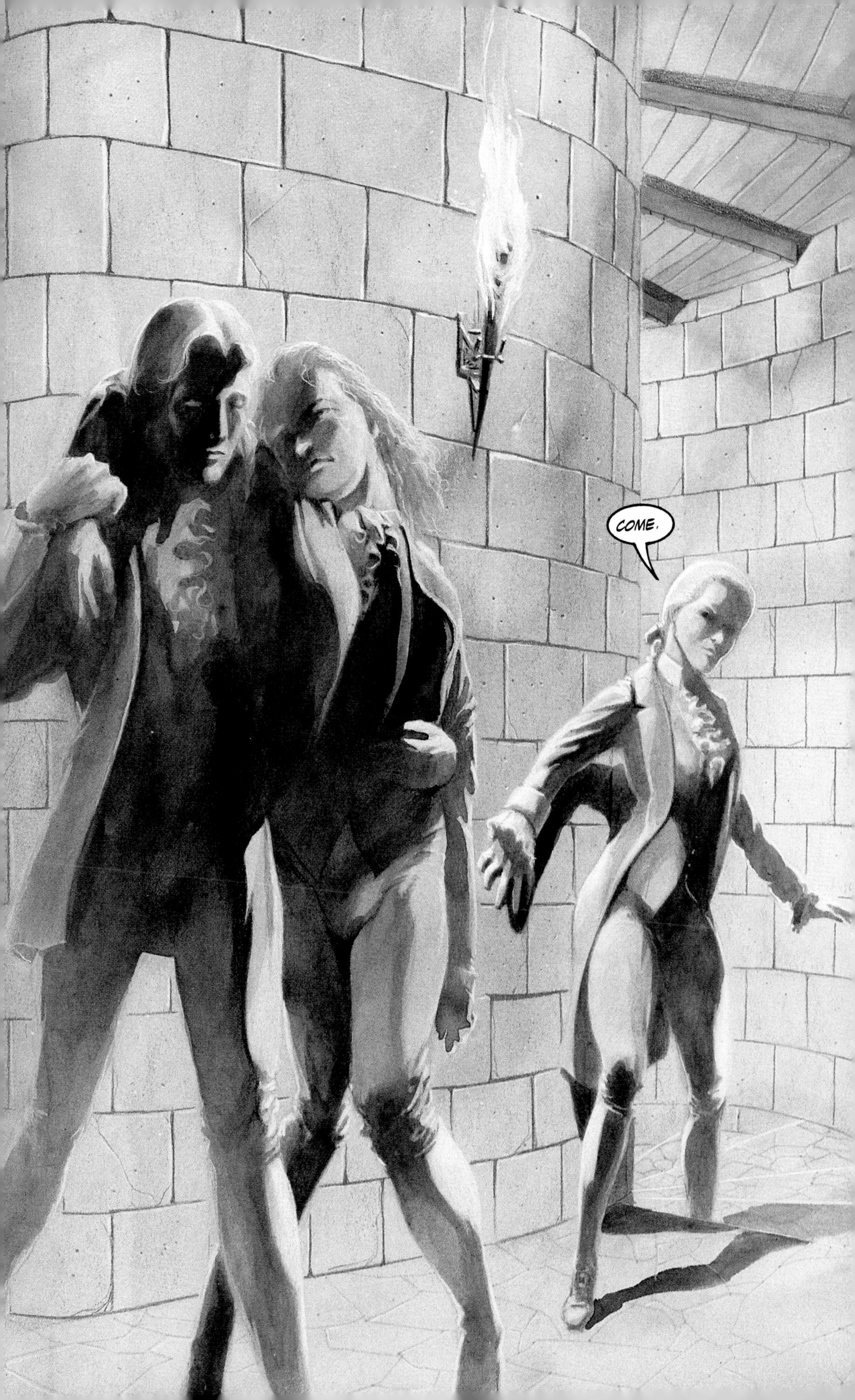
COME.

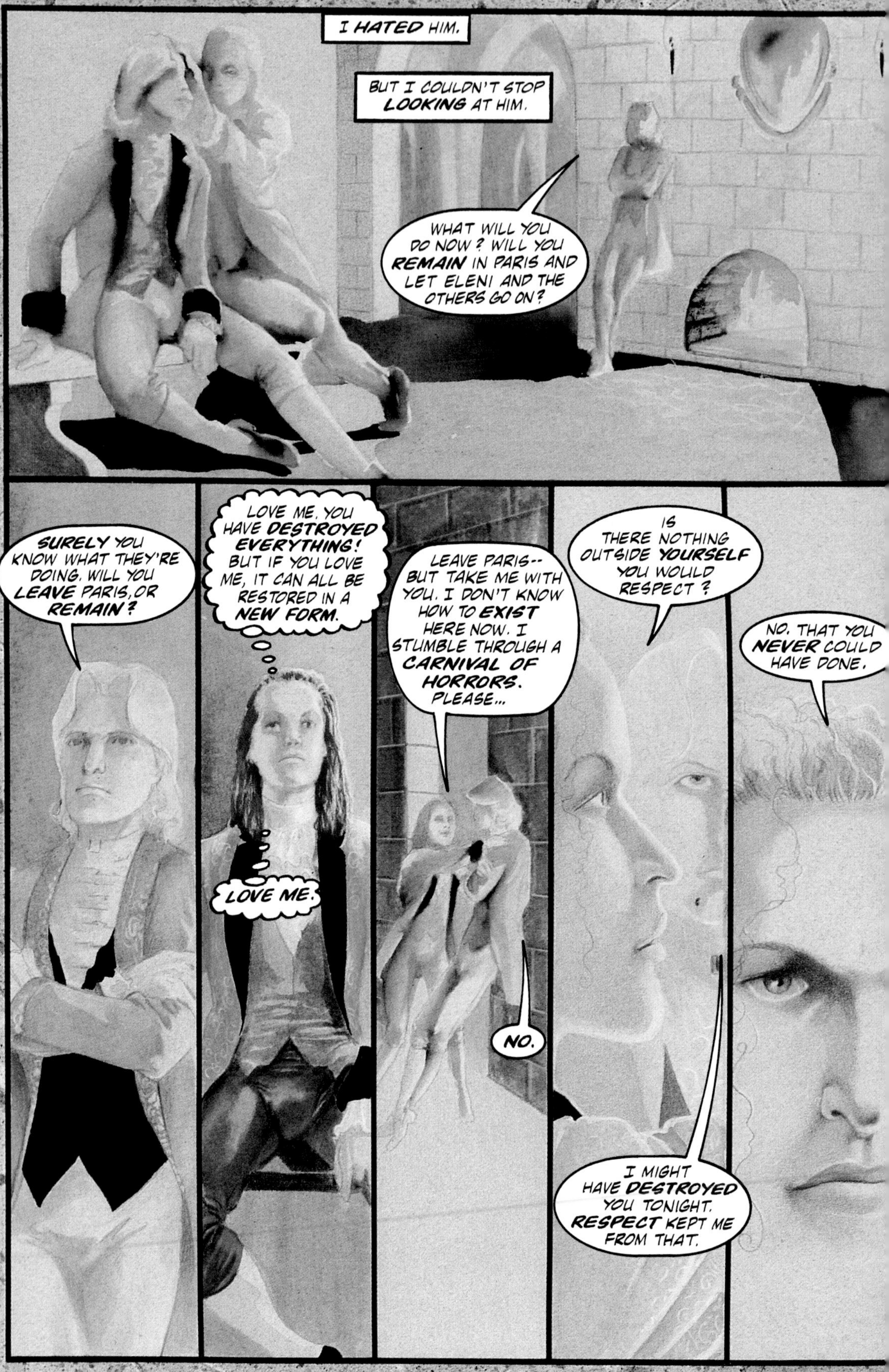
I HATED HIM.
BUT I COULDN'T STOP LOOKING AT HIM.
WHAT WILL YOU DO NOW? WILL YOU REMAIN IN PARIS AND LET ELENI AND THE OTHERS GO ON?
SURELY YOU KNOW WHAT THEY'RE DOING. WILL YOU LEAVE PARIS, OR REMAIN?
LOVE ME. YOU HAVE DESTROYED EVERYTHING! BUT IF YOU LOVE ME, IT CAN ALL BE RESTORED IN A NEW FORM.
LOVE ME.
LEAVE PARIS-- BUT TAKE ME WITH YOU. I DON'T KNOW HOW TO EXIST HERE NOW. I STUMBLE THROUGH A CARNIVAL OF HORRORS. PLEASE...
NO.
IS THERE NOTHING OUTSIDE YOURSELF YOU WOULD RESPECT?
NO. THAT YOU NEVER COULD HAVE DONE.
I MIGHT HAVE DESTROYED YOU TONIGHT. RESPECT KEPT ME FROM THAT.

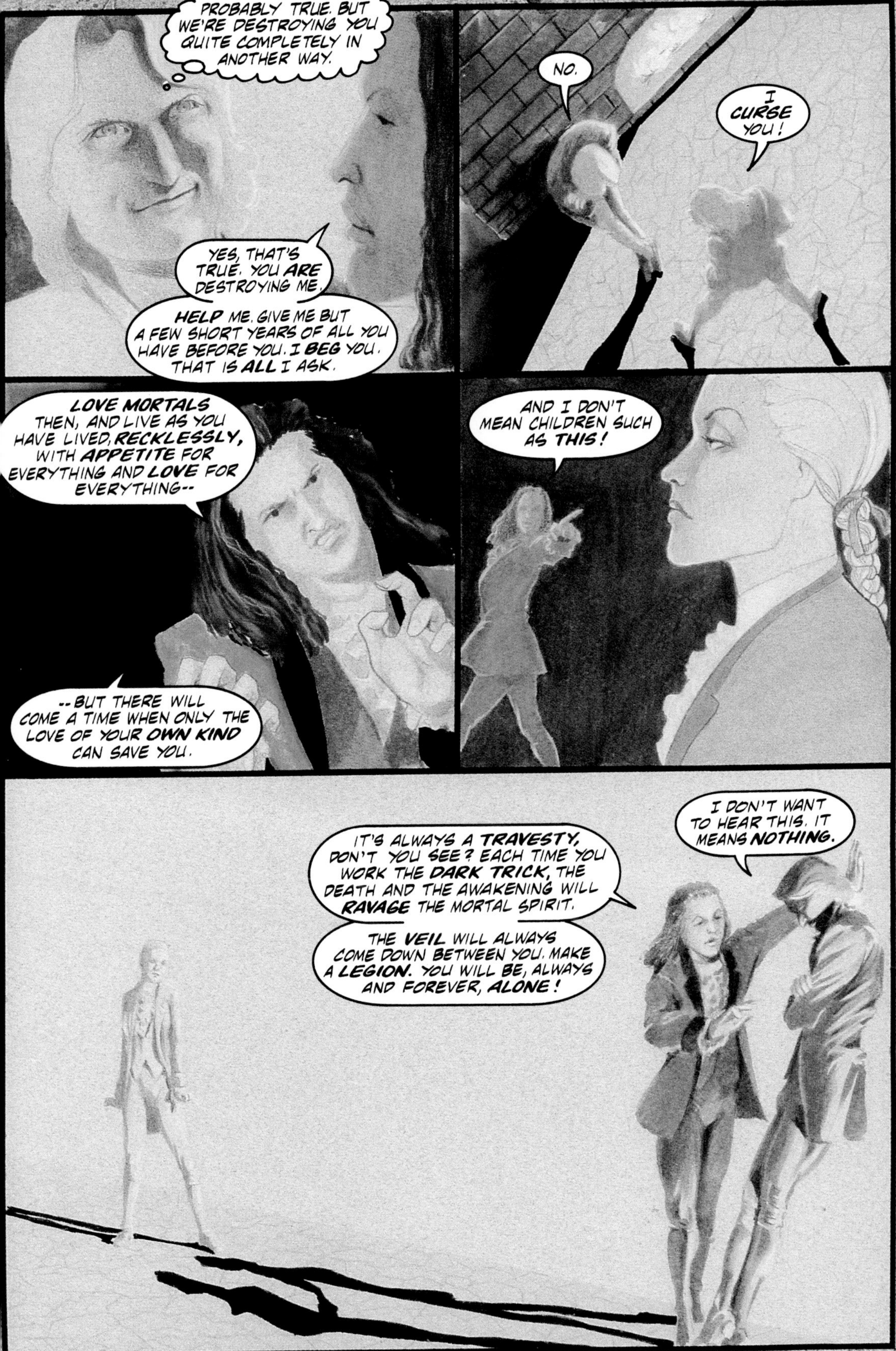
PROBABLY TRUE. BUT WE'RE DESTROYING YOU QUITE COMPLETELY IN ANOTHER WAY.
YES, THAT'S TRUE. YOU ARE DESTROYING ME.
HELP ME. GIVE ME BUT A FEW SHORT YEARS OF ALL YOU HAVE BEFORE YOU. I BEG YOU. THAT IS ALL I ASK.
NO.
I CURSE YOU!
LOVE MORTALS THEN, AND LIVE AS YOU HAVE LIVED, RECKLESSLY, WITH APPETITE FOR EVERYTHING AND LOVE FOR EVERYTHING--
--BUT THERE WILL COME A TIME WHEN ONLY THE LOVE OF YOUR OWN KIND CAN SAVE YOU.
AND I DON'T MEAN CHILDREN SUCH AS THIS!
IT'S ALWAYS A TRAVESTY, DON'T YOU SEE? EACH TIME YOU WORK THE DARK TRICK, THE DEATH AND THE AWAKENING WILL RAVAGE THE MORTAL SPIRIT.
THE VEIL WILL ALWAYS COME DOWN BETWEEN YOU. MAKE A LEGION. YOU WILL BE, ALWAYS AND FOREVER, ALONE!
I DON'T WANT TO HEAR THIS. IT MEANS NOTHING.

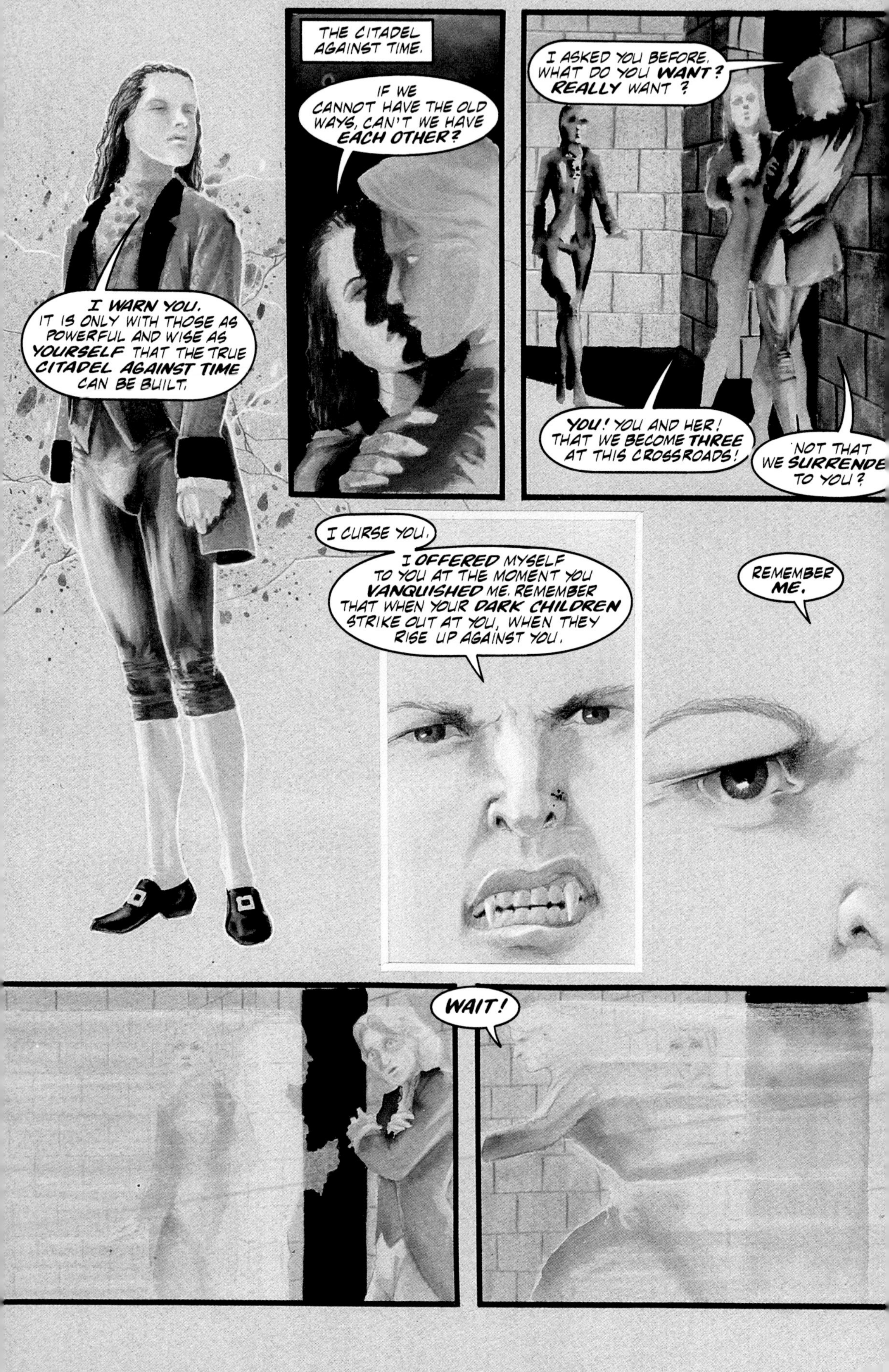
THE CITADEL AGAINST TIME.
IF WE CANNOT HAVE THE OLD WAYS, CAN'T WE HAVE EACH OTHER?
I WARN YOU. IT IS ONLY WITH THOSE AS POWERFUL AND WISE AS YOURSELF THAT THE TRUE CITADEL AGAINST TIME CAN BE BUILT.
I ASKED YOU BEFORE. WHAT DO YOU WANT? REALLY WANT?
YOU! YOU AND HER! THAT WE BECOME THREE AT THIS CROSSROADS!
NOT THAT WE SURRENDE TO YOU?
I CURSE YOU.
I OFFERED MYSELF TO YOU AT THE MOMENT YOU VANQUISHED ME. REMEMBER THAT WHEN YOUR DARK CHILDREN STRIKE OUT AT YOU, WHEN THEY RISE UP AGAINST YOU.
REMEMBER ME.
WAIT!

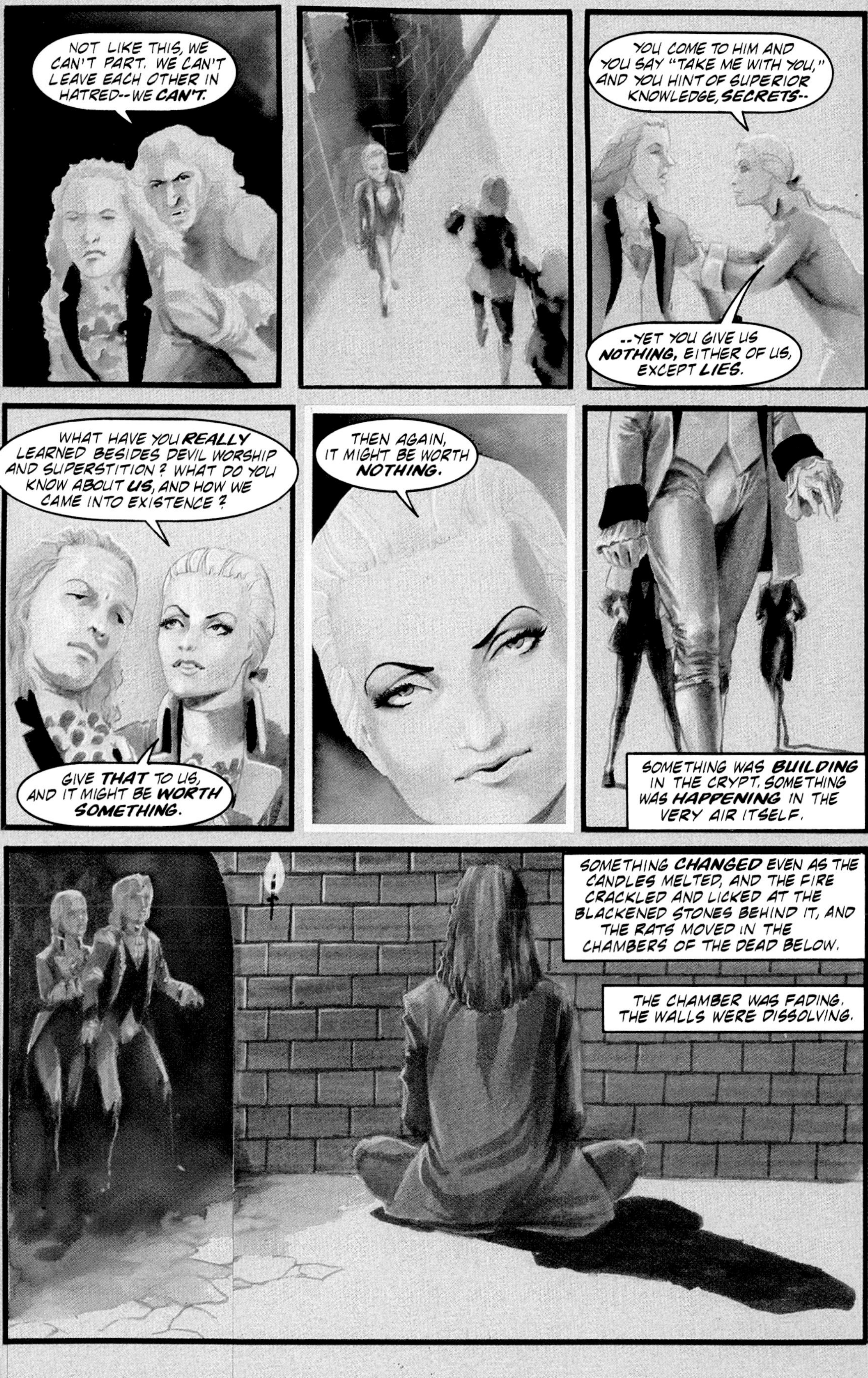
NOT LIKE THIS, WE CAN'T PART. WE CAN'T LEAVE EACH OTHER IN HATRED--WE CAN'T.
YOU COME TO HIM AND YOU SAY "TAKE ME WITH YOU," AND YOU HINT OF SUPERIOR KNOWLEDGE, SECRETS--
--YET YOU GIVE US NOTHING, EITHER OF US, EXCEPT LIES.
WHAT HAVE YOU REALLY LEARNED BESIDES DEVIL WORSHIP AND SUPERSTITION? WHAT DO YOU KNOW ABOUT US, AND HOW WE CAME INTO EXISTENCE?
GIVE THAT TO US, AND IT MIGHT BE WORTH SOMETHING.
THEN AGAIN, IT MIGHT BE WORTH NOTHING.
SOMETHING WAS BUILDING IN THE CRYPT. SOMETHING WAS HAPPENING IN THE VERY AIR ITSELF.
SOMETHING CHANGED EVEN AS THE CANDLES MELTED, AND THE FIRE CRACKLED AND LICKED AT THE BLACKENED STONES BEHIND IT, AND THE RATS MOVED IN THE CHAMBERS OF THE DEAD BELOW.
THE CHAMBER WAS FADING. THE WALLS WERE DISSOLVING.

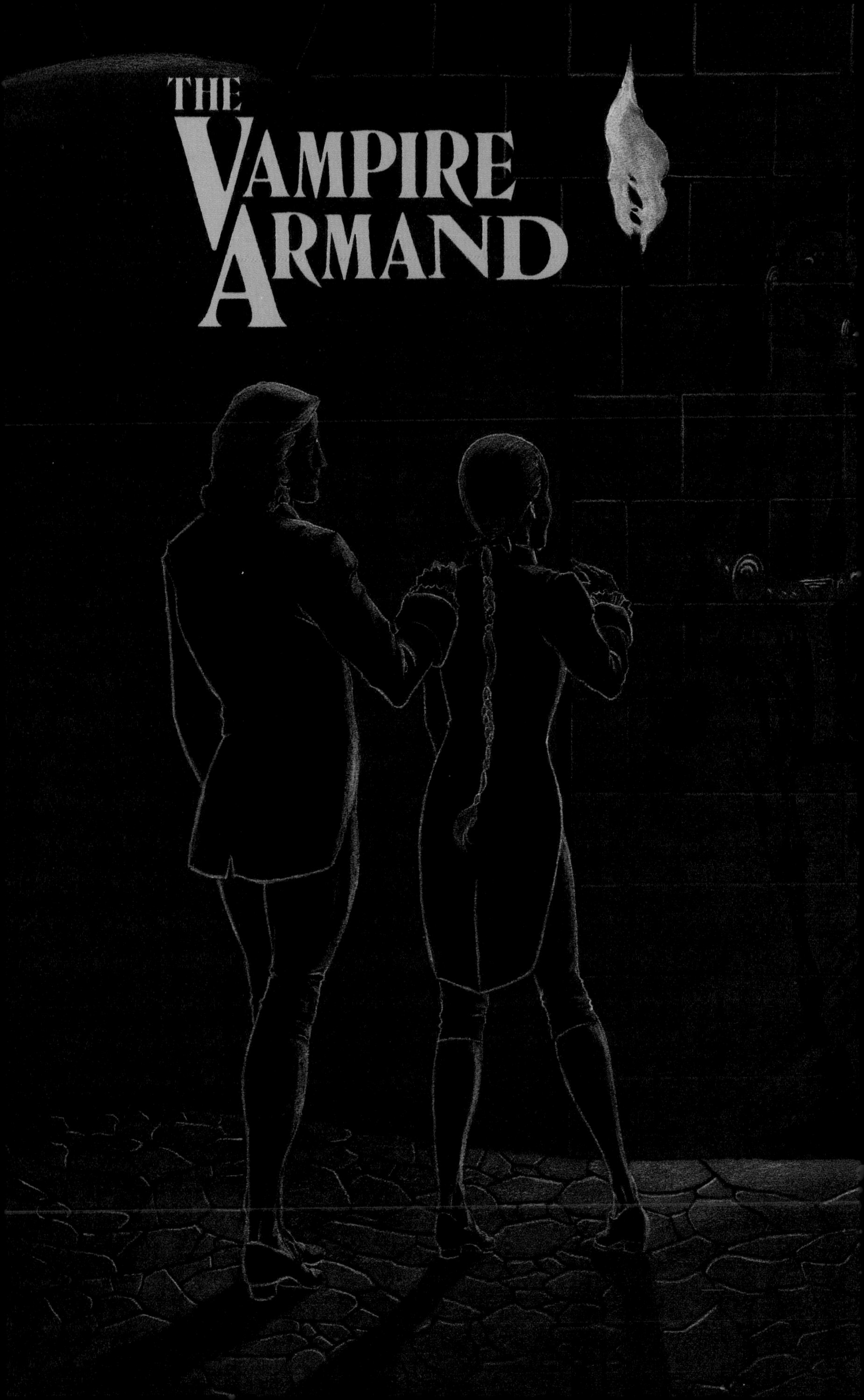
THE
VAMPIRE
ARMAND

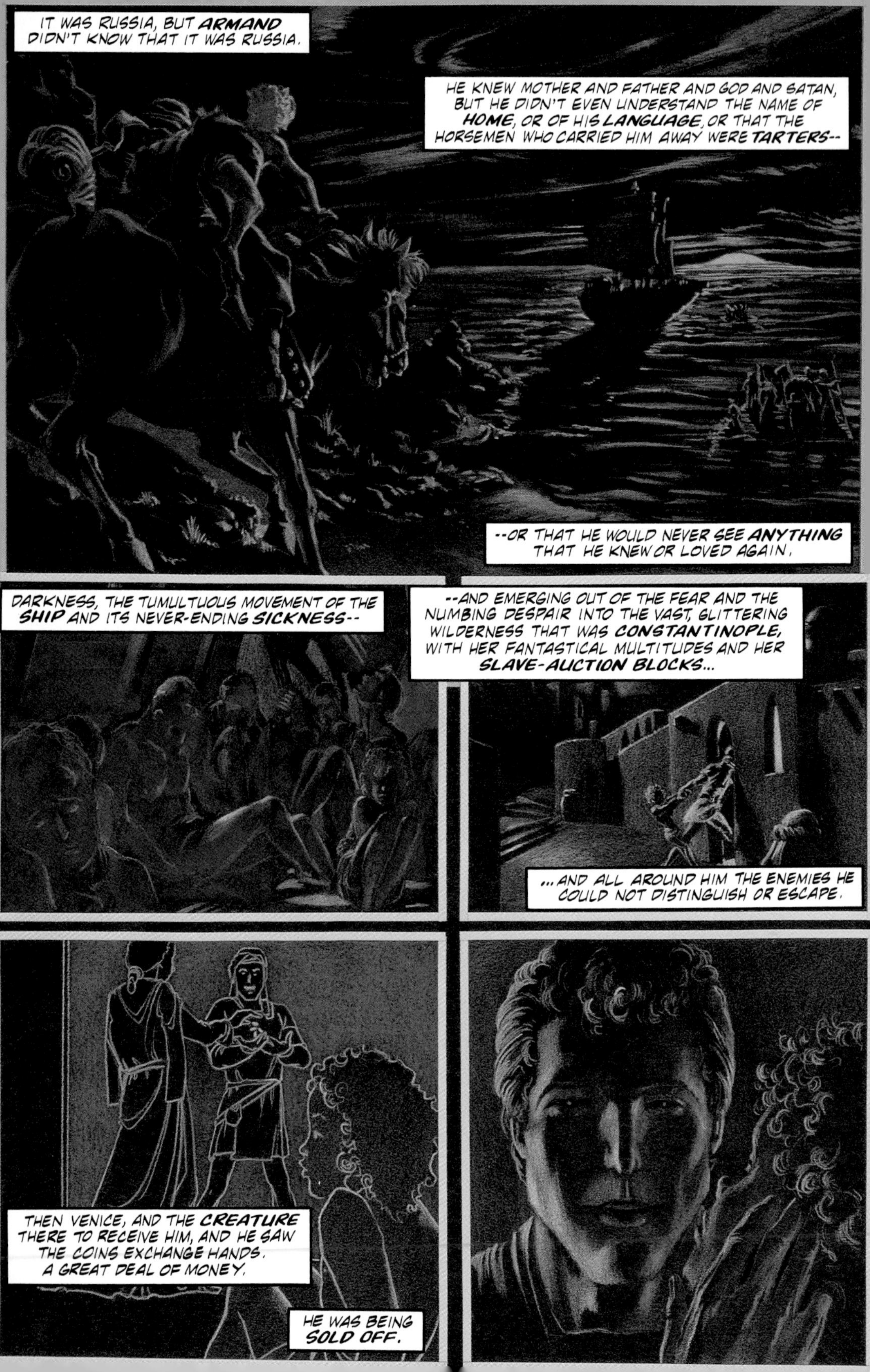
IT WAS RUSSIA, BUT ARMAND DIDN'T KNOW THAT IT WAS RUSSIA.
HE KNEW MOTHER AND FATHER AND GOD AND SATAN, BUT HE DIDN'T EVEN UNDERSTAND THE NAME OF HOME, OR OF HIS LANGUAGE, OR THAT THE HORSEMEN WHO CARRIED HIM AWAY WERE TARTERS--
--OR THAT HE WOULD NEVER SEE ANYTHING THAT HE KNEW OR LOVED AGAIN.
DARKNESS, THE TUMULTUOUS MOVEMENT OF THE SHIP AND ITS NEVER-ENDING SICKNESS--
--AND EMERGING OUT OF THE FEAR AND THE NUMBING DESPAIR INTO THE VAST, GLITTERING WILDERNESS THAT WAS CONSTANTINOPLE, WITH HER FANTASTICAL MULTITUDES AND HER SLAVE-AUCTION BLOCKS...
...AND ALL AROUND HIM THE ENEMIES HE COULD NOT DISTINGUISH OR ESCAPE.
THEN VENICE, AND THE CREATURE THERE TO RECEIVE HIM, AND HE SAW THE COINS EXCHANGE HANDS. A GREAT DEAL OF MONEY.
HE WAS BEING SOLD OFF.

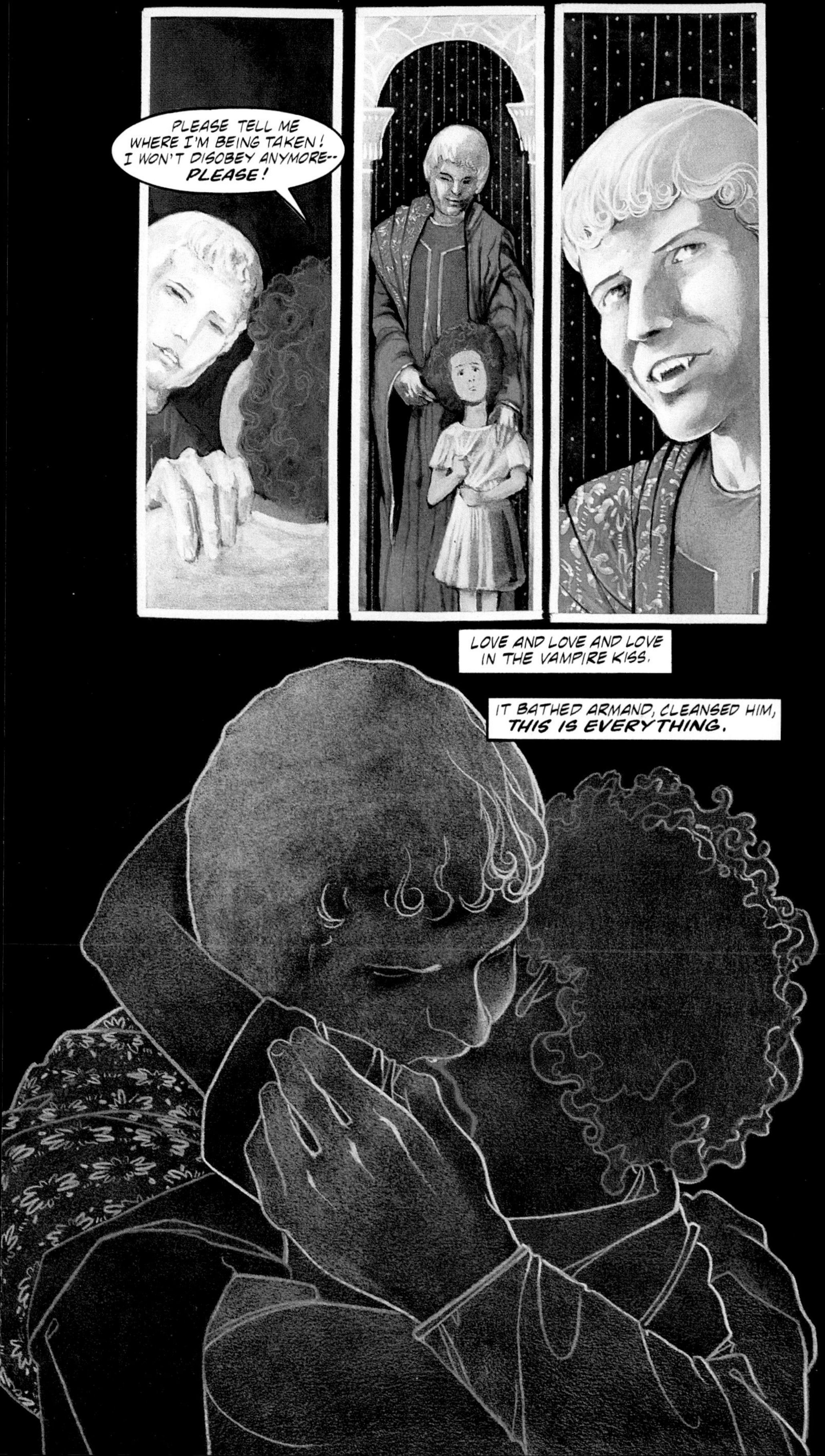
PLEASE TELL ME WHERE I'M BEING TAKEN! I WON'T DISOBEY ANYMORE-- PLEASE!
LOVE AND LOVE AND LOVE IN THE VAMPIRE KISS.
IT BATHED ARMAND, CLEANSED HIM, THIS IS EVERYTHING.

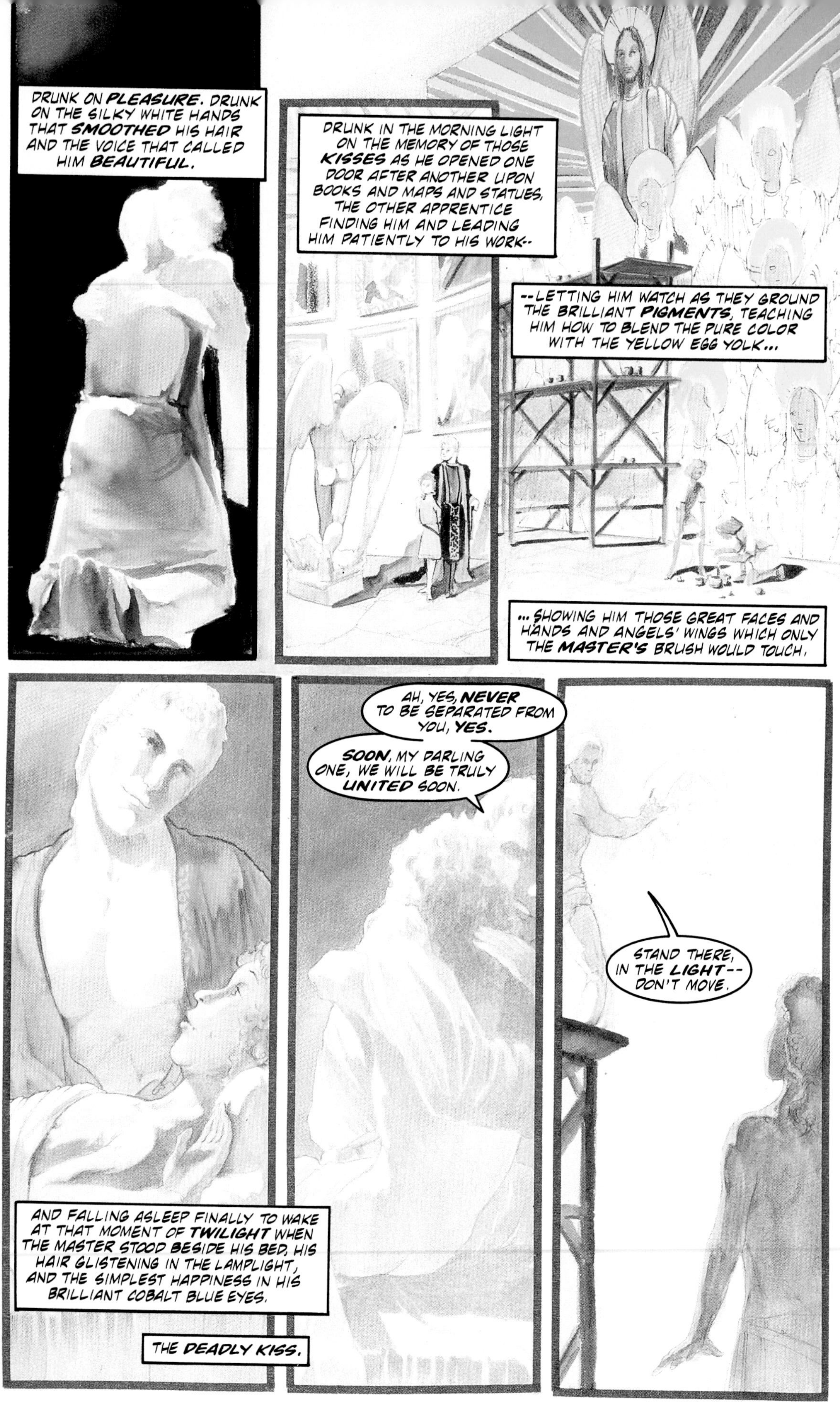
DRUNK ON PLEASURE. DRUNK ON THE SILKY WHITE HANDS THAT SMOOTHED HIS HAIR AND THE VOICE THAT CALLED HIM BEAUTIFUL.
DRUNK IN THE MORNING LIGHT ON THE MEMORY OF THOSE KISSES AS HE OPENED ONE DOOR AFTER ANOTHER UPON BOOKS AND MAPS AND STATUES, THE OTHER APPRENTICE FINDING HIM AND LEADING HIM PATIENTLY TO HIS WORK--
--LETTING HIM WATCH AS THEY GROUND THE BRILLIANT PIGMENTS, TEACHING HIM HOW TO BLEND THE PURE COLOR WITH THE YELLOW EGG YOLK...
...SHOWING HIM THOSE GREAT FACES AND HANDS AND ANGELS' WINGS WHICH ONLY THE MASTER'S BRUSH WOULD TOUCH.
AND FALLING ASLEEP FINALLY TO WAKE AT THAT MOMENT OF TWILIGHT WHEN THE MASTER STOOD BESIDE HIS BED, HIS HAIR GLISTENING IN THE LAMPLIGHT, AND THE SIMPLEST HAPPINESS IN HIS BRILLIANT COBALT BLUE EYES.
THE DEADLY KISS.
AH, YES, NEVER TO BE SEPARATED FROM YOU, YES.
SOON, MY DARLING ONE, WE WILL BE TRULY UNITED SOON.
STAND THERE, IN THE LIGHT-- DON'T MOVE.

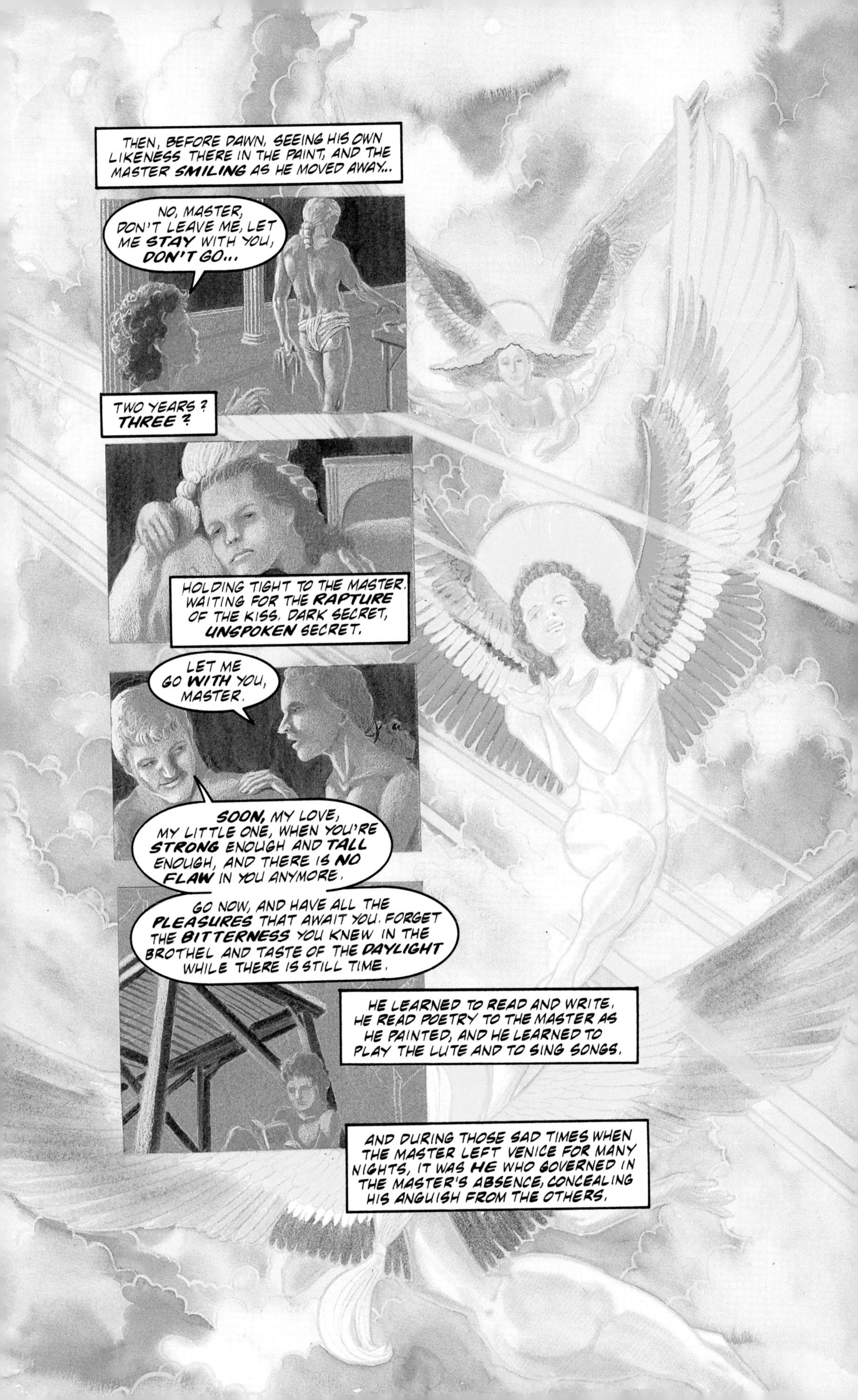
THEN, BEFORE DAWN, SEEING HIS OWN LIKENESS THERE IN THE PAINT, AND THE MASTER SMILING AS HE MOVED AWAY...
NO, MASTER, DON'T LEAVE ME, LET ME STAY WITH YOU, DON'T GO...
TWO YEARS? THREE?
HOLDING TIGHT TO THE MASTER. WAITING FOR THE RAPTURE OF THE KISS. DARK SECRET, UNSPOKEN SECRET.
LET ME GO WITH YOU, MASTER.
SOON, MY LOVE, MY LITTLE ONE, WHEN YOU'RE STRONG ENOUGH AND TALL ENOUGH, AND THERE IS NO FLAW IN YOU ANYMORE.
GO NOW, AND HAVE ALL THE PLEASURES THAT AWAIT YOU. FORGET THE BITTERNESS YOU KNEW IN THE BROTHEL AND TASTE OF THE DAYLIGHT WHILE THERE IS STILL TIME.
HE LEARNED TO READ AND WRITE, HE READ POETRY TO THE MASTER AS HE PAINTED, AND HE LEARNED TO PLAY THE LUTE AND TO SING SONGS.
AND DURING THOSE SAD TIMES WHEN THE MASTER LEFT VENICE FOR MANY NIGHTS, IT WAS HE WHO GOVERNED IN THE MASTER'S ABSENCE, CONCEALING HIS ANGUISH FROM THE OTHERS.

AND ONE NIGHT FINALLY, IN THE SMALL HOURS WHEN EVEN VENICE SLEPT:
THIS IS THE MOMENT, BEAUTIFUL ONE, FOR YOU TO COME TO ME AND BECOME LIKE ME. IS IT WHAT YOU WISH?
YES.
FOREVER TO THRIVE IN SECRET UPON THE BLOOD OF THE EVILDOER AS I THRIVE, AND TO ABIDE WITH THESE SECRETS UNTIL THE END OF THE WORLD.
I TAKE THE VOW, I SURRENDER, I WILL... TO BE WITH YOU, MY MASTER, ALWAYS, YOU ARE THE CREATOR OF ALL THINGS THAT I AM.
THERE HAS NEVER BEEN ANY GREATER DESIRE.
HOW MANY MONTHS WERE THERE AFTER? REELING IN THE POWER OF THE DARK GIFT.

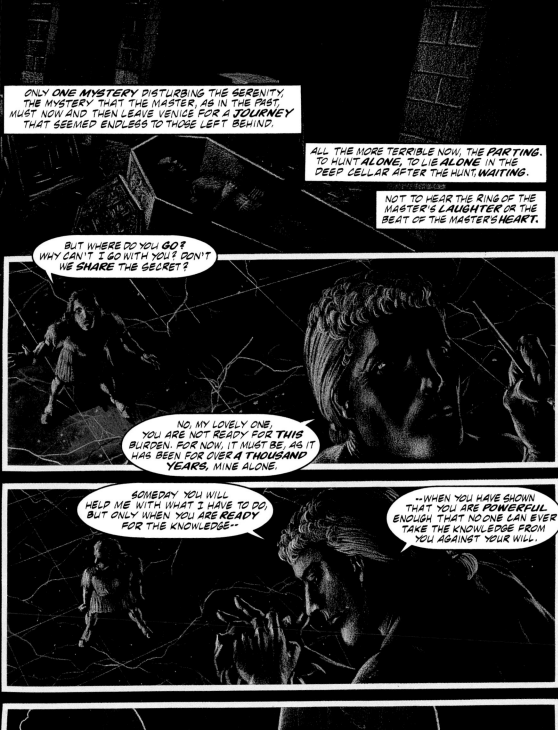

ONLY **ONE MYSTERY** DISTURBING THE SERENITY, THE MYSTERY THAT THE MASTER, AS IN THE PAST, MUST NOW AND THEN LEAVE VENICE FOR A **JOURNEY** THAT SEEMED ENDLESS TO THOSE LEFT BEHIND.

ALL THE MORE TERRIBLE NOW, THE **PARTING.** TO HUNT **ALONE,** TO LIE **ALONE** IN THE DEEP CELLAR AFTER THE HUNT, **WAITING.**

NOT TO HEAR THE RING OF THE MASTER'S **LAUGHTER** OR THE BEAT OF THE MASTER'S **HEART.**

BUT WHERE DO YOU **GO?** WHY CAN'T I GO WITH YOU? DON'T WE **SHARE** THE SECRET?

NO, MY LOVELY ONE, YOU ARE NOT READY FOR **THIS** BURDEN. FOR NOW, IT MUST BE, AS IT HAS BEEN FOR OVER **A THOUSAND YEARS,** MINE ALONE.

SOMEDAY YOU WILL HELP ME WITH WHAT I HAVE TO DO, BUT ONLY WHEN YOU ARE **READY** FOR THE KNOWLEDGE--

--WHEN YOU HAVE SHOWN THAT YOU ARE **POWERFUL** ENOUGH THAT NO ONE CAN EVER TAKE THE KNOWLEDGE FROM YOU AGAINST YOUR WILL.

UNTIL THEN, UNDERSTAND I HAVE **NO CHOICE** BUT TO LEAVE YOU. I GO TO TEND **THOSE WHO MUST BE KEPT** AS I HAVE ALWAYS DONE.

THOSE WHO MUST BE KEPT ARE IN PEACE, OR IN **SILENCE.** MORE THAN THAT WE MAY NEVER KNOW.

THOSE WHO MUST BE KEPT.

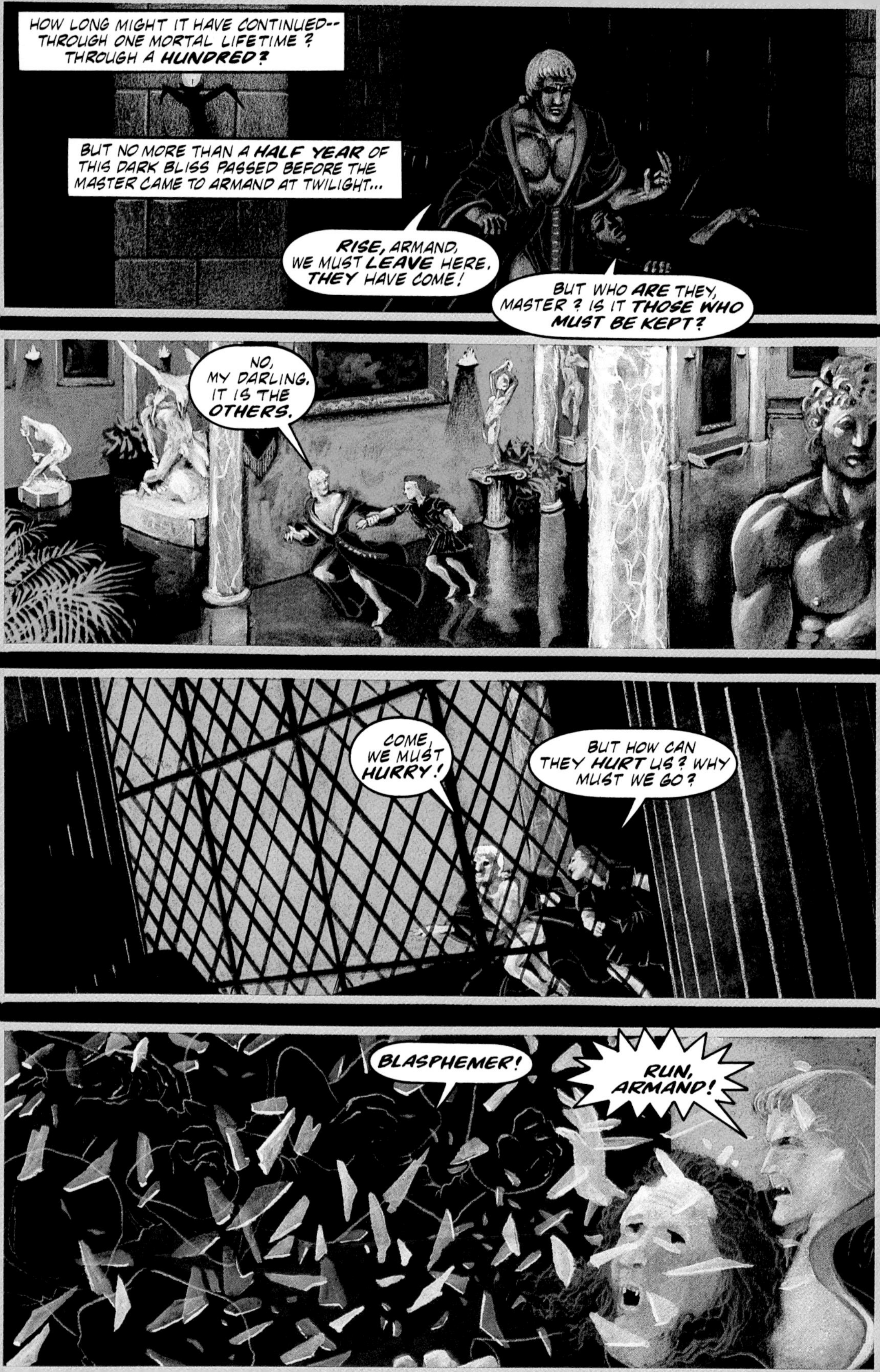
HOW LONG MIGHT IT HAVE CONTINUED-- THROUGH ONE MORTAL LIFETIME? THROUGH A HUNDRED?
BUT NO MORE THAN A HALF YEAR OF THIS DARK BLISS PASSED BEFORE THE MASTER CAME TO ARMAND AT TWILIGHT...
RISE, ARMAND, WE MUST LEAVE HERE. THEY HAVE COME!
BUT WHO ARE THEY, MASTER? IS IT THOSE WHO MUST BE KEPT?
NO, MY DARLING. IT IS THE OTHERS.
COME, WE MUST HURRY!
BUT HOW CAN THEY HURT US? WHY MUST WE GO?
BLASPHEMER!
RUN, ARMAND!

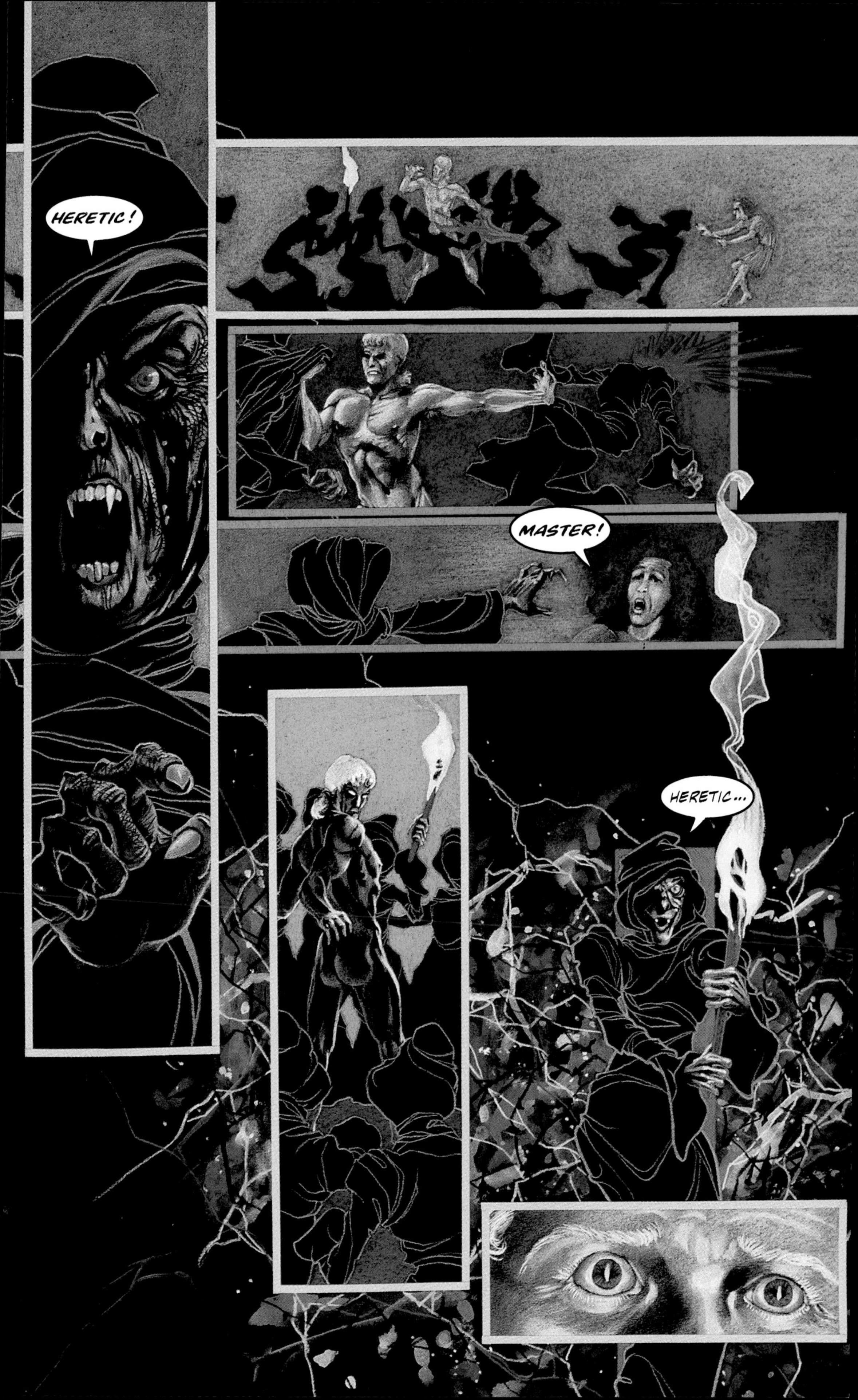
HERETIC!
MASTER!
HERETIC...

NO!

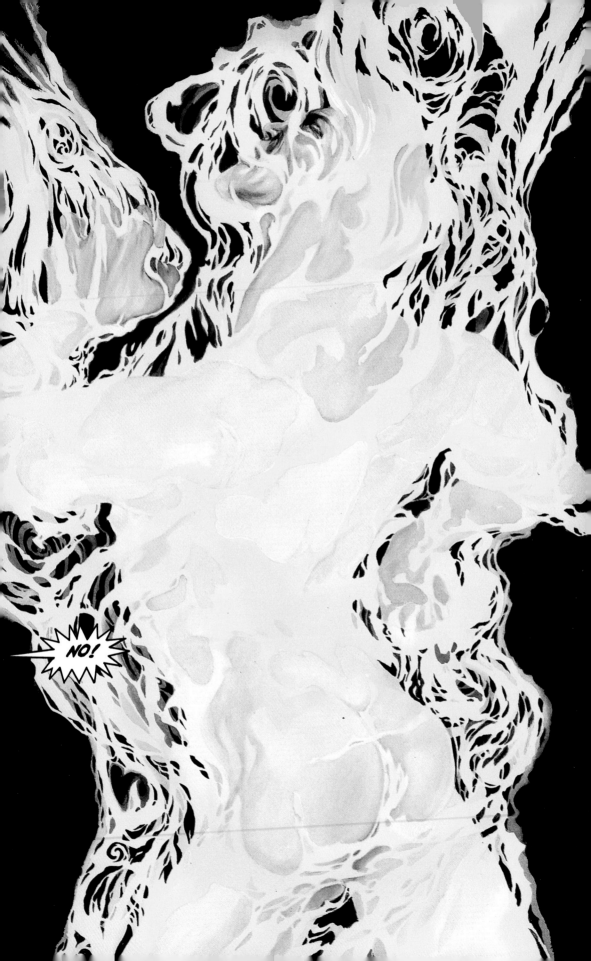

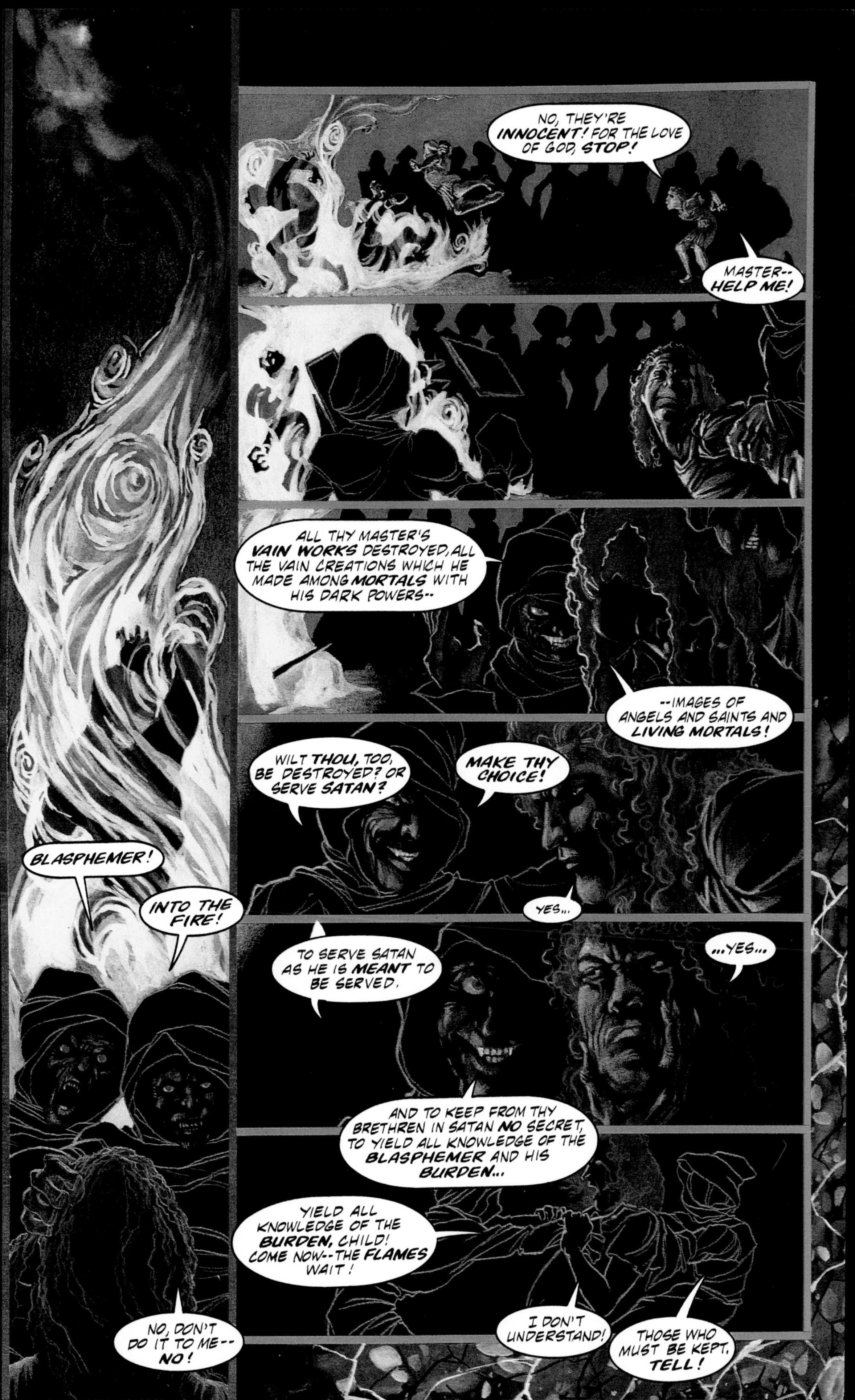
NO, THEY'RE INNOCENT! FOR THE LOVE OF GOD, STOP!
MASTER-- HELP ME!
ALL THY MASTER'S VAIN WORKS DESTROYED, ALL THE VAIN CREATIONS WHICH HE MADE AMONG MORTALS WITH HIS DARK POWERS--
--IMAGES OF ANGELS AND SAINTS AND LIVING MORTALS!
WILT THOU, TOO, BE DESTROYED? OR SERVE SATAN?
MAKE THY CHOICE!
YES...
TO SERVE SATAN AS HE IS MEANT TO BE SERVED.
...YES...
AND TO KEEP FROM THY BRETHREN IN SATAN NO SECRET, TO YIELD ALL KNOWLEDGE OF THE BLASPHEMER AND HIS BURDEN...
YIELD ALL KNOWLEDGE OF THE BURDEN, CHILD! COME NOW--THE FLAMES WAIT!
I DON'T UNDERSTAND!
THOSE WHO MUST BE KEPT. TELL!
BLASPHEMER!
INTO THE FIRE!
NO, DON'T DO IT TO ME-- NO!

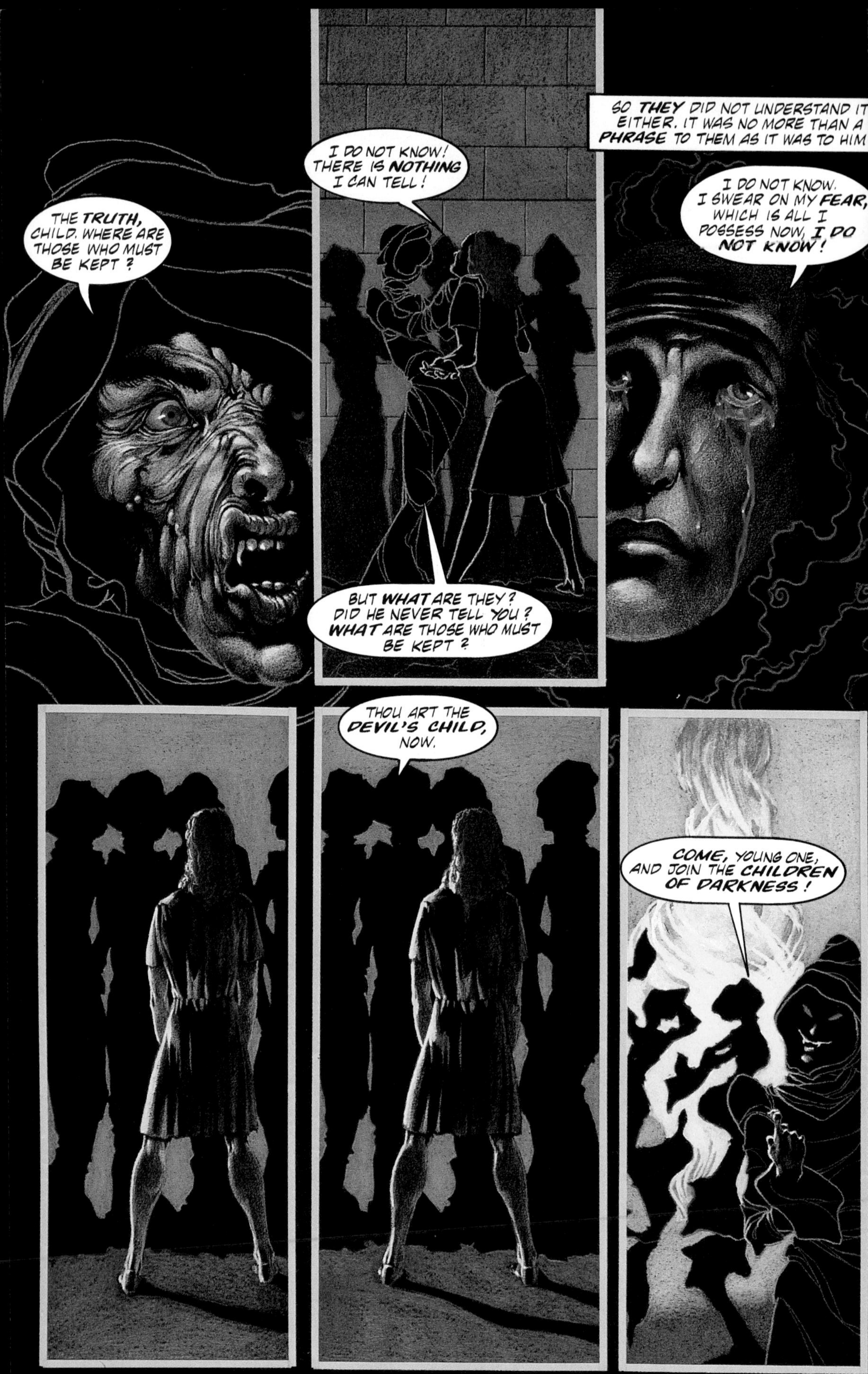

THE TRUTH, CHILD. WHERE ARE THOSE WHO MUST BE KEPT?
I DO NOT KNOW! THERE IS NOTHING I CAN TELL!
BUT WHAT ARE THEY? DID HE NEVER TELL YOU? WHAT ARE THOSE WHO MUST BE KEPT?
SO THEY DID NOT UNDERSTAND IT EITHER. IT WAS NO MORE THAN A PHRASE TO THEM AS IT WAS TO HIM.
I DO NOT KNOW. I SWEAR ON MY FEAR, WHICH IS ALL I POSSESS NOW, I DO NOT KNOW!
THOU ART THE DEVIL'S CHILD, NOW.
COME, YOUNG ONE, AND JOIN THE CHILDREN OF DARKNESS!

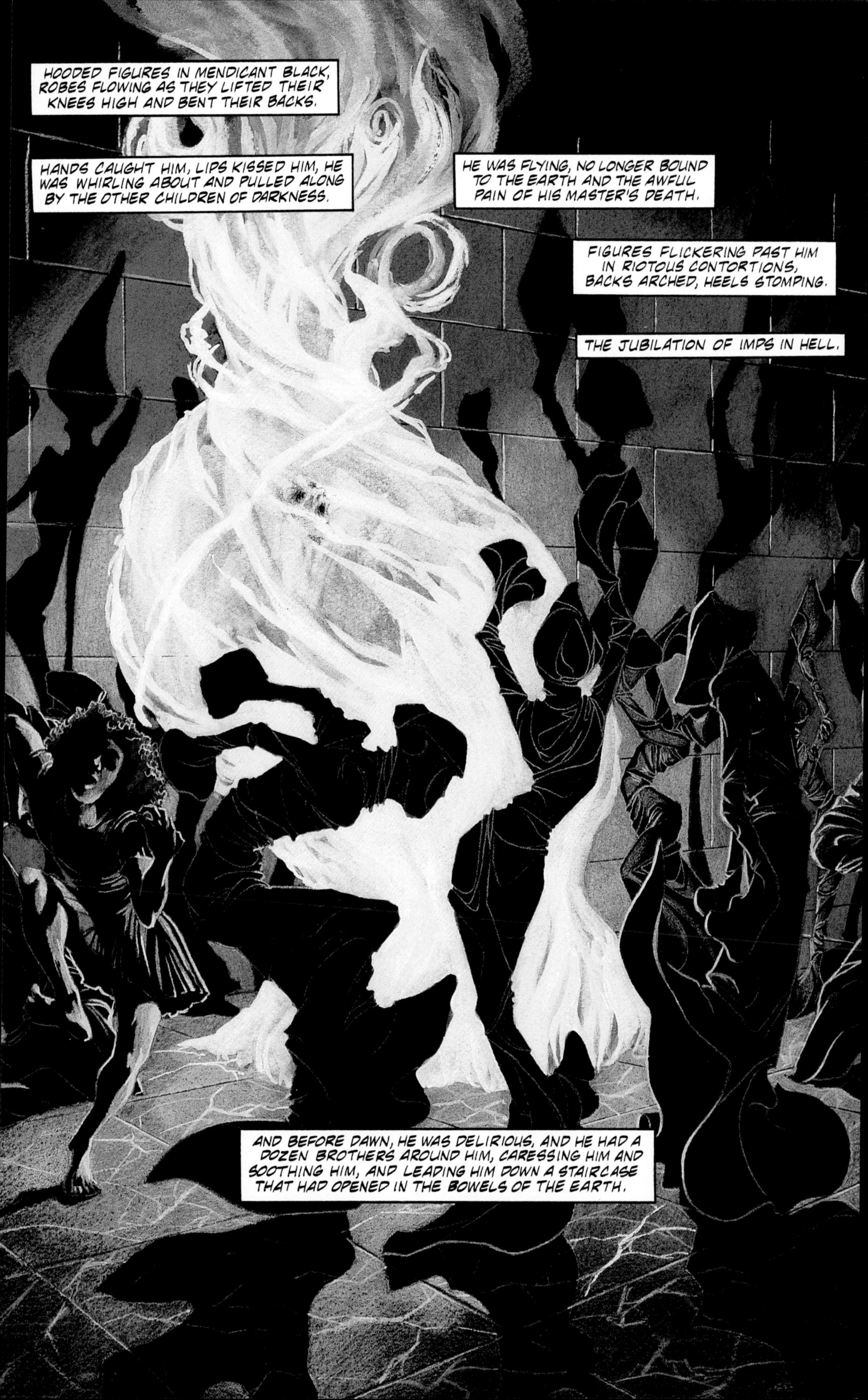
HOODED FIGURES IN MENDICANT BLACK, ROBES FLOWING AS THEY LIFTED THEIR KNEES HIGH AND BENT THEIR BACKS.
HANDS CAUGHT HIM, LIPS KISSED HIM, HE WAS WHIRLING ABOUT AND PULLED ALONG BY THE OTHER CHILDREN OF DARKNESS.
HE WAS FLYING, NO LONGER BOUND TO THE EARTH AND THE AWFUL PAIN OF HIS MASTER'S DEATH.
FIGURES FLICKERING PAST HIM IN RIOTOUS CONTORTIONS, BACKS ARCHED, HEELS STOMPING.
THE JUBILATION OF IMPS IN HELL.
AND BEFORE DAWN, HE WAS DELIRIOUS, AND HE HAD A DOZEN BROTHERS AROUND HIM, CARESSING HIM AND SOOTHING HIM, AND LEADING HIM DOWN A STAIRCASE THAT HAD OPENED IN THE BOWELS OF THE EARTH.

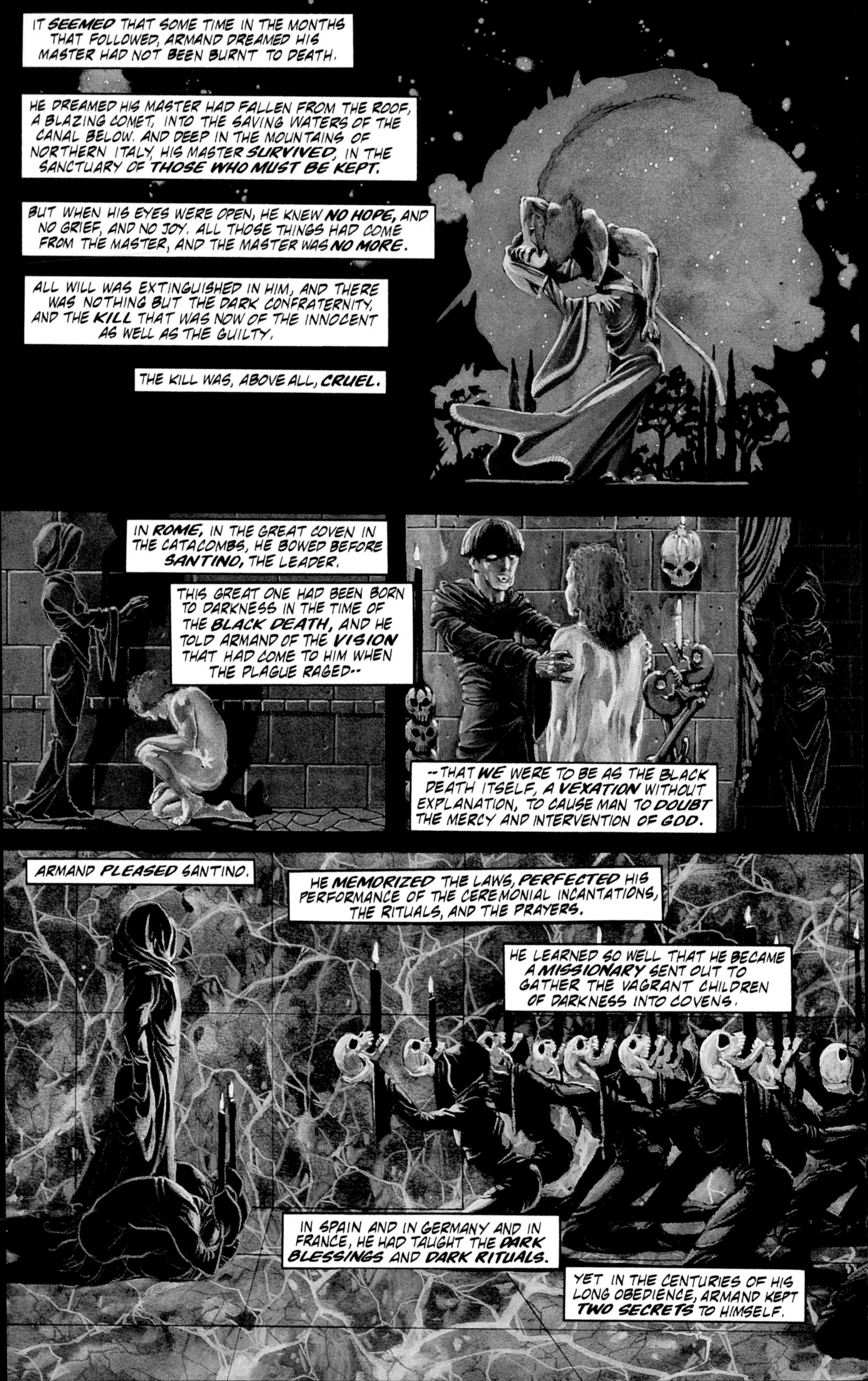
IT SEEMED THAT SOME TIME IN THE MONTHS THAT FOLLOWED, ARMAND DREAMED HIS MASTER HAD NOT BEEN BURNT TO DEATH.
HE DREAMED HIS MASTER HAD FALLEN FROM THE ROOF, A BLAZING COMET, INTO THE SAVING WATERS OF THE CANAL BELOW. AND DEEP IN THE MOUNTAINS OF NORTHERN ITALY, HIS MASTER SURVIVED, IN THE SANCTUARY OF THOSE WHO MUST BE KEPT.
BUT WHEN HIS EYES WERE OPEN, HE KNEW NO HOPE, AND NO GRIEF, AND NO JOY. ALL THOSE THINGS HAD COME FROM THE MASTER, AND THE MASTER WAS NO MORE.
ALL WILL WAS EXTINGUISHED IN HIM, AND THERE WAS NOTHING BUT THE DARK CONFRATERNITY, AND THE KILL THAT WAS NOW OF THE INNOCENT AS WELL AS THE GUILTY.
THE KILL WAS, ABOVE ALL, CRUEL.
IN ROME, IN THE GREAT COVEN IN THE CATACOMBS, HE BOWED BEFORE SANTINO, THE LEADER.
THIS GREAT ONE HAD BEEN BORN TO DARKNESS IN THE TIME OF THE BLACK DEATH, AND HE TOLD ARMAND OF THE VISION THAT HAD COME TO HIM WHEN THE PLAGUE RAGED--
--THAT WE WERE TO BE AS THE BLACK DEATH ITSELF, A VEXATION WITHOUT EXPLANATION, TO CAUSE MAN TO DOUBT THE MERCY AND INTERVENTION OF GOD.
ARMAND PLEASED SANTINO.
HE MEMORIZED THE LAWS, PERFECTED HIS PERFORMANCE OF THE CEREMONIAL INCANTATIONS, THE RITUALS, AND THE PRAYERS.
HE LEARNED SO WELL THAT HE BECAME A MISSIONARY SENT OUT TO GATHER THE VAGRANT CHILDREN OF DARKNESS INTO COVENS.
IN SPAIN AND IN GERMANY AND IN FRANCE, HE HAD TAUGHT THE DARK BLESSINGS AND DARK RITUALS.
YET IN THE CENTURIES OF HIS LONG OBEDIENCE, ARMAND KEPT TWO SECRETS TO HIMSELF.

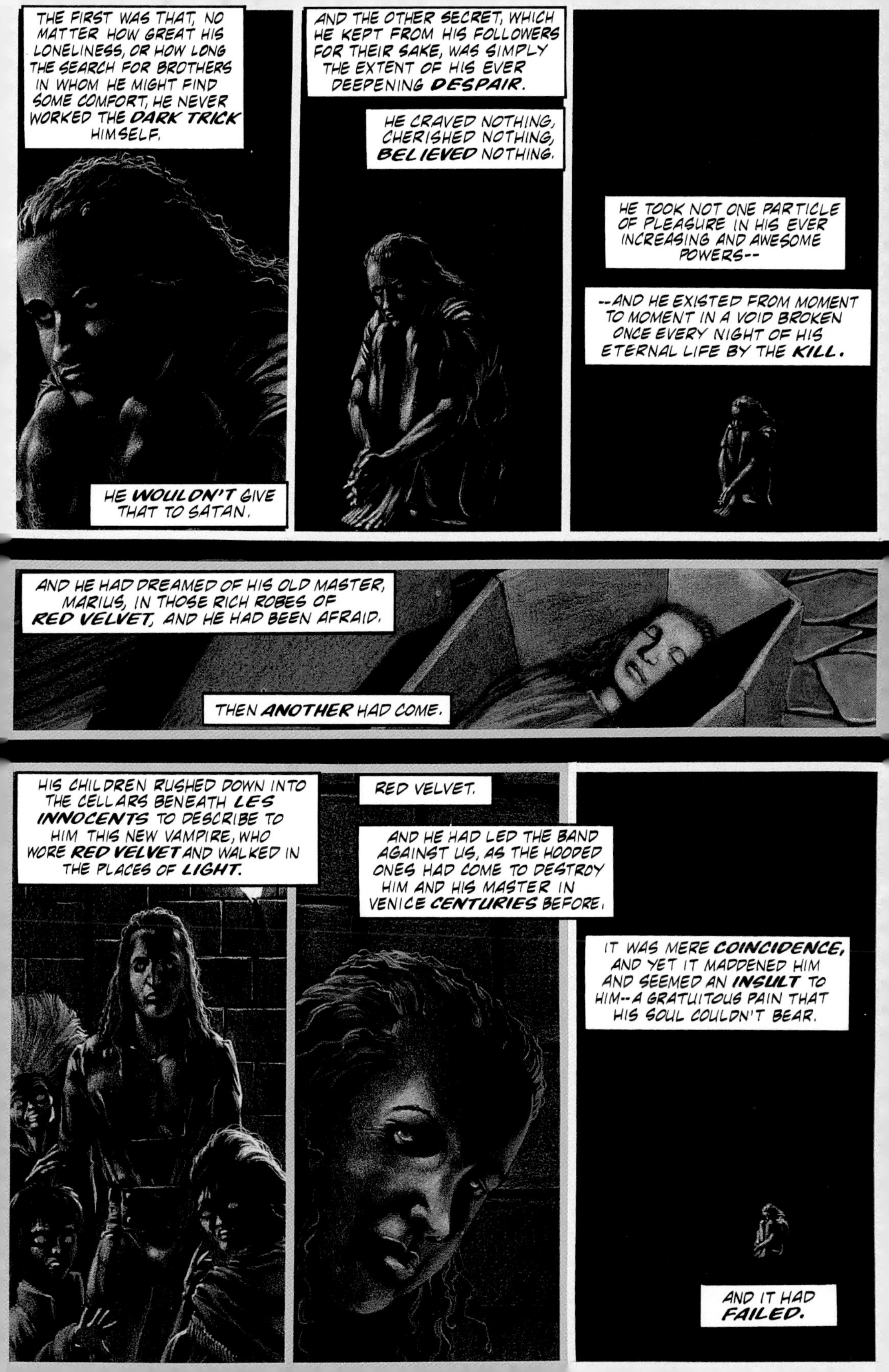
THE FIRST WAS THAT, NO MATTER HOW GREAT HIS LONELINESS, OR HOW LONG THE SEARCH FOR BROTHERS IN WHOM HE MIGHT FIND SOME COMFORT, HE NEVER WORKED THE DARK TRICK HIMSELF.
HE WOULDN'T GIVE THAT TO SATAN.
AND THE OTHER SECRET, WHICH HE KEPT FROM HIS FOLLOWERS FOR THEIR SAKE, WAS SIMPLY THE EXTENT OF HIS EVER DEEPENING DESPAIR.
HE CRAVED NOTHING, CHERISHED NOTHING, BELIEVED NOTHING.
HE TOOK NOT ONE PARTICLE OF PLEASURE IN HIS EVER INCREASING AND AWESOME POWERS--
--AND HE EXISTED FROM MOMENT TO MOMENT IN A VOID BROKEN ONCE EVERY NIGHT OF HIS ETERNAL LIFE BY THE KILL.
AND HE HAD DREAMED OF HIS OLD MASTER, MARIUS, IN THOSE RICH ROBES OF RED VELVET, AND HE HAD BEEN AFRAID.
THEN ANOTHER HAD COME.
HIS CHILDREN RUSHED DOWN INTO THE CELLARS BENEATH LES INNOCENTS TO DESCRIBE TO HIM THIS NEW VAMPIRE, WHO WORE RED VELVET AND WALKED IN THE PLACES OF LIGHT.
RED VELVET.
AND HE HAD LED THE BAND AGAINST US, AS THE HOODED ONES HAD COME TO DESTROY HIM AND HIS MASTER IN VENICE CENTURIES BEFORE.
IT WAS MERE COINCIDENCE, AND YET IT MADDENED HIM AND SEEMED AN INSULT TO HIM--A GRATUITOUS PAIN THAT HIS SOUL COULDN'T BEAR.
AND IT HAD FAILED.

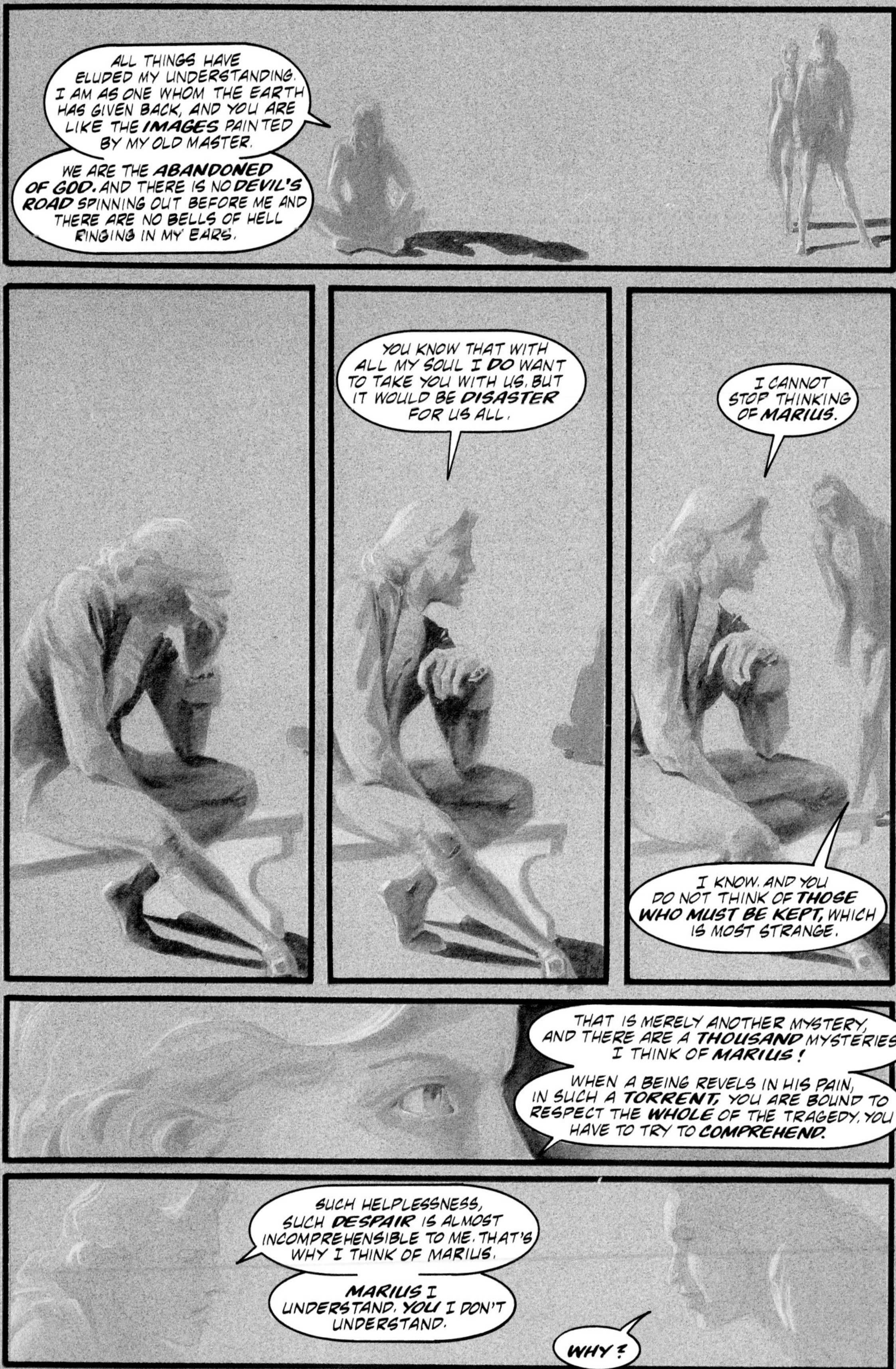

ALL THINGS HAVE ELUDED MY UNDERSTANDING. I AM AS ONE WHOM THE EARTH HAS GIVEN BACK, AND YOU ARE LIKE THE IMAGES PAINTED BY MY OLD MASTER.
WE ARE THE ABANDONED OF GOD. AND THERE IS NO DEVIL'S ROAD SPINNING OUT BEFORE ME AND THERE ARE NO BELLS OF HELL RINGING IN MY EARS.
YOU KNOW THAT WITH ALL MY SOUL I DO WANT TO TAKE YOU WITH US. BUT IT WOULD BE DISASTER FOR US ALL.
I CANNOT STOP THINKING OF MARIUS.
I KNOW. AND YOU DO NOT THINK OF THOSE WHO MUST BE KEPT, WHICH IS MOST STRANGE.
THAT IS MERELY ANOTHER MYSTERY, AND THERE ARE A THOUSAND MYSTERIES I THINK OF MARIUS!
WHEN A BEING REVELS IN HIS PAIN, IN SUCH A TORRENT, YOU ARE BOUND TO RESPECT THE WHOLE OF THE TRAGEDY. YOU HAVE TO TRY TO COMPREHEND.
SUCH HELPLESSNESS, SUCH DESPAIR IS ALMOST INCOMPREHENSIBLE TO ME. THAT'S WHY I THINK OF MARIUS.
MARIUS I UNDERSTAND. YOU I DON'T UNDERSTAND.
WHY?

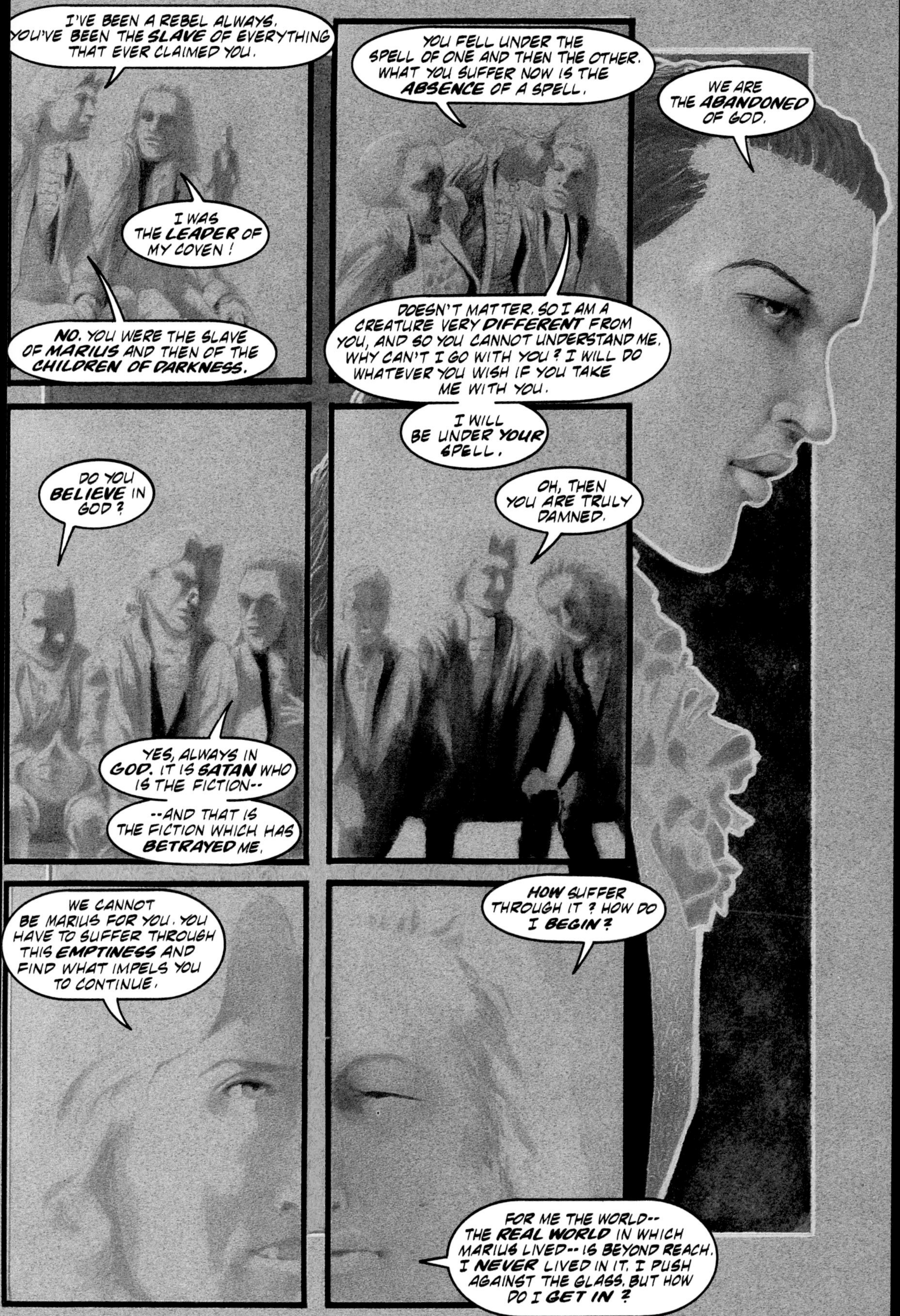
I'VE BEEN A REBEL ALWAYS. YOU'VE BEEN THE SLAVE OF EVERYTHING THAT EVER CLAIMED YOU.
I WAS THE LEADER OF MY COVEN!
NO. YOU WERE THE SLAVE OF MARIUS AND THEN OF THE CHILDREN OF DARKNESS.
YOU FELL UNDER THE SPELL OF ONE AND THEN THE OTHER. WHAT YOU SUFFER NOW IS THE ABSENCE OF A SPELL.
WE ARE THE ABANDONED OF GOD.
DOESN'T MATTER. SO I AM A CREATURE VERY DIFFERENT FROM YOU, AND SO YOU CANNOT UNDERSTAND ME. WHY CAN'T I GO WITH YOU? I WILL DO WHATEVER YOU WISH IF YOU TAKE ME WITH YOU.
I WILL BE UNDER YOUR SPELL.
DO YOU BELIEVE IN GOD?
YES, ALWAYS IN GOD. IT IS SATAN WHO IS THE FICTION--
--AND THAT IS THE FICTION WHICH HAS BETRAYED ME.
OH, THEN YOU ARE TRULY DAMNED.
WE CANNOT BE MARIUS FOR YOU. YOU HAVE TO SUFFER THROUGH THIS EMPTINESS AND FIND WHAT IMPELS YOU TO CONTINUE.
HOW SUFFER THROUGH IT? HOW DO I BEGIN?
FOR ME THE WORLD-- THE REAL WORLD IN WHICH MARIUS LIVED-- IS BEYOND REACH. I NEVER LIVED IN IT. I PUSH AGAINST THE GLASS, BUT HOW DO I GET IN?

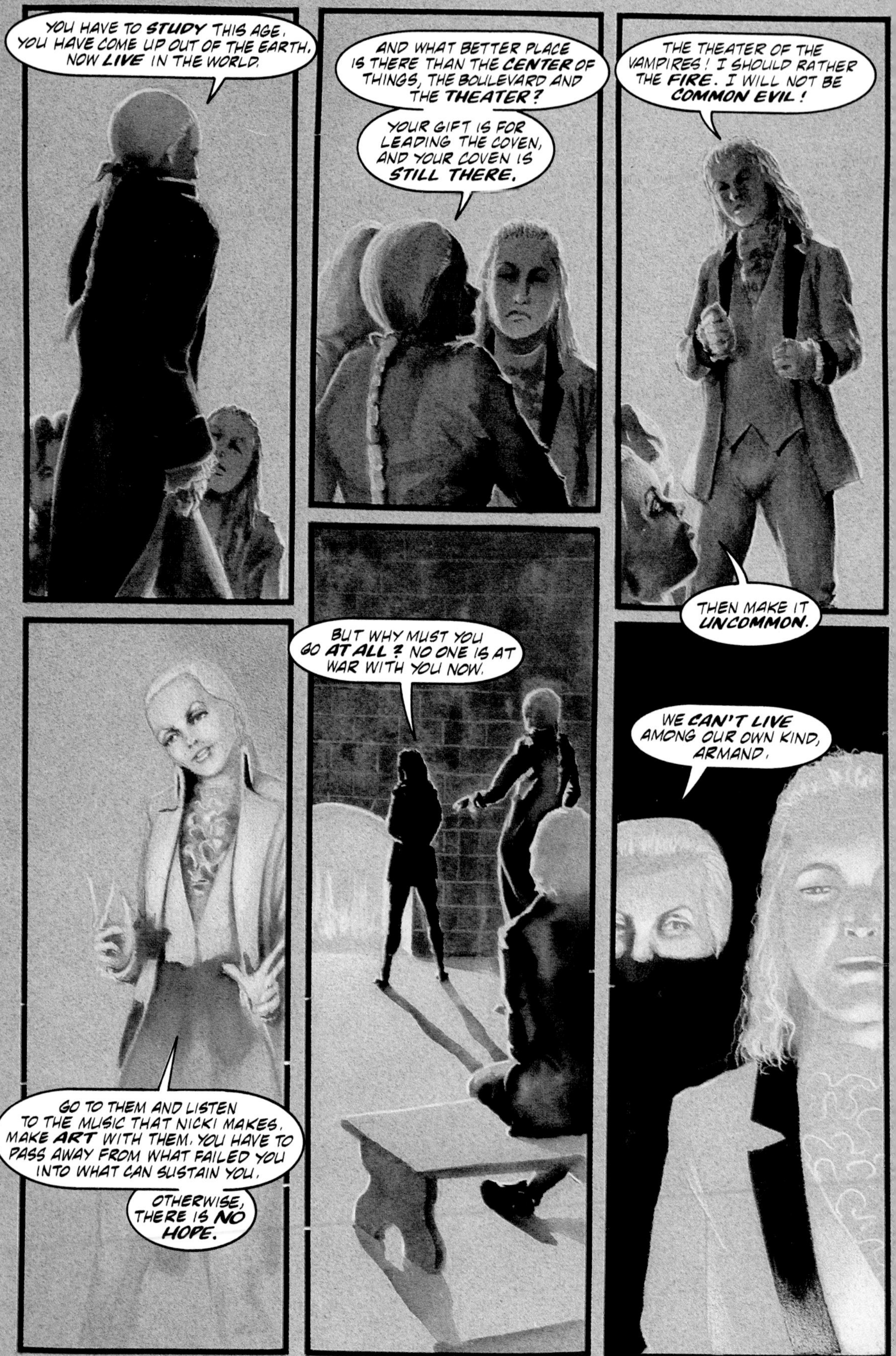
YOU HAVE TO STUDY THIS AGE. YOU HAVE COME UP OUT OF THE EARTH. NOW LIVE IN THE WORLD.
AND WHAT BETTER PLACE IS THERE THAN THE CENTER OF THINGS, THE BOULEVARD AND THE THEATER?
YOUR GIFT IS FOR LEADING THE COVEN, AND YOUR COVEN IS STILL THERE.
THE THEATER OF THE VAMPIRES! I SHOULD RATHER THE FIRE. I WILL NOT BE COMMON EVIL!
THEN MAKE IT UNCOMMON.
GO TO THEM AND LISTEN TO THE MUSIC THAT NICKI MAKES. MAKE ART WITH THEM. YOU HAVE TO PASS AWAY FROM WHAT FAILED YOU INTO WHAT CAN SUSTAIN YOU.
OTHERWISE, THERE IS NO HOPE.
BUT WHY MUST YOU GO AT ALL? NO ONE IS AT WAR WITH YOU NOW.
WE CAN'T LIVE AMONG OUR OWN KIND, ARMAND.

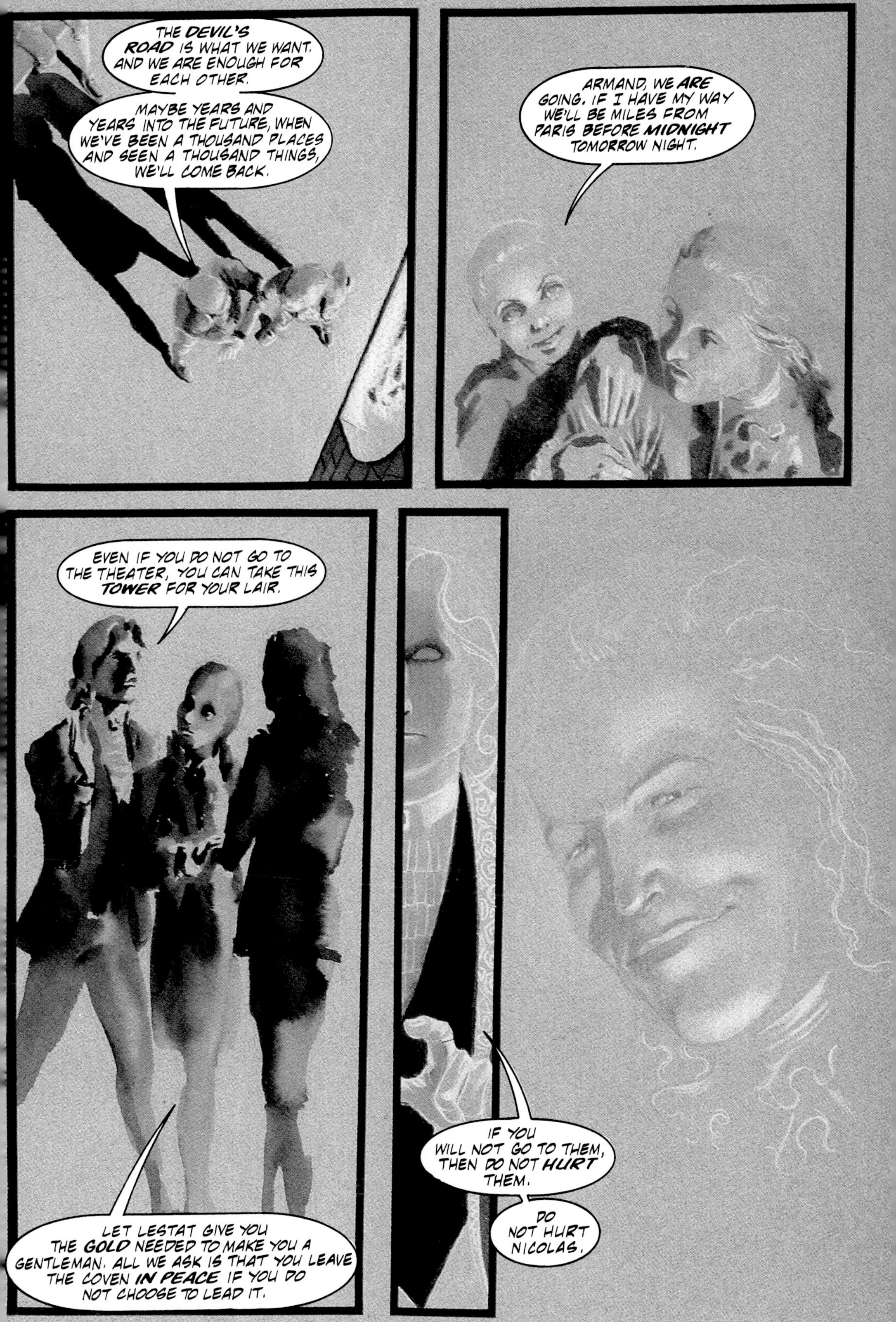
THE DEVIL'S ROAD IS WHAT WE WANT. AND WE ARE ENOUGH FOR EACH OTHER.
MAYBE YEARS AND YEARS INTO THE FUTURE, WHEN WE'VE BEEN A THOUSAND PLACES AND SEEN A THOUSAND THINGS, WE'LL COME BACK.
ARMAND, WE ARE GOING. IF I HAVE MY WAY WE'LL BE MILES FROM PARIS BEFORE MIDNIGHT TOMORROW NIGHT.
EVEN IF YOU DO NOT GO TO THE THEATER, YOU CAN TAKE THIS TOWER FOR YOUR LAIR.
LET LESTAT GIVE YOU THE GOLD NEEDED TO MAKE YOU A GENTLEMAN. ALL WE ASK IS THAT YOU LEAVE THE COVEN IN PEACE IF YOU DO NOT CHOOSE TO LEAD IT.
IF YOU WILL NOT GO TO THEM, THEN DO NOT HURT THEM.
DO NOT HURT NICOLAS.

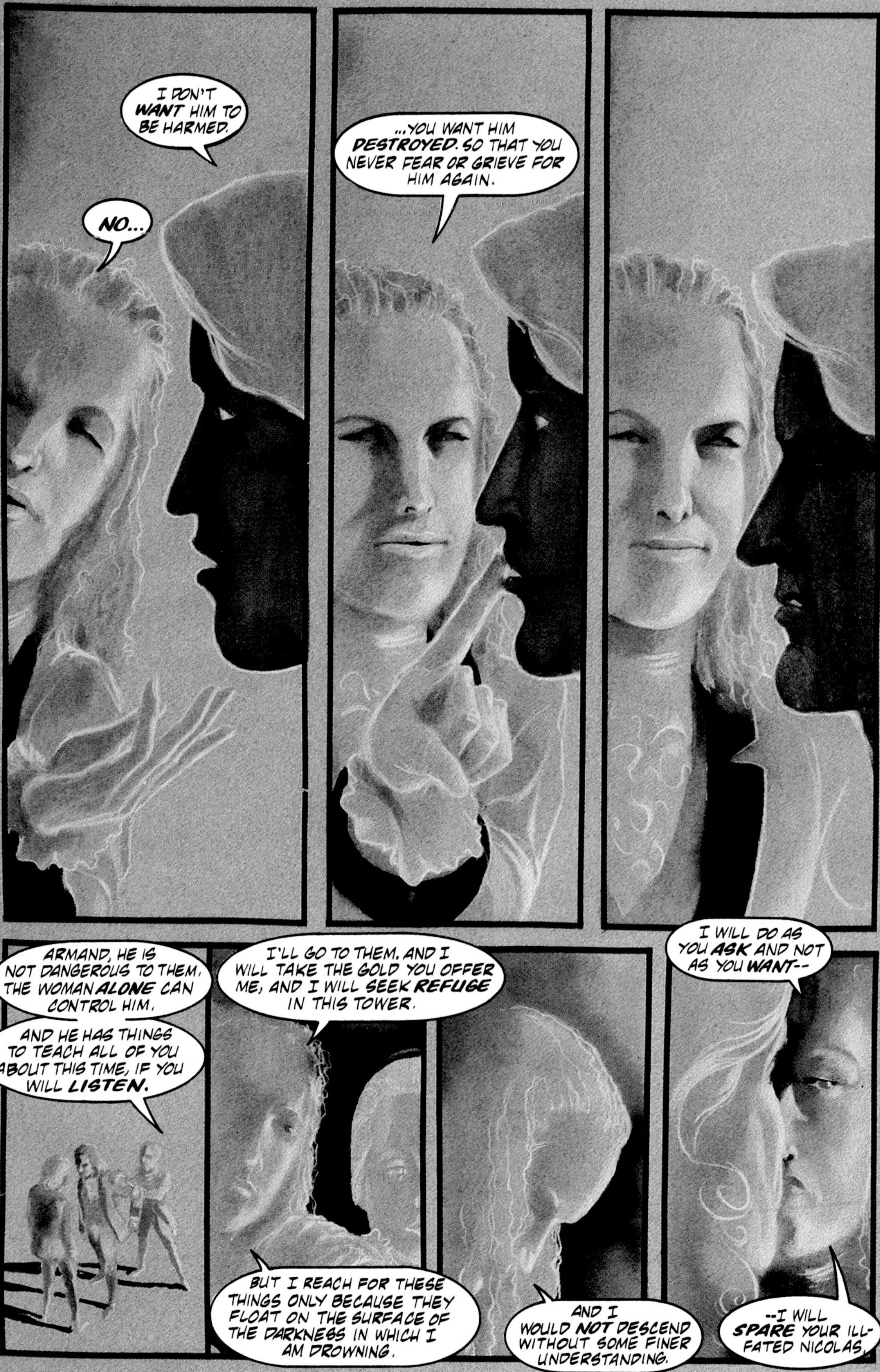
I DON'T WANT HIM TO BE HARMED.
NO...
...YOU WANT HIM DESTROYED. SO THAT YOU NEVER FEAR OR GRIEVE FOR HIM AGAIN.
ARMAND, HE IS NOT DANGEROUS TO THEM. THE WOMAN ALONE CAN CONTROL HIM.
AND HE HAS THINGS TO TEACH ALL OF YOU ABOUT THIS TIME, IF YOU WILL LISTEN.
I'LL GO TO THEM. AND I WILL TAKE THE GOLD YOU OFFER ME, AND I WILL SEEK REFUGE IN THIS TOWER.
BUT I REACH FOR THESE THINGS ONLY BECAUSE THEY FLOAT ON THE SURFACE OF THE DARKNESS IN WHICH I AM DROWNING.
AND I WOULD NOT DESCEND WITHOUT SOME FINER UNDERSTANDING.
I WILL DO AS YOU ASK AND NOT AS YOU WANT--
--I WILL SPARE YOUR ILL-FATED NICOLAS.

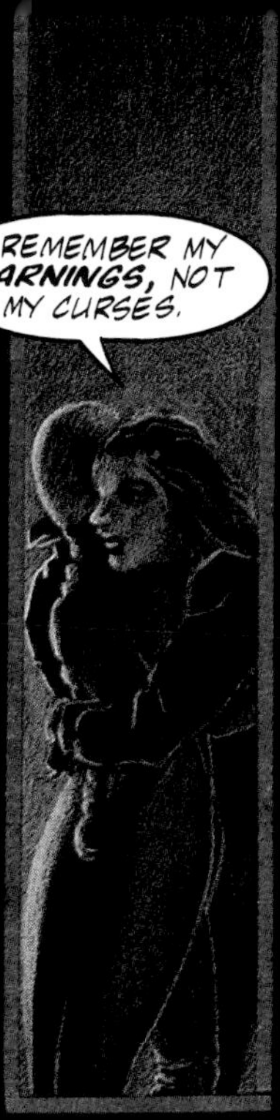
REMEMBER MY **WARNINGS,** NOT MY CURSES.

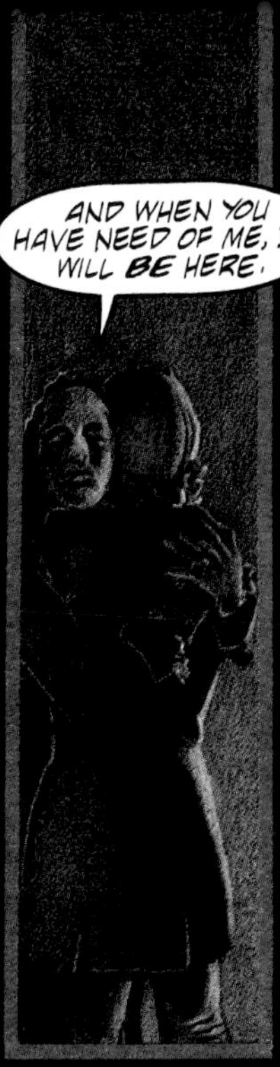
AND WHEN YOU HAVE NEED OF ME, I WILL **BE** HERE.

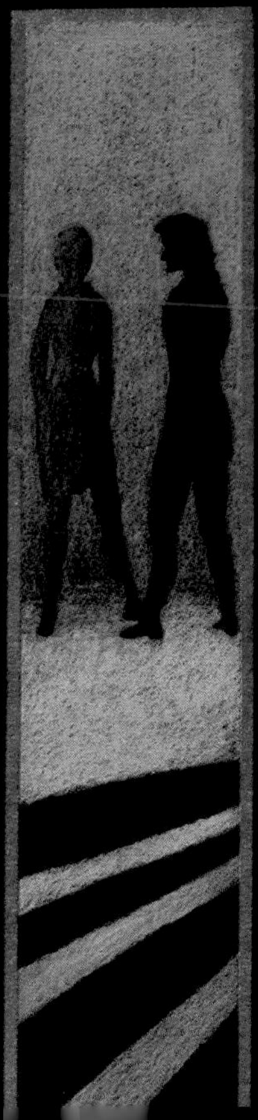

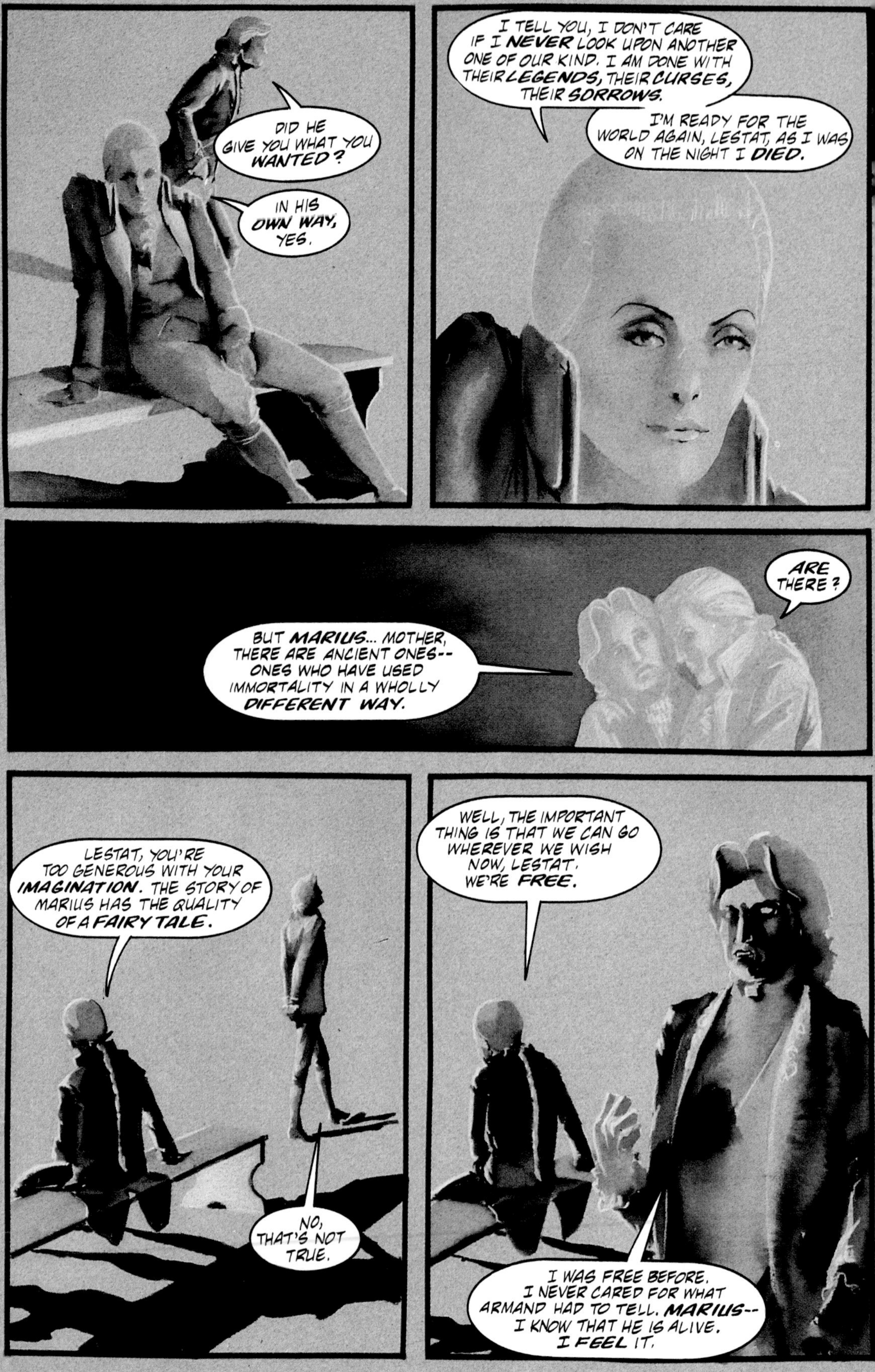

DID HE GIVE YOU WHAT YOU WANTED?
IN HIS OWN WAY, YES.
I TELL YOU, I DON'T CARE IF I NEVER LOOK UPON ANOTHER ONE OF OUR KIND. I AM DONE WITH THEIR LEGENDS, THEIR CURSES, THEIR SORROWS.
I'M READY FOR THE WORLD AGAIN, LESTAT, AS I WAS ON THE NIGHT I DIED.
BUT MARIUS... MOTHER, THERE ARE ANCIENT ONES-- ONES WHO HAVE USED IMMORTALITY IN A WHOLLY DIFFERENT WAY.
ARE THERE?
LESTAT, YOU'RE TOO GENEROUS WITH YOUR IMAGINATION. THE STORY OF MARIUS HAS THE QUALITY OF A FAIRY TALE.
NO, THAT'S NOT TRUE.
WELL, THE IMPORTANT THING IS THAT WE CAN GO WHEREVER WE WISH NOW, LESTAT. WE'RE FREE.
I WAS FREE BEFORE. I NEVER CARED FOR WHAT ARMAND HAD TO TELL. MARIUS-- I KNOW THAT HE IS ALIVE. I FEEL IT.

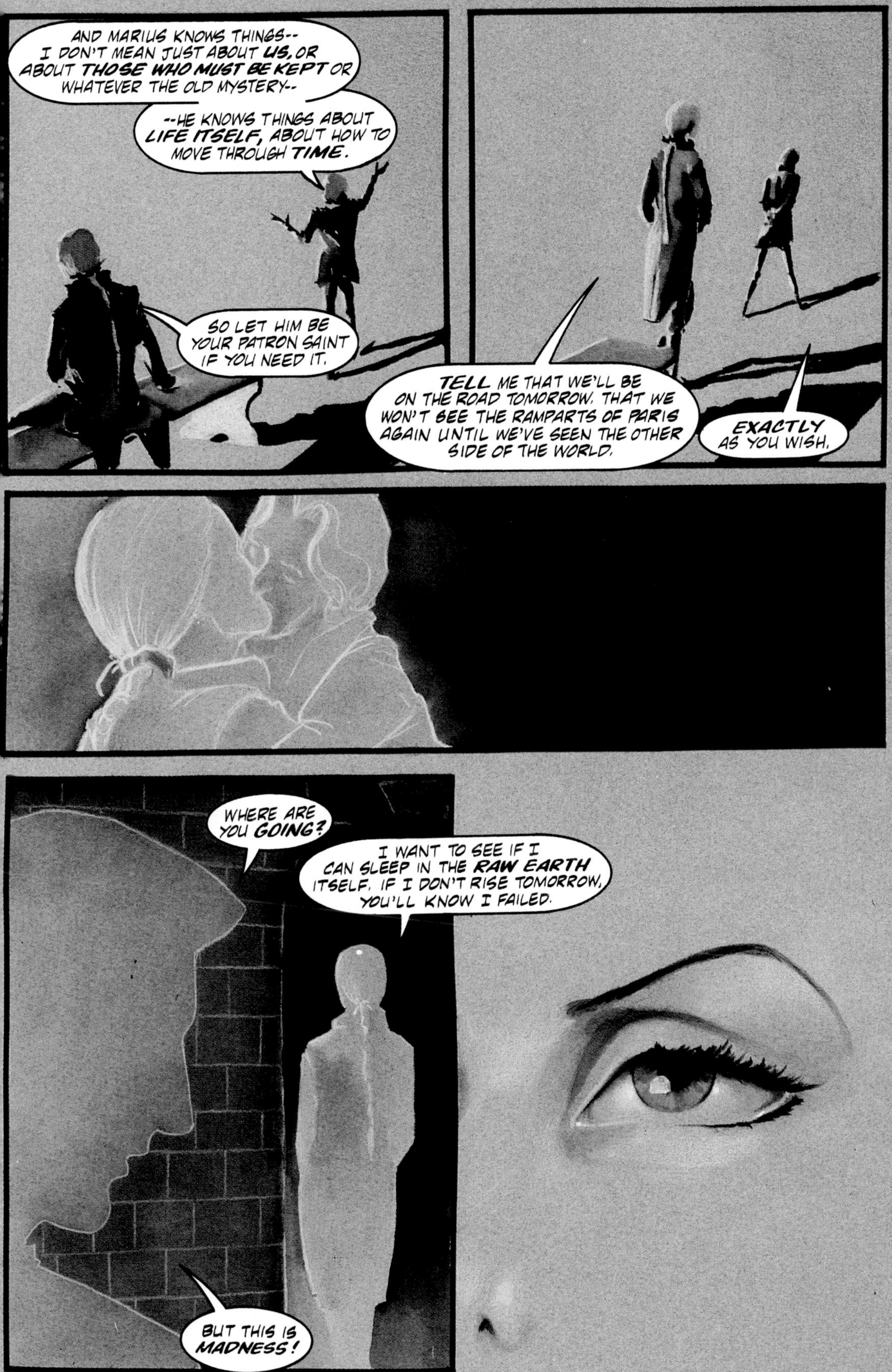
AND MARIUS KNOWS THINGS-- I DON'T MEAN JUST ABOUT US, OR ABOUT THOSE WHO MUST BE KEPT OR WHATEVER THE OLD MYSTERY--
--HE KNOWS THINGS ABOUT LIFE ITSELF, ABOUT HOW TO MOVE THROUGH TIME.
SO LET HIM BE YOUR PATRON SAINT IF YOU NEED IT.
TELL ME THAT WE'LL BE ON THE ROAD TOMORROW. THAT WE WON'T SEE THE RAMPARTS OF PARIS AGAIN UNTIL WE'VE SEEN THE OTHER SIDE OF THE WORLD.
EXACTLY AS YOU WISH.
WHERE ARE YOU GOING?
I WANT TO SEE IF I CAN SLEEP IN THE RAW EARTH ITSELF. IF I DON'T RISE TOMORROW, YOU'LL KNOW I FAILED.
BUT THIS IS MADNESS!

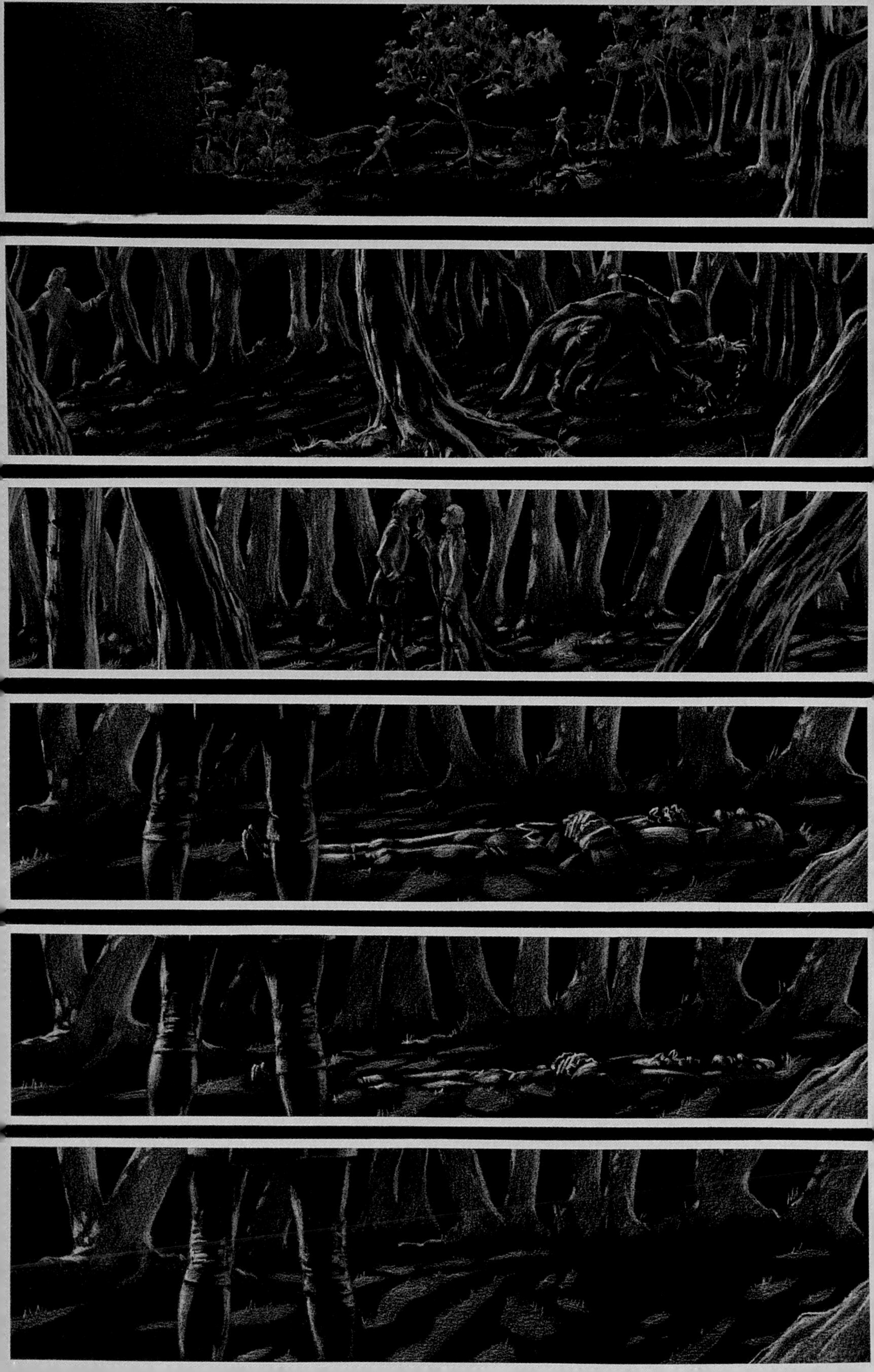

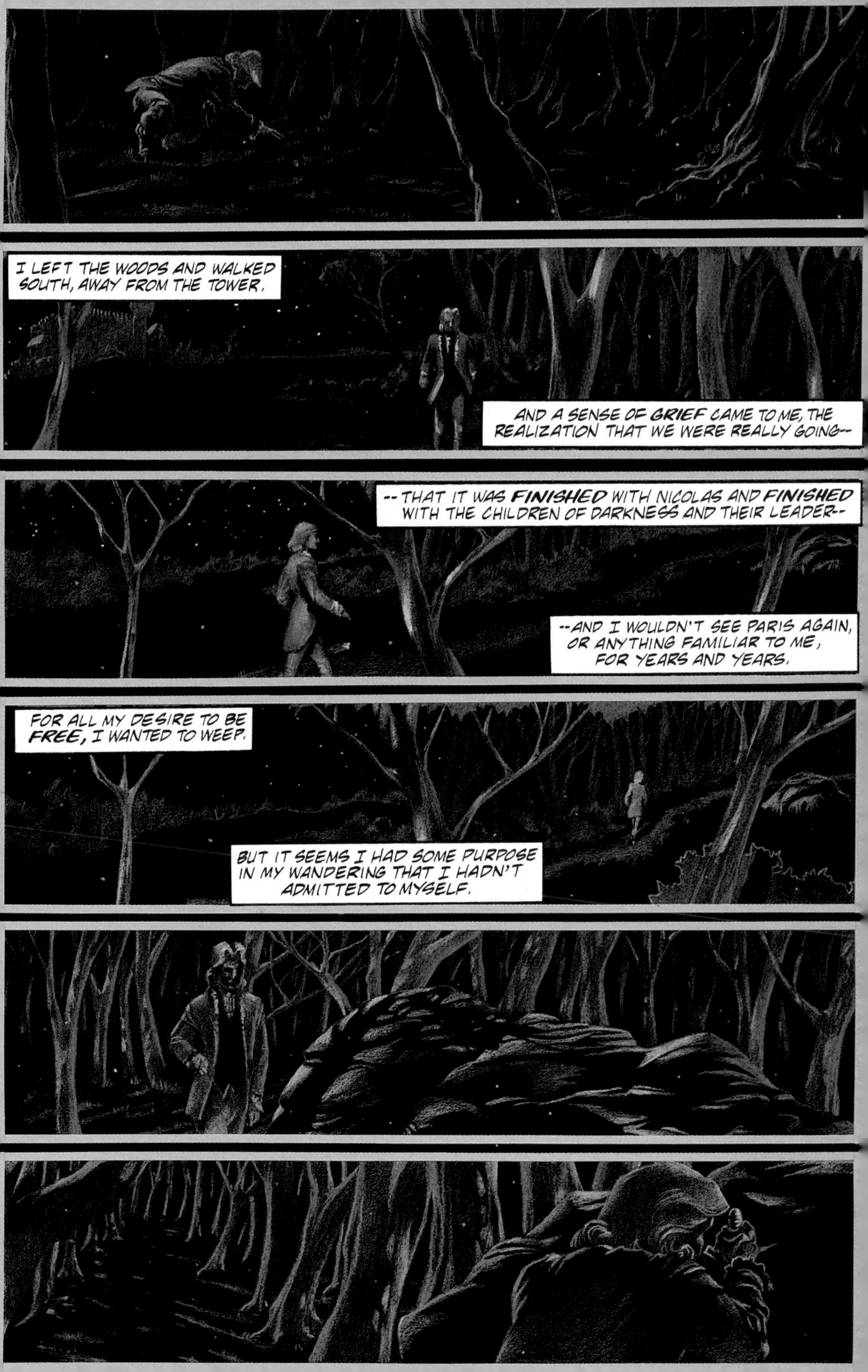

I LEFT THE WOODS AND WALKED SOUTH, AWAY FROM THE TOWER.
AND A SENSE OF GRIEF CAME TO ME, THE REALIZATION THAT WE WERE REALLY GOING--
--THAT IT WAS FINISHED WITH NICOLAS AND FINISHED WITH THE CHILDREN OF DARKNESS AND THEIR LEADER--
--AND I WOULDN'T SEE PARIS AGAIN, OR ANYTHING FAMILIAR TO ME, FOR YEARS AND YEARS.
FOR ALL MY DESIRE TO BE FREE, I WANTED TO WEEP.
BUT IT SEEMS I HAD SOME PURPOSE IN MY WANDERING THAT I HADN'T ADMITTED TO MYSELF.

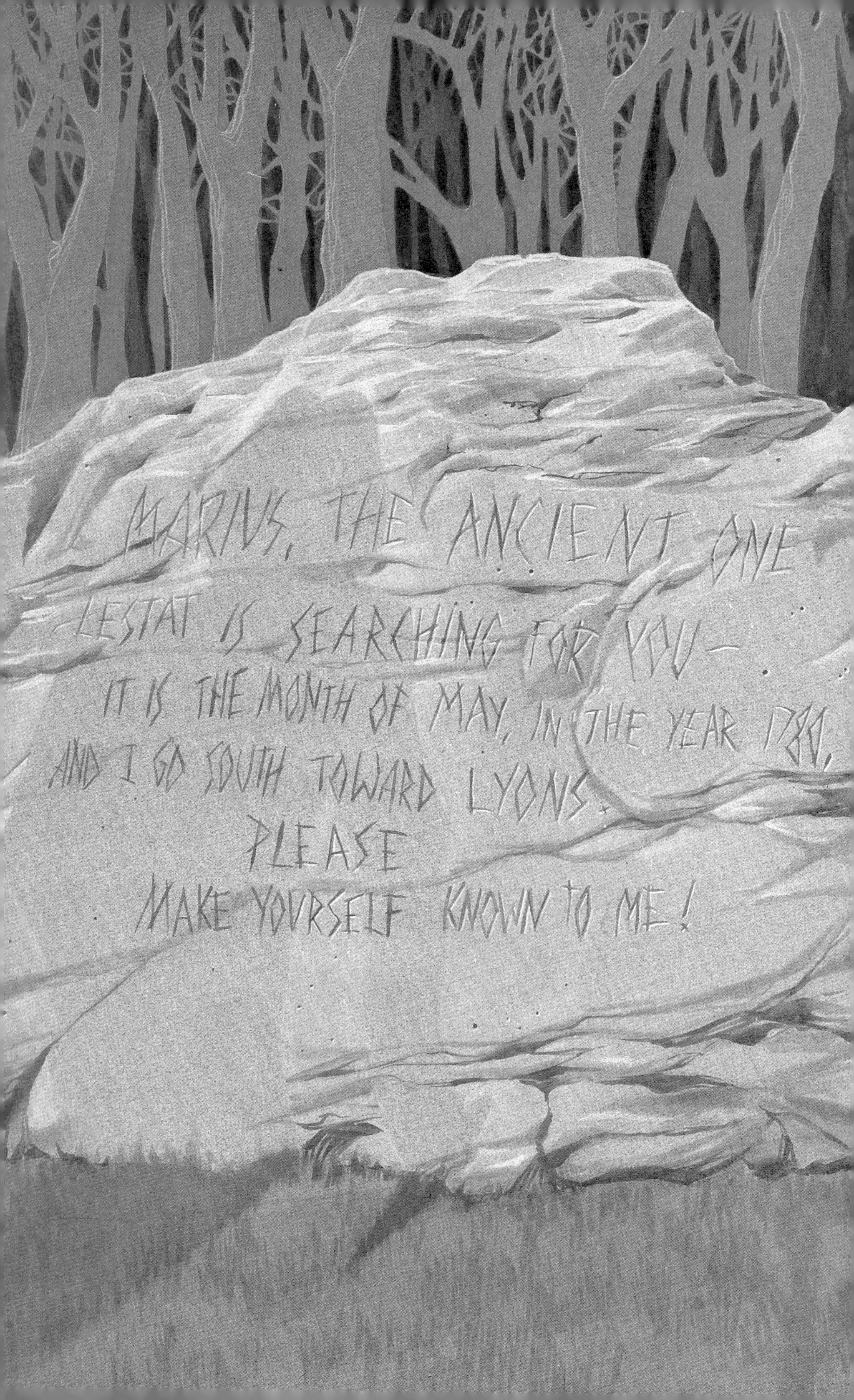
MARIUS, THE ANCIENT ONE
LESTAT IS SEARCHING FOR YOU–
IT IS THE MONTH OF MAY, IN THE YEAR 1780,
AND I GO SOUTH TOWARD LYONS.
PLEASE
MAKE YOURSELF KNOWN TO ME!

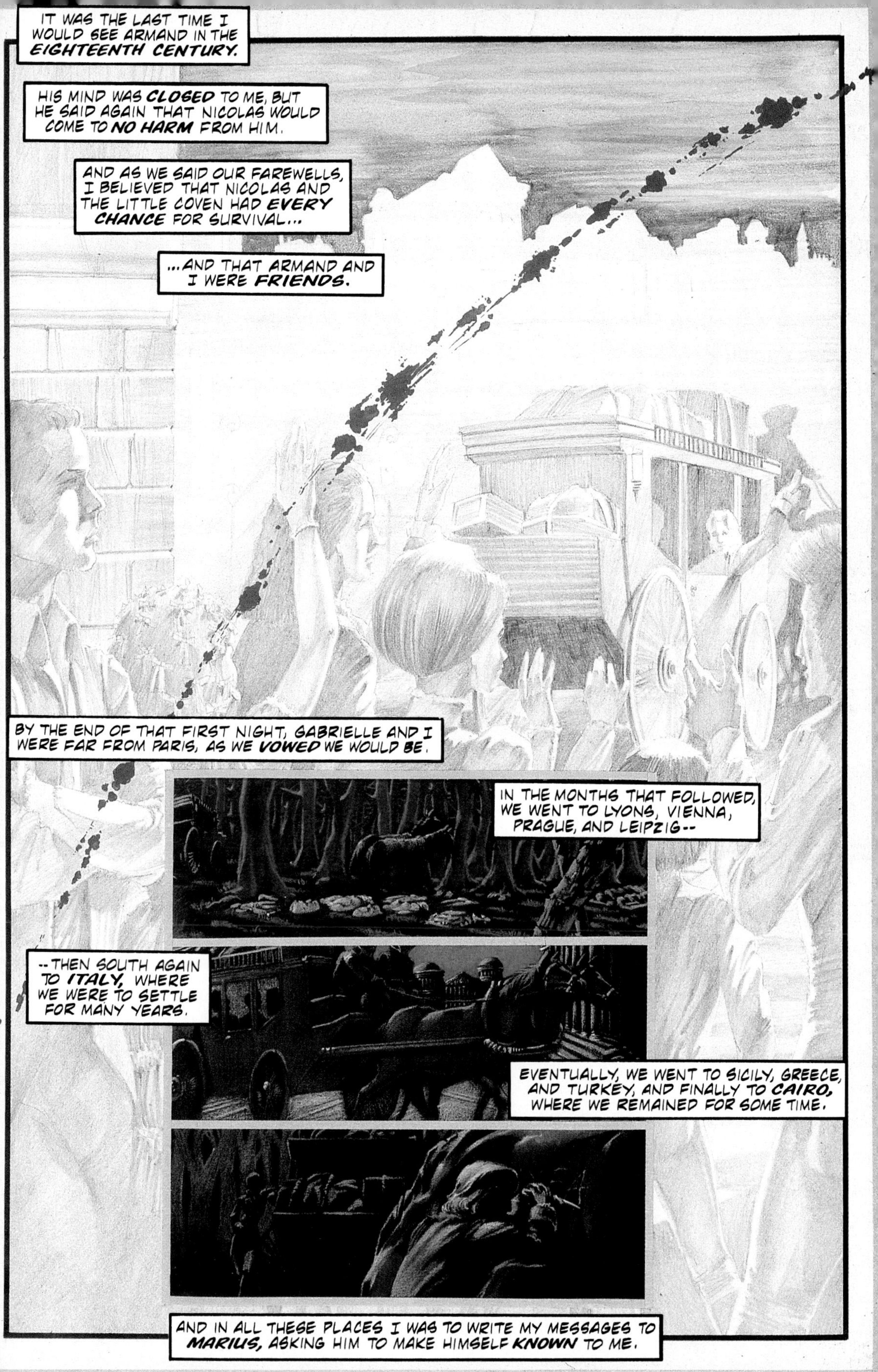
IT WAS THE LAST TIME I WOULD SEE ARMAND IN THE EIGHTEENTH CENTURY.
HIS MIND WAS CLOSED TO ME, BUT HE SAID AGAIN THAT NICOLAS WOULD COME TO NO HARM FROM HIM.
AND AS WE SAID OUR FAREWELLS, I BELIEVED THAT NICOLAS AND THE LITTLE COVEN HAD EVERY CHANCE FOR SURVIVAL...
...AND THAT ARMAND AND I WERE FRIENDS.
BY THE END OF THAT FIRST NIGHT, GABRIELLE AND I WERE FAR FROM PARIS, AS WE VOWED WE WOULD BE.
IN THE MONTHS THAT FOLLOWED, WE WENT TO LYONS, VIENNA, PRAGUE, AND LEIPZIG--
--THEN SOUTH AGAIN TO ITALY, WHERE WE WERE TO SETTLE FOR MANY YEARS.
EVENTUALLY, WE WENT TO SICILY, GREECE, AND TURKEY, AND FINALLY TO CAIRO, WHERE WE REMAINED FOR SOME TIME.
AND IN ALL THESE PLACES I WAS TO WRITE MY MESSAGES TO MARIUS, ASKING HIM TO MAKE HIMSELF KNOWN TO ME.

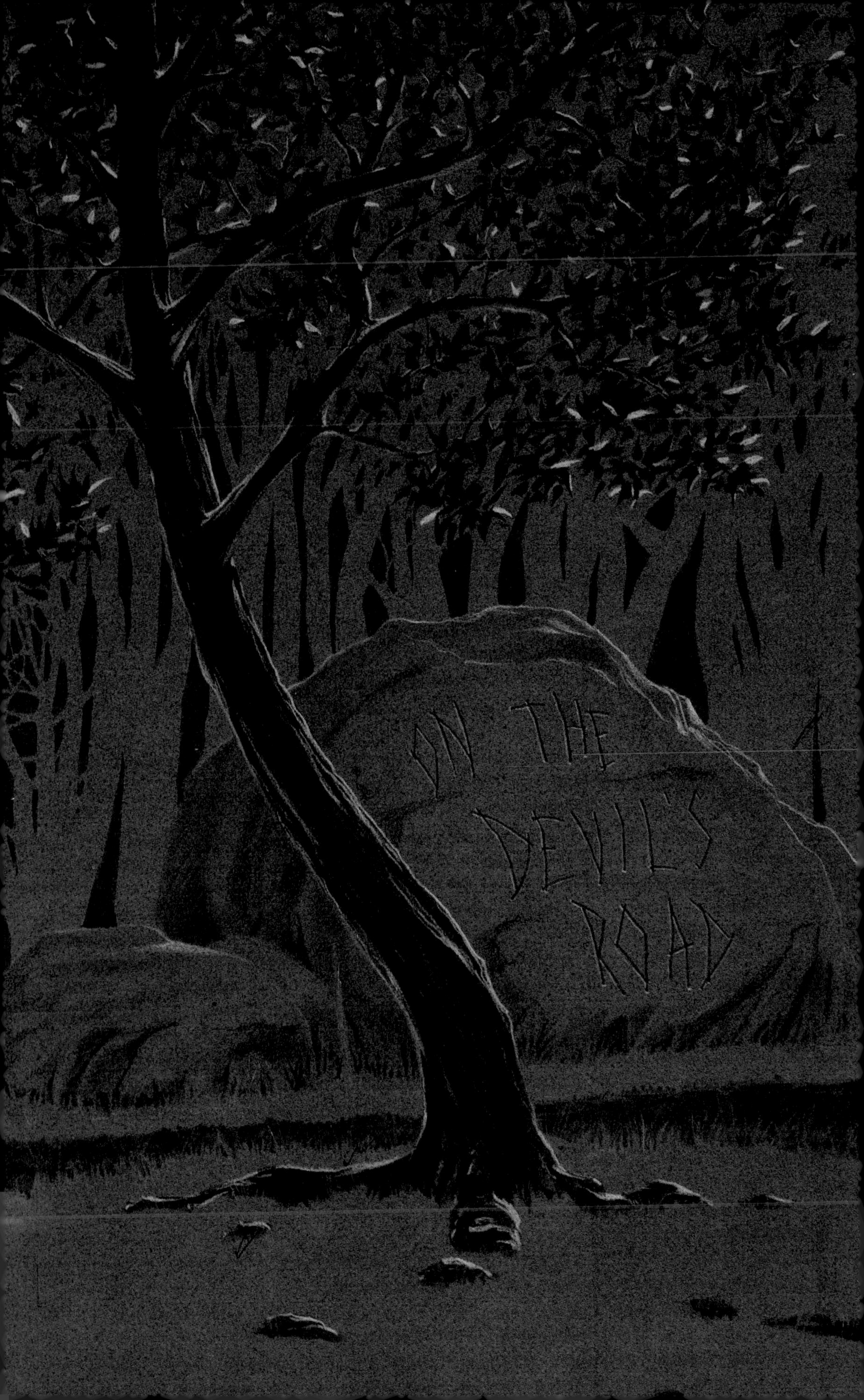
ON THE
DEVIL'S
ROAD

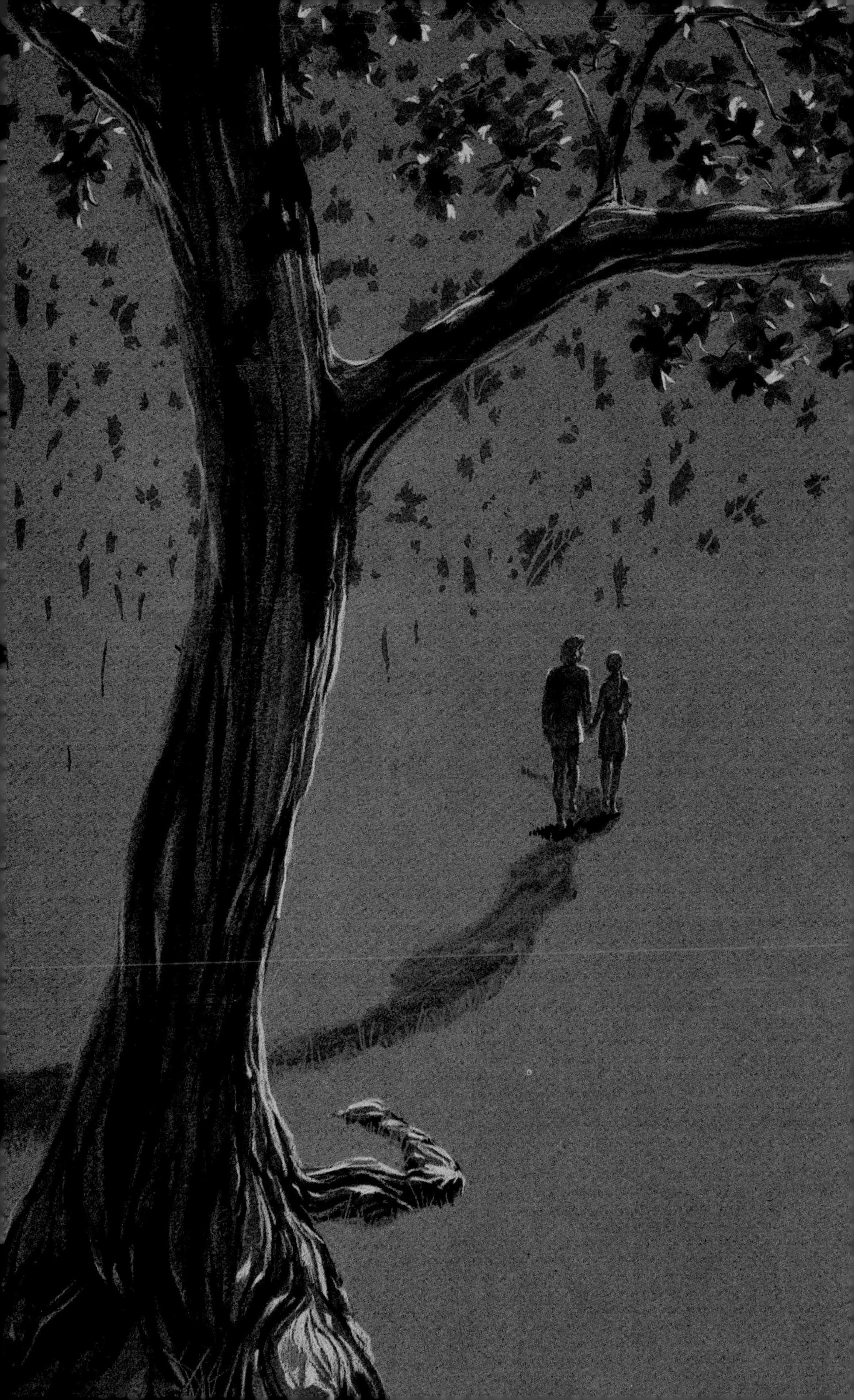

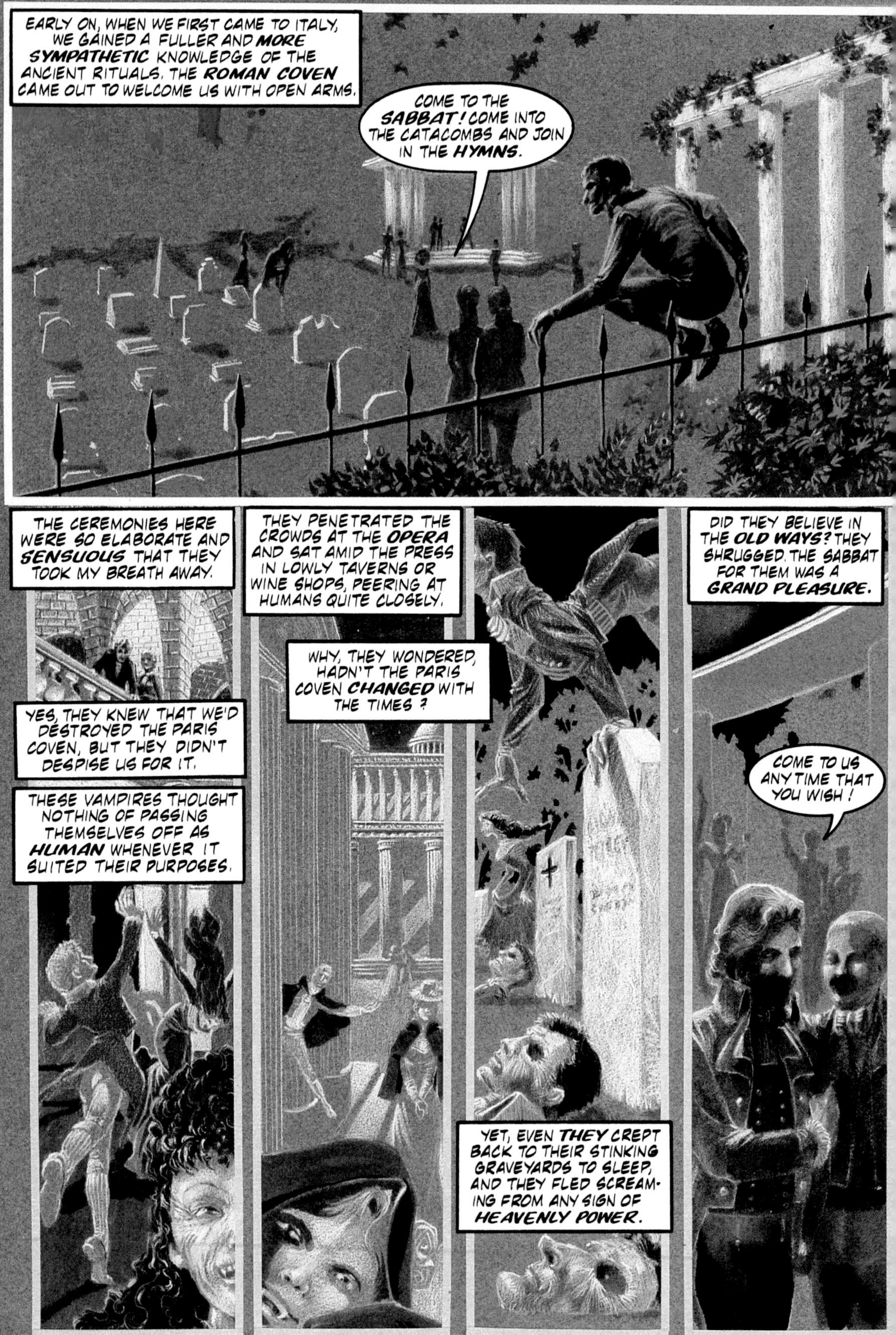
EARLY ON, WHEN WE FIRST CAME TO ITALY, WE GAINED A FULLER AND MORE SYMPATHETIC KNOWLEDGE OF THE ANCIENT RITUALS. THE ROMAN COVEN CAME OUT TO WELCOME US WITH OPEN ARMS.
COME TO THE SABBAT! COME INTO THE CATACOMBS AND JOIN IN THE HYMNS.
THE CEREMONIES HERE WERE SO ELABORATE AND SENSUOUS THAT THEY TOOK MY BREATH AWAY.
YES, THEY KNEW THAT WE'D DESTROYED THE PARIS COVEN, BUT THEY DIDN'T DESPISE US FOR IT.
THESE VAMPIRES THOUGHT NOTHING OF PASSING THEMSELVES OFF AS HUMAN WHENEVER IT SUITED THEIR PURPOSES.
THEY PENETRATED THE CROWDS AT THE OPERA AND SAT AMID THE PRESS IN LOWLY TAVERNS OR WINE SHOPS, PEERING AT HUMANS QUITE CLOSELY.
WHY, THEY WONDERED, HADN'T THE PARIS COVEN CHANGED WITH THE TIMES?
YET, EVEN THEY CREPT BACK TO THEIR STINKING GRAVEYARDS TO SLEEP, AND THEY FLED SCREAMING FROM ANY SIGN OF HEAVENLY POWER.
DID THEY BELIEVE IN THE OLD WAYS? THEY SHRUGGED. THE SABBAT FOR THEM WAS A GRAND PLEASURE.
COME TO US ANY TIME THAT YOU WISH!

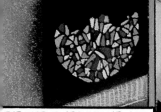

I COULD FILL *VOLUMES* WITH THE THINGS I STUDIED, THE THINGS I STRUGGLED TO *UNDERSTAND.*

I MADE A LIBRARY IN THE OLD *VENETIAN PALAZZO* I HAUNTED, OFTEN READING THE WHOLE NIGHT LONG.

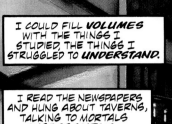

THE WORLD AROUND ME HAD BECOME MY LOVER AND MY TEACHER. I WAS ENRAPTURED WITH THE CATHEDRALS AND CASTLES, THE MUSEUMS AND PALACES THAT I SAW.

I READ THE NEWSPAPERS AND HUNG ABOUT TAVERNS, TALKING TO MORTALS *INCESSANTLY.*

AND OF COURSE IT WAS THE TALE OF *OSIRIS* THAT ENCHANTED ME, BRINGING BACK WITH IT THE ROMANCE OF ARMAND'S STORY AND *MARIUS'* ENIGMATIC WORDS.

AND WHEN I WASN'T OUT ROAMING, I WAS TRAVELING THE REALM OF THE *BOOKS* THAT HAD BELONGED TO GABRIELLE SO *EXCLUSIVELY* ALL THROUGH THOSE DREARY *MORTAL* YEARS AT HOME.

IN EVERY PLACE I VISITED, I WENT TO THE HEART OF THE *SOCIETY*-- I DRANK UP ITS ENTERTAINMENT AND ITS GOSSIP, ITS LITERATURE AND ITS MUSIC, ITS ARCHITECTURE AND ITS ART.

ARMAND HAD TOLD US THAT MARIUS HAD SPOKEN OF THIS MYTH. WHY?

WAS OSIRIS A *VAMPIRE GOD?*

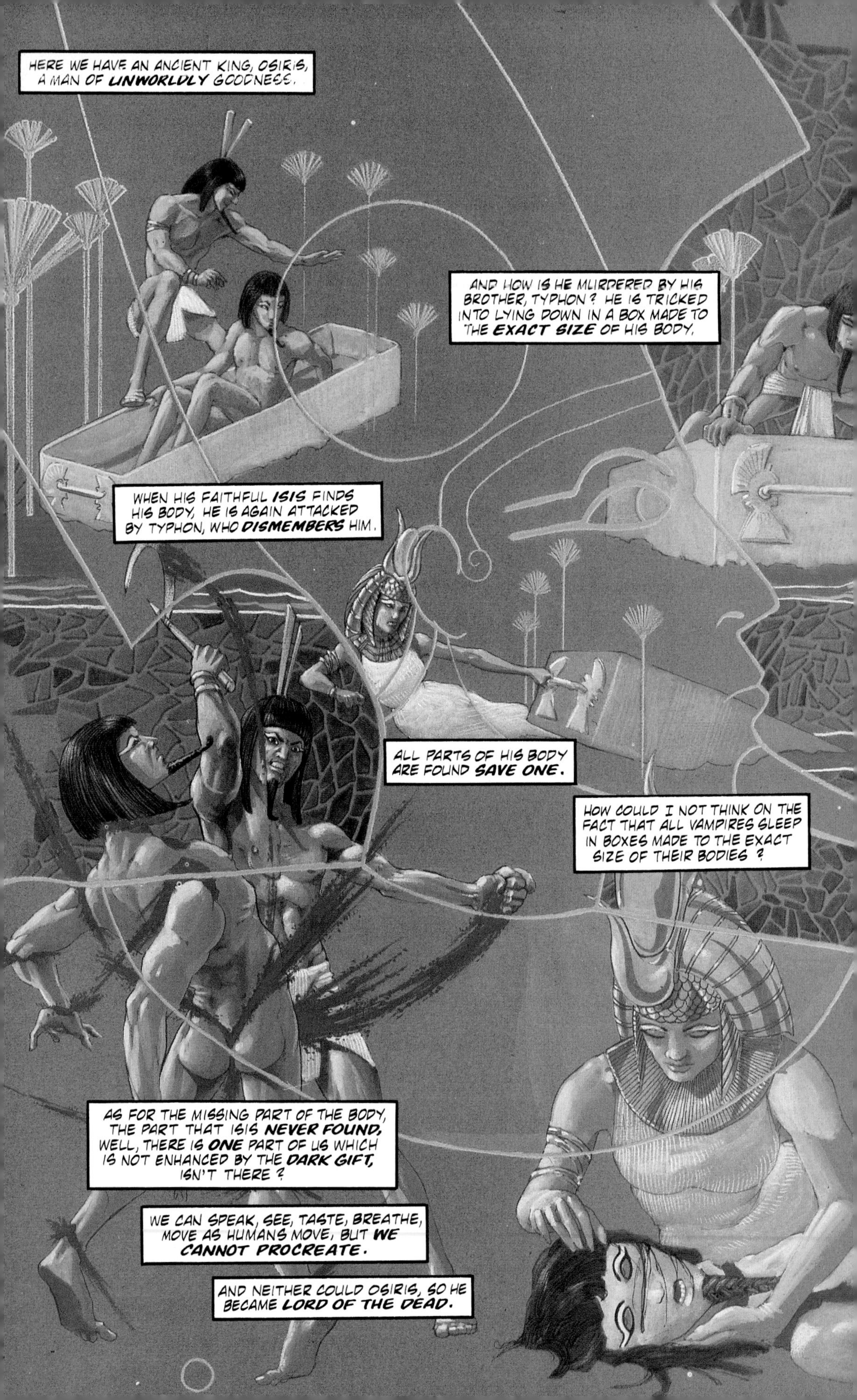
HERE WE HAVE AN ANCIENT KING, OSIRIS, A MAN OF UNWORLDLY GOODNESS.
AND HOW IS HE MURDERED BY HIS BROTHER, TYPHON? HE IS TRICKED INTO LYING DOWN IN A BOX MADE TO THE EXACT SIZE OF HIS BODY.
WHEN HIS FAITHFUL ISIS FINDS HIS BODY, HE IS AGAIN ATTACKED BY TYPHON, WHO DISMEMBERS HIM.
ALL PARTS OF HIS BODY ARE FOUND SAVE ONE.
HOW COULD I NOT THINK ON THE FACT THAT ALL VAMPIRES SLEEP IN BOXES MADE TO THE EXACT SIZE OF THEIR BODIES?
AS FOR THE MISSING PART OF THE BODY, THE PART THAT ISIS NEVER FOUND, WELL, THERE IS ONE PART OF US WHICH IS NOT ENHANCED BY THE DARK GIFT, ISN'T THERE?
WE CAN SPEAK, SEE, TASTE, BREATHE, MOVE AS HUMANS MOVE, BUT WE CANNOT PROCREATE.
AND NEITHER COULD OSIRIS, SO HE BECAME LORD OF THE DEAD.

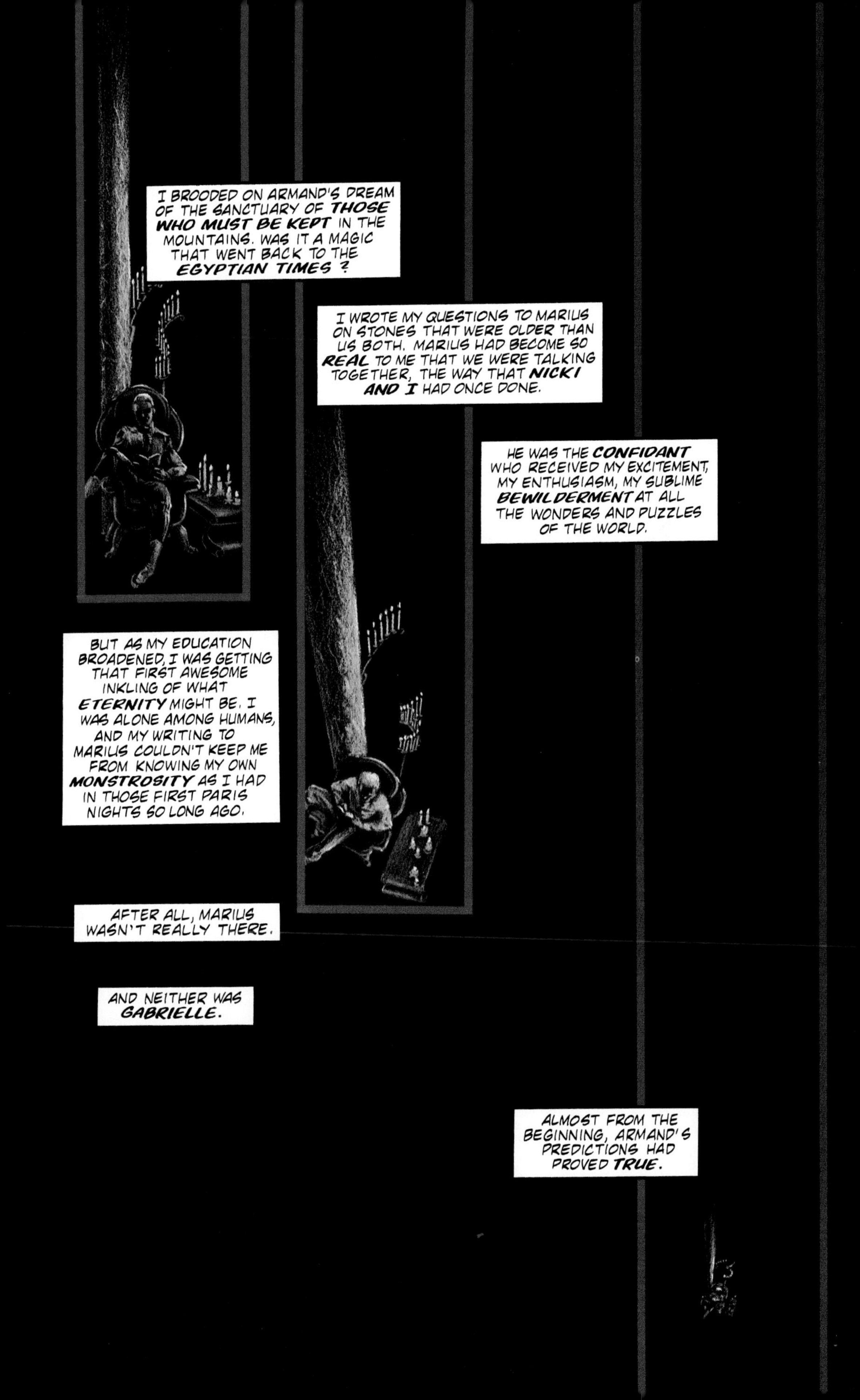
I BROODED ON ARMAND'S DREAM OF THE SANCTUARY OF THOSE WHO MUST BE KEPT IN THE MOUNTAINS. WAS IT A MAGIC THAT WENT BACK TO THE EGYPTIAN TIMES ?
I WROTE MY QUESTIONS TO MARIUS ON STONES THAT WERE OLDER THAN US BOTH. MARIUS HAD BECOME SO REAL TO ME THAT WE WERE TALKING TOGETHER, THE WAY THAT NICKI AND I HAD ONCE DONE.
HE WAS THE CONFIDANT WHO RECEIVED MY EXCITEMENT, MY ENTHUSIASM, MY SUBLIME BEWILDERMENT AT ALL THE WONDERS AND PUZZLES OF THE WORLD.
BUT AS MY EDUCATION BROADENED, I WAS GETTING THAT FIRST AWESOME INKLING OF WHAT ETERNITY MIGHT BE. I WAS ALONE AMONG HUMANS, AND MY WRITING TO MARIUS COULDN'T KEEP ME FROM KNOWING MY OWN MONSTROSITY AS I HAD IN THOSE FIRST PARIS NIGHTS SO LONG AGO.
AFTER ALL, MARIUS WASN'T REALLY THERE.
AND NEITHER WAS GABRIELLE.
ALMOST FROM THE BEGINNING, ARMAND'S PREDICTIONS HAD PROVED TRUE.

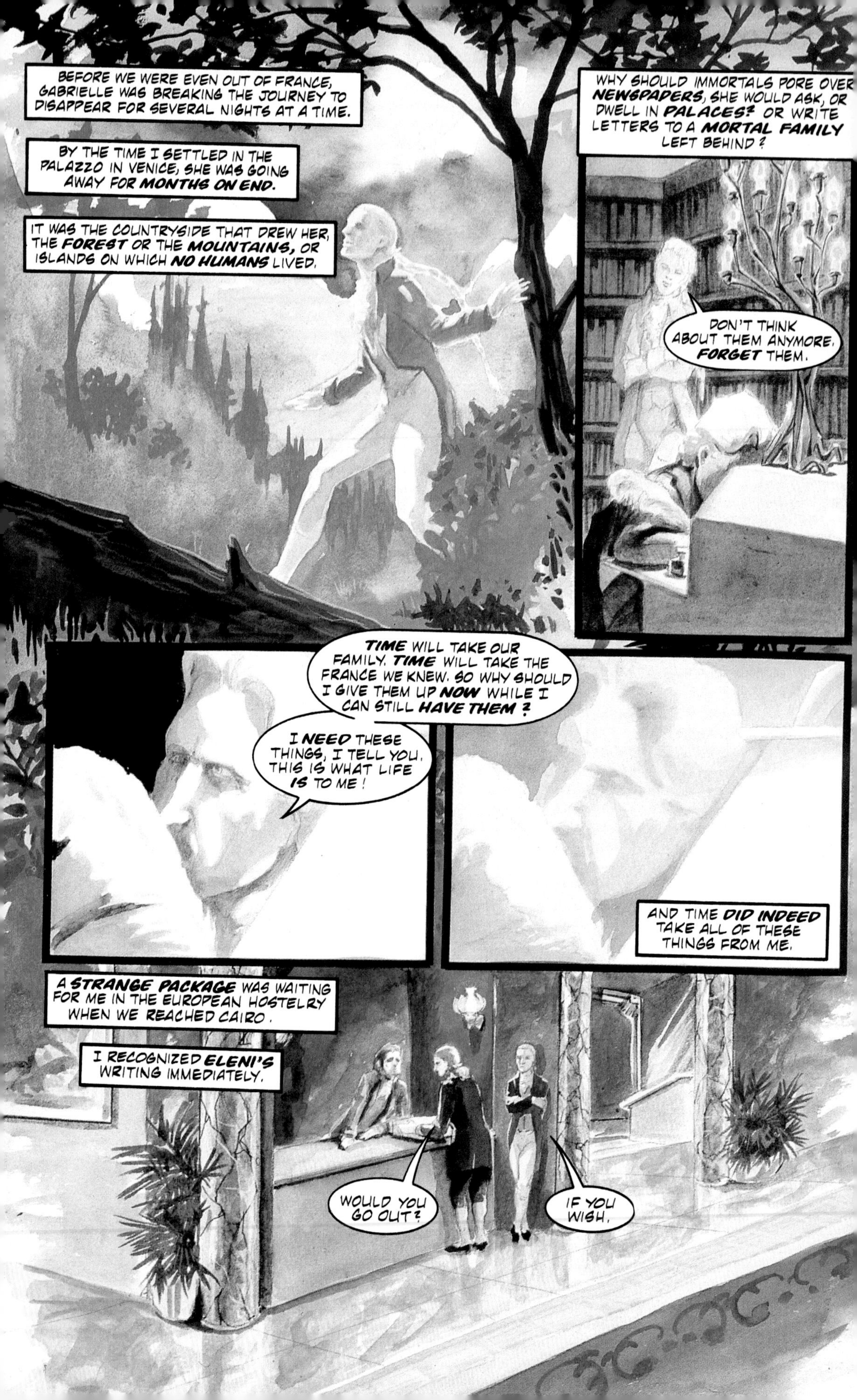

BEFORE WE WERE EVEN OUT OF FRANCE, GABRIELLE WAS BREAKING THE JOURNEY TO DISAPPEAR FOR SEVERAL NIGHTS AT A TIME.
BY THE TIME I SETTLED IN THE PALAZZO IN VENICE, SHE WAS GOING AWAY FOR MONTHS ON END.
IT WAS THE COUNTRYSIDE THAT DREW HER, THE FOREST OR THE MOUNTAINS, OR ISLANDS ON WHICH NO HUMANS LIVED.
WHY SHOULD IMMORTALS PORE OVER NEWSPAPERS, SHE WOULD ASK, OR DWELL IN PALACES? OR WRITE LETTERS TO A MORTAL FAMILY LEFT BEHIND?
DON'T THINK ABOUT THEM ANYMORE. FORGET THEM.
TIME WILL TAKE OUR FAMILY. TIME WILL TAKE THE FRANCE WE KNEW. SO WHY SHOULD I GIVE THEM UP NOW WHILE I CAN STILL HAVE THEM?
I NEED THESE THINGS, I TELL YOU. THIS IS WHAT LIFE IS TO ME!
AND TIME DID INDEED TAKE ALL OF THESE THINGS FROM ME.
A STRANGE PACKAGE WAS WAITING FOR ME IN THE EUROPEAN HOSTELRY WHEN WE REACHED CAIRO.
I RECOGNIZED ELENI'S WRITING IMMEDIATELY.
WOULD YOU GO OUT?
IF YOU WISH.

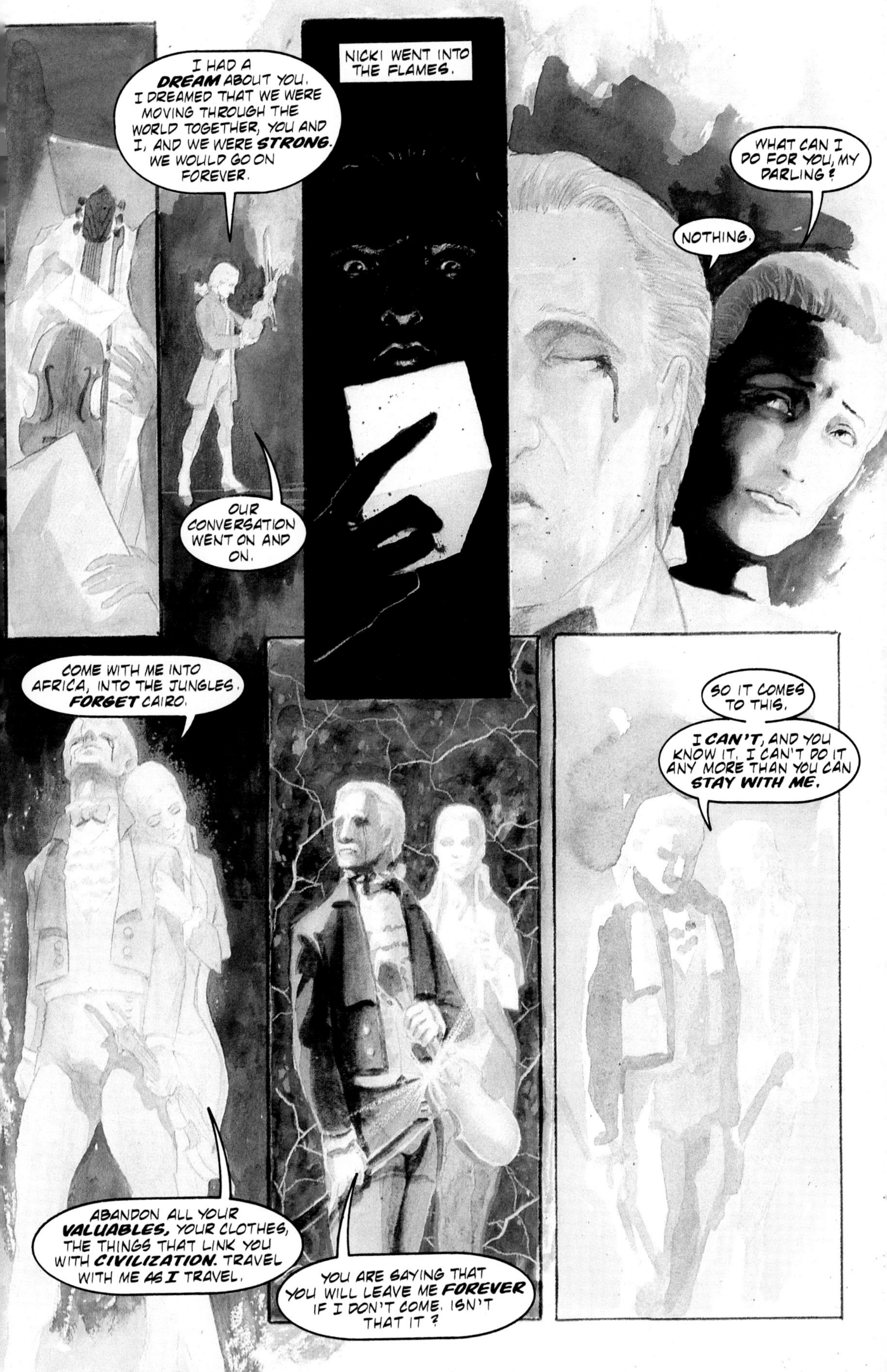
I HAD A DREAM ABOUT YOU. I DREAMED THAT WE WERE MOVING THROUGH THE WORLD TOGETHER, YOU AND I, AND WE WERE STRONG. WE WOULD GO ON FOREVER.
OUR CONVERSATION WENT ON AND ON.
NICKI WENT INTO THE FLAMES.
WHAT CAN I DO FOR YOU, MY DARLING?
NOTHING.
COME WITH ME INTO AFRICA, INTO THE JUNGLES. FORGET CAIRO.
ABANDON ALL YOUR VALUABLES, YOUR CLOTHES, THE THINGS THAT LINK YOU WITH CIVILIZATION. TRAVEL WITH ME AS I TRAVEL.
YOU ARE SAYING THAT YOU WILL LEAVE ME FOREVER IF I DON'T COME. ISN'T THAT IT?
SO IT COMES TO THIS.
I CAN'T, AND YOU KNOW IT. I CAN'T DO IT ANY MORE THAN YOU CAN STAY WITH ME.

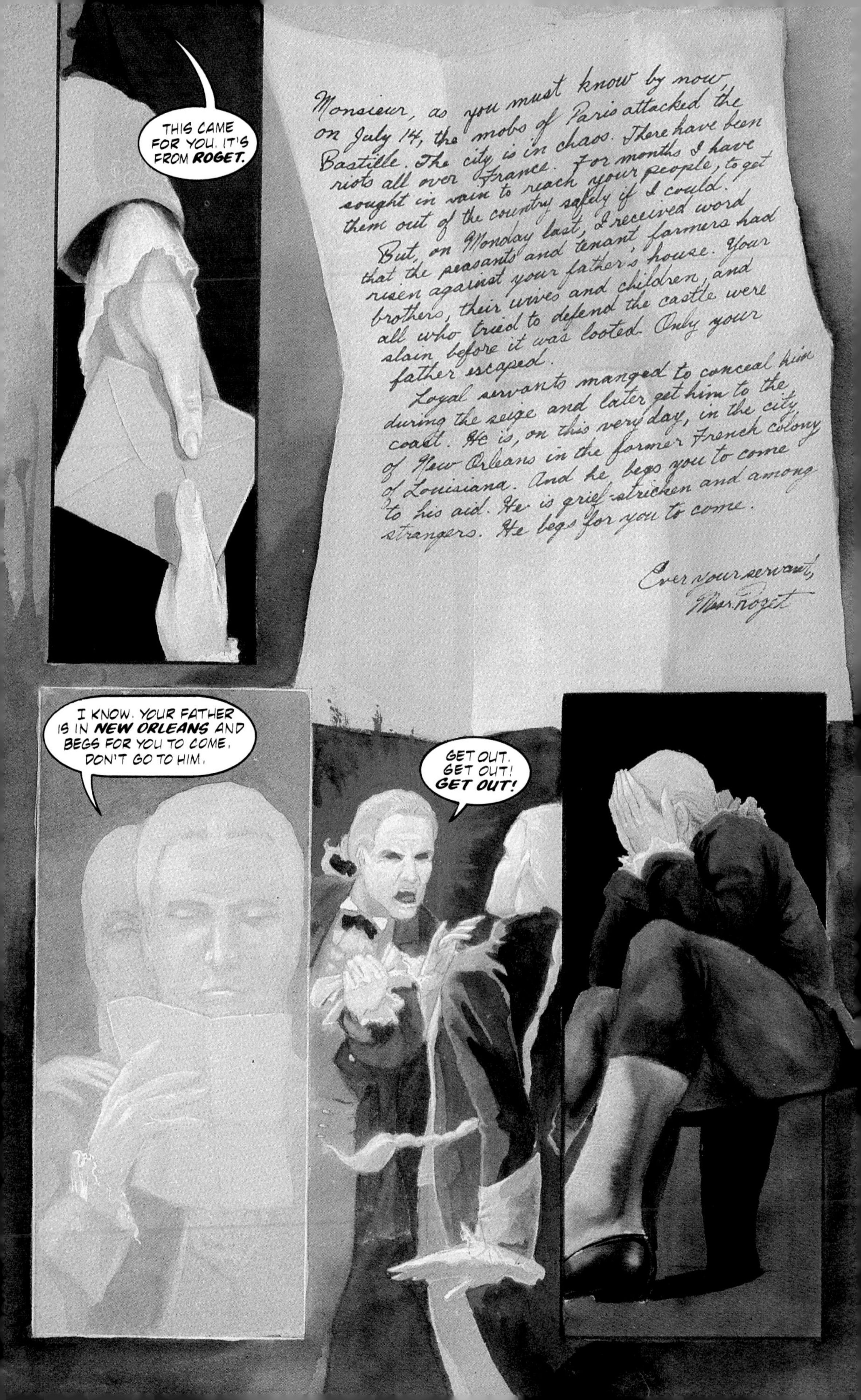
THIS CAME FOR YOU. IT'S FROM ROGET.
Monsieur, as you must know by now, on July 14, the mobs of Paris attacked the Bastille. The city is in chaos. There have been riots all over France. For months I have sought in vain to reach your people, to get them out of the country safely if I could.
But, on Monday last, I received word that the peasants and tenant farmers had risen against your father's house. Your brothers, their wives and children, and all who tried to defend the castle were slain before it was looted. Only your father escaped.
Loyal servants manged to conceal him during the seige and later get him to the coast. He is, on this very day, in the city of New Orleans in the former French colony of Louisiana. And he begs you to come to his aid. He is grief-stricken and among strangers. He begs for you to come.
Ever your servant,
Msr. Roget
I KNOW. YOUR FATHER IS IN NEW ORLEANS AND BEGS FOR YOU TO COME. DON'T GO TO HIM.
GET OUT. GET OUT! GET OUT!

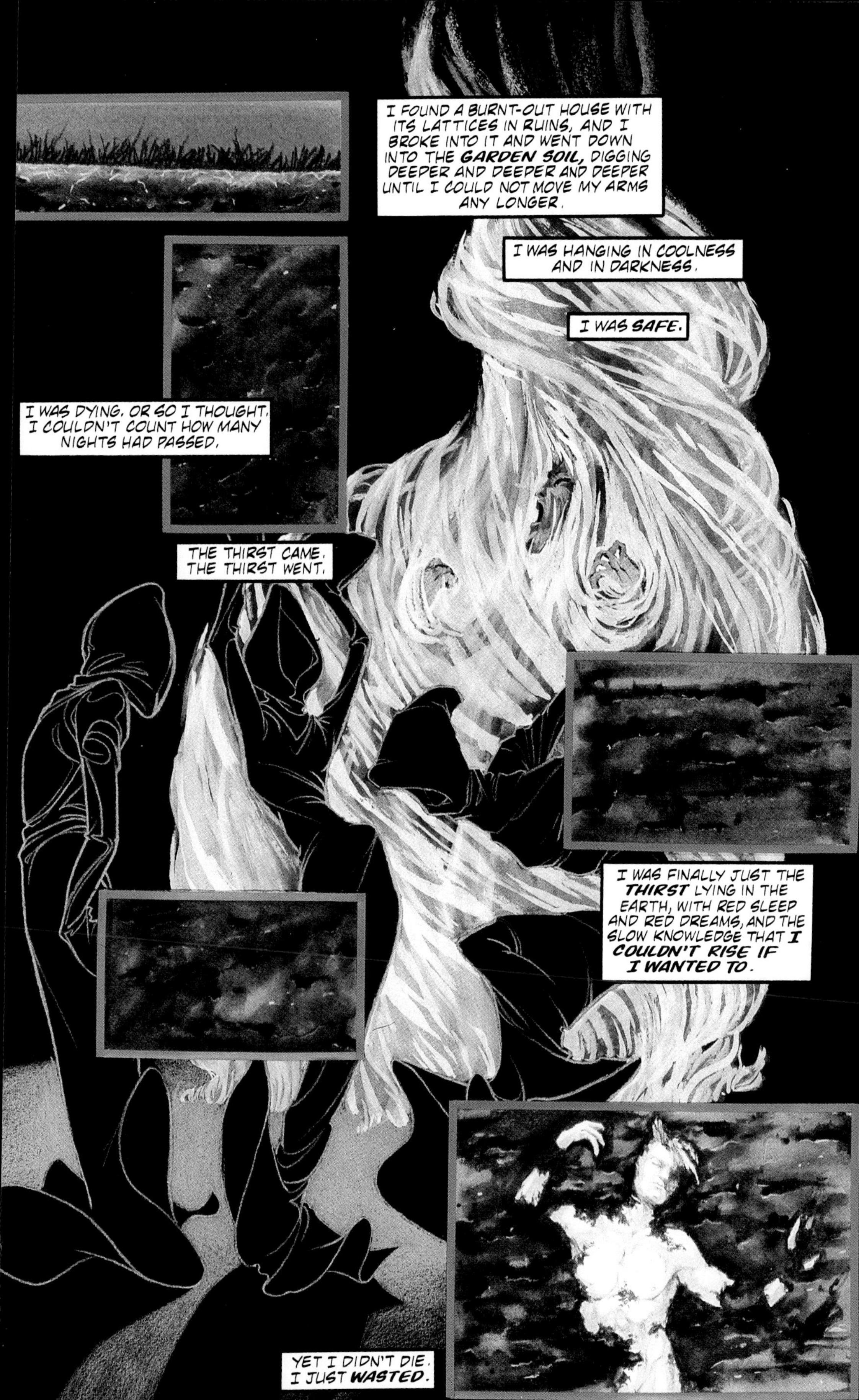
I FOUND A BURNT-OUT HOUSE WITH ITS LATTICES IN RUINS, AND I BROKE INTO IT AND WENT DOWN INTO THE GARDEN SOIL, DIGGING DEEPER AND DEEPER AND DEEPER UNTIL I COULD NOT MOVE MY ARMS ANY LONGER.
I WAS HANGING IN COOLNESS AND IN DARKNESS.
I WAS SAFE.
I WAS DYING. OR SO I THOUGHT. I COULDN'T COUNT HOW MANY NIGHTS HAD PASSED.
THE THIRST CAME. THE THIRST WENT.
I WAS FINALLY JUST THE THIRST LYING IN THE EARTH, WITH RED SLEEP AND RED DREAMS, AND THE SLOW KNOWLEDGE THAT I COULDN'T RISE IF I WANTED TO.
YET I DIDN'T DIE. I JUST WASTED.

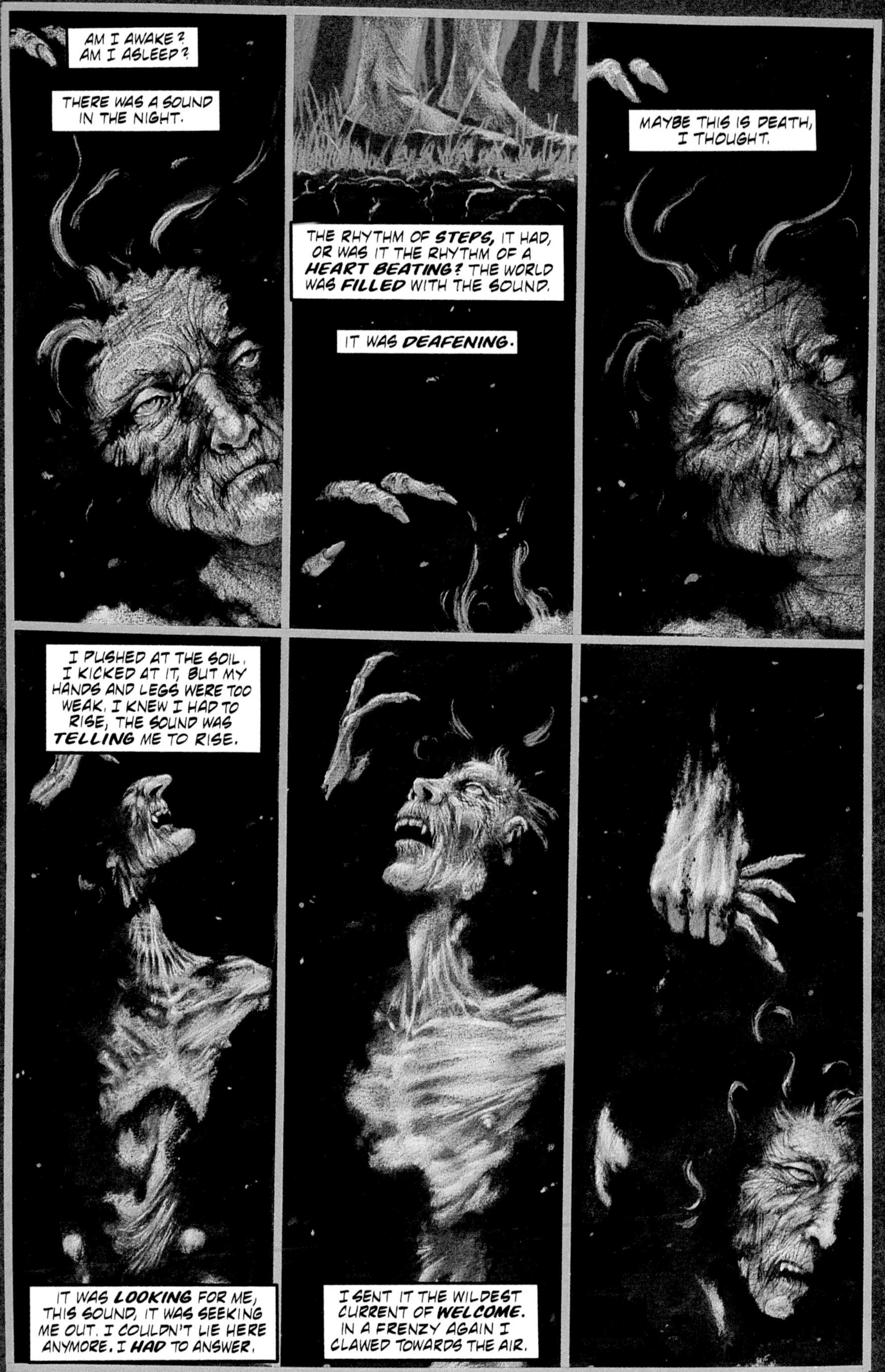
AM I AWAKE? AM I ASLEEP?
THERE WAS A SOUND IN THE NIGHT.
THE RHYTHM OF STEPS, IT HAD, OR WAS IT THE RHYTHM OF A HEART BEATING? THE WORLD WAS FILLED WITH THE SOUND.
IT WAS DEAFENING.
MAYBE THIS IS DEATH, I THOUGHT.
I PUSHED AT THE SOIL. I KICKED AT IT, BUT MY HANDS AND LEGS WERE TOO WEAK. I KNEW I HAD TO RISE, THE SOUND WAS TELLING ME TO RISE.
IT WAS LOOKING FOR ME, THIS SOUND, IT WAS SEEKING ME OUT. I COULDN'T LIE HERE ANYMORE. I HAD TO ANSWER.
I SENT IT THE WILDEST CURRENT OF WELCOME. IN A FRENZY AGAIN I CLAWED TOWARDS THE AIR.

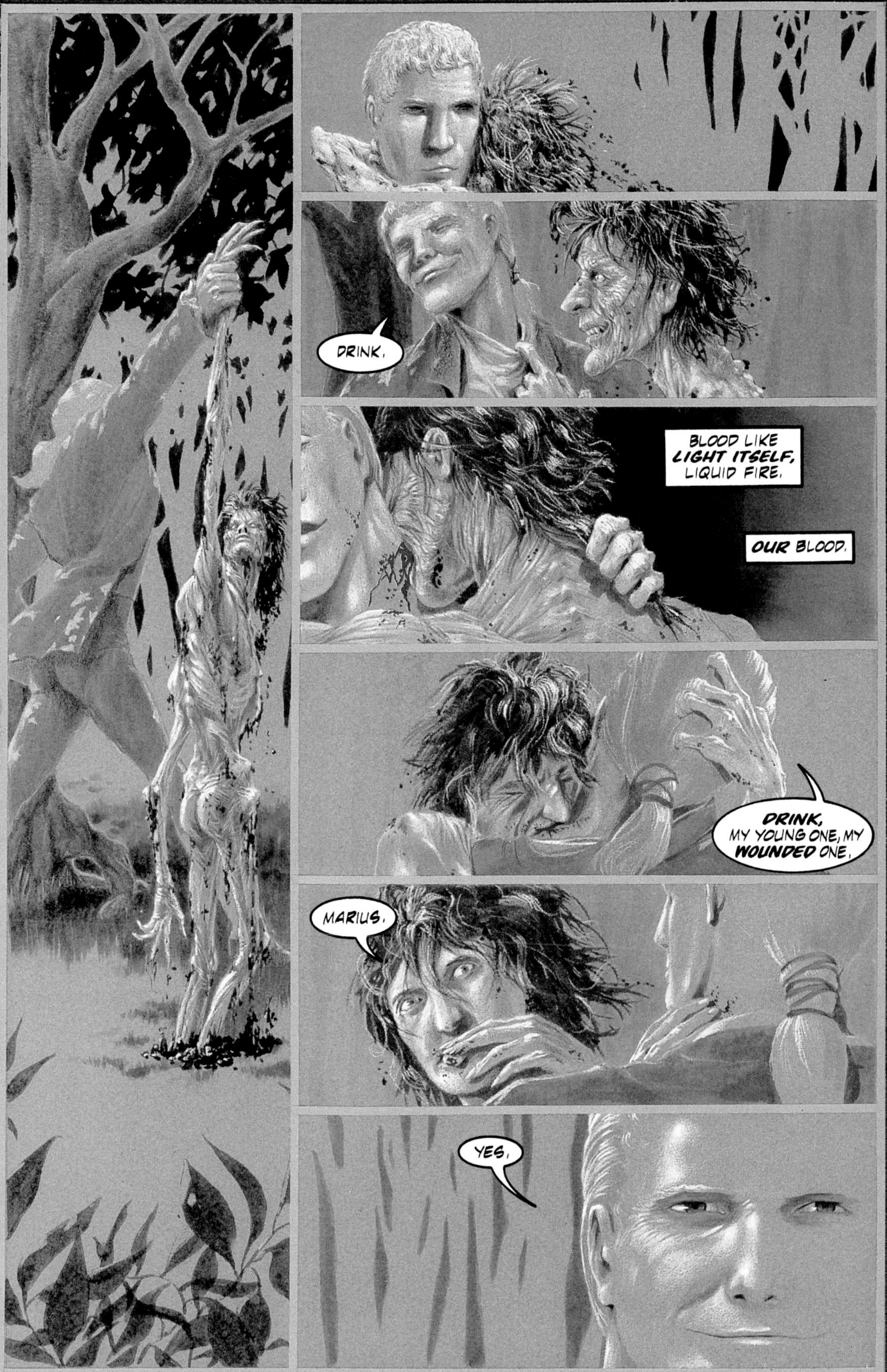

DRINK.
BLOOD LIKE **LIGHT ITSELF,** LIQUID FIRE.
OUR BLOOD.
DRINK, MY YOUNG ONE, MY **WOUNDED** ONE.
MARIUS.
YES.

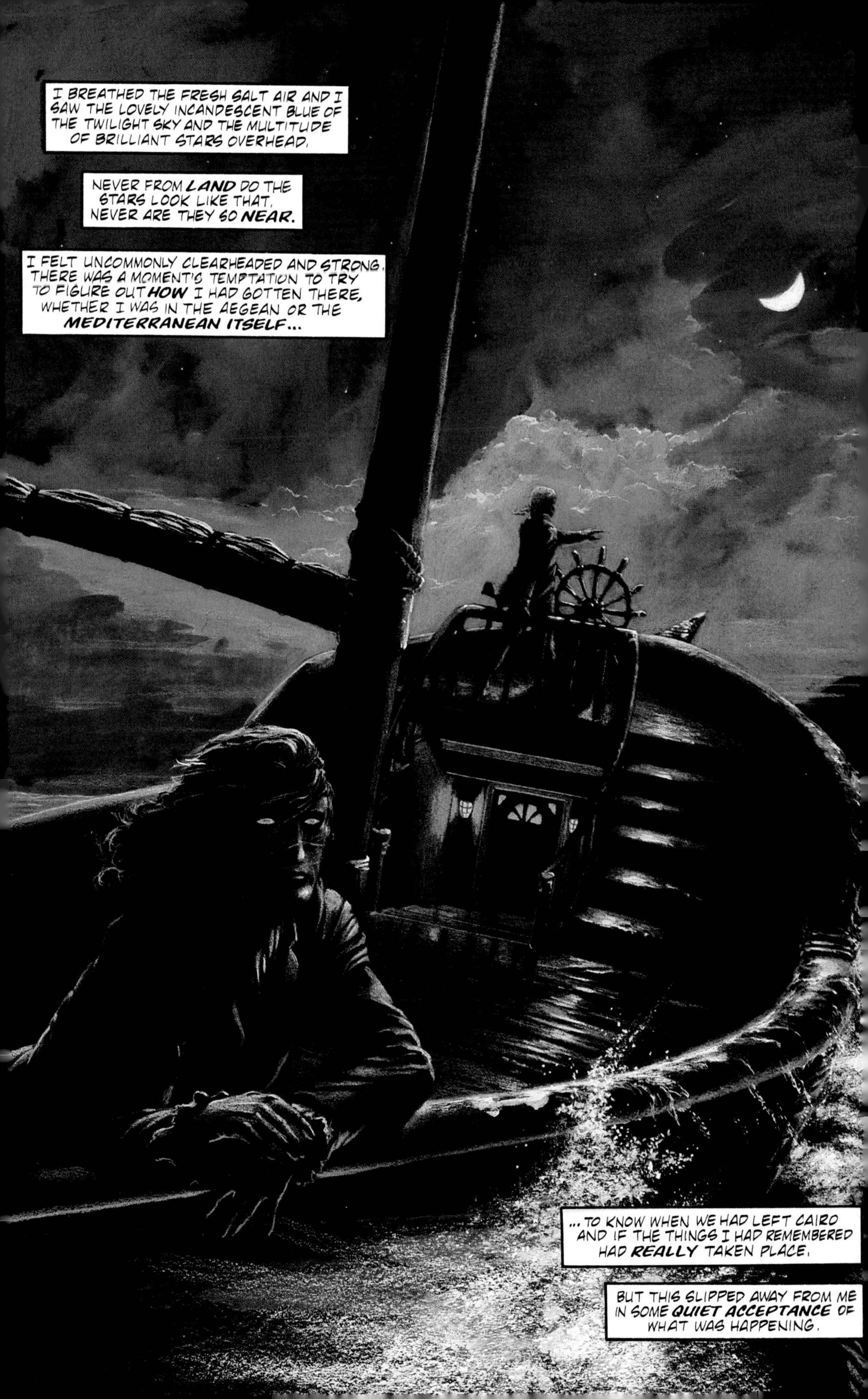
I BREATHED THE FRESH SALT AIR AND I SAW THE LOVELY INCANDESCENT BLUE OF THE TWILIGHT SKY AND THE MULTITUDE OF BRILLIANT STARS OVERHEAD.
NEVER FROM LAND DO THE STARS LOOK LIKE THAT, NEVER ARE THEY SO NEAR.
I FELT UNCOMMONLY CLEARHEADED AND STRONG. THERE WAS A MOMENT'S TEMPTATION TO TRY TO FIGURE OUT HOW I HAD GOTTEN THERE, WHETHER I WAS IN THE AEGEAN OR THE MEDITERRANEAN ITSELF...
...TO KNOW WHEN WE HAD LEFT CAIRO AND IF THE THINGS I HAD REMEMBERED HAD REALLY TAKEN PLACE.
BUT THIS SLIPPED AWAY FROM ME IN SOME QUIET ACCEPTANCE OF WHAT WAS HAPPENING.

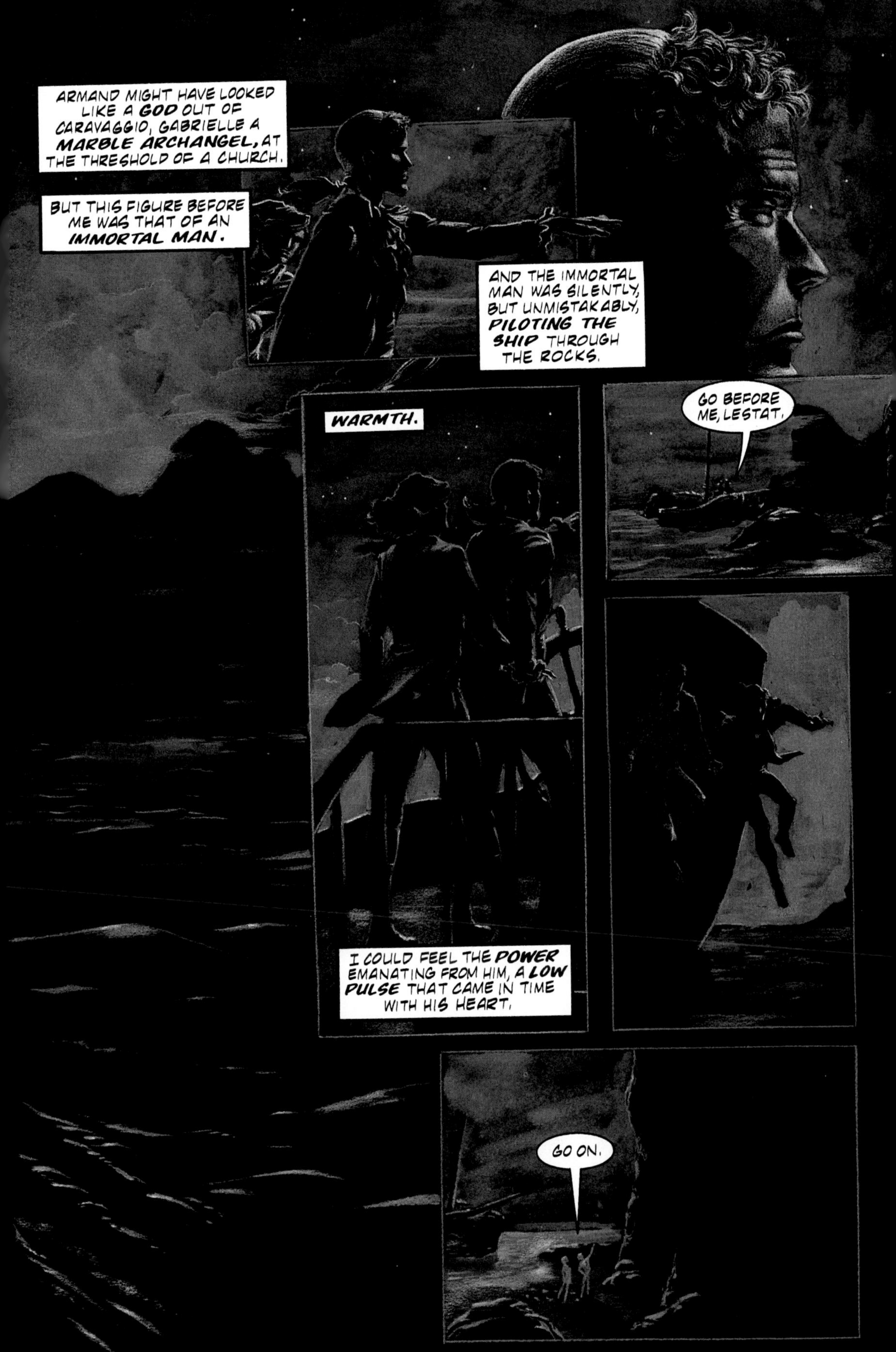
ARMAND MIGHT HAVE LOOKED LIKE A **GOD** OUT OF CARAVAGGIO, GABRIELLE A **MARBLE ARCHANGEL,** AT THE THRESHOLD OF A CHURCH.
BUT THIS FIGURE BEFORE ME WAS THAT OF AN **IMMORTAL MAN.**
AND THE IMMORTAL MAN WAS SILENTLY, BUT UNMISTAKABLY, **PILOTING THE SHIP** THROUGH THE ROCKS.
WARMTH.
I COULD FEEL THE **POWER** EMANATING FROM HIM, A **LOW PULSE** THAT CAME IN TIME WITH HIS HEART.
GO BEFORE ME, LESTAT.
GO ON.

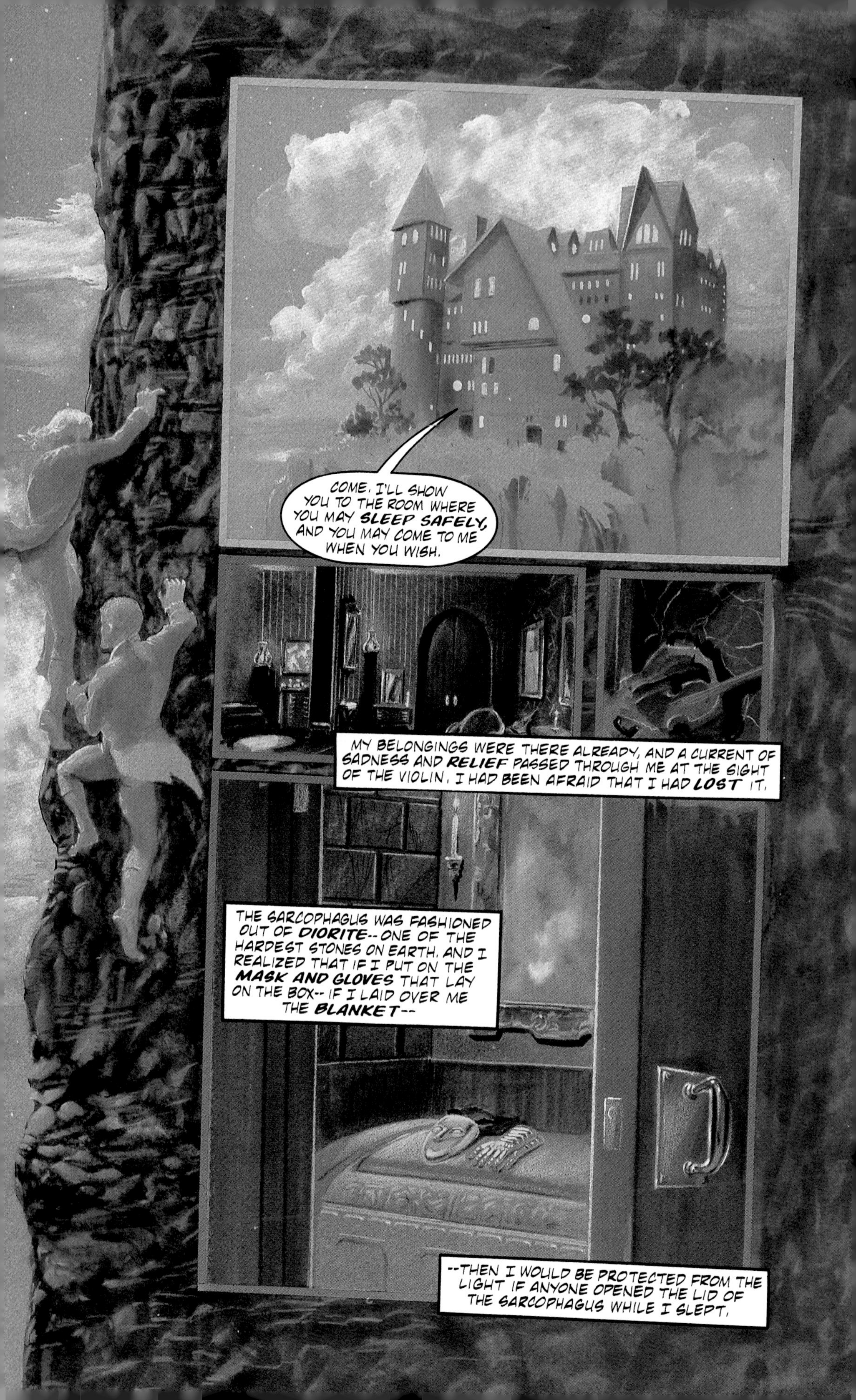
COME. I'LL SHOW YOU TO THE ROOM WHERE YOU MAY SLEEP SAFELY, AND YOU MAY COME TO ME WHEN YOU WISH.
MY BELONGINGS WERE THERE ALREADY, AND A CURRENT OF SADNESS AND RELIEF PASSED THROUGH ME AT THE SIGHT OF THE VIOLIN. I HAD BEEN AFRAID THAT I HAD LOST IT.
THE SARCOPHAGUS WAS FASHIONED OUT OF DIORITE--ONE OF THE HARDEST STONES ON EARTH. AND I REALIZED THAT IF I PUT ON THE MASK AND GLOVES THAT LAY ON THE BOX--IF I LAID OVER ME THE BLANKET--
--THEN I WOULD BE PROTECTED FROM THE LIGHT IF ANYONE OPENED THE LID OF THE SARCOPHAGUS WHILE I SLEPT.

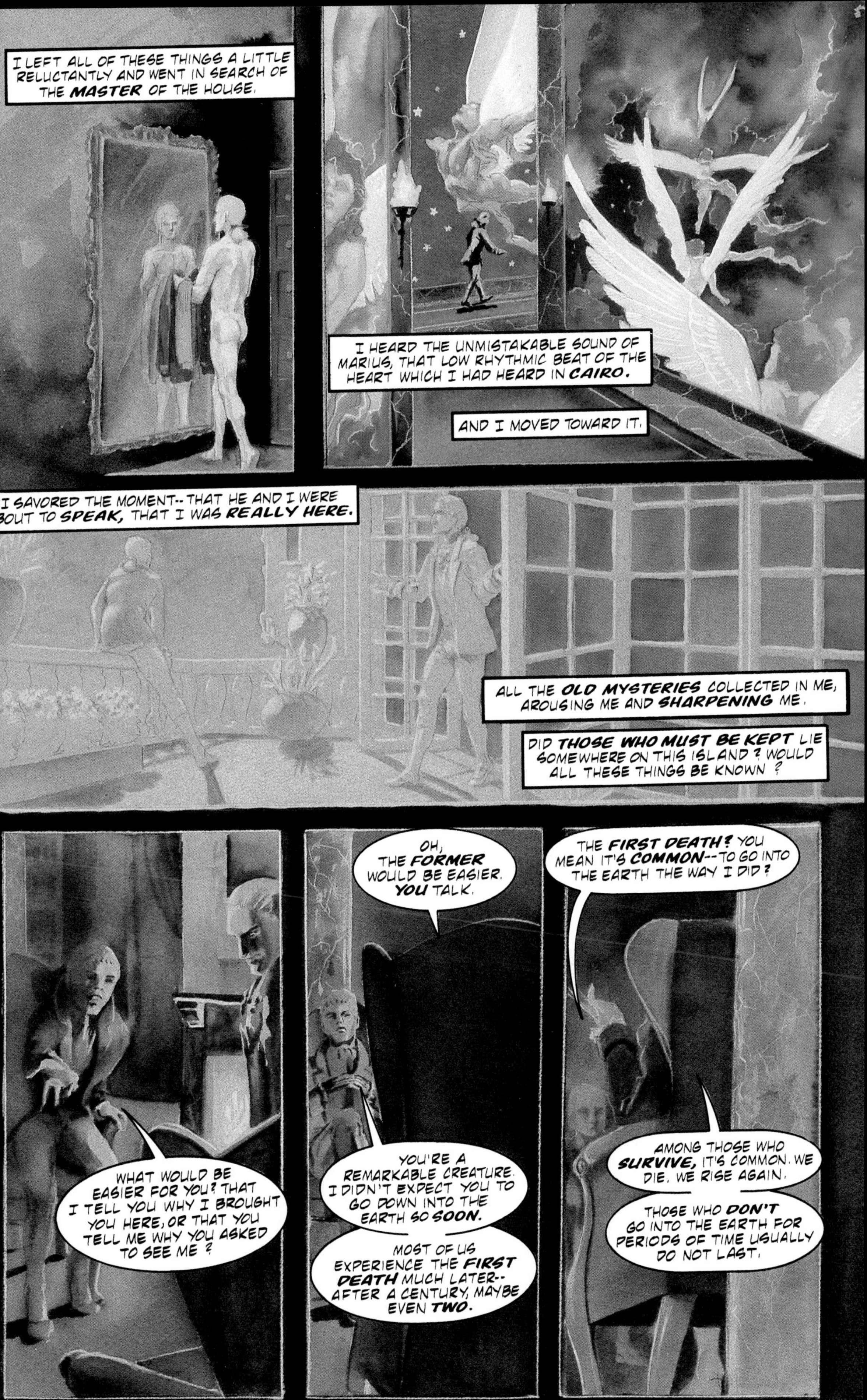
I LEFT ALL OF THESE THINGS A LITTLE RELUCTANTLY AND WENT IN SEARCH OF THE MASTER OF THE HOUSE.
I HEARD THE UNMISTAKABLE SOUND OF MARIUS, THAT LOW RHYTHMIC BEAT OF THE HEART WHICH I HAD HEARD IN CAIRO.
AND I MOVED TOWARD IT.
I SAVORED THE MOMENT-- THAT HE AND I WERE BOUT TO SPEAK, THAT I WAS REALLY HERE.
ALL THE OLD MYSTERIES COLLECTED IN ME, AROUSING ME AND SHARPENING ME.
DID THOSE WHO MUST BE KEPT LIE SOMEWHERE ON THIS ISLAND? WOULD ALL THESE THINGS BE KNOWN ?
WHAT WOULD BE EASIER FOR YOU? THAT I TELL YOU WHY I BROUGHT YOU HERE, OR THAT YOU TELL ME WHY YOU ASKED TO SEE ME ?
OH, THE FORMER WOULD BE EASIER. YOU TALK.
YOU'RE A REMARKABLE CREATURE. I DIDN'T EXPECT YOU TO GO DOWN INTO THE EARTH SO SOON.
MOST OF US EXPERIENCE THE FIRST DEATH MUCH LATER-- AFTER A CENTURY, MAYBE EVEN TWO.
THE FIRST DEATH? YOU MEAN IT'S COMMON-- TO GO INTO THE EARTH THE WAY I DID?
AMONG THOSE WHO SURVIVE, IT'S COMMON. WE DIE. WE RISE AGAIN.
THOSE WHO DON'T GO INTO THE EARTH FOR PERIODS OF TIME USUALLY DO NOT LAST.

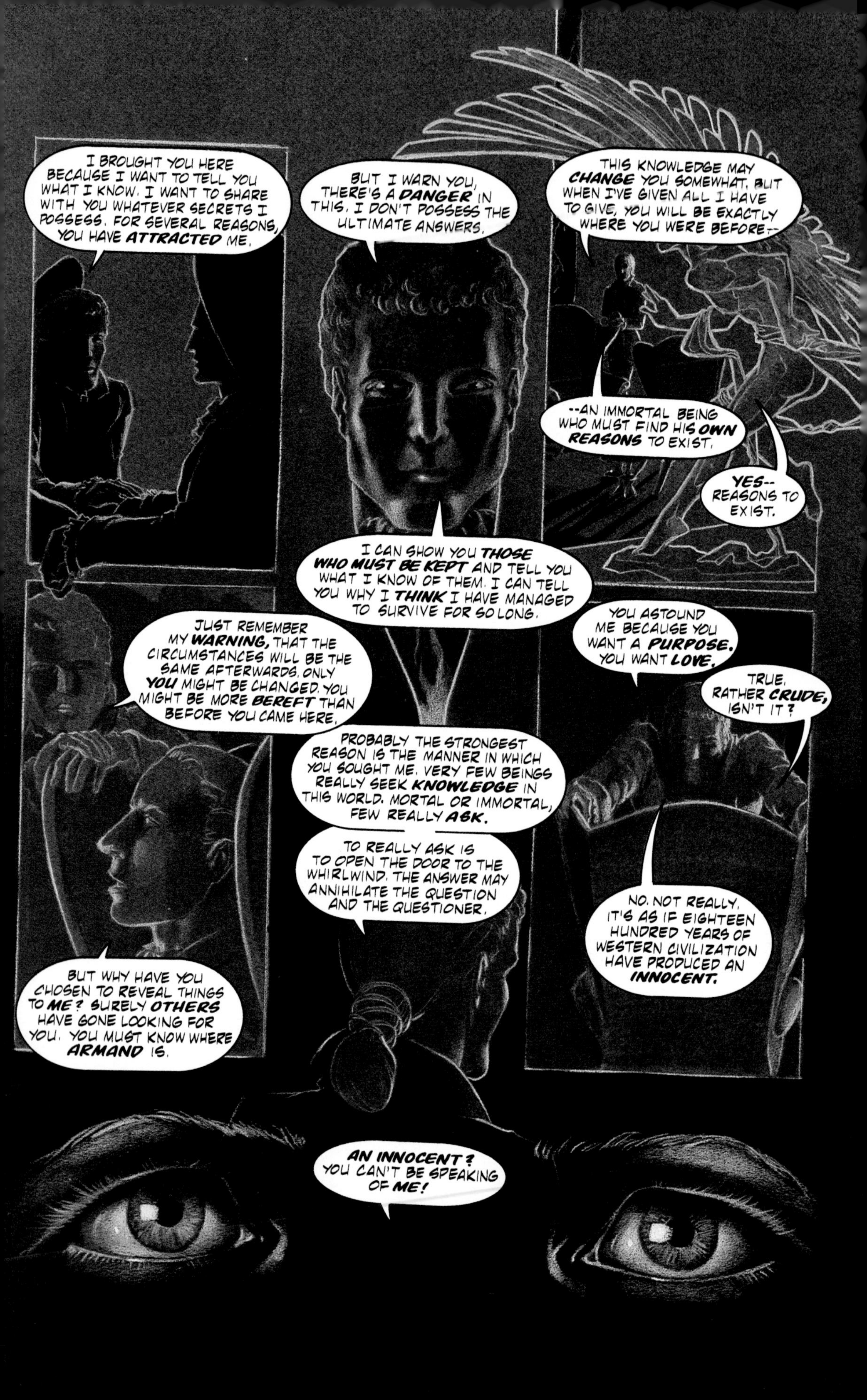
I BROUGHT YOU HERE BECAUSE I WANT TO TELL YOU WHAT I KNOW. I WANT TO SHARE WITH YOU WHATEVER SECRETS I POSSESS. FOR SEVERAL REASONS, YOU HAVE ATTRACTED ME.
BUT I WARN YOU, THERE'S A DANGER IN THIS. I DON'T POSSESS THE ULTIMATE ANSWERS.
THIS KNOWLEDGE MAY CHANGE YOU SOMEWHAT, BUT WHEN I'VE GIVEN ALL I HAVE TO GIVE, YOU WILL BE EXACTLY WHERE YOU WERE BEFORE--
--AN IMMORTAL BEING WHO MUST FIND HIS OWN REASONS TO EXIST.
YES-- REASONS TO EXIST.
I CAN SHOW YOU THOSE WHO MUST BE KEPT AND TELL YOU WHAT I KNOW OF THEM. I CAN TELL YOU WHY I THINK I HAVE MANAGED TO SURVIVE FOR SO LONG.
JUST REMEMBER MY WARNING, THAT THE CIRCUMSTANCES WILL BE THE SAME AFTERWARDS. ONLY YOU MIGHT BE CHANGED. YOU MIGHT BE MORE BEREFT THAN BEFORE YOU CAME HERE.
PROBABLY THE STRONGEST REASON IS THE MANNER IN WHICH YOU SOUGHT ME. VERY FEW BEINGS REALLY SEEK KNOWLEDGE IN THIS WORLD. MORTAL OR IMMORTAL, FEW REALLY ASK.
TO REALLY ASK IS TO OPEN THE DOOR TO THE WHIRLWIND. THE ANSWER MAY ANNIHILATE THE QUESTION AND THE QUESTIONER.
BUT WHY HAVE YOU CHOSEN TO REVEAL THINGS TO ME? SURELY OTHERS HAVE GONE LOOKING FOR YOU. YOU MUST KNOW WHERE ARMAND IS.
YOU ASTOUND ME BECAUSE YOU WANT A PURPOSE. YOU WANT LOVE.
TRUE. RATHER CRUDE, ISN'T IT?
NO. NOT REALLY. IT'S AS IF EIGHTEEN HUNDRED YEARS OF WESTERN CIVILIZATION HAVE PRODUCED AN INNOCENT.
AN INNOCENT? YOU CAN'T BE SPEAKING OF ME!

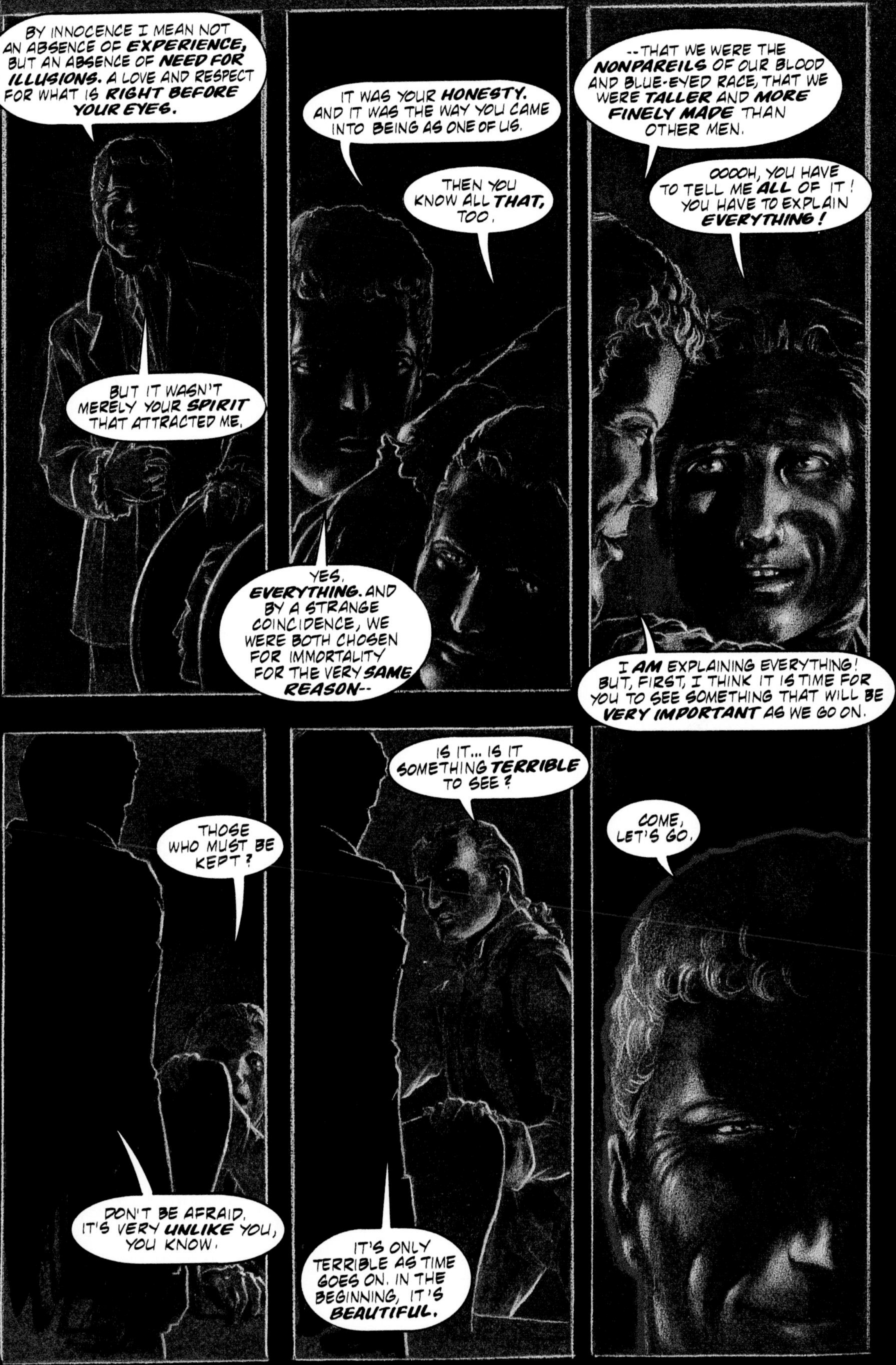
BY INNOCENCE I MEAN NOT AN ABSENCE OF EXPERIENCE, BUT AN ABSENCE OF NEED FOR ILLUSIONS. A LOVE AND RESPECT FOR WHAT IS RIGHT BEFORE YOUR EYES.
BUT IT WASN'T MERELY YOUR SPIRIT THAT ATTRACTED ME.
IT WAS YOUR HONESTY. AND IT WAS THE WAY YOU CAME INTO BEING AS ONE OF US.
THEN YOU KNOW ALL THAT, TOO.
YES. EVERYTHING. AND BY A STRANGE COINCIDENCE, WE WERE BOTH CHOSEN FOR IMMORTALITY FOR THE VERY SAME REASON--
--THAT WE WERE THE NONPAREILS OF OUR BLOOD AND BLUE-EYED RACE, THAT WE WERE TALLER AND MORE FINELY MADE THAN OTHER MEN.
OOOOH, YOU HAVE TO TELL ME ALL OF IT! YOU HAVE TO EXPLAIN EVERYTHING!
I AM EXPLAINING EVERYTHING! BUT, FIRST, I THINK IT IS TIME FOR YOU TO SEE SOMETHING THAT WILL BE VERY IMPORTANT AS WE GO ON.
THOSE WHO MUST BE KEPT?
DON'T BE AFRAID. IT'S VERY UNLIKE YOU, YOU KNOW.
IS IT... IS IT SOMETHING TERRIBLE TO SEE?
IT'S ONLY TERRIBLE AS TIME GOES ON. IN THE BEGINNING, IT'S BEAUTIFUL.
COME, LET'S GO.

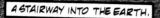

A STAIRWAY INTO THE EARTH.

THIS WAS DEEPER THAN ANY DUNGEON. THIS WAS THE PIT YOU DIG IN CHILDHOOD WHEN YOU BRAG TO YOUR MOTHER AND FATHER THAT YOU WILL MAKE A TUNNEL TO THE VERY *CENTER OF THE EARTH.*

THE *CHILL* WAS RISING THROUGH THE STEPS.

THEY DON'T CAUSE IT. IT WAS HERE LONG BEFORE I BROUGHT THEM.

MANY HAVE COME TO WORSHIP ON THIS ISLAND. MAYBE IT WAS THERE BEFORE THAT, TOO.

DON'T BE AFRAID.

AND THEN I FELT MY BREATHING COME TO A HALT.

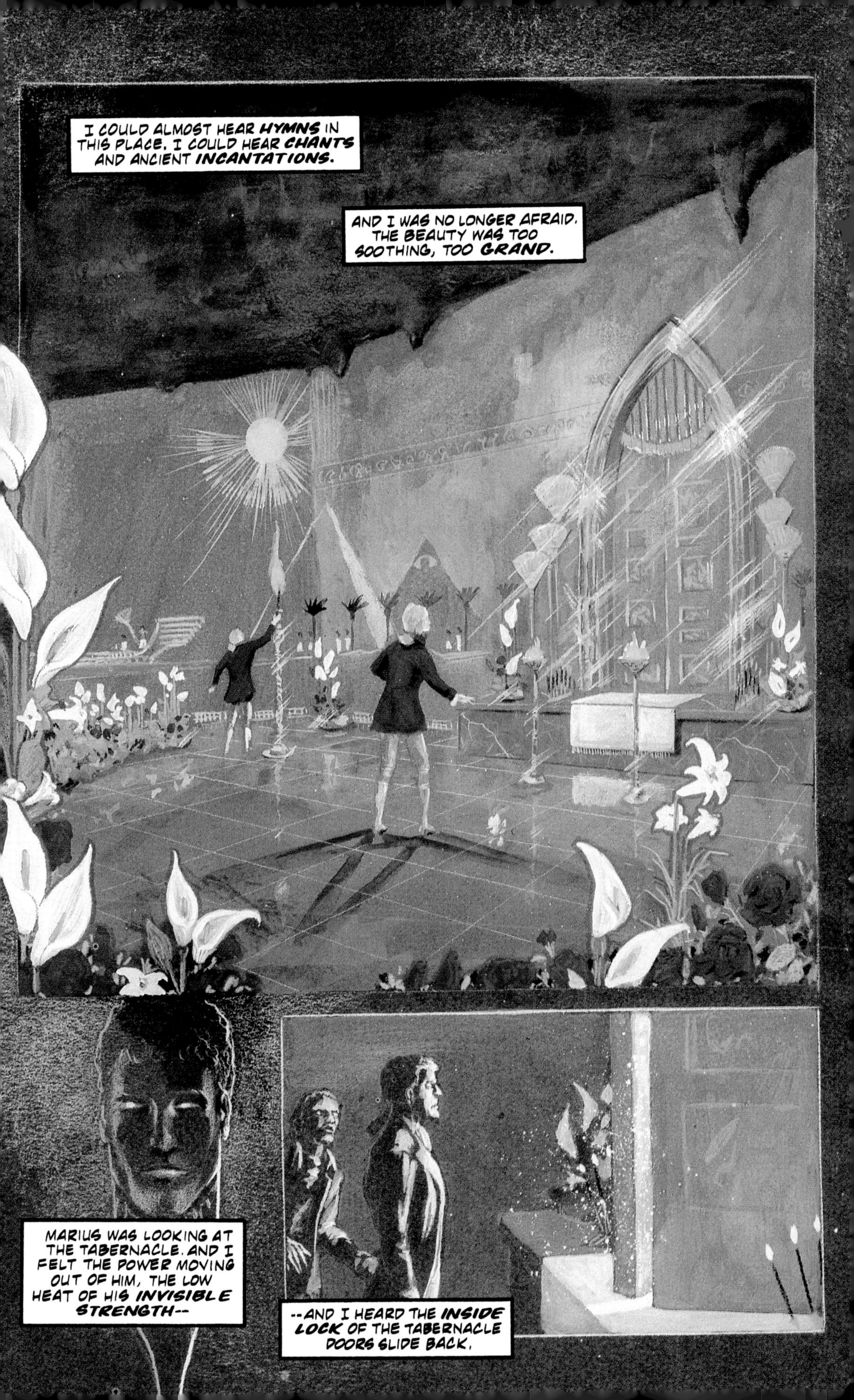
I COULD ALMOST HEAR HYMNS IN THIS PLACE. I COULD HEAR CHANTS AND ANCIENT INCANTATIONS.
AND I WAS NO LONGER AFRAID. THE BEAUTY WAS TOO SOOTHING, TOO GRAND.
MARIUS WAS LOOKING AT THE TABERNACLE. AND I FELT THE POWER MOVING OUT OF HIM, THE LOW HEAT OF HIS INVISIBLE STRENGTH--
--AND I HEARD THE INSIDE LOCK OF THE TABERNACLE DOORS SLIDE BACK.

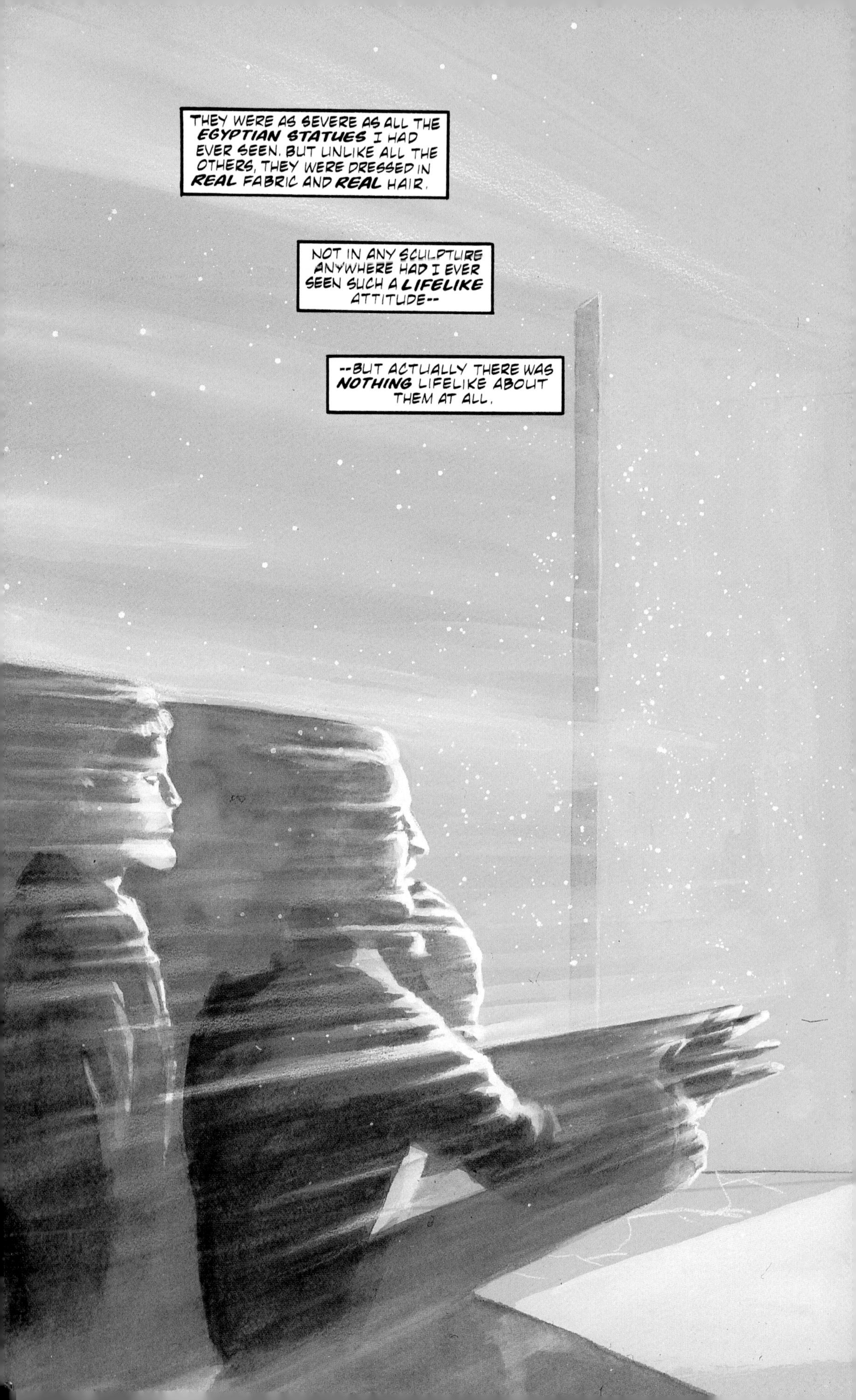
THEY WERE AS SEVERE AS ALL THE EGYPTIAN STATUES I HAD EVER SEEN. BUT UNLIKE ALL THE OTHERS, THEY WERE DRESSED IN REAL FABRIC AND REAL HAIR.
NOT IN ANY SCULPTURE ANYWHERE HAD I EVER SEEN SUCH A LIFELIKE ATTITUDE--
--BUT ACTUALLY THERE WAS NOTHING LIFELIKE ABOUT THEM AT ALL.

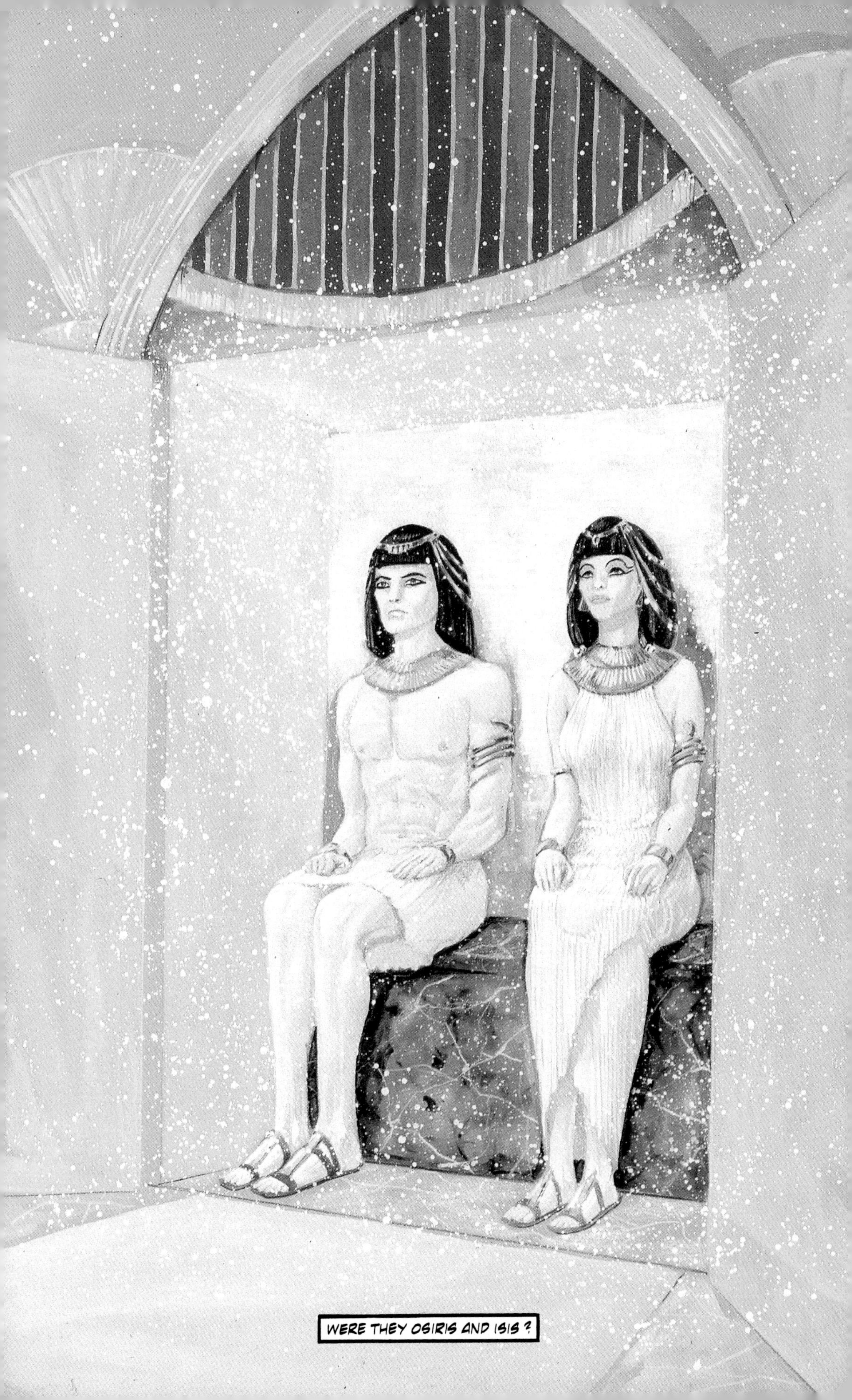
WERE THEY OSIRIS AND ISIS ?

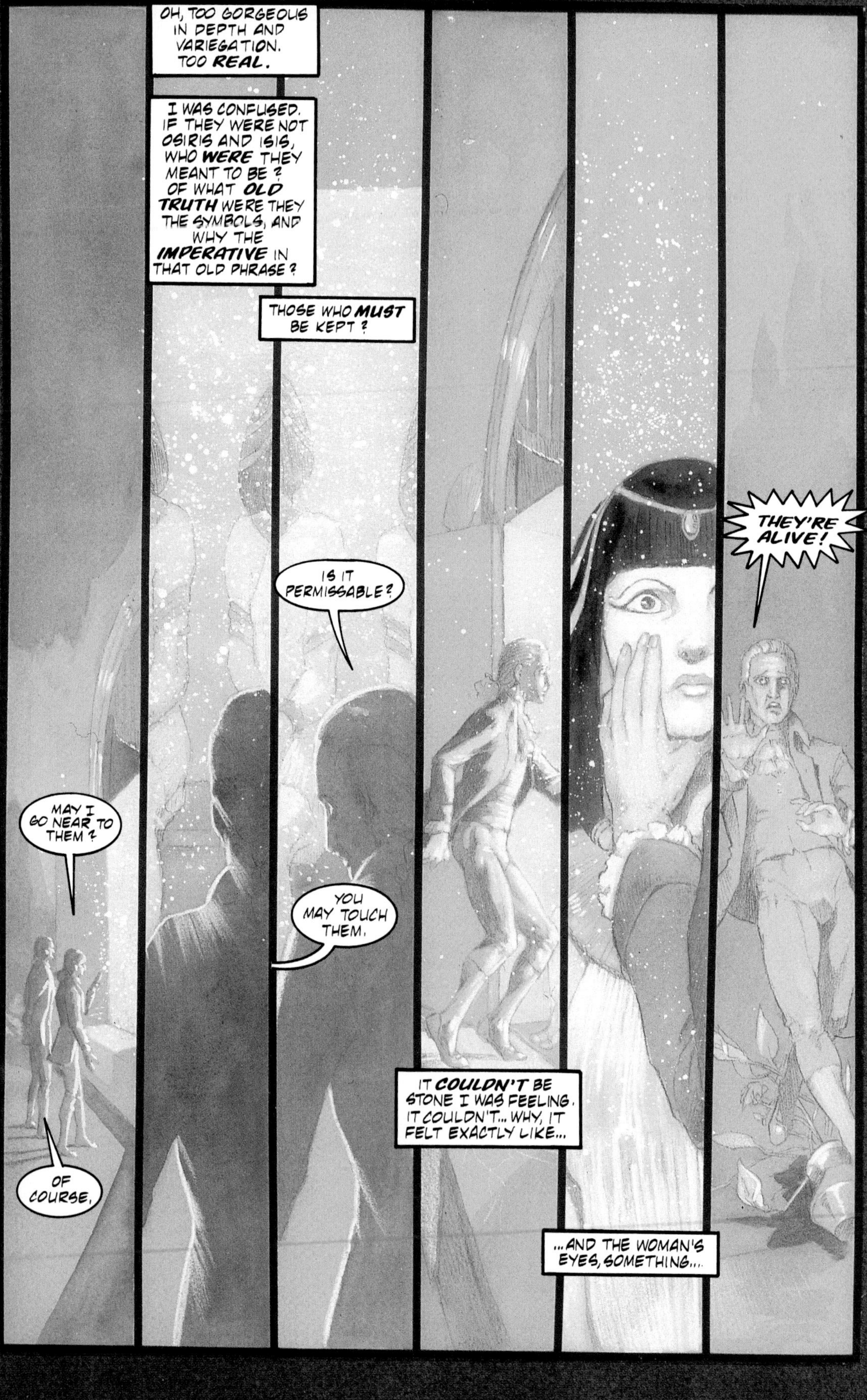
OH, TOO GORGEOUS IN DEPTH AND VARIEGATION. TOO REAL.
I WAS CONFUSED. IF THEY WERE NOT OSIRIS AND ISIS, WHO WERE THEY MEANT TO BE? OF WHAT OLD TRUTH WERE THEY THE SYMBOLS, AND WHY THE IMPERATIVE IN THAT OLD PHRASE?
THOSE WHO MUST BE KEPT?
MAY I GO NEAR TO THEM?
OF COURSE.
IS IT PERMISSABLE?
YOU MAY TOUCH THEM.
IT COULDN'T BE STONE I WAS FEELING. IT COULDN'T... WHY, IT FELT EXACTLY LIKE...
...AND THE WOMAN'S EYES, SOMETHING...
THEY'RE ALIVE!

THEY AREN'T STATUES! THEY'RE VAMPIRES JUST LIKE US!
YES. THAT WORD, HOWEVER, THEY WOULDN'T KNOW.
IT'S QUITE ALL RIGHT. I DON'T THINK THEY DISLIKE YOUR TOUCHING THEM.
YOU MEAN YOU... YOU DON'T KNOW WHETHER... THEY JUST SIT THERE AND... OOOH GOD!
AND HIS WORDS OF HUNDREDS OF YEARS AGO, EMBEDDED IN ARMAND'S TALE, CAME BACK TO ME--
--THOSE WHO MUST BE KEPT ARE AT PEACE, OR IN SILENCE. MORE THAN THAT WE MAY NEVER KNOW.
THEY'RE BREATHING, THINKING, LIVING, AS WE ARE! HOW LONG HAVE THEY BEEN LIKE THIS, HOW LONG?
CALM YOURSELF.
OH GOD, OH GOD, OH GOD...
BUT WHO ARE THEY? ARE THEY OSIRIS AND ISIS?
I DON'T KNOW.
I WANT TO GET AWAY FROM THEM. I WANT TO GET OUT OF HERE!

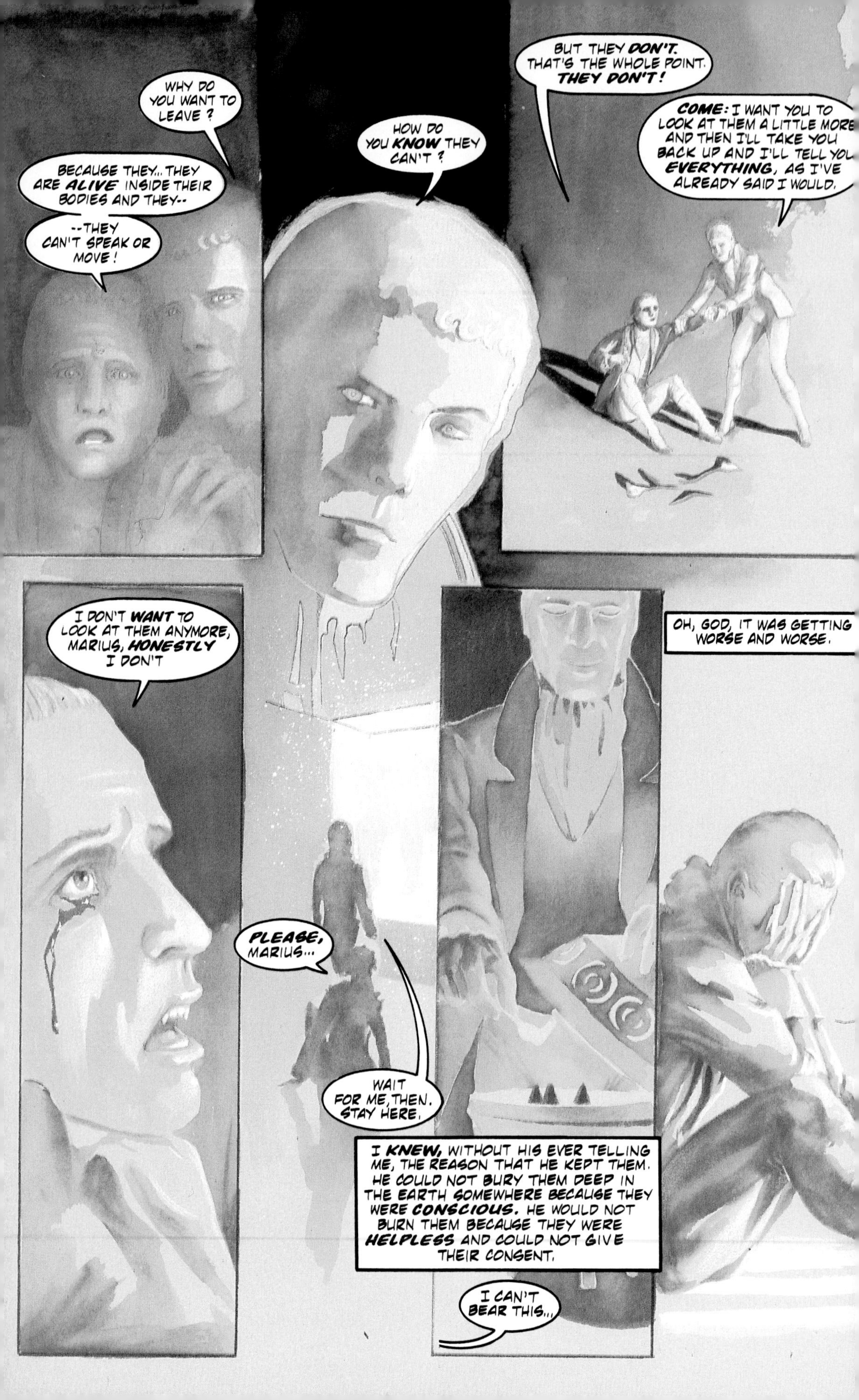
WHY DO YOU WANT TO LEAVE ?
BECAUSE THEY... THEY ARE ALIVE INSIDE THEIR BODIES AND THEY--
--THEY CAN'T SPEAK OR MOVE !
HOW DO YOU KNOW THEY CAN'T ?
BUT THEY DON'T. THAT'S THE WHOLE POINT. THEY DON'T !
COME: I WANT YOU TO LOOK AT THEM A LITTLE MORE AND THEN I'LL TAKE YOU BACK UP AND I'LL TELL YOU EVERYTHING, AS I'VE ALREADY SAID I WOULD.
I DON'T WANT TO LOOK AT THEM ANYMORE, MARIUS, HONESTLY I DON'T
PLEASE, MARIUS...
WAIT FOR ME, THEN. STAY HERE.
OH, GOD, IT WAS GETTING WORSE AND WORSE.
I KNEW, WITHOUT HIS EVER TELLING ME, THE REASON THAT HE KEPT THEM. HE COULD NOT BURY THEM DEEP IN THE EARTH SOMEWHERE BECAUSE THEY WERE CONSCIOUS. HE WOULD NOT BURN THEM BECAUSE THEY WERE HELPLESS AND COULD NOT GIVE THEIR CONSENT.
I CAN'T BEAR THIS...

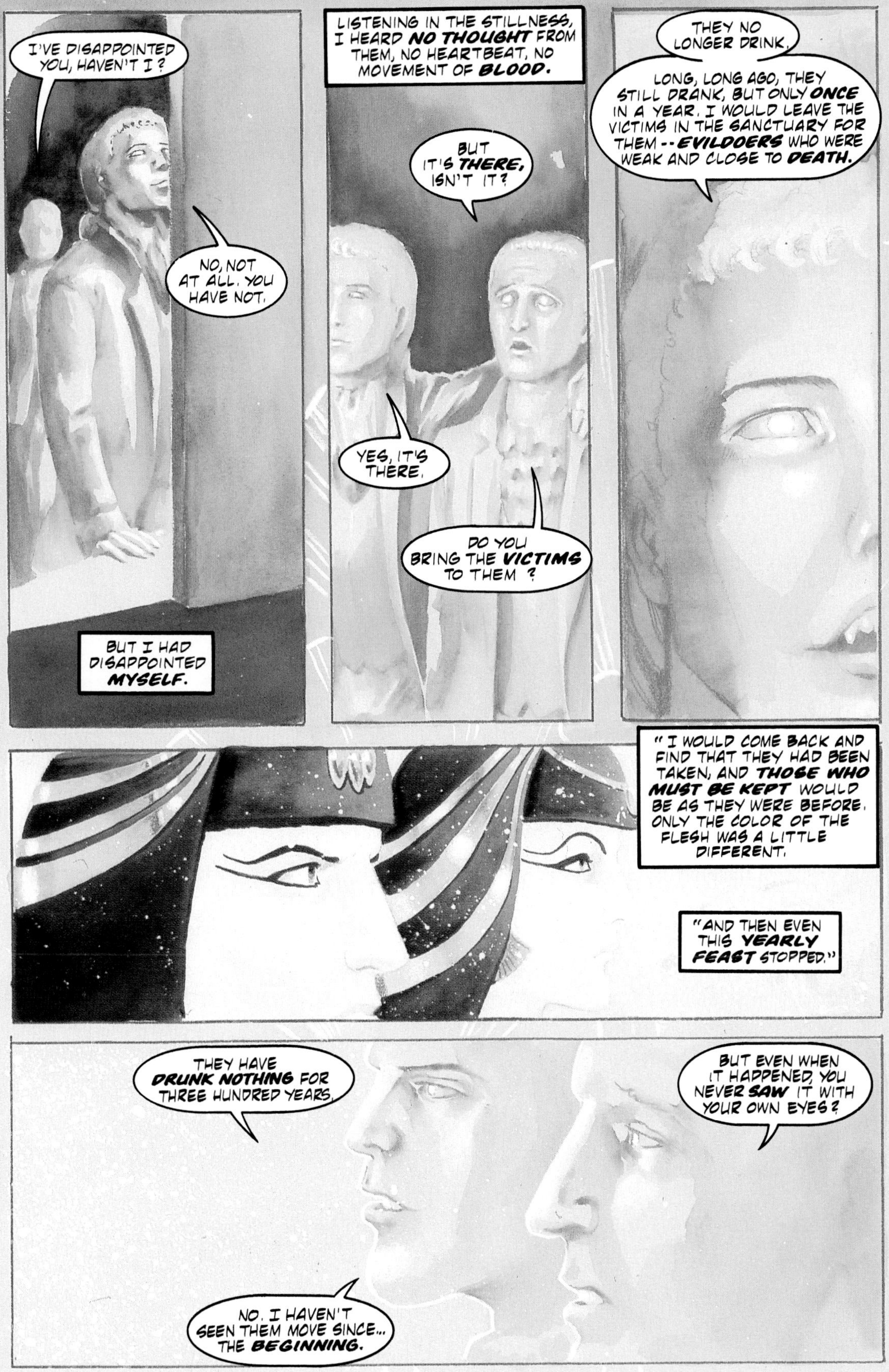
I'VE DISAPPOINTED YOU, HAVEN'T I?
NO, NOT AT ALL. YOU HAVE NOT.
BUT I HAD DISAPPOINTED MYSELF.
LISTENING IN THE STILLNESS, I HEARD NO THOUGHT FROM THEM, NO HEARTBEAT, NO MOVEMENT OF BLOOD.
BUT IT'S THERE, ISN'T IT?
YES, IT'S THERE.
DO YOU BRING THE VICTIMS TO THEM?
THEY NO LONGER DRINK.
LONG, LONG AGO, THEY STILL DRANK, BUT ONLY ONCE IN A YEAR. I WOULD LEAVE THE VICTIMS IN THE SANCTUARY FOR THEM -- EVILDOERS WHO WERE WEAK AND CLOSE TO DEATH.
"I WOULD COME BACK AND FIND THAT THEY HAD BEEN TAKEN, AND THOSE WHO MUST BE KEPT WOULD BE AS THEY WERE BEFORE. ONLY THE COLOR OF THE FLESH WAS A LITTLE DIFFERENT.
"AND THEN EVEN THIS YEARLY FEAST STOPPED."
THEY HAVE DRUNK NOTHING FOR THREE HUNDRED YEARS.
BUT EVEN WHEN IT HAPPENED, YOU NEVER SAW IT WITH YOUR OWN EYES?
NO. I HAVEN'T SEEN THEM MOVE SINCE... THE BEGINNING.

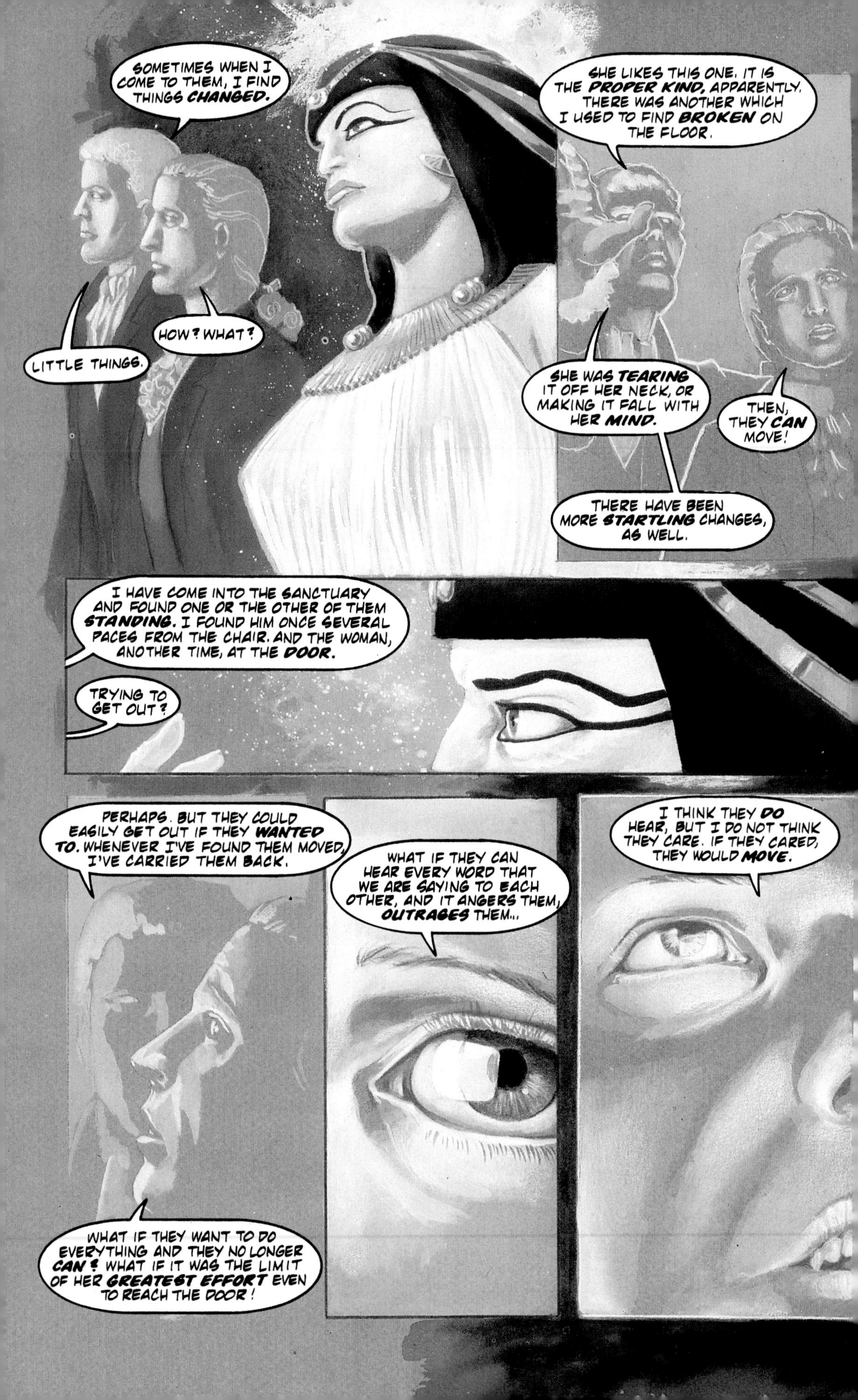
SOMETIMES WHEN I COME TO THEM, I FIND THINGS CHANGED.
HOW? WHAT?
LITTLE THINGS.
SHE LIKES THIS ONE. IT IS THE PROPER KIND, APPARENTLY. THERE WAS ANOTHER WHICH I USED TO FIND BROKEN ON THE FLOOR.
SHE WAS TEARING IT OFF HER NECK, OR MAKING IT FALL WITH HER MIND.
THEN, THEY CAN MOVE!
THERE HAVE BEEN MORE STARTLING CHANGES, AS WELL.
I HAVE COME INTO THE SANCTUARY AND FOUND ONE OR THE OTHER OF THEM STANDING. I FOUND HIM ONCE SEVERAL PACES FROM THE CHAIR. AND THE WOMAN, ANOTHER TIME, AT THE DOOR.
TRYING TO GET OUT?
PERHAPS. BUT THEY COULD EASILY GET OUT IF THEY WANTED TO. WHENEVER I'VE FOUND THEM MOVED, I'VE CARRIED THEM BACK.
WHAT IF THEY WANT TO DO EVERYTHING AND THEY NO LONGER CAN? WHAT IF IT WAS THE LIMIT OF HER GREATEST EFFORT EVEN TO REACH THE DOOR!
WHAT IF THEY CAN HEAR EVERY WORD THAT WE ARE SAYING TO EACH OTHER, AND IT ANGERS THEM, OUTRAGES THEM...
I THINK THEY DO HEAR, BUT I DO NOT THINK THEY CARE. IF THEY CARED, THEY WOULD MOVE.

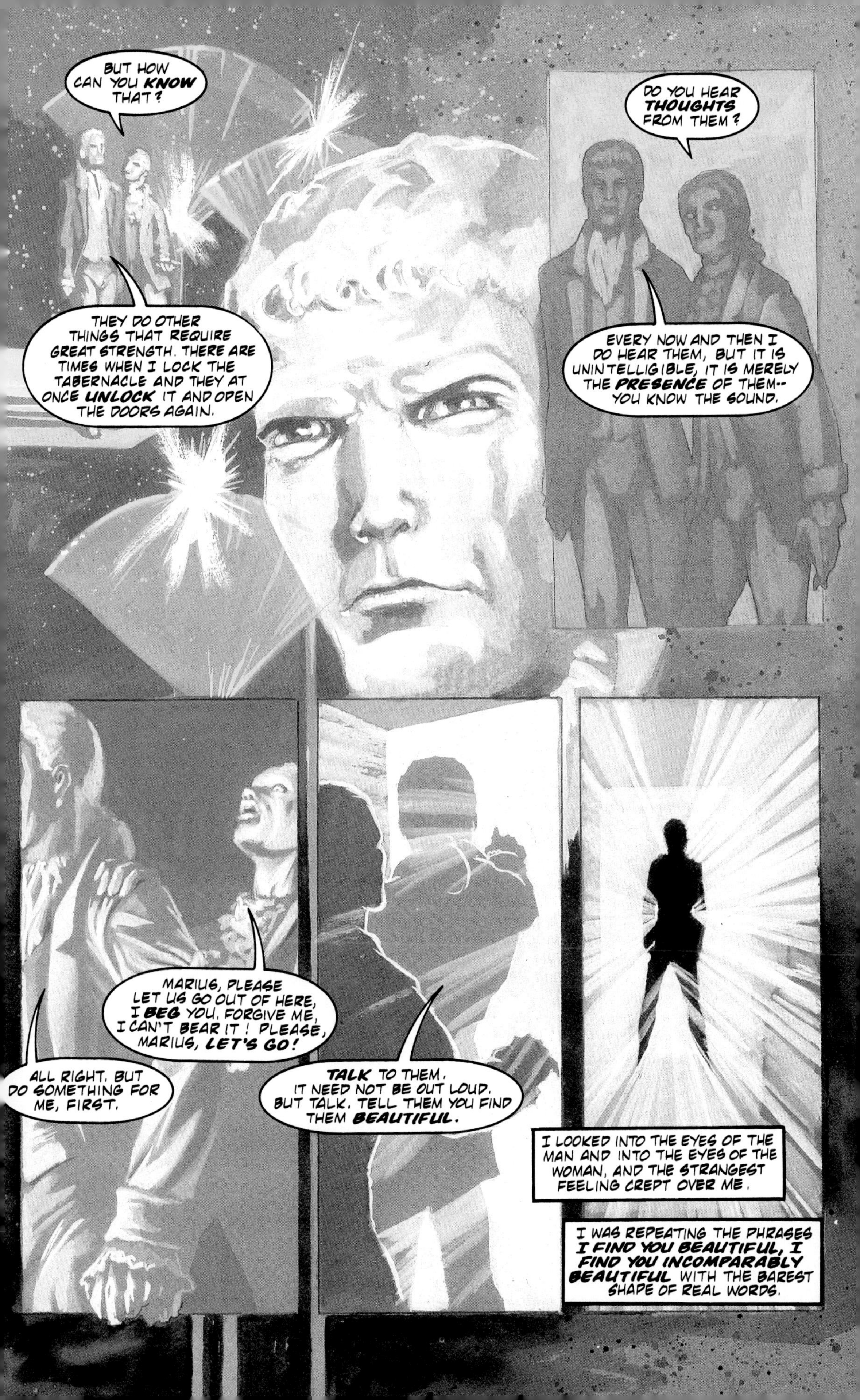

BUT HOW CAN YOU KNOW THAT?
THEY DO OTHER THINGS THAT REQUIRE GREAT STRENGTH. THERE ARE TIMES WHEN I LOCK THE TABERNACLE AND THEY AT ONCE UNLOCK IT AND OPEN THE DOORS AGAIN.
DO YOU HEAR THOUGHTS FROM THEM?
EVERY NOW AND THEN I DO HEAR THEM, BUT IT IS UNINTELLIGIBLE, IT IS MERELY THE PRESENCE OF THEM-- YOU KNOW THE SOUND.
MARIUS, PLEASE LET US GO OUT OF HERE, I BEG YOU. FORGIVE ME, I CAN'T BEAR IT! PLEASE, MARIUS, LET'S GO!
ALL RIGHT. BUT DO SOMETHING FOR ME, FIRST.
TALK TO THEM. IT NEED NOT BE OUT LOUD. BUT TALK. TELL THEM YOU FIND THEM BEAUTIFUL.
I LOOKED INTO THE EYES OF THE MAN AND INTO THE EYES OF THE WOMAN, AND THE STRANGEST FEELING CREPT OVER ME.
I WAS REPEATING THE PHRASES I FIND YOU BEAUTIFUL, I FIND YOU INCOMPARABLY BEAUTIFUL WITH THE BAREST SHAPE OF REAL WORDS.

AKASHA...
I HEARD THE NAME AT THE SAME MOMENT OF SPEAKING IT. THE HAIRS ROSE ALL OVER ME. THE TABERNACLE BECAME LIKE A FLAMING BORDER AROUND HER.
I AM KISSING THE GODDESS ON HER MOUTH, WHAT IS THE MATTER WITH ME! AM I MAD TO THINK OF IT ?

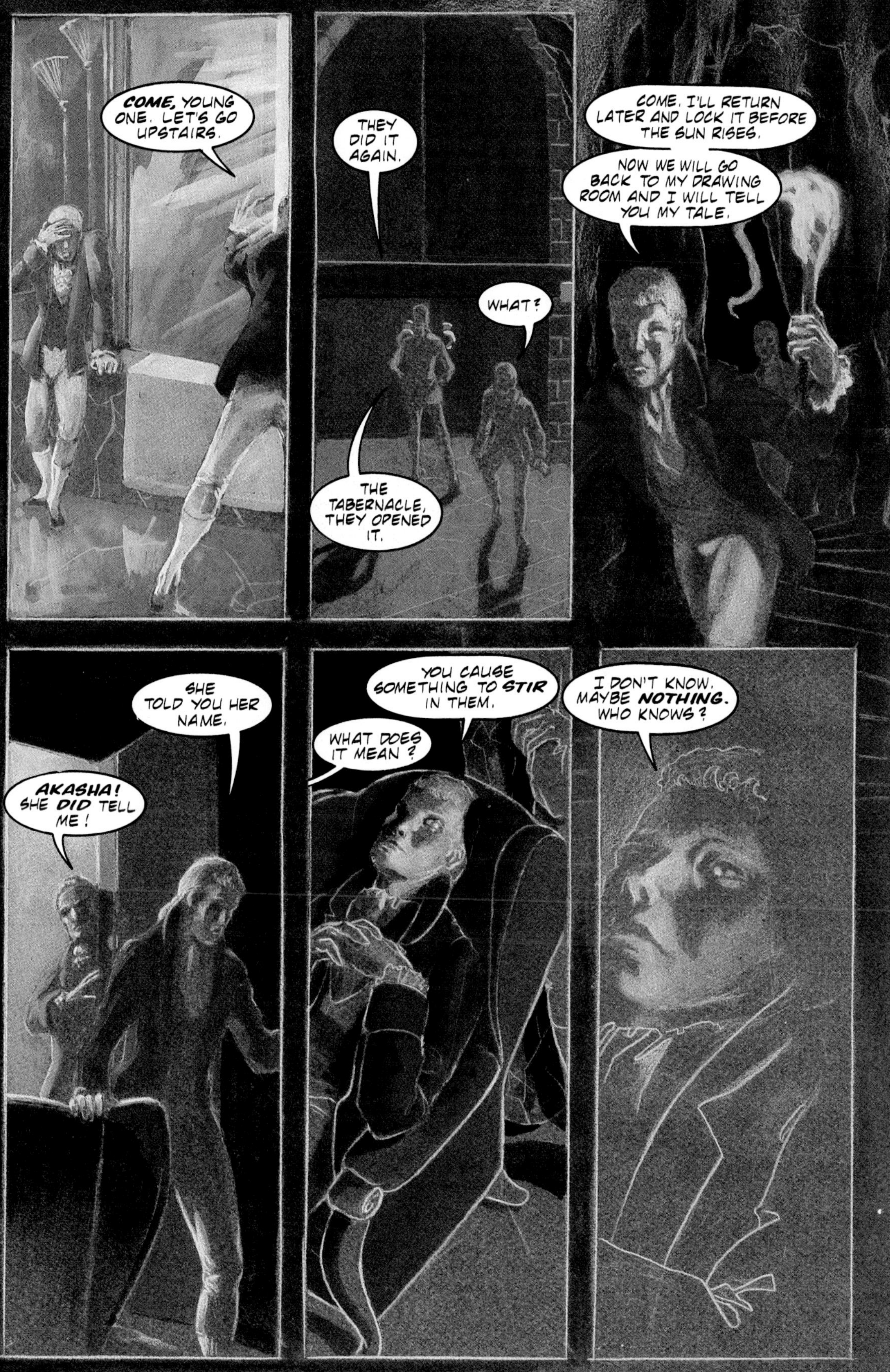

COME, YOUNG ONE. LET'S GO UPSTAIRS.
THEY DID IT AGAIN.
WHAT?
THE TABERNACLE, THEY OPENED IT.
COME. I'LL RETURN LATER AND LOCK IT BEFORE THE SUN RISES.
NOW WE WILL GO BACK TO MY DRAWING ROOM AND I WILL TELL YOU MY TALE.
SHE TOLD YOU HER NAME.
AKASHA! SHE DID TELL ME!
YOU CAUSE SOMETHING TO STIR IN THEM.
WHAT DOES IT MEAN?
I DON'T KNOW. MAYBE NOTHING. WHO KNOWS?

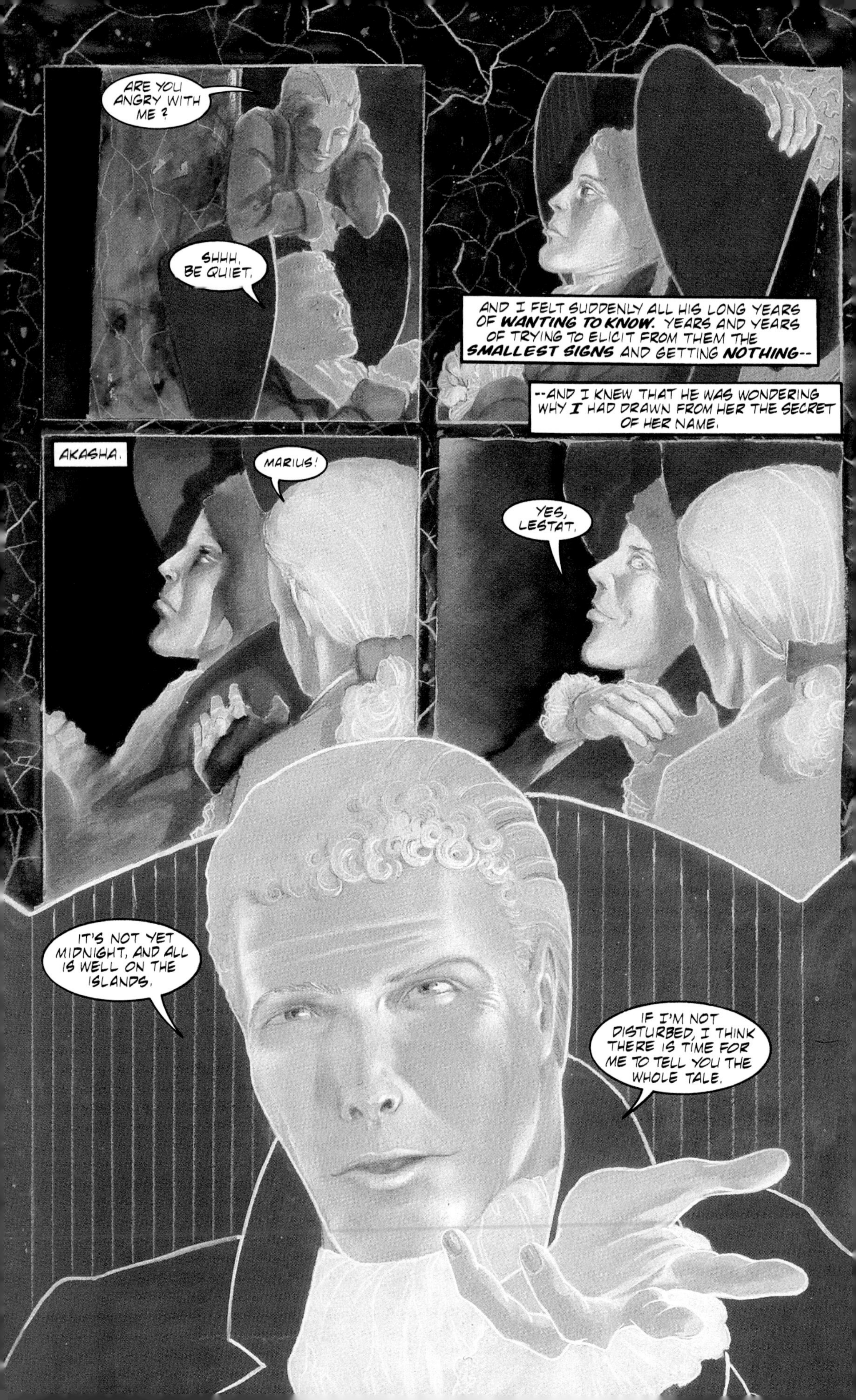
ARE YOU ANGRY WITH ME ?
SHHH. BE QUIET.
AND I FELT SUDDENLY ALL HIS LONG YEARS OF WANTING TO KNOW. YEARS AND YEARS OF TRYING TO ELICIT FROM THEM THE SMALLEST SIGNS AND GETTING NOTHING--
--AND I KNEW THAT HE WAS WONDERING WHY I HAD DRAWN FROM HER THE SECRET OF HER NAME.
AKASHA.
MARIUS!
YES, LESTAT.
IT'S NOT YET MIDNIGHT, AND ALL IS WELL ON THE ISLANDS.
IF I'M NOT DISTURBED, I THINK THERE IS TIME FOR ME TO TELL YOU THE WHOLE TALE.

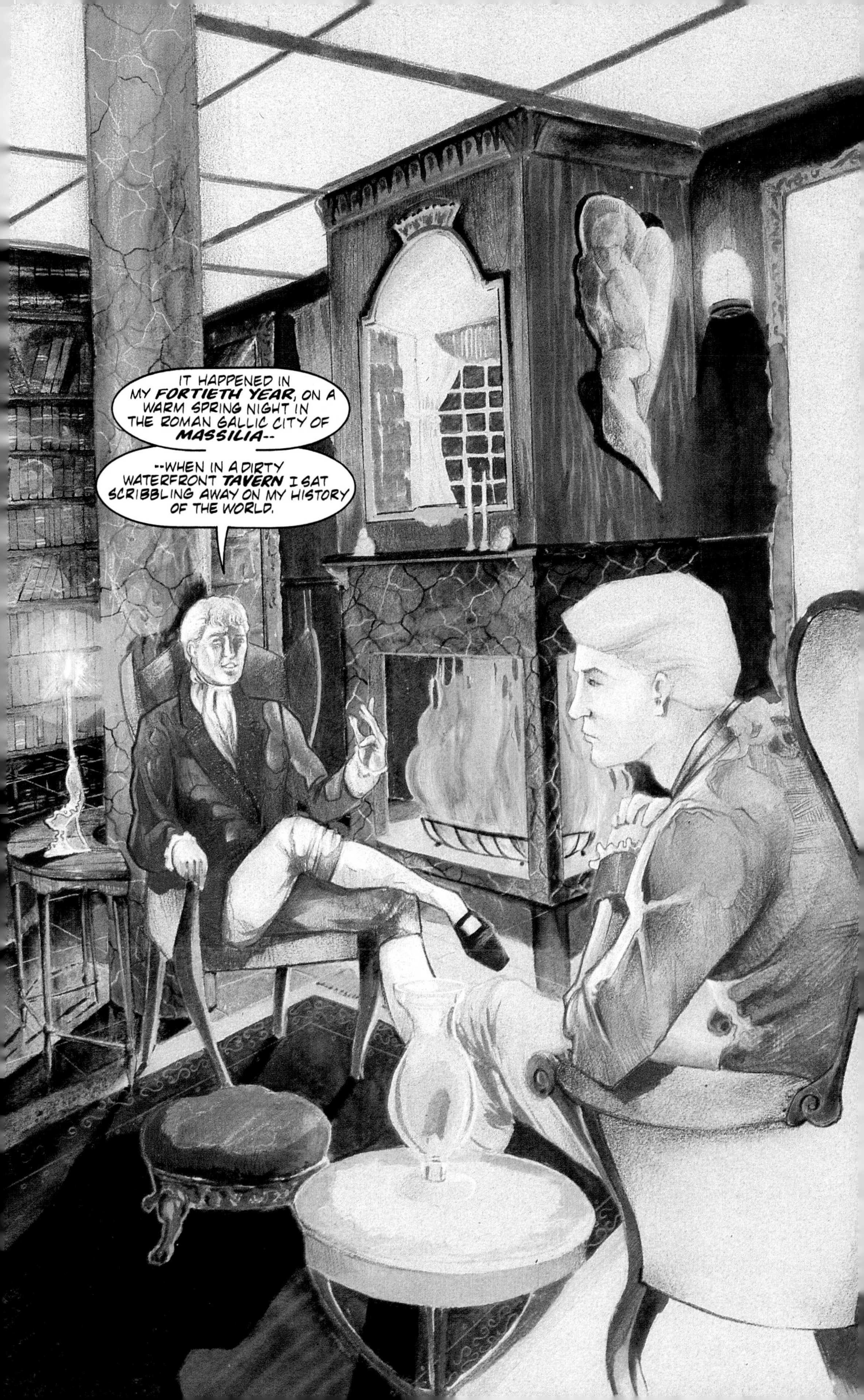
IT HAPPENED IN MY **FORTIETH YEAR**, ON A WARM SPRING NIGHT IN THE ROMAN GALLIC CITY OF **MASSILIA**--
--WHEN IN A DIRTY WATERFRONT **TAVERN** I SAT SCRIBBLING AWAY ON MY HISTORY OF THE WORLD.

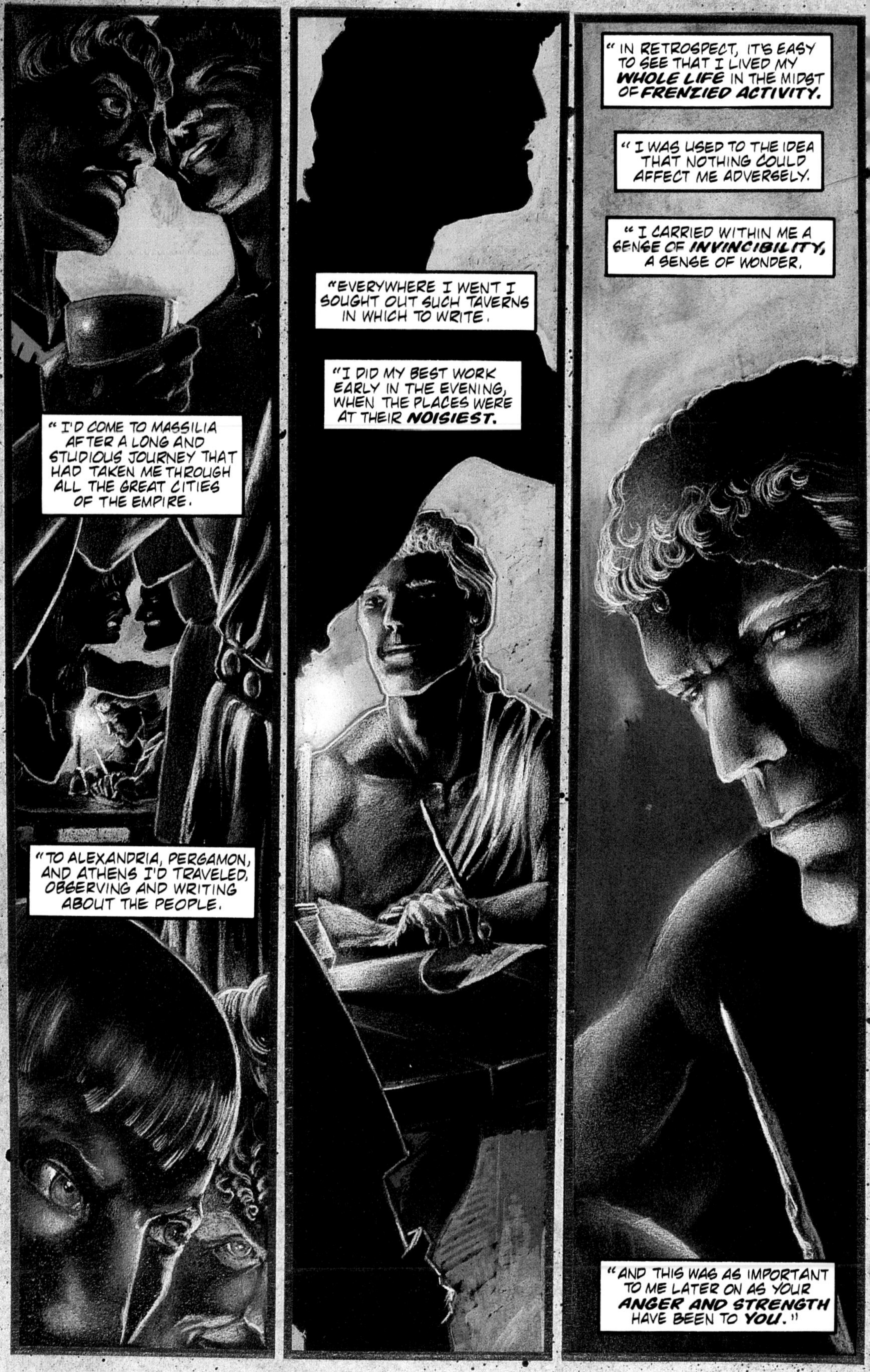
"I'D COME TO MASSILIA AFTER A LONG AND STUDIOUS JOURNEY THAT HAD TAKEN ME THROUGH ALL THE GREAT CITIES OF THE EMPIRE.
"TO ALEXANDRIA, PERGAMON, AND ATHENS I'D TRAVELED, OBSERVING AND WRITING ABOUT THE PEOPLE.
"EVERYWHERE I WENT I SOUGHT OUT SUCH TAVERNS IN WHICH TO WRITE.
"I DID MY BEST WORK EARLY IN THE EVENING, WHEN THE PLACES WERE AT THEIR NOISIEST.
"IN RETROSPECT, IT'S EASY TO SEE THAT I LIVED MY WHOLE LIFE IN THE MIDST OF FRENZIED ACTIVITY.
"I WAS USED TO THE IDEA THAT NOTHING COULD AFFECT ME ADVERSELY.
"I CARRIED WITHIN ME A SENSE OF INVINCIBILITY, A SENSE OF WONDER.
"AND THIS WAS AS IMPORTANT TO ME LATER ON AS YOUR ANGER AND STRENGTH HAVE BEEN TO YOU."

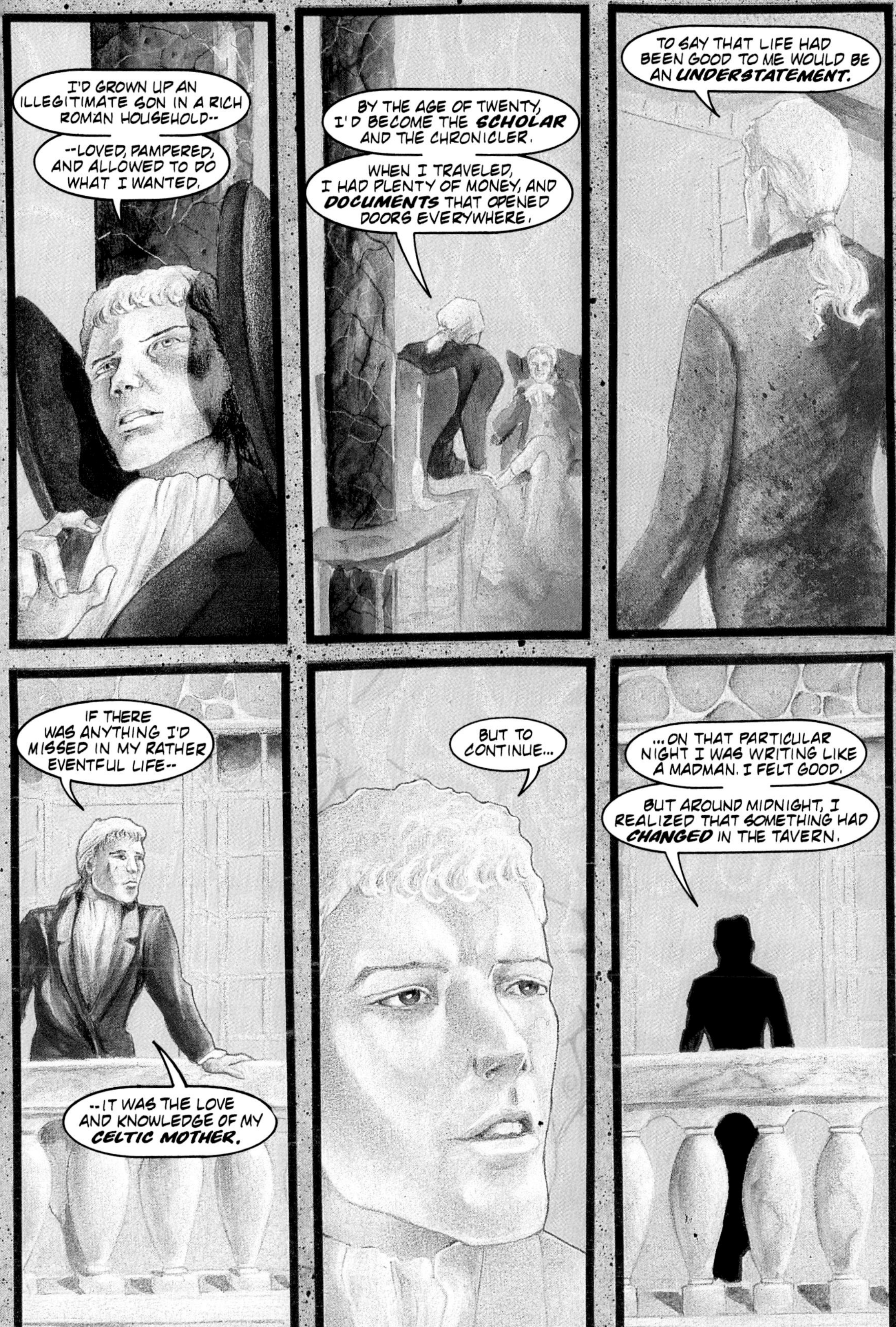
I'D GROWN UP AN ILLEGITIMATE SON IN A RICH ROMAN HOUSEHOLD--
--LOVED, PAMPERED, AND ALLOWED TO DO WHAT I WANTED.
BY THE AGE OF TWENTY, I'D BECOME THE SCHOLAR AND THE CHRONICLER.
WHEN I TRAVELED, I HAD PLENTY OF MONEY, AND DOCUMENTS THAT OPENED DOORS EVERYWHERE.
TO SAY THAT LIFE HAD BEEN GOOD TO ME WOULD BE AN UNDERSTATEMENT.
IF THERE WAS ANYTHING I'D MISSED IN MY RATHER EVENTFUL LIFE--
--IT WAS THE LOVE AND KNOWLEDGE OF MY CELTIC MOTHER.
BUT TO CONTINUE...
...ON THAT PARTICULAR NIGHT I WAS WRITING LIKE A MADMAN. I FELT GOOD.
BUT AROUND MIDNIGHT, I REALIZED THAT SOMETHING HAD CHANGED IN THE TAVERN.

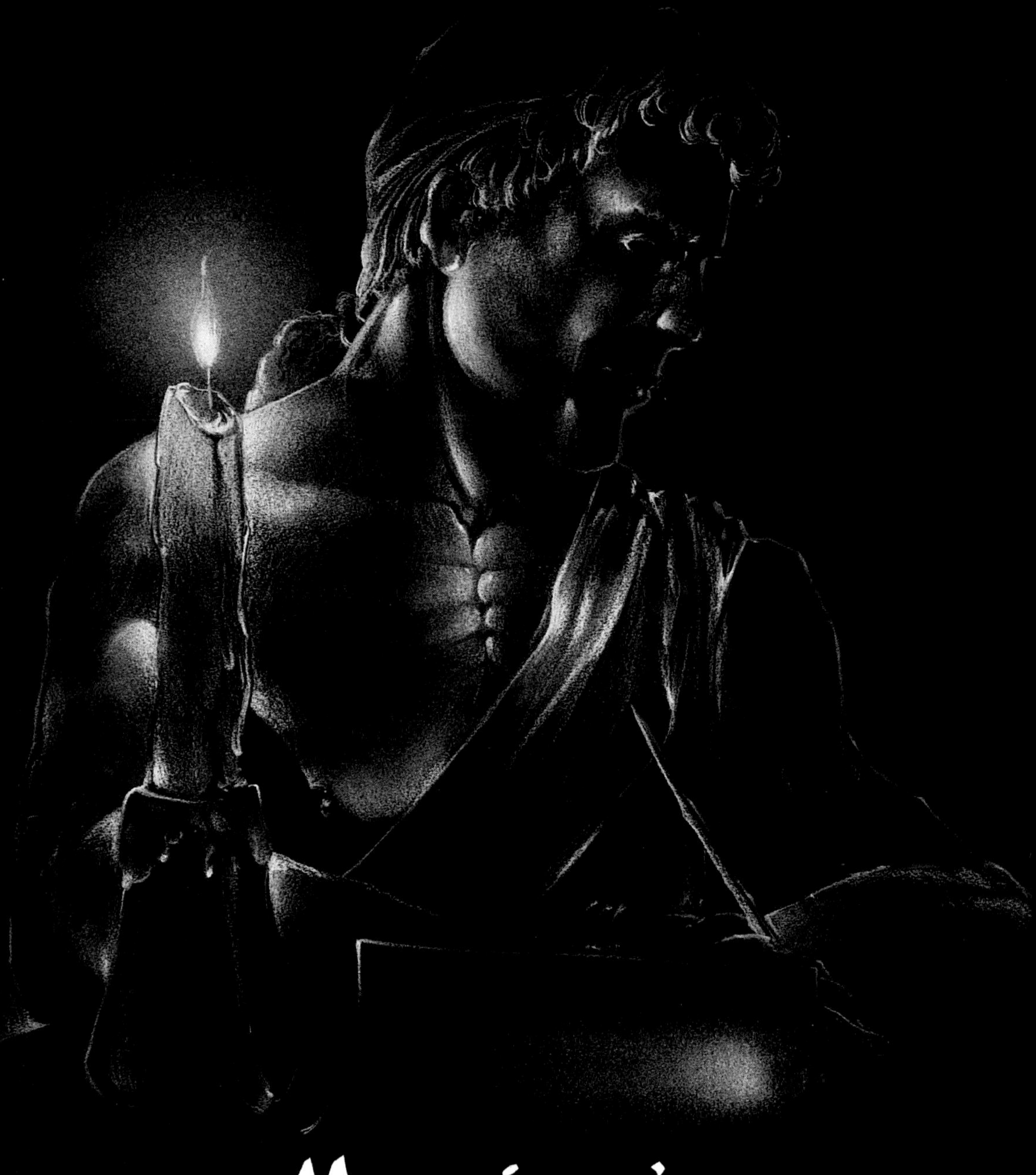

Marius's Story

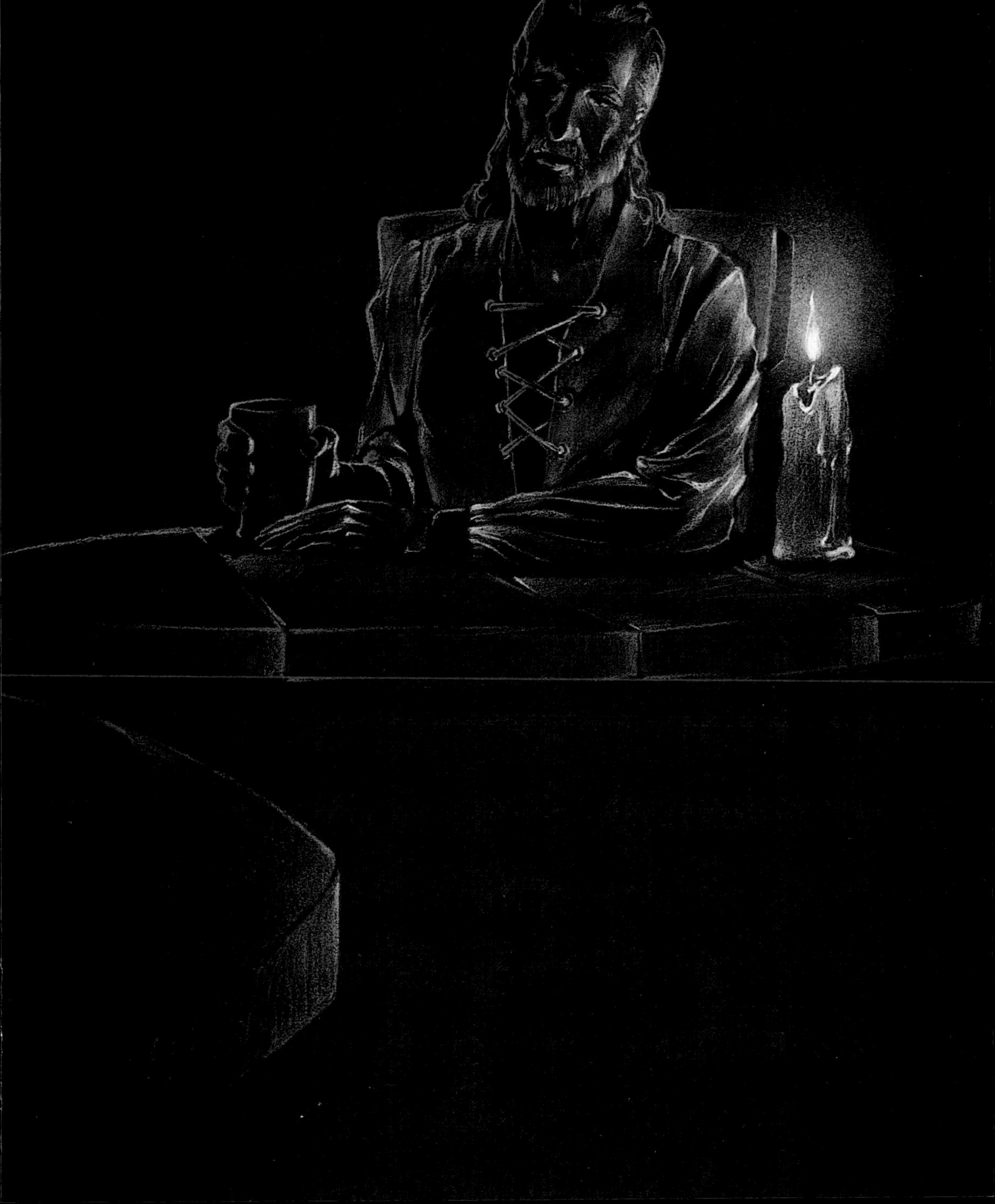

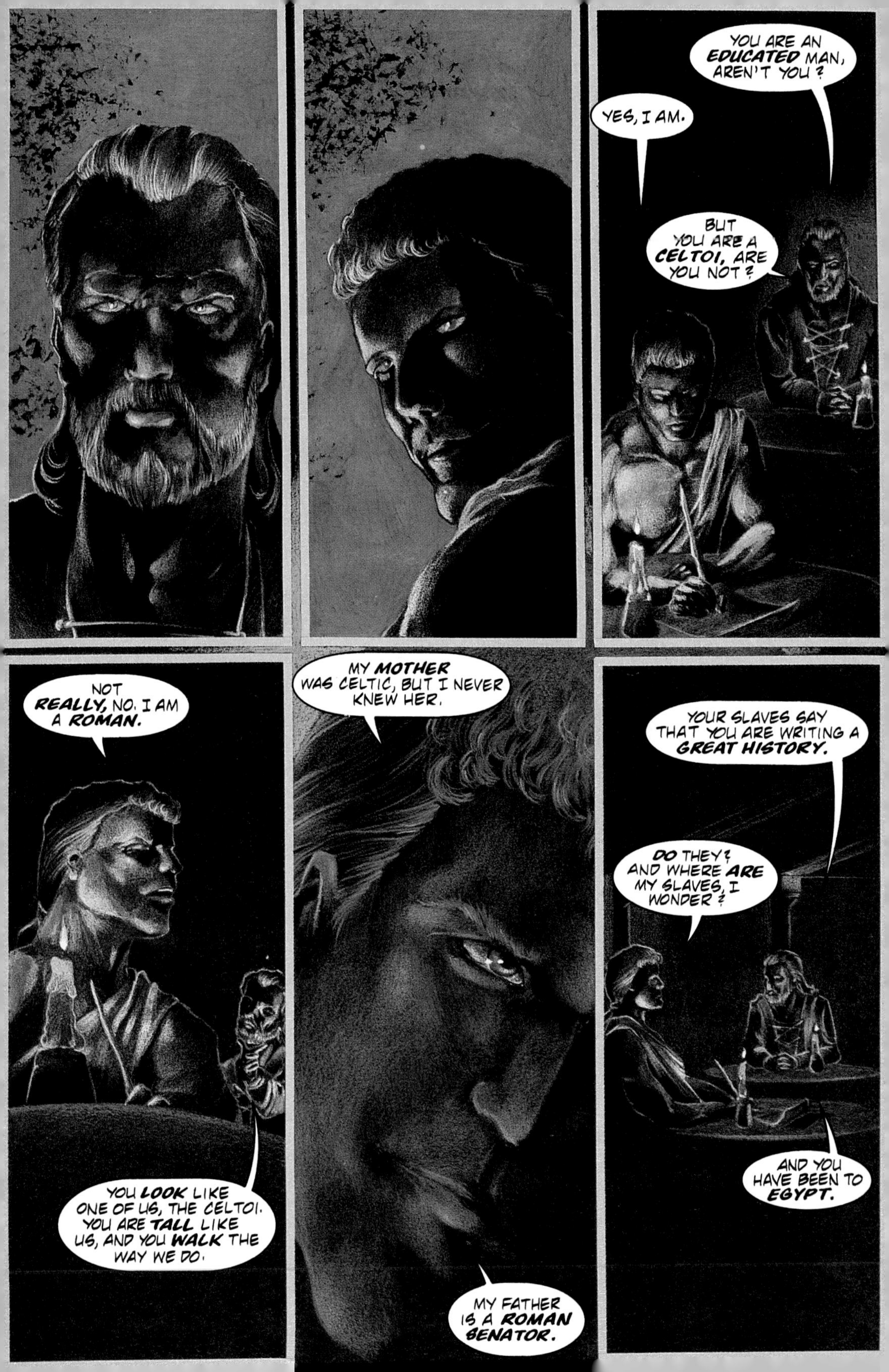
YOU ARE AN EDUCATED MAN, AREN'T YOU?
YES, I AM.
BUT YOU ARE A CELTOI, ARE YOU NOT?
NOT REALLY, NO. I AM A ROMAN.
YOU LOOK LIKE ONE OF US, THE CELTOI. YOU ARE TALL LIKE US, AND YOU WALK THE WAY WE DO.
MY MOTHER WAS CELTIC, BUT I NEVER KNEW HER.
MY FATHER IS A ROMAN SENATOR.
YOUR SLAVES SAY THAT YOU ARE WRITING A GREAT HISTORY.
DO THEY? AND WHERE ARE MY SLAVES, I WONDER?
AND YOU HAVE BEEN TO EGYPT.

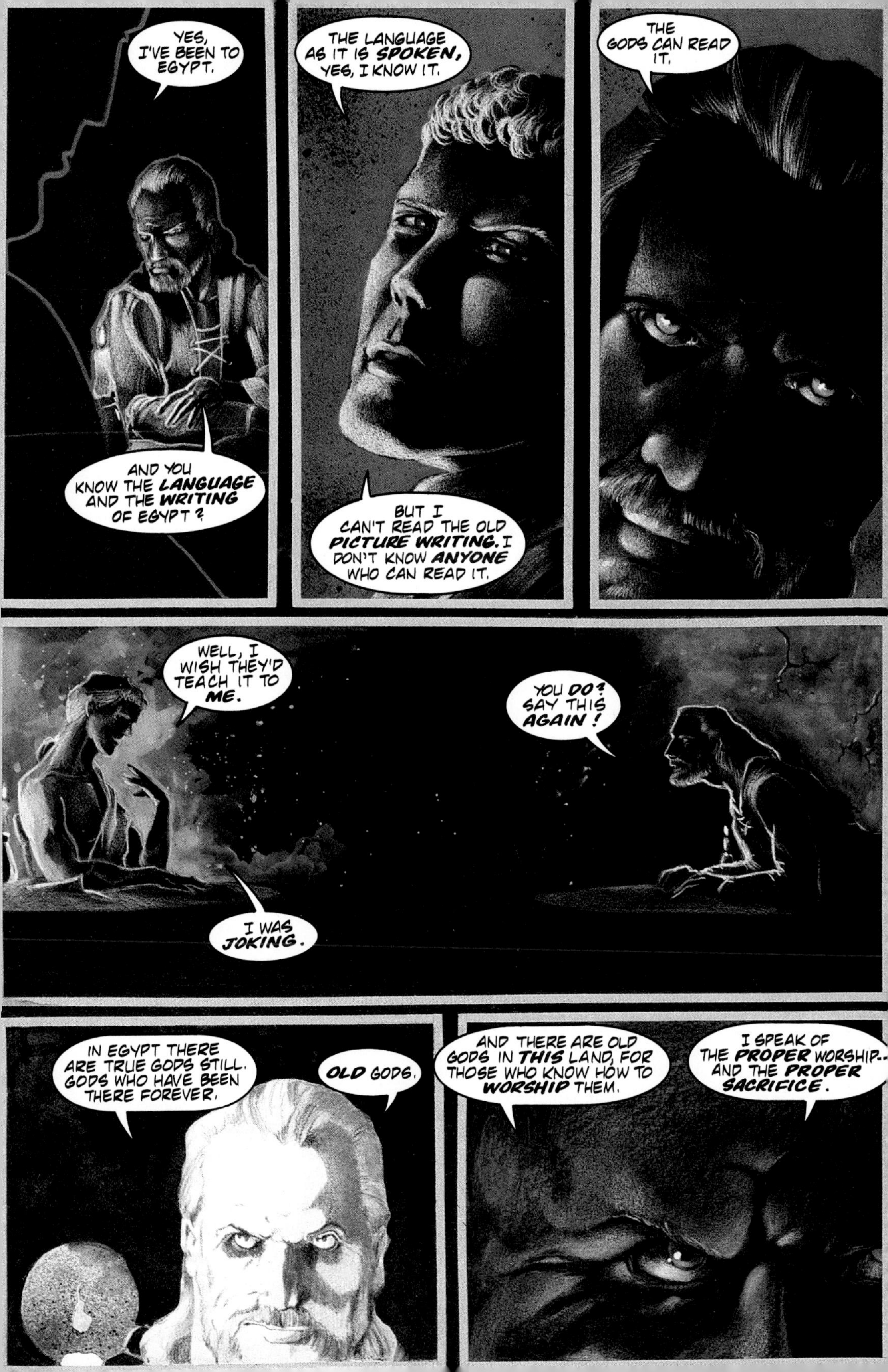
YES, I'VE BEEN TO EGYPT.
AND YOU KNOW THE LANGUAGE AND THE WRITING OF EGYPT?
THE LANGUAGE AS IT IS SPOKEN, YES, I KNOW IT.
BUT I CAN'T READ THE OLD PICTURE WRITING. I DON'T KNOW ANYONE WHO CAN READ IT.
THE GODS CAN READ IT.
WELL, I WISH THEY'D TEACH IT TO ME.
YOU DO? SAY THIS AGAIN!
I WAS JOKING.
IN EGYPT THERE ARE TRUE GODS STILL. GODS WHO HAVE BEEN THERE FOREVER.
OLD GODS.
AND THERE ARE OLD GODS IN THIS LAND, FOR THOSE WHO KNOW HOW TO WORSHIP THEM.
I SPEAK OF THE PROPER WORSHIP... AND THE PROPER SACRIFICE.

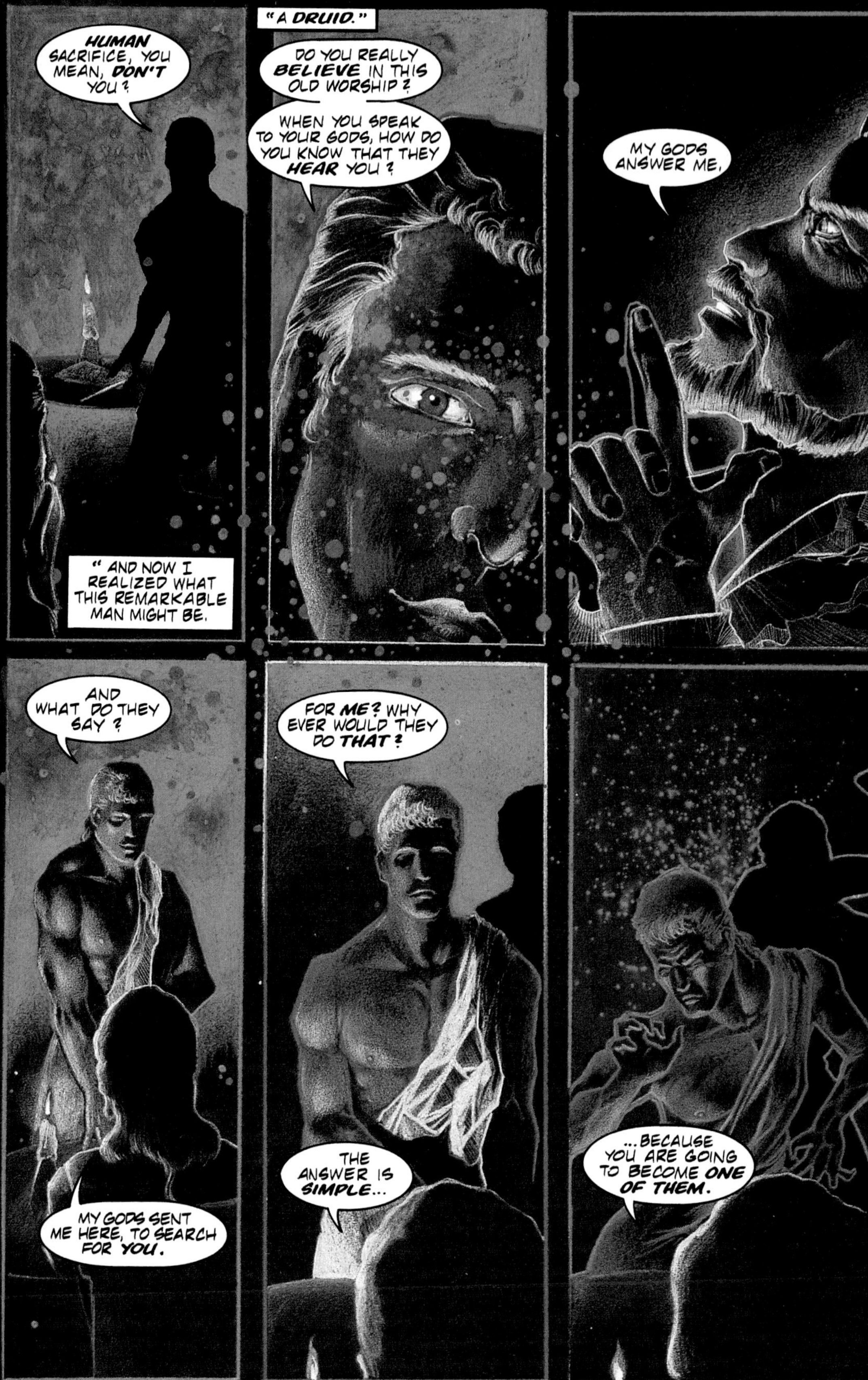
HUMAN SACRIFICE, YOU MEAN, DON'T YOU?
"AND NOW I REALIZED WHAT THIS REMARKABLE MAN MIGHT BE.
"A DRUID."
DO YOU REALLY BELIEVE IN THIS OLD WORSHIP?
WHEN YOU SPEAK TO YOUR GODS, HOW DO YOU KNOW THAT THEY HEAR YOU?
MY GODS ANSWER ME.
AND WHAT DO THEY SAY?
MY GODS SENT ME HERE, TO SEARCH FOR YOU.
FOR ME? WHY EVER WOULD THEY DO THAT?
THE ANSWER IS SIMPLE...
...BECAUSE YOU ARE GOING TO BECOME ONE OF THEM.

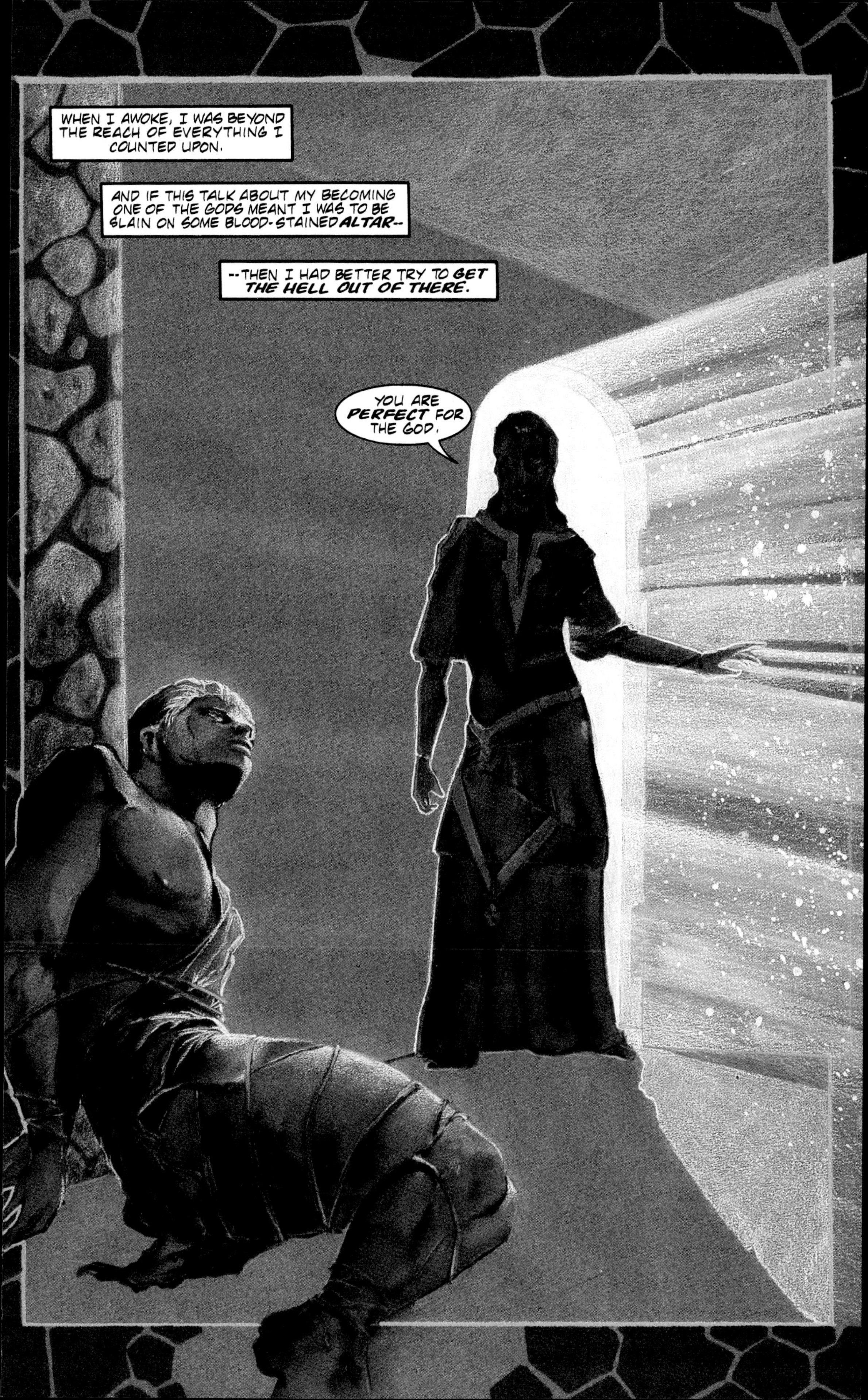

WHEN I AWOKE, I WAS BEYOND THE REACH OF EVERYTHING I COUNTED UPON.
AND IF THIS TALK ABOUT MY BECOMING ONE OF THE GODS MEANT I WAS TO BE SLAIN ON SOME BLOOD-STAINED ALTAR--
--THEN I HAD BETTER TRY TO GET THE HELL OUT OF THERE.
YOU ARE PERFECT FOR THE GOD.

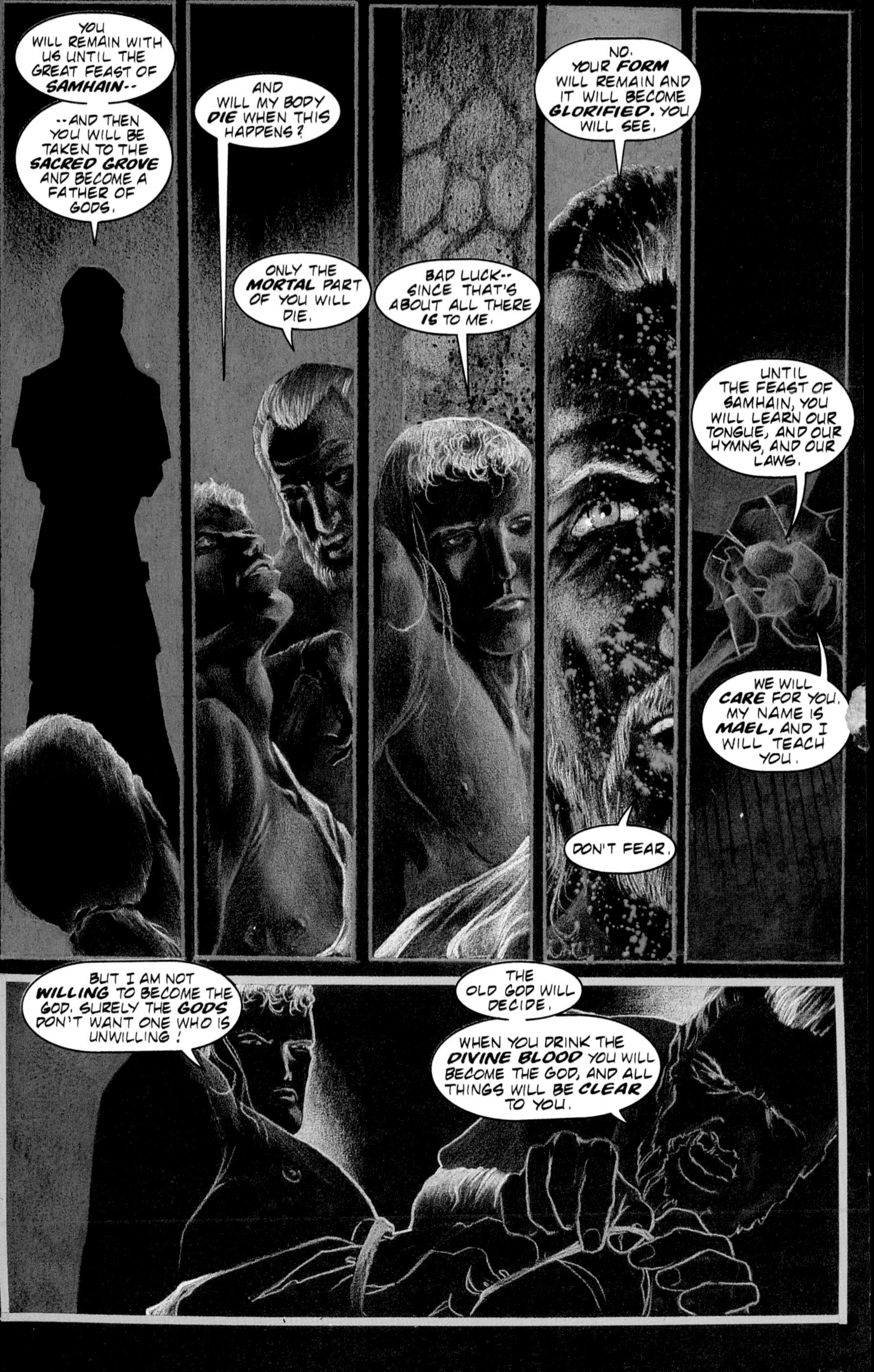
YOU WILL REMAIN WITH US UNTIL THE GREAT FEAST OF SAMHAIN--
--AND THEN YOU WILL BE TAKEN TO THE SACRED GROVE AND BECOME A FATHER OF GODS.
AND WILL MY BODY DIE WHEN THIS HAPPENS?
ONLY THE MORTAL PART OF YOU WILL DIE.
BAD LUCK-- SINCE THAT'S ABOUT ALL THERE IS TO ME.
NO. YOUR FORM WILL REMAIN AND IT WILL BECOME GLORIFIED. YOU WILL SEE.
DON'T FEAR.
UNTIL THE FEAST OF SAMHAIN, YOU WILL LEARN OUR TONGUE, AND OUR HYMNS, AND OUR LAWS.
WE WILL CARE FOR YOU. MY NAME IS MAEL, AND I WILL TEACH YOU.
BUT I AM NOT WILLING TO BECOME THE GOD. SURELY THE GODS DON'T WANT ONE WHO IS UNWILLING!
THE OLD GOD WILL DECIDE.
WHEN YOU DRINK THE DIVINE BLOOD YOU WILL BECOME THE GOD, AND ALL THINGS WILL BE CLEAR TO YOU.

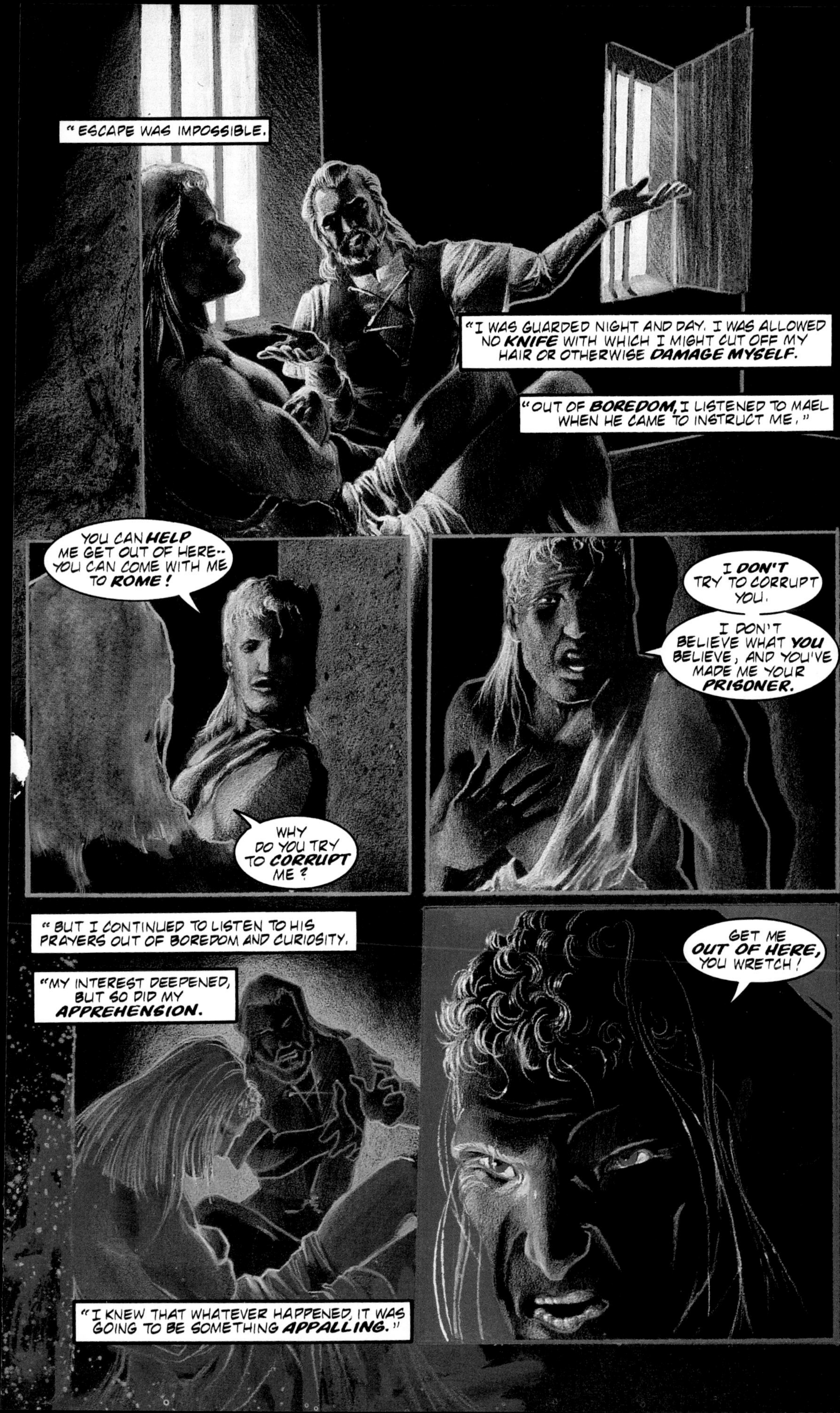
"ESCAPE WAS IMPOSSIBLE.
"I WAS GUARDED NIGHT AND DAY. I WAS ALLOWED NO KNIFE WITH WHICH I MIGHT CUT OFF MY HAIR OR OTHERWISE DAMAGE MYSELF.
"OUT OF BOREDOM, I LISTENED TO MAEL WHEN HE CAME TO INSTRUCT ME."
YOU CAN HELP ME GET OUT OF HERE-- YOU CAN COME WITH ME TO ROME!
WHY DO YOU TRY TO CORRUPT ME?
I DON'T TRY TO CORRUPT YOU.
I DON'T BELIEVE WHAT YOU BELIEVE, AND YOU'VE MADE ME YOUR PRISONER.
"BUT I CONTINUED TO LISTEN TO HIS PRAYERS OUT OF BOREDOM AND CURIOSITY.
"MY INTEREST DEEPENED, BUT SO DID MY APPREHENSION.
"I KNEW THAT WHATEVER HAPPENED, IT WAS GOING TO BE SOMETHING APPALLING."
GET ME OUT OF HERE, YOU WRETCH!

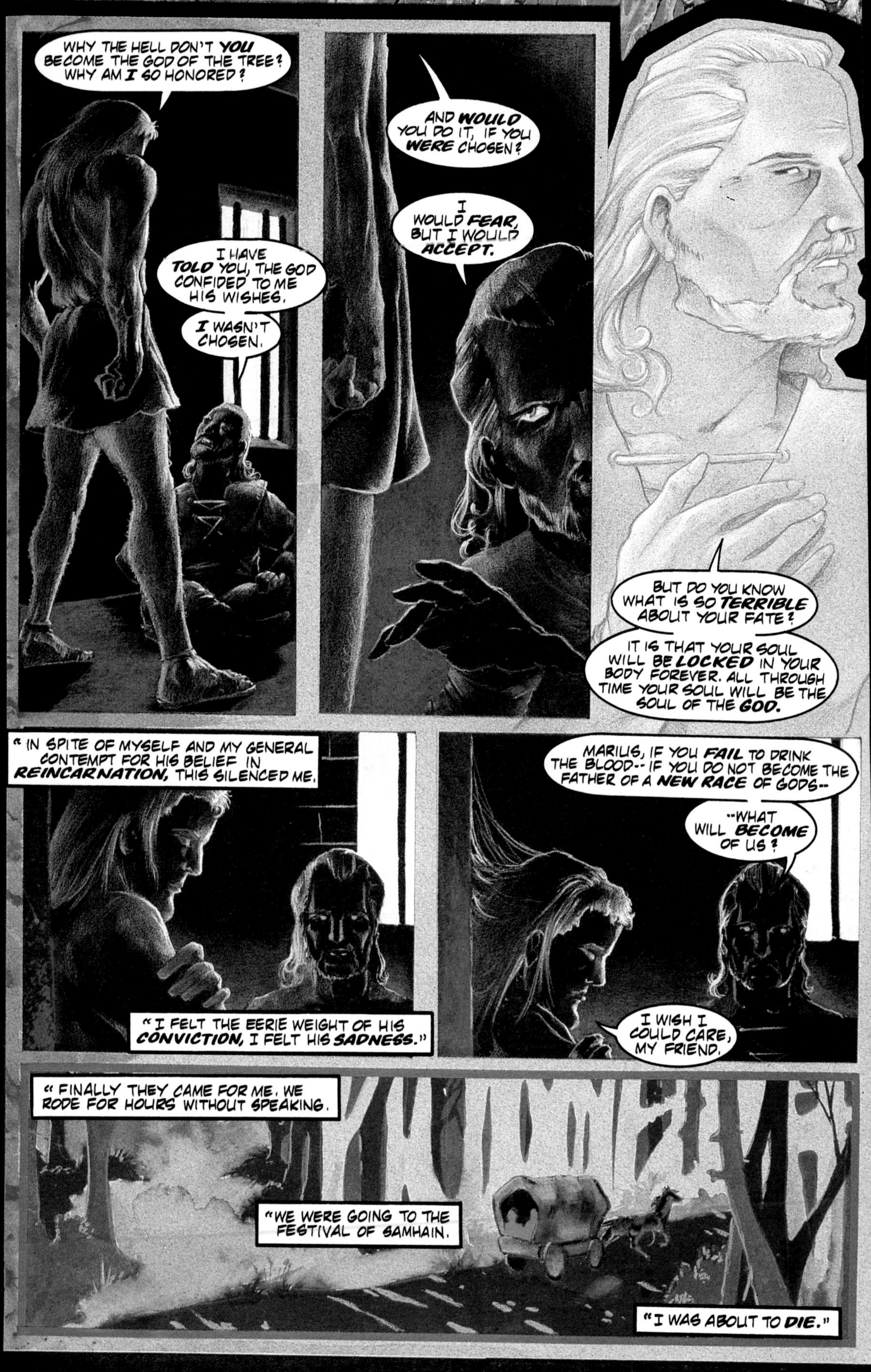

WHY THE HELL DON'T YOU BECOME THE GOD OF THE TREE? WHY AM I SO HONORED?
I HAVE TOLD YOU, THE GOD CONFIDED TO ME HIS WISHES.
I WASN'T CHOSEN.
AND WOULD YOU DO IT, IF YOU WERE CHOSEN?
I WOULD FEAR, BUT I WOULD ACCEPT.
BUT DO YOU KNOW WHAT IS SO TERRIBLE ABOUT YOUR FATE?
IT IS THAT YOUR SOUL WILL BE LOCKED IN YOUR BODY FOREVER. ALL THROUGH TIME YOUR SOUL WILL BE THE SOUL OF THE GOD.
"IN SPITE OF MYSELF AND MY GENERAL CONTEMPT FOR HIS BELIEF IN REINCARNATION, THIS SILENCED ME.
"I FELT THE EERIE WEIGHT OF HIS CONVICTION, I FELT HIS SADNESS."
MARIUS, IF YOU FAIL TO DRINK THE BLOOD-- IF YOU DO NOT BECOME THE FATHER OF A NEW RACE OF GODS--
--WHAT WILL BECOME OF US?
I WISH I COULD CARE, MY FRIEND.
"FINALLY THEY CAME FOR ME. WE RODE FOR HOURS WITHOUT SPEAKING.
"WE WERE GOING TO THE FESTIVAL OF SAMHAIN.
"I WAS ABOUT TO DIE."

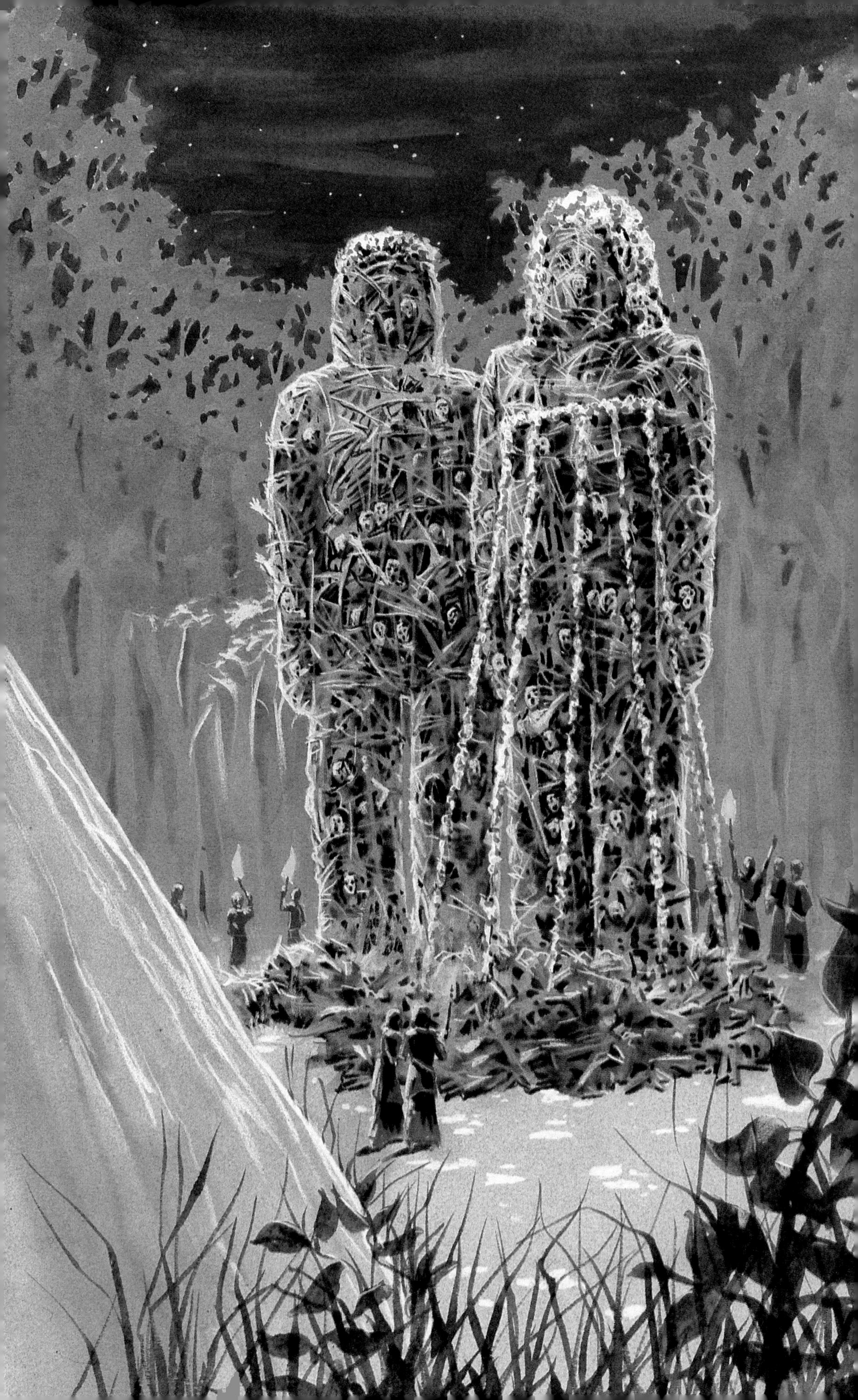

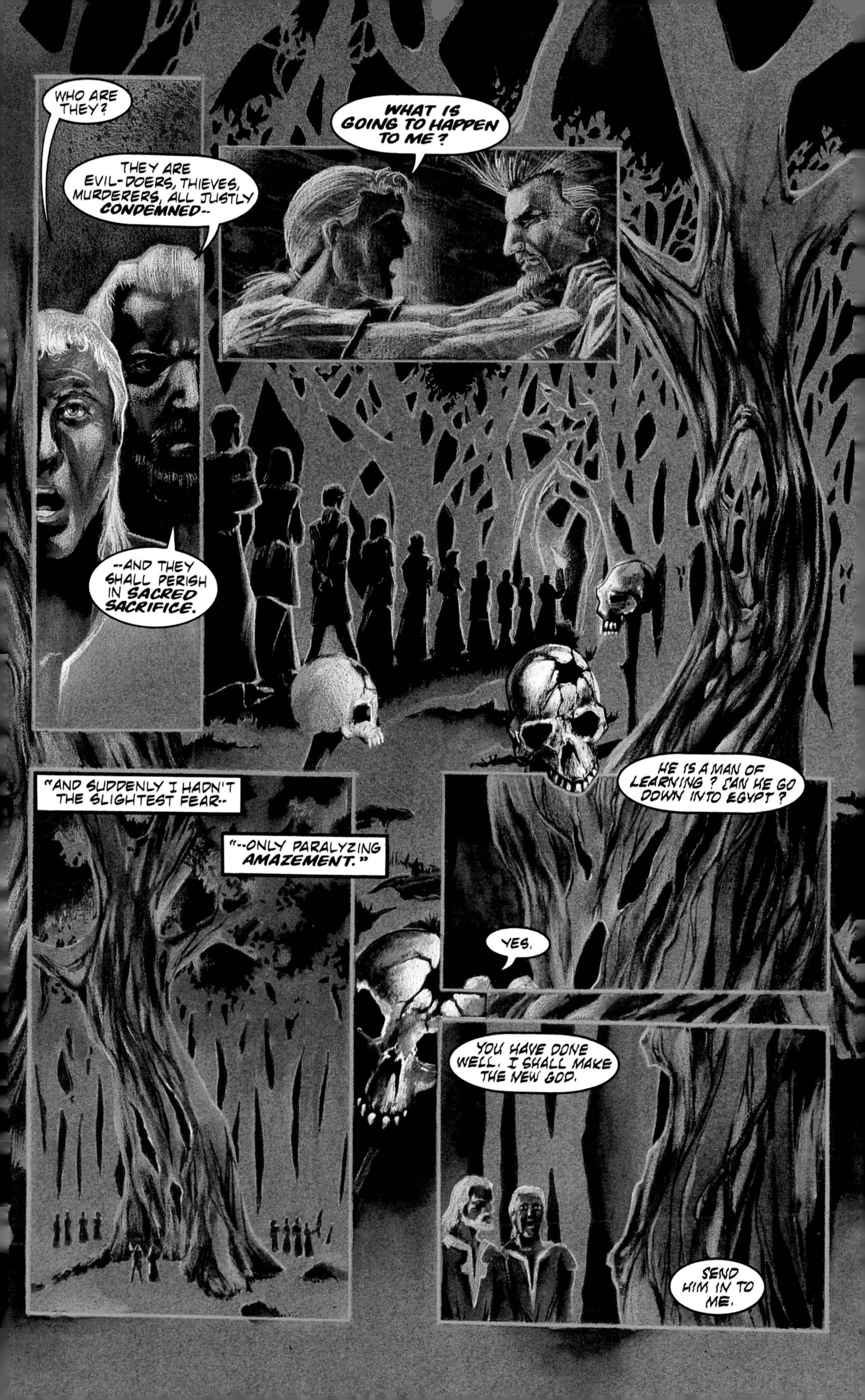
WHO ARE THEY?
WHAT IS GOING TO HAPPEN TO ME?
THEY ARE EVIL-DOERS, THIEVES, MURDERERS, ALL JUSTLY CONDEMNED--
--AND THEY SHALL PERISH IN SACRED SACRIFICE.
"AND SUDDENLY I HADN'T THE SLIGHTEST FEAR--
"--ONLY PARALYZING AMAZEMENT."
HE IS A MAN OF LEARNING ? CAN HE GO DOWN INTO EGYPT ?
YES.
YOU HAVE DONE WELL. I SHALL MAKE THE NEW GOD.
SEND HIM IN TO ME.

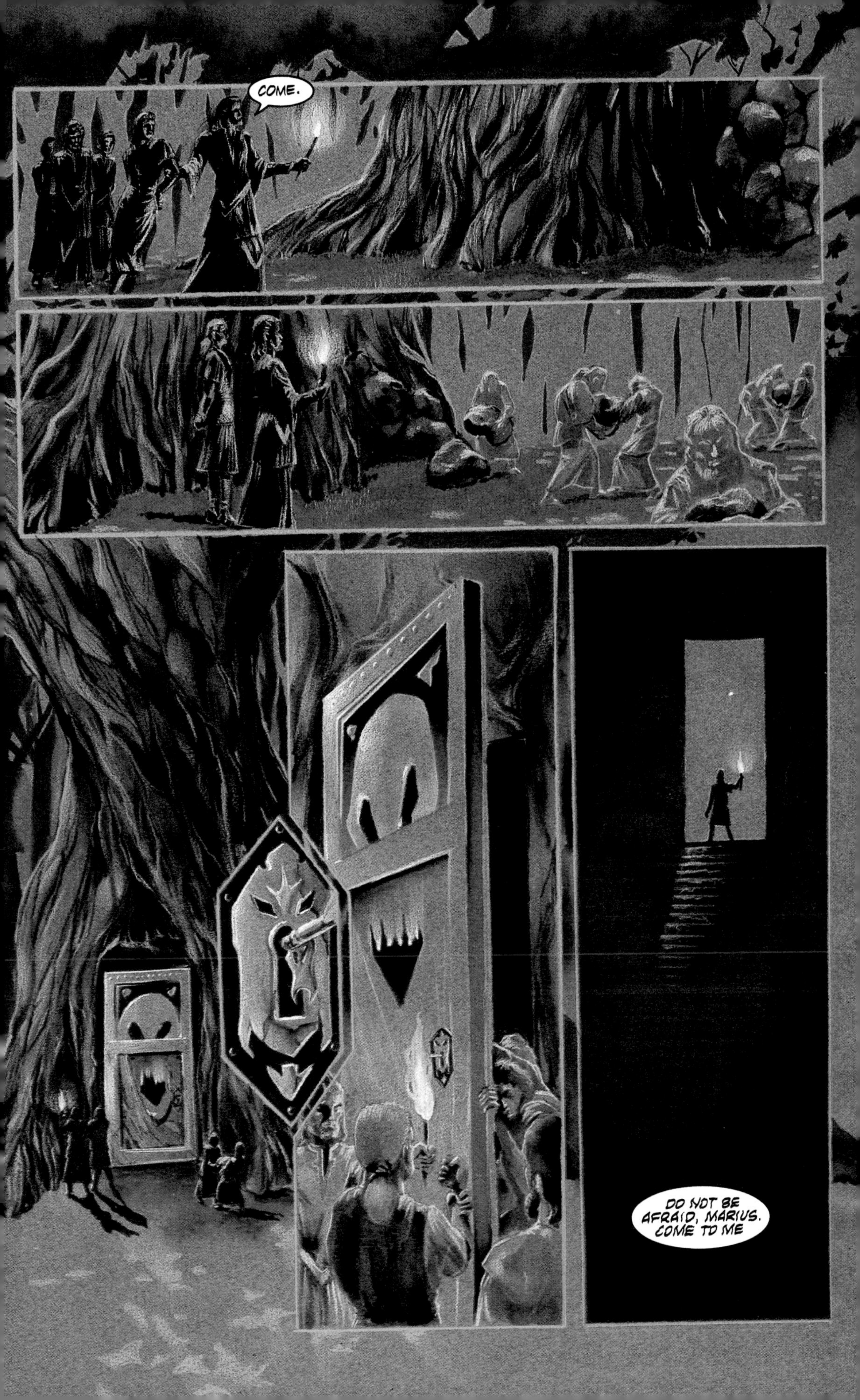
COME.
DO NOT BE AFRAID, MARIUS. COME TO ME

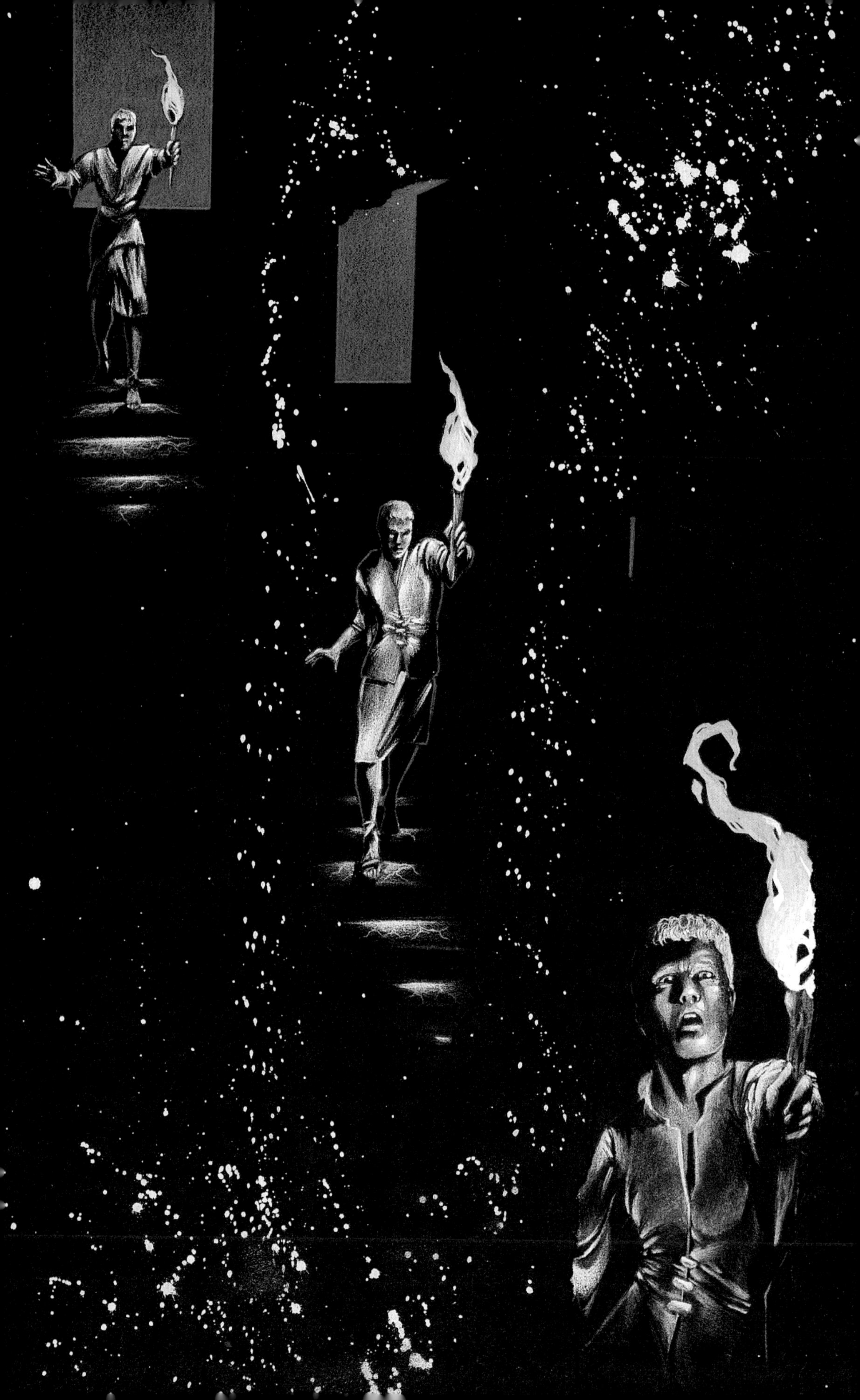

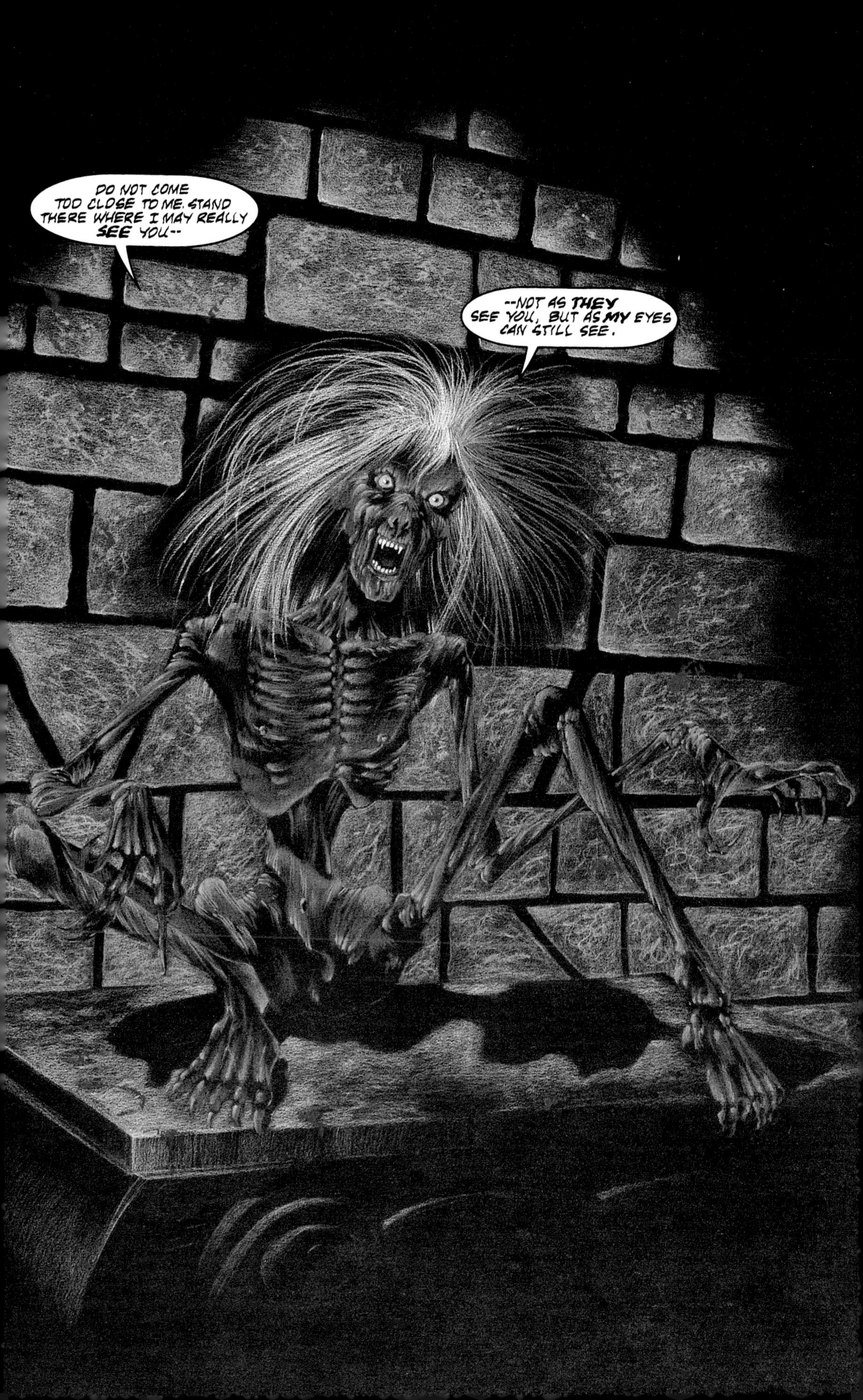
DO NOT COME TOO CLOSE TO ME. STAND THERE WHERE I MAY REALLY **SEE** YOU--
--NOT AS **THEY** SEE YOU, BUT AS **MY** EYES CAN STILL SEE.

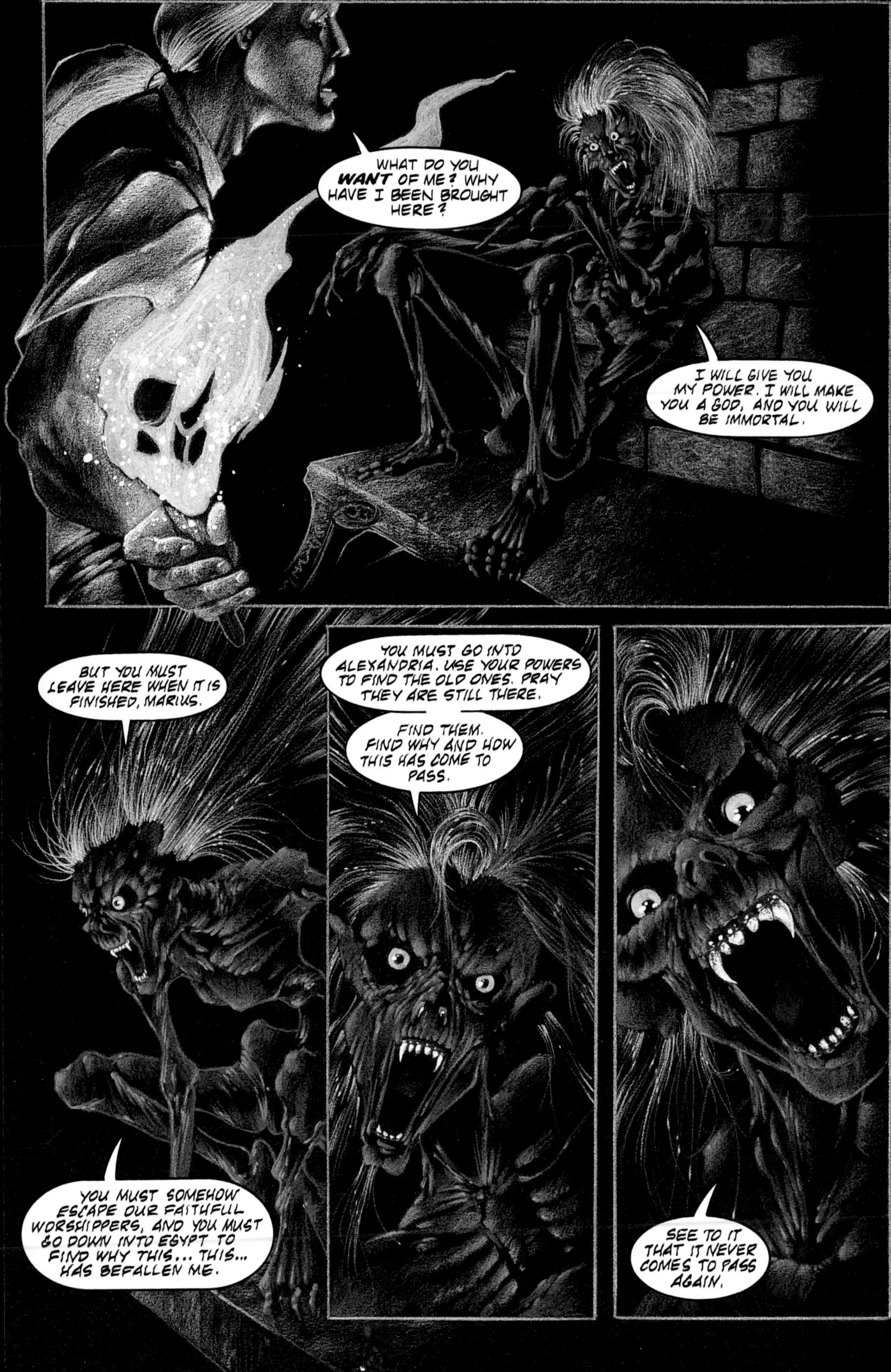
WHAT DO YOU WANT OF ME? WHY HAVE I BEEN BROUGHT HERE?
I WILL GIVE YOU MY POWER. I WILL MAKE YOU A GOD, AND YOU WILL BE IMMORTAL.
BUT YOU MUST LEAVE HERE WHEN IT IS FINISHED, MARIUS.
YOU MUST SOMEHOW ESCAPE OUR FAITHFUL WORSHIPPERS, AND YOU MUST GO DOWN INTO EGYPT TO FIND WHY THIS... THIS... HAS BEFALLEN ME.
YOU MUST GO INTO ALEXANDRIA. USE YOUR POWERS TO FIND THE OLD ONES. PRAY THEY ARE STILL THERE.
FIND THEM. FIND WHY AND HOW THIS HAS COME TO PASS.
SEE TO IT THAT IT NEVER COMES TO PASS AGAIN.

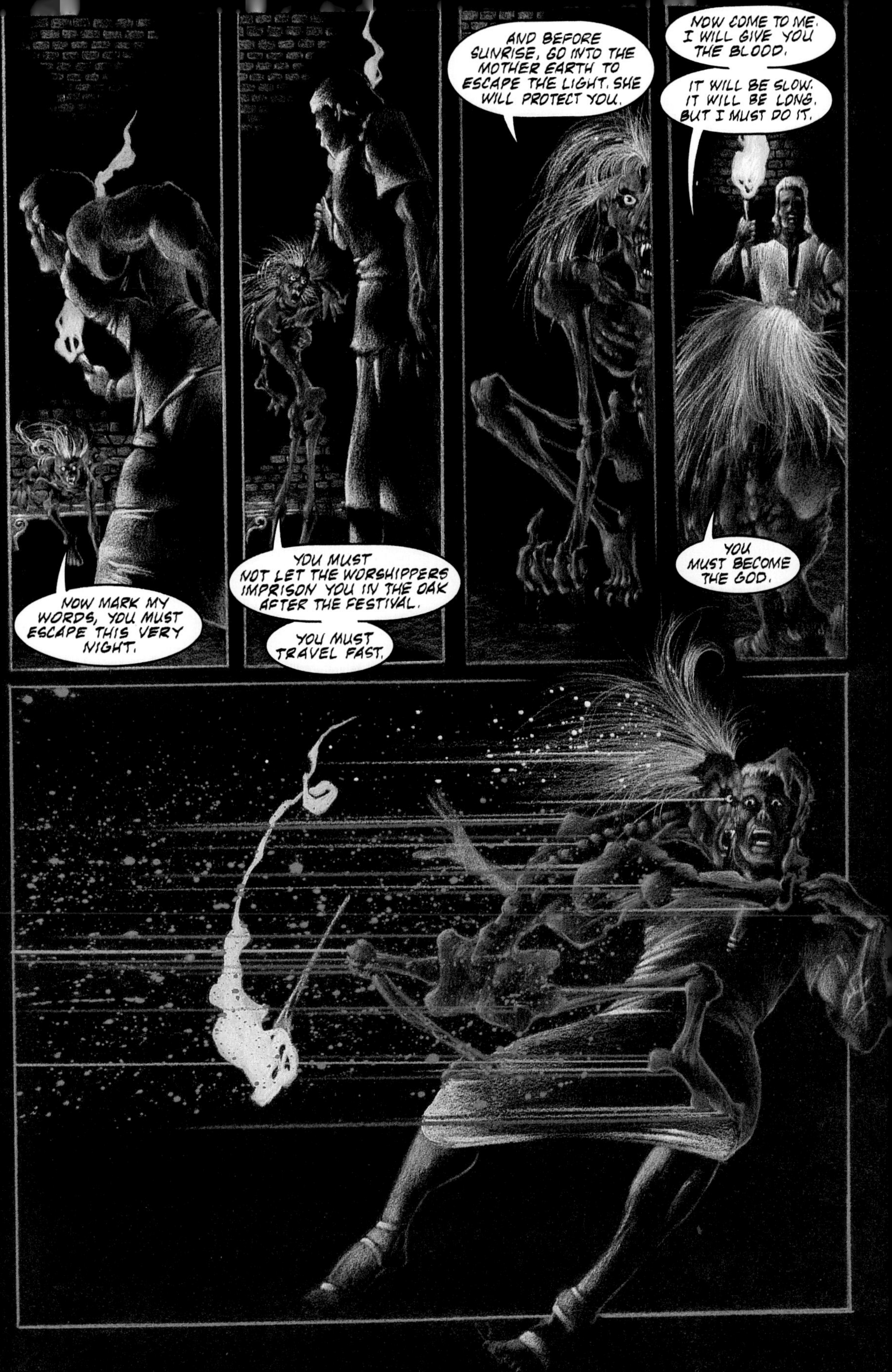
NOW MARK MY WORDS, YOU MUST ESCAPE THIS VERY NIGHT.
YOU MUST NOT LET THE WORSHIPPERS IMPRISON YOU IN THE OAK AFTER THE FESTIVAL.
YOU MUST TRAVEL FAST.
AND BEFORE SUNRISE, GO INTO THE MOTHER EARTH TO ESCAPE THE LIGHT. SHE WILL PROTECT YOU.
NOW COME TO ME. I WILL GIVE YOU THE BLOOD.
IT WILL BE SLOW. IT WILL BE LONG. BUT I MUST DO IT.
YOU MUST BECOME THE GOD.

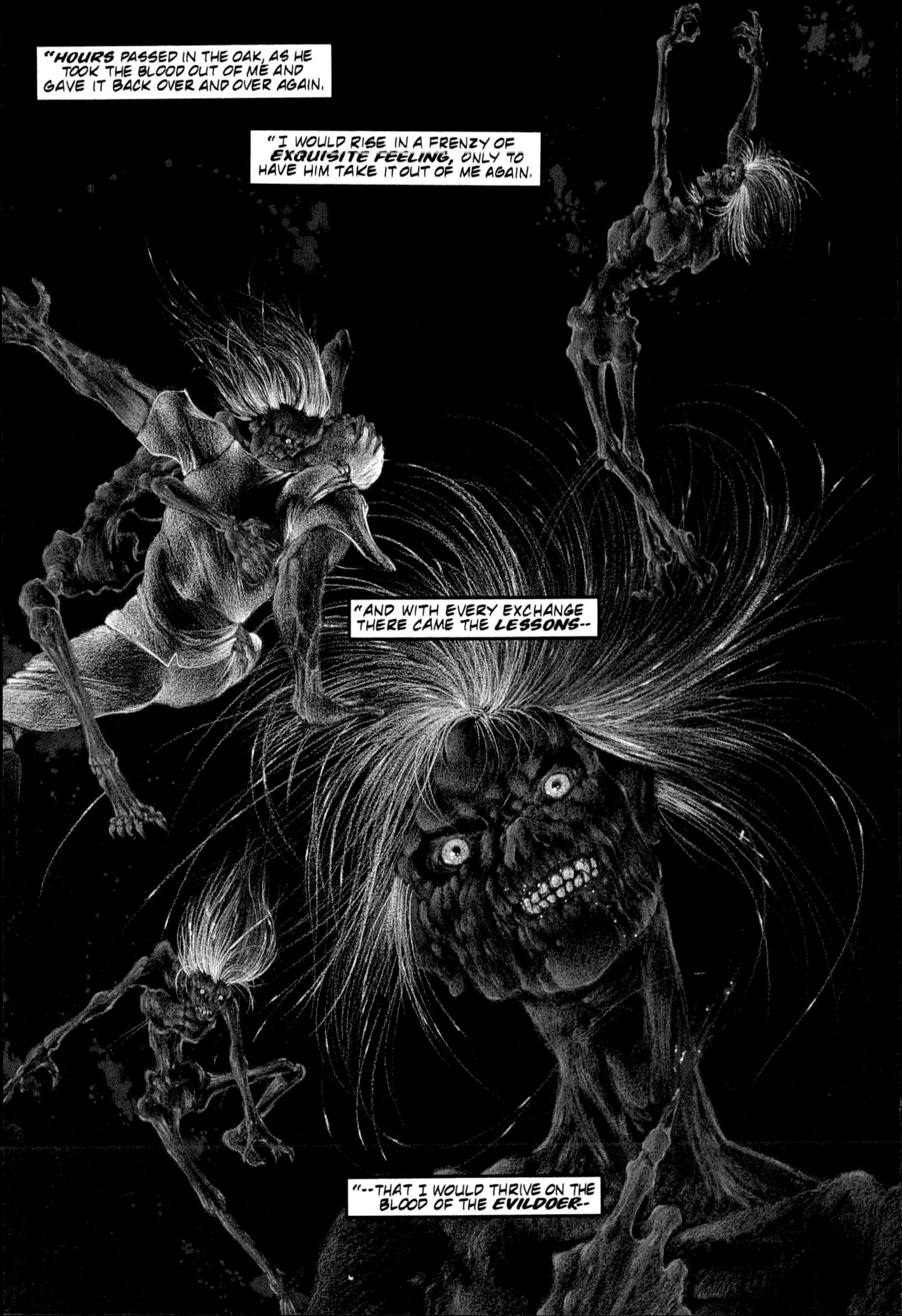
"HOURS PASSED IN THE OAK, AS HE TOOK THE BLOOD OUT OF ME AND GAVE IT BACK OVER AND OVER AGAIN.
"I WOULD RISE IN A FRENZY OF EXQUISITE FEELING, ONLY TO HAVE HIM TAKE IT OUT OF ME AGAIN.
"AND WITH EVERY EXCHANGE THERE CAME THE LESSONS--
"--THAT I WOULD THRIVE ON THE BLOOD OF THE EVILDOER-

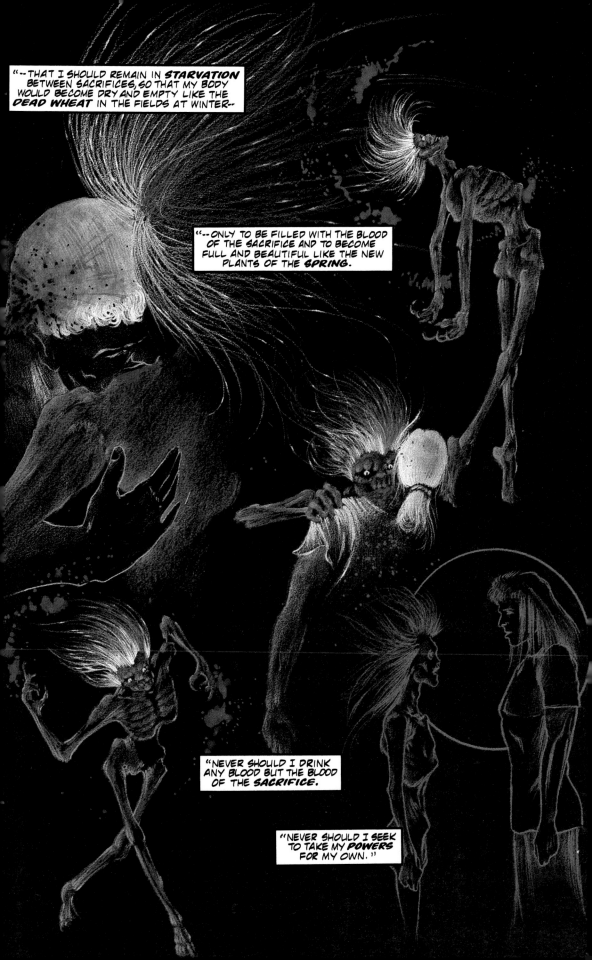

"--THAT I SHOULD REMAIN IN **STARVATION** BETWEEN SACRIFICES, SO THAT MY BODY WOULD BECOME DRY AND EMPTY LIKE THE **DEAD WHEAT** IN THE FIELDS AT WINTER--

"--ONLY TO BE FILLED WITH THE BLOOD OF THE SACRIFICE AND TO BECOME FULL AND BEAUTIFUL LIKE THE NEW PLANTS OF THE **SPRING**.

"NEVER SHOULD I DRINK ANY BLOOD BUT THE BLOOD OF THE **SACRIFICE**.

"NEVER SHOULD I SEEK TO TAKE MY **POWERS** FOR MY OWN."

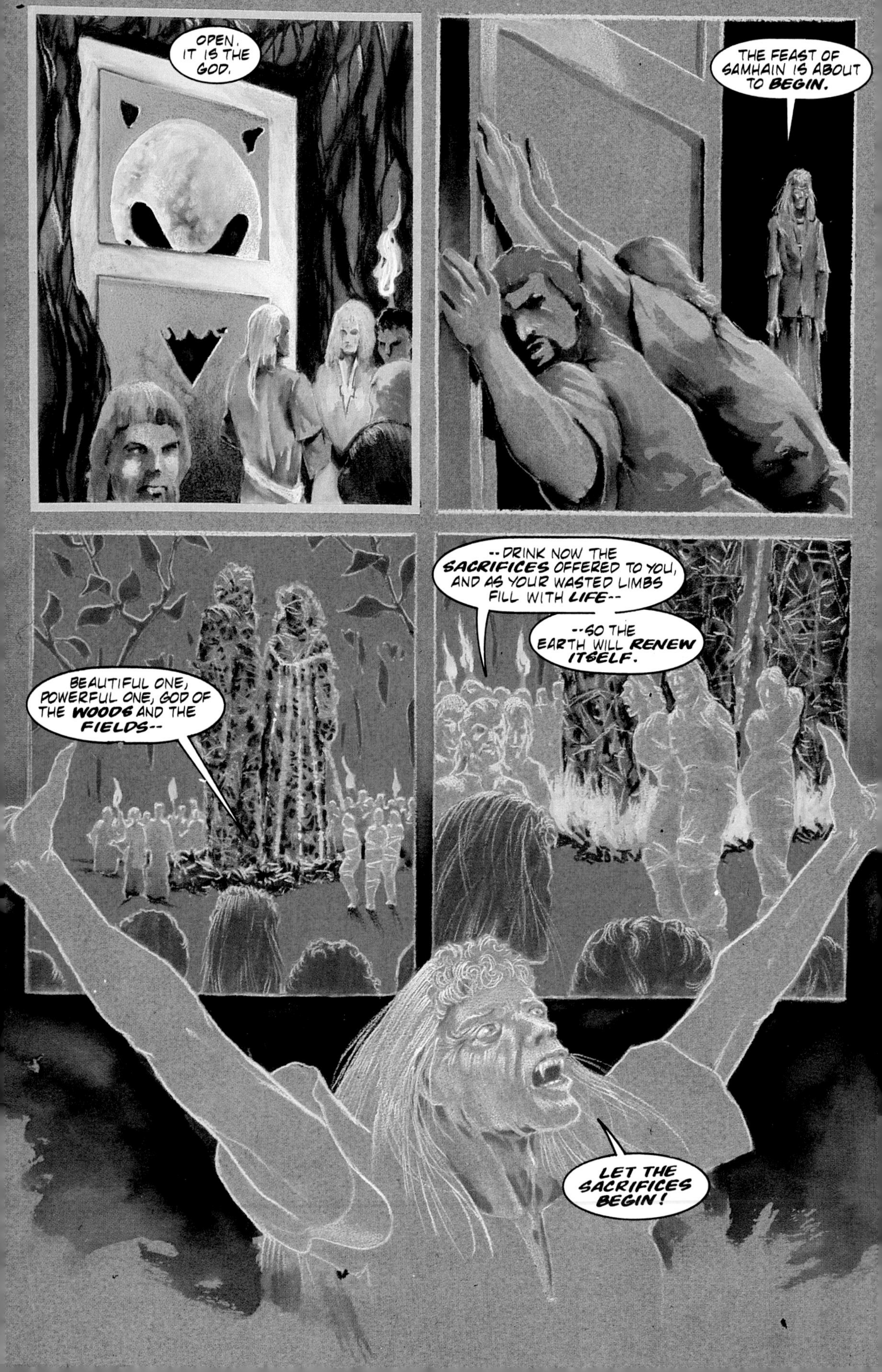
OPEN. IT IS THE GOD.
THE FEAST OF SAMHAIN IS ABOUT TO BEGIN.
BEAUTIFUL ONE, POWERFUL ONE, GOD OF THE WOODS AND THE FIELDS--
--DRINK NOW THE SACRIFICES OFFERED TO YOU, AND AS YOUR WASTED LIMBS FILL WITH LIFE--
--SO THE EARTH WILL RENEW ITSELF.
LET THE SACRIFICES BEGIN!

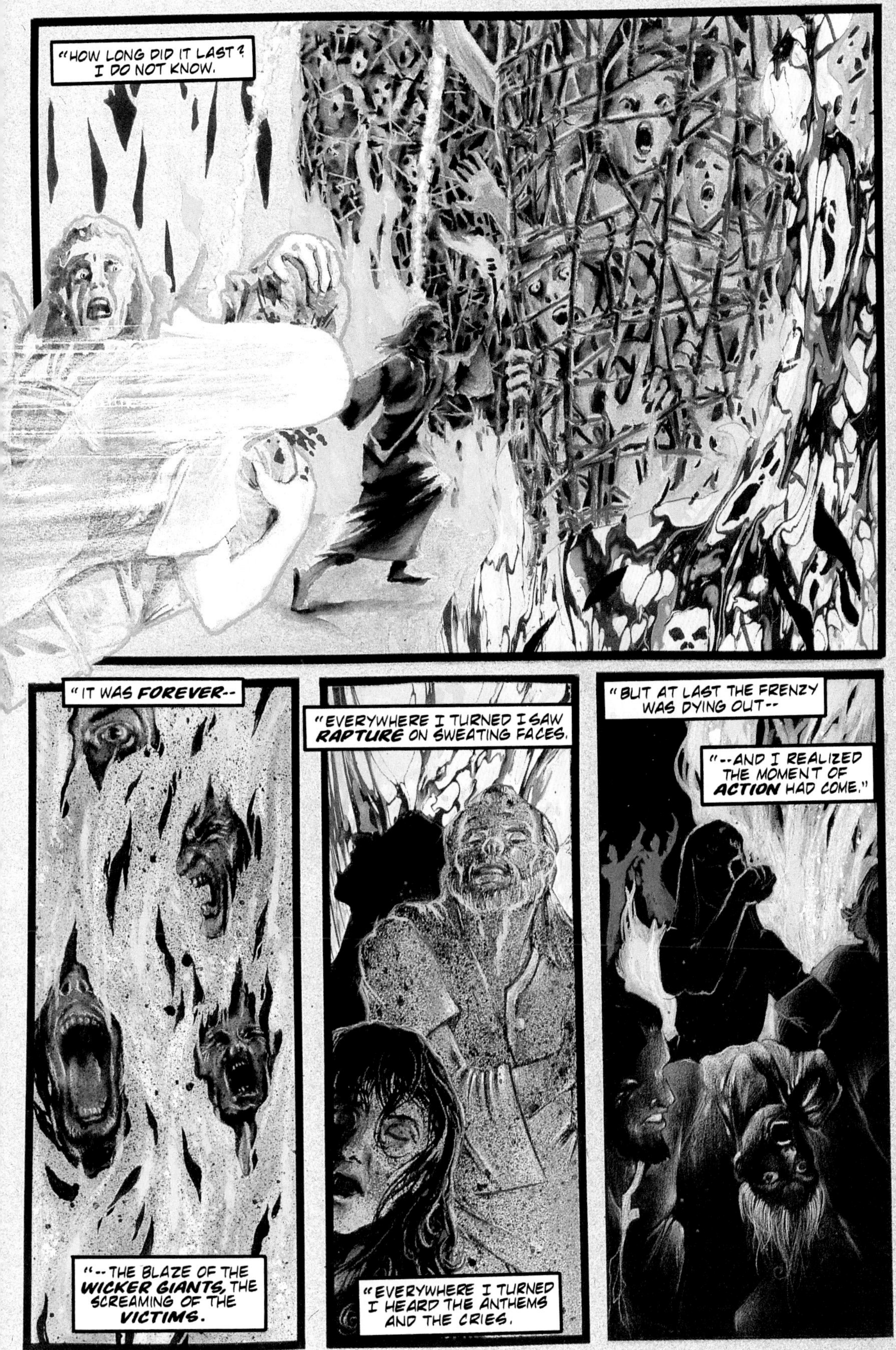
"HOW LONG DID IT LAST? I DO NOT KNOW.
"IT WAS FOREVER--
"--THE BLAZE OF THE WICKER GIANTS, THE SCREAMING OF THE VICTIMS.
"EVERYWHERE I TURNED I SAW RAPTURE ON SWEATING FACES.
"EVERYWHERE I TURNED I HEARD THE ANTHEMS AND THE CRIES.
"BUT AT LAST THE FRENZY WAS DYING OUT--
"--AND I REALIZED THE MOMENT OF ACTION HAD COME."

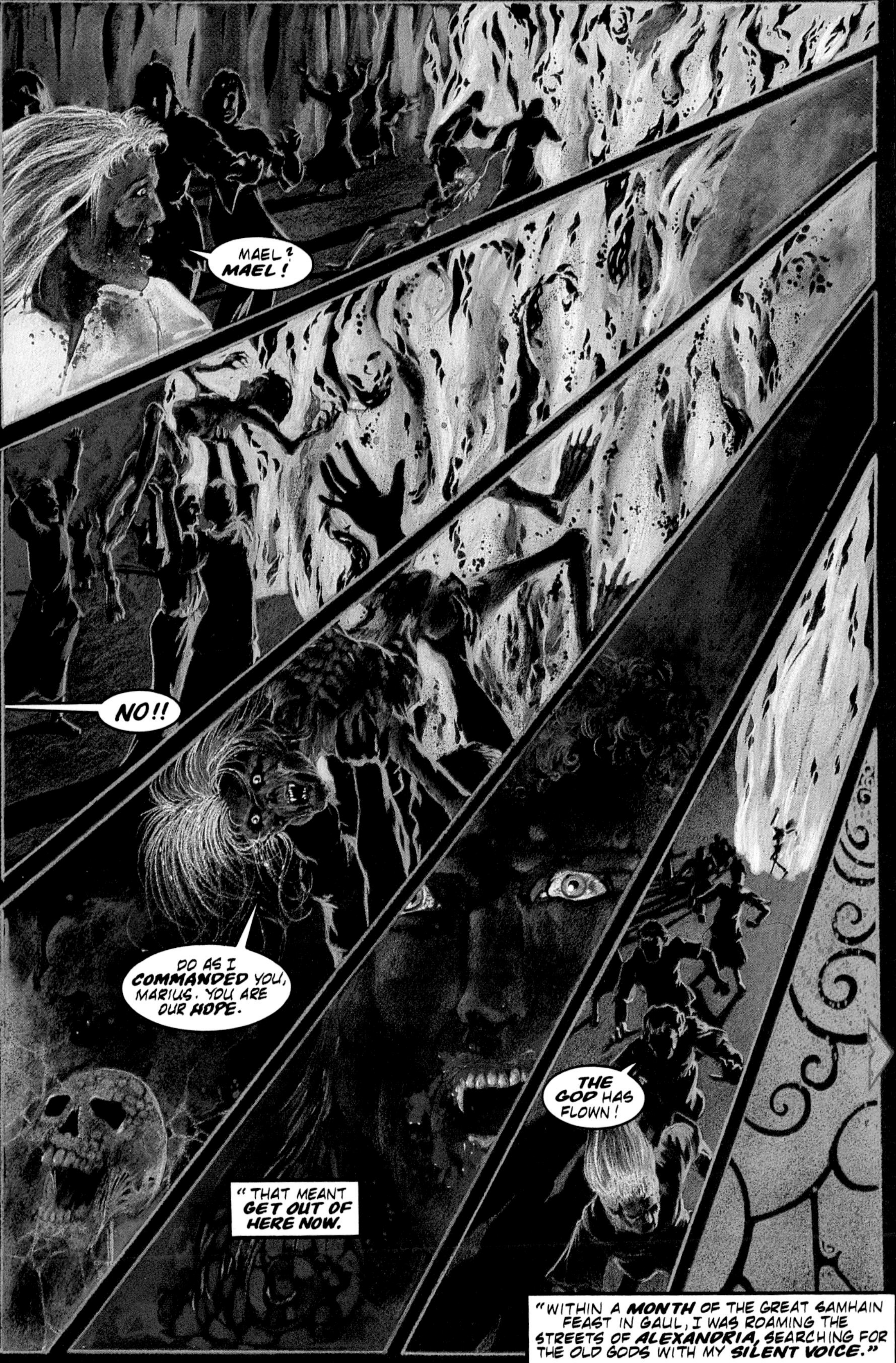

MAEL? MAEL!
NO!!
DO AS I COMMANDED YOU, MARIUS. YOU ARE OUR HOPE.
"THAT MEANT GET OUT OF HERE NOW.
THE GOD HAS FLOWN!
"WITHIN A MONTH OF THE GREAT SAMHAIN FEAST IN GAUL, I WAS ROAMING THE STREETS OF ALEXANDRIA, SEARCHING FOR THE OLD GODS WITH MY SILENT VOICE."

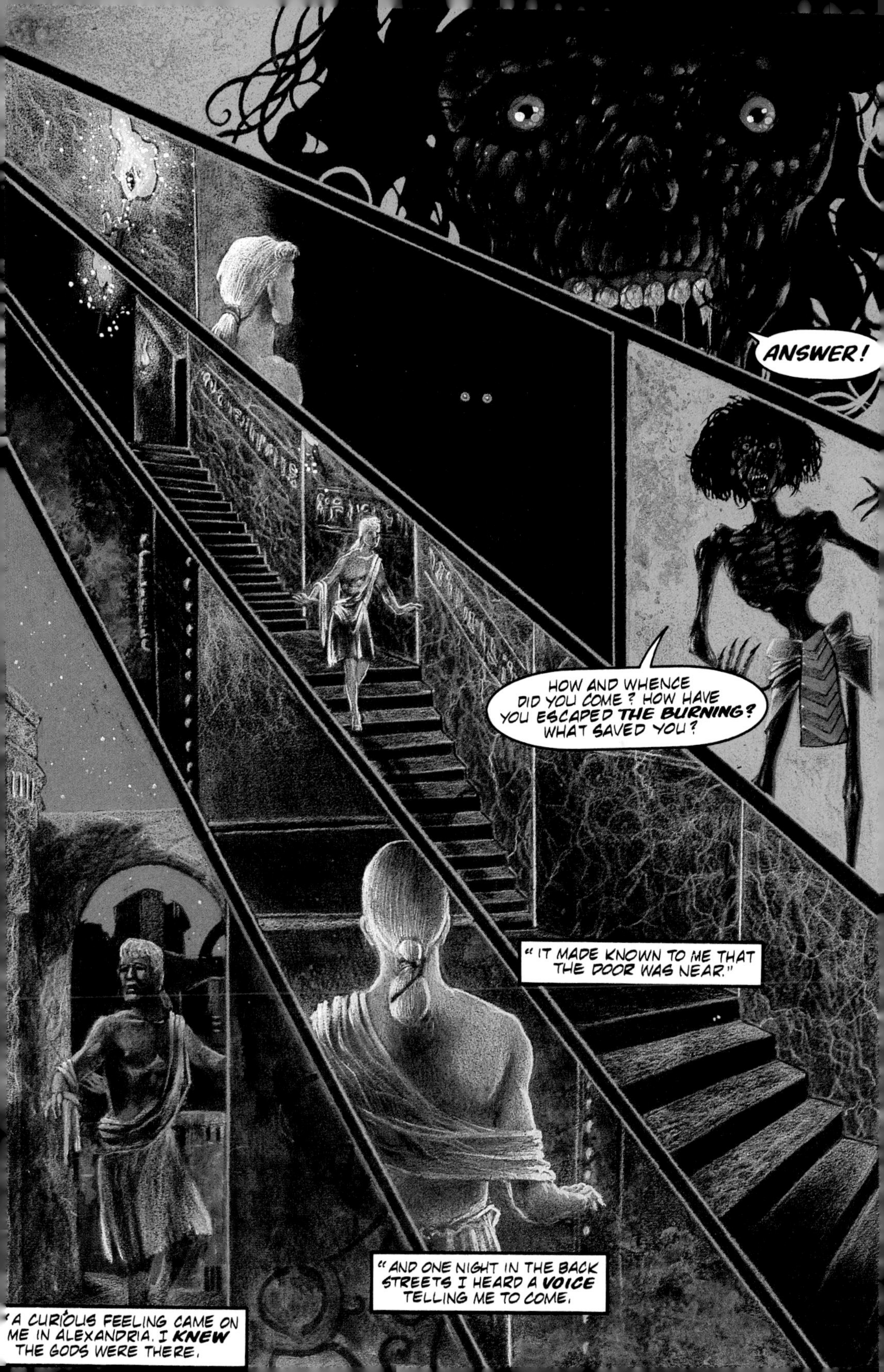
ANSWER!
HOW AND WHENCE DID YOU COME? HOW HAVE YOU ESCAPED THE BURNING? WHAT SAVED YOU?
"IT MADE KNOWN TO ME THAT THE DOOR WAS NEAR."
"AND ONE NIGHT IN THE BACK STREETS I HEARD A VOICE TELLING ME TO COME.
"A CURIOUS FEELING CAME ON ME IN ALEXANDRIA. I KNEW THE GODS WERE THERE.

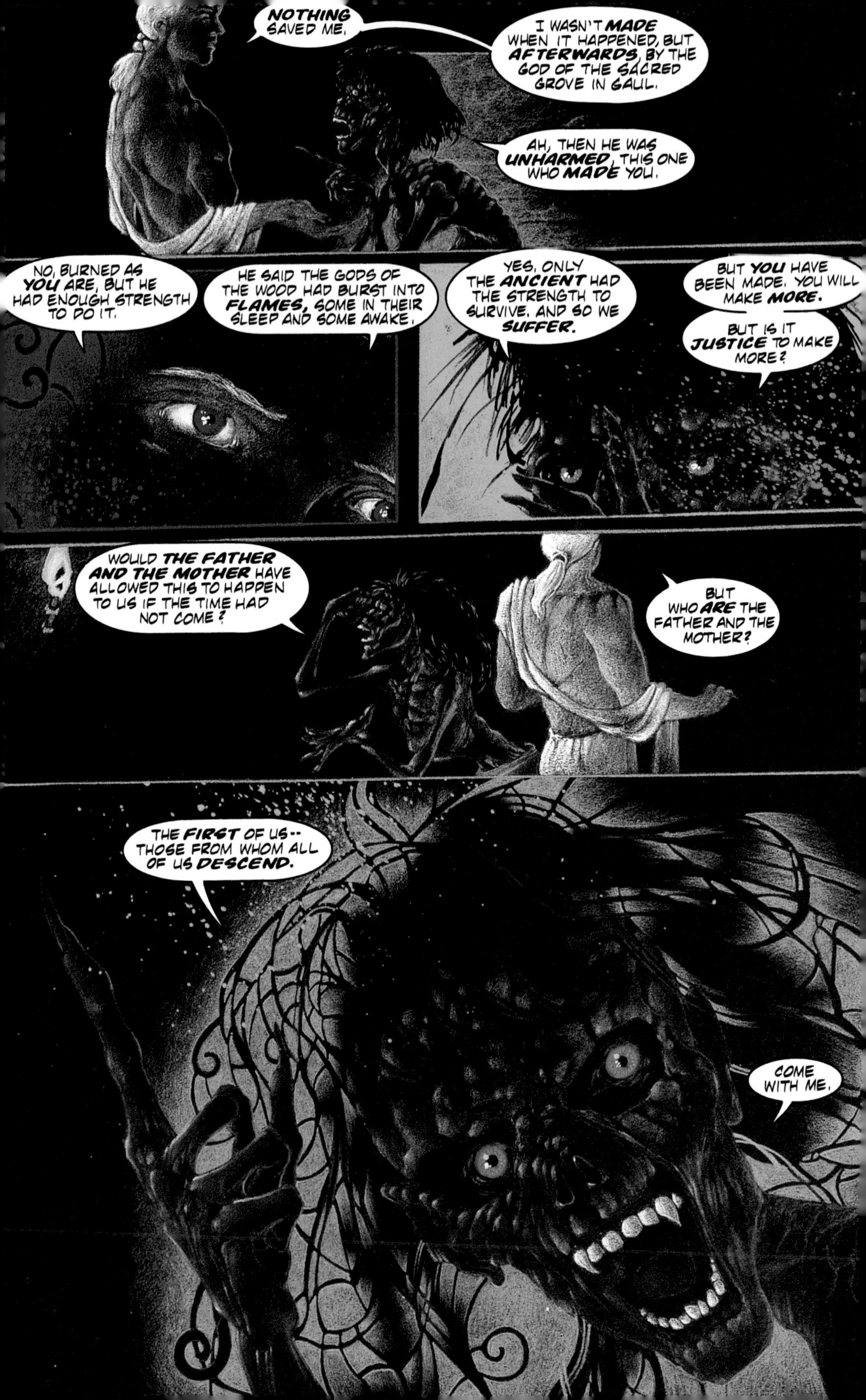
NOTHING SAVED ME.
I WASN'T MADE WHEN IT HAPPENED, BUT AFTERWARDS, BY THE GOD OF THE SACRED GROVE IN GAUL.
AH, THEN HE WAS UNHARMED, THIS ONE WHO MADE YOU.
NO, BURNED AS YOU ARE, BUT HE HAD ENOUGH STRENGTH TO DO IT.
HE SAID THE GODS OF THE WOOD HAD BURST INTO FLAMES, SOME IN THEIR SLEEP AND SOME AWAKE.
YES, ONLY THE ANCIENT HAD THE STRENGTH TO SURVIVE. AND SO WE SUFFER.
BUT YOU HAVE BEEN MADE. YOU WILL MAKE MORE.
BUT IS IT JUSTICE TO MAKE MORE?
WOULD THE FATHER AND THE MOTHER HAVE ALLOWED THIS TO HAPPEN TO US IF THE TIME HAD NOT COME?
BUT WHO ARE THE FATHER AND THE MOTHER?
THE FIRST OF US-- THOSE FROM WHOM ALL OF US DESCEND.
COME WITH ME.

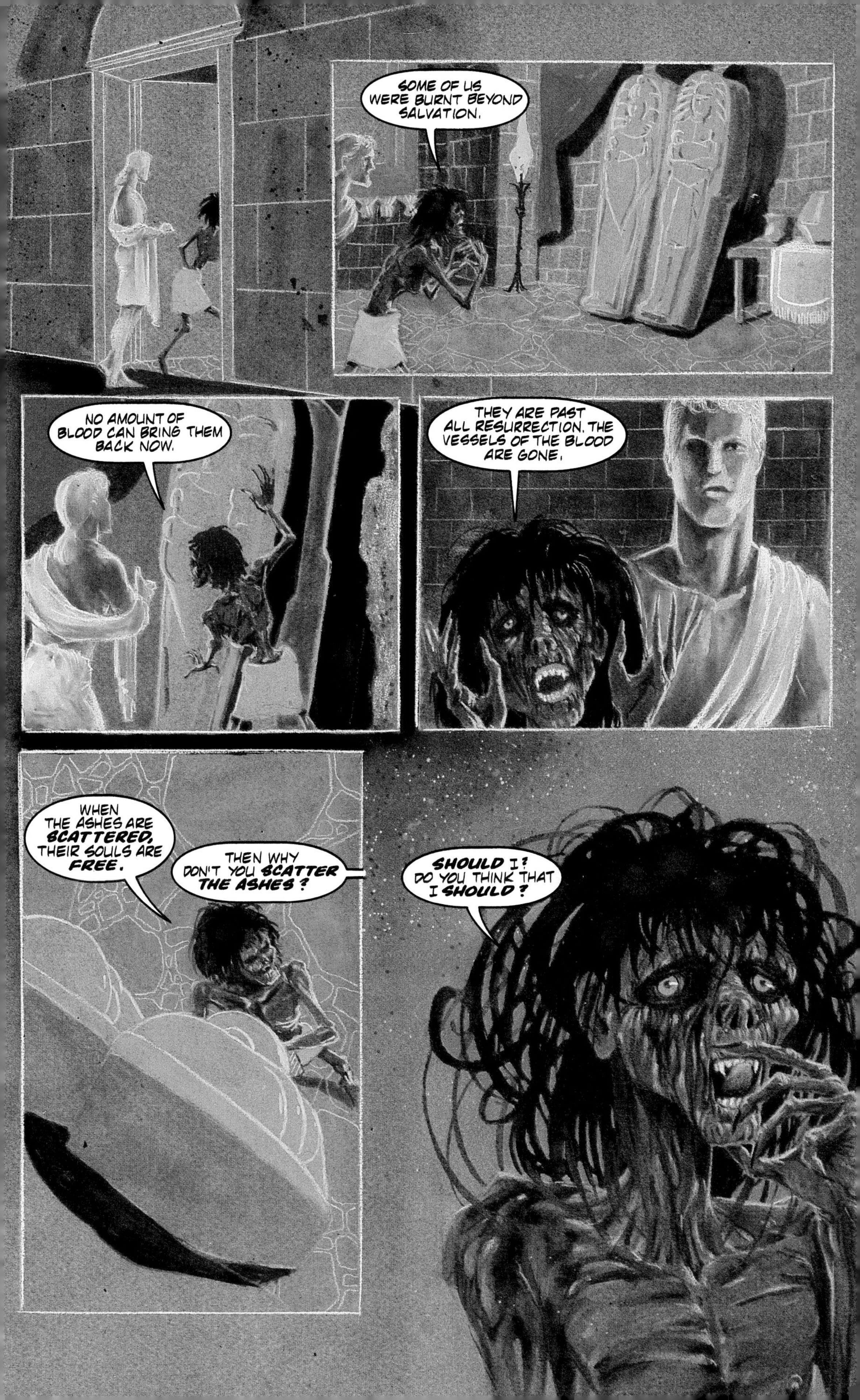
SOME OF US WERE BURNT BEYOND SALVATION.
NO AMOUNT OF BLOOD CAN BRING THEM BACK NOW.
THEY ARE PAST ALL RESURRECTION. THE VESSELS OF THE BLOOD ARE GONE.
WHEN THE ASHES ARE **SCATTERED,** THEIR SOULS ARE **FREE.**
THEN WHY DON'T YOU **SCATTER THE ASHES?**
SHOULD I? DO YOU THINK THAT I **SHOULD?**

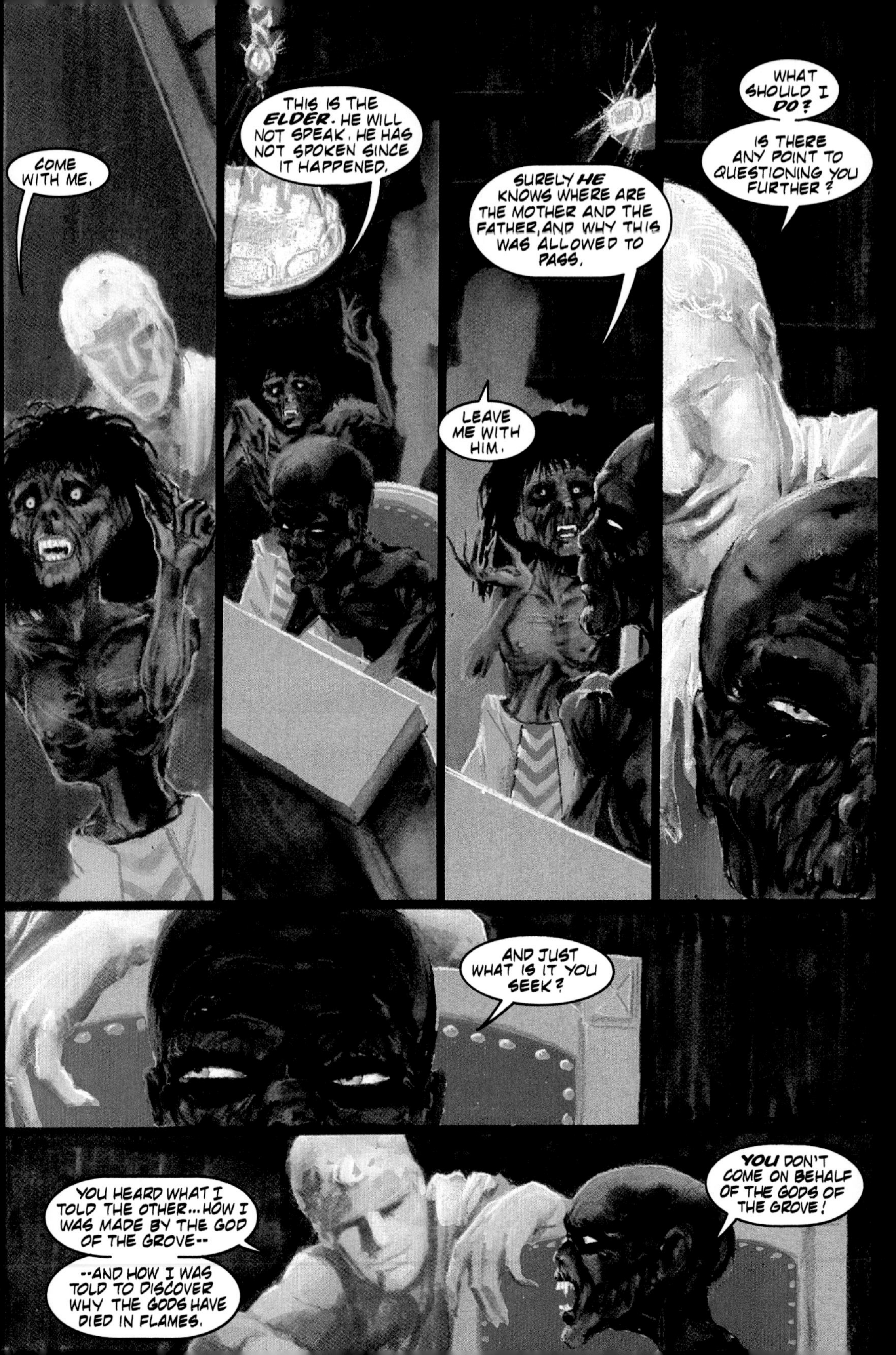
COME WITH ME.
THIS IS THE ELDER. HE WILL NOT SPEAK. HE HAS NOT SPOKEN SINCE IT HAPPENED.
SURELY HE KNOWS WHERE ARE THE MOTHER AND THE FATHER, AND WHY THIS WAS ALLOWED TO PASS.
LEAVE ME WITH HIM.
WHAT SHOULD I DO?
IS THERE ANY POINT TO QUESTIONING YOU FURTHER?
AND JUST WHAT IS IT YOU SEEK?
YOU HEARD WHAT I TOLD THE OTHER... HOW I WAS MADE BY THE GOD OF THE GROVE--
--AND HOW I WAS TOLD TO DISCOVER WHY THE GODS HAVE DIED IN FLAMES.
YOU DON'T COME ON BEHALF OF THE GODS OF THE GROVE!

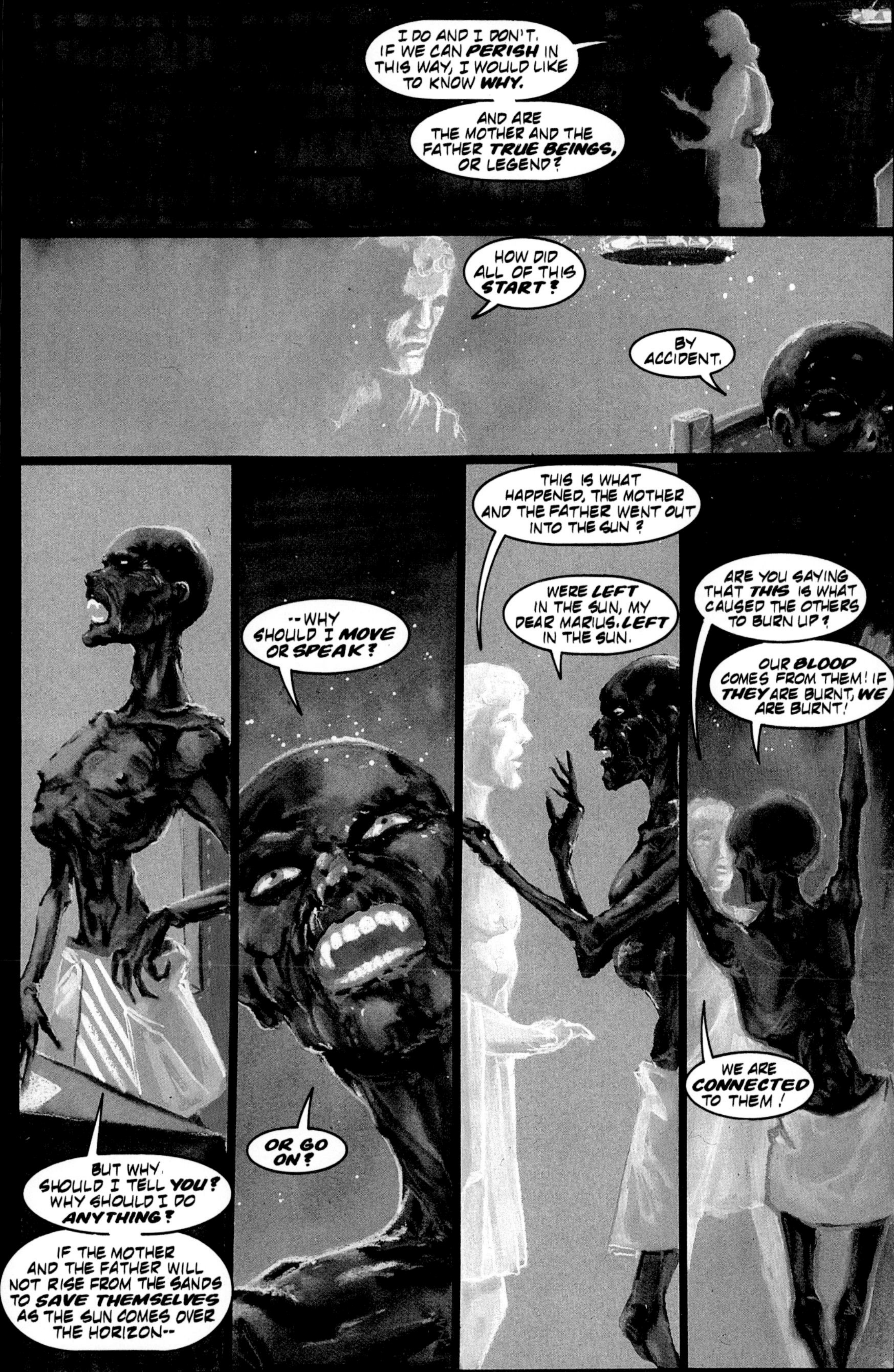
I DO AND I DON'T. IF WE CAN PERISH IN THIS WAY, I WOULD LIKE TO KNOW WHY.
AND ARE THE MOTHER AND THE FATHER TRUE BEINGS, OR LEGEND?
HOW DID ALL OF THIS START?
BY ACCIDENT.
BUT WHY. SHOULD I TELL YOU? WHY SHOULD I DO ANYTHING?
IF THE MOTHER AND THE FATHER WILL NOT RISE FROM THE SANDS TO SAVE THEMSELVES AS THE SUN COMES OVER THE HORIZON--
--WHY SHOULD I MOVE OR SPEAK?
OR GO ON?
THIS IS WHAT HAPPENED, THE MOTHER AND THE FATHER WENT OUT INTO THE SUN?
WERE LEFT IN THE SUN, MY DEAR MARIUS. LEFT IN THE SUN.
ARE YOU SAYING THAT THIS IS WHAT CAUSED THE OTHERS TO BURN UP?
OUR BLOOD COMES FROM THEM! IF THEY ARE BURNT, WE ARE BURNT!
WE ARE CONNECTED TO THEM!

WHO DID IT? WHO PUT THEM IN THE SUN?
THE ONE WHO KEPT THEM. HE COULDN'T ENDURE IT ANY LONGER.
HE LEFT THEM IN THE DESERT, AND THAT NIGHT WHEN HE OPENED HIS EYES AND FOUND HIMSELF A BURNT AND UNRECOGNIZABLE HORROR--
--HE SCREAMED AND SCREAMED.
YOU GOT THEM BACK UNDERGROUND.
YES.
AND THEY ARE BLACKENED AS YOU ARE...
NO. DARKENED TO A GOLDEN BRONZE. NO MORE THAN THAT.
WHERE ARE THEY?
WHY DO YOU WANT TO KNOW? WHY SHOULD I GIVE YOU THE SECRET?

WHERE ARE THEY?
WHY SHOULD I NOT SINK THEM INTO THE VERY DEPTHS OF THE SEA?
WHY SHOULD I NOT BURY THEM IN THE DEPTHS OF THE EARTH AND LET THEM LIE IN SILENCE THERE--
--NO MATTER WHAT THEY THINK AND FEEL?
TELL ME HOW THEY BECAME THE MOTHER AND THE FATHER.
WHY?
I WANT TO KNOW! I CAME HERE TO KNOW AND YOU MUST TELL ME!
ALL RIGHT, SO THAT YOU CAN UNDERSTAND THE FUTILITY OF IT--
--SO THAT YOU CAN UNDERSTAND THE SILENCE OF THE MOTHER AND THE FATHER--
--I WILL TELL.
BUT MARK MY WORDS, I MAY YET BRING US ALL DOWN. I MAY YET BURN THE MOTHER AND FATHER IN THE HEAT OF A KILN!
BUT WE WILL DISPENSE WITH LENGTHY INITIATIONS AND HIGH BLOWN LANGUAGE.

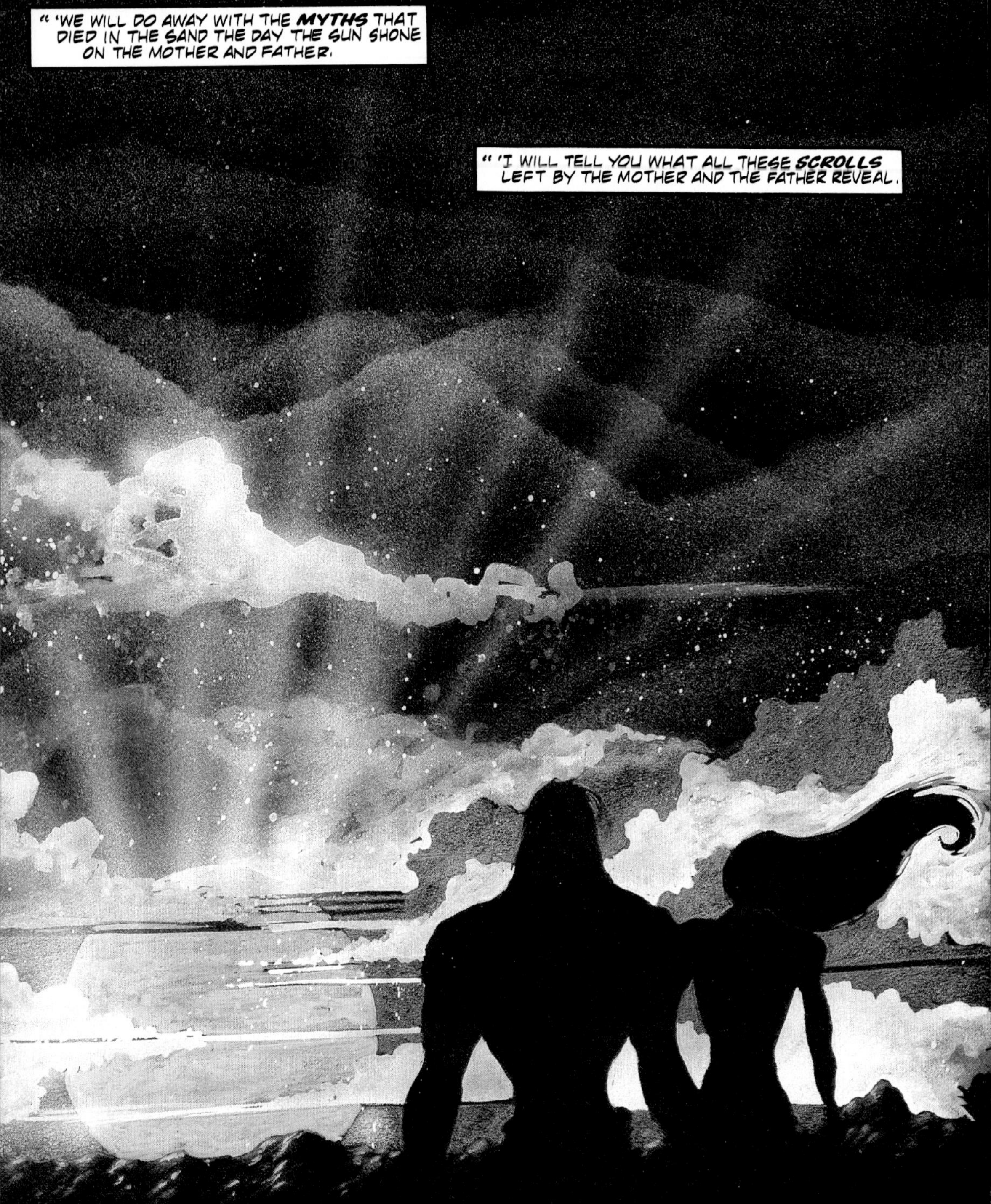
" 'WE WILL DO AWAY WITH THE MYTHS THAT DIED IN THE SAND THE DAY THE SUN SHONE ON THE MOTHER AND FATHER.
" 'I WILL TELL YOU WHAT ALL THESE SCROLLS LEFT BY THE MOTHER AND THE FATHER REVEAL.

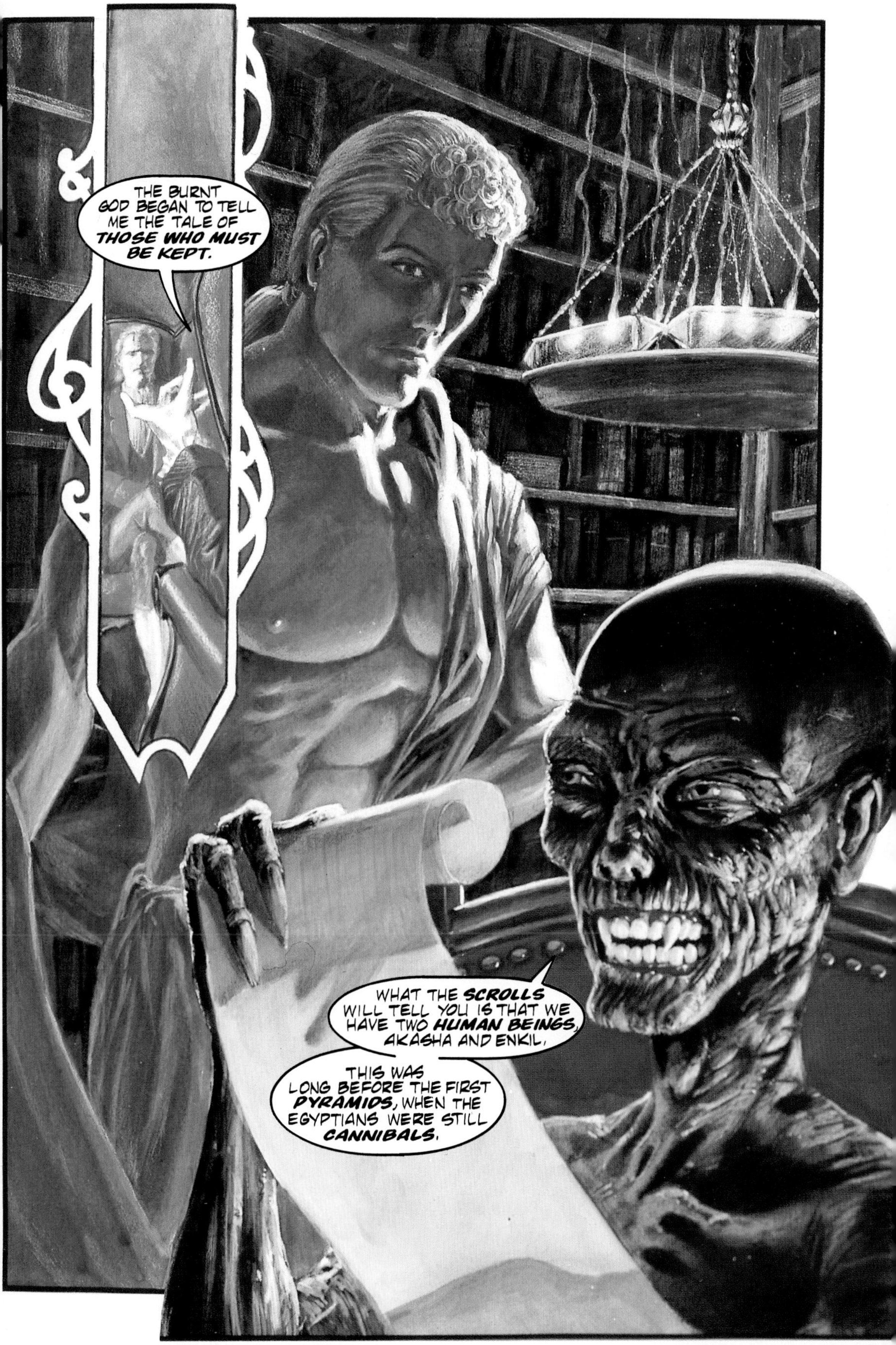
THE BURNT GOD BEGAN TO TELL ME THE TALE OF **THOSE WHO MUST BE KEPT.**
WHAT THE **SCROLLS** WILL TELL YOU IS THAT WE HAVE TWO **HUMAN BEINGS,** AKASHA AND ENKIL.
THIS WAS LONG BEFORE THE FIRST **PYRAMIDS,** WHEN THE EGYPTIANS WERE STILL **CANNIBALS.**

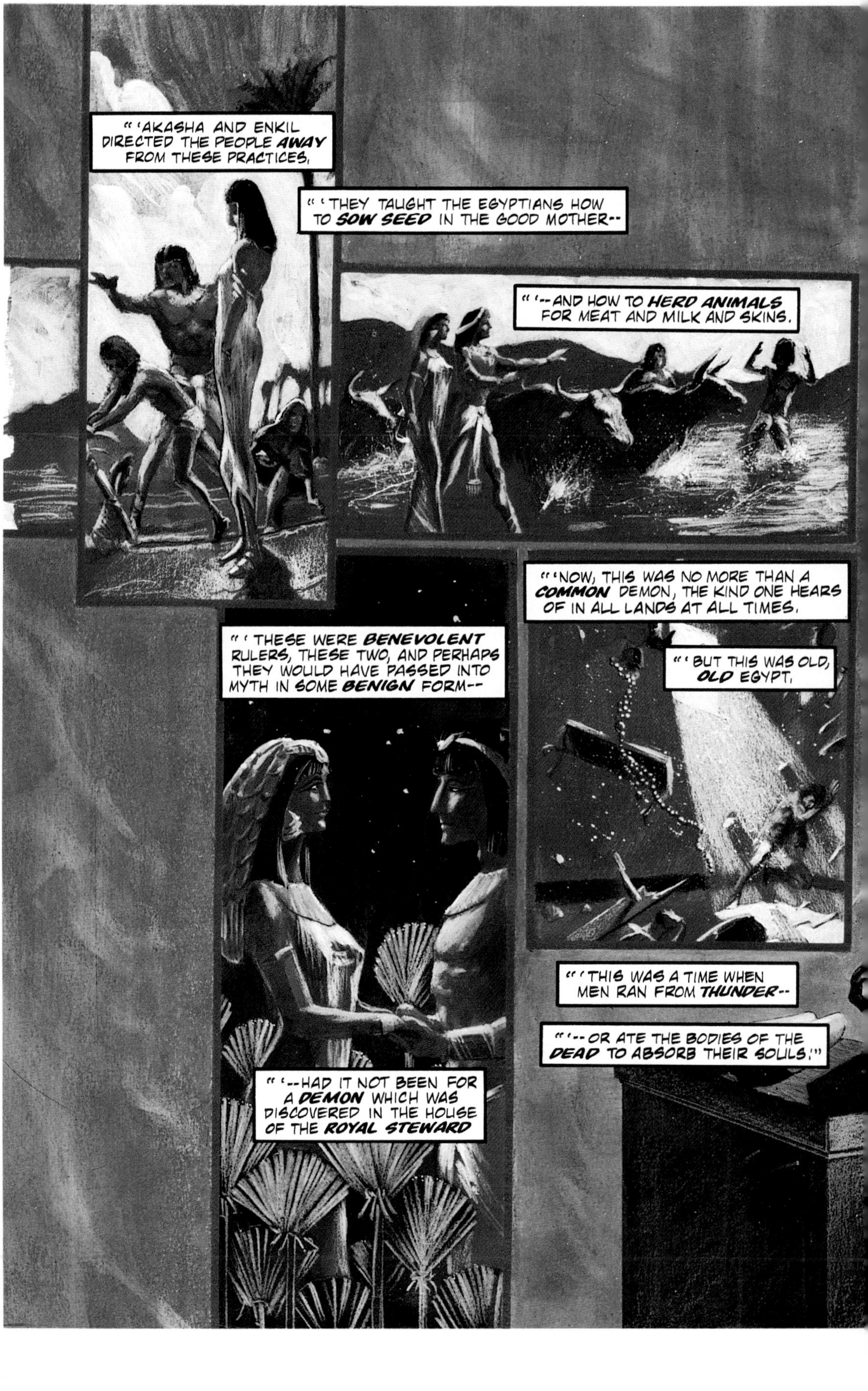
"'AKASHA AND ENKIL DIRECTED THE PEOPLE AWAY FROM THESE PRACTICES.
"'THEY TAUGHT THE EGYPTIANS HOW TO SOW SEED IN THE GOOD MOTHER--
"'--AND HOW TO HERD ANIMALS FOR MEAT AND MILK AND SKINS.
"'THESE WERE BENEVOLENT RULERS, THESE TWO, AND PERHAPS THEY WOULD HAVE PASSED INTO MYTH IN SOME BENIGN FORM--
"'--HAD IT NOT BEEN FOR A DEMON WHICH WAS DISCOVERED IN THE HOUSE OF THE ROYAL STEWARD
"'NOW, THIS WAS NO MORE THAN A COMMON DEMON, THE KIND ONE HEARS OF IN ALL LANDS AT ALL TIMES.
"'BUT THIS WAS OLD, OLD EGYPT.
"'THIS WAS A TIME WHEN MEN RAN FROM THUNDER--
"'--OR ATE THE BODIES OF THE DEAD TO ABSORB THEIR SOULS.'"

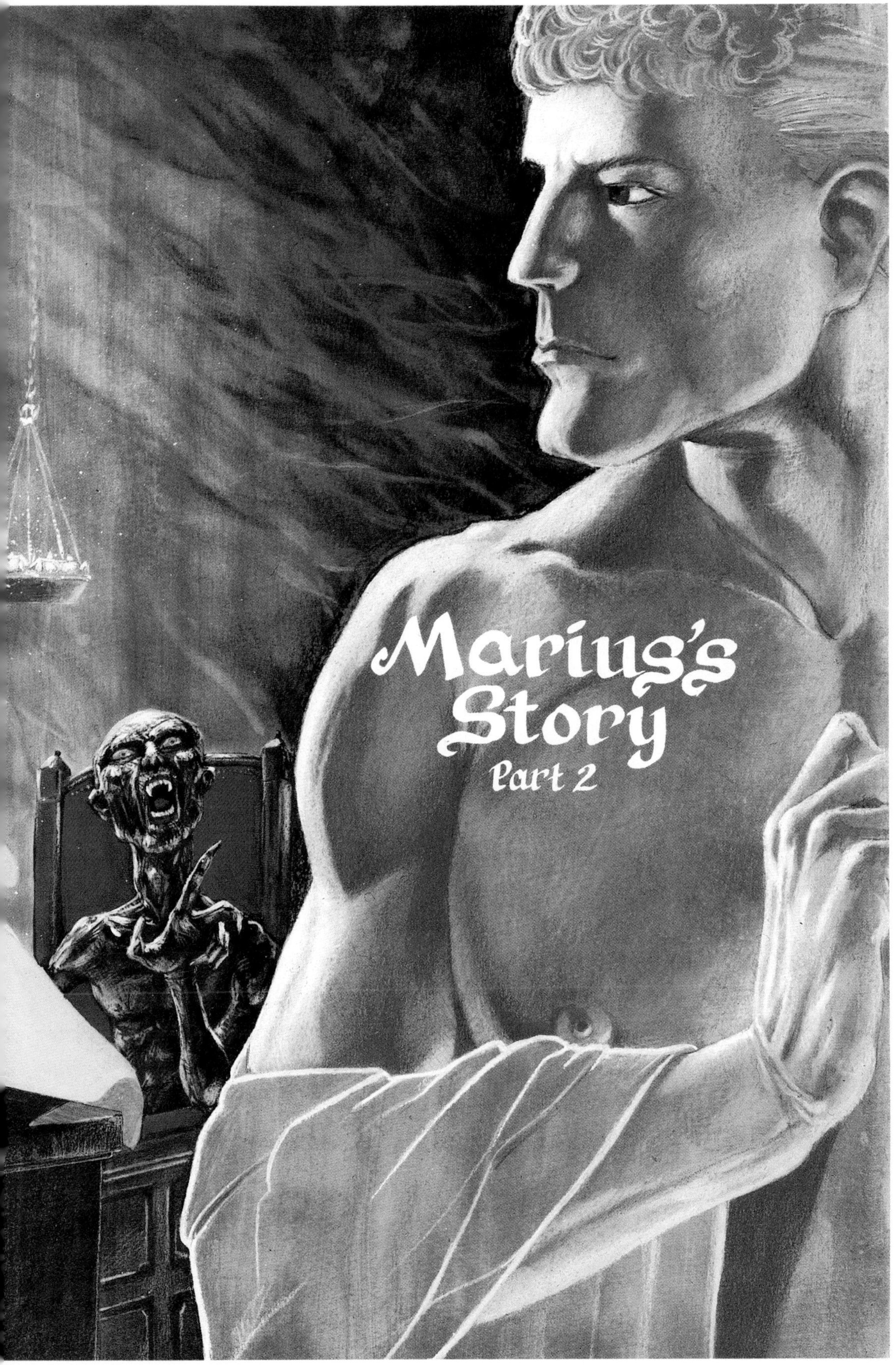
Marius's Story
Part 2

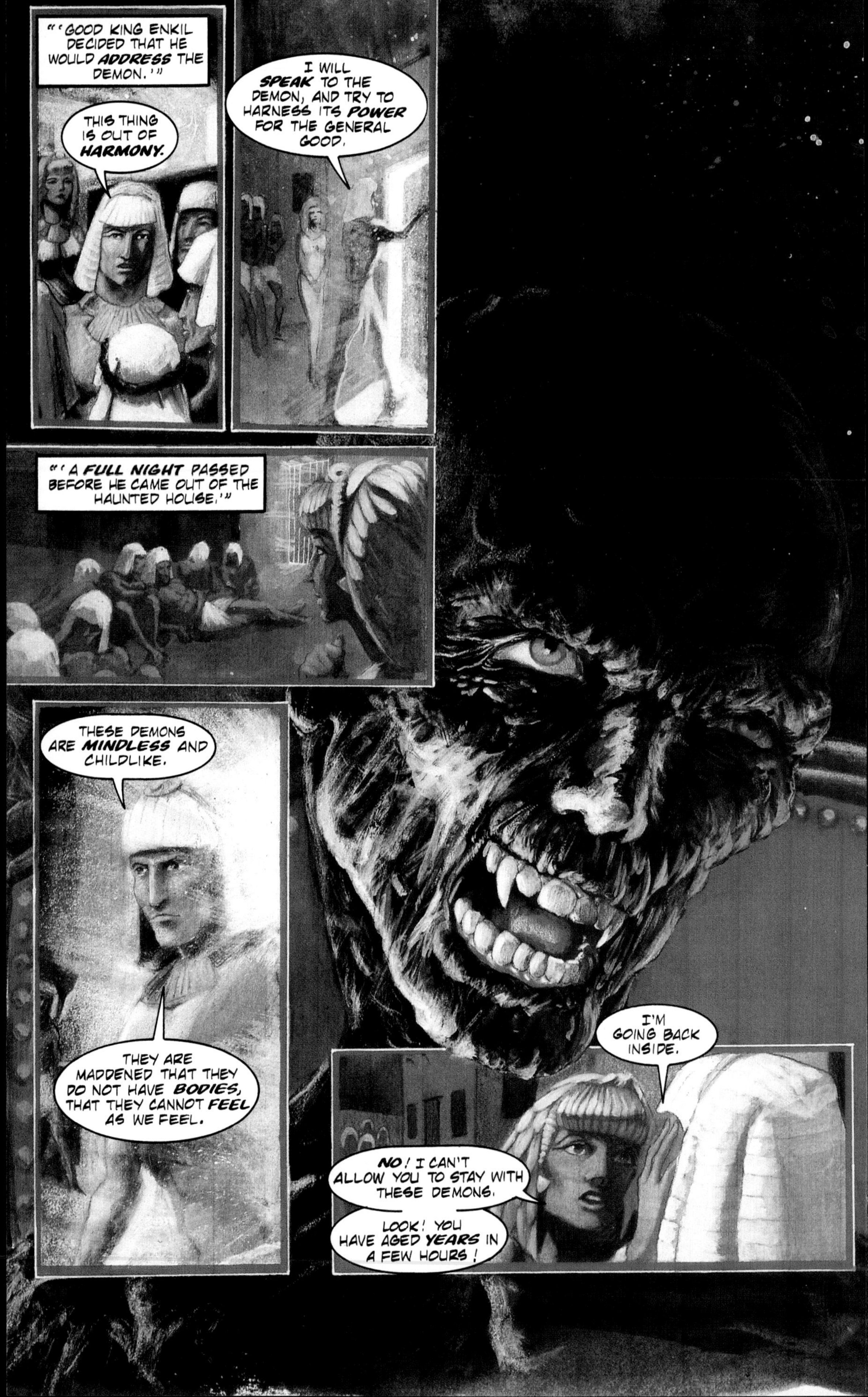
"'GOOD KING ENKIL DECIDED THAT HE WOULD ADDRESS THE DEMON.'"
THIS THING IS OUT OF HARMONY.
I WILL SPEAK TO THE DEMON, AND TRY TO HARNESS ITS POWER FOR THE GENERAL GOOD.
"'A FULL NIGHT PASSED BEFORE HE CAME OUT OF THE HAUNTED HOUSE.'"
THESE DEMONS ARE MINDLESS AND CHILDLIKE.
THEY ARE MADDENED THAT THEY DO NOT HAVE BODIES, THAT THEY CANNOT FEEL AS WE FEEL.
I'M GOING BACK INSIDE.
NO! I CAN'T ALLOW YOU TO STAY WITH THESE DEMONS.
LOOK! YOU HAVE AGED YEARS IN A FEW HOURS!

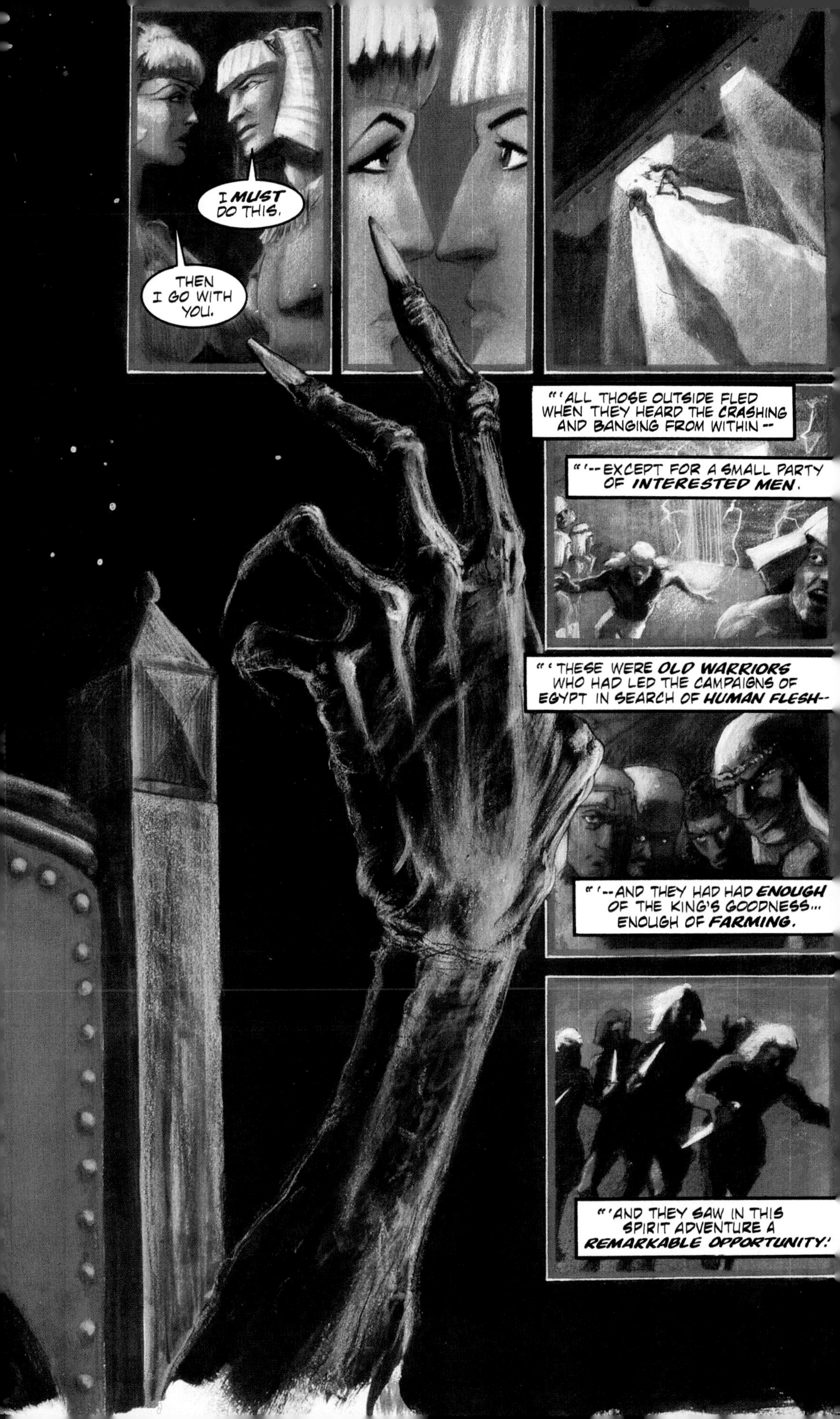
I MUST DO THIS.
THEN I GO WITH YOU.
"'ALL THOSE OUTSIDE FLED WHEN THEY HEARD THE CRASHING AND BANGING FROM WITHIN--
"'--EXCEPT FOR A SMALL PARTY OF INTERESTED MEN.
"'THESE WERE OLD WARRIORS WHO HAD LED THE CAMPAIGNS OF EGYPT IN SEARCH OF HUMAN FLESH--
"'--AND THEY HAD HAD ENOUGH OF THE KING'S GOODNESS... ENOUGH OF FARMING.
"'AND THEY SAW IN THIS SPIRIT ADVENTURE A REMARKABLE OPPORTUNITY.'

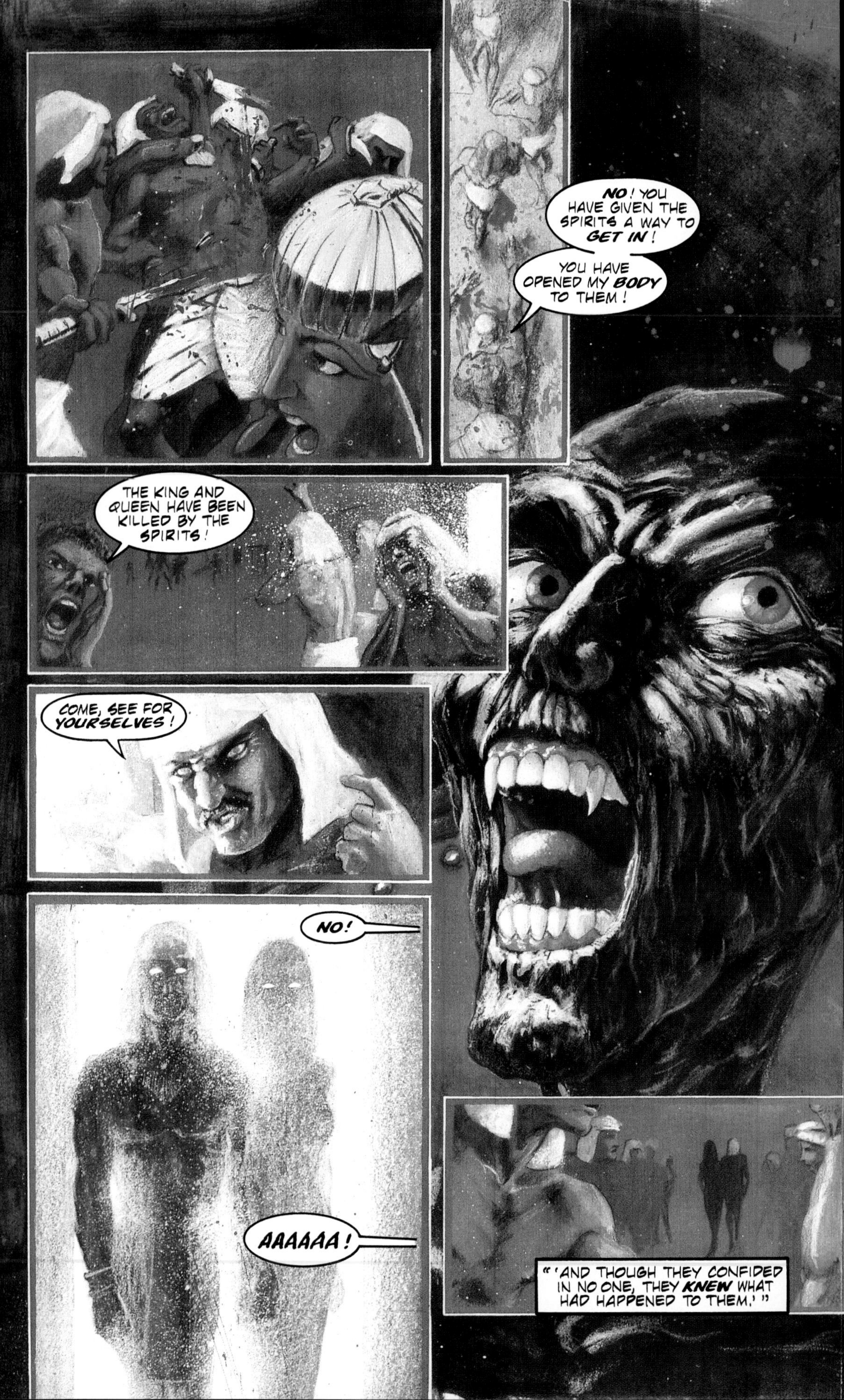
NO! YOU HAVE GIVEN THE SPIRITS A WAY TO GET IN!
YOU HAVE OPENED MY BODY TO THEM!
THE KING AND QUEEN HAVE BEEN KILLED BY THE SPIRITS!
COME, SEE FOR YOURSELVES!
NO!
AAAAAA!
"'AND THOUGH THEY CONFIDED IN NO ONE, THEY KNEW WHAT HAD HAPPENED TO THEM.'"

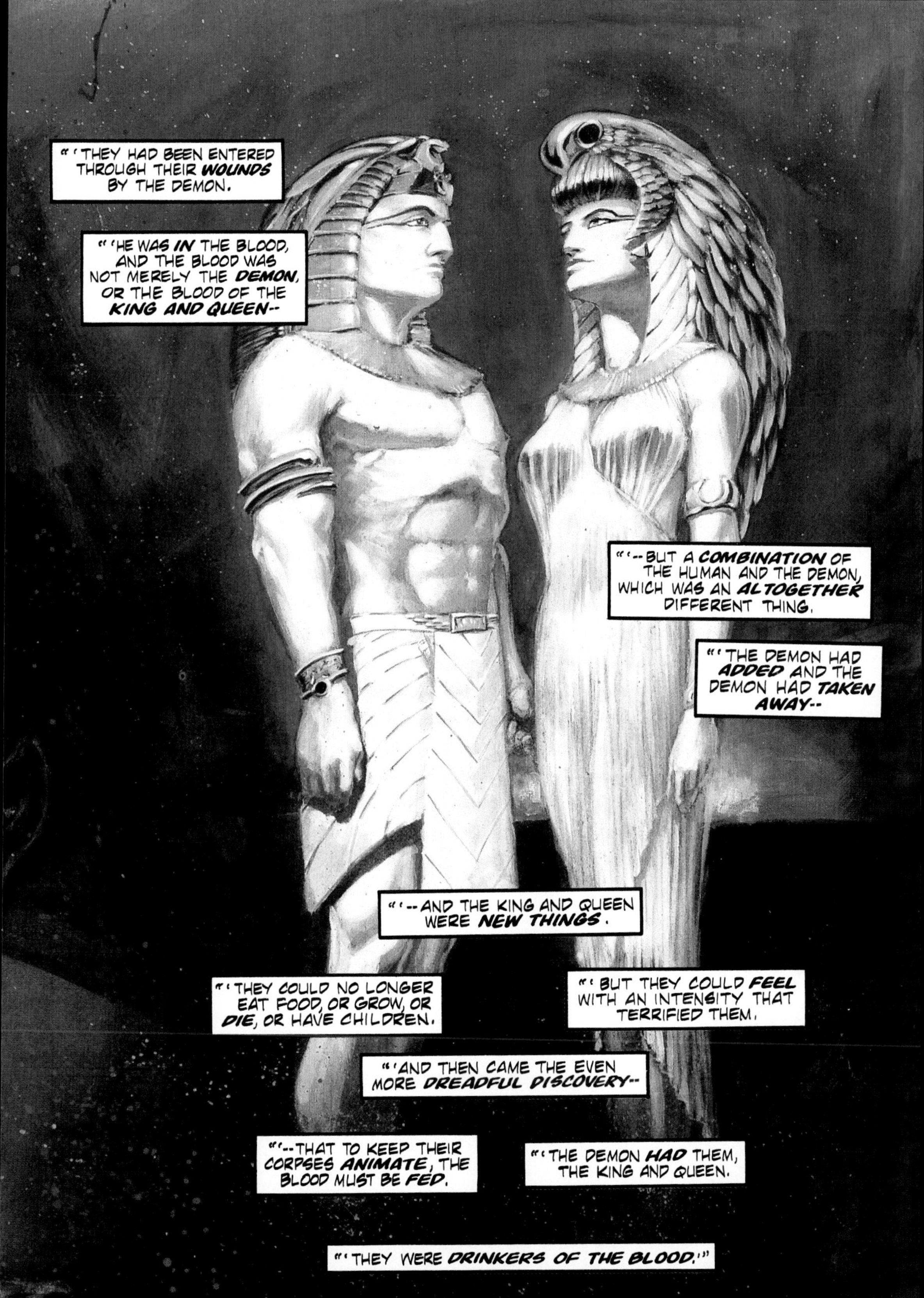
"'THEY HAD BEEN ENTERED THROUGH THEIR WOUNDS BY THE DEMON.
"'HE WAS IN THE BLOOD, AND THE BLOOD WAS NOT MERELY THE DEMON, OR THE BLOOD OF THE KING AND QUEEN--
"'--BUT A COMBINATION OF THE HUMAN AND THE DEMON, WHICH WAS AN ALTOGETHER DIFFERENT THING.
"'THE DEMON HAD ADDED AND THE DEMON HAD TAKEN AWAY--
"'--AND THE KING AND QUEEN WERE NEW THINGS.
"'THEY COULD NO LONGER EAT FOOD, OR GROW, OR DIE, OR HAVE CHILDREN.
"'BUT THEY COULD FEEL WITH AN INTENSITY THAT TERRIFIED THEM.
"'AND THEN CAME THE EVEN MORE DREADFUL DISCOVERY--
"'--THAT TO KEEP THEIR CORPSES ANIMATE, THE BLOOD MUST BE FED.
"'THE DEMON HAD THEM, THE KING AND QUEEN.
"'THEY WERE DRINKERS OF THE BLOOD.'"

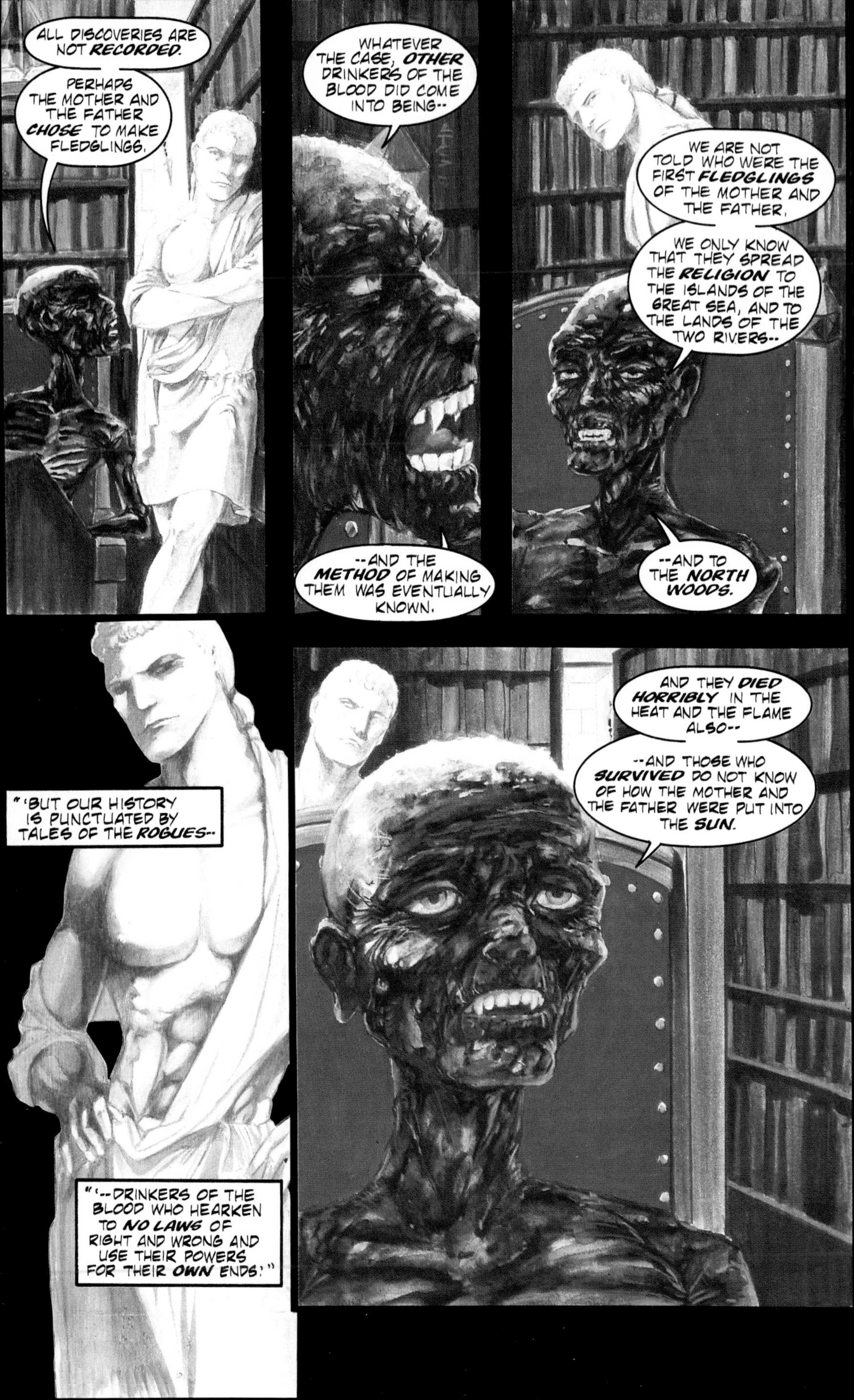
ALL DISCOVERIES ARE NOT RECORDED.
PERHAPS THE MOTHER AND THE FATHER CHOSE TO MAKE FLEDGLINGS.
WHATEVER THE CASE, OTHER DRINKERS OF THE BLOOD DID COME INTO BEING--
--AND THE METHOD OF MAKING THEM WAS EVENTUALLY KNOWN.
WE ARE NOT TOLD WHO WERE THE FIRST FLEDGLINGS OF THE MOTHER AND THE FATHER.
WE ONLY KNOW THAT THEY SPREAD THE RELIGION TO THE ISLANDS OF THE GREAT SEA, AND TO THE LANDS OF THE TWO RIVERS--
--AND TO THE NORTH WOODS.
"'BUT OUR HISTORY IS PUNCTUATED BY TALES OF THE ROGUES--
"'--DRINKERS OF THE BLOOD WHO HEARKEN TO NO LAWS OF RIGHT AND WRONG AND USE THEIR POWERS FOR THEIR OWN ENDS.'"
AND THEY DIED HORRIBLY IN THE HEAT AND THE FLAME ALSO--
--AND THOSE WHO SURVIVED DO NOT KNOW OF HOW THE MOTHER AND THE FATHER WERE PUT INTO THE SUN.

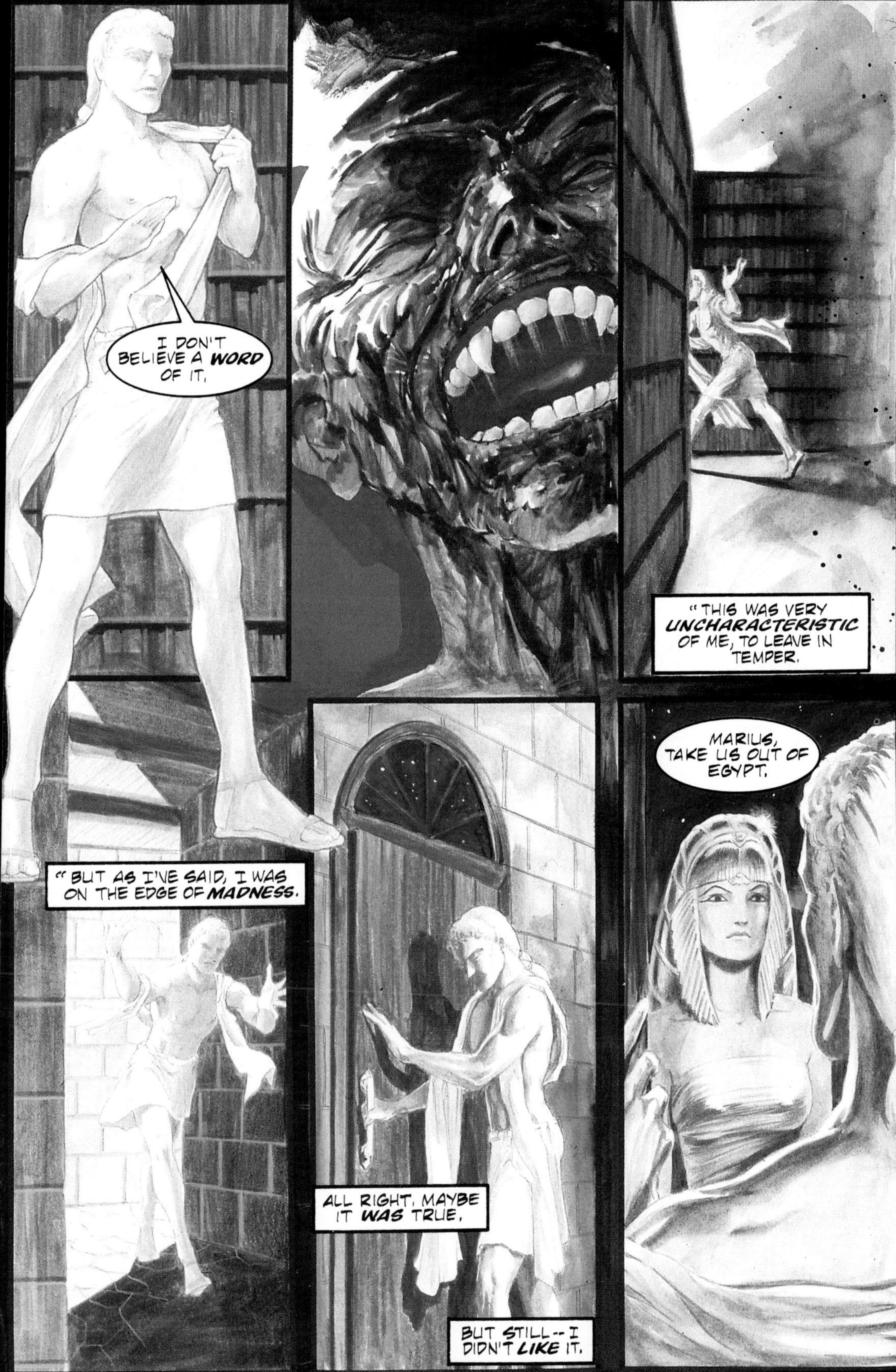
I DON'T BELIEVE A WORD OF IT.
"THIS WAS VERY UNCHARACTERISTIC OF ME, TO LEAVE IN TEMPER.
"BUT AS I'VE SAID, I WAS ON THE EDGE OF MADNESS.
ALL RIGHT, MAYBE IT WAS TRUE.
BUT STILL -- I DIDN'T LIKE IT.
MARIUS, TAKE US OUT OF EGYPT.

"AKASHA HAD SILENTLY *SPOKEN* TO ME!

" I WAS *DELIRIOUS*, BUT I KNEW THAT IF I WENT OUT OF THE CITY AND INTO THE SANDS I COULD *FIND* HER.

"SHE WAS *LEADING* ME TO WHERE SHE WAS.

" IN THE HOUR THAT FOLLOWED, I WAS TO REMEMBER THE *STRENGTH* AND THE SPEED I'D KNOWN IN THE FORESTS OF GAUL.

" I WENT OUT FROM THE CITY TO WHERE THE *STARS* PROVIDED THE ONLY LIGHT.

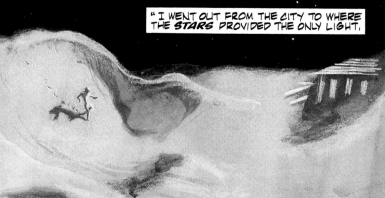

" IT WOULD HAVE TAKEN A BAND OF MORTALS *SEVERAL HOURS* TO DISCOVER THE TRAP DOOR--

"--BUT I FOUND IT *QUICKLY*...

"...AND I WAS ABLE TO *LIFT* IT, WHICH MORTALS *COULDN'T HAVE DONE*."

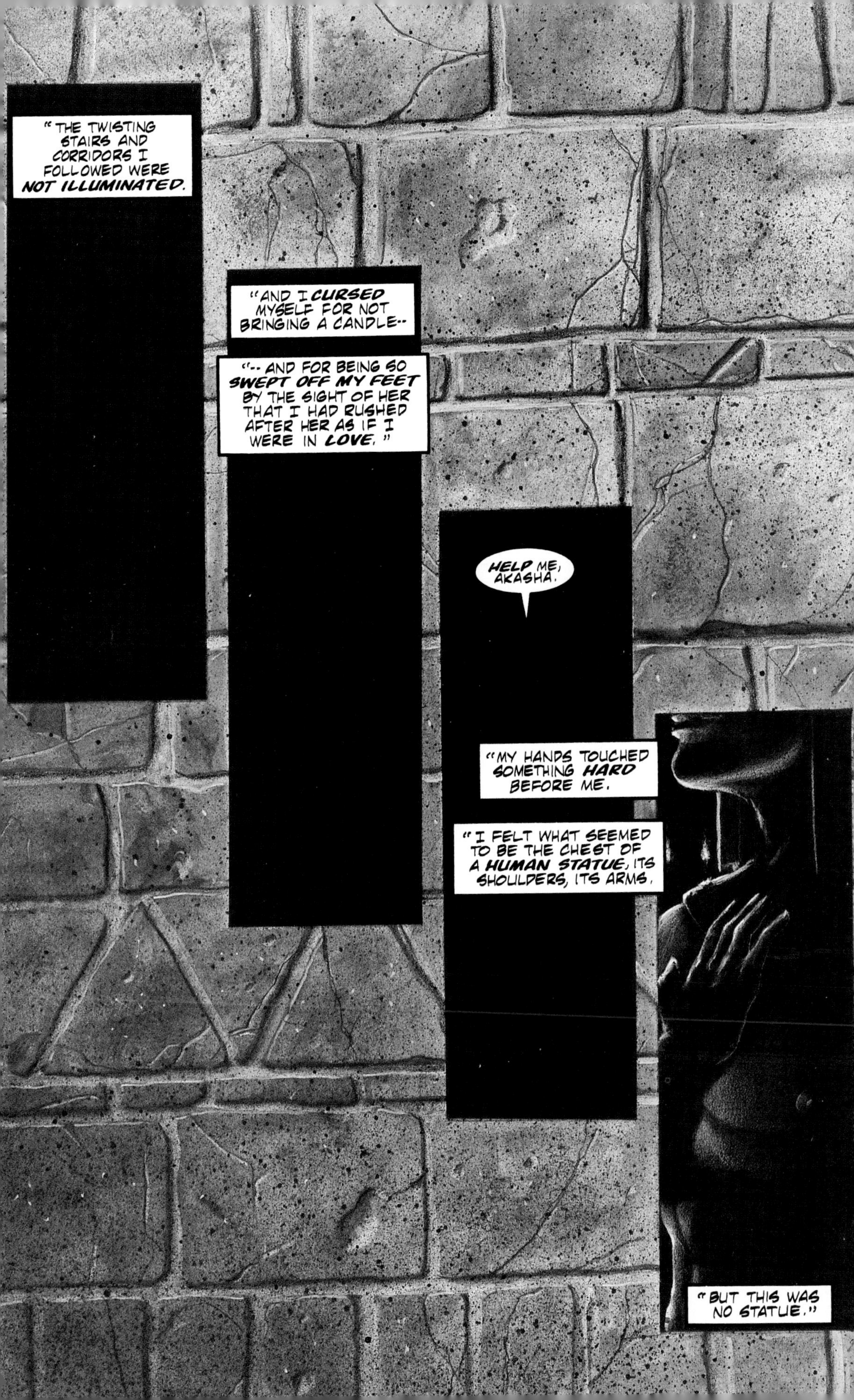
"THE TWISTING STAIRS AND CORRIDORS I FOLLOWED WERE NOT ILLUMINATED.
"AND I CURSED MYSELF FOR NOT BRINGING A CANDLE--
"-- AND FOR BEING SO SWEPT OFF MY FEET BY THE SIGHT OF HER THAT I HAD RUSHED AFTER HER AS IF I WERE IN LOVE."
HELP ME, AKASHA.
"MY HANDS TOUCHED SOMETHING HARD BEFORE ME.
"I FELT WHAT SEEMED TO BE THE CHEST OF A HUMAN STATUE, ITS SHOULDERS, ITS ARMS.
"BUT THIS WAS NO STATUE."

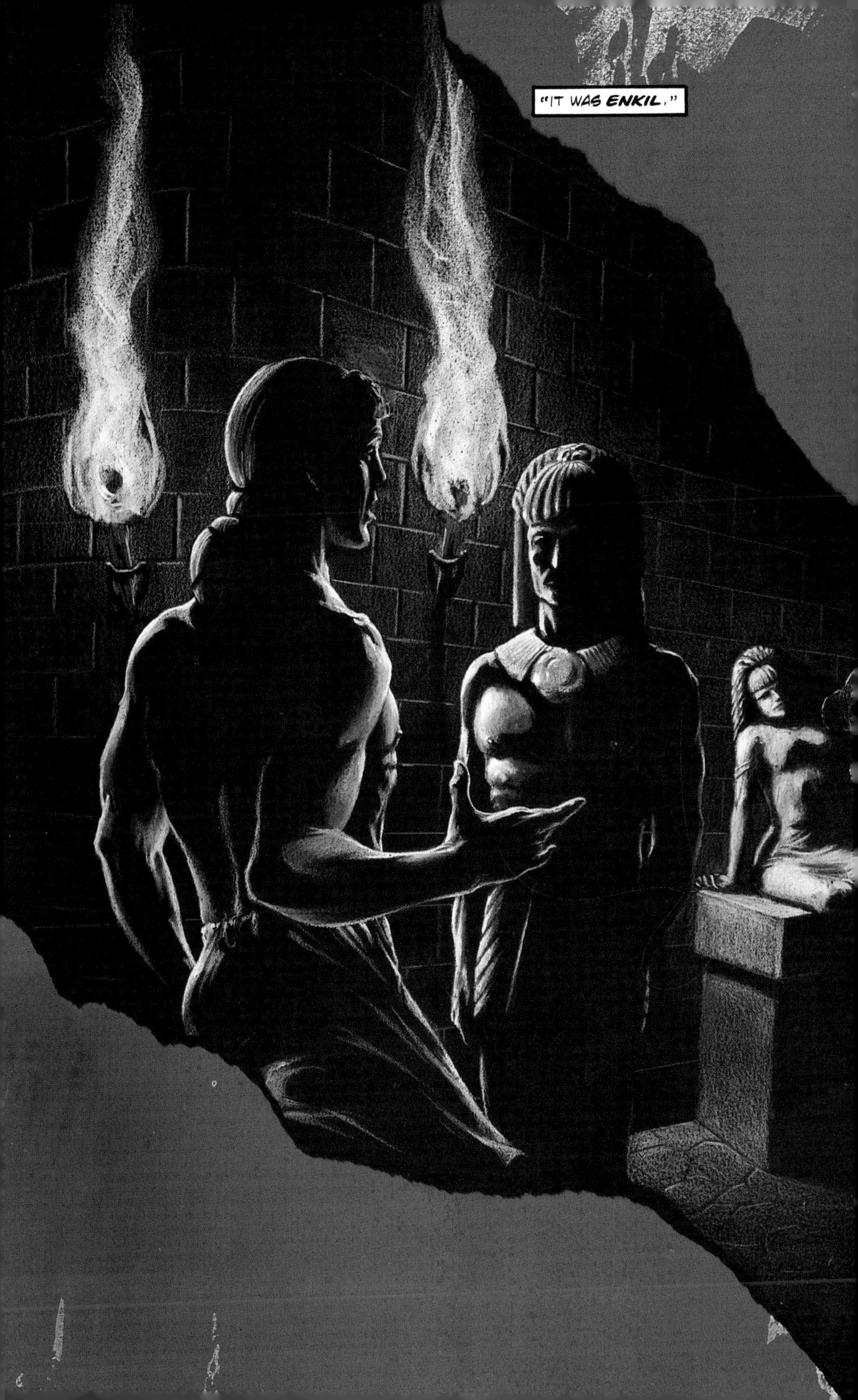
"IT WAS ENKIL."

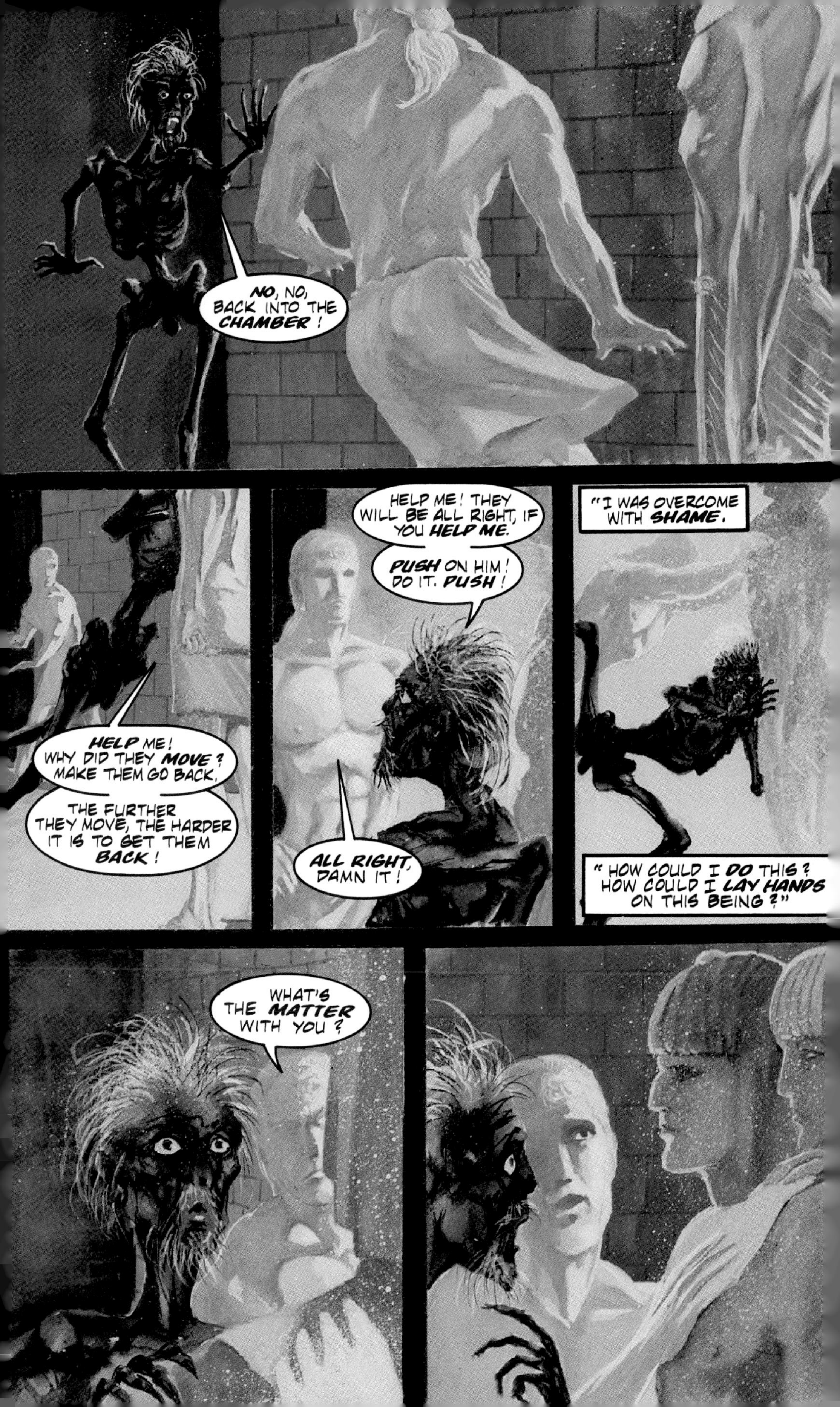
NO, NO, BACK INTO THE CHAMBER!
HELP ME! WHY DID THEY MOVE? MAKE THEM GO BACK.
THE FURTHER THEY MOVE, THE HARDER IT IS TO GET THEM BACK!
HELP ME! THEY WILL BE ALL RIGHT, IF YOU HELP ME.
PUSH ON HIM! DO IT. PUSH!
ALL RIGHT, DAMN IT!
"I WAS OVERCOME WITH SHAME.
"HOW COULD I DO THIS? HOW COULD I LAY HANDS ON THIS BEING?"
WHAT'S THE MATTER WITH YOU?

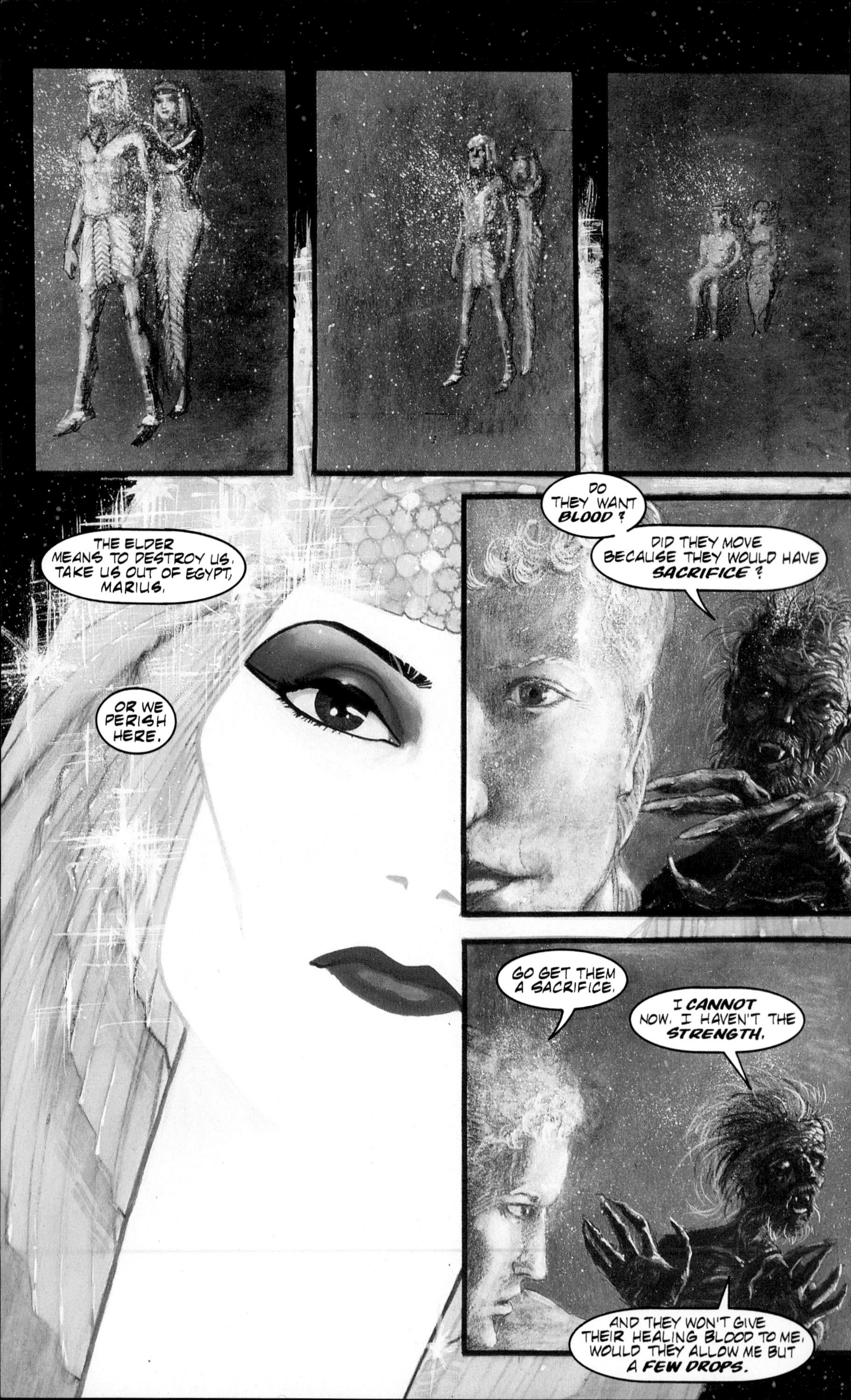
THE ELDER MEANS TO DESTROY US, TAKE US OUT OF EGYPT, MARIUS.
OR WE PERISH HERE.
DO THEY WANT BLOOD?
DID THEY MOVE BECAUSE THEY WOULD HAVE SACRIFICE?
GO GET THEM A SACRIFICE.
I CANNOT NOW. I HAVEN'T THE STRENGTH.
AND THEY WON'T GIVE THEIR HEALING BLOOD TO ME, WOULD THEY ALLOW ME BUT A FEW DROPS.

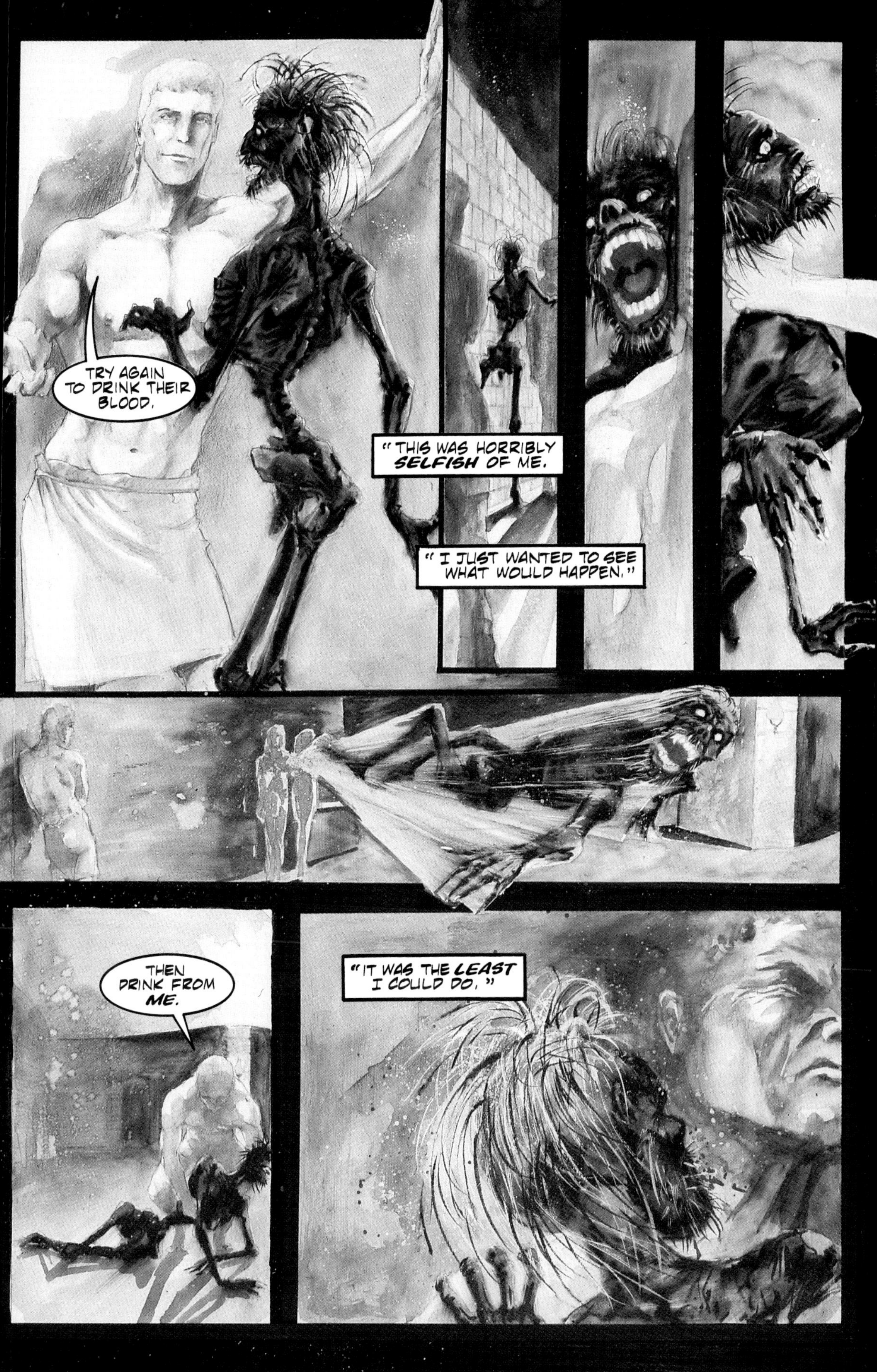
TRY AGAIN TO DRINK THEIR BLOOD.
"THIS WAS HORRIBLY SELFISH OF ME.
"I JUST WANTED TO SEE WHAT WOULD HAPPEN."
THEN DRINK FROM ME.
"IT WAS THE LEAST I COULD DO."

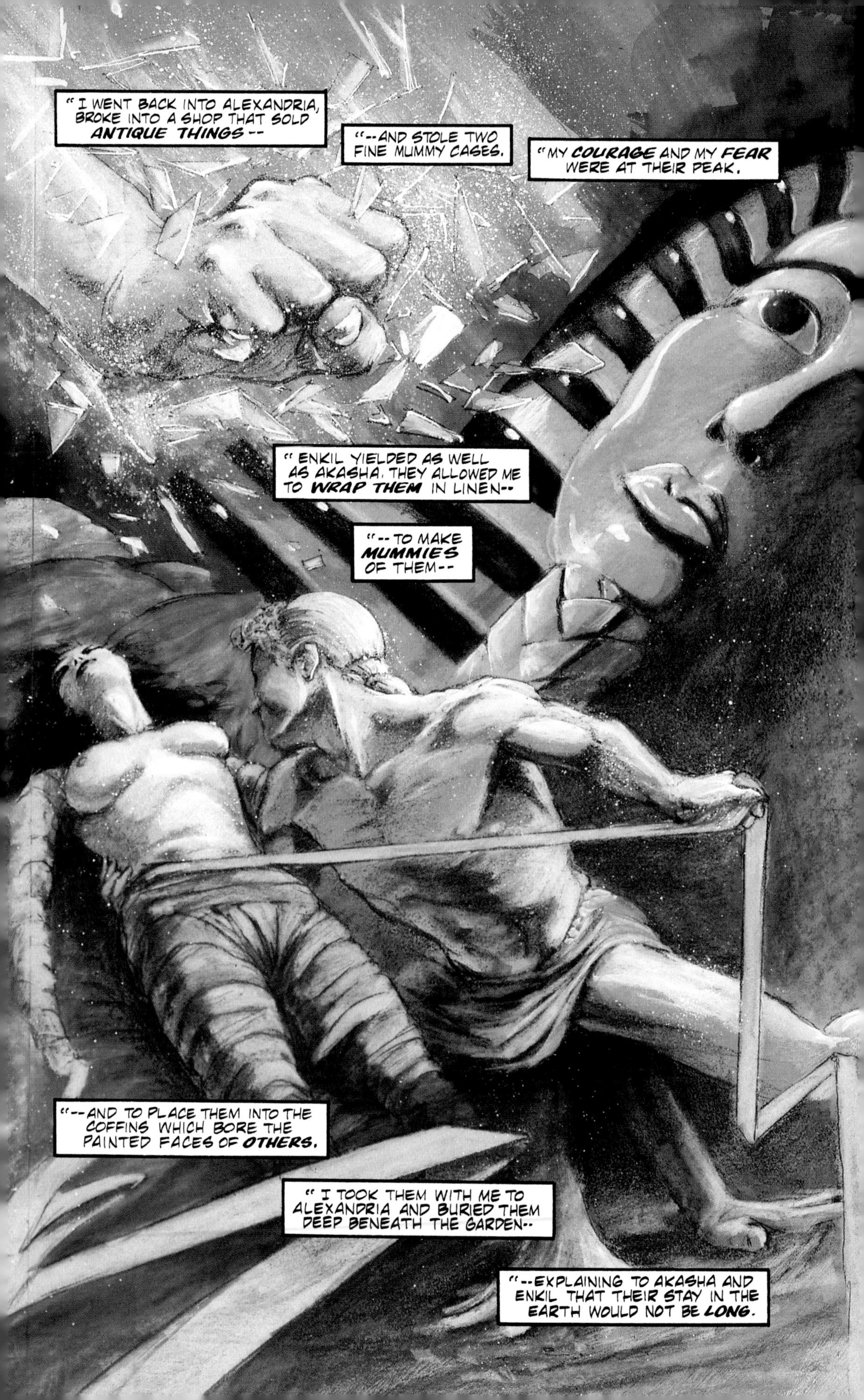
"I WENT BACK INTO ALEXANDRIA, BROKE INTO A SHOP THAT SOLD ANTIQUE THINGS--
"--AND STOLE TWO FINE MUMMY CASES.
"MY COURAGE AND MY FEAR WERE AT THEIR PEAK.
"ENKIL YIELDED AS WELL AS AKASHA. THEY ALLOWED ME TO WRAP THEM IN LINEN--
"--TO MAKE MUMMIES OF THEM--
"--AND TO PLACE THEM INTO THE COFFINS WHICH BORE THE PAINTED FACES OF OTHERS.
"I TOOK THEM WITH ME TO ALEXANDRIA AND BURIED THEM DEEP BENEATH THE GARDEN--
"--EXPLAINING TO AKASHA AND ENKIL THAT THEIR STAY IN THE EARTH WOULD NOT BE LONG.

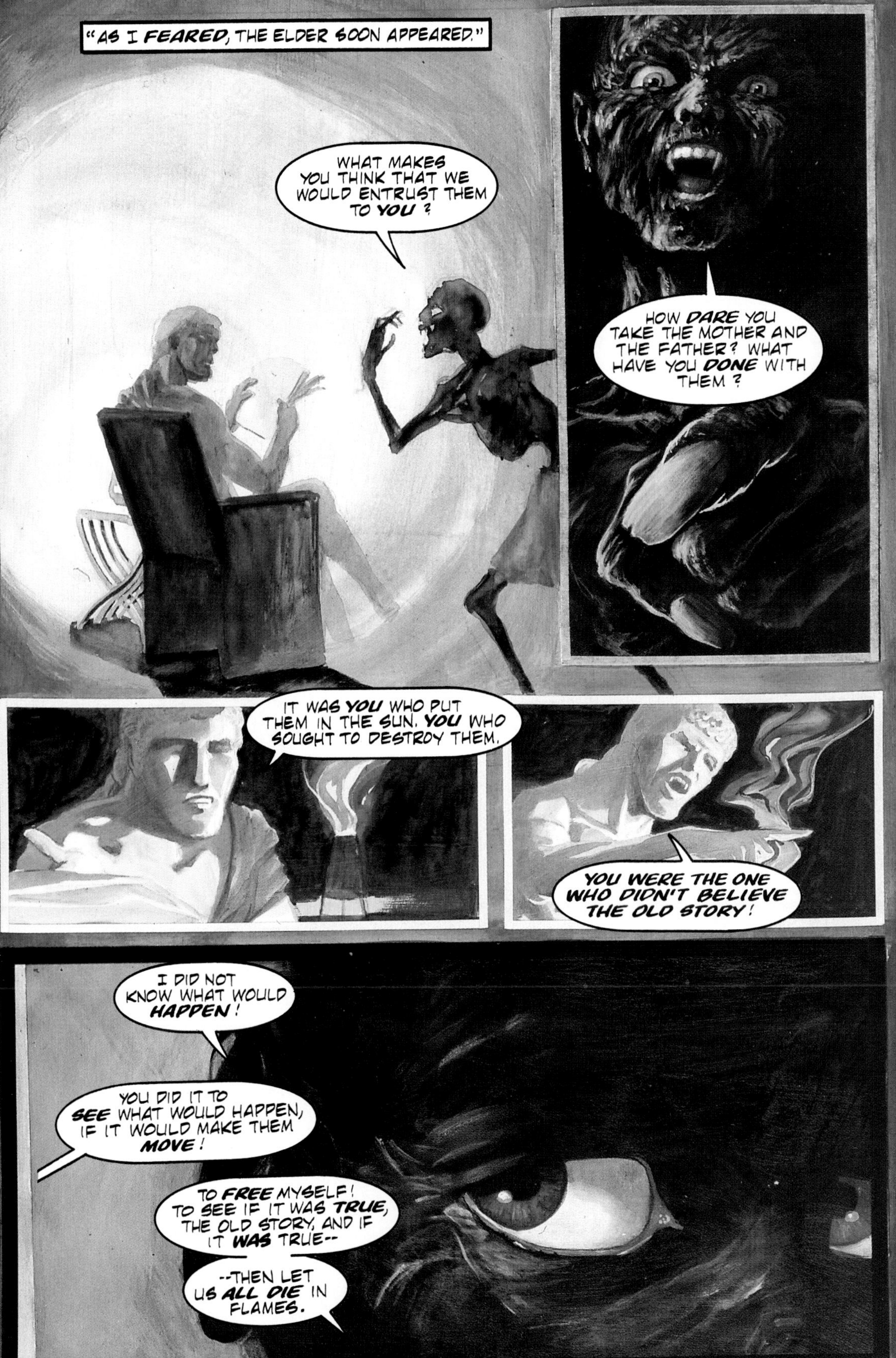
"AS I FEARED, THE ELDER SOON APPEARED."
WHAT MAKES YOU THINK THAT WE WOULD ENTRUST THEM TO YOU?
HOW DARE YOU TAKE THE MOTHER AND THE FATHER? WHAT HAVE YOU DONE WITH THEM?
IT WAS YOU WHO PUT THEM IN THE SUN. YOU WHO SOUGHT TO DESTROY THEM.
YOU WERE THE ONE WHO DIDN'T BELIEVE THE OLD STORY!
I DID NOT KNOW WHAT WOULD HAPPEN!
YOU DID IT TO SEE WHAT WOULD HAPPEN, IF IT WOULD MAKE THEM MOVE!
TO FREE MYSELF! TO SEE IF IT WAS TRUE, THE OLD STORY, AND IF IT WAS TRUE--
--THEN LET US ALL DIE IN FLAMES.

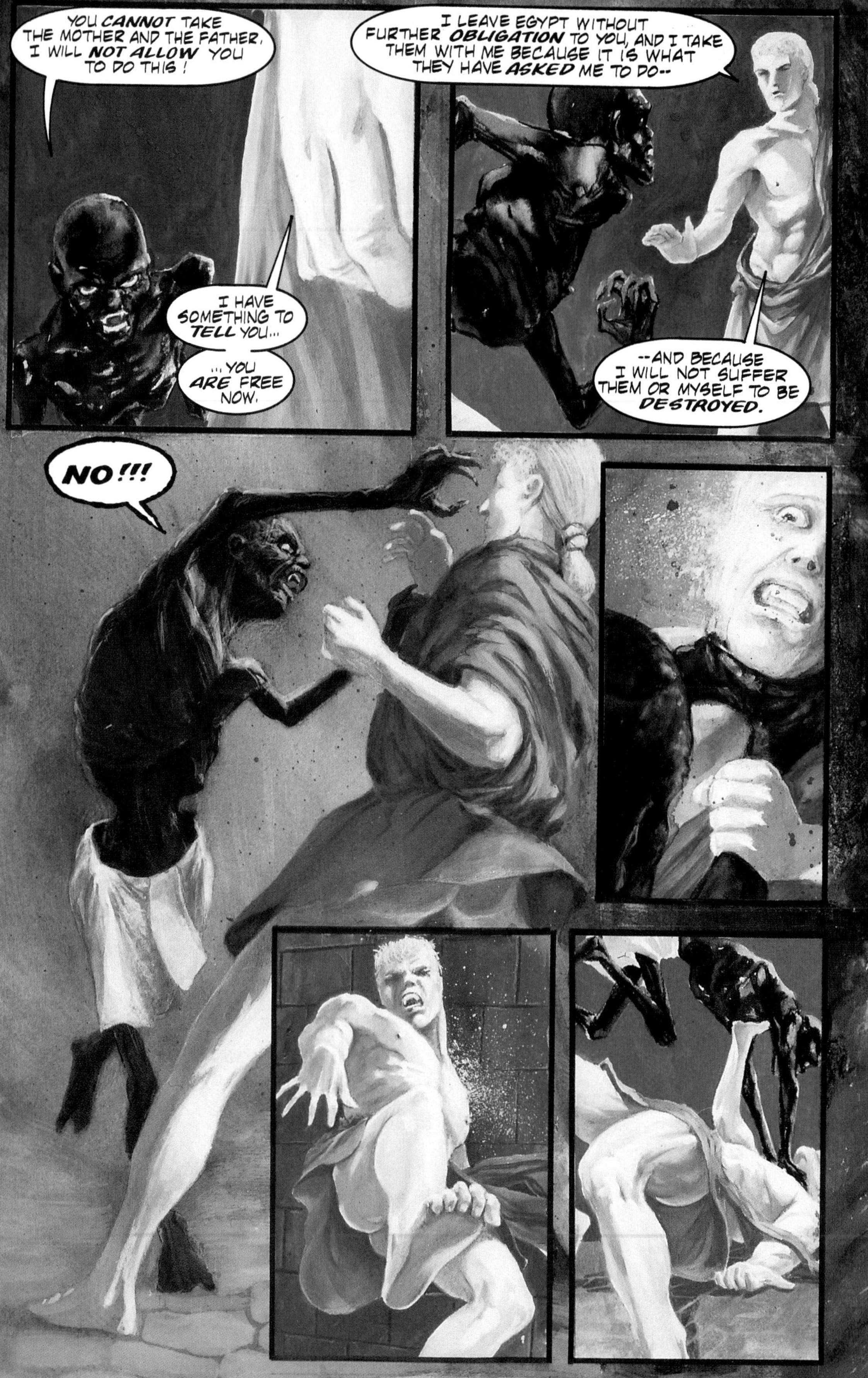
YOU CANNOT TAKE THE MOTHER AND THE FATHER, I WILL NOT ALLOW YOU TO DO THIS!
I HAVE SOMETHING TO TELL YOU...
...YOU ARE FREE NOW.
I LEAVE EGYPT WITHOUT FURTHER OBLIGATION TO YOU, AND I TAKE THEM WITH ME BECAUSE IT IS WHAT THEY HAVE ASKED ME TO DO--
--AND BECAUSE I WILL NOT SUFFER THEM OR MYSELF TO BE DESTROYED.
NO!!!

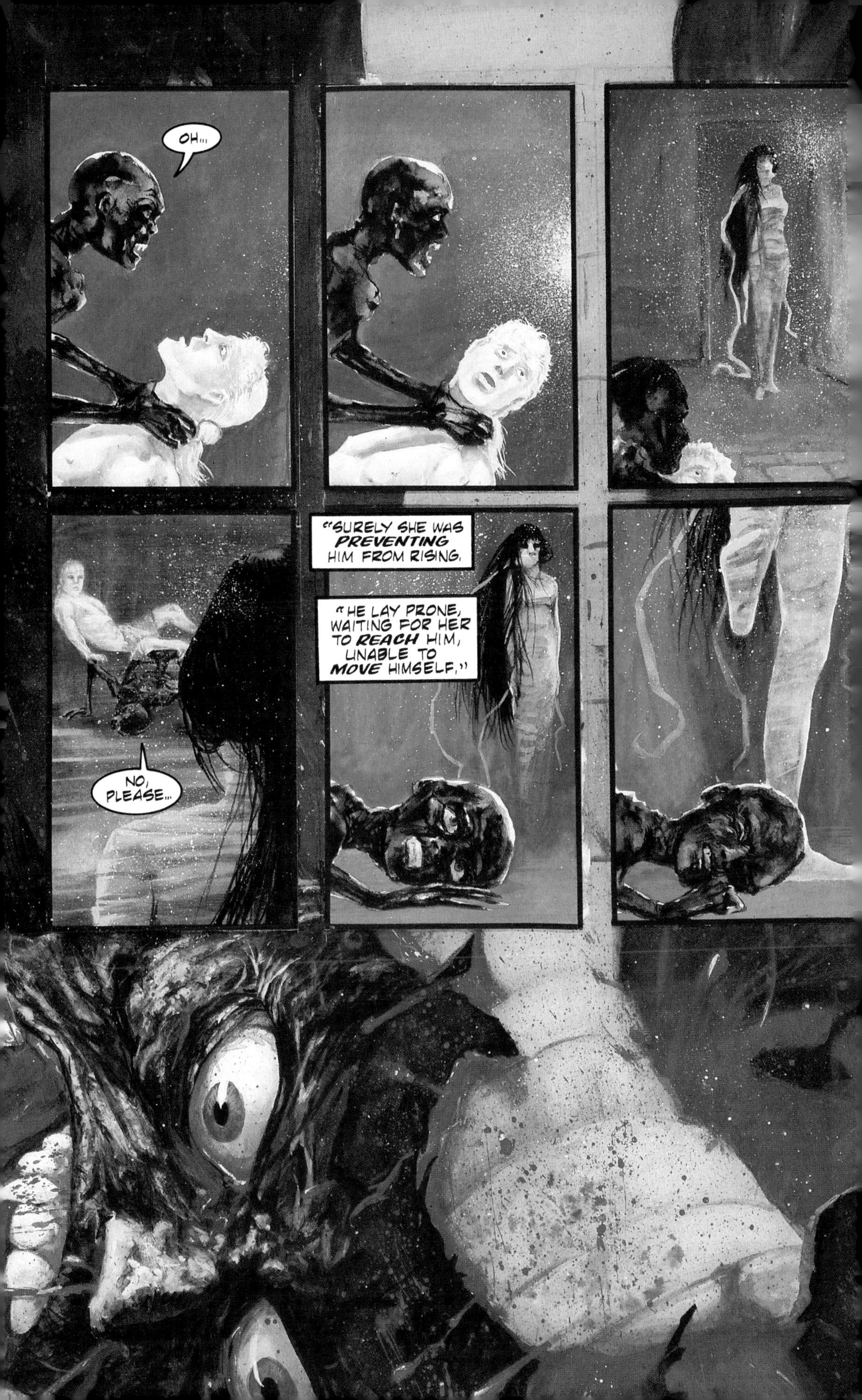
OH...
NO, PLEASE...
"SURELY SHE WAS PREVENTING HIM FROM RISING.
"HE LAY PRONE, WAITING FOR HER TO REACH HIM, UNABLE TO MOVE HIMSELF."

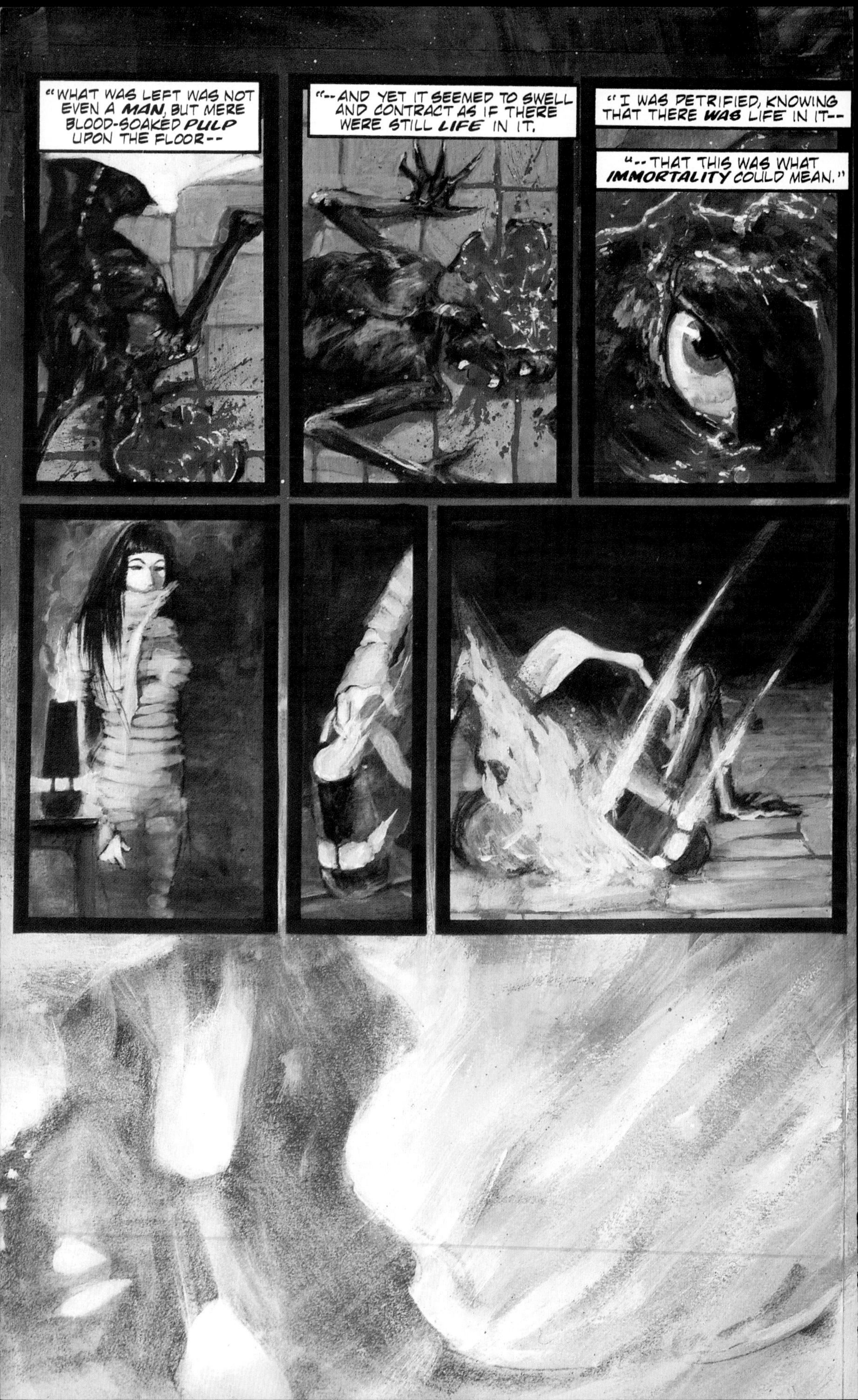
"WHAT WAS LEFT WAS NOT EVEN A MAN, BUT MERE BLOOD-SOAKED PULP UPON THE FLOOR--
"--AND YET IT SEEMED TO SWELL AND CONTRACT AS IF THERE WERE STILL LIFE IN IT.
"I WAS PETRIFIED, KNOWING THAT THERE WAS LIFE IN IT--
"--THAT THIS WAS WHAT IMMORTALITY COULD MEAN."

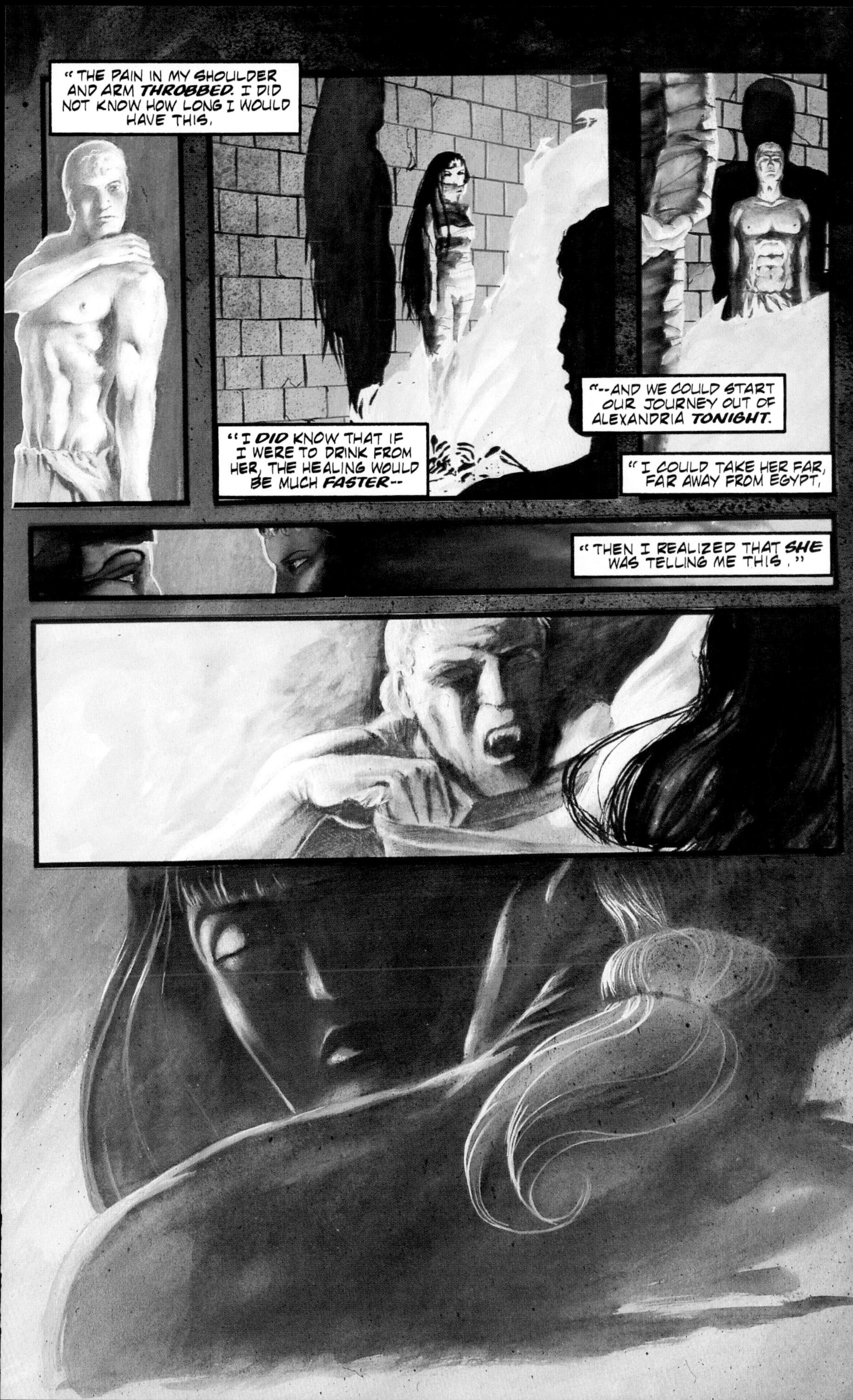
"THE PAIN IN MY SHOULDER AND ARM THROBBED. I DID NOT KNOW HOW LONG I WOULD HAVE THIS.
"I DID KNOW THAT IF I WERE TO DRINK FROM HER, THE HEALING WOULD BE MUCH FASTER--
"--AND WE COULD START OUR JOURNEY OUT OF ALEXANDRIA TONIGHT.
"I COULD TAKE HER FAR, FAR AWAY FROM EGYPT.
"THEN I REALIZED THAT SHE WAS TELLING ME THIS."

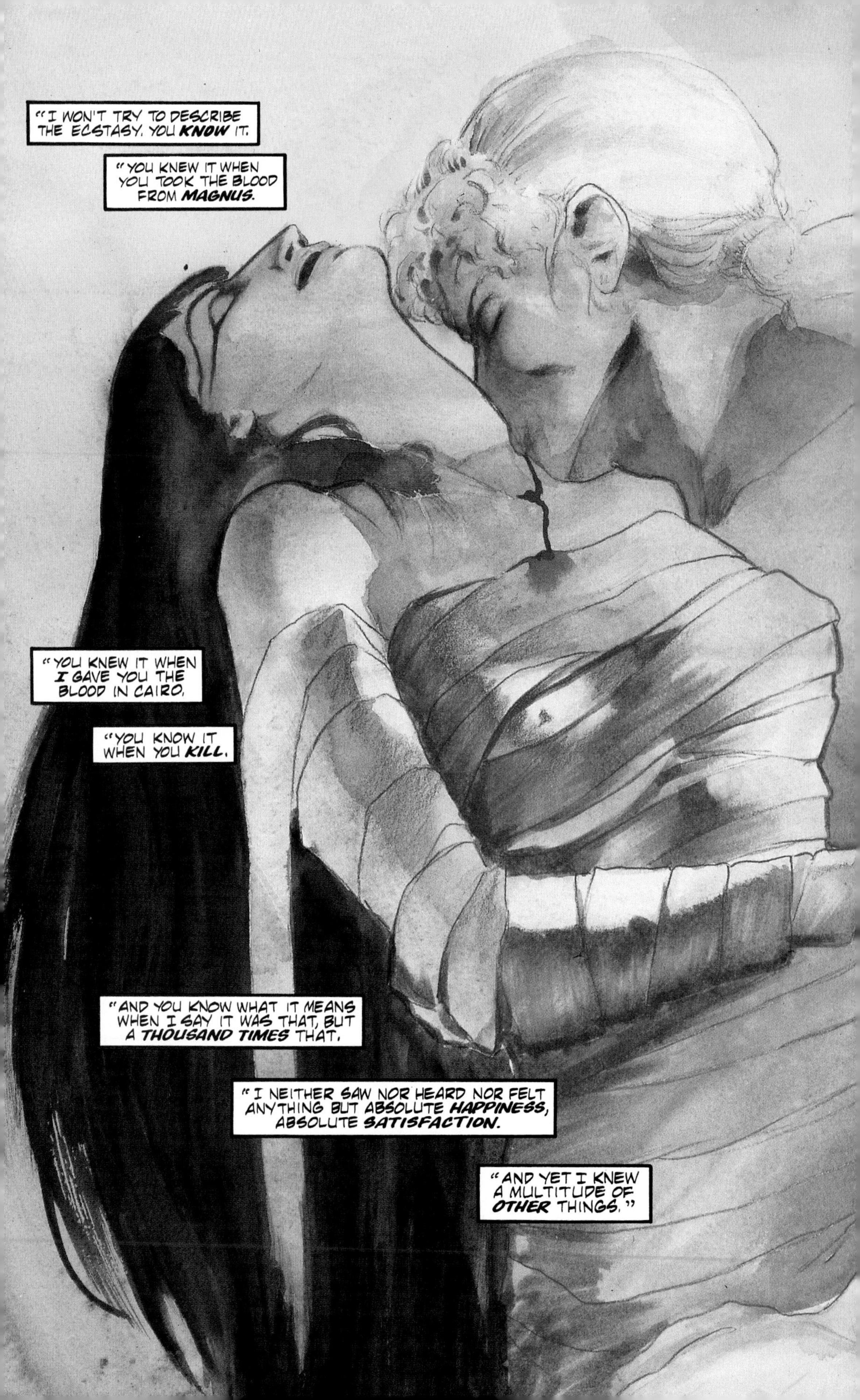
"I WON'T TRY TO DESCRIBE THE ECSTASY. YOU KNOW IT.
"YOU KNEW IT WHEN YOU TOOK THE BLOOD FROM MAGNUS.
"YOU KNEW IT WHEN I GAVE YOU THE BLOOD IN CAIRO.
"YOU KNOW IT WHEN YOU KILL.
"AND YOU KNOW WHAT IT MEANS WHEN I SAY IT WAS THAT, BUT A THOUSAND TIMES THAT.
"I NEITHER SAW NOR HEARD NOR FELT ANYTHING BUT ABSOLUTE HAPPINESS, ABSOLUTE SATISFACTION.
"AND YET I KNEW A MULTITUDE OF OTHER THINGS."

" I KNEW THAT THOUSANDS OF YEARS AGO THERE HAD BEEN *GREAT BATTLES* AMONG THE DRINKERS OF THE BLOOD--

"-- AND MANY OF THEM HAD BECOME RUTHLESS AND PROFANE BRINGERS OF *DEATH*.

" THESE WERE *DEATH ANGELS* WHO BELIEVED THAT NO INDIVIDUAL HUMAN LIFE MATTERED,

" AND THOUGH THESE GODS HAD BEEN REVEALED TO ME BY AKASHA IN ALL THEIR GRANDEUR AND MYSTERY...

"... I FOUND THEM *APPALLING*.

" THE PHILOSOPHIES THAT PROCEEDED FROM THEM WOULD NEVER JUSTIFY MY *KILLING*--

"-- OR GIVE ME *CONSOLATION* AS A DRINKER OF THE BLOOD.

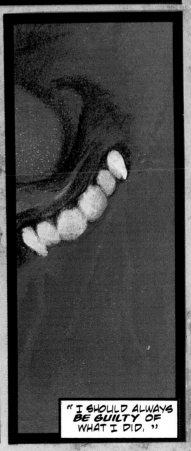

" I SHOULD ALWAYS *BE GUILTY* OF WHAT I DID, "

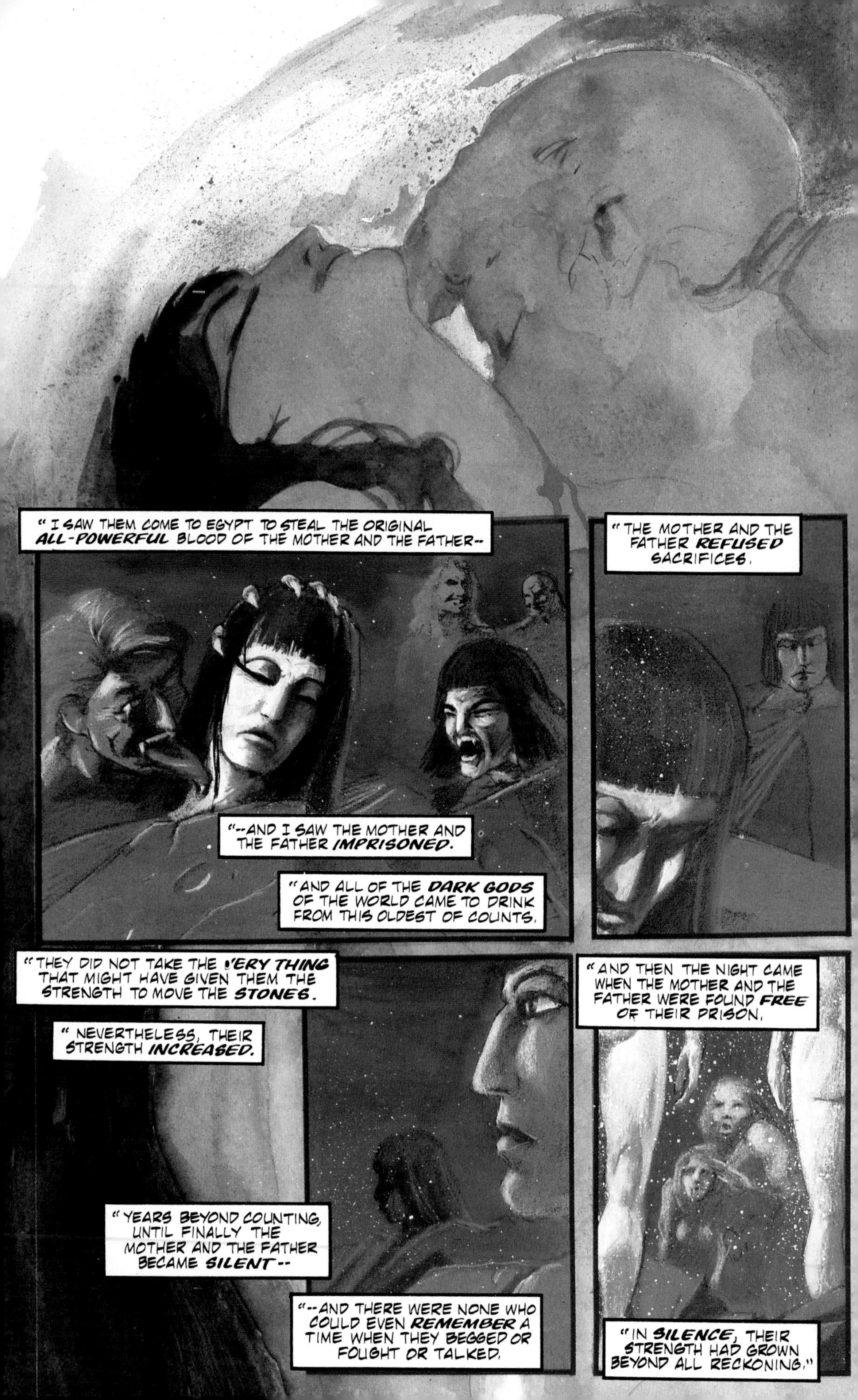
"I SAW THEM COME TO EGYPT TO STEAL THE ORIGINAL ALL-POWERFUL BLOOD OF THE MOTHER AND THE FATHER--
"--AND I SAW THE MOTHER AND THE FATHER IMPRISONED.
"AND ALL OF THE DARK GODS OF THE WORLD CAME TO DRINK FROM THIS OLDEST OF COUNTS.
"THE MOTHER AND THE FATHER REFUSED SACRIFICES.
"THEY DID NOT TAKE THE VERY THING THAT MIGHT HAVE GIVEN THEM THE STRENGTH TO MOVE THE STONES.
"NEVERTHELESS, THEIR STRENGTH INCREASED.
"YEARS BEYOND COUNTING, UNTIL FINALLY THE MOTHER AND THE FATHER BECAME SILENT--
"--AND THERE WERE NONE WHO COULD EVEN REMEMBER A TIME WHEN THEY BEGGED OR FOUGHT OR TALKED.
"AND THEN THE NIGHT CAME WHEN THE MOTHER AND THE FATHER WERE FOUND FREE OF THEIR PRISON.
"IN SILENCE, THEIR STRENGTH HAD GROWN BEYOND ALL RECKONING."

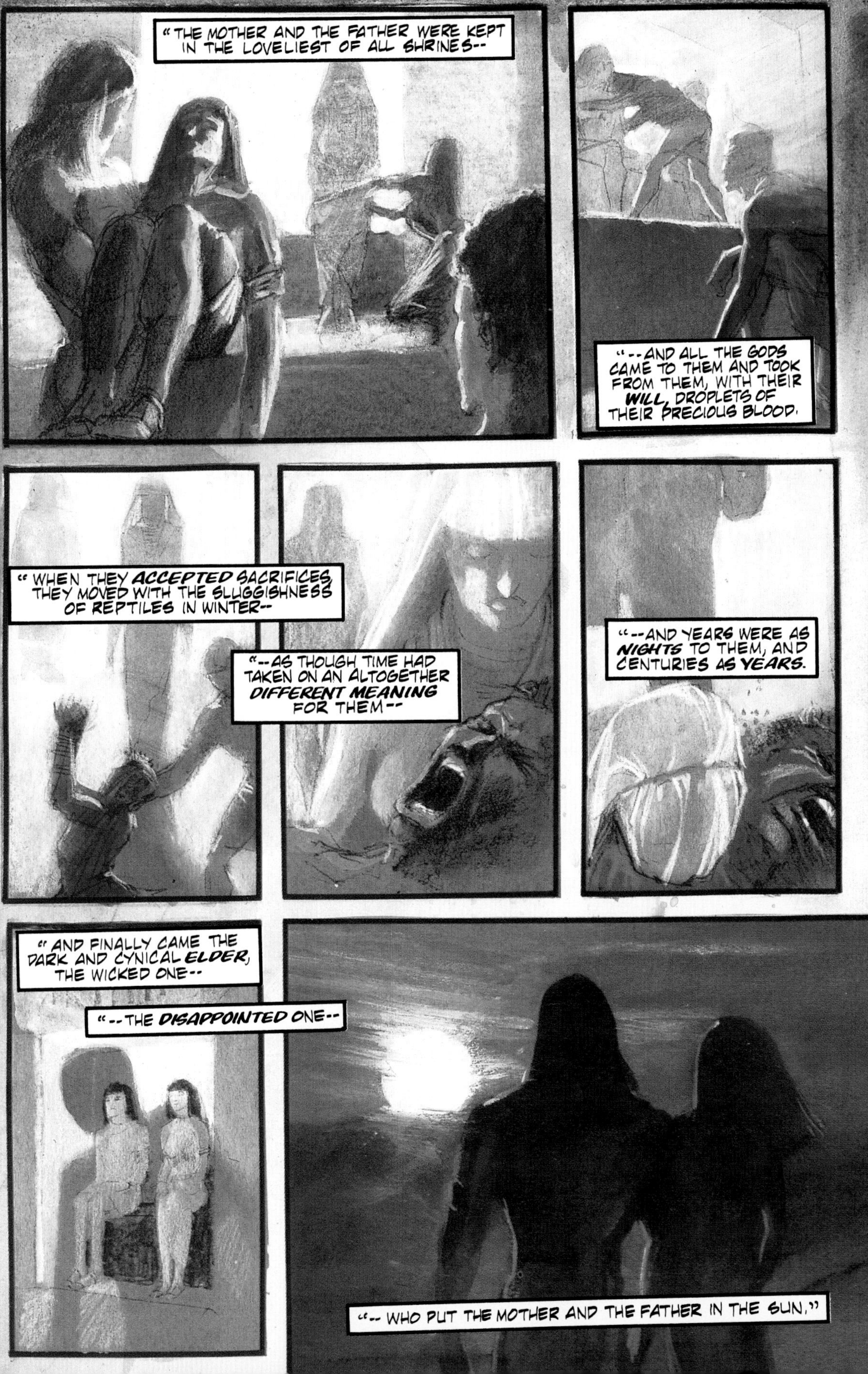
"THE MOTHER AND THE FATHER WERE KEPT IN THE LOVELIEST OF ALL SHRINES--
"--AND ALL THE GODS CAME TO THEM AND TOOK FROM THEM, WITH THEIR WILL, DROPLETS OF THEIR PRECIOUS BLOOD.
"WHEN THEY ACCEPTED SACRIFICES, THEY MOVED WITH THE SLUGGISHNESS OF REPTILES IN WINTER--
"--AS THOUGH TIME HAD TAKEN ON AN ALTOGETHER DIFFERENT MEANING FOR THEM--
"--AND YEARS WERE AS NIGHTS TO THEM, AND CENTURIES AS YEARS.
"AND FINALLY CAME THE DARK AND CYNICAL ELDER, THE WICKED ONE--
"--THE DISAPPOINTED ONE--
"-- WHO PUT THE MOTHER AND THE FATHER IN THE SUN."

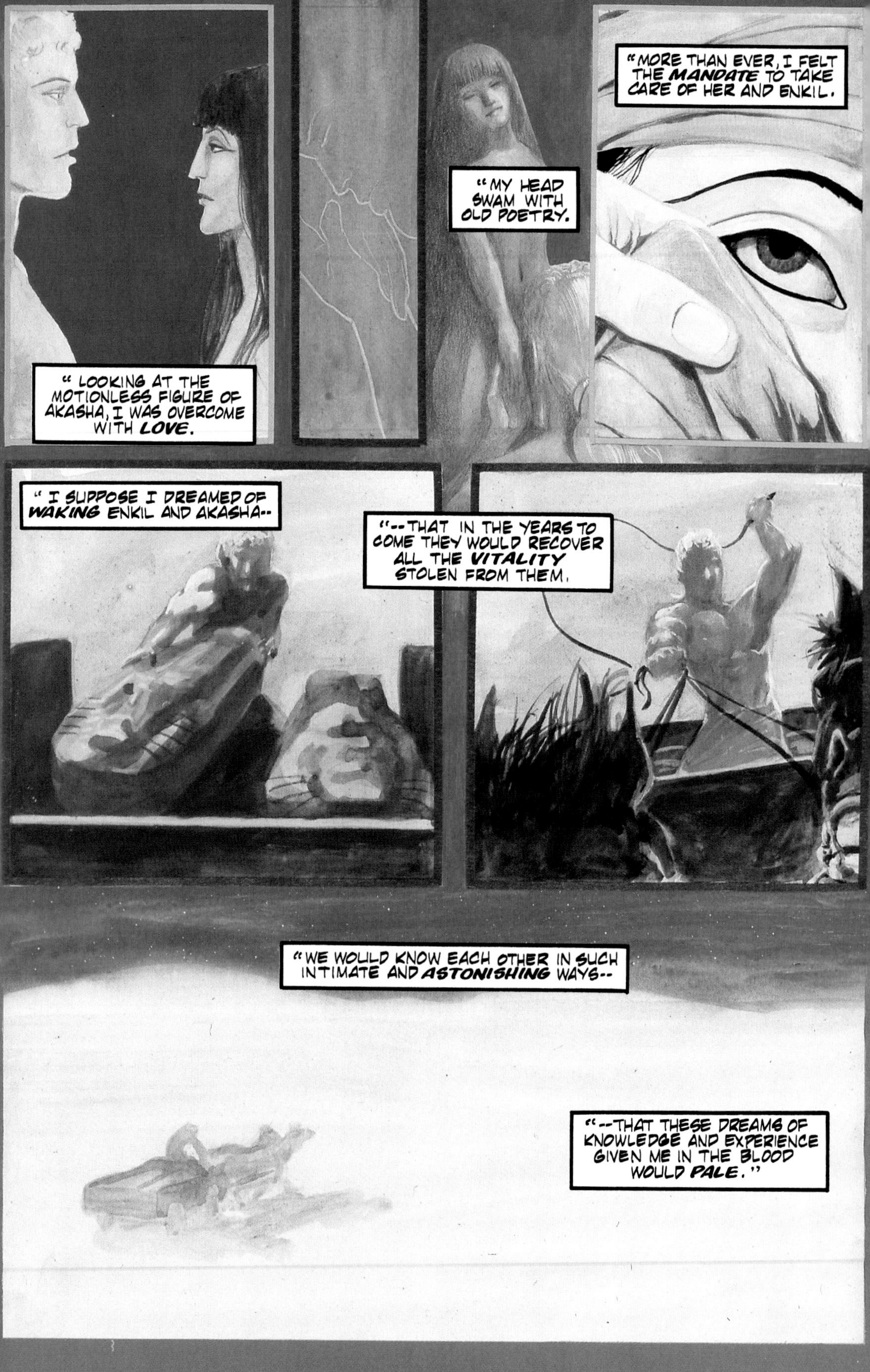
"LOOKING AT THE MOTIONLESS FIGURE OF AKASHA, I WAS OVERCOME WITH LOVE.
"MY HEAD SWAM WITH OLD POETRY.
"MORE THAN EVER, I FELT THE MANDATE TO TAKE CARE OF HER AND ENKIL.
"I SUPPOSE I DREAMED OF WAKING ENKIL AND AKASHA--
"--THAT IN THE YEARS TO COME THEY WOULD RECOVER ALL THE VITALITY STOLEN FROM THEM.
"WE WOULD KNOW EACH OTHER IN SUCH INTIMATE AND ASTONISHING WAYS--
"--THAT THESE DREAMS OF KNOWLEDGE AND EXPERIENCE GIVEN ME IN THE BLOOD WOULD PALE."

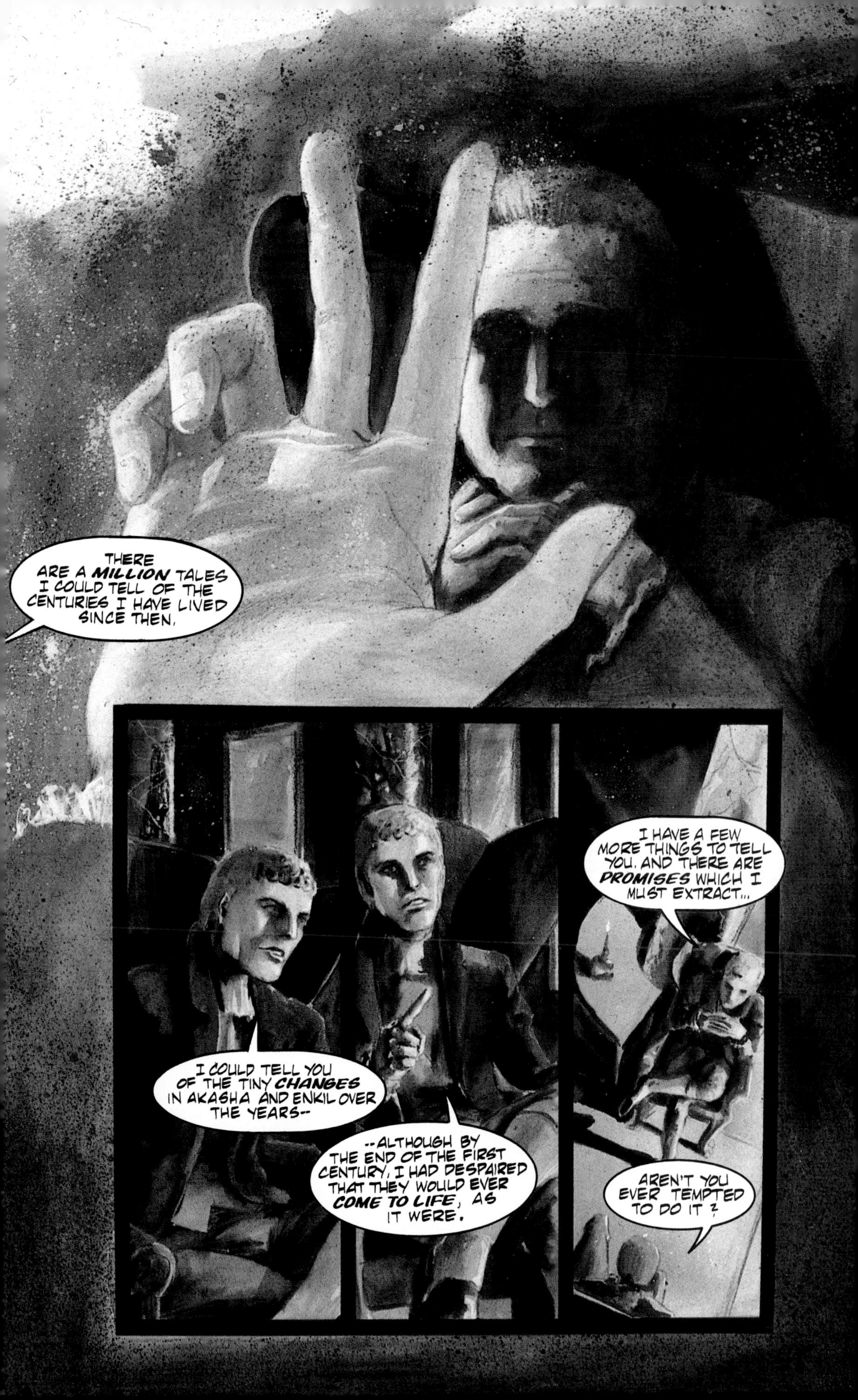
THERE ARE A **MILLION** TALES I COULD TELL OF THE CENTURIES I HAVE LIVED SINCE THEN.
I COULD TELL YOU OF THE TINY **CHANGES** IN AKASHA AND ENKIL OVER THE YEARS--
--ALTHOUGH BY THE END OF THE FIRST CENTURY, I HAD DESPAIRED THAT THEY WOULD EVER **COME TO LIFE**, AS IT WERE.
I HAVE A FEW MORE THINGS TO TELL YOU. AND THERE ARE **PROMISES** WHICH I MUST EXTRACT...
AREN'T YOU EVER TEMPTED TO DO IT?

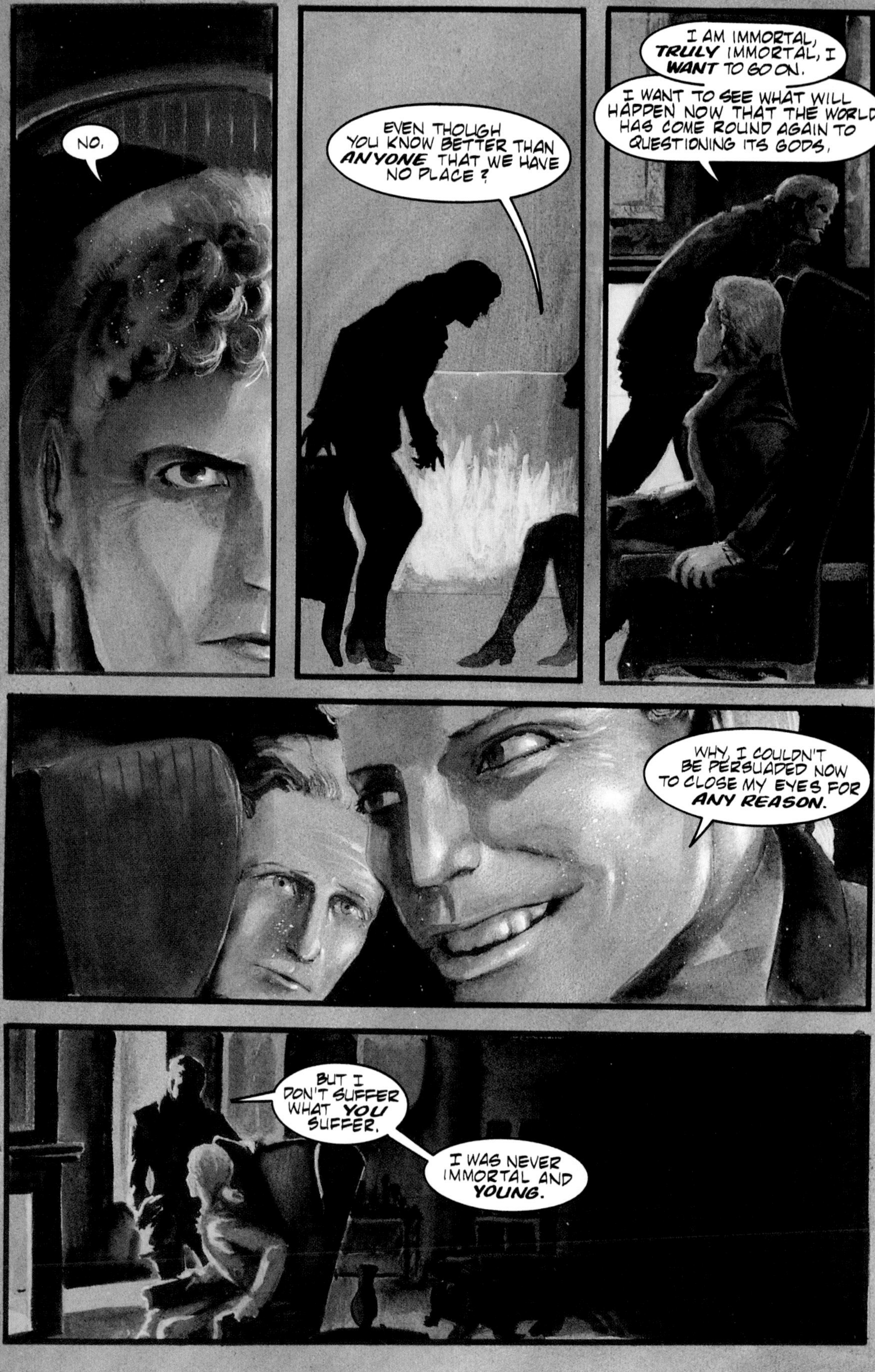
NO.
EVEN THOUGH YOU KNOW BETTER THAN ANYONE THAT WE HAVE NO PLACE?
I AM IMMORTAL, TRULY IMMORTAL, I WANT TO GO ON.
I WANT TO SEE WHAT WILL HAPPEN NOW THAT THE WORLD HAS COME ROUND AGAIN TO QUESTIONING ITS GODS.
WHY, I COULDN'T BE PERSUADED NOW TO CLOSE MY EYES FOR ANY REASON.
BUT I DON'T SUFFER WHAT YOU SUFFER.
I WAS NEVER IMMORTAL AND YOUNG.

I HAVE DONE OVER AND OVER WHAT YOU HAVE *YET* TO DO--

--THE THING THAT MUST TAKE YOU AWAY FROM ME *VERY SOON.*

TAKE ME *AWAY?* BUT I DON'T *WANT* TO!

YOU *HAVE* TO GO, LESTAT, AND VERY SOON, AS I SAID.

MARIUS, I CAN'T *IMAGINE* LEAVING NOW!

LISTEN TO ME. BEFORE I WAS TAKEN BY THE GAULS, I HAD LIVED A GOOD *LIFETIME.*

AND HAVING *HAD* THAT LIFETIME, I HAD THE STRENGTH FOR *OTHERS* LATER ON.

YOU, LIKE MANY WHO GO EARLY INTO THE FIRE OR THE SUN, HAVE HAD NO *REAL LIFE* AT ALL.

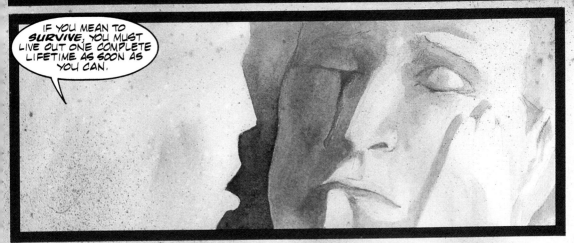

IF YOU MEAN TO *SURVIVE,* YOU MUST LIVE OUT ONE COMPLETE LIFETIME AS SOON AS YOU CAN.

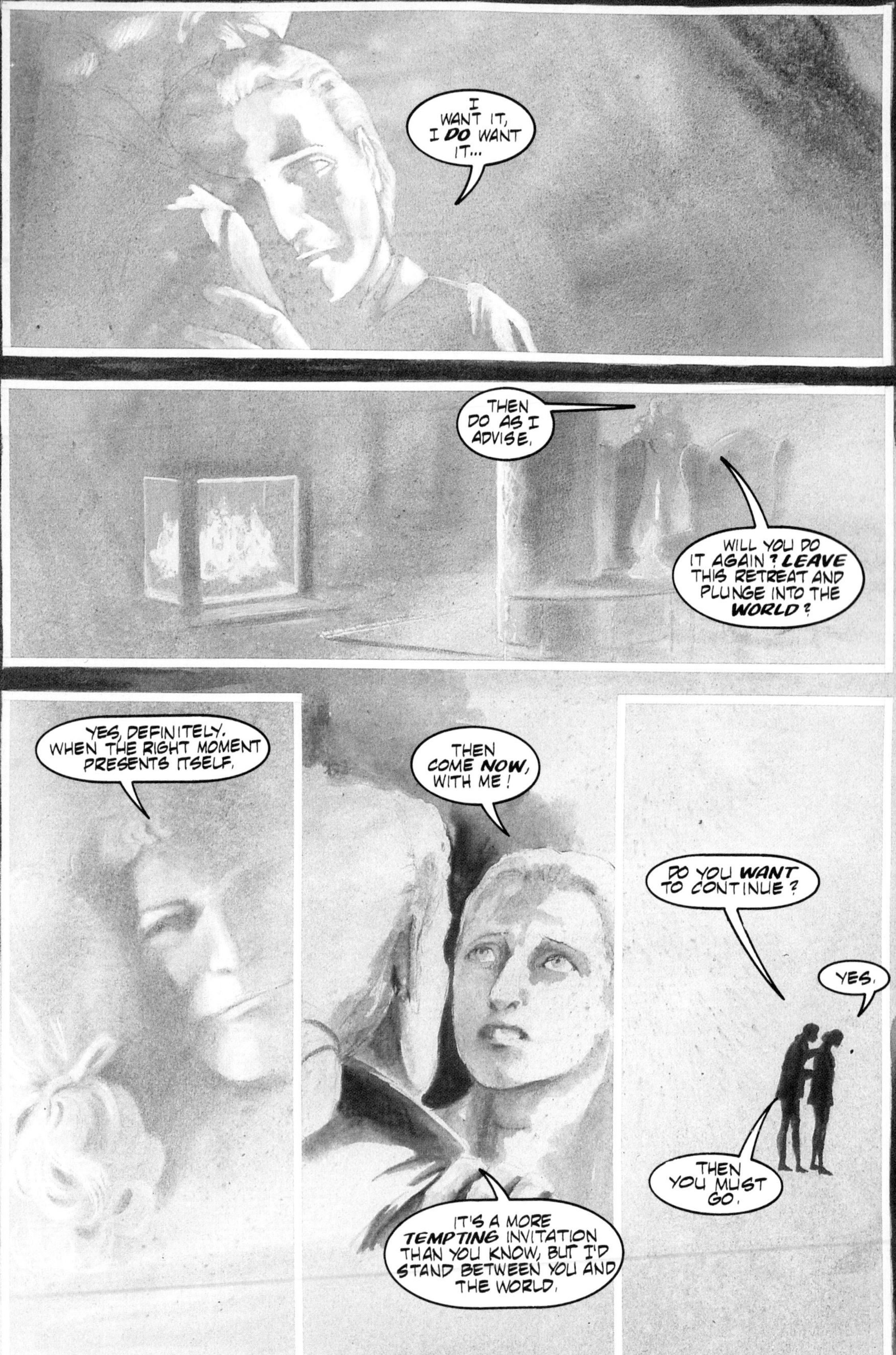
I WANT IT, I DO WANT IT...
THEN DO AS I ADVISE.
WILL YOU DO IT AGAIN? LEAVE THIS RETREAT AND PLUNGE INTO THE WORLD?
YES, DEFINITELY. WHEN THE RIGHT MOMENT PRESENTS ITSELF.
THEN COME NOW, WITH ME!
IT'S A MORE TEMPTING INVITATION THAN YOU KNOW, BUT I'D STAND BETWEEN YOU AND THE WORLD.
DO YOU WANT TO CONTINUE?
YES.
THEN YOU MUST GO.

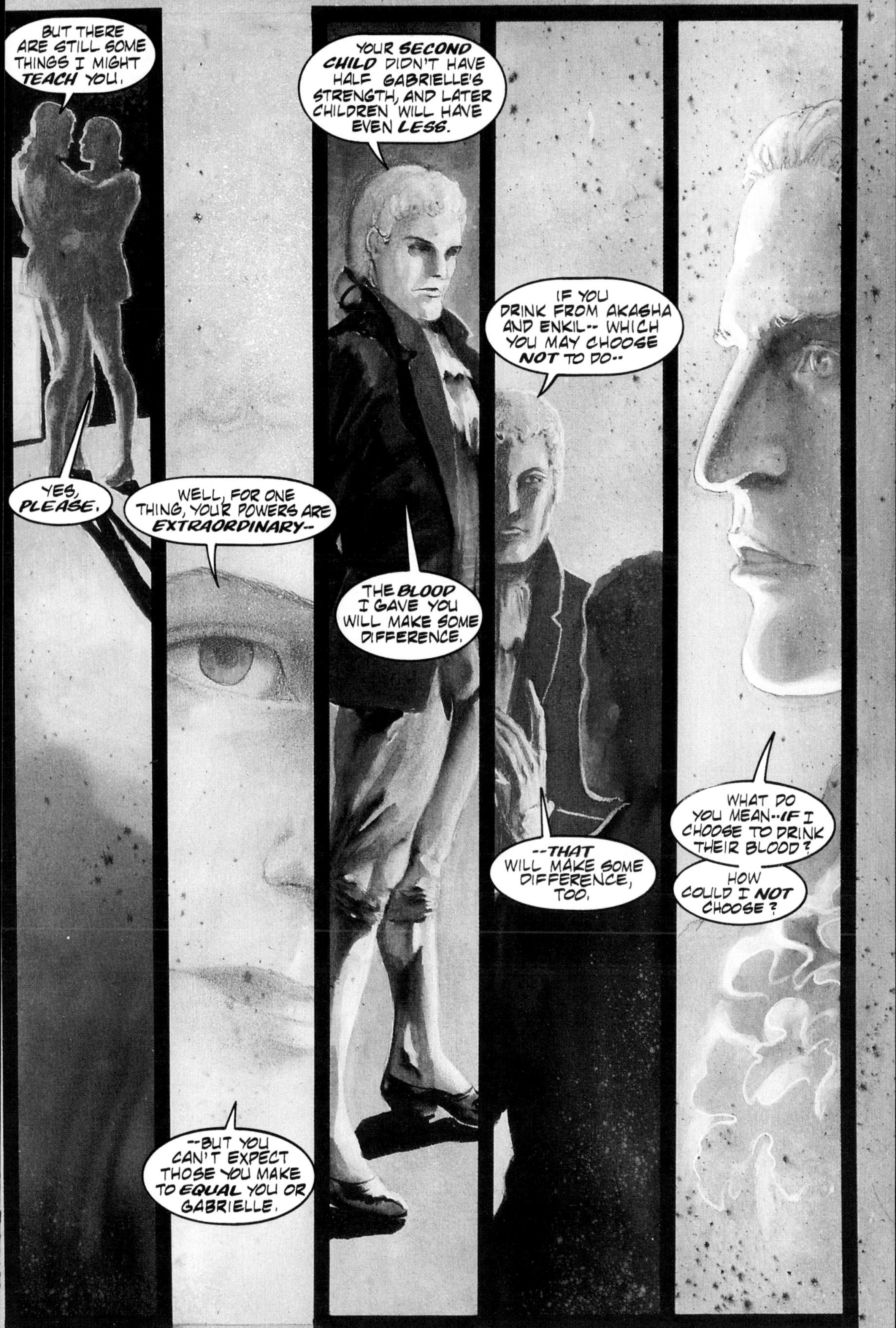
BUT THERE ARE STILL SOME THINGS I MIGHT TEACH YOU.
YES, PLEASE.
WELL, FOR ONE THING, YOUR POWERS ARE EXTRAORDINARY--
--BUT YOU CAN'T EXPECT THOSE YOU MAKE TO EQUAL YOU OR GABRIELLE.
YOUR SECOND CHILD DIDN'T HAVE HALF GABRIELLE'S STRENGTH, AND LATER CHILDREN WILL HAVE EVEN LESS.
THE BLOOD I GAVE YOU WILL MAKE SOME DIFFERENCE.
IF YOU DRINK FROM AKASHA AND ENKIL-- WHICH YOU MAY CHOOSE NOT TO DO--
--THAT WILL MAKE SOME DIFFERENCE, TOO.
WHAT DO YOU MEAN--IF I CHOOSE TO DRINK THEIR BLOOD?
HOW COULD I NOT CHOOSE?

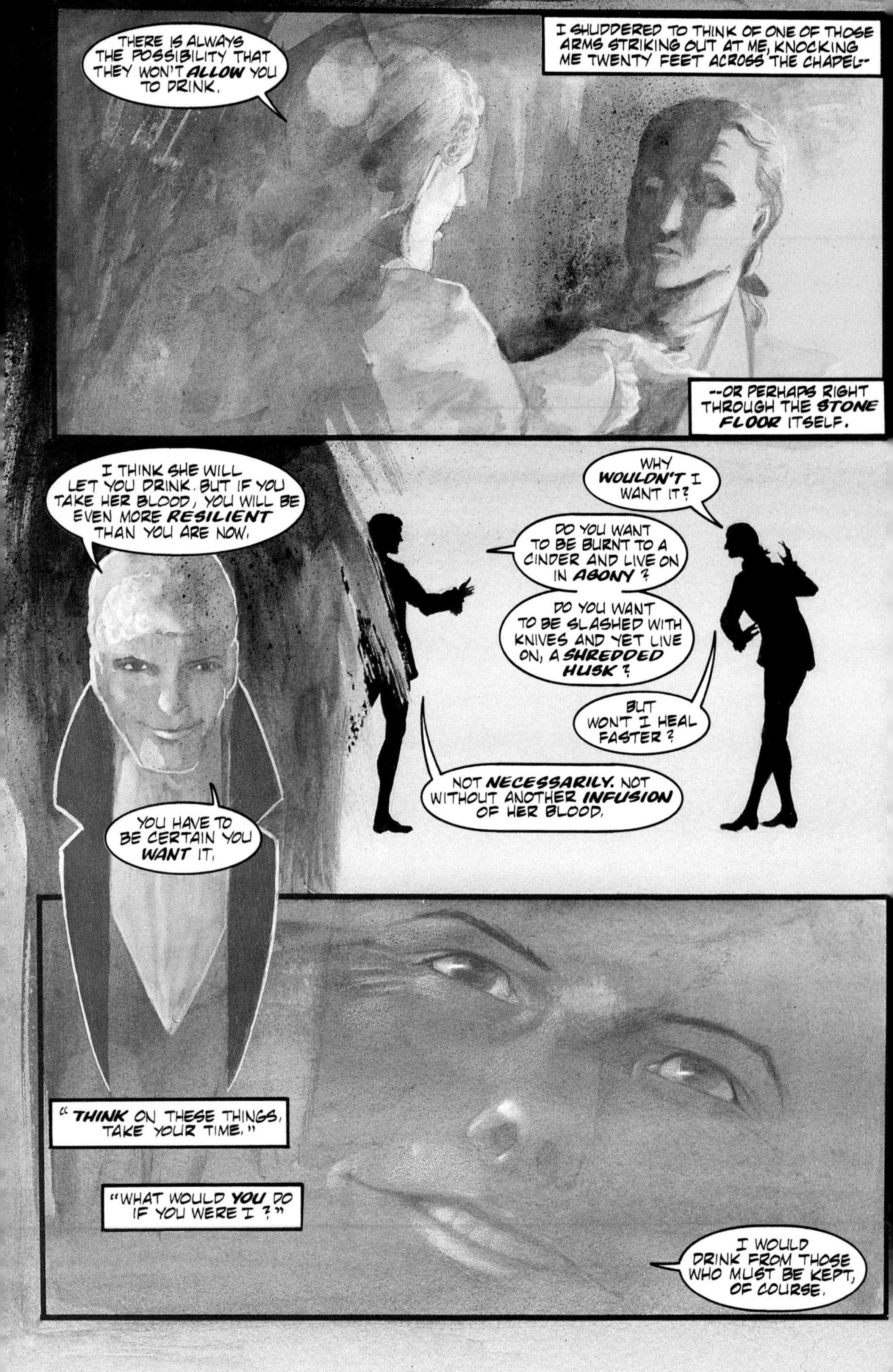
THERE IS ALWAYS THE POSSIBILITY THAT THEY WON'T ALLOW YOU TO DRINK.
I SHUDDERED TO THINK OF ONE OF THOSE ARMS STRIKING OUT AT ME, KNOCKING ME TWENTY FEET ACROSS THE CHAPEL--
--OR PERHAPS RIGHT THROUGH THE STONE FLOOR ITSELF.
I THINK SHE WILL LET YOU DRINK. BUT IF YOU TAKE HER BLOOD, YOU WILL BE EVEN MORE RESILIENT THAN YOU ARE NOW.
YOU HAVE TO BE CERTAIN YOU WANT IT.
WHY WOULDN'T I WANT IT?
DO YOU WANT TO BE BURNT TO A CINDER AND LIVE ON IN AGONY?
DO YOU WANT TO BE SLASHED WITH KNIVES AND YET LIVE ON, A SHREDDED HUSK?
BUT WON'T I HEAL FASTER?
NOT NECESSARILY. NOT WITHOUT ANOTHER INFUSION OF HER BLOOD.
"THINK ON THESE THINGS, TAKE YOUR TIME."
"WHAT WOULD YOU DO IF YOU WERE I?"
I WOULD DRINK FROM THOSE WHO MUST BE KEPT, OF COURSE.

AND NOW... MORE ANSWERS?
TELL ME WHAT YOU WISH TO KNOW.
I'VE SEEN GHOSTS... SEEN THE PESTY DEMONS YOU DESCRIBED.
I'VE SEEN THEM POSSESS MORTALS AND DWELLINGS.
I KNOW NO MORE THAN YOU DO. WHAT CAN I ADD TO ENKIL'S ANCIENT EXPLANATION?
THEY RAGE BECAUSE THEY DO NOT HAVE BODIES.
BUT THERE ARE OTHER IMMORTALS THAT ARE MORE INTERESTING.
WHAT ARE THEY?

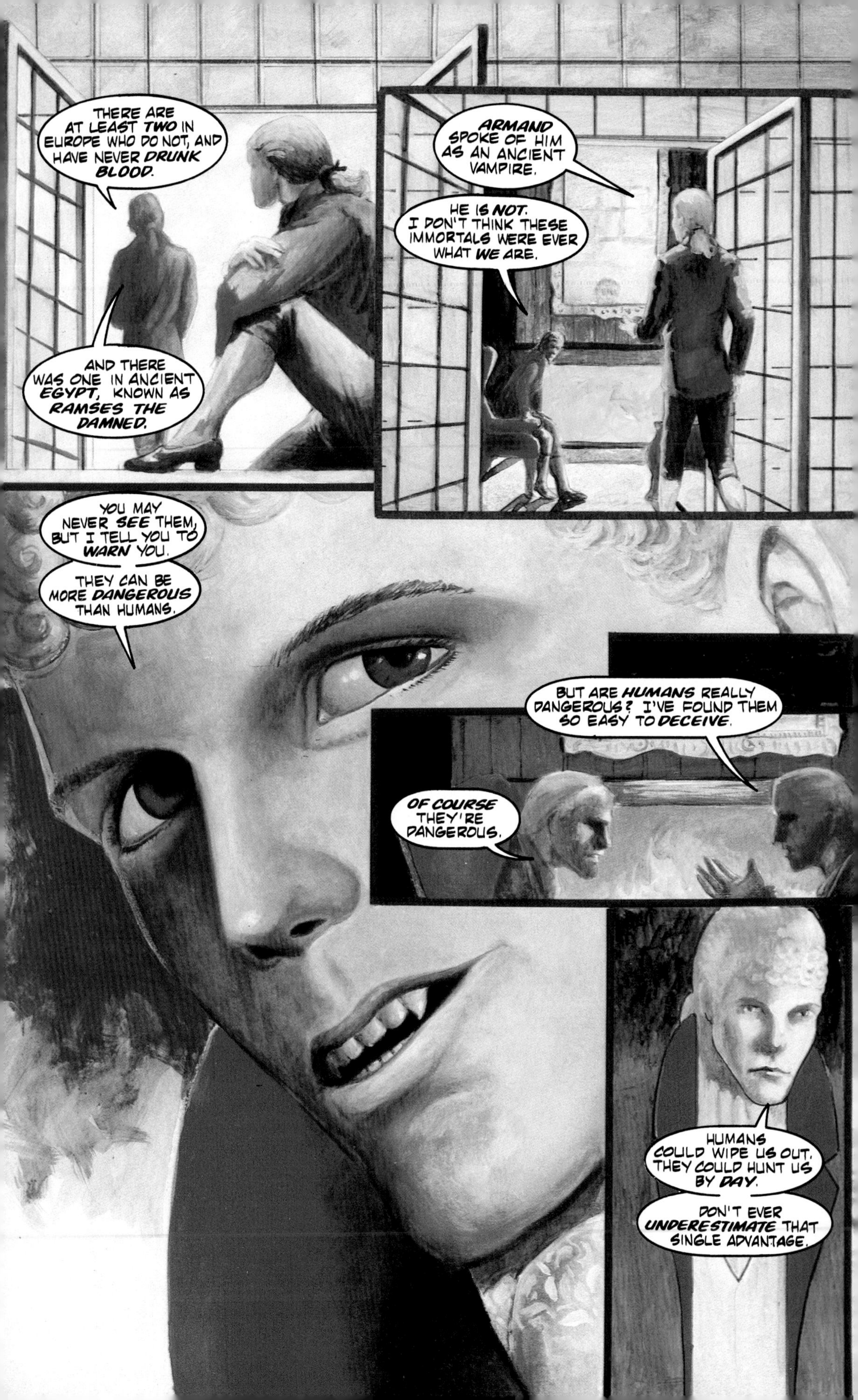
THERE ARE AT LEAST TWO IN EUROPE WHO DO NOT, AND HAVE NEVER DRUNK BLOOD.
AND THERE WAS ONE IN ANCIENT EGYPT, KNOWN AS RAMSES THE DAMNED.
ARMAND SPOKE OF HIM AS AN ANCIENT VAMPIRE.
HE IS NOT. I DON'T THINK THESE IMMORTALS WERE EVER WHAT WE ARE.
YOU MAY NEVER SEE THEM, BUT I TELL YOU TO WARN YOU.
THEY CAN BE MORE DANGEROUS THAN HUMANS.
BUT ARE HUMANS REALLY DANGEROUS? I'VE FOUND THEM SO EASY TO DECEIVE.
OF COURSE THEY'RE DANGEROUS.
HUMANS COULD WIPE US OUT. THEY COULD HUNT US BY DAY.
DON'T EVER UNDERESTIMATE THAT SINGLE ADVANTAGE.

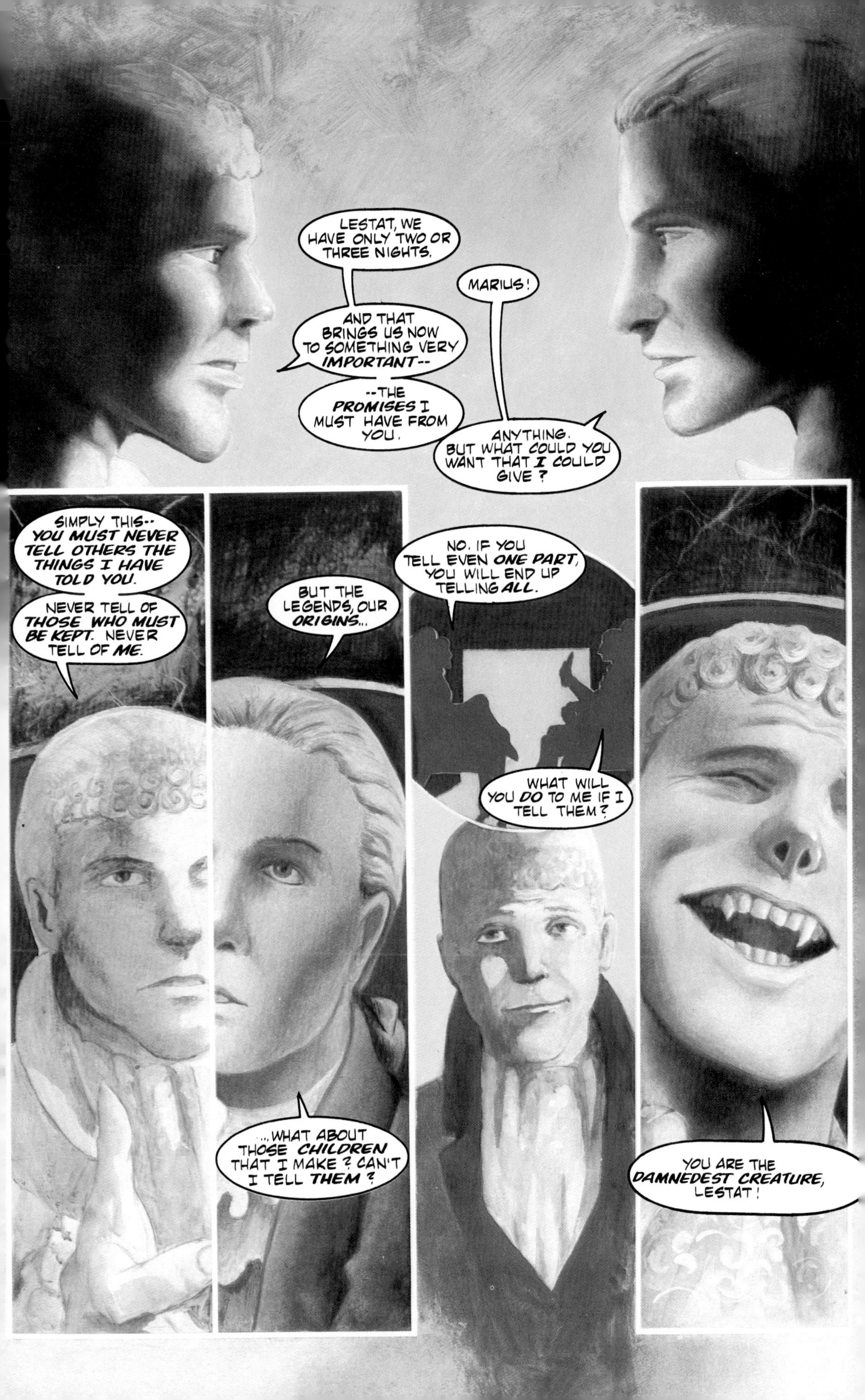
LESTAT, WE HAVE ONLY TWO OR THREE NIGHTS.
MARIUS!
AND THAT BRINGS US NOW TO SOMETHING VERY IMPORTANT--
--THE PROMISES I MUST HAVE FROM YOU.
ANYTHING. BUT WHAT COULD YOU WANT THAT I COULD GIVE?
SIMPLY THIS-- YOU MUST NEVER TELL OTHERS THE THINGS I HAVE TOLD YOU.
NEVER TELL OF THOSE WHO MUST BE KEPT. NEVER TELL OF ME.
BUT THE LEGENDS, OUR ORIGINS...
...WHAT ABOUT THOSE CHILDREN THAT I MAKE? CAN'T I TELL THEM?
NO. IF YOU TELL EVEN ONE PART, YOU WILL END UP TELLING ALL.
WHAT WILL YOU DO TO ME IF I TELL THEM?
YOU ARE THE DAMNEDEST CREATURE, LESTAT!

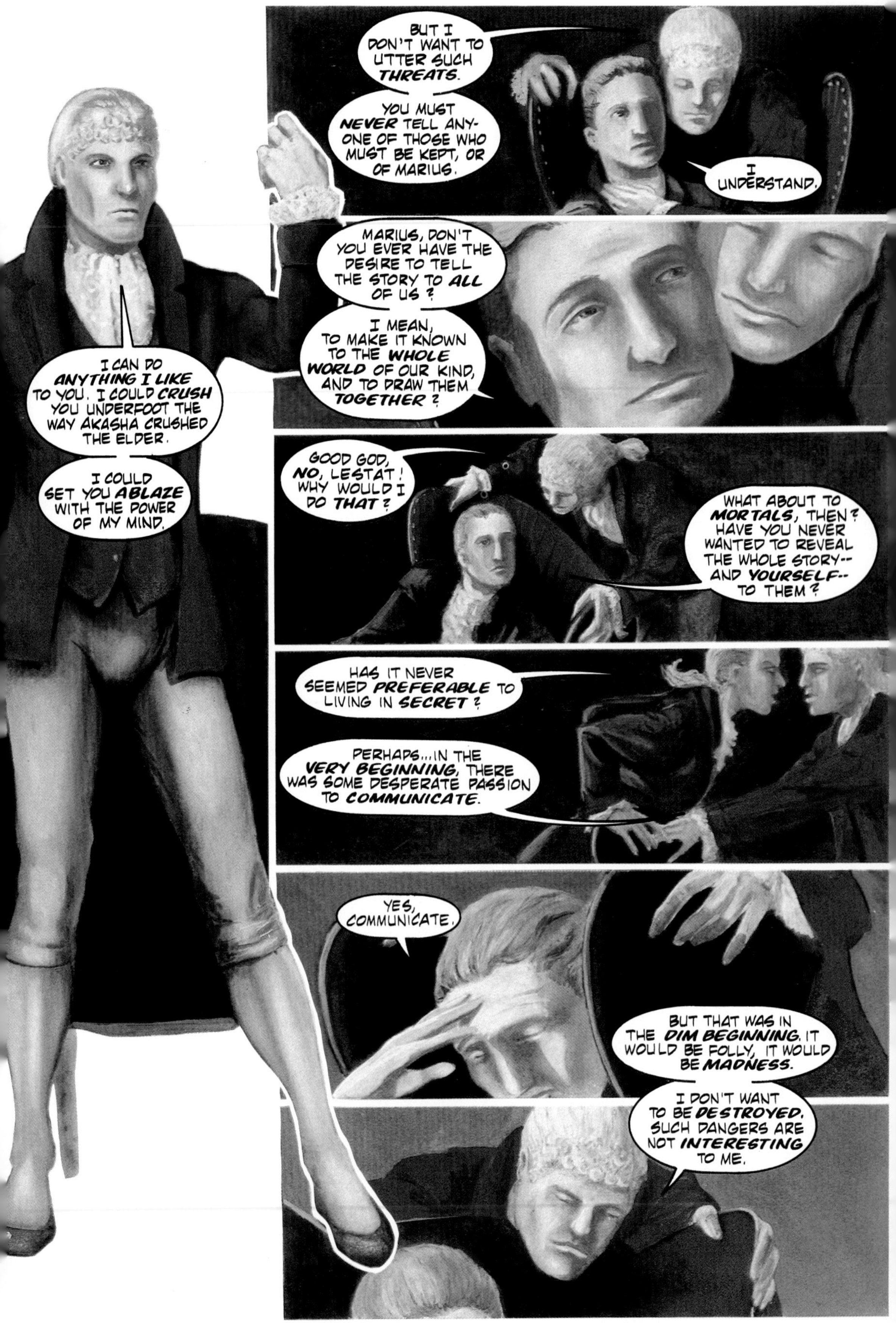
BUT I DON'T WANT TO UTTER SUCH THREATS.
YOU MUST NEVER TELL ANY-ONE OF THOSE WHO MUST BE KEPT, OR OF MARIUS.
I UNDERSTAND.
I CAN DO ANYTHING I LIKE TO YOU. I COULD CRUSH YOU UNDERFOOT THE WAY AKASHA CRUSHED THE ELDER.
I COULD SET YOU ABLAZE WITH THE POWER OF MY MIND.
MARIUS, DON'T YOU EVER HAVE THE DESIRE TO TELL THE STORY TO ALL OF US?
I MEAN, TO MAKE IT KNOWN TO THE WHOLE WORLD OF OUR KIND, AND TO DRAW THEM TOGETHER?
GOOD GOD, NO, LESTAT! WHY WOULD I DO THAT?
WHAT ABOUT TO MORTALS, THEN? HAVE YOU NEVER WANTED TO REVEAL THE WHOLE STORY-- AND YOURSELF-- TO THEM?
HAS IT NEVER SEEMED PREFERABLE TO LIVING IN SECRET?
PERHAPS...IN THE VERY BEGINNING, THERE WAS SOME DESPERATE PASSION TO COMMUNICATE.
YES, COMMUNICATE.
BUT THAT WAS IN THE DIM BEGINNING. IT WOULD BE FOLLY, IT WOULD BE MADNESS.
I DON'T WANT TO BE DESTROYED. SUCH DANGERS ARE NOT INTERESTING TO ME.

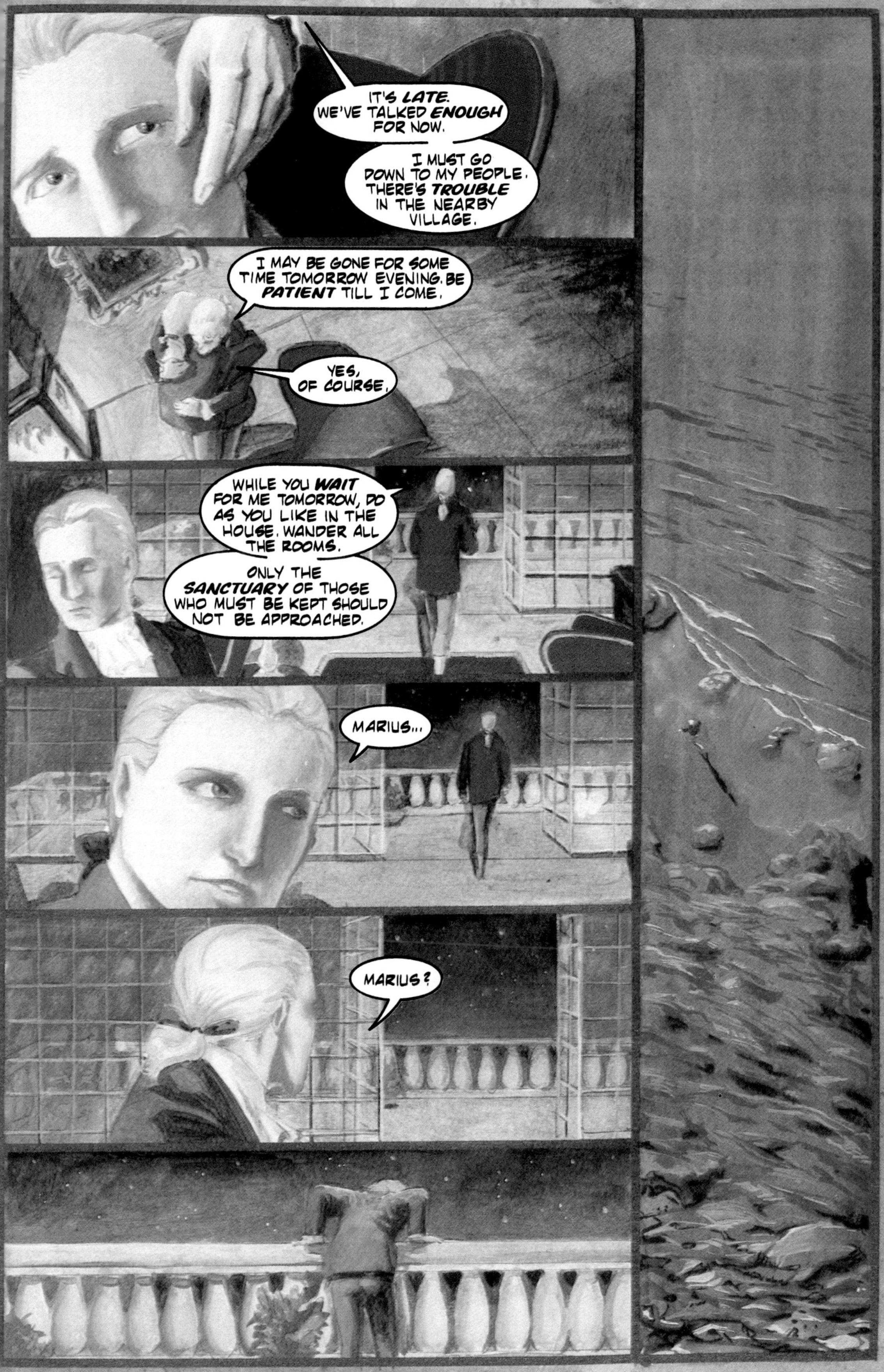
IT'S LATE. WE'VE TALKED ENOUGH FOR NOW.
I MUST GO DOWN TO MY PEOPLE. THERE'S TROUBLE IN THE NEARBY VILLAGE.
I MAY BE GONE FOR SOME TIME TOMORROW EVENING. BE PATIENT TILL I COME.
YES, OF COURSE.
WHILE YOU WAIT FOR ME TOMORROW, DO AS YOU LIKE IN THE HOUSE. WANDER ALL THE ROOMS.
ONLY THE SANCTUARY OF THOSE WHO MUST BE KEPT SHOULD NOT BE APPROACHED.
MARIUS...
MARIUS?

WHEN I OPENED MY EYES THE NEXT NIGHT, I HAD AN *IDEA*.

IT IMMEDIATELY *OBSESSED* ME.

NO, *FORGET* ABOUT IT. MARIUS SAID TO *STAY AWAY* FROM THE SANCTUARY.

NO. DON'T DO IT. AFTER ALL, IT WON'T DO ANY *GOOD*.

NOTHING WILL HAPPEN.

BUT IF *THAT'S* THE CASE, WHY *NOT* DO IT?

WHY NOT DO IT *NOW*?

THE DOOR TO THE STAIRWAY DOWN TO THOSE WHO MUST BE KEPT *WASN'T* LOCKED.

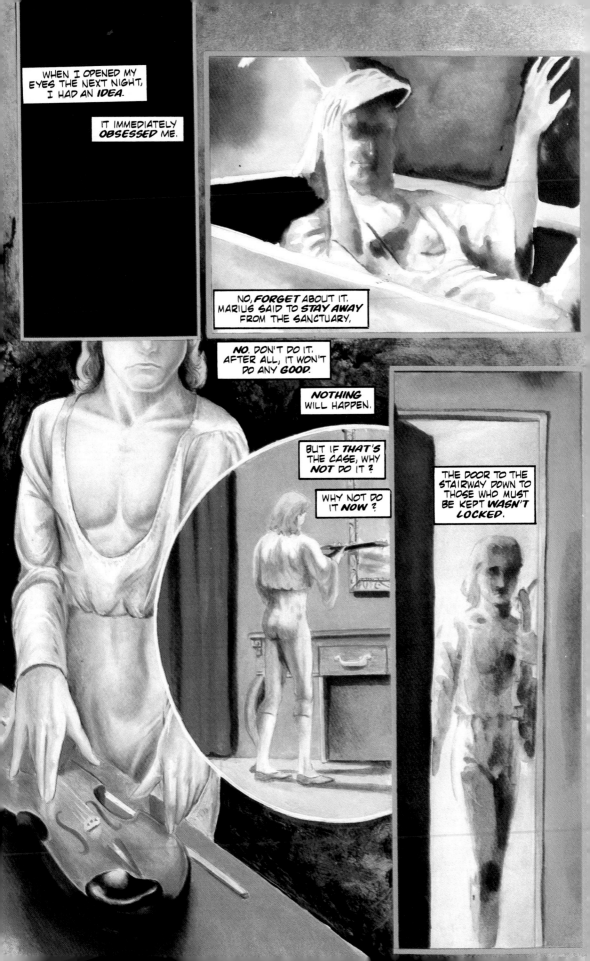

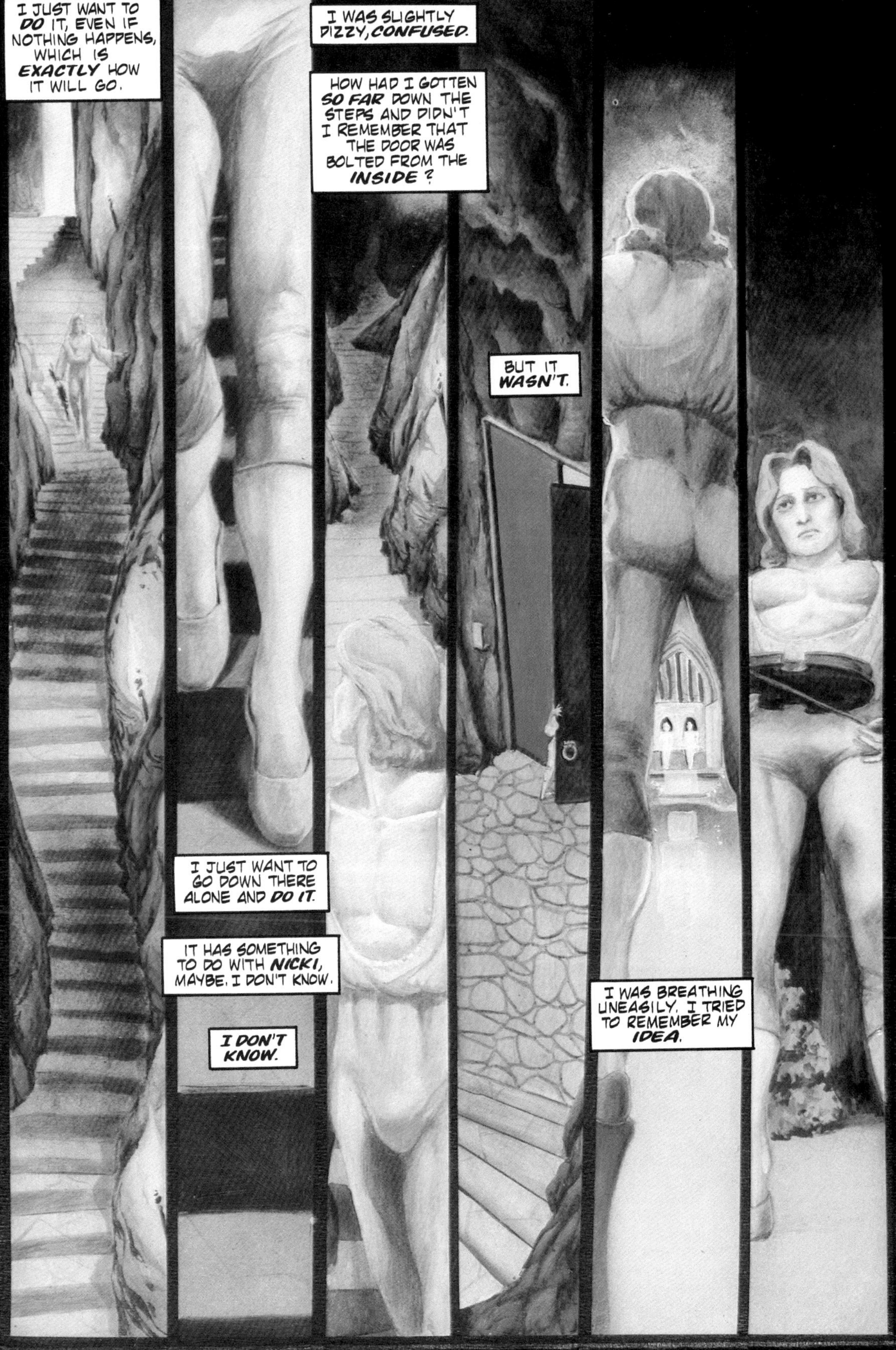

I JUST WANT TO DO IT, EVEN IF NOTHING HAPPENS, WHICH IS EXACTLY HOW IT WILL GO.
I JUST WANT TO GO DOWN THERE ALONE AND DO IT.
IT HAS SOMETHING TO DO WITH NICKI, MAYBE. I DON'T KNOW.
I DON'T KNOW.
I WAS SLIGHTLY DIZZY, CONFUSED.
HOW HAD I GOTTEN SO FAR DOWN THE STEPS AND DIDN'T I REMEMBER THAT THE DOOR WAS BOLTED FROM THE INSIDE?
BUT IT WASN'T.
I WAS BREATHING UNEASILY. I TRIED TO REMEMBER MY IDEA.

Those
Who Must Be
Kept

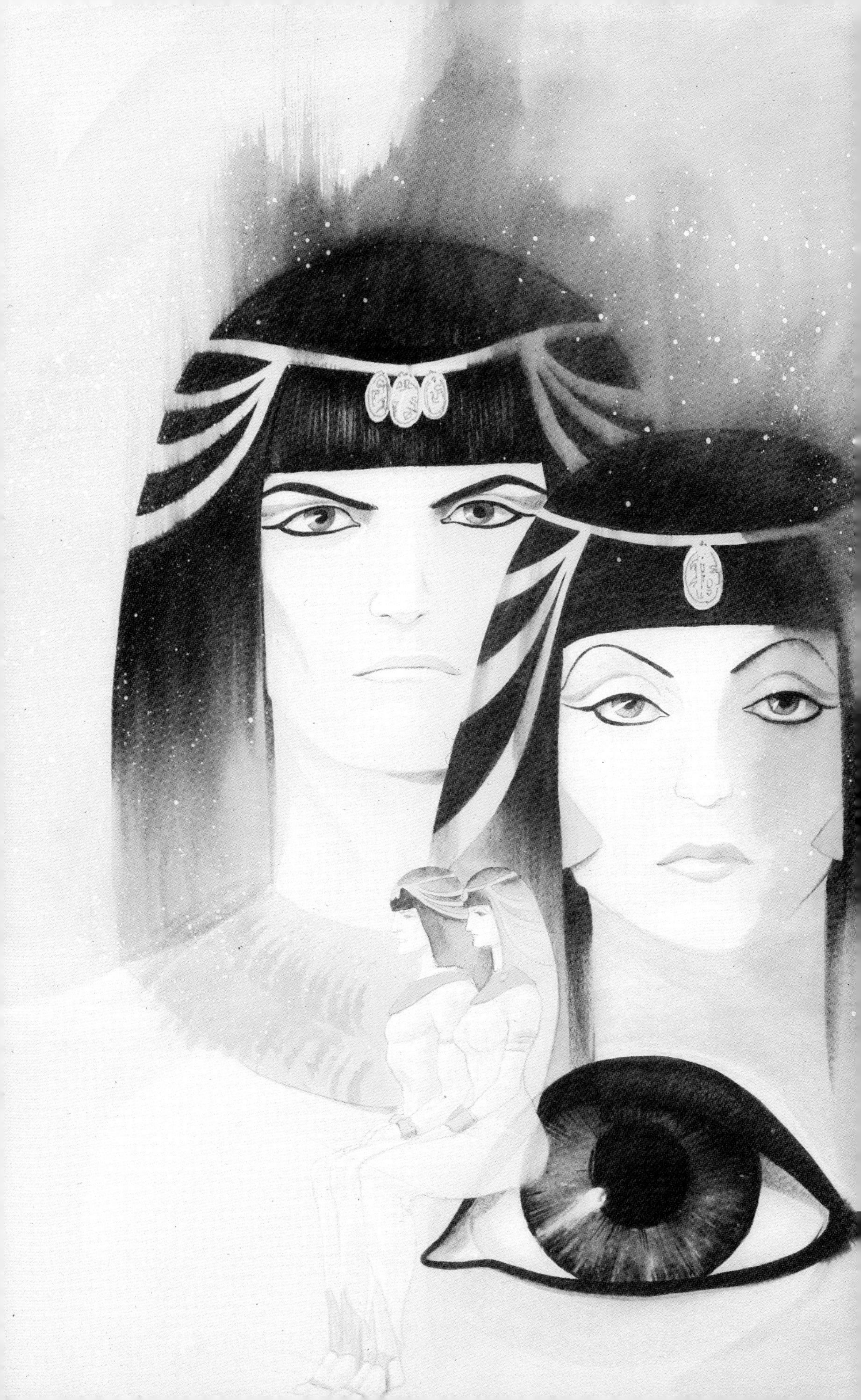

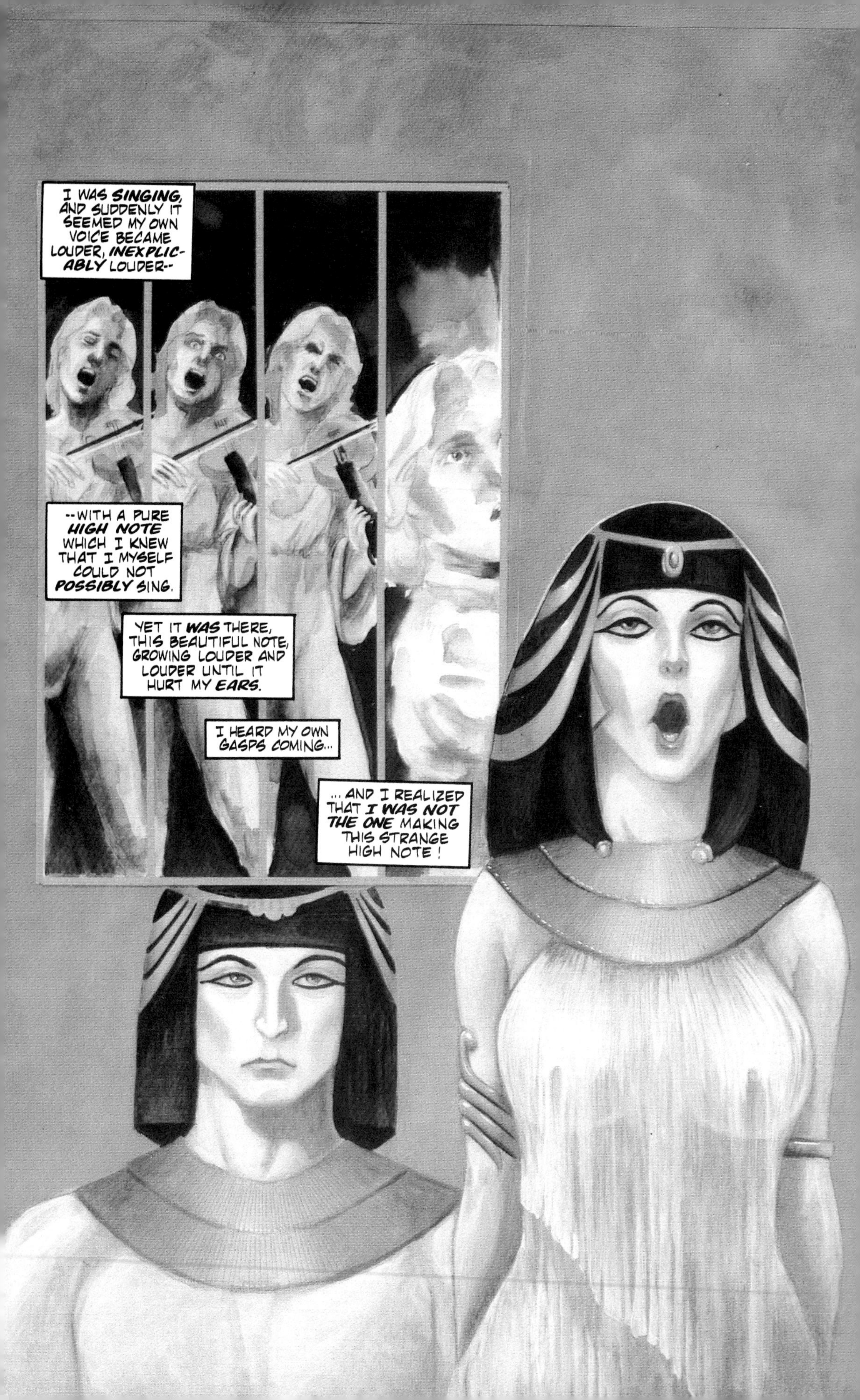
I WAS SINGING, AND SUDDENLY IT SEEMED MY OWN VOICE BECAME LOUDER, INEXPLICABLY LOUDER--
--WITH A PURE HIGH NOTE WHICH I KNEW THAT I MYSELF COULD NOT POSSIBLY SING.
YET IT WAS THERE, THIS BEAUTIFUL NOTE, GROWING LOUDER AND LOUDER UNTIL IT HURT MY EARS.
I HEARD MY OWN GASPS COMING...
...AND I REALIZED THAT I WAS NOT THE ONE MAKING THIS STRANGE HIGH NOTE!

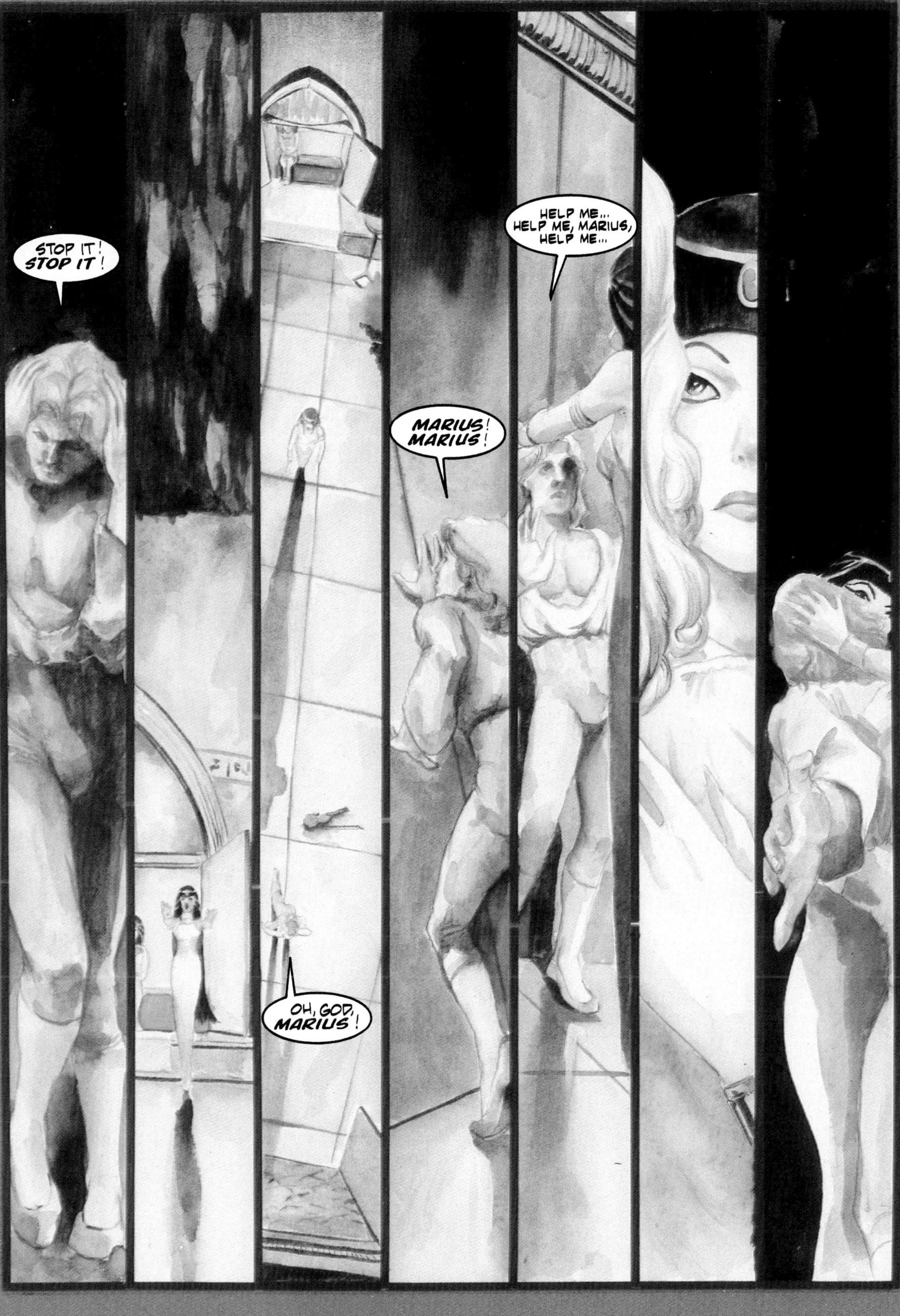
STOP IT! STOP IT!
OH, GOD, MARIUS!
MARIUS! MARIUS!
HELP ME... HELP ME, MARIUS, HELP ME...

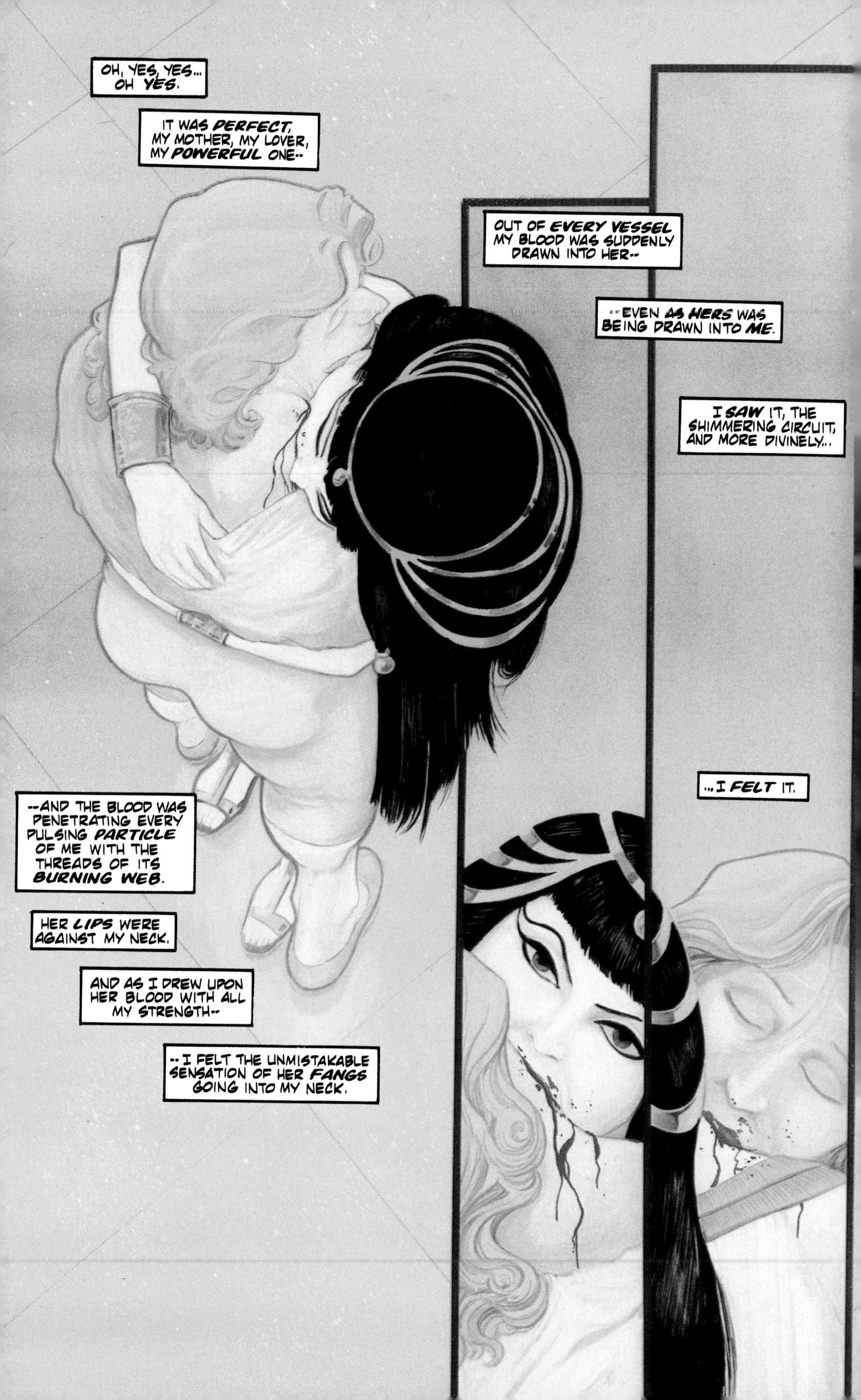
OH, YES, YES... OH YES.
IT WAS PERFECT, MY MOTHER, MY LOVER, MY POWERFUL ONE--
OUT OF EVERY VESSEL MY BLOOD WAS SUDDENLY DRAWN INTO HER--
--EVEN AS HERS WAS BEING DRAWN INTO ME.
I SAW IT, THE SHIMMERING CIRCUIT, AND MORE DIVINELY...
...I FELT IT.
--AND THE BLOOD WAS PENETRATING EVERY PULSING PARTICLE OF ME WITH THE THREADS OF ITS BURNING WEB.
HER LIPS WERE AGAINST MY NECK.
AND AS I DREW UPON HER BLOOD WITH ALL MY STRENGTH--
--I FELT THE UNMISTAKABLE SENSATION OF HER FANGS GOING INTO MY NECK.

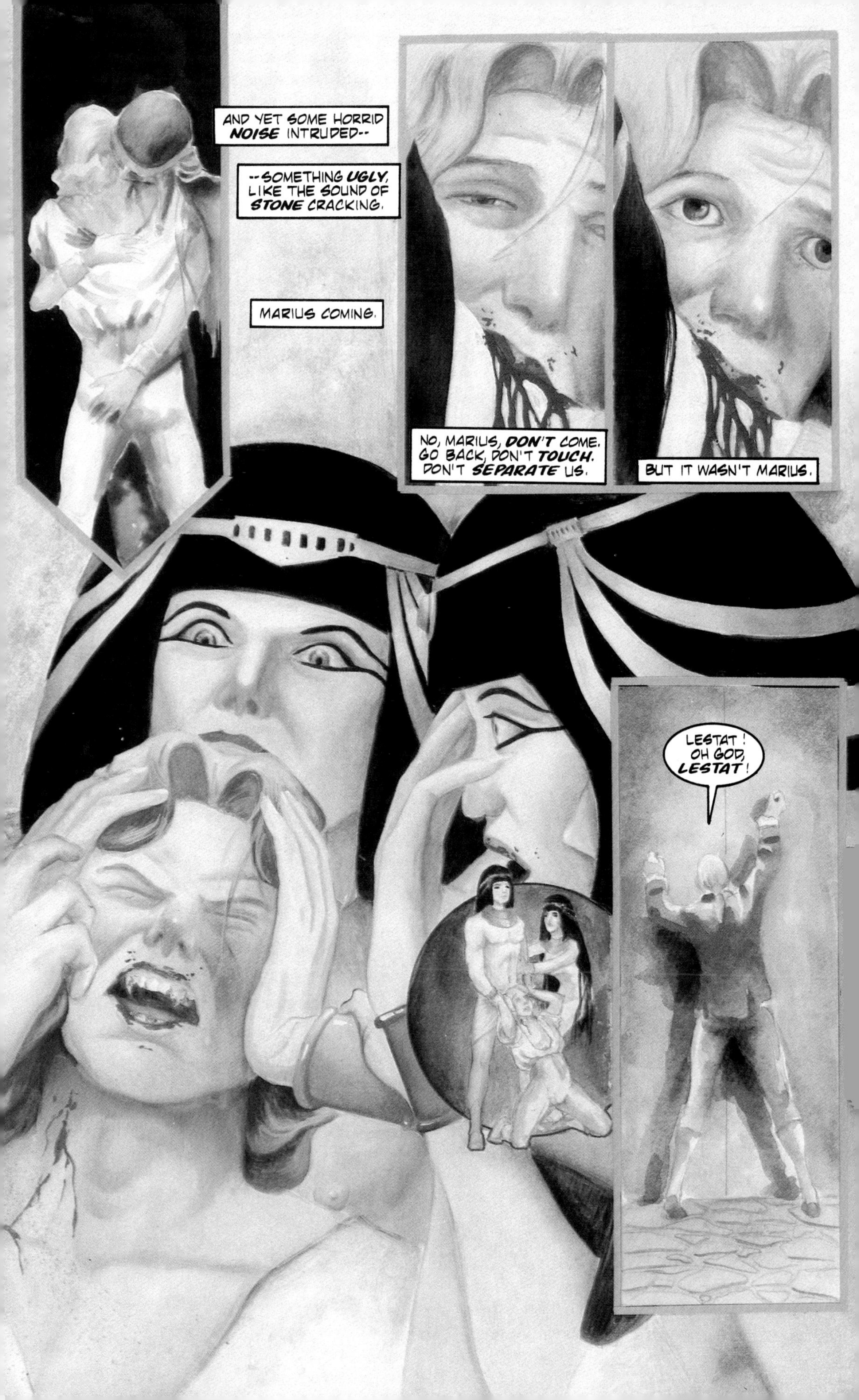
AND YET SOME HORRID **NOISE** INTRUDED--
--SOMETHING **UGLY**, LIKE THE SOUND OF **STONE** CRACKING.
MARIUS COMING.
NO, MARIUS, **DON'T** COME. GO BACK, DON'T **TOUCH**. DON'T **SEPARATE** US.
BUT IT WASN'T MARIUS.
LESTAT! OH GOD, **LESTAT**!

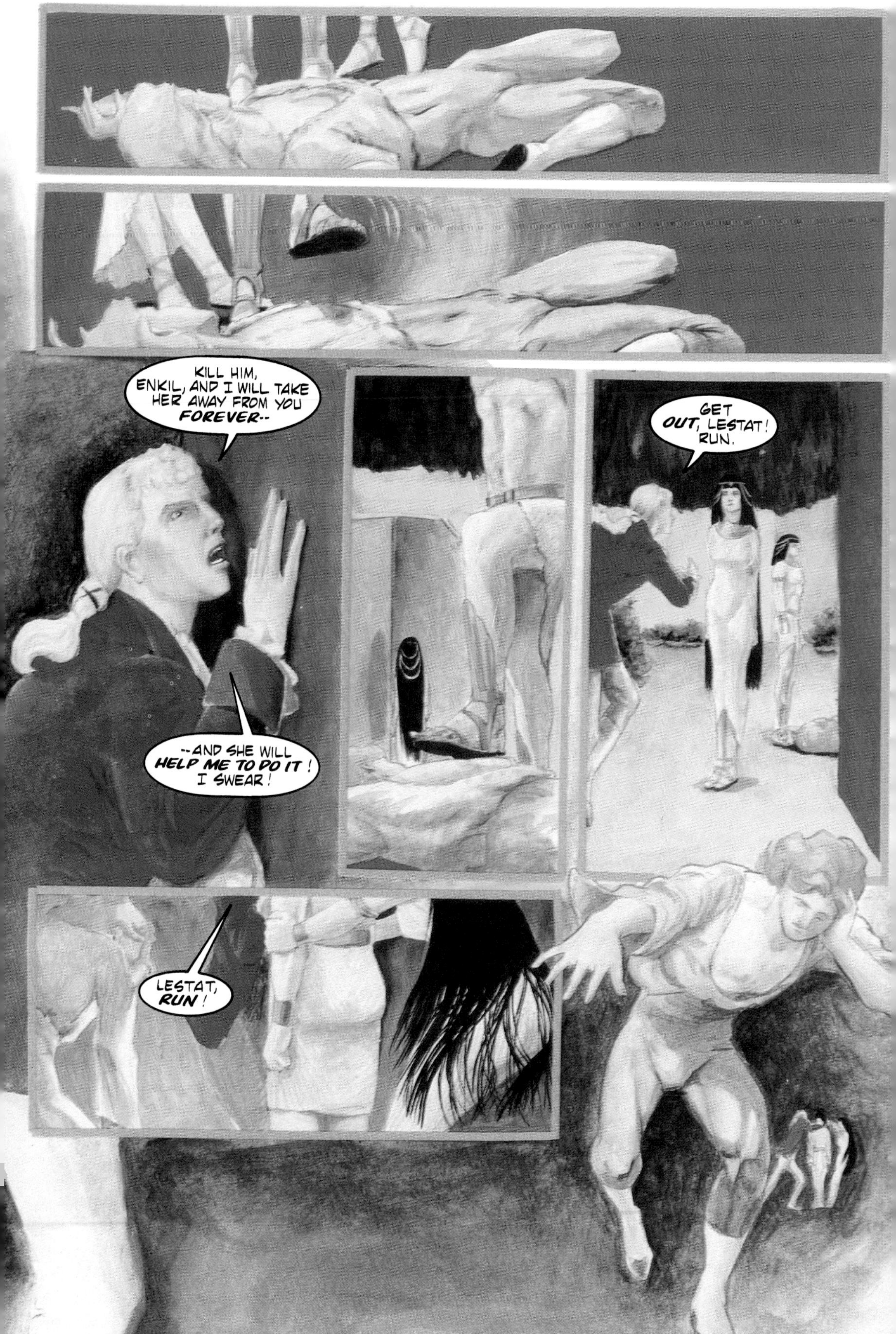
KILL HIM, ENKIL, AND I WILL TAKE HER AWAY FROM YOU FOREVER--
--AND SHE WILL HELP ME TO DO IT! I SWEAR!
GET OUT, LESTAT! RUN.
LESTAT, RUN!

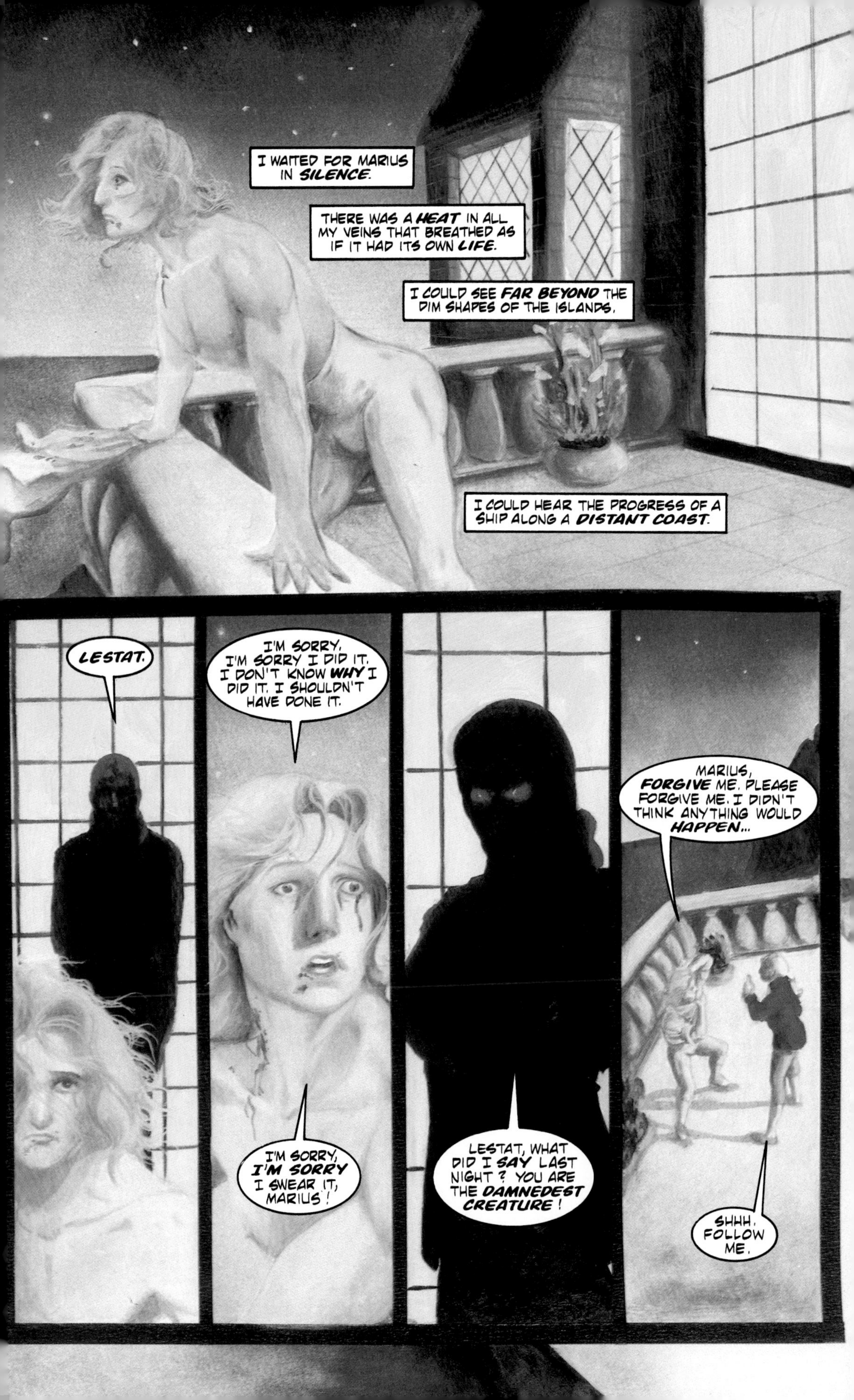
I WAITED FOR MARIUS IN SILENCE.
THERE WAS A HEAT IN ALL MY VEINS THAT BREATHED AS IF IT HAD ITS OWN LIFE.
I COULD SEE FAR BEYOND THE DIM SHAPES OF THE ISLANDS.
I COULD HEAR THE PROGRESS OF A SHIP ALONG A DISTANT COAST.
LESTAT.
I'M SORRY. I'M SORRY I DID IT. I DON'T KNOW WHY I DID IT. I SHOULDN'T HAVE DONE IT.
I'M SORRY, I'M SORRY I SWEAR IT, MARIUS!
LESTAT, WHAT DID I SAY LAST NIGHT? YOU ARE THE DAMNEDEST CREATURE!
MARIUS, FORGIVE ME. PLEASE FORGIVE ME. I DIDN'T THINK ANYTHING WOULD HAPPEN...
SHHH. FOLLOW ME.

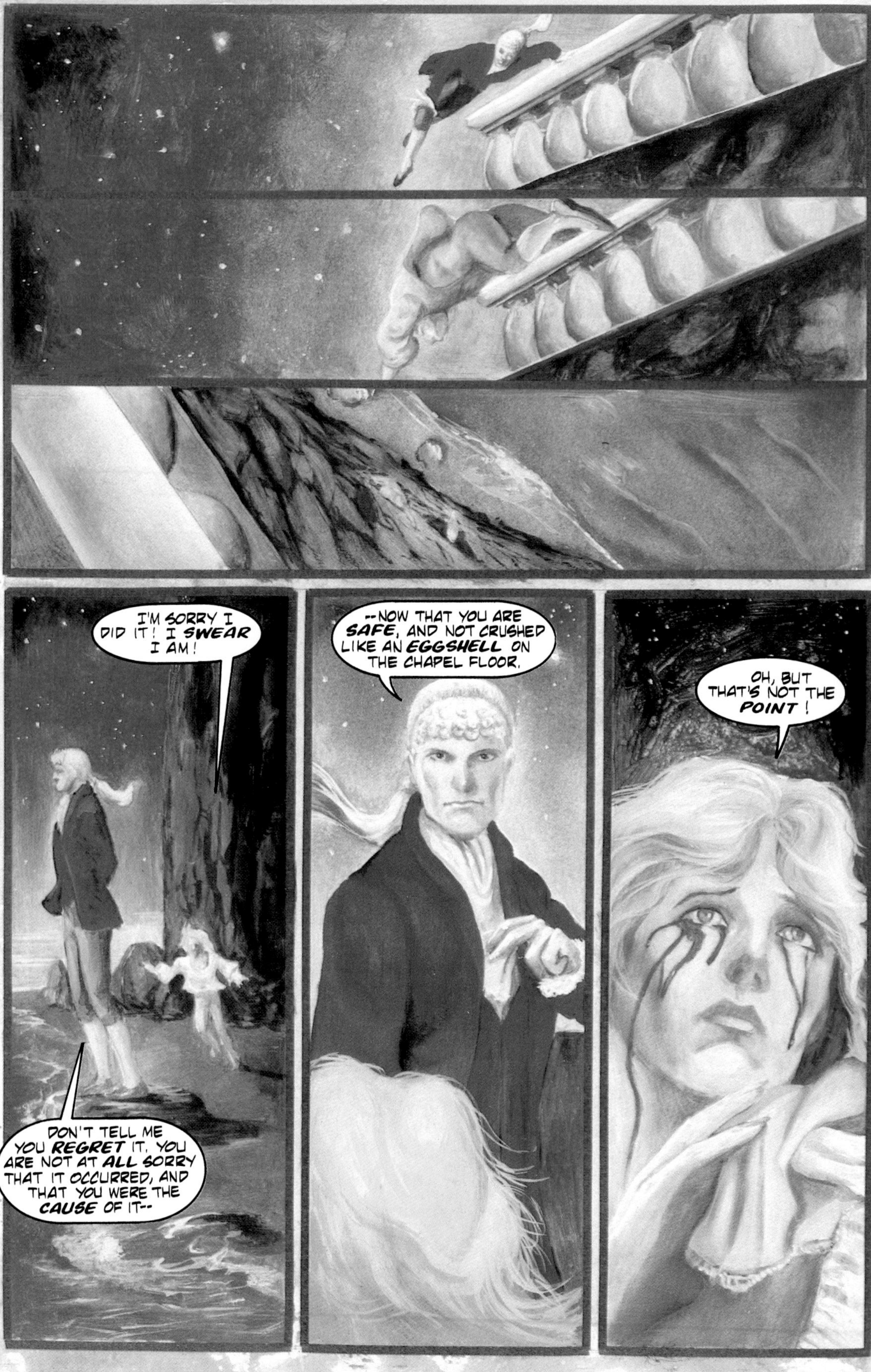
I'M SORRY I DID IT! I SWEAR I AM!
DON'T TELL ME YOU REGRET IT. YOU ARE NOT AT ALL SORRY THAT IT OCCURRED, AND THAT YOU WERE THE CAUSE OF IT--
--NOW THAT YOU ARE SAFE, AND NOT CRUSHED LIKE AN EGGSHELL ON THE CHAPEL FLOOR.
OH, BUT THAT'S NOT THE POINT!

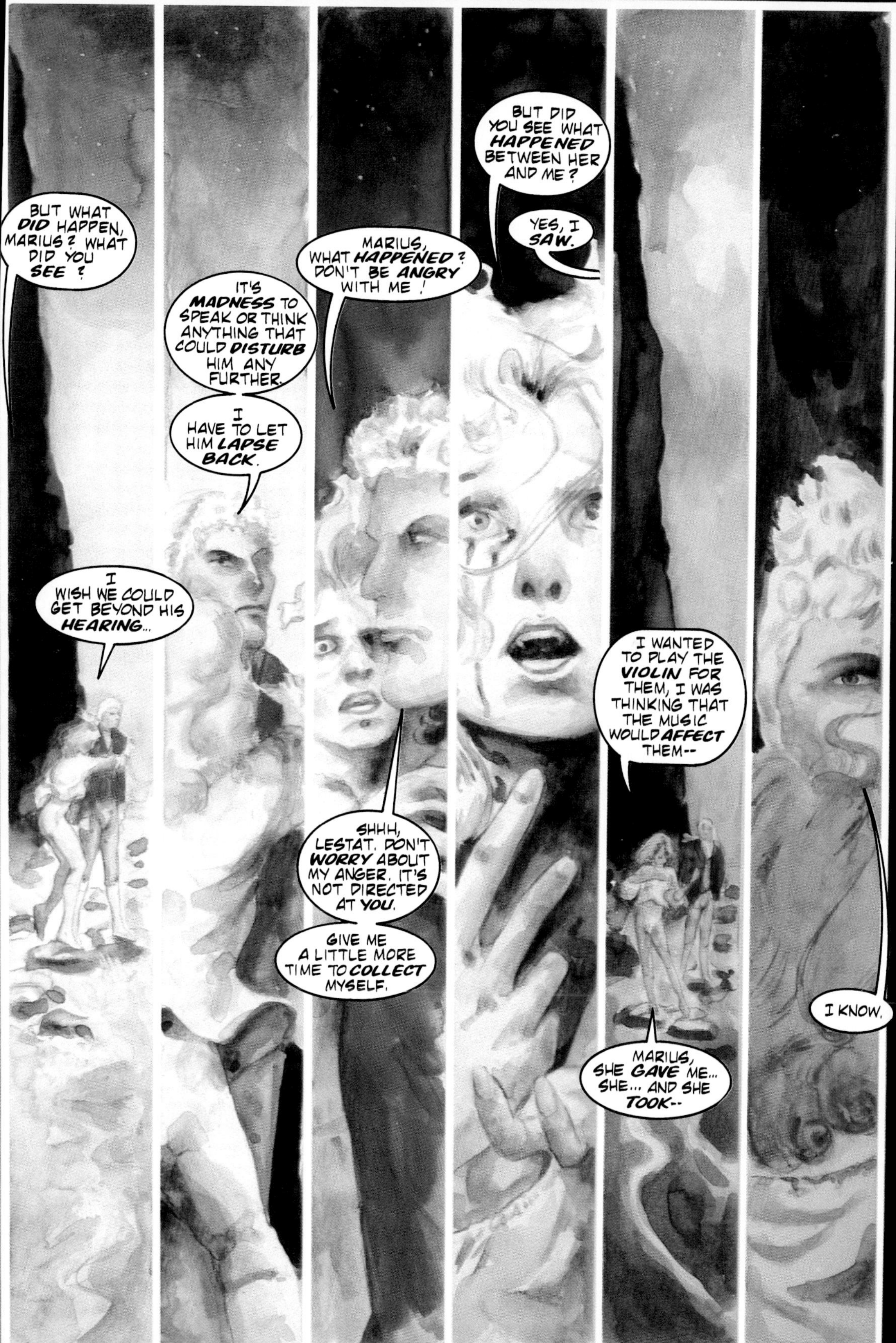
BUT WHAT DID HAPPEN, MARIUS? WHAT DID YOU SEE?
I WISH WE COULD GET BEYOND HIS HEARING...
IT'S MADNESS TO SPEAK OR THINK ANYTHING THAT COULD DISTURB HIM ANY FURTHER.
I HAVE TO LET HIM LAPSE BACK.
MARIUS, WHAT HAPPENED? DON'T BE ANGRY WITH ME!
SHHH, LESTAT. DON'T WORRY ABOUT MY ANGER. IT'S NOT DIRECTED AT YOU.
GIVE ME A LITTLE MORE TIME TO COLLECT MYSELF.
BUT DID YOU SEE WHAT HAPPENED BETWEEN HER AND ME?
YES, I SAW.
I WANTED TO PLAY THE VIOLIN FOR THEM, I WAS THINKING THAT THE MUSIC WOULD AFFECT THEM--
MARIUS, SHE GAVE ME... SHE... AND SHE TOOK--
I KNOW.

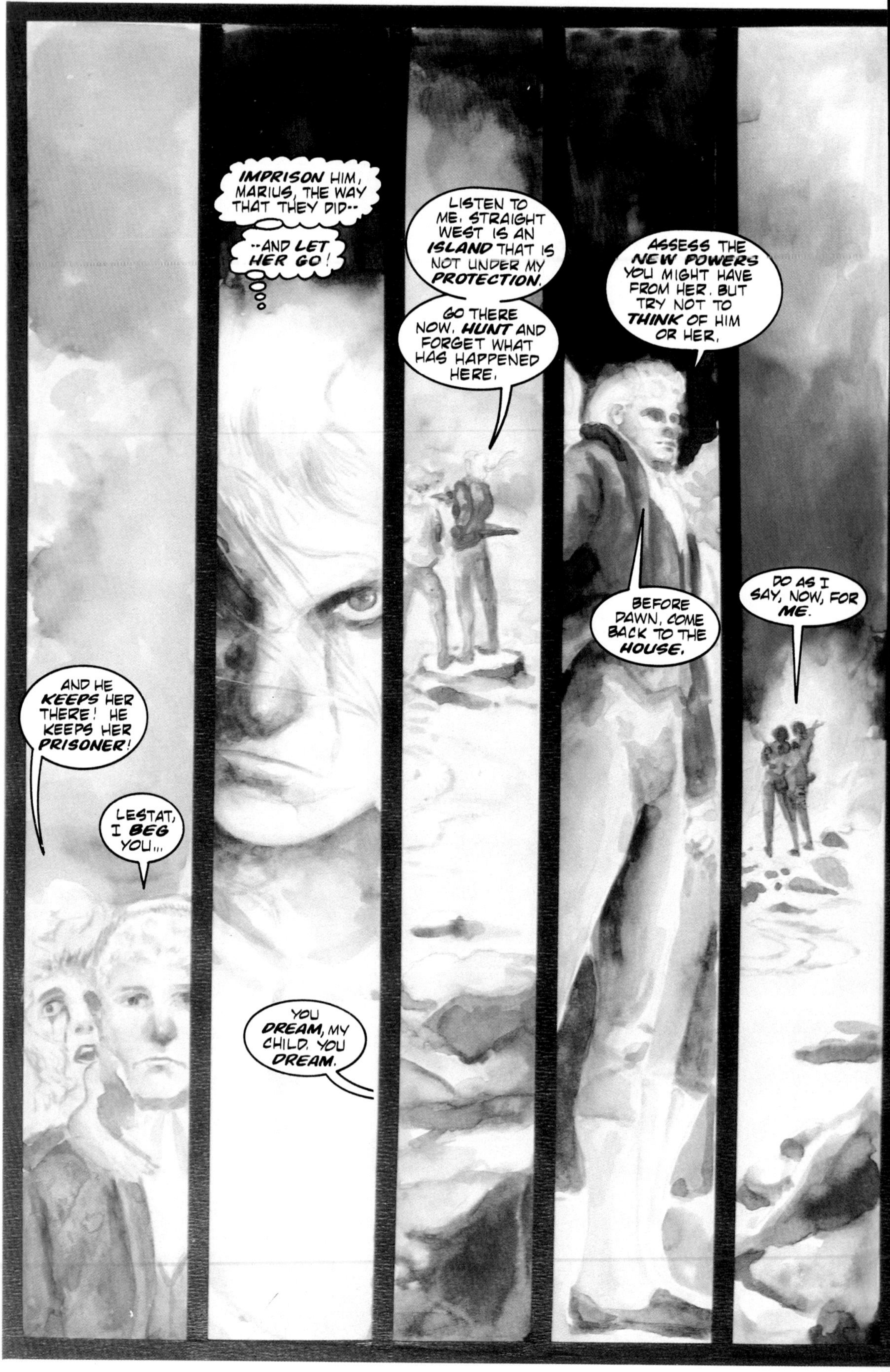
AND HE KEEPS HER THERE! HE KEEPS HER PRISONER!
LESTAT, I BEG YOU...
IMPRISON HIM, MARIUS, THE WAY THAT THEY DID--
--AND LET HER GO!
YOU DREAM, MY CHILD. YOU DREAM.
LISTEN TO ME. STRAIGHT WEST IS AN ISLAND THAT IS NOT UNDER MY PROTECTION.
GO THERE NOW. HUNT AND FORGET WHAT HAS HAPPENED HERE.
ASSESS THE NEW POWERS YOU MIGHT HAVE FROM HER. BUT TRY NOT TO THINK OF HIM OR HER.
BEFORE DAWN, COME BACK TO THE HOUSE.
DO AS I SAY, NOW, FOR ME.

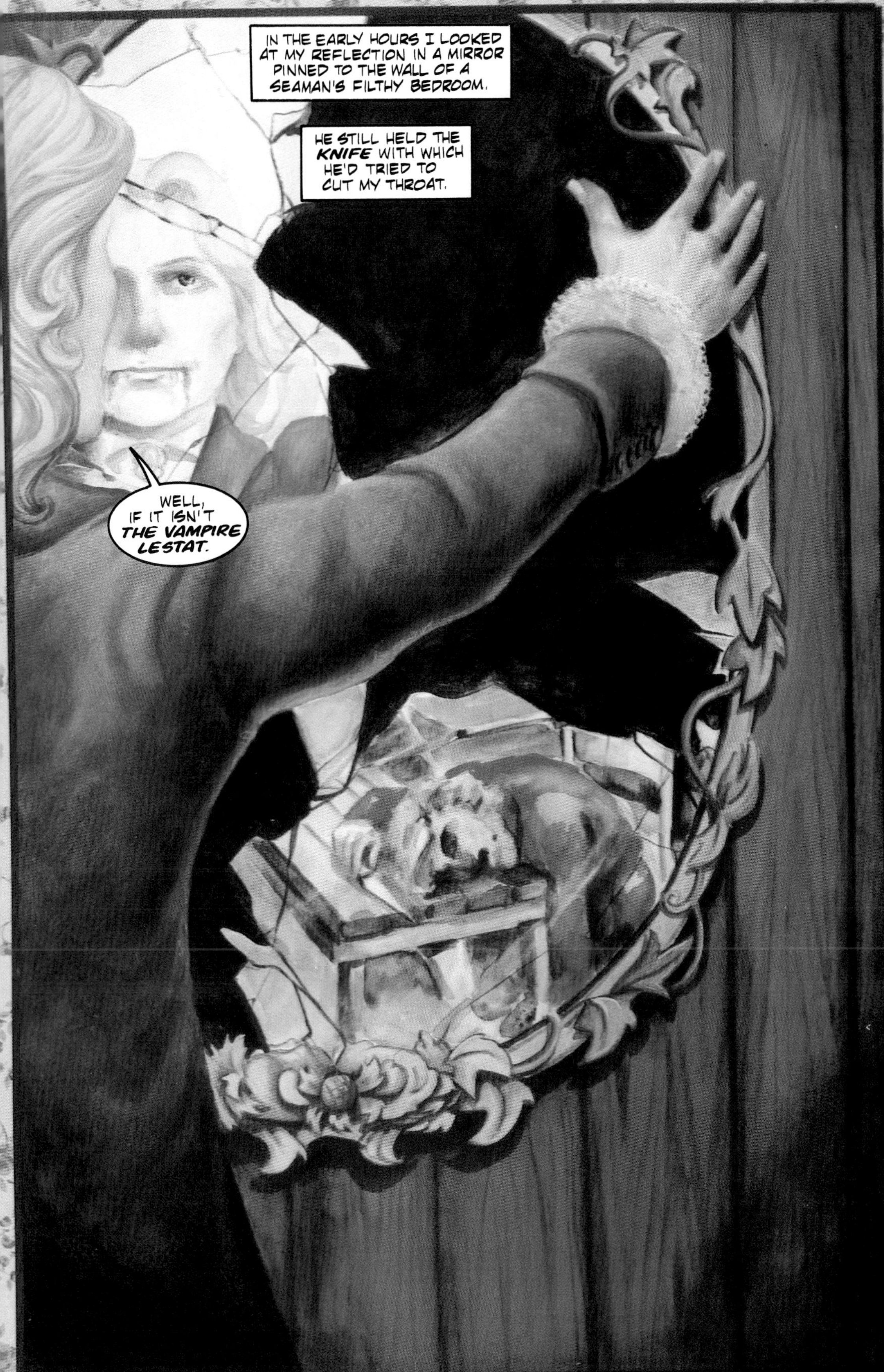
IN THE EARLY HOURS I LOOKED AT MY REFLECTION IN A MIRROR PINNED TO THE WALL OF A SEAMAN'S FILTHY BEDROOM.
HE STILL HELD THE KNIFE WITH WHICH HE'D TRIED TO CUT MY THROAT.
WELL, IF IT ISN'T THE VAMPIRE LESTAT.

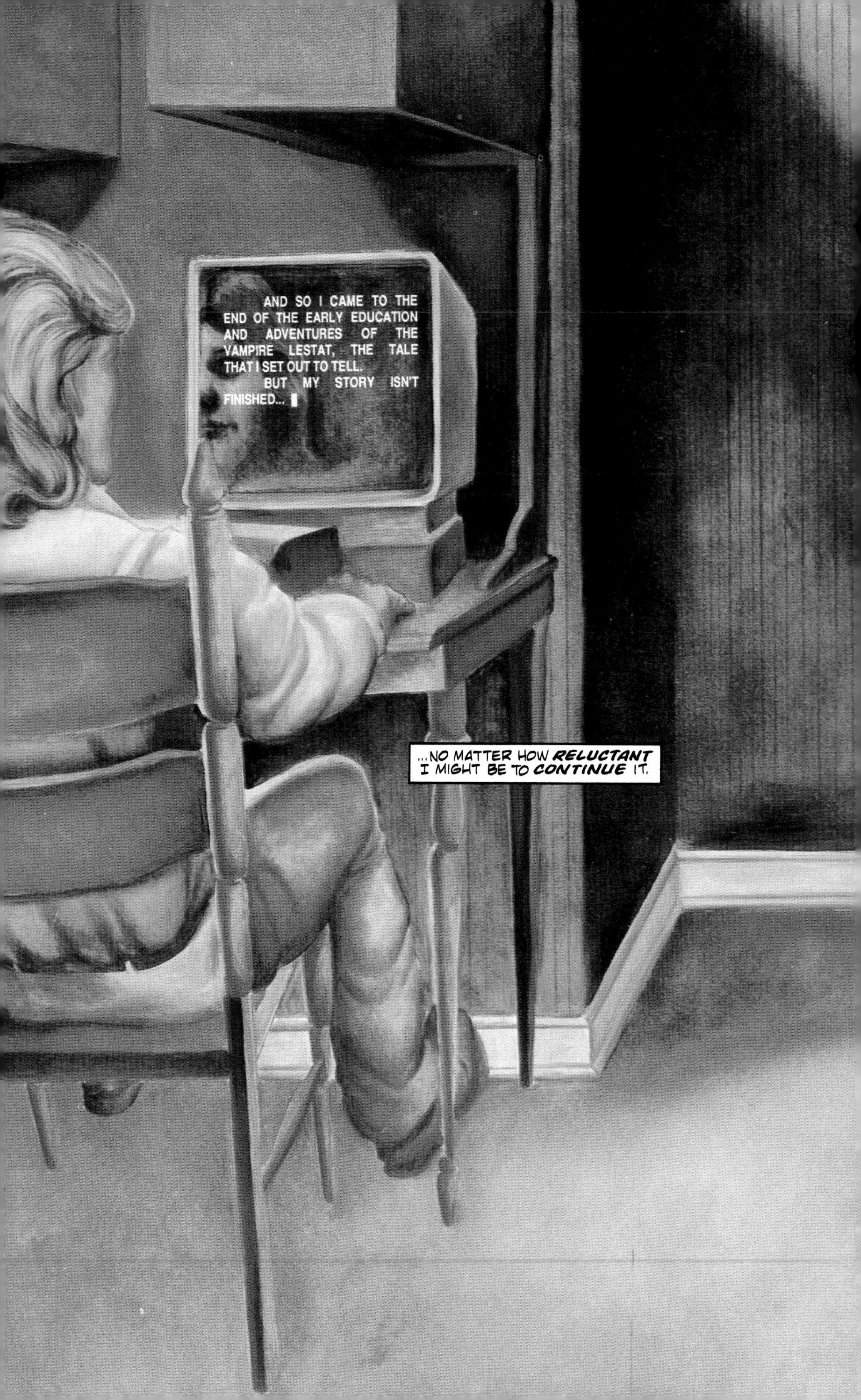
AND SO I CAME TO THE END OF THE EARLY EDUCATION AND ADVENTURES OF THE VAMPIRE LESTAT, THE TALE THAT I SET OUT TO TELL.
BUT MY STORY ISN'T FINISHED...
...NO MATTER HOW *RELUCTANT* I MIGHT BE TO *CONTINUE* IT.

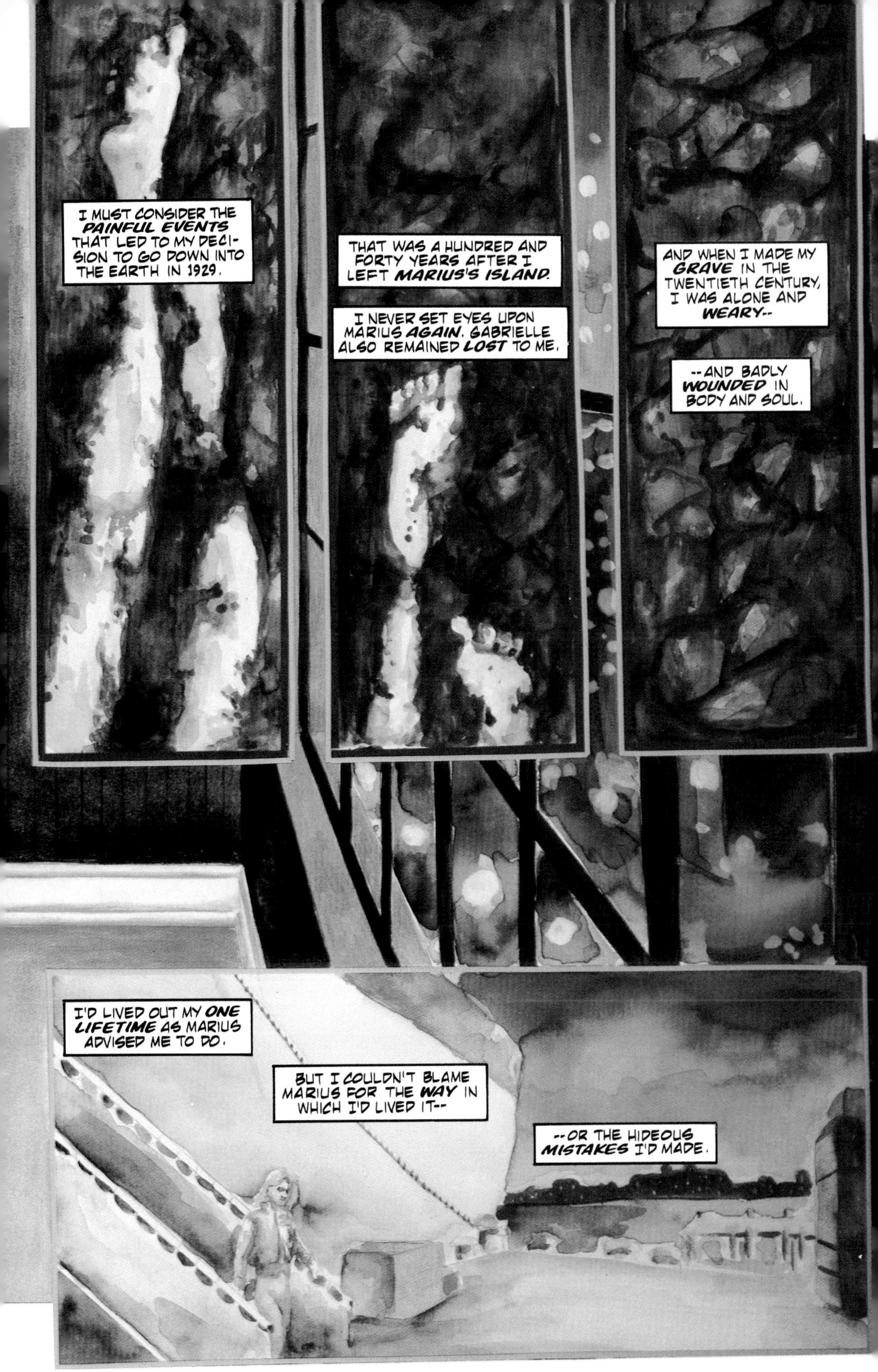
I MUST CONSIDER THE PAINFUL EVENTS THAT LED TO MY DECISION TO GO DOWN INTO THE EARTH IN 1929.
THAT WAS A HUNDRED AND FORTY YEARS AFTER I LEFT MARIUS'S ISLAND.
I NEVER SET EYES UPON MARIUS AGAIN. GABRIELLE ALSO REMAINED LOST TO ME.
AND WHEN I MADE MY GRAVE IN THE TWENTIETH CENTURY, I WAS ALONE AND WEARY--
--AND BADLY WOUNDED IN BODY AND SOUL.
I'D LIVED OUT MY ONE LIFETIME AS MARIUS ADVISED ME TO DO.
BUT I COULDN'T BLAME MARIUS FOR THE WAY IN WHICH I'D LIVED IT--
--OR THE HIDEOUS MISTAKES I'D MADE.

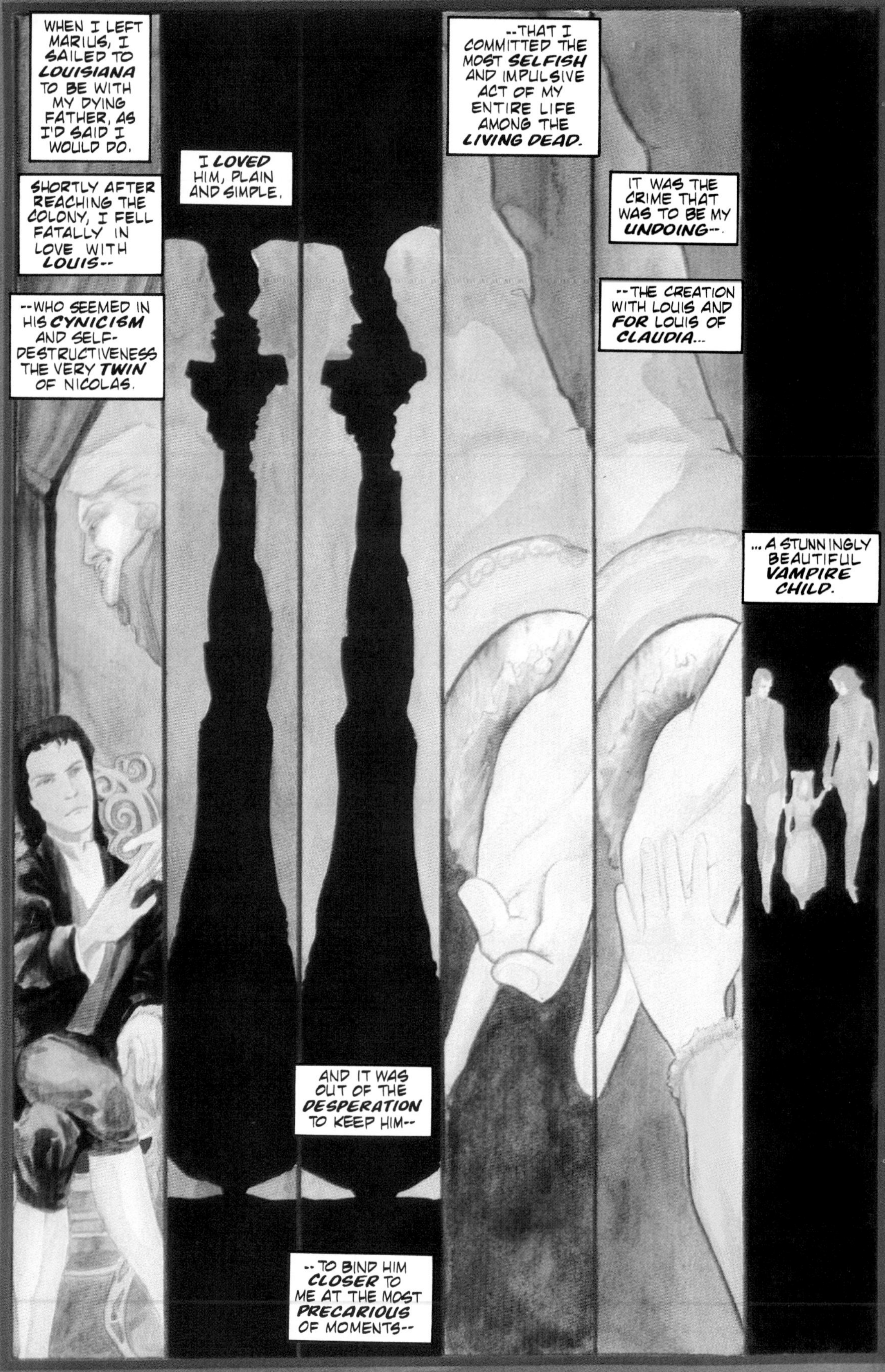
WHEN I LEFT MARIUS, I SAILED TO LOUISIANA TO BE WITH MY DYING FATHER, AS I'D SAID I WOULD DO.
SHORTLY AFTER REACHING THE COLONY, I FELL FATALLY IN LOVE WITH LOUIS--
--WHO SEEMED IN HIS CYNICISM AND SELF-DESTRUCTIVENESS THE VERY TWIN OF NICOLAS.
I LOVED HIM, PLAIN AND SIMPLE.
AND IT WAS OUT OF THE DESPERATION TO KEEP HIM--
--TO BIND HIM CLOSER TO ME AT THE MOST PRECARIOUS OF MOMENTS--
--THAT I COMMITTED THE MOST SELFISH AND IMPULSIVE ACT OF MY ENTIRE LIFE AMONG THE LIVING DEAD.
IT WAS THE CRIME THAT WAS TO BE MY UNDOING--.
--THE CREATION WITH LOUIS AND FOR LOUIS OF CLAUDIA...
...A STUNNINGLY BEAUTIFUL VAMPIRE CHILD.

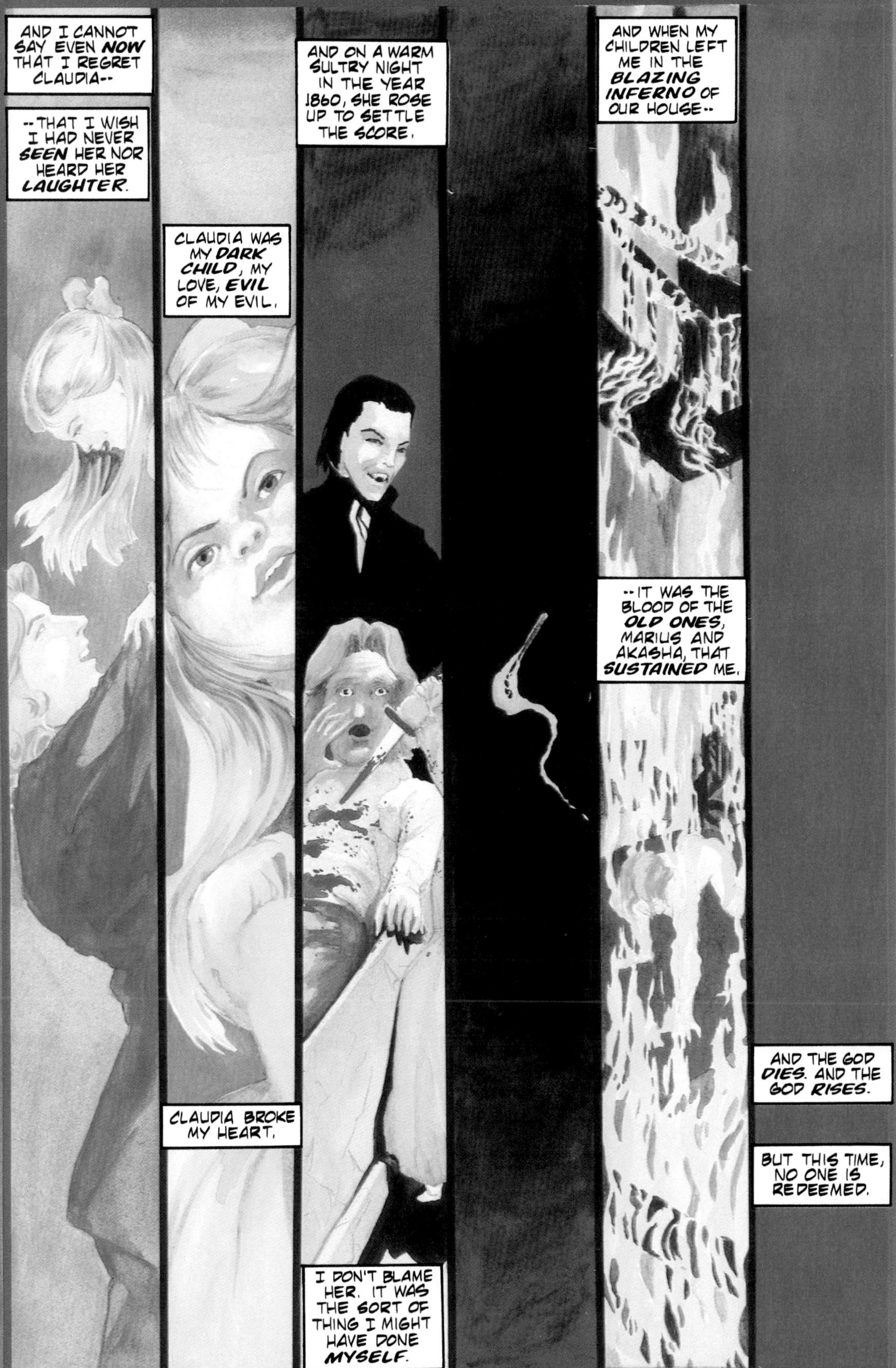
AND I CANNOT SAY EVEN NOW THAT I REGRET CLAUDIA--
--THAT I WISH I HAD NEVER SEEN HER NOR HEARD HER LAUGHTER.
CLAUDIA WAS MY DARK CHILD, MY LOVE, EVIL OF MY EVIL.
CLAUDIA BROKE MY HEART.
AND ON A WARM SULTRY NIGHT IN THE YEAR 1860, SHE ROSE UP TO SETTLE THE SCORE.
I DON'T BLAME HER. IT WAS THE SORT OF THING I MIGHT HAVE DONE MYSELF.
AND WHEN MY CHILDREN LEFT ME IN THE BLAZING INFERNO OF OUR HOUSE--
--IT WAS THE BLOOD OF THE OLD ONES, MARIUS AND AKASHA, THAT SUSTAINED ME.
AND THE GOD DIES. AND THE GOD RISES.
BUT THIS TIME, NO ONE IS REDEEMED.

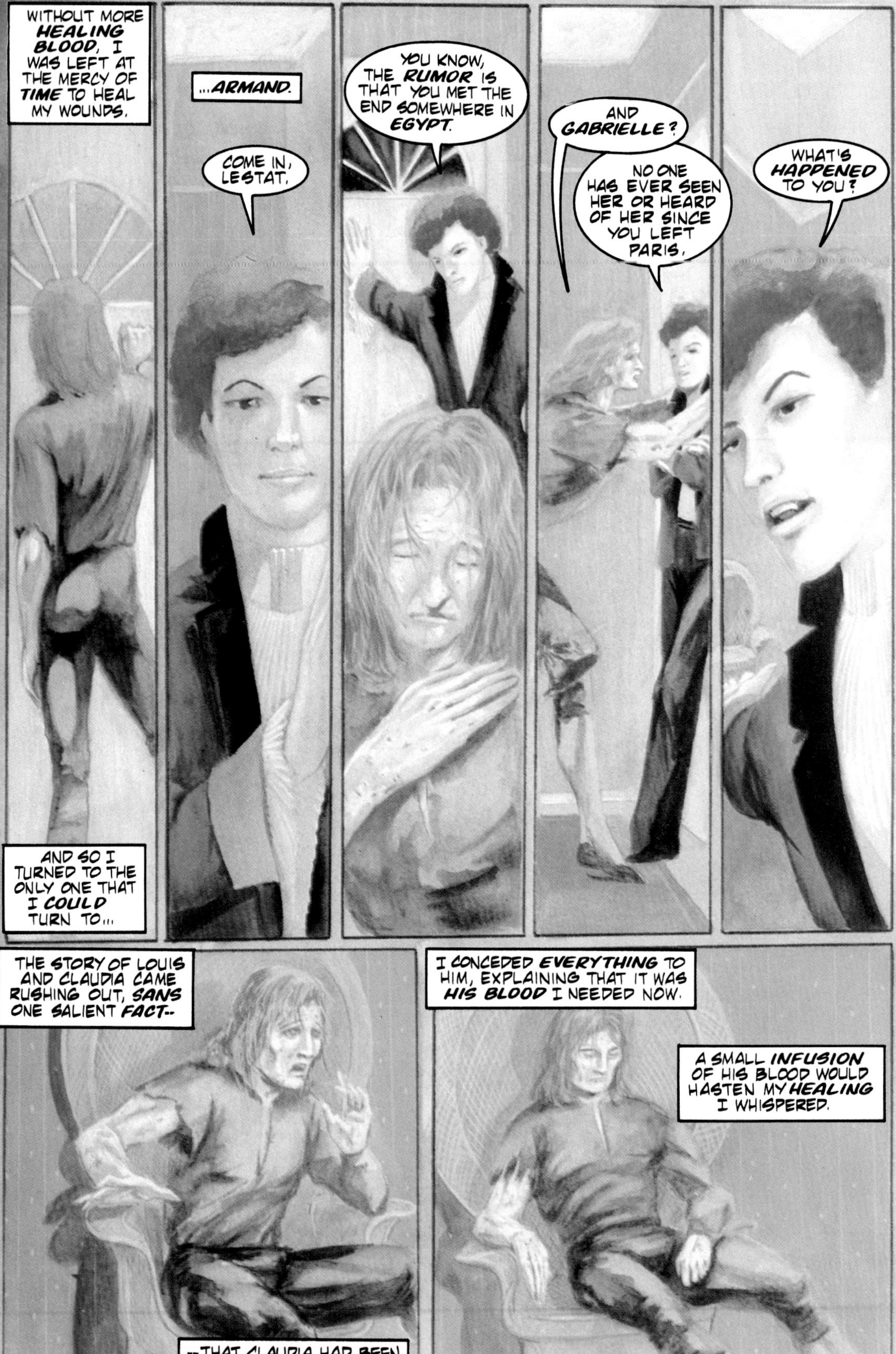

WITHOUT MORE HEALING BLOOD, I WAS LEFT AT THE MERCY OF TIME TO HEAL MY WOUNDS.
AND SO I TURNED TO THE ONLY ONE THAT I COULD TURN TO...
...ARMAND.
COME IN, LESTAT.
YOU KNOW, THE RUMOR IS THAT YOU MET THE END SOMEWHERE IN EGYPT.
AND GABRIELLE?
NO ONE HAS EVER SEEN HER OR HEARD OF HER SINCE YOU LEFT PARIS.
WHAT'S HAPPENED TO YOU?
THE STORY OF LOUIS AND CLAUDIA CAME RUSHING OUT, SANS ONE SALIENT FACT--
--THAT CLAUDIA HAD BEEN ONLY... A CHILD.
I CONCEDED EVERYTHING TO HIM, EXPLAINING THAT IT WAS HIS BLOOD I NEEDED NOW.
A SMALL INFUSION OF HIS BLOOD WOULD HASTEN MY HEALING I WHISPERED.

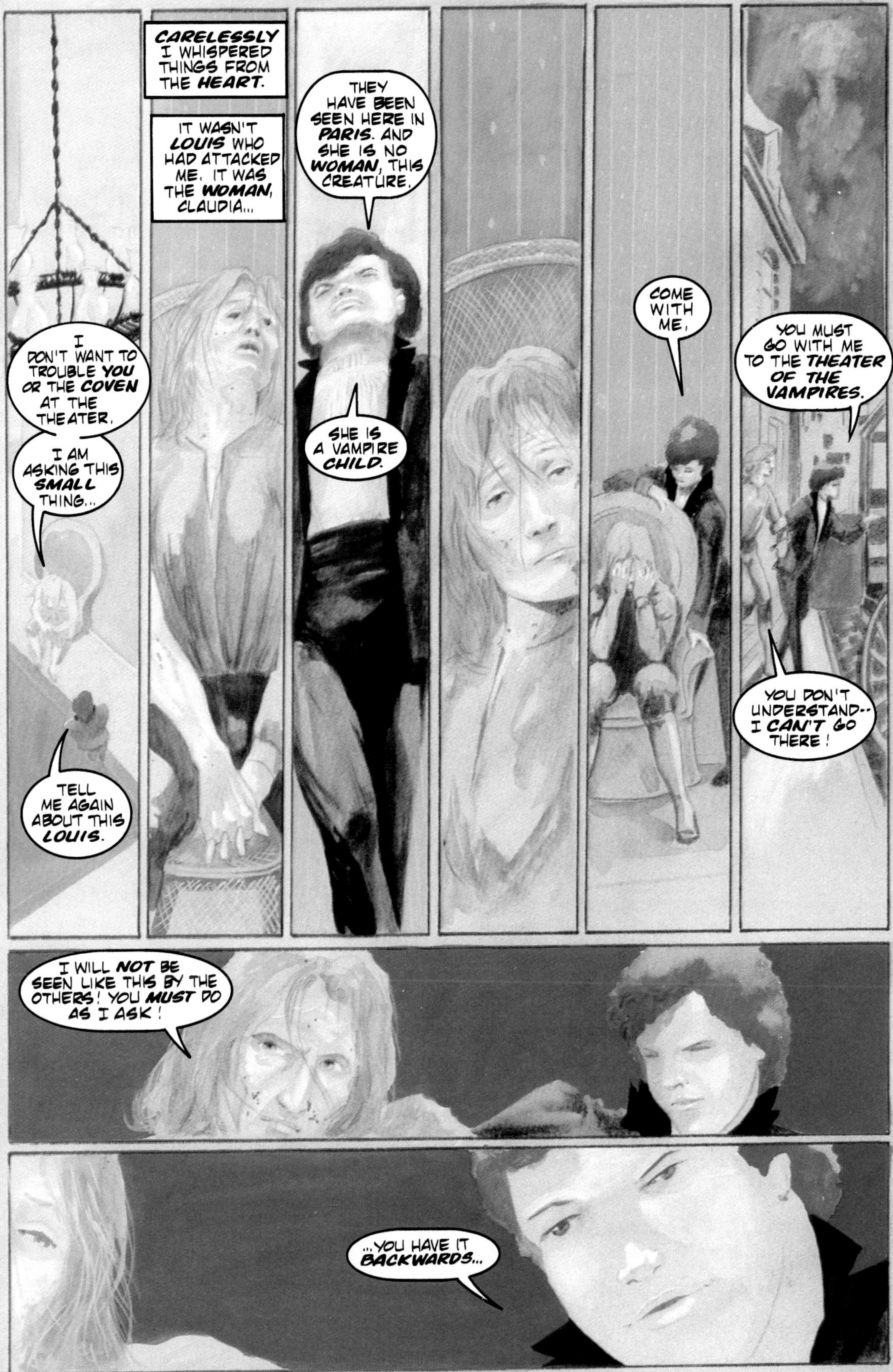
CARELESSLY I WHISPERED THINGS FROM THE HEART.
IT WASN'T LOUIS WHO HAD ATTACKED ME. IT WAS THE WOMAN, CLAUDIA...
I DON'T WANT TO TROUBLE YOU OR THE COVEN AT THE THEATER.
I AM ASKING THIS SMALL THING...
TELL ME AGAIN ABOUT THIS LOUIS.
THEY HAVE BEEN SEEN HERE IN PARIS. AND SHE IS NO WOMAN, THIS CREATURE.
SHE IS A VAMPIRE CHILD.
COME WITH ME.
YOU MUST GO WITH ME TO THE THEATER OF THE VAMPIRES.
YOU DON'T UNDERSTAND-- I CAN'T GO THERE!
I WILL NOT BE SEEN LIKE THIS BY THE OTHERS! YOU MUST DO AS I ASK!
...YOU HAVE IT BACKWARDS...

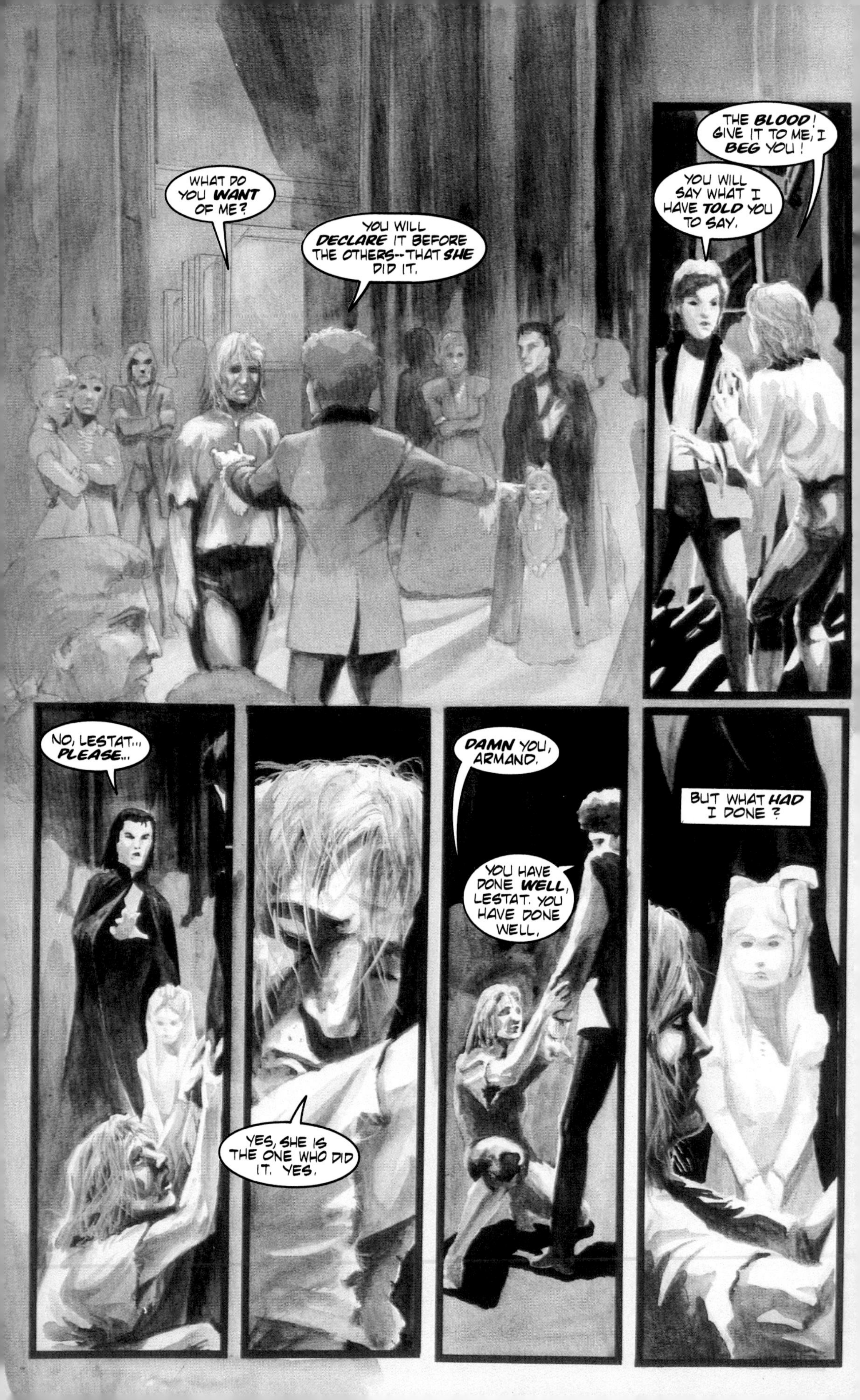
WHAT DO YOU WANT OF ME?
YOU WILL DECLARE IT BEFORE THE OTHERS--THAT SHE DID IT.
THE BLOOD! GIVE IT TO ME, I BEG YOU!
YOU WILL SAY WHAT I HAVE TOLD YOU TO SAY.
NO, LESTAT... PLEASE...
YES, SHE IS THE ONE WHO DID IT. YES.
DAMN YOU, ARMAND.
YOU HAVE DONE WELL, LESTAT. YOU HAVE DONE WELL.
BUT WHAT HAD I DONE?

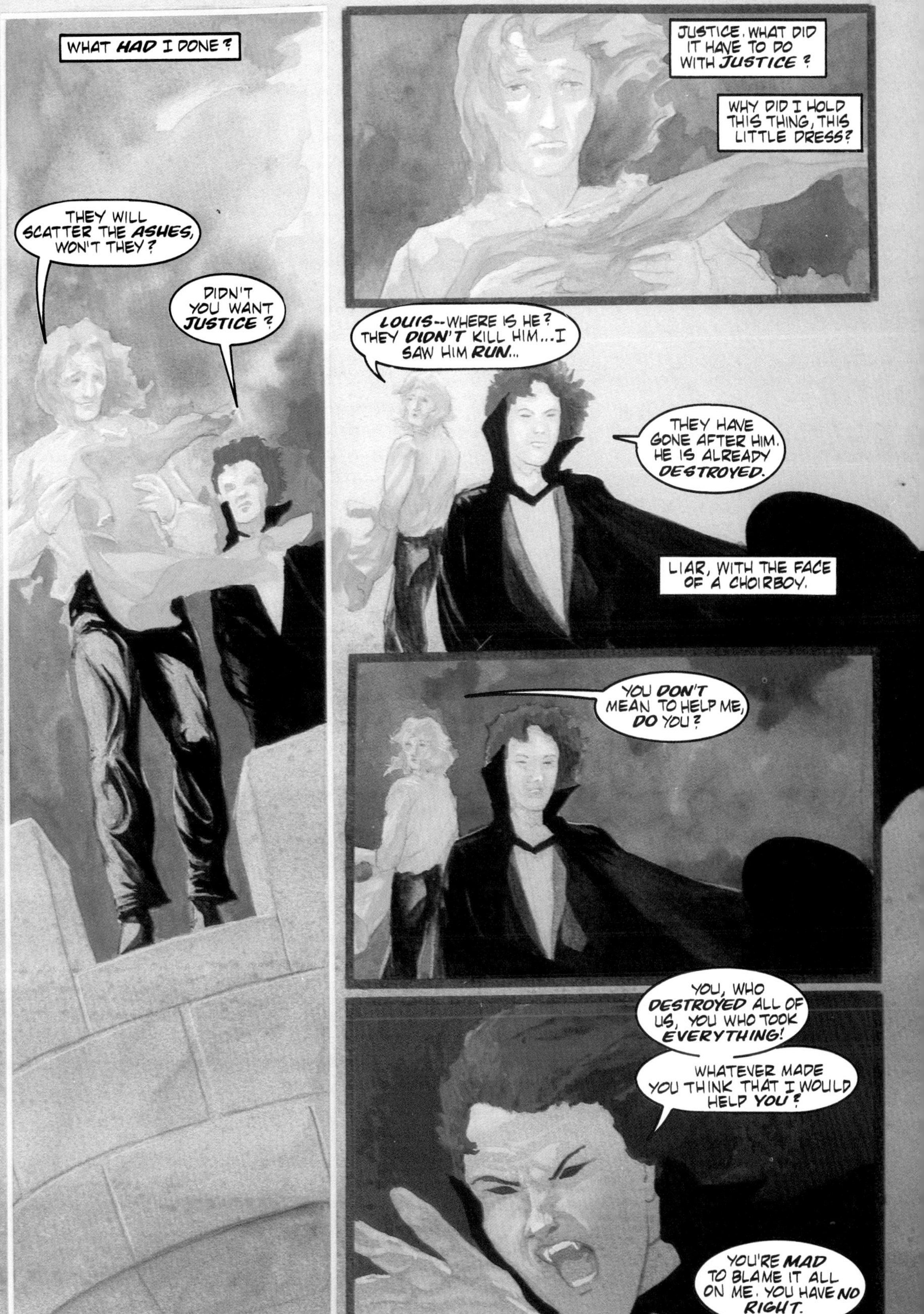
WHAT HAD I DONE?
THEY WILL SCATTER THE ASHES, WON'T THEY?
DIDN'T YOU WANT JUSTICE?
JUSTICE. WHAT DID IT HAVE TO DO WITH JUSTICE?
WHY DID I HOLD THIS THING, THIS LITTLE DRESS?
LOUIS--WHERE IS HE? THEY DIDN'T KILL HIM... I SAW HIM RUN...
THEY HAVE GONE AFTER HIM. HE IS ALREADY DESTROYED.
LIAR, WITH THE FACE OF A CHOIRBOY.
YOU DON'T MEAN TO HELP ME, DO YOU?
YOU, WHO DESTROYED ALL OF US, YOU WHO TOOK EVERYTHING!
WHATEVER MADE YOU THINK THAT I WOULD HELP YOU?
YOU'RE MAD TO BLAME IT ALL ON ME. YOU HAVE NO RIGHT.

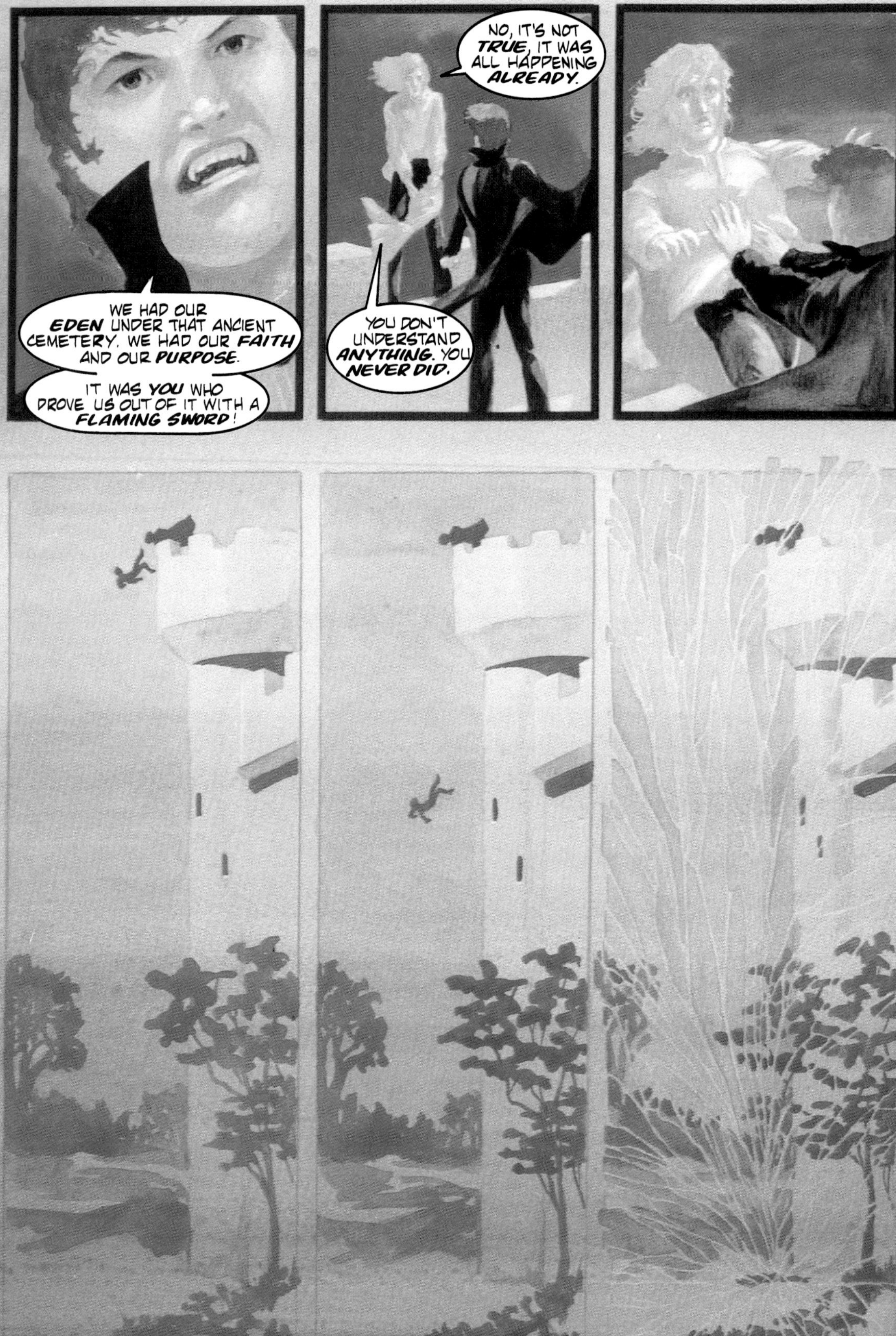
WE HAD OUR EDEN UNDER THAT ANCIENT CEMETERY. WE HAD OUR FAITH AND OUR PURPOSE.
IT WAS YOU WHO DROVE US OUT OF IT WITH A FLAMING SWORD!
NO, IT'S NOT TRUE, IT WAS ALL HAPPENING ALREADY.
YOU DON'T UNDERSTAND ANYTHING. YOU NEVER DID.

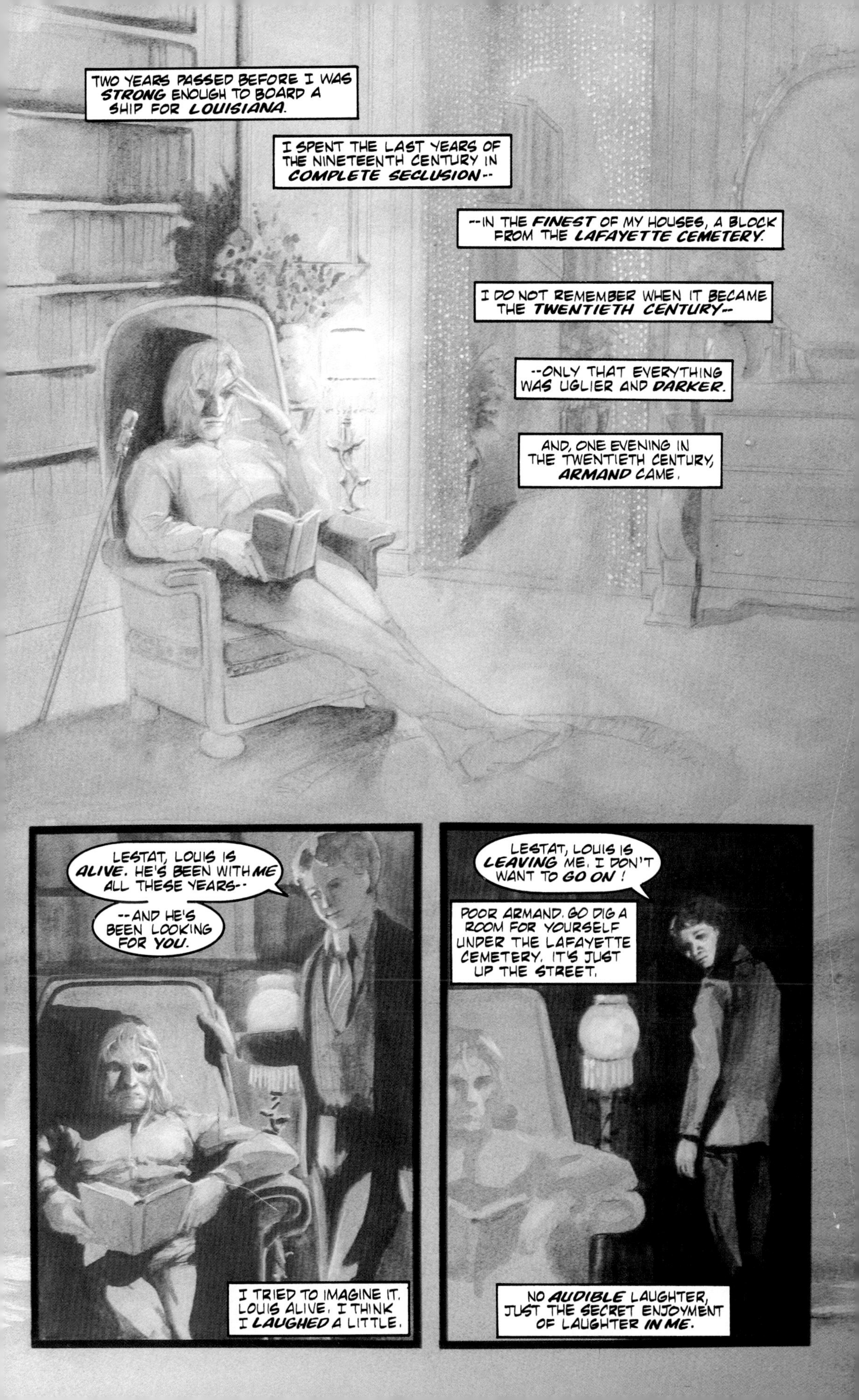
TWO YEARS PASSED BEFORE I WAS STRONG ENOUGH TO BOARD A SHIP FOR LOUISIANA.
I SPENT THE LAST YEARS OF THE NINETEENTH CENTURY IN COMPLETE SECLUSION--
--IN THE FINEST OF MY HOUSES, A BLOCK FROM THE LAFAYETTE CEMETERY.
I DO NOT REMEMBER WHEN IT BECAME THE TWENTIETH CENTURY--
--ONLY THAT EVERYTHING WAS UGLIER AND DARKER.
AND, ONE EVENING IN THE TWENTIETH CENTURY, ARMAND CAME.
LESTAT, LOUIS IS ALIVE. HE'S BEEN WITH ME ALL THESE YEARS--
--AND HE'S BEEN LOOKING FOR YOU.
I TRIED TO IMAGINE IT. LOUIS ALIVE. I THINK I LAUGHED A LITTLE.
LESTAT, LOUIS IS LEAVING ME. I DON'T WANT TO GO ON!
POOR ARMAND. GO DIG A ROOM FOR YOURSELF UNDER THE LAFAYETTE CEMETERY. IT'S JUST UP THE STREET.
NO AUDIBLE LAUGHTER, JUST THE SECRET ENJOYMENT OF LAUGHTER IN ME.

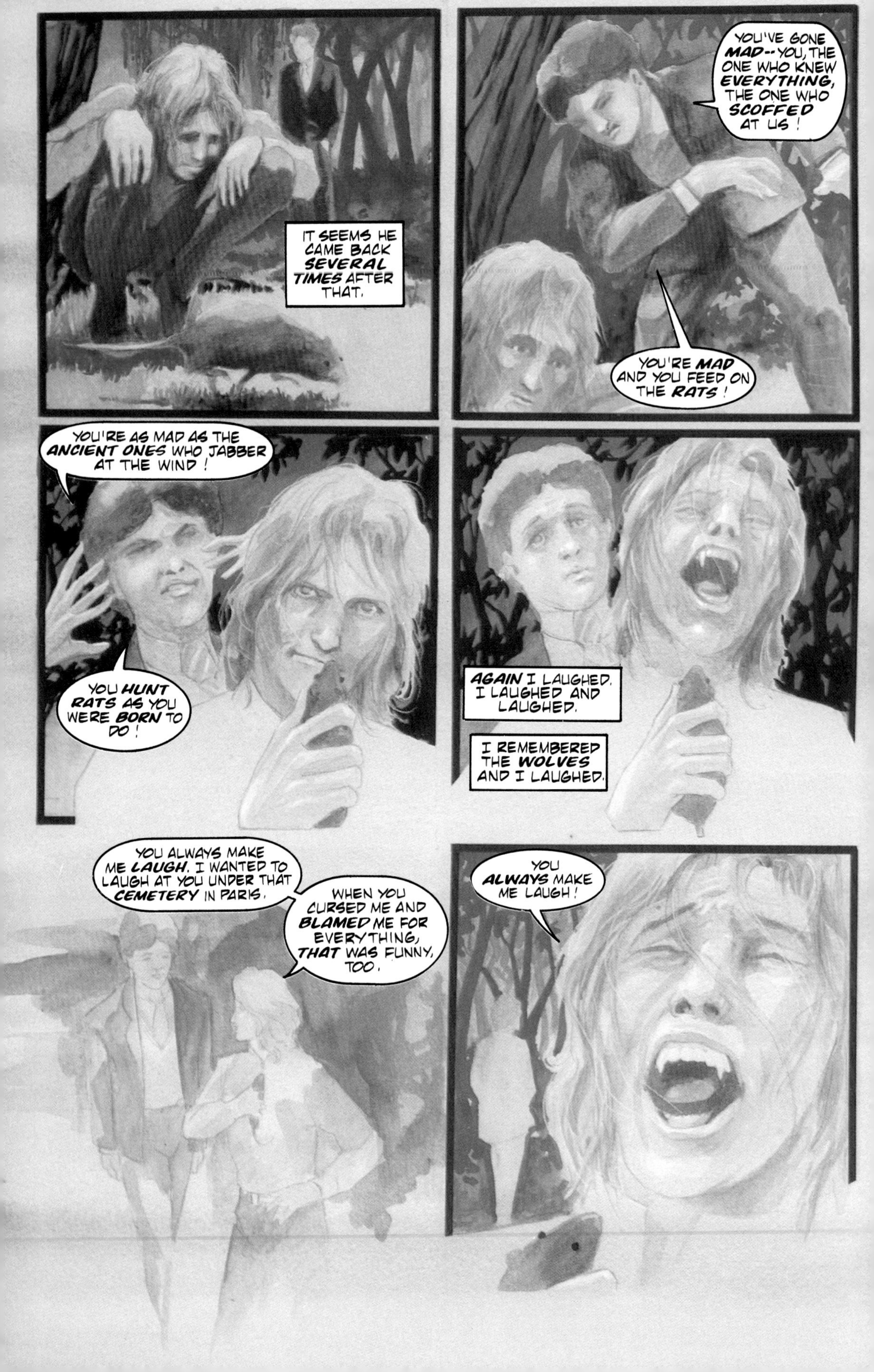
IT SEEMS HE CAME BACK SEVERAL TIMES AFTER THAT.
YOU'VE GONE MAD-- YOU, THE ONE WHO KNEW EVERYTHING, THE ONE WHO SCOFFED AT US !
YOU'RE MAD AND YOU FEED ON THE RATS !
YOU'RE AS MAD AS THE ANCIENT ONES WHO JABBER AT THE WIND !
YOU HUNT RATS AS YOU WERE BORN TO DO !
AGAIN I LAUGHED. I LAUGHED AND LAUGHED.
I REMEMBERED THE WOLVES AND I LAUGHED.
YOU ALWAYS MAKE ME LAUGH. I WANTED TO LAUGH AT YOU UNDER THAT CEMETERY IN PARIS.
WHEN YOU CURSED ME AND BLAMED ME FOR EVERYTHING, THAT WAS FUNNY, TOO.
YOU ALWAYS MAKE ME LAUGH !

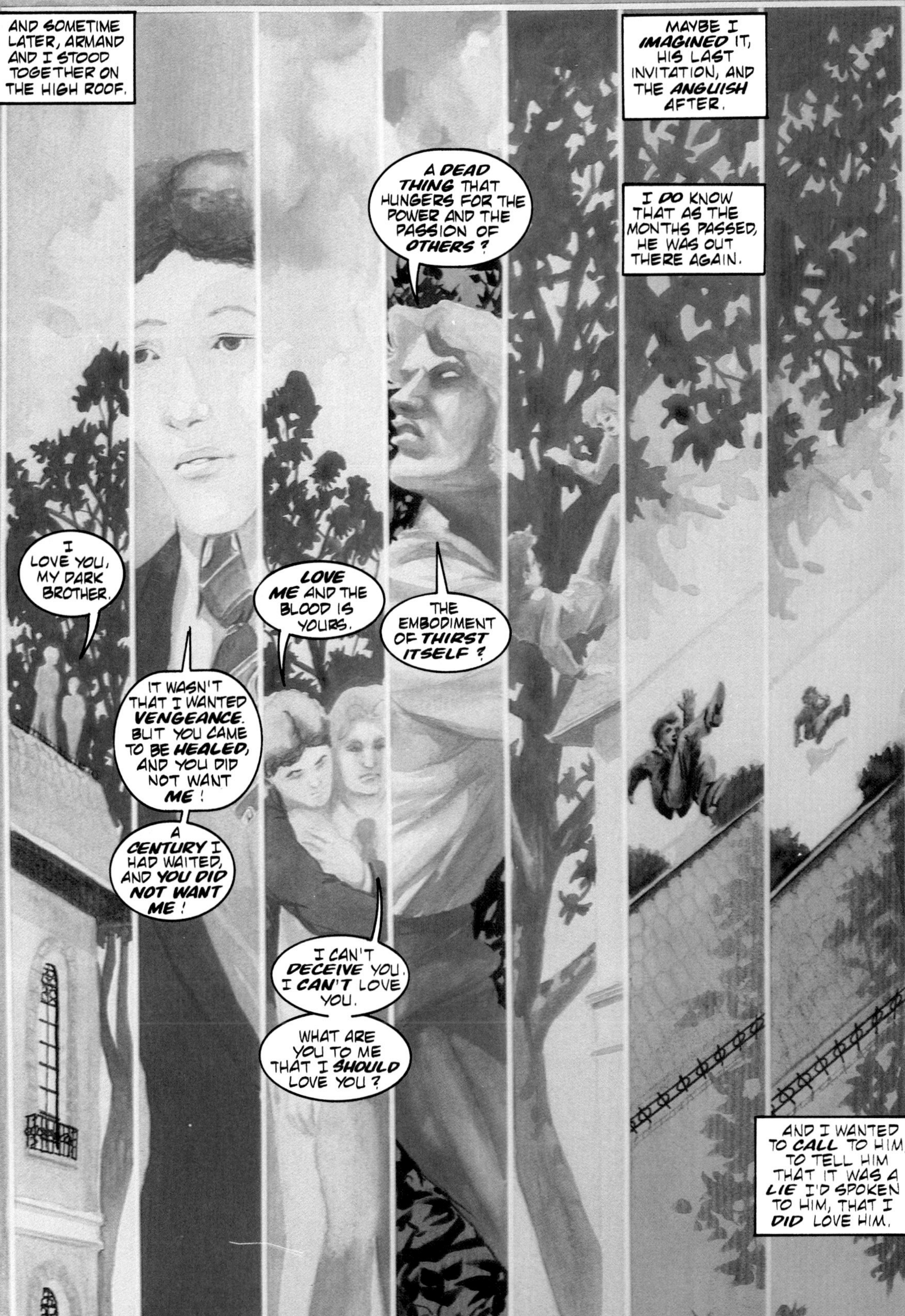
AND SOMETIME LATER, ARMAND AND I STOOD TOGETHER ON THE HIGH ROOF.
I LOVE YOU, MY DARK BROTHER.
IT WASN'T THAT I WANTED VENGEANCE. BUT YOU CAME TO BE HEALED, AND YOU DID NOT WANT ME!
A CENTURY I HAD WAITED, AND YOU DID NOT WANT ME!
LOVE ME AND THE BLOOD IS YOURS.
I CAN'T DECEIVE YOU. I CAN'T LOVE YOU.
WHAT ARE YOU TO ME THAT I SHOULD LOVE YOU?
A DEAD THING THAT HUNGERS FOR THE POWER AND THE PASSION OF OTHERS?
THE EMBODIMENT OF THIRST ITSELF?
MAYBE I IMAGINED IT, HIS LAST INVITATION, AND THE ANGUISH AFTER.
I DO KNOW THAT AS THE MONTHS PASSED, HE WAS OUT THERE AGAIN.
AND I WANTED TO CALL TO HIM, TO TELL HIM THAT IT WAS A LIE I'D SPOKEN TO HIM, THAT I DID LOVE HIM.
I DID.

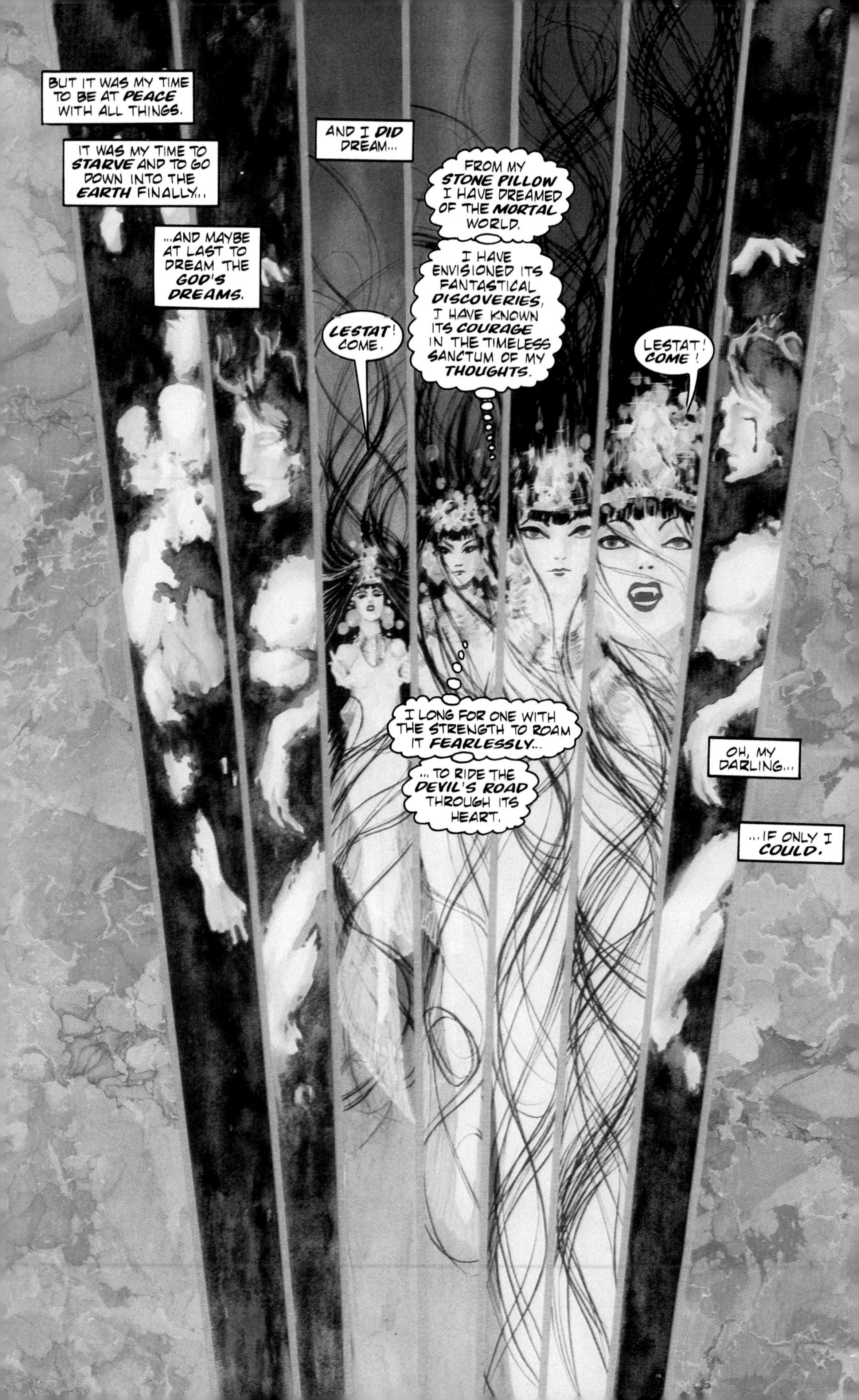
BUT IT WAS MY TIME TO BE AT PEACE WITH ALL THINGS.
IT WAS MY TIME TO STARVE AND TO GO DOWN INTO THE EARTH FINALLY...
...AND MAYBE AT LAST TO DREAM THE GOD'S DREAMS.
AND I DID DREAM...
FROM MY STONE PILLOW I HAVE DREAMED OF THE MORTAL WORLD.
I HAVE ENVISIONED ITS FANTASTICAL DISCOVERIES, I HAVE KNOWN ITS COURAGE IN THE TIMELESS SANCTUM OF MY THOUGHTS.
LESTAT! COME.
LESTAT! COME!
I LONG FOR ONE WITH THE STRENGTH TO ROAM IT FEARLESSLY...
...TO RIDE THE DEVIL'S ROAD THROUGH ITS HEART.
OH, MY DARLING...
...IF ONLY I COULD.

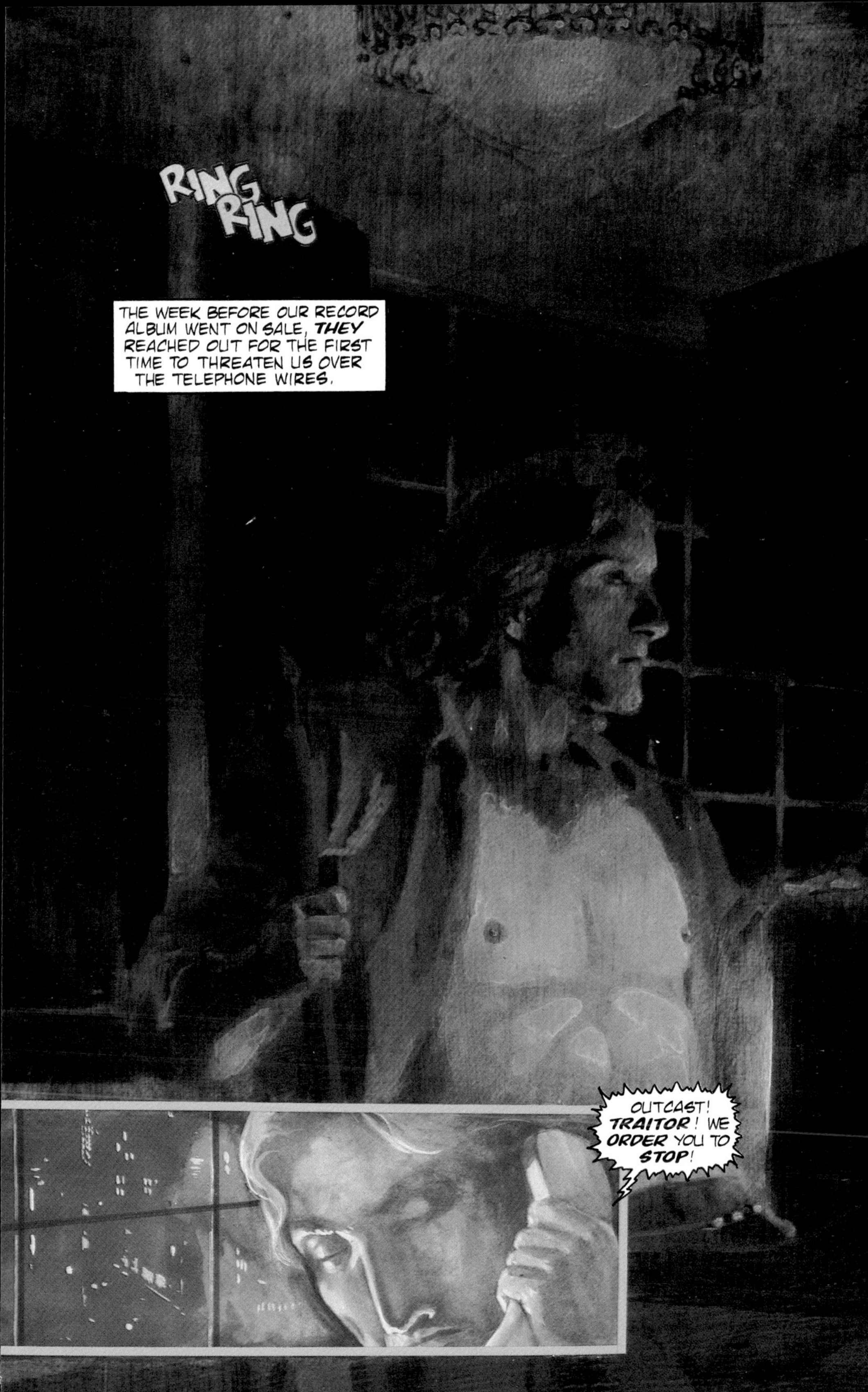
RING RING
THE WEEK BEFORE OUR RECORD ALBUM WENT ON SALE, THEY REACHED OUT FOR THE FIRST TIME TO THREATEN US OVER THE TELEPHONE WIRES.
OUTCAST! TRAITOR! WE ORDER YOU TO STOP!

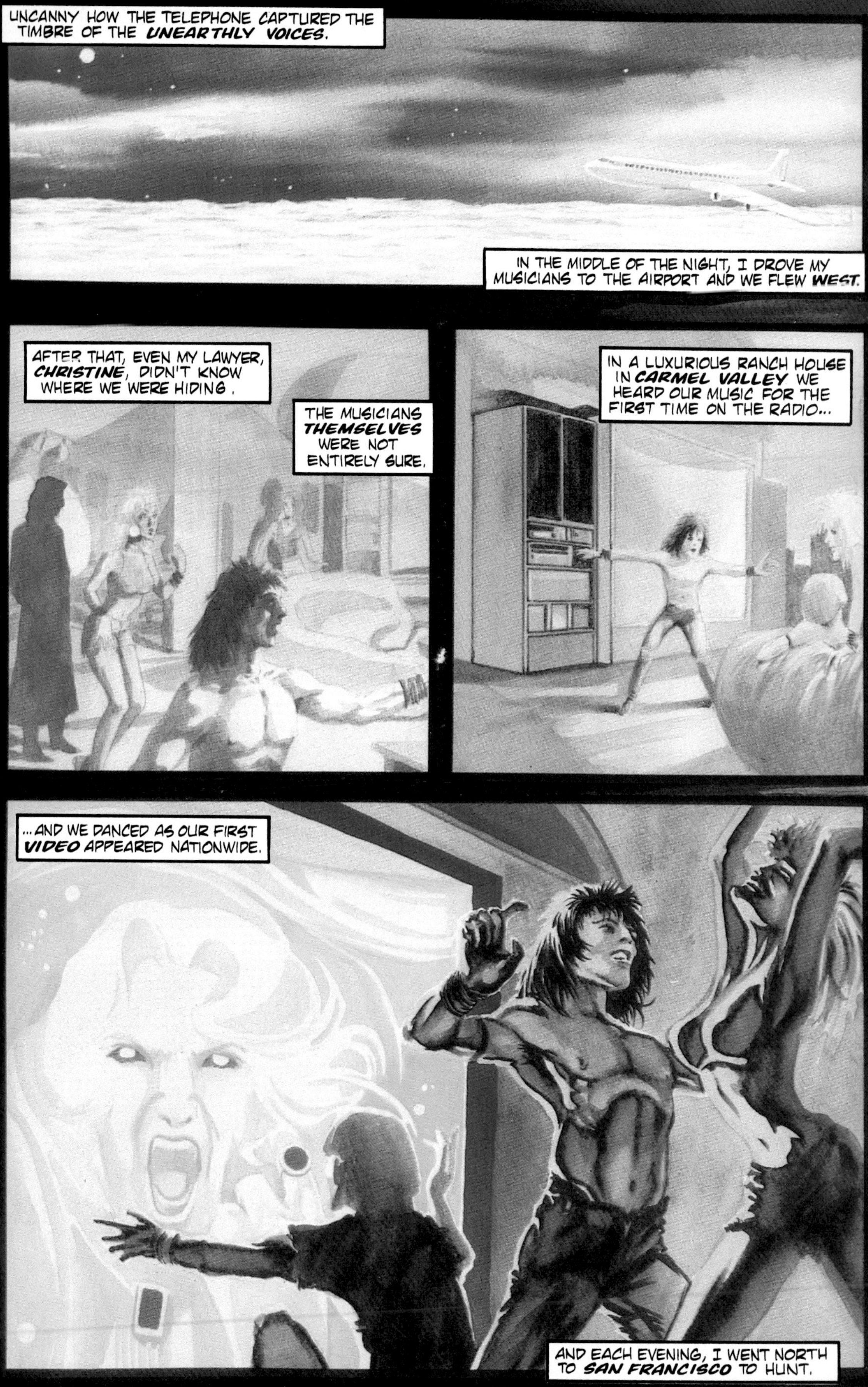
UNCANNY HOW THE TELEPHONE CAPTURED THE TIMBRE OF THE **UNEARTHLY VOICES**.
IN THE MIDDLE OF THE NIGHT, I DROVE MY MUSICIANS TO THE AIRPORT AND WE FLEW **WEST**.
AFTER THAT, EVEN MY LAWYER, **CHRISTINE**, DIDN'T KNOW WHERE WE WERE HIDING.
THE MUSICIANS **THEMSELVES** WERE NOT ENTIRELY SURE.
IN A LUXURIOUS RANCH HOUSE IN **CARMEL VALLEY** WE HEARD OUR MUSIC FOR THE FIRST TIME ON THE RADIO...
...AND WE DANCED AS OUR FIRST **VIDEO** APPEARED NATIONWIDE.
AND EACH EVENING, I WENT NORTH TO **SAN FRANCISCO** TO HUNT.

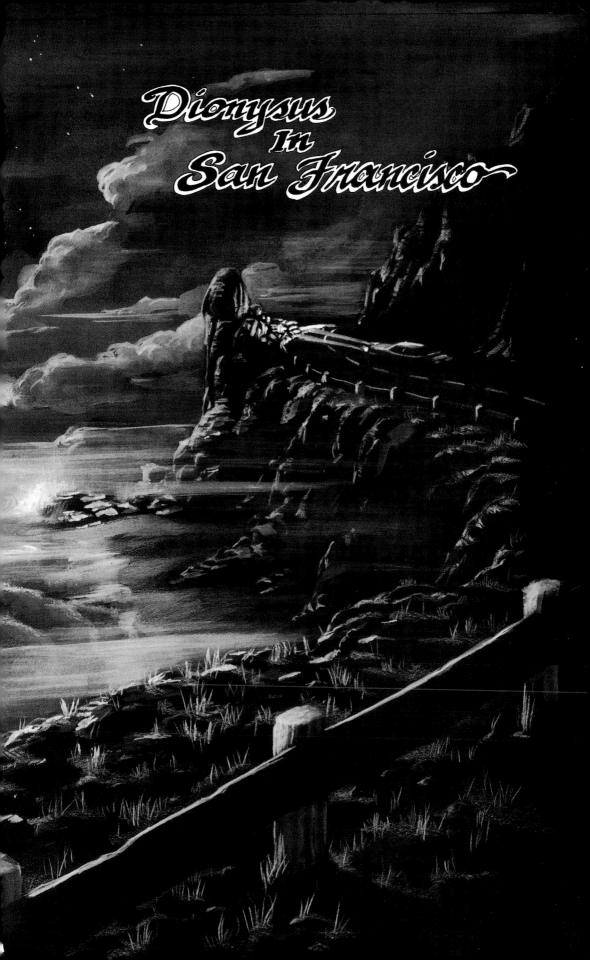

Dionysus In San Francisco

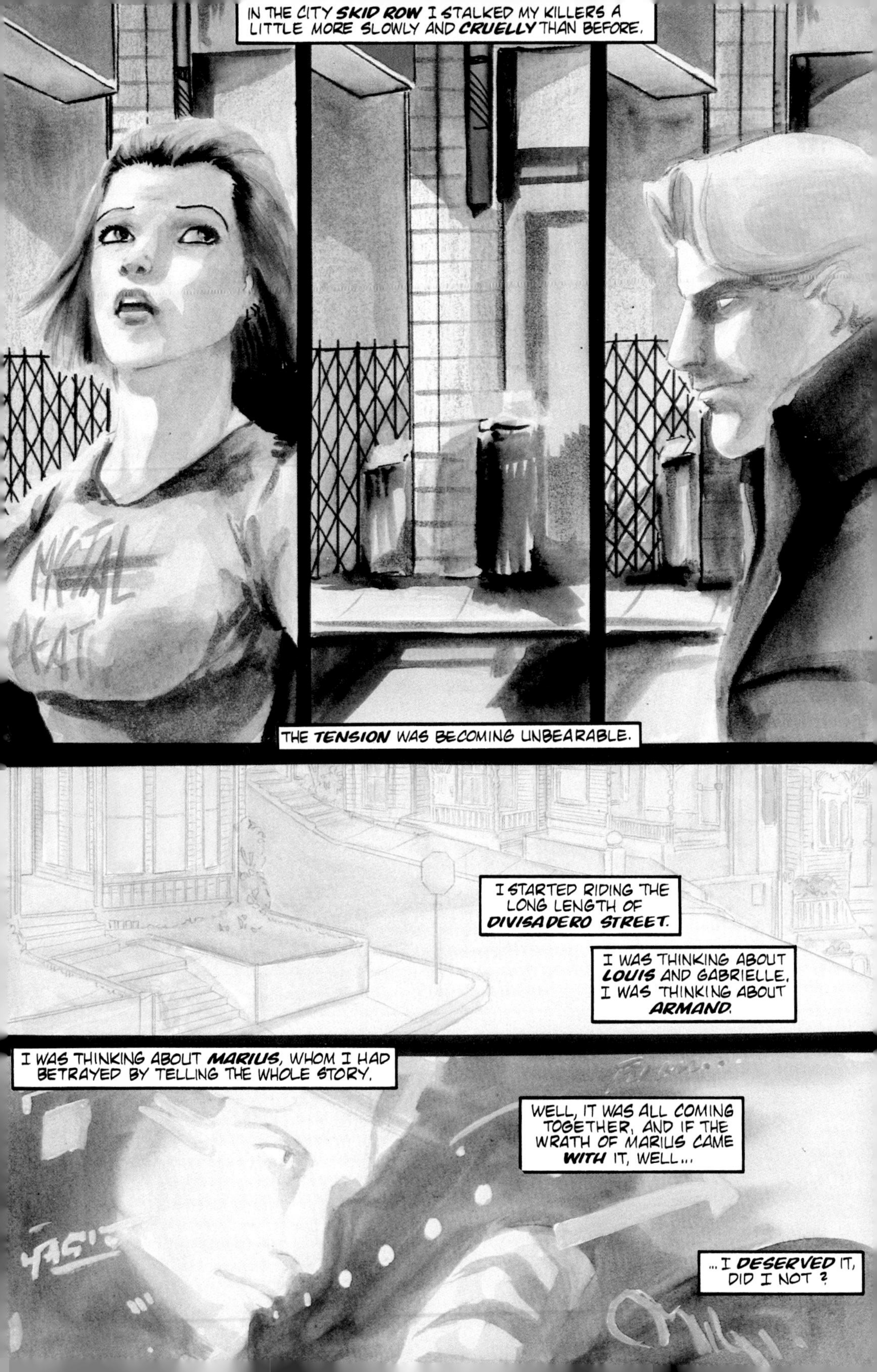
IN THE CITY SKID ROW I STALKED MY KILLERS A LITTLE MORE SLOWLY AND CRUELLY THAN BEFORE.
THE TENSION WAS BECOMING UNBEARABLE.
I STARTED RIDING THE LONG LENGTH OF DIVISADERO STREET.
I WAS THINKING ABOUT LOUIS AND GABRIELLE. I WAS THINKING ABOUT ARMAND.
I WAS THINKING ABOUT MARIUS, WHOM I HAD BETRAYED BY TELLING THE WHOLE STORY.
WELL, IT WAS ALL COMING TOGETHER, AND IF THE WRATH OF MARIUS CAME WITH IT, WELL...
...I DESERVED IT, DID I NOT ?

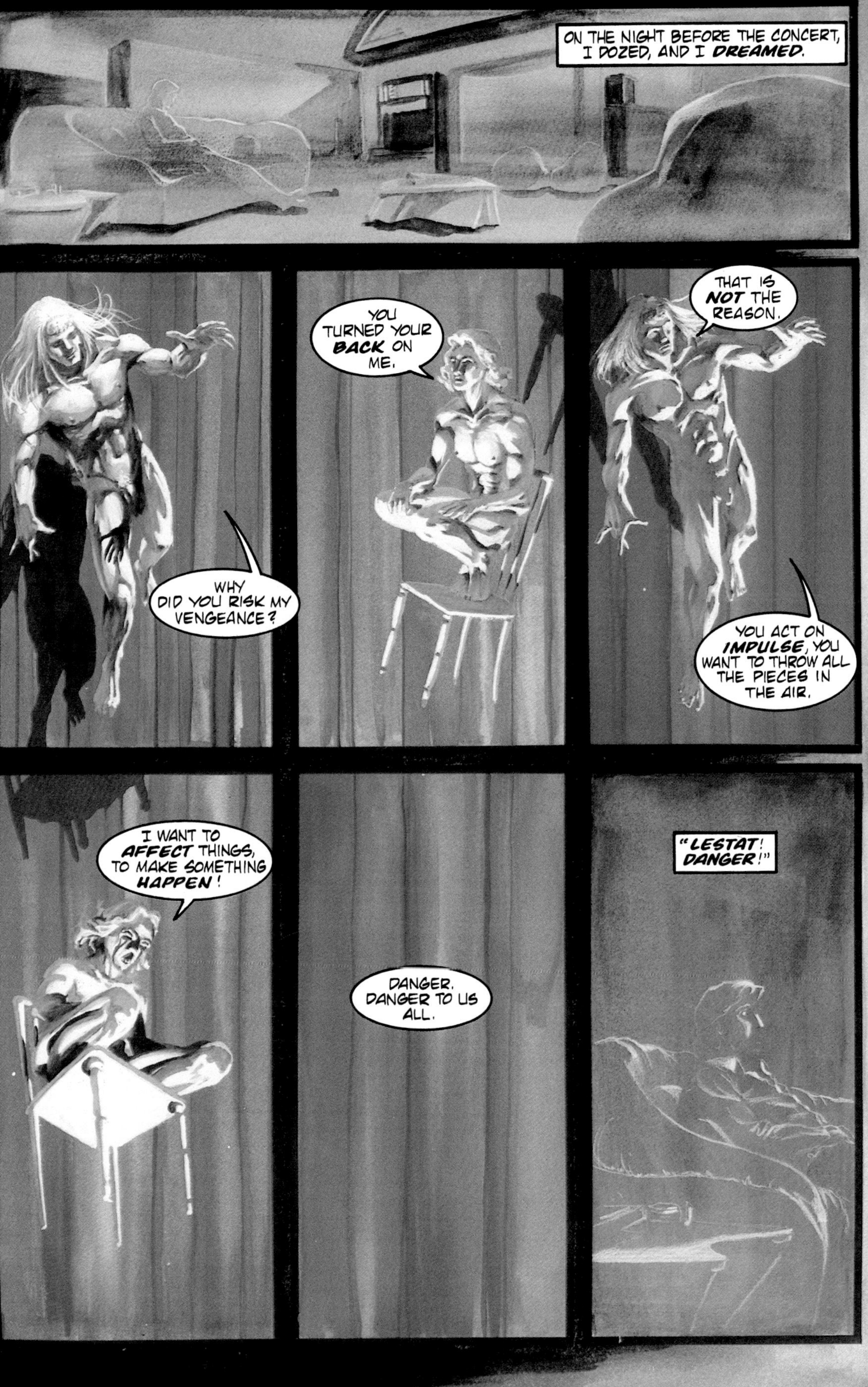

ON THE NIGHT BEFORE THE CONCERT, I DOZED, AND I DREAMED.
WHY DID YOU RISK MY VENGEANCE?
YOU TURNED YOUR BACK ON ME.
THAT IS NOT THE REASON.
YOU ACT ON IMPULSE, YOU WANT TO THROW ALL THE PIECES IN THE AIR.
I WANT TO AFFECT THINGS, TO MAKE SOMETHING HAPPEN!
DANGER. DANGER TO US ALL.
"LESTAT! DANGER!"

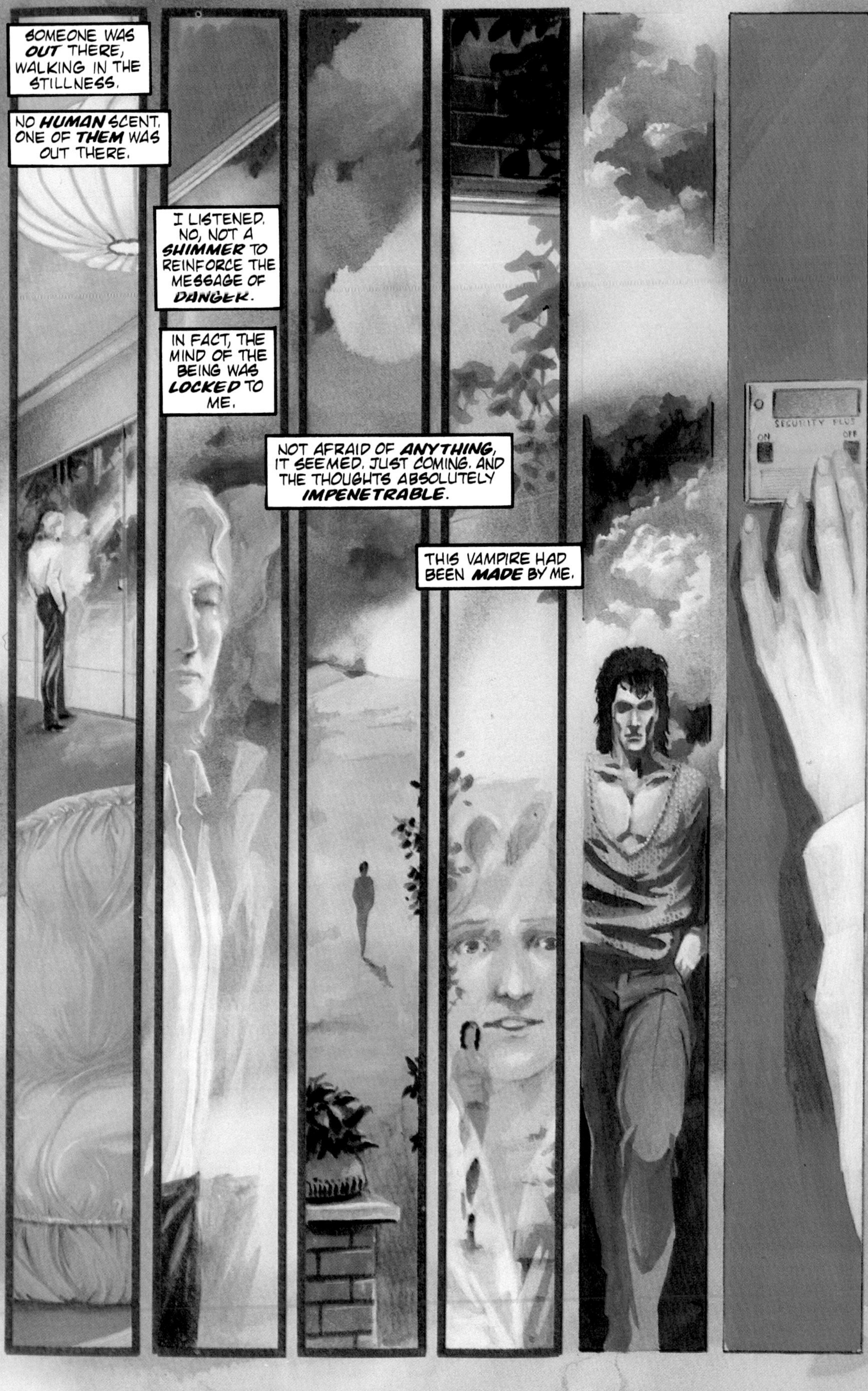
SOMEONE WAS OUT THERE, WALKING IN THE STILLNESS.
NO HUMAN SCENT. ONE OF THEM WAS OUT THERE.
I LISTENED. NO, NOT A SHIMMER TO REINFORCE THE MESSAGE OF DANGER.
IN FACT, THE MIND OF THE BEING WAS LOCKED TO ME.
NOT AFRAID OF ANYTHING, IT SEEMED. JUST COMING. AND THE THOUGHTS ABSOLUTELY IMPENETRABLE.
THIS VAMPIRE HAD BEEN MADE BY ME.
SECURITY PLUS
ON
OFF

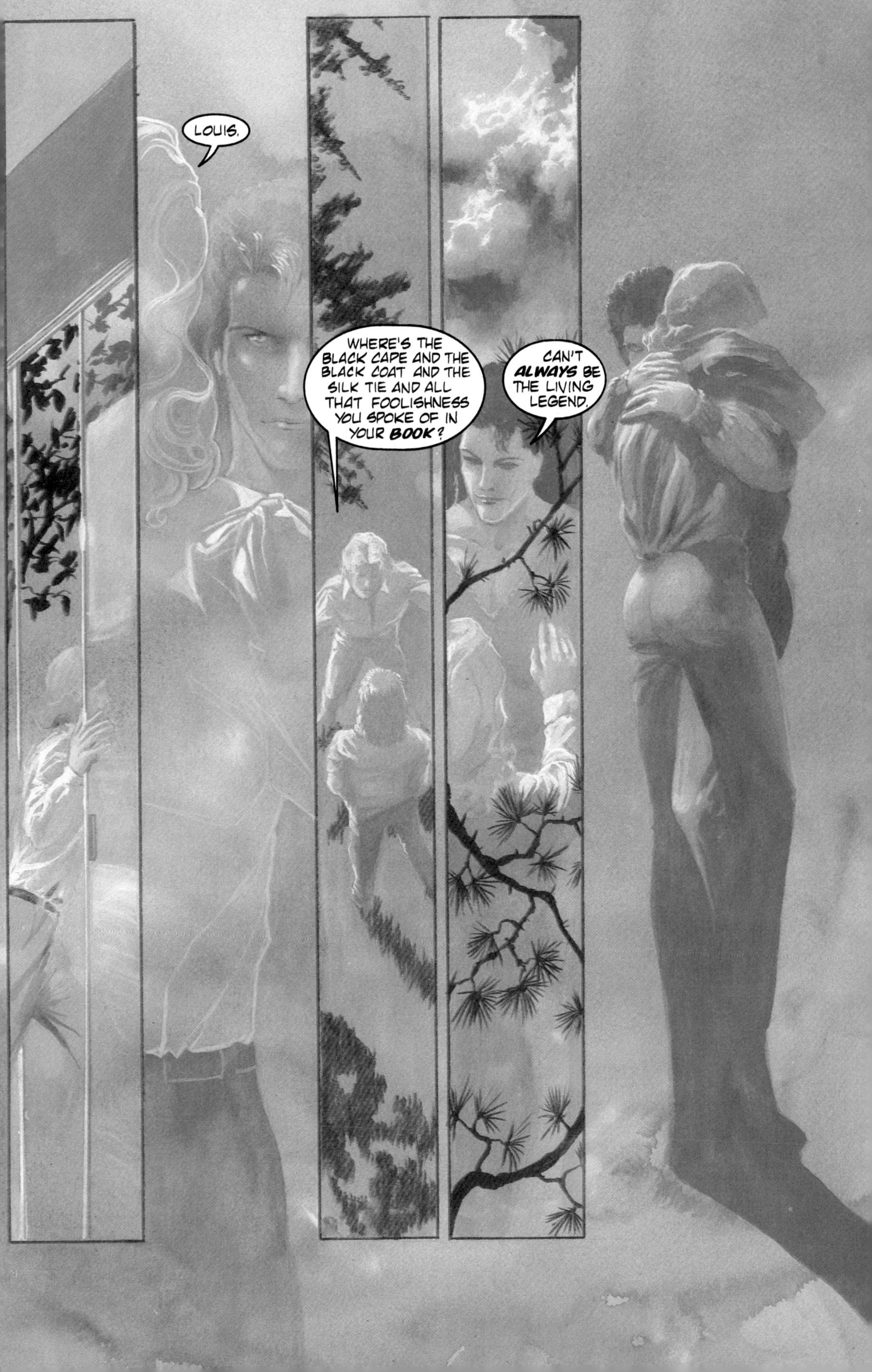
LOUIS.
WHERE'S THE BLACK CAPE AND THE BLACK COAT AND THE SILK TIE AND ALL THAT FOOLISHNESS YOU SPOKE OF IN YOUR **BOOK**?
CAN'T **ALWAYS** BE THE LIVING LEGEND.

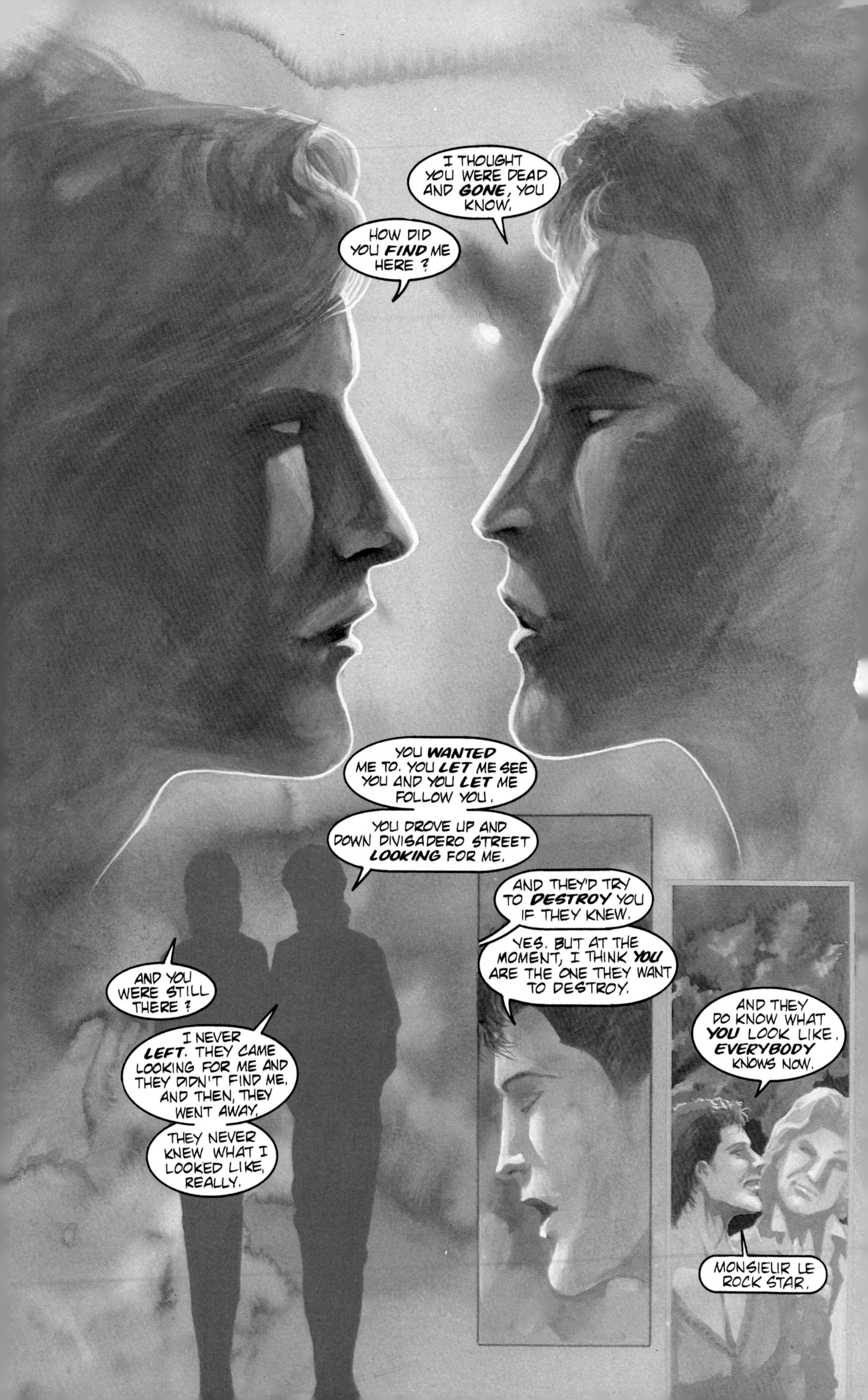

I THOUGHT YOU WERE DEAD AND GONE, YOU KNOW.
HOW DID YOU FIND ME HERE ?
YOU WANTED ME TO. YOU LET ME SEE YOU AND YOU LET ME FOLLOW YOU.
YOU DROVE UP AND DOWN DIVISADERO STREET LOOKING FOR ME.
AND YOU WERE STILL THERE ?
I NEVER LEFT. THEY CAME LOOKING FOR ME AND THEY DIDN'T FIND ME. AND THEN, THEY WENT AWAY.
THEY NEVER KNEW WHAT I LOOKED LIKE, REALLY.
AND THEY'D TRY TO DESTROY YOU IF THEY KNEW.
YES. BUT AT THE MOMENT, I THINK YOU ARE THE ONE THEY WANT TO DESTROY.
AND THEY DO KNOW WHAT YOU LOOK LIKE. EVERYBODY KNOWS NOW.
MONSIEUR LE ROCK STAR.

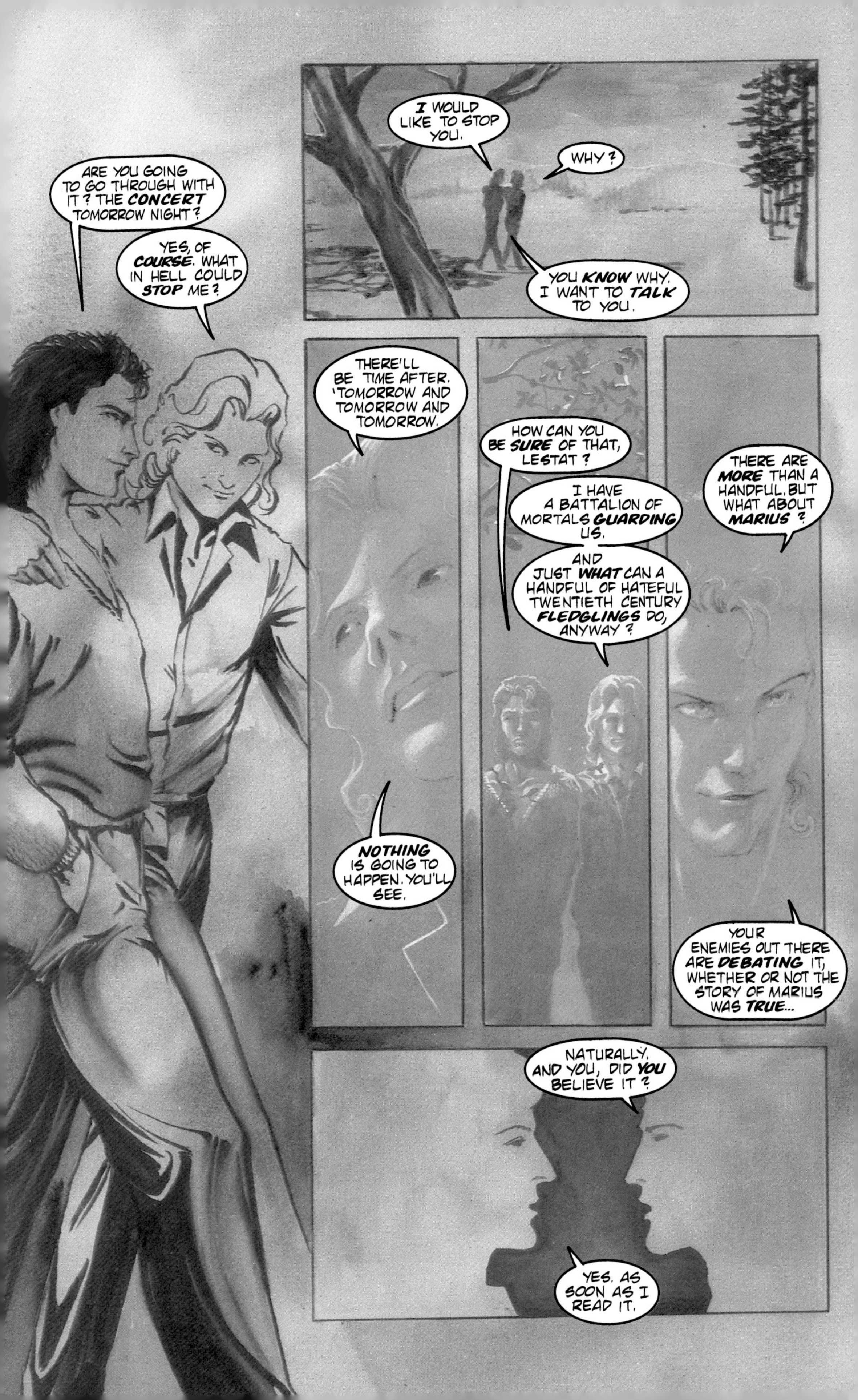
ARE YOU GOING TO GO THROUGH WITH IT? THE CONCERT TOMORROW NIGHT?
YES, OF COURSE. WHAT IN HELL COULD STOP ME?
I WOULD LIKE TO STOP YOU.
WHY?
YOU KNOW WHY. I WANT TO TALK TO YOU.
THERE'LL BE TIME AFTER. 'TOMORROW AND TOMORROW AND TOMORROW.
NOTHING IS GOING TO HAPPEN. YOU'LL SEE.
HOW CAN YOU BE SURE OF THAT, LESTAT?
I HAVE A BATTALION OF MORTALS GUARDING US.
AND JUST WHAT CAN A HANDFUL OF HATEFUL TWENTIETH CENTURY FLEDGLINGS DO, ANYWAY?
THERE ARE MORE THAN A HANDFUL, BUT WHAT ABOUT MARIUS?
YOUR ENEMIES OUT THERE ARE DEBATING IT, WHETHER OR NOT THE STORY OF MARIUS WAS TRUE...
NATURALLY. AND YOU, DID YOU BELIEVE IT?
YES. AS SOON AS I READ IT.

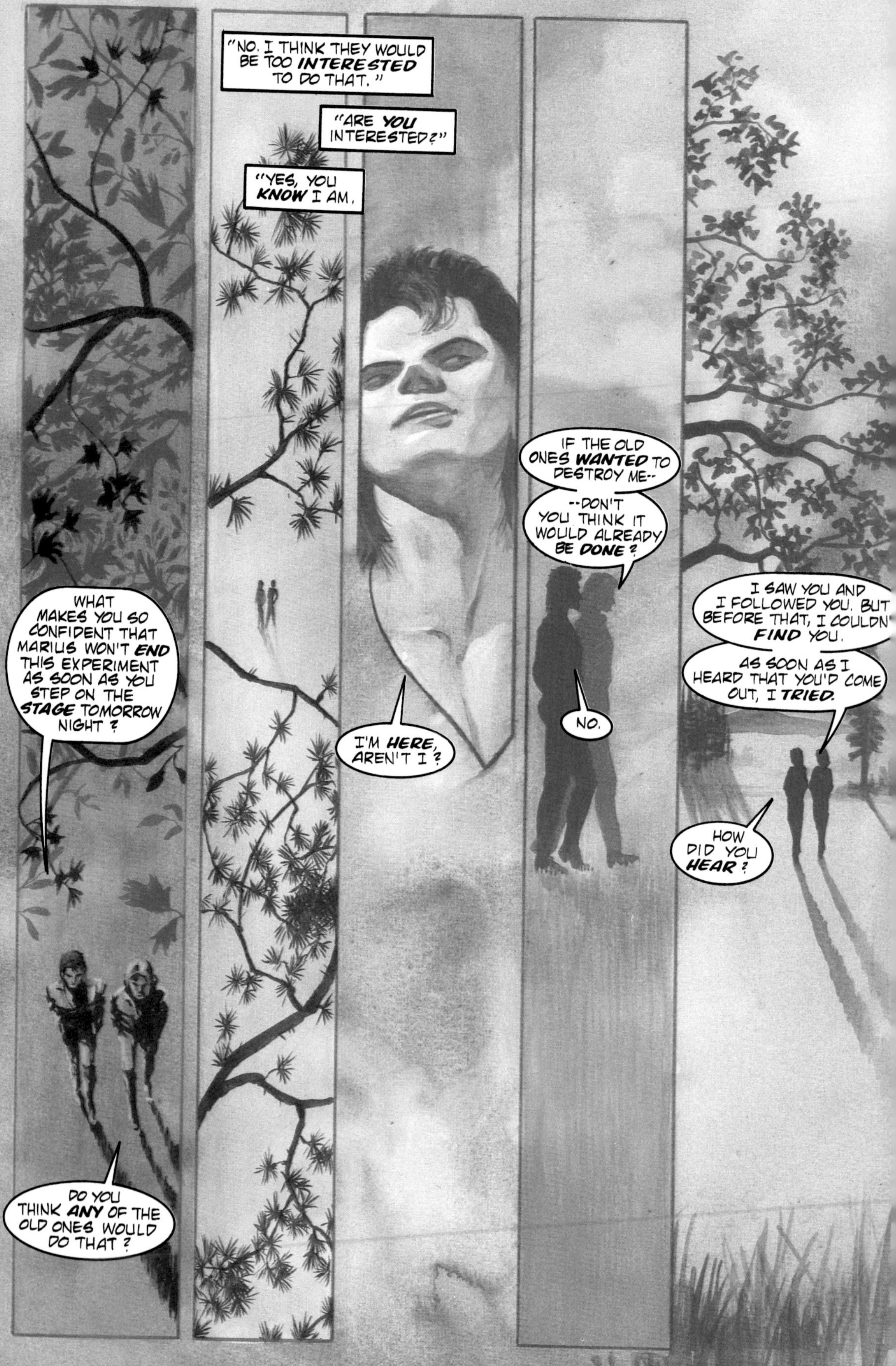
"NO. I THINK THEY WOULD BE TOO INTERESTED TO DO THAT."
"ARE YOU INTERESTED?"
"YES, YOU KNOW I AM.
WHAT MAKES YOU SO CONFIDENT THAT MARIUS WON'T END THIS EXPERIMENT AS SOON AS YOU STEP ON THE STAGE TOMORROW NIGHT?
DO YOU THINK ANY OF THE OLD ONES WOULD DO THAT?
I'M HERE, AREN'T I?
IF THE OLD ONES WANTED TO DESTROY ME--
--DON'T YOU THINK IT WOULD ALREADY BE DONE?
NO.
I SAW YOU AND I FOLLOWED YOU. BUT BEFORE THAT, I COULDN' FIND YOU.
AS SOON AS I HEARD THAT YOU'D COME OUT, I TRIED.
HOW DID YOU HEAR?

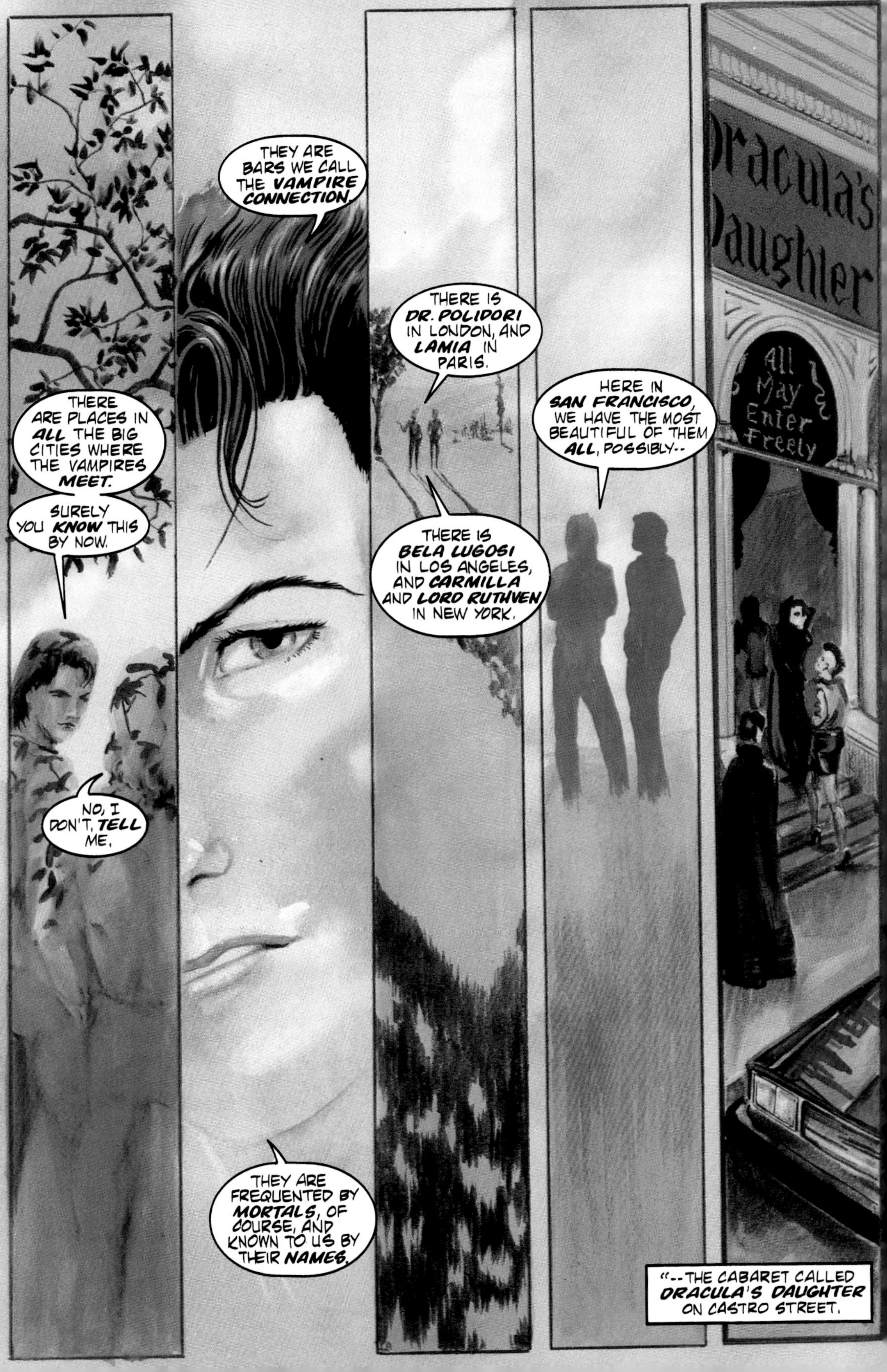

THERE ARE PLACES IN ALL THE BIG CITIES WHERE THE VAMPIRES MEET.
SURELY YOU KNOW THIS BY NOW.
NO, I DON'T. TELL ME.
THEY ARE BARS WE CALL THE VAMPIRE CONNECTION.
THEY ARE FREQUENTED BY MORTALS, OF COURSE, AND KNOWN TO US BY THEIR NAMES.
THERE IS DR. POLIDORI IN LONDON, AND LAMIA IN PARIS.
THERE IS BELA LUGOSI IN LOS ANGELES, AND CARMILLA AND LORD RUTHVEN IN NEW YORK.
HERE IN SAN FRANCISCO, WE HAVE THE MOST BEAUTIFUL OF THEM ALL, POSSIBLY--
Dracula's Daughter
All May Enter Freely
"--THE CABARET CALLED DRACULA'S DAUGHTER ON CASTRO STREET.

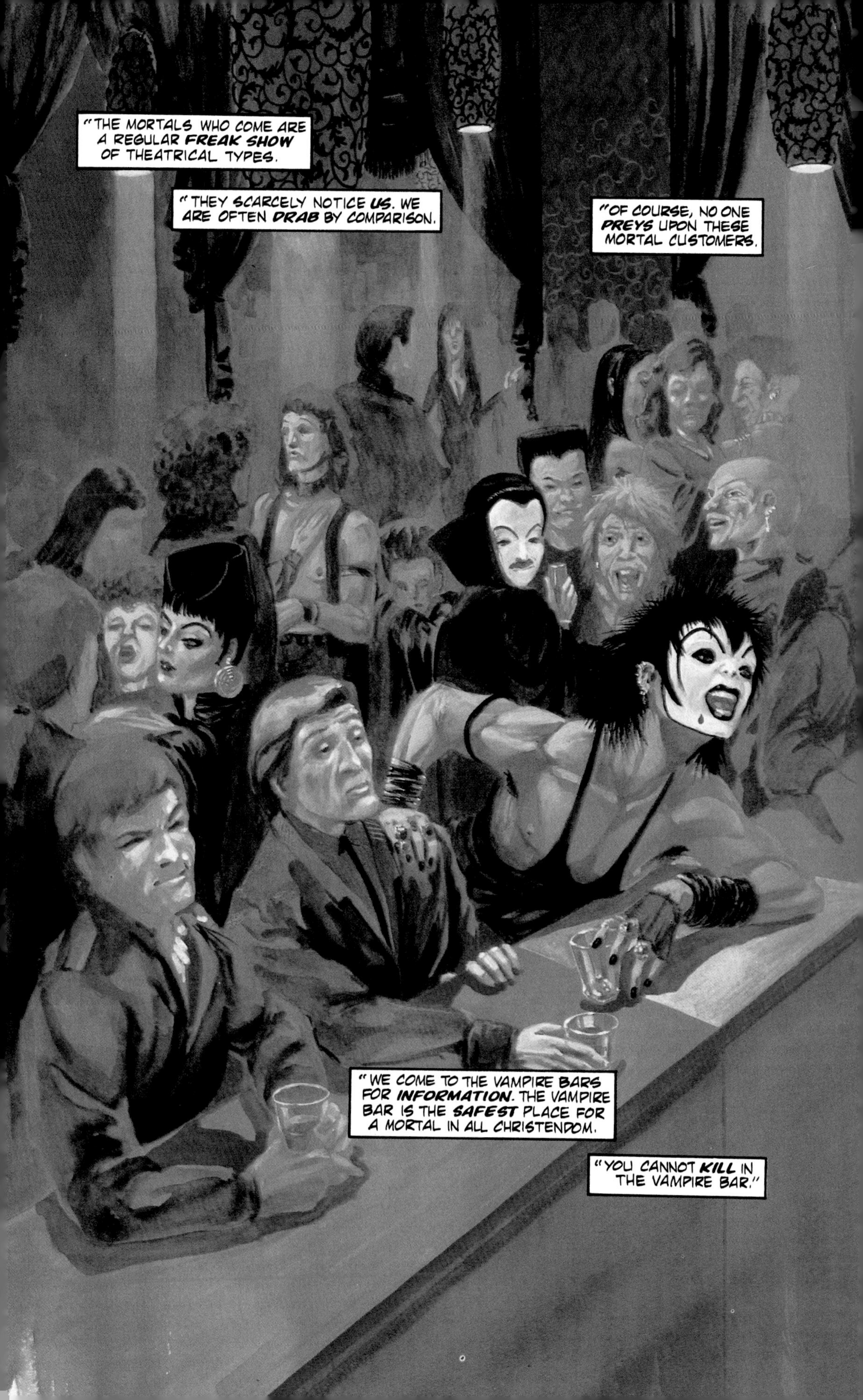
"THE MORTALS WHO COME ARE A REGULAR FREAK SHOW OF THEATRICAL TYPES.
"THEY SCARCELY NOTICE US. WE ARE OFTEN DRAB BY COMPARISON.
"OF COURSE, NO ONE PREYS UPON THESE MORTAL CUSTOMERS.
"WE COME TO THE VAMPIRE BARS FOR INFORMATION. THE VAMPIRE BAR IS THE SAFEST PLACE FOR A MORTAL IN ALL CHRISTENDOM.
"YOU CANNOT KILL IN THE VAMPIRE BAR."

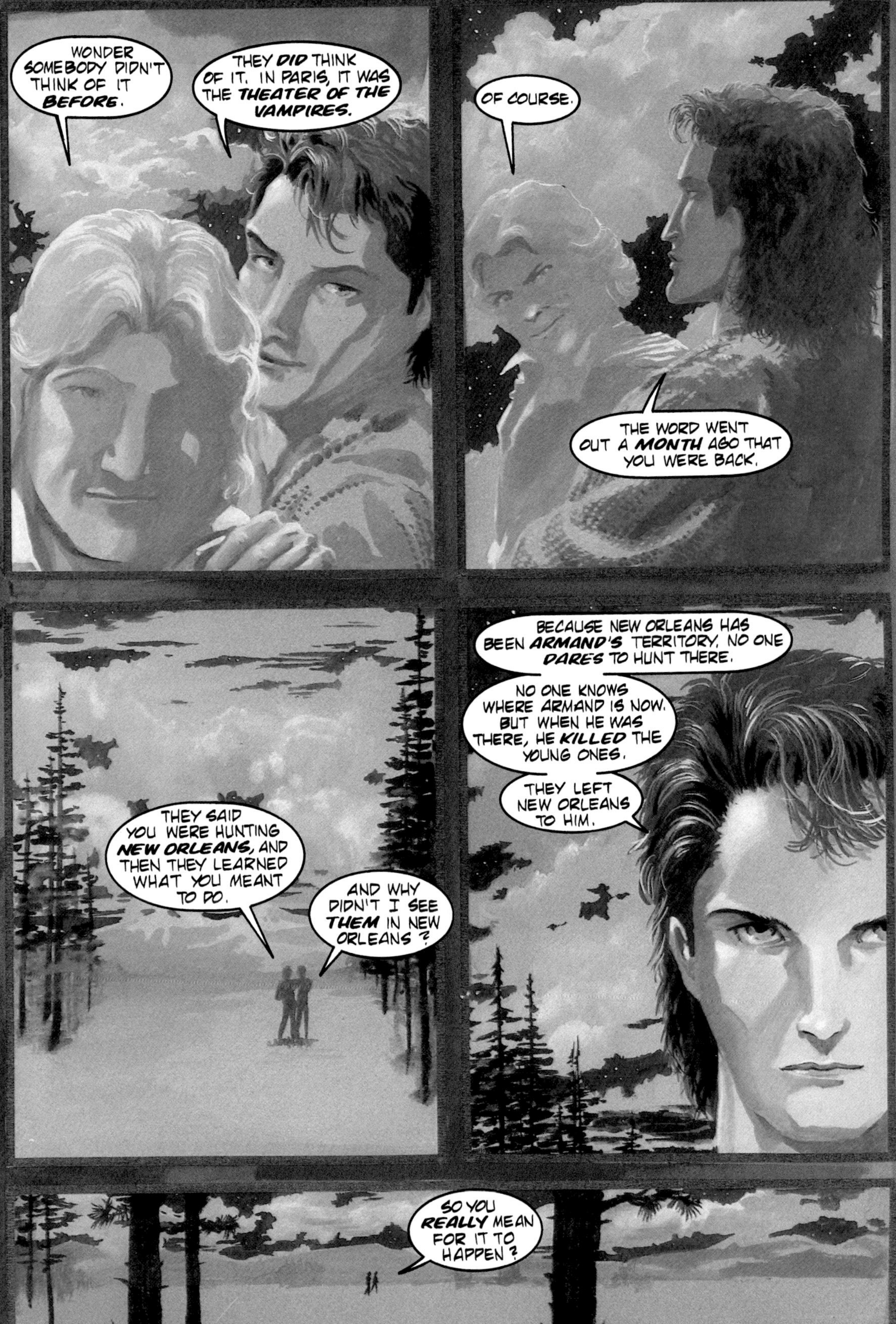
WONDER SOMEBODY DIDN'T THINK OF IT BEFORE.
THEY DID THINK OF IT. IN PARIS, IT WAS THE THEATER OF THE VAMPIRES.
OF COURSE.
THE WORD WENT OUT A MONTH AGO THAT YOU WERE BACK.
THEY SAID YOU WERE HUNTING NEW ORLEANS, AND THEN THEY LEARNED WHAT YOU MEANT TO DO.
AND WHY DIDN'T I SEE THEM IN NEW ORLEANS?
BECAUSE NEW ORLEANS HAS BEEN ARMAND'S TERRITORY, NO ONE DARES TO HUNT THERE.
NO ONE KNOWS WHERE ARMAND IS NOW. BUT WHEN HE WAS THERE, HE KILLED THE YOUNG ONES.
THEY LEFT NEW ORLEANS TO HIM.
SO YOU REALLY MEAN FOR IT TO HAPPEN?

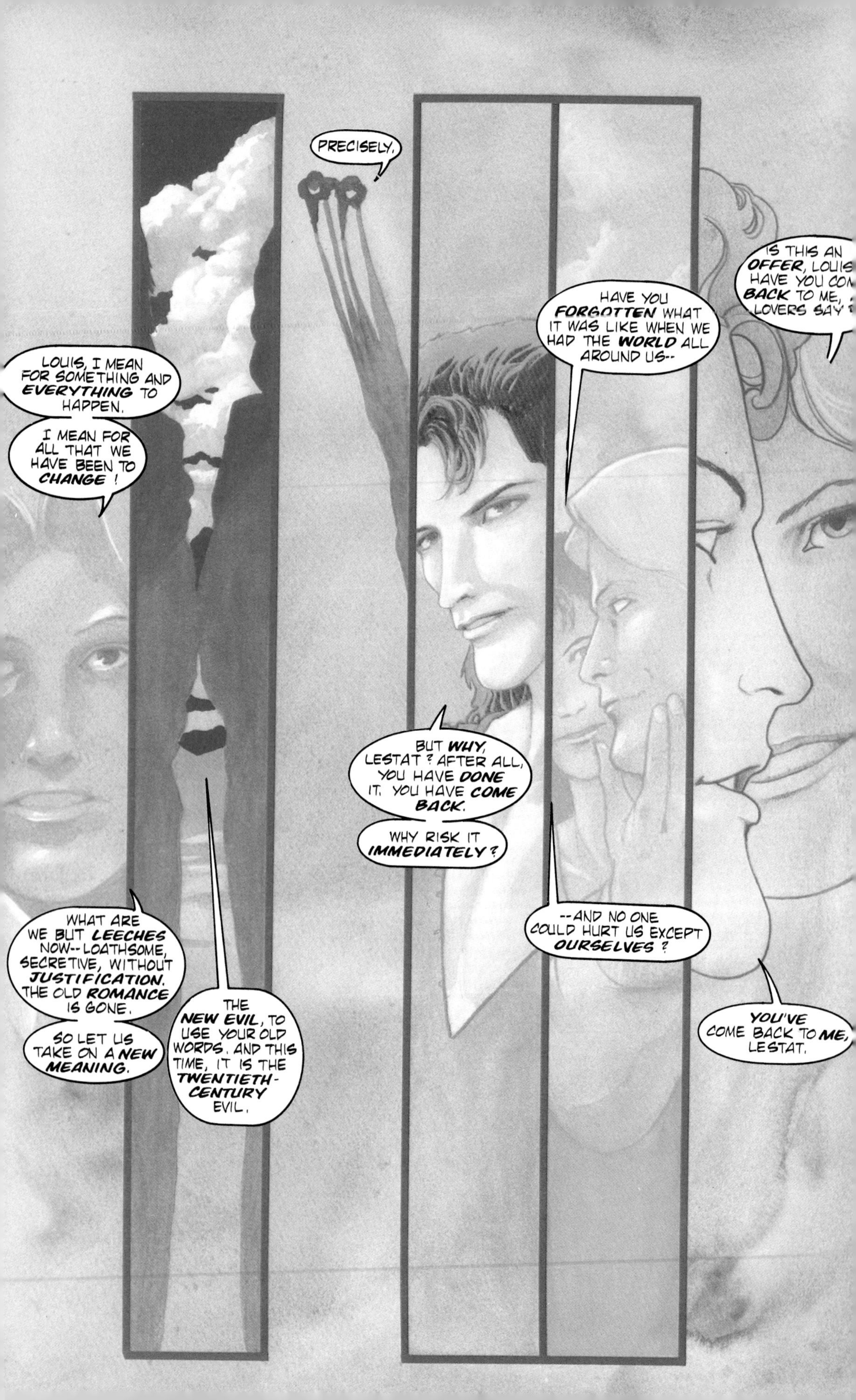

LOUIS, I MEAN FOR SOMETHING AND EVERYTHING TO HAPPEN.
I MEAN FOR ALL THAT WE HAVE BEEN TO CHANGE !
WHAT ARE WE BUT LEECHES NOW--LOATHSOME, SECRETIVE, WITHOUT JUSTIFICATION. THE OLD ROMANCE IS GONE.
SO LET US TAKE ON A NEW MEANING.
THE NEW EVIL, TO USE YOUR OLD WORDS. AND THIS TIME, IT IS THE TWENTIETH-CENTURY EVIL.
PRECISELY.
BUT WHY, LESTAT ? AFTER ALL, YOU HAVE DONE IT. YOU HAVE COME BACK.
WHY RISK IT IMMEDIATELY ?
HAVE YOU FORGOTTEN WHAT IT WAS LIKE WHEN WE HAD THE WORLD ALL AROUND US--
--AND NO ONE COULD HURT US EXCEPT OURSELVES ?
IS THIS AN OFFER, LOUIS HAVE YOU COM BACK TO ME, LOVERS SAY
YOU'VE COME BACK TO ME, LESTAT.

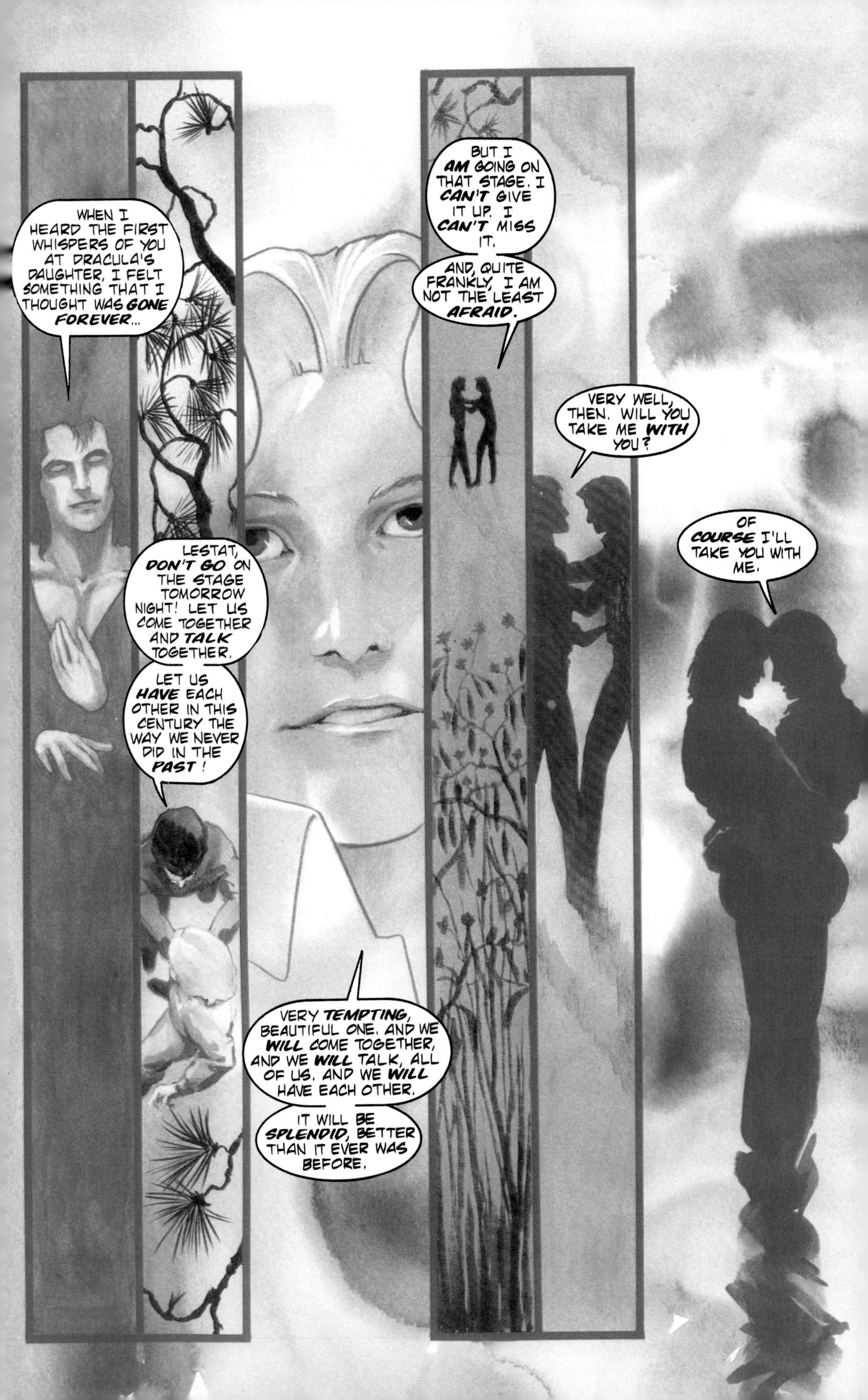
WHEN I HEARD THE FIRST WHISPERS OF YOU AT DRACULA'S DAUGHTER, I FELT SOMETHING THAT I THOUGHT WAS GONE FOREVER...
LESTAT, DON'T GO ON THE STAGE TOMORROW NIGHT! LET US COME TOGETHER AND TALK TOGETHER.
LET US HAVE EACH OTHER IN THIS CENTURY THE WAY WE NEVER DID IN THE PAST!
VERY TEMPTING, BEAUTIFUL ONE. AND WE WILL COME TOGETHER, AND WE WILL TALK, ALL OF US. AND WE WILL HAVE EACH OTHER.
IT WILL BE SPLENDID, BETTER THAN IT EVER WAS BEFORE.
BUT I AM GOING ON THAT STAGE. I CAN'T GIVE IT UP. I CAN'T MISS IT.
AND, QUITE FRANKLY, I AM NOT THE LEAST AFRAID.
VERY WELL, THEN. WILL YOU TAKE ME WITH YOU?
OF COURSE I'LL TAKE YOU WITH ME.

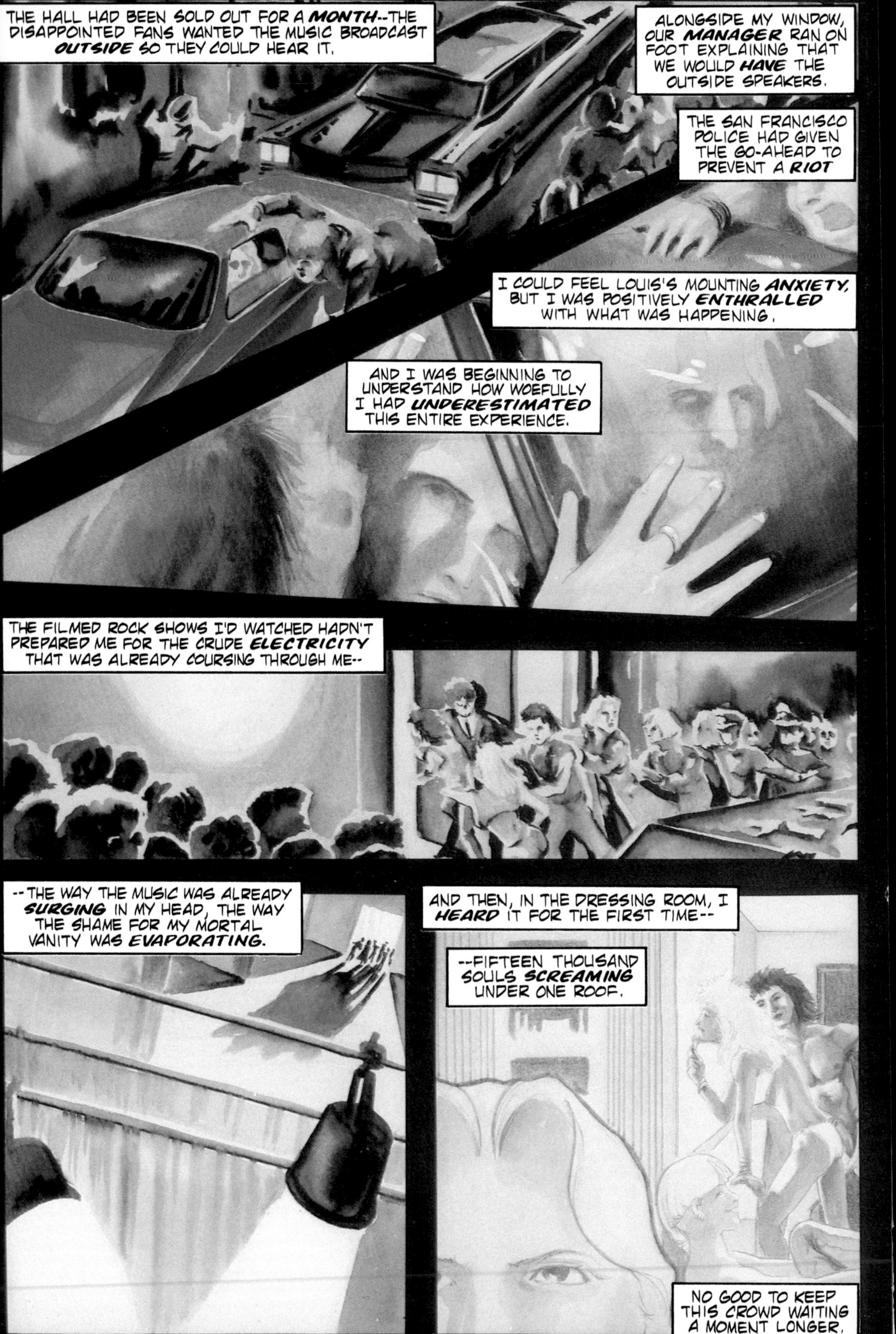
THE HALL HAD BEEN SOLD OUT FOR A MONTH--THE DISAPPOINTED FANS WANTED THE MUSIC BROADCAST OUTSIDE SO THEY COULD HEAR IT.
ALONGSIDE MY WINDOW, OUR MANAGER RAN ON FOOT EXPLAINING THAT WE WOULD HAVE THE OUTSIDE SPEAKERS.
THE SAN FRANCISCO POLICE HAD GIVEN THE GO-AHEAD TO PREVENT A RIOT
I COULD FEEL LOUIS'S MOUNTING ANXIETY, BUT I WAS POSITIVELY ENTHRALLED WITH WHAT WAS HAPPENING.
AND I WAS BEGINNING TO UNDERSTAND HOW WOEFULLY I HAD UNDERESTIMATED THIS ENTIRE EXPERIENCE.
THE FILMED ROCK SHOWS I'D WATCHED HADN'T PREPARED ME FOR THE CRUDE ELECTRICITY THAT WAS ALREADY COURSING THROUGH ME--
--THE WAY THE MUSIC WAS ALREADY SURGING IN MY HEAD, THE WAY THE SHAME FOR MY MORTAL VANITY WAS EVAPORATING.
AND THEN, IN THE DRESSING ROOM, I HEARD IT FOR THE FIRST TIME--
--FIFTEEN THOUSAND SOULS SCREAMING UNDER ONE ROOF.
NO GOOD TO KEEP THIS CROWD WAITING A MOMENT LONGER.

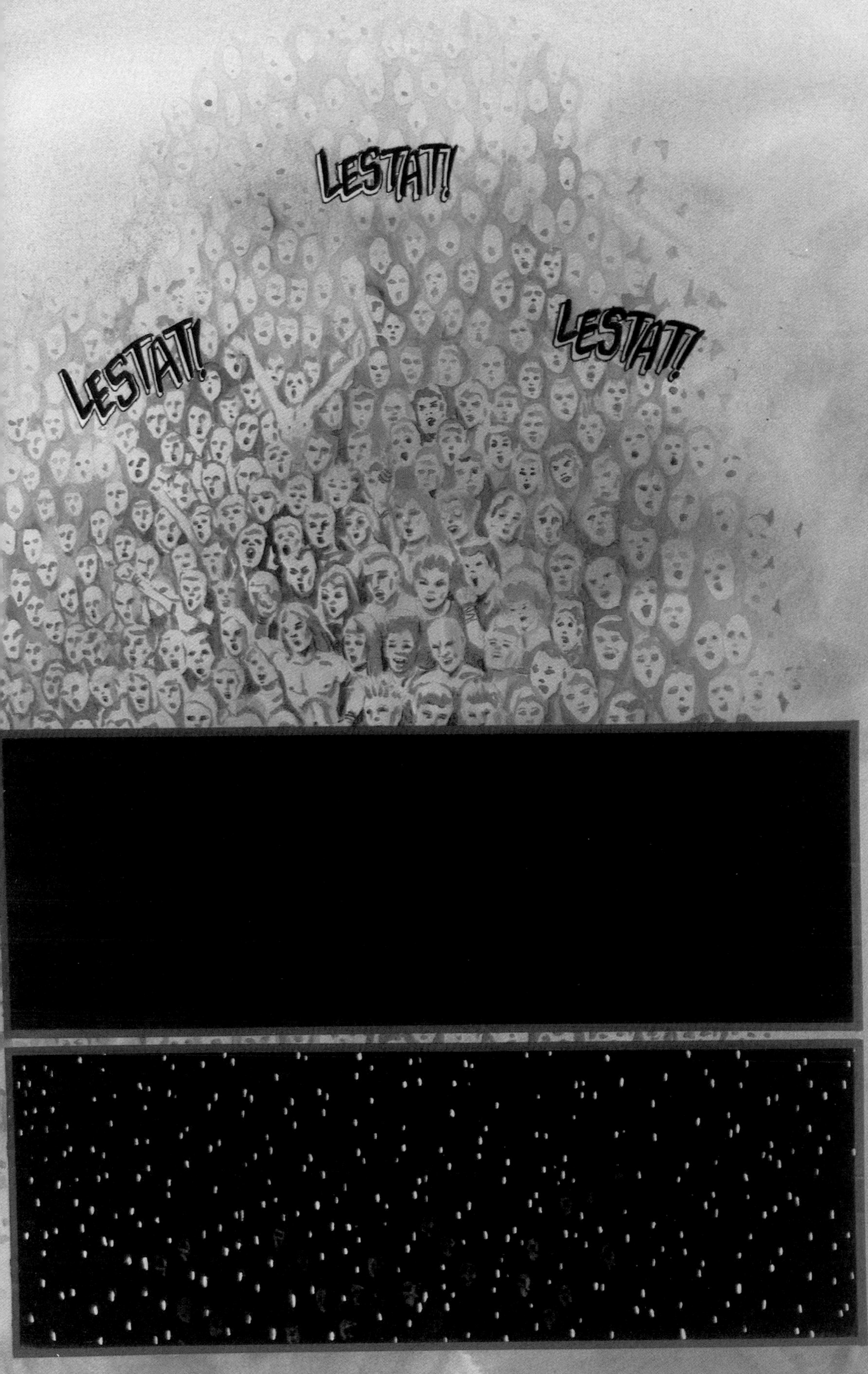
LESTAT!
LESTAT!
LESTAT!

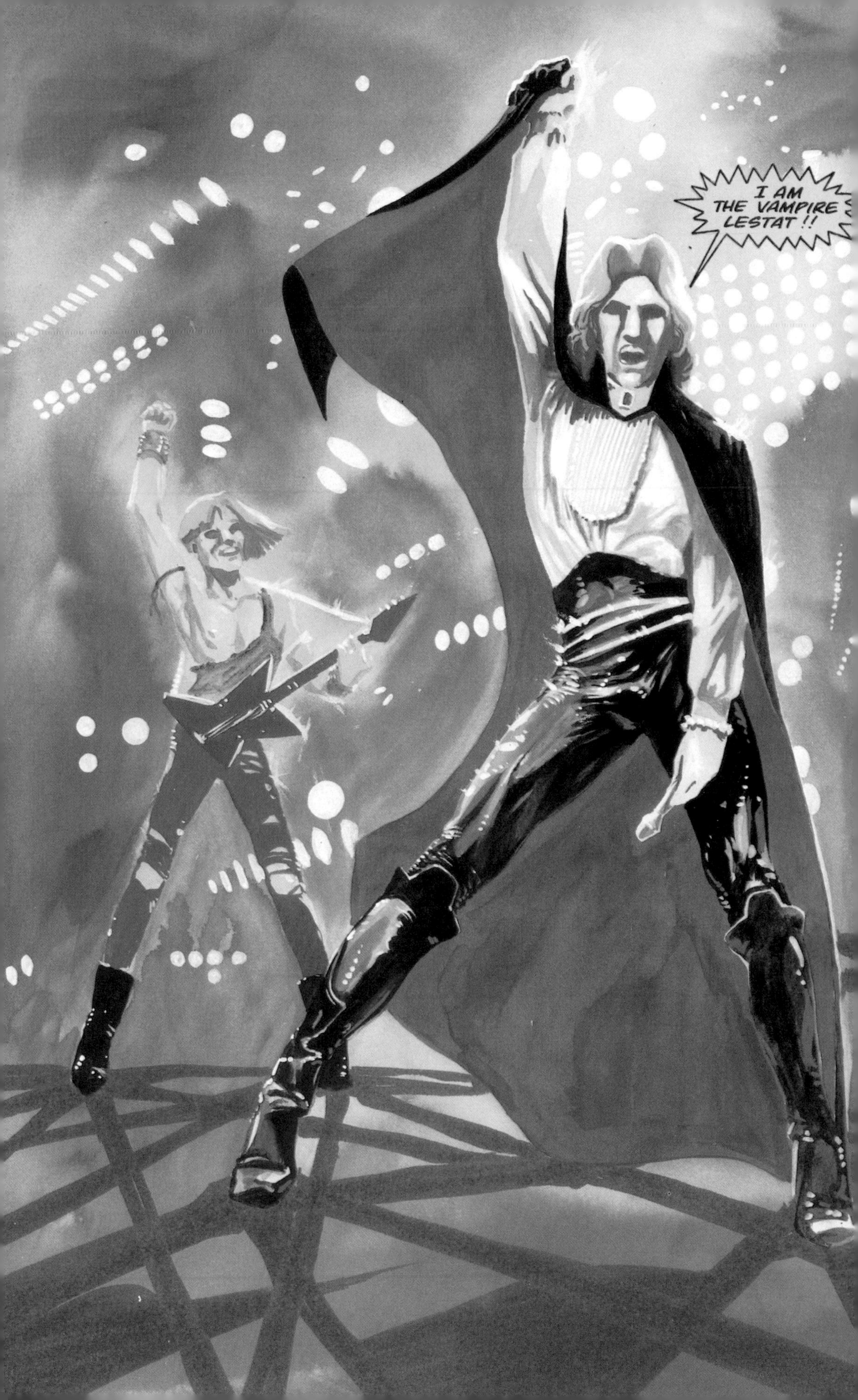
I AM THE VAMPIRE LESTAT !!

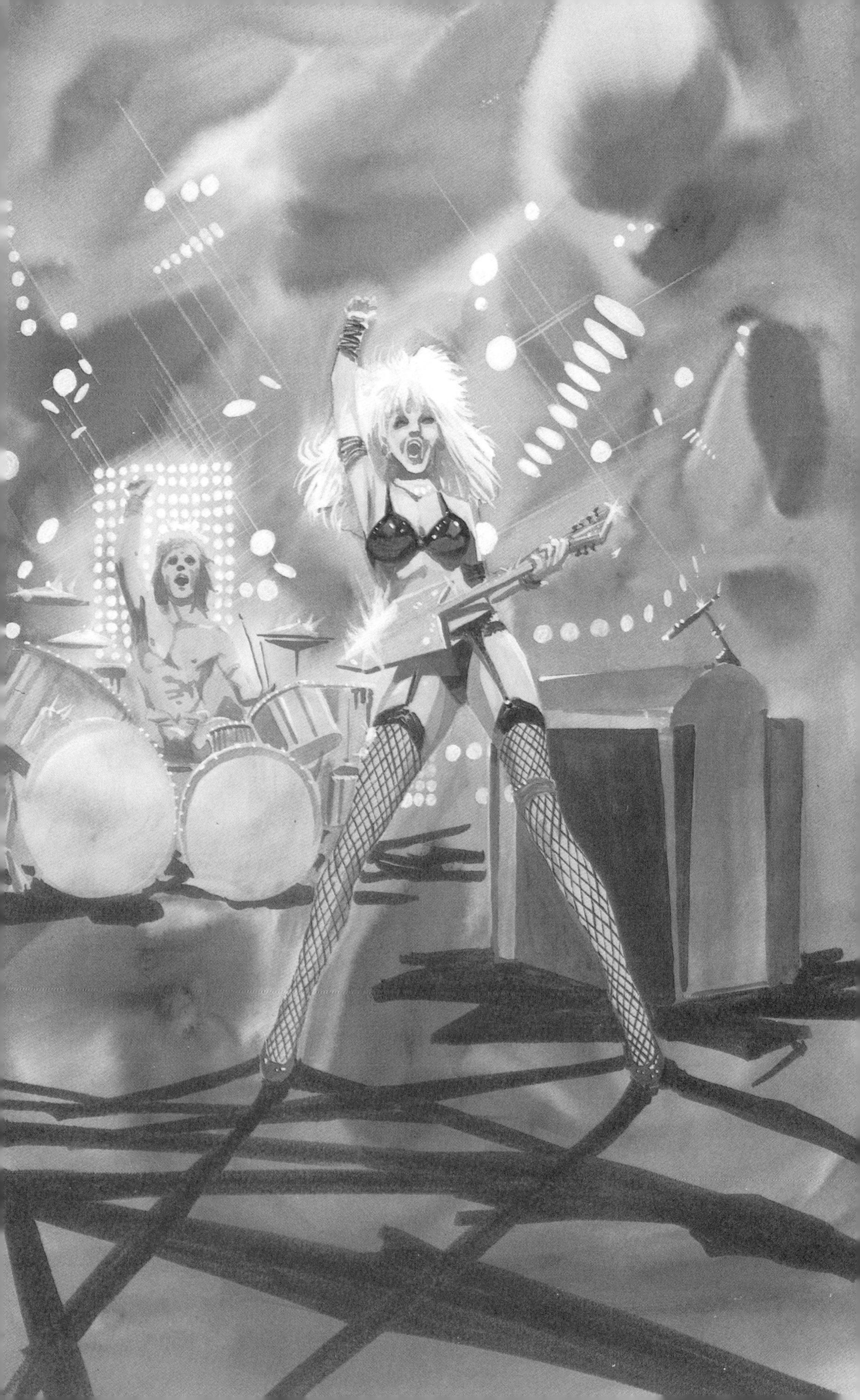

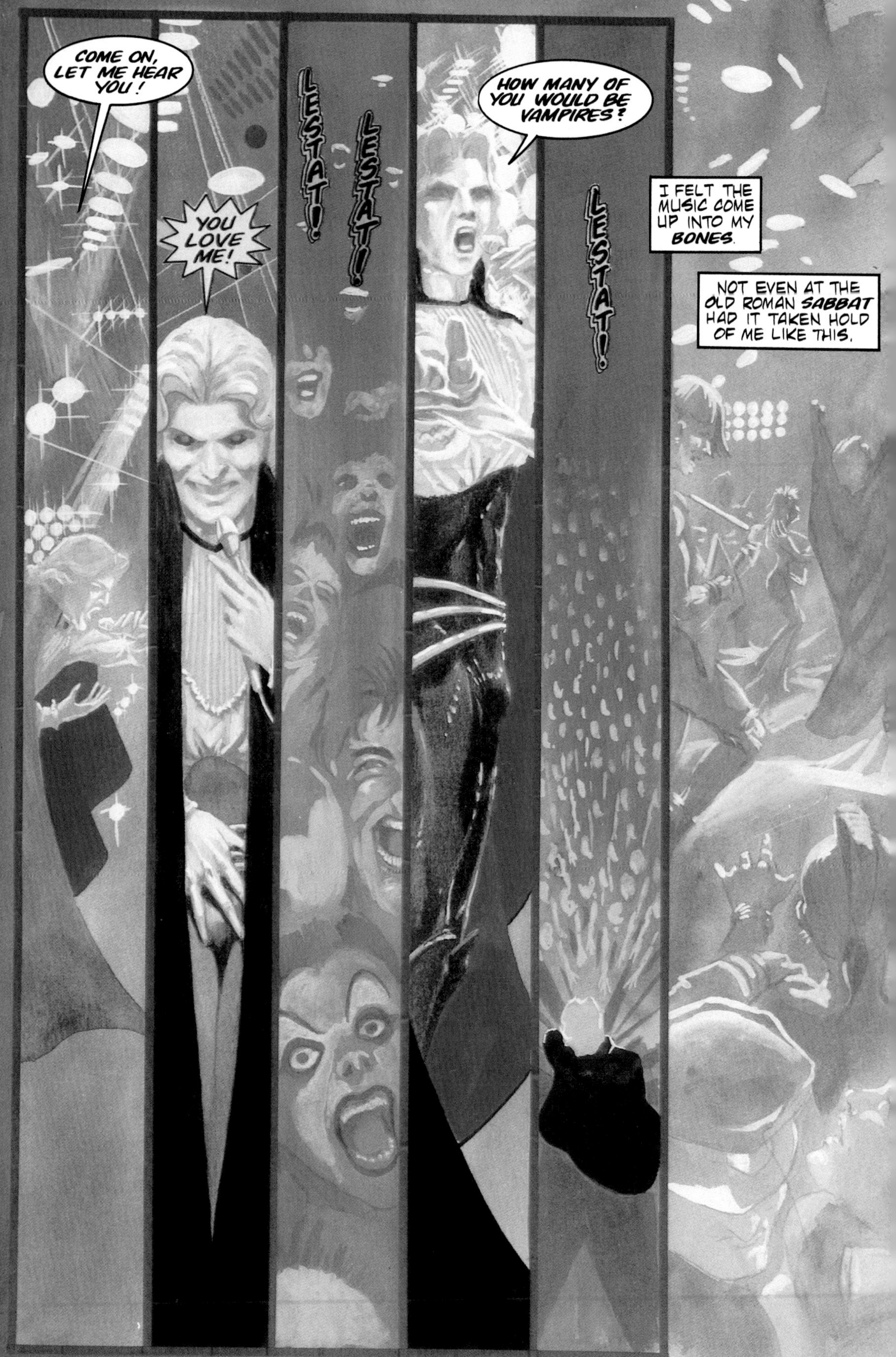
COME ON, LET ME HEAR YOU!
YOU LOVE ME!
LESTAT!
LESTAT!
HOW MANY OF YOU WOULD BE VAMPIRES?
LESTAT!
I FELT THE MUSIC COME UP INTO MY BONES.
NOT EVEN AT THE OLD ROMAN SABBAT HAD IT TAKEN HOLD OF ME LIKE THIS.

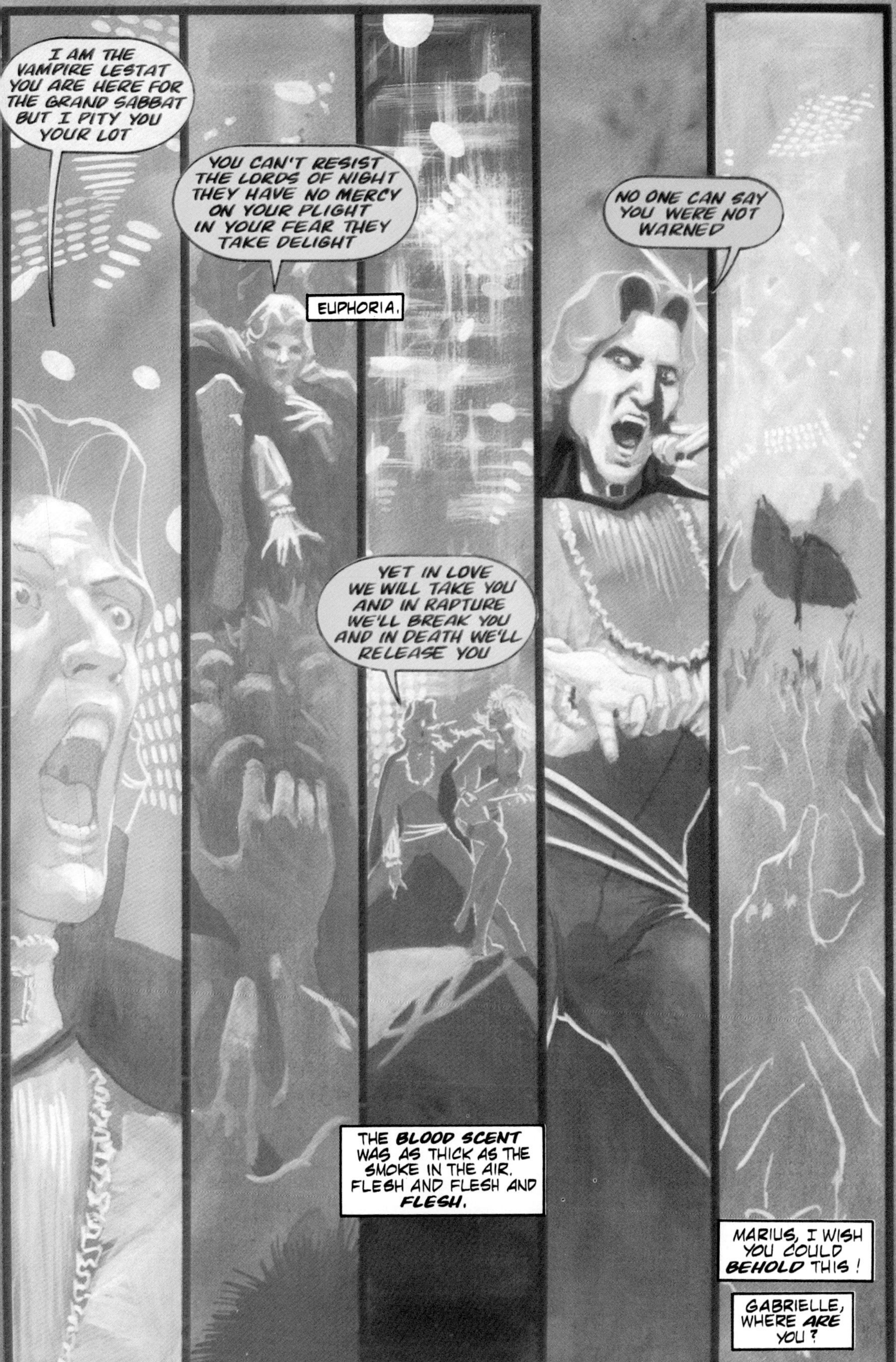
I AM THE VAMPIRE LESTAT YOU ARE HERE FOR THE GRAND SABBAT BUT I PITY YOU YOUR LOT
YOU CAN'T RESIST THE LORDS OF NIGHT THEY HAVE NO MERCY ON YOUR PLIGHT IN YOUR FEAR THEY TAKE DELIGHT
EUPHORIA.
YET IN LOVE WE WILL TAKE YOU AND IN RAPTURE WE'LL BREAK YOU AND IN DEATH WE'LL RELEASE YOU
THE BLOOD SCENT WAS AS THICK AS THE SMOKE IN THE AIR. FLESH AND FLESH AND FLESH.
NO ONE CAN SAY YOU WERE NOT WARNED
MARIUS, I WISH YOU COULD BEHOLD THIS!
GABRIELLE, WHERE ARE YOU?

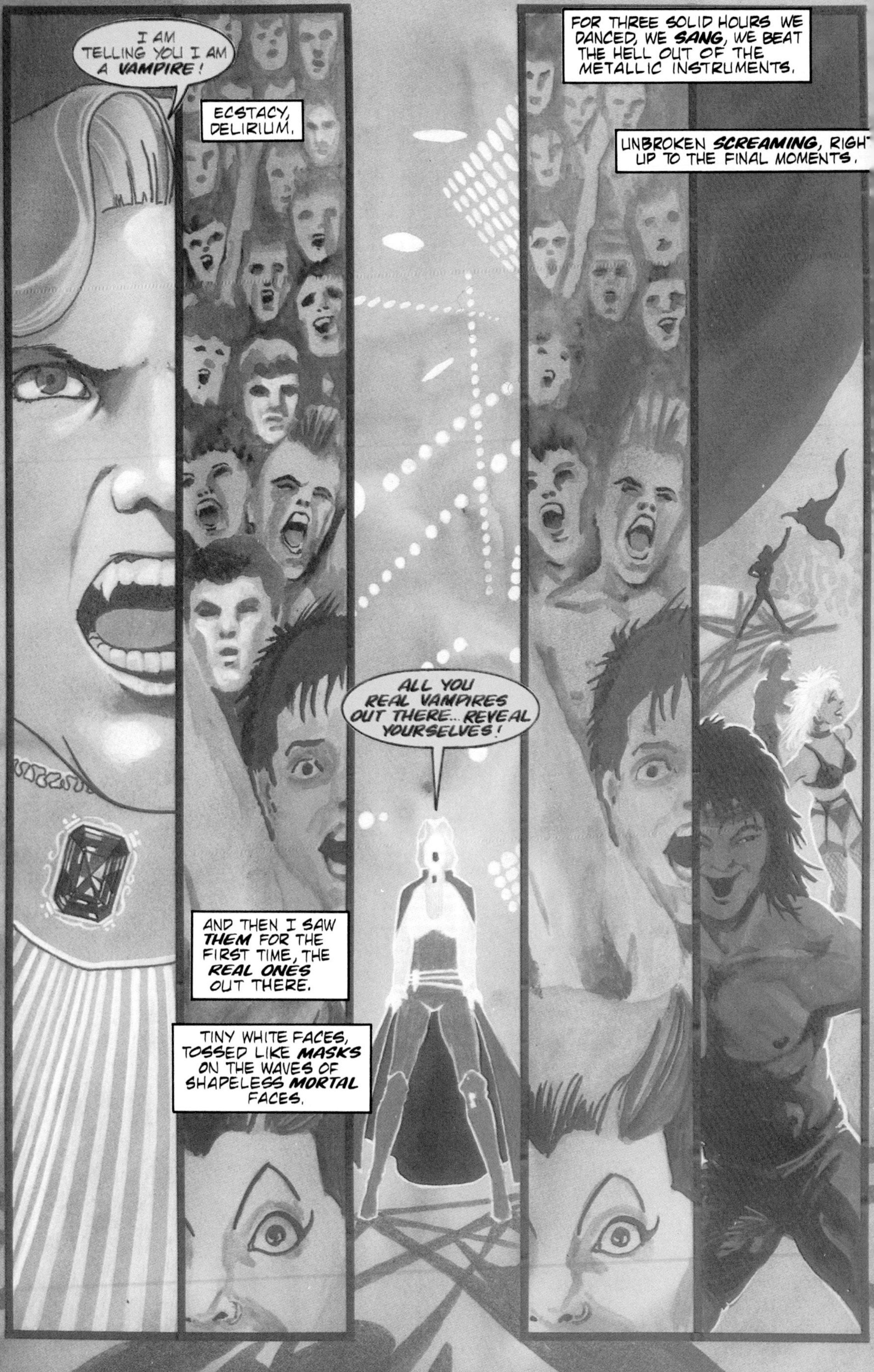
I AM TELLING YOU I AM A VAMPIRE!
ECSTACY, DELIRIUM.
AND THEN I SAW THEM FOR THE FIRST TIME, THE REAL ONES OUT THERE.
TINY WHITE FACES, TOSSED LIKE MASKS ON THE WAVES OF SHAPELESS MORTAL FACES.
ALL YOU REAL VAMPIRES OUT THERE... REVEAL YOURSELVES!
FOR THREE SOLID HOURS WE DANCED, WE SANG, WE BEAT THE HELL OUT OF THE METALLIC INSTRUMENTS.
UNBROKEN SCREAMING, RIGHT UP TO THE FINAL MOMENTS.

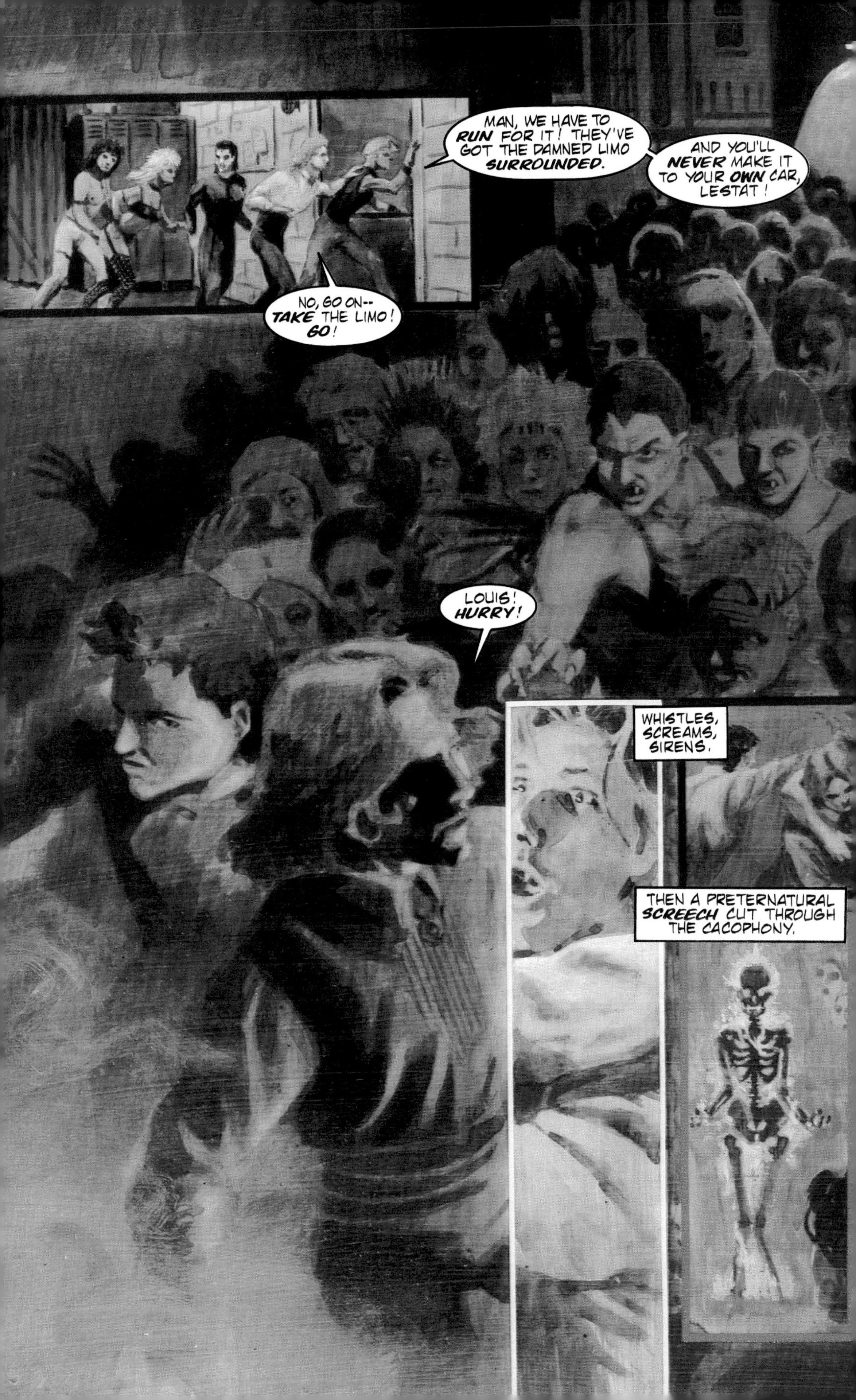
MAN, WE HAVE TO RUN FOR IT! THEY'VE GOT THE DAMNED LIMO SURROUNDED.
AND YOU'LL NEVER MAKE IT TO YOUR OWN CAR, LESTAT!
NO, GO ON-- TAKE THE LIMO! GO!
LOUIS! HURRY!
WHISTLES, SCREAMS, SIRENS.
THEN A PRETERNATURAL SCREECH CUT THROUGH THE CACOPHONY.

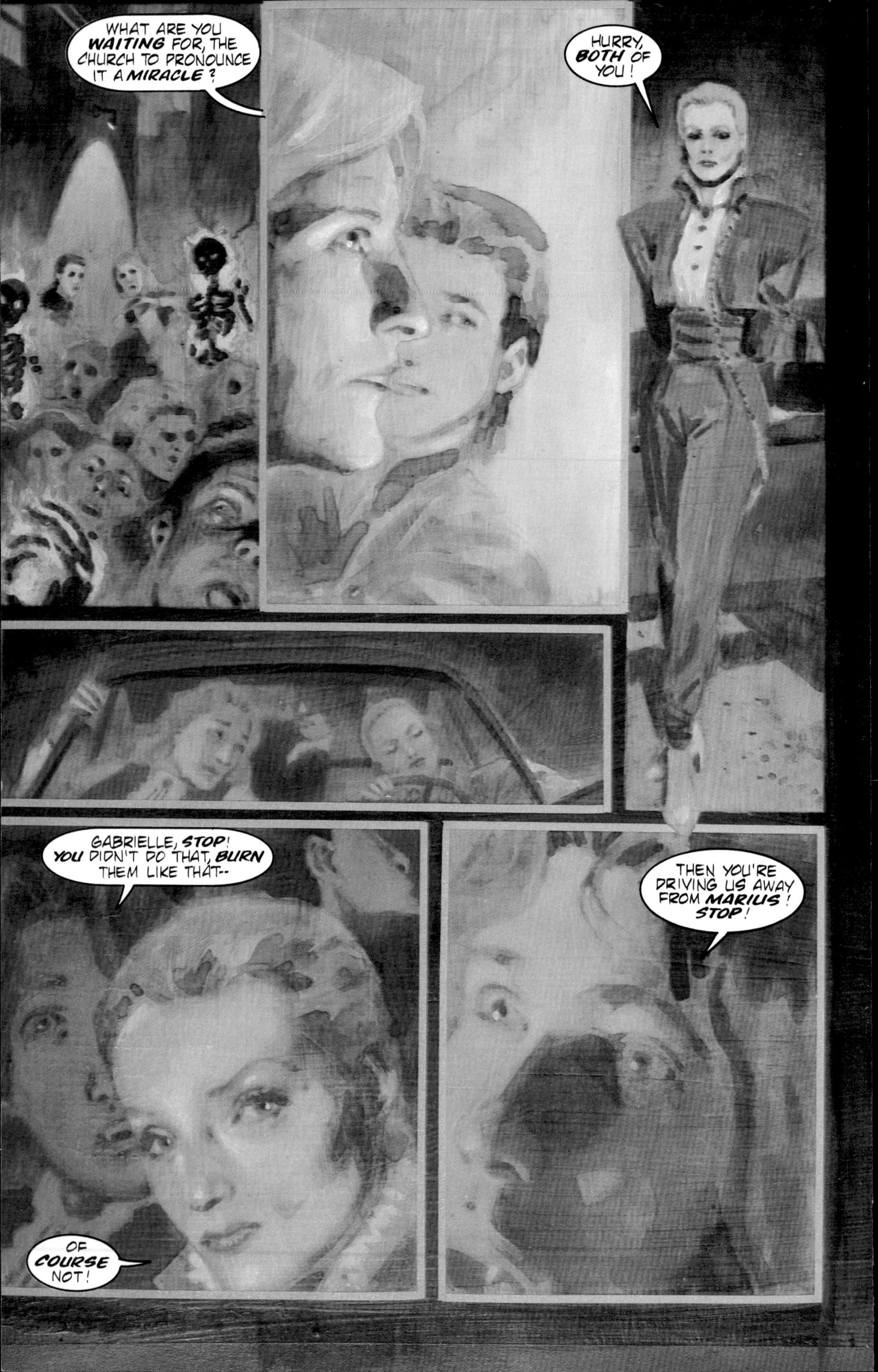
WHAT ARE YOU WAITING FOR, THE CHURCH TO PRONOUNCE IT A MIRACLE?
HURRY, BOTH OF YOU!
GABRIELLE, STOP! YOU DIDN'T DO THAT, BURN THEM LIKE THAT--
THEN YOU'RE DRIVING US AWAY FROM MARIUS! STOP!
OF COURSE NOT!

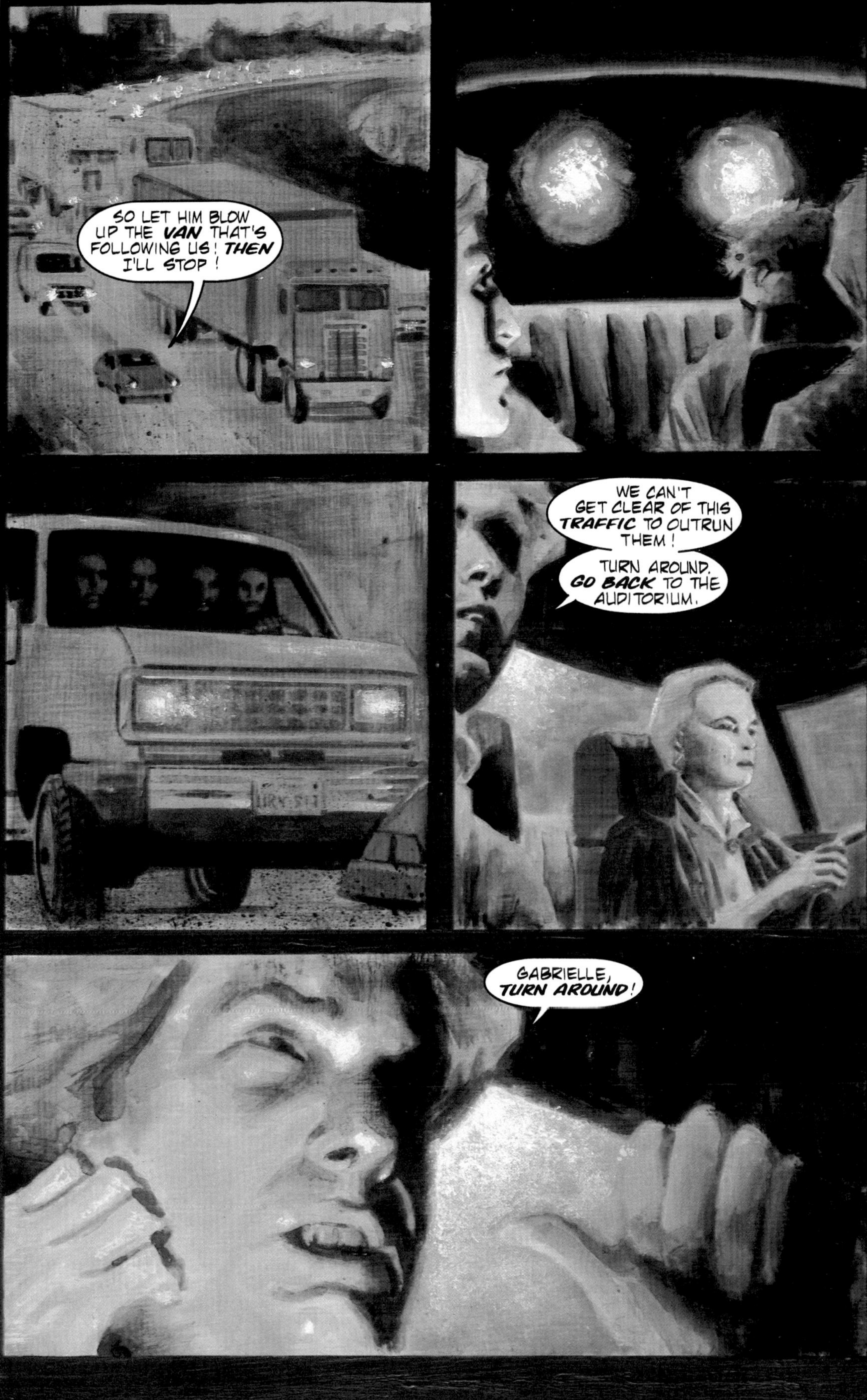
SO LET HIM BLOW UP THE **VAN** THAT'S FOLLOWING US! **THEN** I'LL STOP!
WE CAN'T GET CLEAR OF THIS **TRAFFIC** TO OUTRUN THEM!
TURN AROUND. **GO BACK** TO THE AUDITORIUM.
GABRIELLE, **TURN AROUND**!

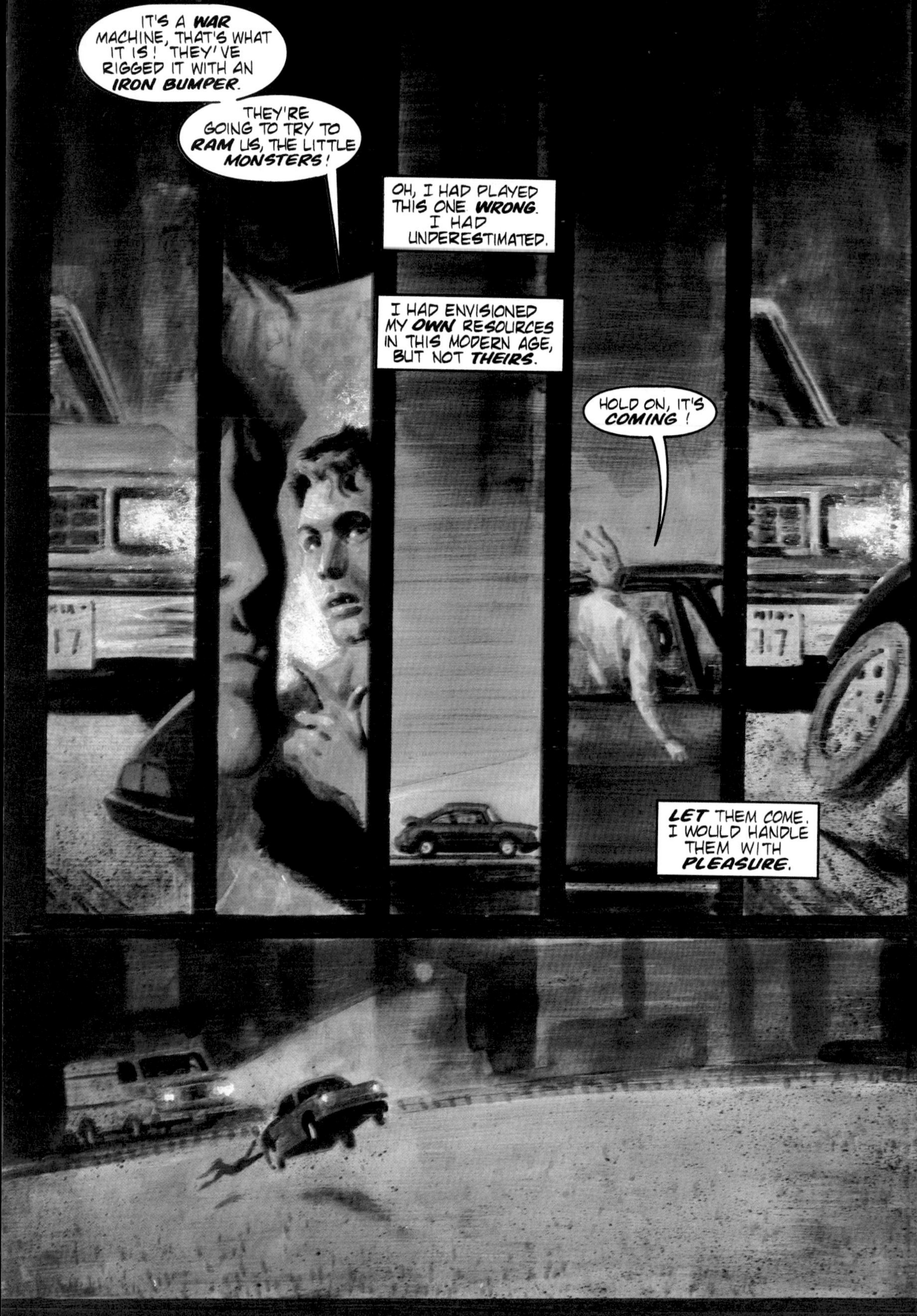
IT'S A WAR MACHINE, THAT'S WHAT IT IS! THEY'VE RIGGED IT WITH AN IRON BUMPER.
THEY'RE GOING TO TRY TO RAM US, THE LITTLE MONSTERS!
OH, I HAD PLAYED THIS ONE WRONG. I HAD UNDERESTIMATED.
I HAD ENVISIONED MY OWN RESOURCES IN THIS MODERN AGE, BUT NOT THEIRS.
HOLD ON, IT'S COMING!
LET THEM COME. I WOULD HANDLE THEM WITH PLEASURE.

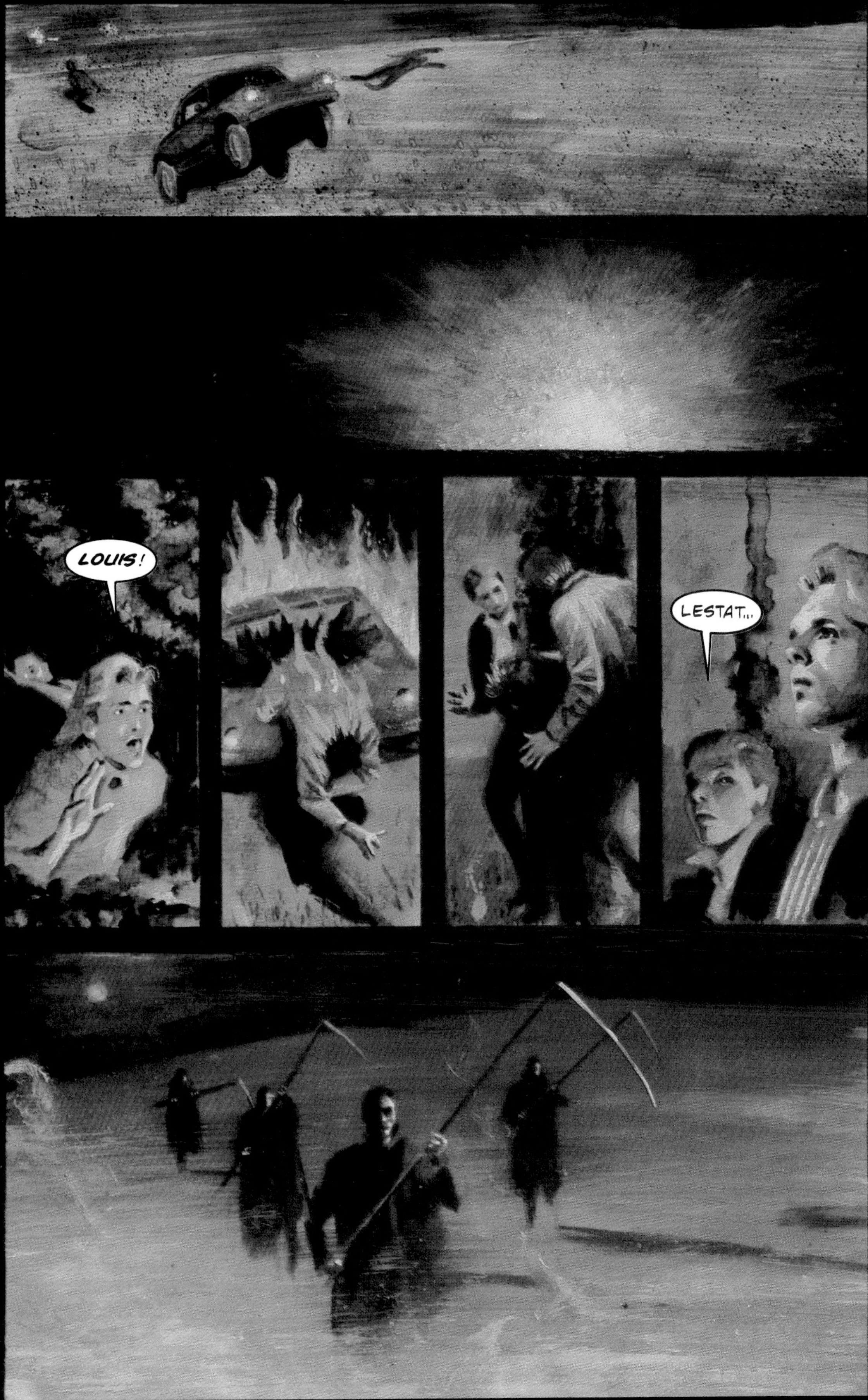
LOUIS!
LESTAT...

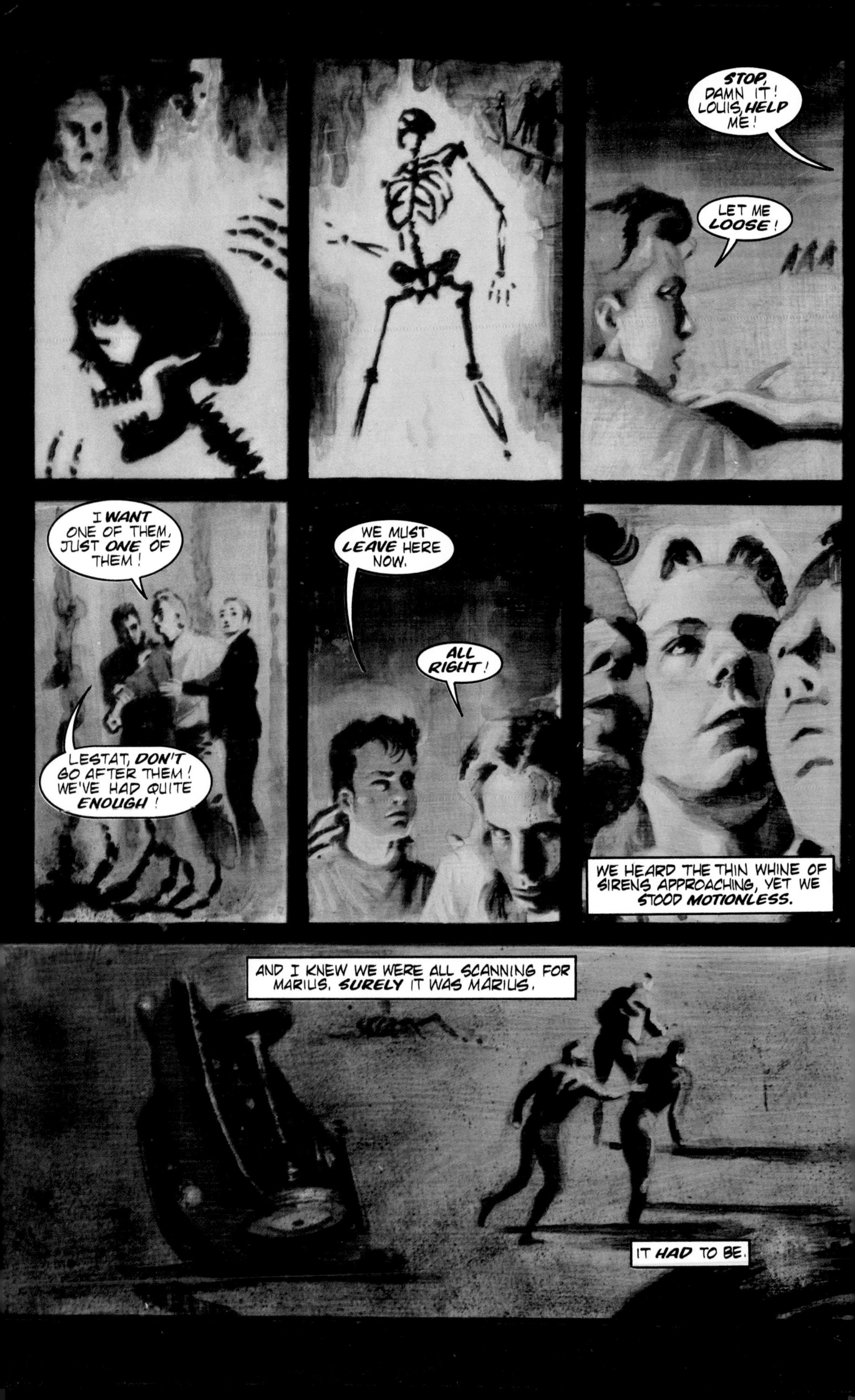
STOP, DAMN IT! LOUIS, HELP ME!
LET ME LOOSE!
I WANT ONE OF THEM, JUST ONE OF THEM!
LESTAT, DON'T GO AFTER THEM! WE'VE HAD QUITE ENOUGH!
WE MUST LEAVE HERE NOW.
ALL RIGHT!
WE HEARD THE THIN WHINE OF SIRENS APPROACHING, YET WE STOOD MOTIONLESS.
AND I KNEW WE WERE ALL SCANNING FOR MARIUS. SURELY IT WAS MARIUS.
IT HAD TO BE.

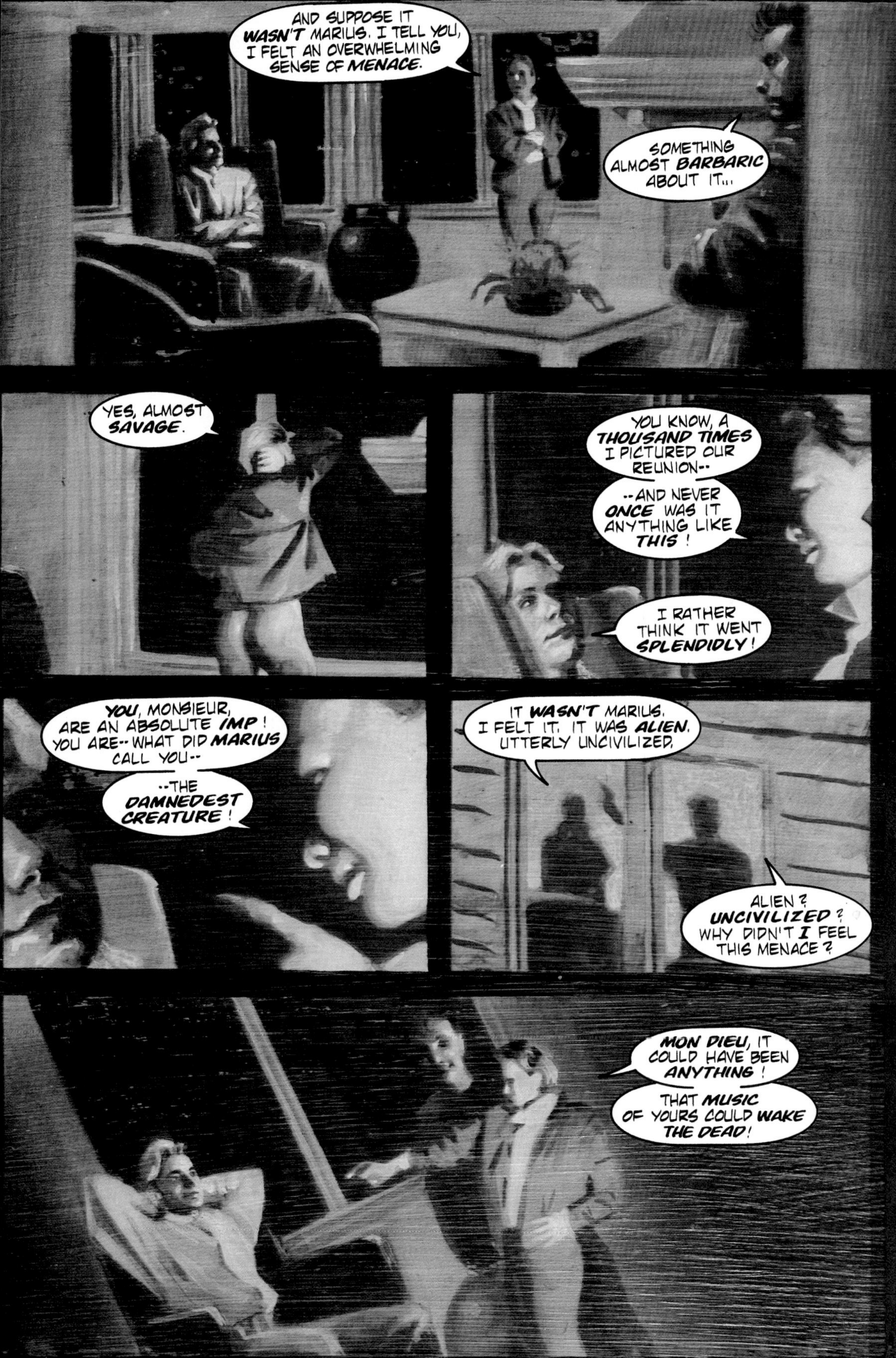
AND SUPPOSE IT WASN'T MARIUS. I TELL YOU, I FELT AN OVERWHELMING SENSE OF MENACE.
SOMETHING ALMOST BARBARIC ABOUT IT...
YES, ALMOST SAVAGE.
YOU KNOW, A THOUSAND TIMES I PICTURED OUR REUNION--
--AND NEVER ONCE WAS IT ANYTHING LIKE THIS!
I RATHER THINK IT WENT SPLENDIDLY!
YOU, MONSIEUR, ARE AN ABSOLUTE IMP! YOU ARE-- WHAT DID MARIUS CALL YOU--
--THE DAMNEDEST CREATURE!
IT WASN'T MARIUS. I FELT IT. IT WAS ALIEN. UTTERLY UNCIVILIZED.
ALIEN? UNCIVILIZED? WHY DIDN'T I FEEL THIS MENACE?
MON DIEU, IT COULD HAVE BEEN ANYTHING!
THAT MUSIC OF YOURS COULD WAKE THE DEAD!

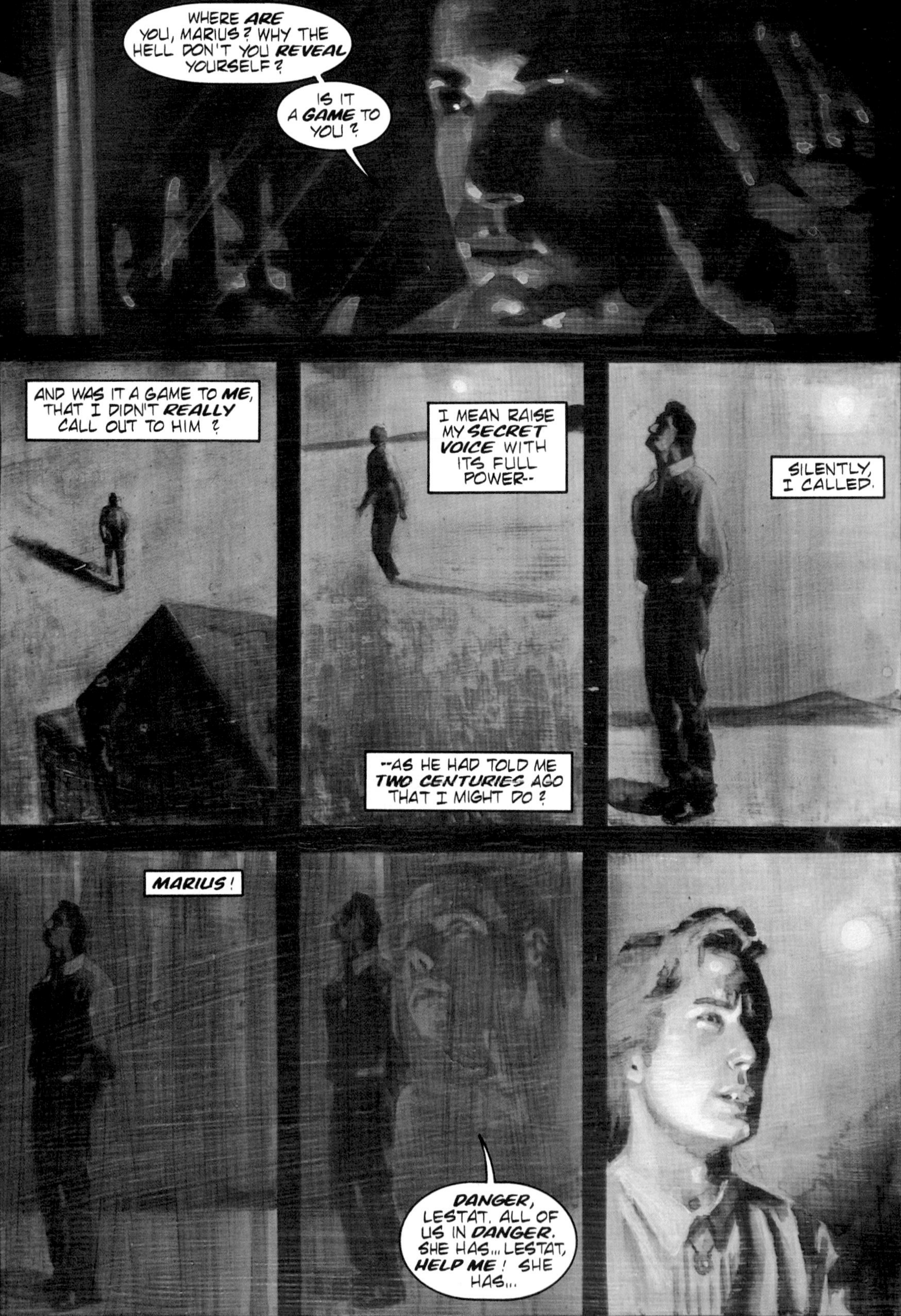

WHERE ARE YOU, MARIUS? WHY THE HELL DON'T YOU REVEAL YOURSELF?
IS IT A GAME TO YOU?
AND WAS IT A GAME TO ME, THAT I DIDN'T REALLY CALL OUT TO HIM?
I MEAN RAISE MY SECRET VOICE WITH ITS FULL POWER--
--AS HE HAD TOLD ME TWO CENTURIES AGO THAT I MIGHT DO?
SILENTLY, I CALLED.
MARIUS!
DANGER, LESTAT. ALL OF US IN DANGER. SHE HAS... LESTAT, HELP ME! SHE HAS...

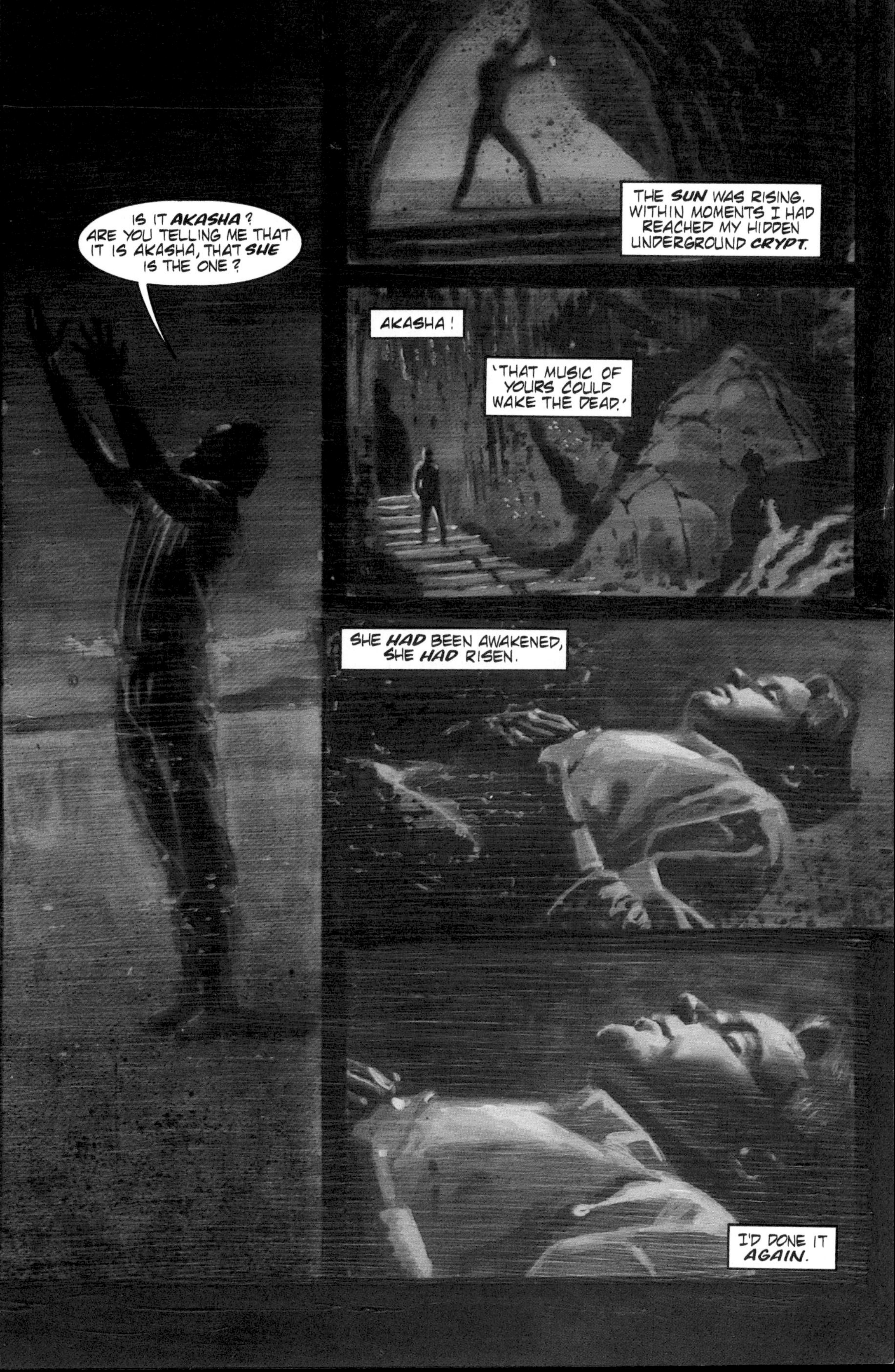

IS IT AKASHA? ARE YOU TELLING ME THAT IT IS AKASHA, THAT SHE IS THE ONE?
THE SUN WAS RISING. WITHIN MOMENTS I HAD REACHED MY HIDDEN UNDERGROUND CRYPT.
AKASHA!
'THAT MUSIC OF YOURS COULD WAKE THE DEAD.'
SHE HAD BEEN AWAKENED, SHE HAD RISEN.
I'D DONE IT AGAIN.

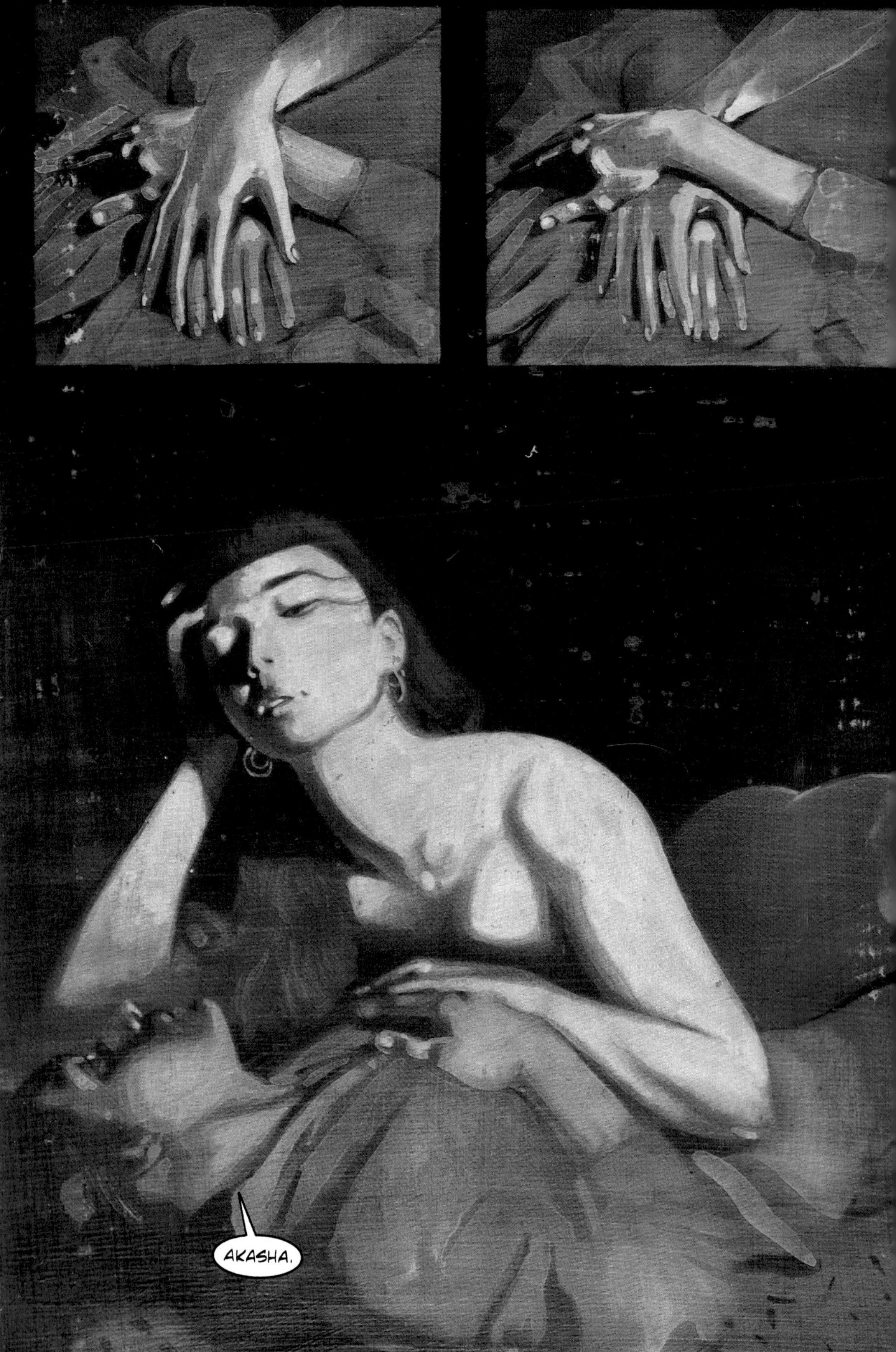
AKASHA.